BIRDWATCHING IN MAINE

Edited by Derek Lovitch

Birdwatching in Maine

A SITE GUIDE

University Press of New England · Hanover and London

University Press of New England
www.upne.com
© 2017 University Press of New England
All rights reserved
Manufactured in the United States of
America
Typeset in Calluna

Library of Congress Cataloging-in-
Publication Data

Names: Lovitch, Derek, 1977– editor.

Title: Birdwatching in Maine: a site guide
/ Derek Lovitch.

Other titles: Bird watching in Maine

Description: Hanover: University Press
of New England, [2017] | Includes
bibliographical references and index.

Identifiers: LCCN 2016035693 (print) | LCCN
2016037788 (ebook) | ISBN 9781611687224
(pbk.: alk. paper) | ISBN 9781512600391
(epub, mobi & pdf) Subjects: LCSH: Bird
watching—Maine—Guidebooks. | Birds—
Maine—Identification.

Classification: LCC QL677.5 .L678 2017
(print) | LCC QL677.5 (ebook) | DDC
598.072/34741—dc23

LC record available at https://lccn.loc
.gov/2016035693

5 4 3 2 1

FOR JEANNETTE AND OUR DOG, SASHA—

MY FAVORITE BIRDING COMPANIONS

The Birds of Maine, by Luke Seitz.

Contents

3   OXFORD COUNTY   107
   Kirk Betts

Preface

Jeannette and I moved to Portland in 2003, relocating from Whitefish Point in Michigan's Upper Peninsula. We signed a three-month lease, found some jobs, and planned to figure things out. Three months turned into a year, and a year turned into Freeport Wild Bird Supply—which we originally opened in Yarmouth in 2004.

Finding excuses not to take jobs or return to school elsewhere, we realized Maine had sucked us in: the seasons (no complaints about winter, we had just moved from the UP!), the landscape, and certainly the birding. The burgeoning food and beer scene has been a further welcoming development. We were hooked.

For us, the store was the vehicle from which to do what we really wanted: share our passion for birds, make a career of it, and work to further the birding community and develop its commitment to conservation. From free Saturday Morning Birdwalks to my role as a senior leader for WINGS Birding Inc., I bird a lot, and I love birding in Maine.

Maine offers a tremendous wealth of birding opportunities for all levels of interest and experience. From those looking beyond their backyards for the first time to the worldly visitor looking to plug a hole in a life list, Maine offers it all. Four distinct weather seasons offer four distinct birding seasons. The state's wealth of undeveloped land, extensive coastline, countless islands, and diverse habitat combine for an impressive diversity of birds at all times of the year.

No small part of the reason Jeannette and I stayed in Maine is the reason you are reading this book. Whether you are looking for a new "patch," looking to add a life bird, or just wondering "what else is out there," I hope this book will guide you in your search. I hope you too will discover the wonders of birding in Maine!

First and foremost, I would like to thank my wife, Jeannette. No project—or much of anything else—would happen or succeed without her support, assistance, and patience. She was my sounding board, proofreader, and therapist, and assisted in everything from refining directions to organizing maps. And, of course, she afforded me the time to bury myself in front of my laptop or wander the countryside collecting "data."

I couldn't have accomplished this vision without the efforts and support of my contributors. My sincerest thanks to Seth Benz, John Berry, Kirk Betts, Ron Joseph, Kristen Lindquist, Rich MacDonald, Dan Nickerson, Luke Seitz, Jeff and Allison Wells, and Herb Wilson. They all worked hard to fulfill the vision of this project, dealing with deadlines, demands, and occasionally my wrath! Luke was instrumental in the production of the bar graphs in the Species Accounts, and without Jeannette I would still be working on maps.

I also thank all the birders I have learned from since I moved to Maine, in particular Lysle Brinker, who first introduced me to some of the best sites southern Maine has to offer. I couldn't possibly list all the birders I have learned from, and learned with, over the years, but I do want to thank several in particular: Chris Bartlett, Rich Eakin, Ed Hess, Robby Lambert, Kristen Lindquist, Don Mairs, Pat Moynahan, Luke Seitz, and Bill Sheehan.

I also offer my thanks to a host of birding companions, "assistants," and everyone else who, during the course of this project, offered information, support, or otherwise made this book possible, including, but by no means limited to, Serena Doose, Katrina Fenton, Lois Gerke, Kristen Lindquist, Phil McCormack, Evan Obercian, and Andrew Wolgang. I would also like to thank Fritz Appleby, Lysle Brinker, Andre Brousseau, Greg Caron, Don Green, Gerard Kiladjian, Jeannette Lovitch, Julia McLeod, Lena Moser, Pat Moynahan, Bill Needleman, Heather Printup, Scott Richardson, Luke Seitz, and Alison Truesdale for their assistance with edits, information, permissions, or other details that greatly enhanced the entries for York and Cumberland Counties.

And last but most certainly not least, I would like to thank Phyllis Deutsch and the staff of the University Press of New England for believing in the vision for this project and guiding it to its completion and success.

BIRDWATCHING IN MAINE

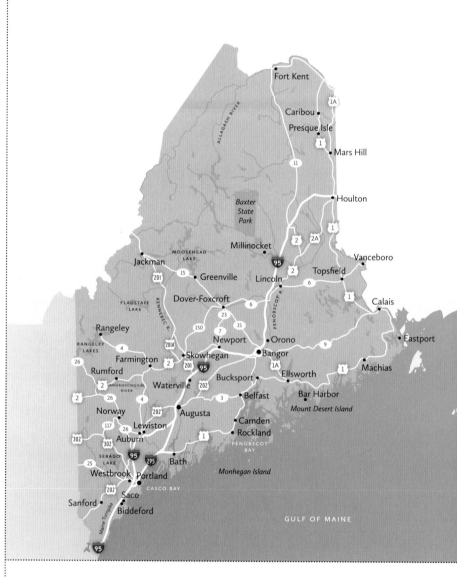

MAINE ROAD AND TOWN REFERENCES

Introduction

WHY GO BIRDING IN MAINE?

Nearly 450 species have been recorded in the 33,215 square miles (nearly as large as all other New England states combined), over six thousand lakes and large ponds, over three thousand coastal islands, and thirty-five hundred miles of coastline of the state of Maine. Over 200 species breed in the state, including many species reaching the northern limits of their breeding range, sometimes alongside species at the southern and eastern limits of their range.

Yellow-throated Vireos in the silver maple–lined riverbanks of the coastal plain are just an hour's drive from Philadelphia Vireos in steep creek-side slopes thick with quaking aspen. Louisiana Waterthrushes occupy eastern hemlock–shaded bubbling brooks in the foothills, while American Pipits occupy alpine tundra atop Mount Katahdin.

Saltmarsh Sparrows breed in the southern coastal salt marshes, just in-shore from barrier islands hosting Piping Plovers and Least Terns. Up in the mountains, and right up to the coast in far "Downeast" Maine, boreal forest approaches its southeastern limits, home to a suite of charismatic, enigmatic, and much-sought-after boreal specialties that include Spruce Grouse, Black-backed Woodpecker, Gray Jay, Boreal Chickadee, and a bunch of warblers.

The boreal and high-latitude Arctic and sub-Arctic habitats are highly cyclical. Cycles of boom and bust in food resources result in boom-and-bust cycles for the birds that depend on them. When these enigmatic northern birds move south (and/or east) in pursuit of food (owing either to a lack of food in their usual range or to a bumper crop of youngsters), "irruptions" occur, bringing some of the most desired of North American birds, from Snowy Owls to Bohemian Waxwings, to all corners of the state.

Geography, from mountains to the complex coastline, directs and con-centrates "neotropical migrants" (species that move from tropical America northward to breed in the forests of North America to take advantage of seasonal abundances in insect-food resources) that are flowing to and from the boreal—often referred to as North America's bird factory. From urban parks to Monhegan Island, migration watchers stationed around the state can observe a portion of one of the planet's great natural spectacles.

Bird migration simply defies the imagination. The mechanisms that cause it, direct it, and occasionally misdirect it are complex, and in some cases still unexplained. For now, I will direct you to some great resources about migration. One of my favorite books is Scott Weidensaul's *Living on the Wind: Across the Hemisphere with Migratory Birds*. And to delve deeper, give books such as *The Migration Ecology of Birds* by Ian Newton a try.

But my job is to get you to the places you need to be to observe migration. And migration is not a short-term phenomenon; it's nearly always going on. While the bulk of long-distance neotropical migrants pass through in May and again in September, there's always something on the move. As the last truant shorebirds are still moseying north in mid-to-late June, the first southbound shorebirds (failed breeders or nonbreeders) begin to return. As American Robins and Bohemian Waxwings are still wandering south in February as fruit resources are depleted, a warm spell of southern winds will deliver the first few Red-winged Blackbirds and Turkey Vultures prospecting north in anticipation of the thaw.

While migration is not caused by weather (instead, it's triggered by the need to find food and directed by hormonal changes triggered by the lengthening and shortening days), weather does greatly affect it, and affects the observation of it. I will plug my first book, *How to Be a Better Birder* (2012) and its sections on birding by geography, birding by habitat, and birding by weather. Hopefully that will offer some background to many of the topics that we cover throughout *Birdwatching in Maine.*

I readily admit I have much to learn about so many corners of the state. Therefore I chose to invite regional experts to work with me on this project. There is no way I, or any other single individual, can accumulate the amount of local information that local birders amass over a lifetime of birding their home territory and local patches.

I wanted to tap this local expertise and finally provide Maine with a definitive treatment of its birding opportunities. While some counties have received (and in most cases deserve) more thorough treatment than others, all geographic regions are covered. No matter where you live or visit in Maine, there is fantastic birding to be found—if you know where to look!

Basics of Birding in Maine

To fully appreciate the wonders of Maine's birds and nature, we need to be prepared. Comfort and safety go a long way in helping you enjoy and maximize your birding day. To put it simply, in Maine we have bugs, and we have "weathah." Being prepared for both will help ensure happy birding memories.

WEATHER

There are a lot of jokes about Maine's seasons: "Early winter, winter, late winter, and the Fourth of July"; "Winter, mud season, bug season, and the Fourth of July"; "Winter and road construction." I think you get the idea. But no matter what you call each season, you will want to be prepared for a range of conditions. Between high mountains, islands surrounded by chilly waters, and storms arriving from most any direction, our weather is dynamic and ever changing.

In all seasons, proper layering is critical. Summertime visitors can be caught off guard by chilly mornings, especially in the mountains, or cold and damp days along the coast. The Gulf of Maine, although one of the fastest-warming bodies of water on the planet, is still a cold-water system, and you'll want to be prepared for boat rides with air temperatures barely warmer than the water you are cruising through (which usually peaks off the southern coasts in August in the low 60s Fahrenheit. Summertime temperatures range from lows in the 40s to highs in the 90s (increasingly regular). But for an example, the average high/low for Portland in July is 79/59 degrees Fahrenheit (26/15 Celsius).

In winter it can get bitterly cold, but thanks to the moderating influence of the ocean, true Arctic air masses are usually short-lived. Snow is plentiful in most winters, but don't be shocked to wake up to a coating at your mountaintop campsite in June or September. In winter, plan extra time for driving, as although the state and municipal road crews have a lot of practice, keeping our roads clear can be a challenge. No matter how good the bird is, be sure to take your time and drive carefully. And dress warm! Winter temperatures range from an average high/low in January of 20/1F (–6/–17C) in Caribou to 31/13F (0/–10C) in Portland. To help plan your trip and what conditions you might expect, visit usclimatedata.com for monthly averages, and for forecasts, the National Weather Service at www.weather.gov/car/ for northern Maine, and www.weather.gov/gyx/ for southern Maine.

Other than a few reports of timber rattlesnakes, Maine has no poisonous snakes. Black bears, especially sows with cubs, should be given wide berth and avoided. But the most dangerous animal in Maine is the iconic moose. Young males in particular can be aggressive, but the biggest threat is finding a thousand-pound animal standing in the middle of the road on a foggy morning as you come driving around a bend. Please use the utmost caution when traveling in regions known for higher densities of moose, and be sure to pay attention to posted "moose crossing" signs that mark areas with high rates of collisions. Sadly, many collisions with moose result in fatalities, especially for people in low cars.

INSECTS

We have a lot of bugs (one of the reasons we have so many birds!), and some of them bite. A lot. Mosquitoes are ubiquitous, from the boreal forest to the coastal salt marshes. There are over forty species of mosquitoes in Maine, and just about all of them bite. Hatches occur at various times of year, but early June through early August tends to see the most activity from these nuisances. However, mosquito-borne illnesses are exceedingly rare.

Maine might be more famous for its blackflies, however. Slightly larger than what most people refer to as a gnat, members of this large family of blood-sucking flies can occur (mostly in bogs and mountainous areas) in massive clouds that send you running back to the car. Blackflies usually start appearing on warm days in early May and peak in early June. Luckily, the peak season is usually short-lived, and they are actually an important part of the food chain and an important water-quality indicator species. There's even a Maine Blackfly Breeders Association (www.maineblackfly.org)—a tongue-in-cheek group that happily doesn't breed them, but uses events and unique blackfly-themed products to raise money for charity.

Moose flies, nearly the size of a quarter, hurt like heck, but they are big and slow and are usually easily swatted away. Deerflies are a little wilier and can be overwhelming in some locations. They peak in July, just after we get a respite from mosquitoes and blackflies. Fierce greenhead flies are only found in small numbers in the coastal salt marshes, mostly in the southern reaches of the state.

And we do have ticks, including the "deer" or black-legged tick that carries

Lyme disease. Increasingly common in the southern two-thirds of the state, they are still less abundant than the relatively harmless, if rather annoying, wood or "dog" tick. For ticks, I simply wear light-colored clothing, tuck my pants into my socks, and check frequently in the field, and immediately upon my return home. I find insect repellent to be only marginally helpful—I prefer to just pick them off my clothes and vigilantly check after every outing.

For mosquitoes and the biting flies, long pants, a light-colored field shirt, and a ball cap (especially helpful with deerflies) are usually sufficient for me. I then cover the limited exposed parts (hand and face) with repellent. Since I have moved to Maine, I have relied solely on repellents with 30 percent oil of lemon eucalyptus, the only plant-based repellent certified by the Centers for Disease Control and Prevention. I find with liberal and frequent application, it is just as effective as DEET, a chemical that I now avoid as much as possible.

HUNTING

Hunting is a way of life for many in Maine, even in suburban environs. Folks heading out into the woods should be aware of hunting seasons and plan accordingly. Most public land, along with the vast majority of private property, is open to hunting. Blaze orange is highly recommended. Looking for ducks in a popular hunting spot on the first weekend of the season would not be recommended—for one thing, you're not going to see many birds sitting still! Thankfully, Maine still does not permit hunting on Sunday, so the woods and fields are a little more peaceful, if nothing else. For a listing of the hunting seasons see www.maine.gov/ifw/hunting_trapping/.

How to Use This Book

So let's get down to business.

Birdwatching in Maine is broken down into sixteen chapters, one for each county. Of course, birds, habitats, and even parks don't always follow political boundaries, but I think you will find that this format gets you to where you need to go. The counties are listed from south to north, using the southernmost corner of the county as the rough guide. For locales that straddle county lines, I include a cross-reference to the site's entry (or main entry) within one of the county site listings.

Each county begins with a **county overview**. This is my personal account of birding the county, my recommendations and preferences, and a summary

MAINE COUNTIES

of the best birding that each county has to offer throughout the season. I'll also introduce the authors for the fourteen counties that I didn't write and give them a chance to tell you a little about themselves.

We then get to the meat of the book, the **site entries**. These are ordered (very) roughly from south to north, west to east. They are *not* ranked in any way here (see the county overview for top sites). I've used a one- or two-letter abbreviation for the county, followed by a number for every site for ease of cross-referencing. So, for example, site number one in York County is Y1; site number twelve in Sagadahoc County is SA12.

The **site number** is then followed by the **site name**, the **town or towns** the site is located in, and the **coordinates** on the DeLorme *Maine Atlas and Gazetteer*. This iconic Maine resource is no less useful now than it was before the advent of GPS and navigational apps. This is a must-have for all Maine birders, especially when you find yourself in some remote corner of the state with no cell phone coverage or a mountain blocking a GPS signal. Furthermore, maps have a lot more to teach us. Look at the coastline—do you see any features that look as if they might concentrate migrants? Notice that road in the "middle of nowhere" that looks as though it offers a view of a lake. I wonder what waterfowl might touch down there? "Birding by geography" is a constant theme of my writing and birding efforts, and a map is the first crucial place to start.

Next up is the **season**. This is offered as a general guide to the most productive time to visit the location or locations. Months in boldface are the prime times. One of the great things about birding is that there are birds everywhere all the time. Don't ignore a convenient local site just because this book recommends it only in winter—it's always worth a check to see what unconventional seasons have to offer. You just might discover the next big migrant trap hot spot or a rarity!

Visitation is a catch-all for pertinent information regarding your exploration of the site. We start with a rough estimation of the time you should devote to the area, the always important location (or lack thereof) of restroom facilities of any kind, and fee information. All Maine state parks have a rather nominal entry fee per person, per day, but parks are free to Maine residents over sixty-five years of age. Current fees can be found at www.maine.gov/dacf/parks/park_passes_fees_rules/index.shtml. I cannot recommend the annual pass enough—it's a great deal and well worth it for any residents or visitors who plan on doing some park exploration. After fee information, if applicable, we list the hours and days that a location is open to access. If no dates or times are listed, you can assume that the site is open seven days a week from dawn to dusk. A wheelchair icon signifies locations that are at least partially accessible to those with limited mobility (including vehicle tour loops), while a canoe icon references sites that are at least partially birdable by canoe or kayak.

The **highlights** section is a very brief overview of the most interesting species, groups of species, or avian highlights that the site might afford. This is by no means complete. Instead, it provides just a sampling of what a site has to offer, in addition to quickly directing you to some of the most sought-after species you might be looking for.

Each site's text then begins with a short introduction to offer some general information, expand on the highlights list, and get you excited for your visit to each spot.

Then, at last, we come to the important stuff: how to get here and how to bird it. I've chosen not to separate the driving directions from the birding directions. Instead, the directions section is designed not only to get you where you need to go, but to get you around once you are there.

I had each author start the directions at a major highway (mostly I-95, the southern part of which is the Maine Turnpike, a toll road; I-295; or US Route 1). More remote areas are referenced to the most practical starting point, usually a major state highway or a town center with state highway crossroads.

Directions are offered to the tenth of a mile. We had to round up or down in some instances, and in any case odometers can vary from vehicle to vehicle, and even a pause to check the rearview mirror at an intersection before you glance down to see or resent the mileage could affect the exact reading. Should any of the directions steer you slightly wrong, I sincerely apologize in advance—and if they do, please let me know!

Often—just because of the practical aspects of producing a comprehensive guide for a state as large as Maine—I have decided to forgo extensive listing of common species that will be encountered at each site. Instead, I often restrict myself to generalities such as "common birds of mixed forest habitats" or a selection of representative species. Of course, for the species of note and your "target birds," we will get as specific as possible.

At the conclusion of each entry, I offer a list of rarities that have been encountered (and in almost all cases, documented) at a particular site through June 1, 2016. For the most part, I have limited the list to genuine out-of-range vagrants (rarely, unseasonable birds when they are particularly significant) and note that these are in no way complete lists of all the "good" birds that have been recorded at a site. And with the exception of first state records, I have mostly limited the listing to the last ten years. Instead, it's merely a sample for a representation of the great birds that might be encountered, the types of vagrants that have shown up (often a direct measure of habitat and/or geography), and a little whetting of the appetite for those of you who—like me—love to look for vagrants.

And finally, there are Web addresses to sites with useful information or helpful trail maps when appropriate. Fee or reservation information (such as for boat trips) can be found at the listed links as well.

Now, let's go birding!

American Birding Association Code of Birding Ethics

As birding grows in popularity, conflicts between property owners, birders, and even the birds themselves continue to grow. Especially for rare birds and endangered species, birders and photographers can negatively affect an individual, or in extreme cases, a species, by overzealousness, carelessness, or simple selfishness. Please, when looking at birds—of any kind, at any time— put the bird and its well-being first and foremost. Always have consideration for your fellow birders and private property, and use common sense.

CODE OF BIRDING ETHICS

1. Promote the welfare of birds and their environment.
   a. Support the protection of important bird habitat.
   b. To avoid stressing birds or exposing them to danger, exercise restraint and caution during observation, photography, sound recording, or filming.

   Limit the use of recordings and other methods of attracting birds, and never use such methods in heavily birded areas, or for attracting any species that is Threatened, Endangered, or of Special Concern, or is rare in your local area;

   Keep well back from nests and nesting colonies, roosts, display areas, and important feeding sites. In such sensitive areas, if there is a need for extended observation, photography, filming, or recording, try to use a blind or hide, and take advantage of natural cover.

   Use artificial light sparingly for filming or photography, especially for close-ups.

c. Before advertising the presence of a rare bird, evaluate the potential for disturbance to the bird, its surroundings, and other people in the area, and proceed only if access can be controlled, disturbance minimized, and permission has been obtained from private land owners. The sites of rare nesting birds should be divulged only to the proper conservation authorities.

d. Stay on roads, trails, and paths where they exist; otherwise keep habitat disturbance to a minimum.

2. Respect the law, and the rights of others.

a. Do not enter private property without the owner's explicit permission.

b. Follow all laws, rules, and regulations governing use of roads and public areas, both at home and abroad.

c. Practice common courtesy in contacts with other people. Your exemplary behavior will generate goodwill with birders and non-birders alike.

3. Ensure that feeders, nest structures, and other artificial bird environments are safe.

a. Keep dispensers, water, and food clean and free of decay or disease. It is important to feed birds continually during harsh weather.

b. Maintain and clean nest structures regularly.

c. If you are attracting birds to an area, ensure the birds are not exposed to predation from cats and other domestic animals, or dangers posed by artificial hazards.

4. Group birding, whether organized or impromptu, requires special care.

Each individual in the group, in addition to the obligations spelled out in Items #1 and #2, has responsibilities as a group member.

a. Respect the interests, rights, and skills of fellow birders, as well as people participating in other legitimate outdoor activities. Freely share your knowledge and experience, except where code 1(c) applies. Be especially helpful to beginning birders.

b. If you witness unethical birding behavior, assess the situation, and intervene if you think it prudent. When interceding, inform the person(s) of the inappropriate action, and attempt, within reason, to have it stopped. If the behavior continues, document it, and notify appropriate individuals or organizations.

Group Leader Responsibilities [amateur and professional trips and tours]

c. Be an exemplary ethical role model for the group. Teach through word and example.

d. Keep groups to a size that limits impact on the environment, and does not interfere with others using the same area.

e. Ensure everyone in the group knows of and practices this code.

f. Learn and inform the group of any special circumstances applicable to the areas being visited (e.g., no tape recorders allowed).

g. Acknowledge that professional tour companies bear a special responsibility to place the welfare of birds and the benefits of public knowledge ahead of the company's commercial interests. Ideally, leaders should keep track of tour sightings, document unusual occurrences, and submit records to appropriate organizations.

Please follow this code and distribute and teach it to others. And for more information, please visit www.aba.org.

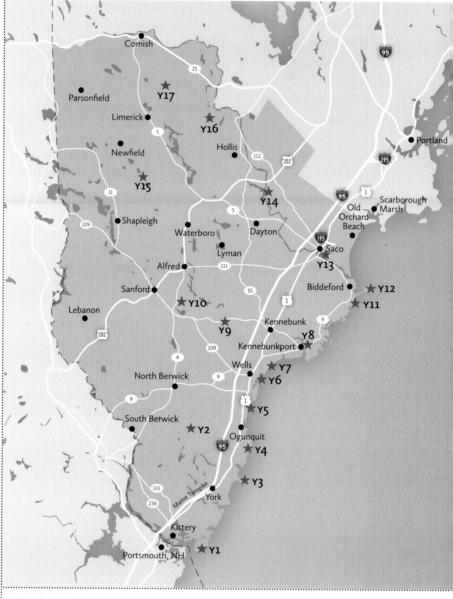

Cornish

Parsonfield

Y17

Limerick

Y16

Newfield

Hollis

25

5

112

202

Portland

Y15

95

1

Scarborough
Marsh

Old
Orchard
Beach

11

Shapleigh

Y14

5

Dayton

109

Waterboro

Lyman

195

Saco

Alfred

111

Y13

Sanford

35

Biddeford

Y12

Lebanon

Y10

1

Y11

202

Y9

9

Kennebunk

Kennebunkport

Y8

4

109

Wells

Y7

North Berwick

9

Y6

9

1

Y5

South Berwick

Y2

Ogunquit

101

95

Y4

236

Maine Turnpike

York

Y3

Kittery

Portsmouth, NH

Y1

YORK COUNTY

1 York County

DEREK LOVITCH

The second-most-populous county in the state stretches from sandy barrier islands and salt marsh to the foothills of the White Mountains, with a wide range of habitats in between. Dense coastal development, including well-known travel destinations such as Wells Beach and Kennebunkport, bring throngs of visitors to the coast each summer. However, some wonderful protected areas also attract a wide array of birds in between.

Biddeford Pool (site Y12) is an exceptional year-round birding destination. Whether it's migrant fallouts, the chance at exceptional vagrants, summer sea watching, large concentrations of wintering waterbirds, or more, Biddeford Pool has something to offer at every season.

During migration, the north-south coastline of York County is less conducive to geographic concentration than the other coastal counties, but those features that do stick out in the ocean, such as the Biddeford Pool peninsula, the Nubble (Y3), and Kittery's Fort Foster (Y1), offer opportunities to witness fallouts, concentrations of migrants after good flights, and to search for rarities. Spring or fall, Fort Foster is a top destination for migrant land birds, with other hot spots including the Wells Reserve at Laudholm (Y7) and Timber Point (Y11). Waterbird migration can be spectacular, while in early spring and late fall the Sanford Lagoons (Y10) become a prime destination.

In summer, breeding birds abound, from Saltmarsh Sparrows and Eastern Willets in the coastal marshes (such as Webhannet Marsh, at site Y6) to up to nineteen species of warblers over the wide range of habitats. In addition to being a good time to catch shorebird migration along the coast, including oversummering migrants, June and July are the time to seek rare or local breeders, such as Piping Plover and Least Terns at Laudholm Farms, and grassland birds at the Kennebunk Plains (Y9), where many of the state's remaining Upland Sandpipers and Grasshopper Sparrows might be found.

As fall progresses, the state's "banana belt" has a more moderated climate, allowing lingering or pioneering birds to persist and concentrate at prime locations, such as Biddeford Pool, Fort Foster, and the Saco "Yacht Club" and Riverwalk (Y13). And in winter, Harlequin Ducks and alcids (e.g., site Y4) captivate us along the coast. —*Derek Lovitch*

SITE Y1 Fort Foster and Seapoint Beach

TOWN Kittery. DeLorme Map 1: C4. **SEASON** All year. **VISITATION** 1–4 hrs. Restrooms open May–September (but see below). Fee at Fort Foster in summer. **HIGHLIGHTS** Migration hot spot; rarities; waterfowl and winter waterbirds.

Fort Foster is under-birded and underappreciated yet has a track record that suggests it should be a major destination for birders in Maine and New Hampshire alike. Four-seasons birding at the southernmost point in Maine (not including limited-access Appledore Island) should attract hordes from both sides of the bridge. An impressive array of rarities, migration "fallouts," and charismatic wintering birds combine to make this one of my favorite places to bird in the entire state—if I lived closer, I'd bird it nearly every day. Mitigated by the surrounding water and featuring various important food sources (unfortunately including an increasing domination by less nutritionally valuable invasive fruiting plants), Fort Foster is a top destination for vagrant-hunters in the later fall "rarity season" in particular.

DIRECTIONS

From I-95 take Exit 2 and head south on Route 236 toward Kittery and into the rotary. Take the third exit onto Route 236 South. Continue for a total of 3.5 miles as 236 ends and becomes Route 103 East, to a soft right onto Chauncey Creek Road. At the four-way intersection make a right onto Pocahontas Road, and just over the bridge bear right to stay on Pocahontas. Follow it to its end at the entrance to **Fort Foster**.

Prior to 10 a.m. May through sometime in October and in other seasons, park in the wide dirt shoulders and walk down the paved entrance road. There's no right or wrong way to bird this park, and especially in migration, certain corners are hot one day and not the next. Therefore, take your time to explore, checking all corners of the park. The oaks along the entrance road can be excellent for migrant warblers, and the brushy trails are perfect for migrant sparrows and what I like to call "scrubby migrants." The freshwater pond is always worth a check and often hosts Black-crowned Night-Herons May–September (and rarely into the winter).

Thoroughly check the shoreline for migrant shorebirds at low tide, and in winter, Purple Sandpipers (any tide, but most often seen at high or incoming). In winter, Great Cormorants line the offshore islets, and one or two young birds occasionally oversummer among the Double-crested Cormorants. Common Eiders are abundant all year, and from mid-fall through early spring impressive numbers of all the regularly occurring sea ducks are expected, along with both loons and Red-necked and Horned Grebes. Snowy Owls occasionally roost on the offshore islets as well, as do Peregrine Falcons.

Breeding birds include plentiful Yellow Warblers, often several pairs of Carolina Wrens and Blue-gray Gnatcatchers, and a good mix of the usual woodland species. Fall migration can be very productive, including noteworthy flights of raptors, especially on a moderate northwest breeze. A combination of habitat and especially geography has produced an impressive array of rarities; expect the unexpected here, especially in the late October and early November rarity season.

But perhaps most important, Fort Foster is one of the premier spring migration destinations in the state. Especially when rain or fog impede migrants heading north (on southerly winds or calm conditions prior to weather events), "fallouts" can occur, affording the birder the opportunity to see as many as twenty species of warblers and southern vagrant "overshoots."

After birding Fort Foster, I usually check nearby **Seapoint Beach** (no restrooms, but there is an outhouse at the Cutt's Island Trail, on the north side of the road after crossing a wide creek). Backtrack to Chauncey Creek Road and make a right. Follow it to the end at the parking area for the town beach. Pay attention to signage; it seems to change nearly annually. Currently, between May 15 and September 15, nonresidents are limited to the first few spaces on the right as you approach the end of the road (just before a fork, with a private road to the left; park here and then walk the last 200 or so yards to the end). Otherwise, proceed to the end of the road and a gravel parking lot. Activity, especially dog walkers, can affect the shorebird numbers here, but especially from August to October you'll want to carefully scan the north end of the beach where copious amounts of seaweed build up. The piles of wrack host numerous "seaweed flies" that also attract late-lingering passerines and the occasional vagrant. White-rumped Sandpipers are regu-

Purple Sandpipers, Seapoint Beach. © Jeannette Lovitch

lar and often linger well into the late fall here; and keep an eye out for the occasional Baird's or Buff-breasted Sandpipers among the masses, especially in September. Walk along the beach (good for "Ipswich" Savannah Sparrow, Snow Bunting (with the occasional Lapland Longspur), and American Pipit in late fall, and the small scrub point can host various migrants. Saltmarsh Sparrows and Willets breed in the marsh; and in winter, Purple Sandpipers and Great Cormorants often spend the high tide along the rocky peninsula at the south end of the beach. This is also a great spot for all the regularly occurring winter waterbirds.

Afterward, you can return to Kittery, perhaps for lunch at Loco Coco's Tacos, or follow Route 103 east into York Harbor, where you can make a right onto Route 1A and continue along for a coastal tour (see Cape Neddick and the Nubble, Y3).

RARITIES

Fort Foster unless otherwise noted. Cave Swallow, November 2005, and at Seapoint Beach, November 2005 and November 2008; Worm-eating Warbler (three records); Western Reef-Heron, August 2006 (Kittery town landing); Western Kingbird, October 2007; Acadian Flycatcher, May 2013; two Connecticut Warblers, September 2013; "Audubon's" Yellow-rumped Warbler, October–November 2013; Yellow-throated Warbler, May 2015.

Mount Agamenticus

TOWNS York and South Berwick. DeLorme Map 1: A4. **SEASON** May–July, September–November. **VISITATION** 1 hr. to all day (for hawk watching). Seasonal restroom facilities. ♿ **HIGHLIGHTS** Fall hawk migration; land-bird migration; typical breeding birds.

"Mount A" rises 691 feet above the coastal plain, with recent clear-cutting of the summit restoring a 180-degree view from the Presidential Mountains of New Hampshire to the city of Boston. Best known as a fall hawk-watching location, Mount A is a good spot for a hike through deciduous-dominated, mature forest with the breeding species expected in the habitat. Depending on how the summit is managed in the future, it could provide improved habitat for migrants, especially sparrows and other scrub-loving species.

DIRECTIONS

From I-95 take Exit 7 and follow the signs for US Route 1. At the light, make a left onto Route 1 North and follow for 3.7 miles to a left onto Mountain Road (opposite the famous Flo's Hot Dogs, where I almost always stop for lunch). In 1.4 miles, after crossing I-95, make a right at the stop sign to remain on Mountain Road. In 2.6 miles you'll find a trailhead on your right to hike up the mountain, and just beyond, a paved road (gate open 7 a.m.–sunset) that winds up to the summit. Check the posted trail maps, or print out your own, and explore the extensive trail system. Wood Thrushes and Scarlet Tanagers, at least twelve species of breeding warblers, Black-billed Cuckoos, and much more are found in these woods, and it is an excellent place for studying your reptiles and amphibians.

At the summit, check the recently clear-cut open areas for breeding Indigo Buntings, Prairie Warblers, and Eastern Towhees, and sparrows in migration. The Ring Trail provides a nice, easy loop to sample the woodland birds. From September through early November scan the skies for migrant raptors. A small cadre of devoted hawk watchers may be found on weekends especially, and some single-day counts have been very impressive. However, since Mount A is just a bump in the coastal plain, it does not concentrate birds very much, and raptors are often very high and far. Moderate north-westerly winds (often 15–25 mph) are usually necessary to produce a good flight. It's definitely hit-or-miss here, and southern Maine is still in search of a prime fall hawk-watching location that has consistently strong flights and

17

good views of migrants. Perhaps the newly reopened views at the summit, combined with a renewed interest in hawk watching and increased observer effort, could prove me wrong, however. And it would be fascinating to see what an entire season of daily coverage could produce.

Visit the website of the Mount Agamenticus Conservation Region, www .agamenticus.org, for trail guides, map, and information about ecology, history, and conservation.

SITE Y3 The Nubble (Cape Neddick)

TOWN York. DeLorme Map 1: A–B5. SEASON All year, but especially October–May. VISITATION 15 min. to half day. Restrooms from Memorial Day through at least Columbus Day at Sohier Park; all year at Long Sands Beach. ♿ HIGHLIGHTS Waterbirds; Harlequin Duck, alcids (including Dovekie), Great Cormorant; Purple Sandpiper in winter; sea watching, migrants.

"The Nubble" is not only one of the most photographed lighthouses in the United States, but also the home of some fine, four-seasons birding. In summer, check the rocks for the occasional Great Cormorant among the masses of Double-crested; this is one of the best spots in southern Maine for oversummering Greats (always immatures). In winter, Harlequin Ducks and Purple Sandpipers are common, "white-winged gulls" (Iceland and Glaucous) are regular, and all the regular wintering waterbirds are usually seen; it's a good spot for all three scoters. On flat-calm days, especially after a good easterly blow, this is one of the best spots to check for alcids on the water near to shore in winter. Razorbills can be common, and carefully check for both Common (very rare) and Thick-billed Murre, and especially Dovekie (the latter two species rare but regular). During migration, anything is possible in the neighborhood, including fallouts and vagrants. All year long, onshore winds can often yield productive sea watching (as long as there is no fog, of course), with shearwaters in the summer and alcids in the winter, and impressive flights of migrant waterbirds in spring and fall.

DIRECTIONS

From I-95 take Exit 7 and follow signs to US Route 1. At the light make a left onto Route 1 North. In 1.2 miles turn right at the light onto Old Post Road.

In 0.9 miles make a left onto Ridge Road. In another 0.5 miles turn right onto Webber Road. At its end make a left on Route 1A, where you can check **Long Sands Beach**. Park now and again, scanning the water and beach for waterbirds, gulls, and shorebirds. Note the restroom on your right.

Make your first right after the end of the beach onto Nubble Road and follow along the edge of the peninsula until you see the entrance for **Sohier Park** on your right. Park here and scan the Nubble and all the surrounding waters. Any scoter, both loons, and occasionally Red-necked Grebe can be found here in summer and are common here in winter. This is also one of the premier sea-watching sites in Maine (and the only one that can be productive from the shelter of a vehicle during inclement weather), so be sure to spend some time scanning the open water.

During migration, especially after periods of southwesterly winds in May and early June, and again after westerly winds in the fall, the neighborhood can be very productive. I usually leave my car at Sohier Park, cross the street, and enter the neighborhood via Cycad Street. Depending on time and birdiness, I can spend hours walking through the neighborhood, making various-length loops (a street map or a map app on a smartphone is helpful) to check some of my favorite thickets and yards (but please, do not trespass; remain on the road edge). I've enjoyed impressive fallouts on several occasions, and a wide variety of rarities can be expected, especially the rare-but-regular stuff like Yellow-breasted Chat, Orange-crowned Warbler, Lark and Clay-colored Sparrows, etc.

After at least sampling the neighborhood by foot or by car, continue rounding the cape on Nubble Road, until it ends back at Route 1A. Make a right and pull into the large parking lot on the right for **Short Sands Beach**. This is another spot to check for all sorts of waterbirds, especially gulls, and be sure to scan the rocky edges on both sides of the cove for more Harlequin Ducks in winter.

Many birders will make a brief stop here during their visits to the area, but to make a nice half to full day, consider heading here after birding Fort Foster (site Y1), or head north. In winter, this is your starting point for the Winter Alcid and Harlequin Duck Tour (Y4).

RARITIES

Sage Thrasher, November–December 2001 (only state record)

SITE Y4 Winter Alcid and Harlequin Duck Tour

TOWNS York and Ogunquit. DeLorme Map 1: A–B5. **SEASON** November, December–March, April. **VISITATION** 3 hrs. to half day. Portable toilets at Short Sands Beach and Perkins Cove. ♿ **HIGHLIGHTS** Harlequin Duck, King Eider, alcids, Purple Sandpiper, Great Cormorant, wintering waterbirds.

A thorough check of this stretch of rocky coastline—one of my favorite birding routes in midwinter—can often yield fifty or more Harlequin Ducks and hundreds of Purple Sandpipers. Great Cormorants are sprinkled throughout; all regularly occurring waterbirds can usually be seen (including particularly large numbers of all three scoters); and this is the place to check for alcids, especially after winter storms.

DIRECTIONS

Begin the tour at **Sohier Park** at the Nubble, as described in site Y3. After checking **Short Sands Beach**, continue north on Route 1A, squiggling through the center of York Beach, where the road once again becomes two-way. Make a right, then a left, and in 0.6 miles bear right onto **Shore Road**. You'll soon cross the Cape Neddick River, which is worth a scan at all seasons. Continue north on Shore Road, carefully stopping (shoulder space is woefully limited) where you see water. A few groups of Harlequin Ducks and Purple Sandpipers can often be spotted here, and check the large flocks of Common Eider carefully for a rare King. When you reach the freshwater ponds on your left, opposite Phillips Cove, check carefully if there is open water for lingering dabblers and scan the ocean for Harlequin Ducks and eiders.

A mile past the end of the pond, turn right into the driveway for the **Cliff House** at Bald Head. Although the property is private, the owners have been gracious in allowing birders access for decades. Please respect the property to continue this tradition. Follow the entrance road around the rotary in front of the main entrance and make a right to head down to the water. Park in the designated spots and ask at the front desk what areas you are able to access after current construction.

This is another one of the best sea-watching locations in Maine and one of the few where you can bird from the car in inclement weather. However, it is best to get out and scan the entire shoreline for Harlequin Ducks and Purple Sandpipers. A flock of twenty to forty "Harlies" is not uncommon here, and numbers can swell to sixty or more birds in early spring. Great Cormorants are often sitting on rocks, especially just to the north, and all wintering waterbirds are regular here, including both loons and grebes. Pacific Loon is reported annually here, although most reports unfortunately go undocumented. It's also one of the most regular spots to host a King Eider.

This is one of the best spots in the state for Razorbill and Black-legged Kittiwake; look for both in any conditions, although strong westerly winds are usually not fruitful. On easterly winds, especially after a big nor'easter storm, this is a great spot to sea watch for the rarer alcids, including both murres and especially Dovekie. Spend as much time as temperatures allow here.

After leaving the Cliff House, turn right onto Shore Road and continue for another 1.7 miles. Bear right to turn onto Perkins Cove Road and continue to its end at the parking lot (fee in summer) for **Perkins Cove**. Check the cove on your right for any odd ducks with the local Mallards. There are year-round public restroom facilities (portable toilets in winter) at the end of the shopping area ahead of you (follow signs).

Back at the parking area, carefully scan the water to the north and walk toward the restaurant on the western end of the lot to pick up **Marginal Way**. This pedestrian walkway (it can be very icy in winter) is worth walking in its entirety all year but is most popular for birding in winter when Harlequin Ducks, Purple Sandpipers, and white-winged gulls are regular, and look for alcids (especially Dovekies after strong storms). Large rafts of scoters are common, especially Black Scoters, which are rather local in midwinter. On a calm day, listen for their plaintive but whiny whistle, which is commonly heard from this species throughout the winter. Pay attention to the thickets and yards along the way, as they can host overwintering "half hardies," and sometimes even a rarity. I often walk to the end of Marginal Way and then return to the car by walking through the neighborhood (take a left onto Stearns Road, then a left onto Cherry Road; turn right at its end at Frazier Pasture, where you'll see the entrance to Marginal Way on your left), which can produce passerines, including Carolina Wren, and, in finch years, both crossbills.

Although this tour concludes here, you can easily make a full day by grabbing a lunch in town (I am particularly fond of the grilled veggie sandwich or treats at the Village Food Market, or I head back south on Route 1 to the iconic Flo's Hot Dogs or the Jamaican Jerk Center) and then continuing north to **Moody-Ogunquit Beach**, as described in site Y5.

Cave Swallow, November 2005 (first state record, Marginal Way); Gray Kingbird, October 2010 (only state record)

SITE Y5 Moody-Ogunquit Beach and Beach Plum Farm

TOWNS Ogunquit and Wells. DeLorme Map 2: E5, and Map 3: E1.
SEASON All year, but especially **September–December**. **VISITATION** 1 hr.
to half day. Various restroom facilities in the warmer months; gas stations
and the like in the winter. **HIGHLIGHTS** Diverse habitats, waterbirds, rarities.

Salt marsh, barrier island, scrubby uplands, and wooded neighborhoods
combine to make this small stretch of coastline productive to birding at any
season. Favorable microclimates and patchy habitat concentrate lingering
"half hardies" and vagrants in late fall into early winter. More thorough coverage would likely yield even more rarities. This tour nicely combines with
the Winter Alcid and Harlequin Duck Tour (site Y4) by continuing north on
Route 1 from the center of Ogunquit (after departing Marginal Way/Perkins
Cove) or by beginning here and continuing north and picking up the Wells
Marshes and Beaches Tour (site Y6).

DIRECTIONS

From I-95 take Exit 19 and make a left at the light after the tollbooths, onto
Route 9/109. Make a right at the next light onto Chapel Road and follow it
to its end at US Route 1. Make a right onto Route 1 South and continue for
3.4 miles to **Beach Plum Farm** on the left. Enter the parking lot and walk
toward the community garden.

Bird the edges of the property, especially the lower fields accessed by a
trail on your right just beyond the buildings, compost heap, and community
garden. Sparrow migration can be exciting here in late September and October, with various seasonal rarities lingering into December. Look for late
warblers, Dickcissels, Blue Grosbeaks, and other rare-but-regular excitement.
Although spring migration is usually less eventful here, it's definitely worth
a check. Midsummer is usually less interesting, and in deep winter, once
there's a lot of snow on the ground covering food sources, you might want
to skip the walk, but the adjacent neighborhood often hosts lingering "half
hardies," especially Pine Warbler.

Next, head north on US Route 1 for 0.8 miles to a light and turn right onto Bourne Avenue. As you enter **Moody Marsh**, check for shorebirds and waterfowl in season. Concentrations of dabbling ducks and Canada Geese in late fall and early spring can be impressive. At the end, make a right and continue to the end of the road at the large public parking lot. Check the marsh, the pitch pine forest (it can have crossbills in irruption winters), and walk the trail past the sewage plant to bird the bayberry-covered dunes. This is one of the few spots in the state that still hosts Yellow-rumped Warblers in winter, and the marsh margins here are good for Horned Lark in spring and fall. I usually walk as far as the footbridge, cross over the dunes, and return to the parking area via **Moody/Ogunquit Beach**, looking for Snowy Owls and Sanderlings in winter, "Ipswich" Savannah Sparrows and Snow Buntings in late fall, and scanning the often-productive waters all year for waterbirds.

Returning to your car, travel north on Ocean, past Bourne Road, to the next stop sign at Furbish Road. Make a left and reenter the marsh. A dirt parking area on your right makes a good place to stop to scan the marsh from the road. When done, continue back to US Route 1 and make a right to head north. In half a mile make a right onto Eldridge Road. On the right in 0.4 miles is the **Wells water treatment plant**. Enter the plant, make a right, and park in the designated spaces in the front of the building. Slowly walk the periphery of the property, especially in fall rarity season. Highlights for me here included a Western Tanager and Northern Shrike in the same tree (December 2007) and a hardy Clay-colored Sparrow, both on the York County Christmas Bird Count. Sightings like this strongly suggest this place should be checked more often.

When you're done, return to Eldridge Road, make a right, and continue to its end at Webhannet Drive. Make a right, then a left at the next stop sign. Curve around to **Moody Point**, which can be good for sea watching at all seasons (I usually park on a nearby side street). From mid-fall through mid-spring, this is a good spot for Red-throated Loon and Red-necked Grebe, and Purple Sandpiper in winter. After—or instead of—sea watching, return to the intersection of Webhannet and Eldridge. Make a left to return to Route 1, or stay straight to its end at Mile Road. By making a right, you can pick up the Wells Beach tour (site Y6).

Throughout the tour, check thickets, feeders, and other promising patches for migrants and rarities, especially after the weather first turns truly cold for the season in late fall or early winter.

Western Tanager, December 2007, Clay-colored Sparrow and Brown Thrasher, December 2013, at the sewage treatment plant—all first CBC records; Lark Sparrow (several records from Beach Plum Farm); Barnacle Goose, March 2012 (Moody Marsh)

SITE Y6 Wells Marshes and Beaches

TOWN Wells. DeLorme Map 3: E1. SEASON All year. VISITATION 2 hrs. to half day. Restroom facilities at various locations in warmer months, plenty of gas stations, etc., for the winter months. ⚓ HIGHLIGHTS Purple Sandpipers, Snowy Owls, and waterbirds in winter; shorebirds (May and July–September); Least Terns (June–July); Saltmarsh and Nelson's Sparrows (late May–September); sea watching all year; Fish Crow (summer).

A rich array of important coastal habitats can be found in the midst of some of the densest shoreline development in the state. While most of the salt marsh and shoreline edge is protected as part of Rachel Carson National Wildlife Refuge, wall-to-wall development covers the barrier island and uplands. Wide sand beaches, extensive mud-sand flats, salt pannes (depressions within salt or brackish marshes that retain water independently of tides), and a sheltered harbor can combine to produce a wide array of waterbirds and shorebirds at all seasons.

DIRECTIONS

Follow the directions in site Y5 above to reach US Route 1. Make a right onto Route 1 South, and in 0.3 miles make a left onto Mile Road (you'll probably want to stop for breakfast or doughnuts for later at Congdon's Donuts). If pull-off opportunities and traffic allow, check the **Webhannet Marsh** (both Saltmarsh and a few Nelson's Sparrows breed; shorebirds; wading birds) on either side of the causeway (or park in the public lot at the east end of the marsh for a safe place to view) then continue into **Wells Beach**. Stay straight into a public parking lot at the end of the road and begin your searching of the water here. Check the beach between here and the jetty (see below) for Sanderlings (except in June and rare in July) and other shorebirds, and in winter check the offshore rocks at low tide for Purple Sandpipers. Snowy Owls are sometimes seen roosting here, as well as on rooftops (especially at high tide) along the road as you drive north to the jetty. Check the ocean from October to April for all three scoters, Common and Red-throated Loons, Horned and Red-necked Grebes, and so on.

Leaving the parking lot, make a right onto Atlantic Avenue and follow it to its end at another public parking lot (fee in summer). Check **Wells Harbor** and walk the sandy path to the beach and the jetty. Purple Sandpipers frequent the jetty in winter, and the harbor and river mouth can be full of Common Eiders and other waterfowl. Check flocks of Bonaparte's Gulls for Little and Black-headed Gulls (both very rare; spring and fall), and sea watching from the end of the jetty can be very rewarding, especially in easterly winds. One of my all-time birding highlights in Maine was an adult Long-tailed Jaeger that flew right over me at the end of the jetty and out into the harbor one lovely spring morning.

When you've had your fill, backtrack to US Route 1 and head north. In 1.3 miles make a right onto **Harbor Road** (at the fire station, immediately past the light at Route 9/109). As you reenter the marsh, check the salt pannes on your right for shorebirds—especially at high tide. Then proceed down the road to **Community Park** on your right. Park at the far end of the sandy loop road, past the gazebo, and take the diffuse sandy trail into the woods (check for migrants). Follow the trail to the marsh (Nelson's and Saltmarsh Sparrows May to September; most easily observed on flood tides), and around the bayberry thickets (one of the few places in the state that sometimes host Yellow-rumped Warblers all winter) to the river. At low tide, scan the sand/mudflats for shorebirds, and check the docks, channel, markers, etc. (looking toward the end of Wells Beach as described above) for terns in summer and gulls in winter. This is a good spot for Least Terns from late May to July, and Forster's Tern is rare but regular, especially in August.

I usually continue along the shore to the dock, scan the harbor, and then take the paved road back to Community Park for a nice, short loop. After retrieving your car, take Harbor Road back up to Route 1. You can make a right onto Route 1 North and continue on to the Wells Reserve (site Y7) or beyond. Heading south on Route 1, check for Fish Crows (end of March to September) around the fast-food restaurants, and especially the Hannaford parking lot, within the next half mile or so, from mid-to-late March through September.

RARITIES

Long-tailed Jaeger, May 2004 (Wells Beach); King Eider, winter 2005 (harbor); Wood Thrush, January 2007 (Community Park—Maine's only winter record); American Avocet, November 2005 (Webhannet Marsh); Sabine's Gull, October 2011 (harbor); Gyrfalcon, January–March 2015

SITE Y7 Wells Reserve at Laudholm

TOWN Wells. DeLorme Map 3: D1. **SEASON** April, **May–November,** December. **VISITATION** 2–4 hrs. Bathrooms. Entrance fee Memorial Day through Columbus Day. Open 7 a.m.–sunset. & **HIGHLIGHTS** Migrants; diversity of breeding birds from Bobolinks and Brown Thrashers to a variety of warblers and Piping Plovers and Least Terns; migrant shorebirds; late lingering migrants.

This National Estuarine Research Reserve, with sixteen hundred acres of a wide variety of habitats, is worth a visit at any time of year. Although the proliferation of invasive plants has taken a toll on the quality of the habitat—especially its suitability for breeding birds—a diversity of species can still be encountered on most visits. The reserve has an excellent track record of producing rarities, and the total of 277 species recorded on the property is a testament to the quality of the birding here.

DIRECTIONS

From I-95 take Exit 19. At the light after the tollbooth make a left onto Route 9/109 East into Wells. At the end of the road turn left onto US Route 1 North. In 1.5 miles, at the second blinking light, turn right onto Laudholm Farm Road. In 0.4 miles turn left onto Skinner Mill Road, and then turn right into the reserve entrance.

At the kiosk, grab a trail map to the over 7 miles of trails. Various loops can be taken, depending on your time and interest. The Knight Trail travels across hayfields where Bobolinks breed, while the Cart Path passes through shrub-scrub habitat that can be particularly productive in fall migration, especially as the season progresses. The Laird Norton Trail through damp red-maple woods can be good in migration, especially when the maple is budding in the spring, and a couple of marsh overlooks should be checked for roosting wading birds and shorebirds.

Follow the Barrier Beach Trail, checking the salt marsh as you go. Once at the beach, head north. Shorebirding can be productive here, especially at the mouth of the Little River. Piping Plovers and one of the largest colonies of Least Terns in the state breeds here, safely observed from the south shore of the river (most of the colony is on the north side, but obey all signage and fencing). Mud/sand flats at low tide and dry beach (often on the north side of the Little River) at high tide often attract roosting terns and gulls, and the area should be checked carefully for rarities. Mid-tide is usually best for migrant shorebirds. Lesser Black-backed Gull is fairly regular in April and September–October (occasionally later), and southern strays such as Royal Tern and Black Skimmer have been found in July and August. Wrack lines in September can produce Baird's and Buff-breasted Sandpiper. If Bonaparte's Gulls are present, check them carefully for the rare Little or Black-headed Gull.

Meanwhile, keep an eye out overhead in September and October. Northwesterly winds can produce decent hawk flights here, especially of more coastal migrants such as falcons and immature accipiters. In winter, Northern Shrike is occasional, Snowy Owl is rare, and the waters can be teeming with sea ducks, including both loons and all three scoters. Sanderlings are also sometimes seen here, a surprisingly local bird in the winter along the Maine coast.

RARITIES

White-winged Tern, June 2003 (only state record); Cerulean Warbler, August 2004; Scissor-tailed Flycatcher, June 2014

The Wells Reserve offers a variety of tours, programs, and educational activities, along with a gift shop. Visit its website, www.wellsreserve.org, for more information and to download a trail map.

SITE Y8 First Chance Whale Watch

TOWN Kennebunkport. DeLorme Map 3: D2. SEASON June–September.
VISITATION See website for current schedule, reservations, and parking details. HIGHLIGHTS Pelagic birds including Great, Sooty, and Cory's Shearwater, Wilson's Storm-Petrel, etc.; rarely Leach's Storm-Petrel and Manx Shearwater; Northern Gannet; whales, other sea life.

Leaving from the southernmost departure point for whale watching in Maine, this trip is usually more productive on a regular basis, for both birds and whales, than departures from Portland or Boothbay Harbor. Because of the speed of the boat and the departure location, the boat can either head northeast to the small ledges off Portland and points east, or east and southeast to the usually more-productive Jeffrey's Ledge. Few birders have reported from the boat over the years, so records proving the trips' potential are still rather scant.

Simply because more "data" exist for the Odyssey Whalewatch from Portland in Cumberland County (site C10), likely species and their timing are covered for that site instead of here. However, I think the Kennebunkport-based trip has more potential, because of its ability to cover more ocean and having more productive areas to choose from, based on where whales have been seen.

DIRECTIONS

From I-95 take Exit 25. Follow the signage for Route 35 South toward Kennebunk. In just over a mile, make a left onto US Route 1 North and an immediate right to remain on Route 35 South/9A East. In 3.4 miles make a left onto Route 9, and before the bridge pull into the parking lot for the First Chance Whale Watch.

For more information and reservations (recommended), visit the website for First Chance Whale Watch at www.firstchancewhalewatch.com.

SITE Y9 Kennebunk Plains

TOWN Kennebunk. DeLorme Map 3: D5.   **SEASON** April, **May–July**, August–September.   **VISITATION** 1 hr. to half day. Portable toilet at adjacent Nedeau Park.   **HIGHLIGHTS** Grassland specialties Upland Sandpiper, Grasshopper Sparrow, Vesper Sparrow, etc.; plus Eastern Whip-poor-will. A territorial Clay-colored Sparrow or two is nearly annual; breeding has been recorded.

This is one of the premier birding destinations in the state. A number of species occur in greater densities here (including state-listed endangered Upland Sandpiper and Grasshopper Sparrow) than anywhere else. They are also relatively easy to enjoy, especially when you arrive early. Each year, the hot spots for each species vary based on current conditions of the habitat, particularly how recently controlled burns were conducted. Thorough birding here will usually yield all desired species, but in some years nothing more than a "quick hit" is required for most of the targets, depending on where they are most active. In midsummer, listen from the roads and slowly drive

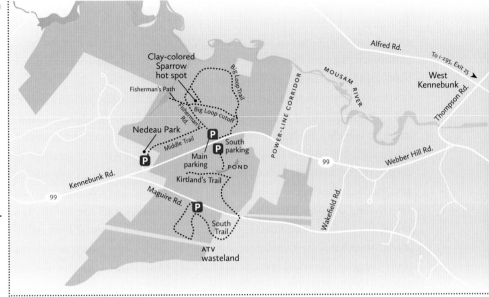

KENNEBUNK PLAINS

around for Eastern Whip-poor-wills and Common Nighthawks, while in spring, listen at edges for American Woodcock.

DIRECTIONS

From I-95 take Exit 25. From the north, make a left at the end of the off-ramp access road, behind the rest area (best bathroom option) onto Alewive Road (Route 35 South). At the light make a right onto Alfred Road. From the south, make a right at the end of the off-ramp onto Route 35 (Fletcher Street). Cross over I-95 and continue straight through the light onto Alfred Road.

Follow Alfred Road for 0.8 miles to a four-way stop and make a left onto Mill Street. In 0.6 miles bear right, then another right at the stop sign to turn onto Route 99 West (Webber Hill Road). In 2.1 miles you'll see the parking area on the right. From this main parking area we begin our tour. I have made up names for each trail and some of the prime patches, but keep in mind trails—although obvious and well defined—are not named or signed here.

Upland Sandpipers seem to prefer the most recently burned areas, with Grasshopper Sparrows soon taking up residence. As patches become shrubbier and studded with small trees, Eastern Towhees and Brown Thrasher become more common, and this is where to look for Clay-colored Sparrow and, rarely, Blue-winged Warbler. Vesper and Field Sparrows like the partially shrubby stuff in between, while Prairie Warblers are abundant at the edges, along with plentiful Pine Warblers, Chipping Sparrows, Chestnut-sided Warblers, and scattered Indigo Buntings.

Using the map above as an important reference, I usually begin by walking the Fisherman's Road north through the center of the plains. While this is open to vehicles, birding is best without a car and without the chance to crush any baby Upland Sandpipers or snakes, both of which sometimes get caught in the deep tire ruts in the roads here. For a quick spin, I follow this road to the Fisherman's Path, past the "Clay-colored Sparrow hot spot," and take the Big Loop back to the car. Otherwise, I usually walk the Middle Trail to the far tree line and cross into Lloyd G. Nedeau Memorial Park (which sometimes has Clay-colored Sparrow and Upland Sandpiper as well and more shrub specialists at its edges) before returning to the Fisherman's Road. I then take the Fisherman's Path to the pond (Alder Flycatcher; Black-billed Cuckoo) before continuing on the Big Loop.

After returning to my car, I walk or drive across the street to the South Lot and walk straight back to the pond (Alder Flycatcher). Next, I drive to Maguire Road, which traverses the southern chunk of the plains. Here roadside birding is safer and more fruitful, but as usual, I prefer to walk it. First, I walk the Kirtland's Trail, so dubbed since it was the young pitch pines near the back side (the opposite shore of the pond we visited from the South Lot) that hosted a shocking Kirtland's Warbler one spring. Then I check the power-line corridor along the eastern boundary of the plains (Blue-winged Warbler on occasion, although recent widening and de-vegetating has diminished the frequency of occurrences), before crossing Maguire Road and following the power-line corridor access road to the southern tree line. There I follow the South Trail along the boundaries and back to the car—a long but often rewarding walk.

The plains are also one of the last reliable spots in the state for the declining Eastern Whip-poor-will. To hear and perhaps even see these nocturnal birds, slowly drive the roads—especially Maguire Road—after dusk and before dawn. When the birds are singing in June, I often find them along the roadside, singing from the ground. Look for their orange eye-shine in your headlights or flashlight. Great Horned Owl is often heard as well, and listen for booming Common Nighthawks—a few might still breed around here.

Grasshopper Sparrow, Kennebunk Plains. © Luke Seitz

The breeding residents of note begin to arrive in late April but reach their peak in the latter half of May through June. Things quiet down quicker in the day in July, but breeding activity is in full swing. Birds—mostly in molt—are shier and harder to find in August, but activity picks up again in September, and October sparrow migration is uncharted here. Winter is often barren, but Northern Shrike and Snow Bunting are occasional, and it's worth looking for Rough-legged Hawk.

After a morning at the "Kenny Plains," I usually visit the Sanford Sewerage Treatment Facility by heading west on Route 99 to its end at Route 109. Make a right and follow to a light in 1.1 miles. Take a right onto Jagger Mill Road, and at its end make a right onto Route 4 North. In 0.3 miles turn right at the blinking light onto Gavel Road and pick up the directions for site Y10.

RARITIES

Kirtland's Warbler, June 2008 (yes, you read that correctly, only state record)

SITE Y10 Sanford Lagoons

TOWN Sanford. DeLorme Map 2: C4. **SEASON** March, **April**, May–September, **October–December**. **VISITATION** 45 min. to 2 hrs. No restroom facilities. Open Monday–Friday, 6 a.m.–4:30 p.m., and Saturday and Sunday, 7:00–8:30 a.m. ♿ **HIGHLIGHTS** Migrant waterfowl and shorebirds, breeding rails, swallow aggregations (July–August), Louisiana Waterthrush (April–July).

One of the few "open water" wastewater treatment plants in Maine, the Sanford Sewerage Treatment Facility has a great tradition of welcoming birders. In fact, despite being mostly closed on the weekends, the facility has opened special "birding hours" for those who can't make it out during the work week! A sincere thanks to Andre Brousseau and the staff of the facility for being so welcoming to birders. Andy Aldrich deserves credit for his work at improving birding opportunities here and keeping people informed of sightings.

Primary settling now occurs indoors, and water levels are no longer manipulated in the holding ponds, so shorebird habitat is limited. However, an expanding cattail marsh holds breeding Sora and Virginia Rail, and waterbird migration can be outstanding. Hunting is not permitted, making the ponds a refuge during fall waterfowl season. From the onset of fall through freeze-up, concentrations of a variety of ducks can be impressive here, and the facility has become known for its rarities and rare breeding (or at least attempted breeding) records. Over two hundred species have been recorded here.

DIRECTIONS

From I-95 take Exit 32. At the light after the tollbooth make a right onto Route 111 West (Alfred Road). Follow for 11.4 miles and make a left onto Route 4 South. Follow it for 3.7 miles to the blinking light and make a left onto Gavel Road.

Follow Gavel Road past the entrance gate (if you get there before the gate opens, it is worth birding the edge of the road for passerines). Pass through the next gate and take a soft left/stay straight toward the front of the building. Park in the designated spaces in front of the building (to the right of the entrance) or, if those are full, around the left side of the building. *You must sign in.* Enter the double doors and note the visiting station at the window on your right. Sign in, and if it is your first visit, sign the waiver form as well. Also note the sightings book for recent observations, and when you return to sign out, please add your own observations.

After signing in, walk clockwise around the building and approach the settling ponds through the open gate. For a quicker check, take the inner loop around the central pond. To be more thorough, take the outer loop all the way around the edge of the property. Louisiana Waterthrush and Blue-gray Gnatcatcher breed along the edge of the Mousam River on the other side of the fence. The edge can also be very good in migration for the expected warblers and other visitors.

Large numbers of Red-winged Blackbird breed in the cattails, and probably so do Virginia Rail and Sora. Breeding Mallards, American Black Ducks, and Canada Geese are joined by impressive numbers of Wood Duck broods in the summer into fall. Spotted Sandpipers and Killdeer breed, and other shorebirds will drop in based on water levels. Common Gallinule has bred, and the ponds hosted the state's southernmost attempted breeding record of Ruddy Duck. Waterfowl migration includes good numbers of Green-winged Teal and Ring-necked Ducks, and almost anything ducky is possible. By mid-to-late July into August, clouds of swallows form, dominated by Tree, but also including impressive numbers of Barn, Bank, and Cliff, with fewer Northern Rough-winged. Throughout the year—except when the ponds are frozen solid—anything is possible here, and daily coverage would likely result in an even more impressive list of rarities.

RARITIES

Eared Grebe, May–September 2009; Purple Gallinule, June 2009; Black-bellied Whistling-Duck, June 2010 (first state record); Red Phalarope, May 2011; Mississippi Kite, June 2015

A bird list for the site can be found on York County Audubon's website at www.yorkcountyaudubon.org/birds-birding/york-county-birding-trail /sanford-sewer-ponds.

SITE Y11 Timber Point and Fortunes Rocks Beach

TOWN Biddeford. DeLorme Map 3: C–D3.   SEASON All year, but especially May and October–December.   VISITATION 1–3 hrs. Portable toilets at Fortunes Rocks Beach in warmer months. Partially & HIGHLIGHTS Migrant passerines and rarities, shorebirds, migrant waterfowl.

Acquired by Rachel Carson National Wildlife Refuge only in 2011, the Timber Point Trail is rapidly becoming a local hot spot for spring and fall migration. But get there early, as it doesn't seem to "hold" migrants as often as other nearby migrant traps. A quick check here before continuing on to Biddeford Pool is a good way to start the birding day. Meanwhile, the ponds at Fortunes Rocks Beach have been known for a long time as a good spot for waterfowl in season but are probably worth a check now and again outside traditional duck times.

DIRECTIONS

Follow the directions to Biddeford Pool (site Y12), but after turning left onto Route 9 East from West Street, make a right in 0.3 miles onto Granite Point Road. In 0.6 miles there's a pull-off on the right where you can scan the salt pannes, especially for shorebirds in summer and fall. To extend your visit, you can walk all the way to the point from here, checking woodlands and thickets, marsh and beach, along the way. Otherwise, drive the 0.8 miles to the parking area on your right, just before the paved road ends. Walk the dirt road and bird the scrub and marsh edges. The wrack line along the beach can be very good for "lingering" migrants in late fall. Check the overlooks of the Little River marsh, and watch for mixed-species foraging flocks in the woods. Exiting the woods, you'll find some fields that are good for sparrows, and migrants along the edge.

Scan Goose Rocks Beach (a scope is helpful) for shorebirds, including breeding Piping Plovers, and check the water and channel for the expected waterbird species. At low tide, you can make the short walk to Timber Island, but be careful not to get caught out there by the rising tide. A tide clock is posted near the end of the trail for you to consult, but having your own tide chart is always recommended. If you do cross to Timber Island, check the woods for migrants, and sea watching from the southern end of the island can be rewarding. Wintering and migrant flocks of all three scoters can be impressive here, and (especially late-) summertime sea watching can produce many of the expected nearshore seabirds such as Northern Gannets, Wilson's Storm-Petrel, and Great and Sooty Shearwaters.

After returning to your car, drive back up Granite Point Road and make a right onto Route 9. Take your first right onto Fortunes Rocks Road and follow it to the water. A series of ponds on the west side of the road, paralleling the shoreline, deserve to be checked from ice-out in spring through early May, and in fall until freeze-up. Scan from the roadside, but at the second pond (Etherington), park in the designated spaces and also check the beach for shorebirds in migration and waterbirds in winter. A couple of Piping Plovers usually nest along the beach to the northeast of here as well.

Continuing northeast along Fortunes Rocks Road, check Lord's Pond, and pishing at some of the more promising thickets in late fall and early winter can produce a surprise now and again. With salt marsh once again on your left, you'll rejoin Route 208. Making a left will take you on Bridge Street and back out to Route 9. Making a right onto Mile Stretch will allow you to pick up the Biddeford Pool tour, site Y12.

RARITIES

Trumpeter Swan, April 2011 (Fortunes Rocks Beach ponds, unknown provenance); Prothonotary Warbler, August 2014 and 2015 (Timber Point Trail)

SITE Y12 Biddeford Pool

TOWN Biddeford. DeLorme Map 3: C3. **SEASON** All year. **VISITATION** 2 hrs. to all day. Portable toilet most of year only at Biddeford Pool Beach. ♿ **HIGHLIGHTS** Migrants of all sorts, especially shorebirds and waterbirds; wintering waterbirds; Snowy Owl; vagrants; Fish Crow (summer).

One of the premier birding destinations in all of New England, Biddeford Pool offers often-exceptional birding all year long. A narrow peninsula sticking out perpendicular to the rest of the coast would be prime enough geography to attract a wide range of species. Add to that a surprising array of habitats in a small area, including a tidal lagoon, beaches, rocky outcroppings, salt marsh, and well-vegetated neighborhoods, and you have a recipe for a great birding destination. All sites are easily accessible, affording visiting birders the chance to hit a few hot spots quickly, or immerse themselves in a full-day exhaustive search of all nooks and crannies.

Most birders refer to this entire area as Biddeford Pool. However, most maps will show you that only the neighborhood at the eastern end of the southern peninsula is "Biddeford Pool," while the shallow lagoon (bordered on the north by the Hill's Beach peninsula) is usually labeled simply as "the Pool."

I usually begin my visit based on what I am looking for at a given season. If I am beginning with passerines or sea watching, I will begin at East Point. If I am in the midst of shorebird season(s), I will begin at the Pool or one of the beaches, depending on the tide. You'll want to start your visit at the proper place at the proper time to maximize your birding, especially when it comes to shorebirds. For example, I often start at Hill's Beach at dead low, moving on to the Pool for the mid-tide, then over to Biddeford Pool Beach,

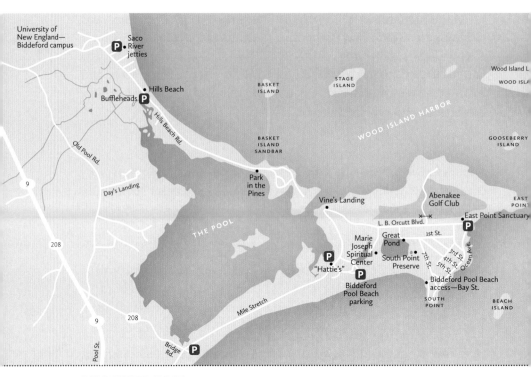

BIDDEFORD POOL

followed by walking Ocean Avenue at high tide for roosting shorebirds (and vice versa if you start at the high tide).

Here I will describe a "generic" visit, based on my usual routine outside of when I am focusing on shorebirds. Especially in summer, I prefer to park once and walk for up to several hours, thoroughly checking every nook and cranny. Parking is limited here, so I find it easier just to hoof it. Your interest, time, and energy will vary, so plan accordingly. Regardless of how you tackle the area, we'll begin at East Point at high tide, and/or as close to dawn as possible.

DIRECTIONS

Maine Audubon's **East Point Sanctuary** encompasses the easternmost point of the larger, southern peninsula, and this is where I like to start my birding visit. To reach it from I-95 (the Maine Turnpike) take Exit 32 for Biddeford. After the toll plaza, make a left at the traffic light onto Route 111 East. Get into the right lane to stay straight at the fourth light onto West Street. Keep an eye out for Fish Crows that often feed around the dumpsters of the fast-food joints here from late March through September.

In 4.5 miles you'll see fields on the left. These are worth checking for waterfowl in early spring and late fall. At the end of the road make a left onto Route 9 East. In 1.7 miles make a right onto Water Tower Way and then an immediate right onto Route 208 South (Bridge Road). At its end, make a left onto Mile Stretch. In winter, keep an eye out for Snowy Owls on rooftops and near dunes along this road. Continue on the main, yellow centerline-striped road for several curves, as the road becomes L. B. Orcutt Boulevard. East Point Sanctuary is on the left, just before the end of the road at the shoreline. I usually park on the right, in the wide, dirt shoulder, and leave my car here for the duration of my visit.

To check the sanctuary, enter the trail on the north side of the road and follow it as it enters the woods adjacent to the golf course (scan for shorebirds, especially in or after rain, and check for geese in fall and early winter). Once you reach the scrub, bird it thoroughly: all sorts of passerines can be seen here in migration, especially at dawn following a "morning flight" of birds returning to land and/or reorienting after an overnight flight; Yellow Warblers are common breeders. The mowed field near the point can harbor Snow Buntings in late fall and early spring. Check the shoreline for Purple Sandpipers in winter, when Great Cormorants will be seen offshore and roosting on nearby rocky islets.

The tip of the point is best for sea watching—Black Guillemots are common all year, but this is a great spot to scan for Razorbills and other alcids, along with Black-legged Kittiwake from October through April, and for seabirds in summer, especially with an easterly wind. There's not much shelter in a gale, but if you can find a place to tuck yourself in along the bank of the shoreline, the sea watching can be phenomenal. Meanwhile, we're beginning to learn that in summer, late afternoon/early evenings can produce nearshore Manx Shearwaters here—perhaps suggestive of prospecting nesters.

In winter, Common and Red-throated Loons and Horned and Red-necked Grebes are joined by all three scoters; and often-impressive numbers of other sea ducks, especially Common Eider (search carefully for the rare King), and Brant, are often seen in the area in March and April. From the north side of the point, scan Wood Island in late fall through early spring for Snowy Owl (often sitting on the lighthouse building) and Rough-legged Hawk. Even in non-irruption years, this is one of the most reliable places in the southern half of the state for either of these species. Harlequin Ducks are rarely seen here, but one actually oversummered in 2006. In summer, a colony of Double-crested Cormorants fights for space along with hundreds of pairs of Herring and Great Black-backed Gulls on Wood Island and other nearby islets, especially Gooseberry Island in the middle of the channel.

After having your fill at East Point, return to your car or begin walking south along **Ocean Avenue**, following the shoreline. Beach Island, which is exposed at all but the highest tides, is another good spot to check for Snowy Owls, Purple Sandpipers, and almost always Great Cormorants in winter. Meanwhile, the nearshore rocks can host feeding Purples, and this is one of only two spots in the state that has Ruddy Turnstones (usually just a handful) in the winter. During spring (mostly late May through early June), but especially "fall" shorebird migration (mid-July through September), shorebirds will often roost on exposed rocks along Ocean Avenue at high tide. Avoid disturbing them (many of these birds had enough trouble with people and dogs on the beach while feeding), but scan the flocks carefully.

I prefer to stay on foot the whole time, rounding the corner, scanning the waters to the south (particularly good for Red-necked Grebe and Red-throated Loon in winter), even in summer as a few scoters (usually White-winged) or other "winter" waterbirds are often found lingering. Walk the road until you reach the beach access path down through the rocks at the corner of Bay Street.

As the tide falls, birds leave their roosts and begin to arrive on this stretch of sand, usually referred to as **Biddeford Pool Beach.** It's the first place to feed on the receding tide, and the last place to grab a bite on the incoming tide. It's one of the more reliable locations in the state for Baird's and Buff-breasted Sandpipers, along with uncommon American Golden-Plovers (late August–early October), but numbers of many other shorebird species can be very impressive here. Western Sandpiper is annual, and several dozen White-rumped Sandpipers can be present, with Semipalmated Sandpipers and Plovers dominating. I like to sit on the sand, allowing the shorebirds arriving on the beach to get used to me. Often, with patience, quiet, and limited motion, I will have thousands of shorebirds feeding within a few yards of me in a matter of minutes, offering fantastic photo ops.

As the tide goes out, you'll notice shorebirds will begin to leave the beach and fly over land. They're heading to the Pool. I'll often walk the length of the beach until I reach the bathhouse, cross the dunes, and walk the entrance road to the parking lot until I get to the Pool (see "Hattie's Deli" below) to continue working the shorebirds. Otherwise, I head back into the woods to look for passerines.

From the beach, look toward the grove of pitch pines to the right of the Marie Joseph Spiritual Retreat Center. Find the public path (the nonpublic ones are clearly marked), which will lead into the woods of the **South Point Preserve**. This small land trust property includes a shallow pond at a corner of Great Pond. Scan the trees carefully for roosting Black-crowned Night-Herons (Yellow-crowned Night-Heron is rare, but almost annual here) and bird the trees and scrubs for migrants and, in late fall, lingering migrants and rarities.

Exit the woods via the trail to the right (when facing the pond), between two yards, and up to Seventh Street. When I have seen a lot of passerines at any of the spots so far, I will work this neighborhood thoroughly, walking up and down many of the roads, checking yards and the few remaining undeveloped lots, especially in late fall. Following a strong southerly blow and rain on April 24, 2012, my wife and I found a Hooded Warbler, Summer Tanager, and Blue Grosbeak within the course of an hour!

For a quicker "sample," make a left onto Seventh, and at its end make a left onto First. Scan **Great Pond** (all seasons, even in winter, when gulls often roost on the ice), carefully checking the shoreline trees for night-herons and other roosting waders. Then backtrack along First Street, until its end at Ocean Avenue.

After returning to your car, backtrack along L. B. Orcutt, forking to the right (past the fire station) to remain on Orcutt until it ends at a boat launch. Park here at **Vine's Landing** and check the channel (especially at outgoing and incoming tides) and scan the water and shorelines to the northeast (Brant in migration, Snowy Owl in winter, etc.).

Make a right out of the parking lot, curve around on Yates Street, and at its end make a left back onto Mile Stretch. If you had not yet checked **Biddeford Pool Beach**, the parking lot area, and Elphis Pond, make your second left (Gilbert Place) and follow the dirt road into the parking lot for the beach (permit only in summer). This is the alternative way to check the beach for shorebirds or waterbirds. Meanwhile, take the small paths on the east side of the lot to check **Elphis Pond** and its shoreline scrub, which is another great place for migrants; Willow Flycatcher and Green Heron breed here.

Exit the parking lot, make a left onto Mile Stretch, and pull into the paved parking area on your right at the edge of the marsh. Nostalgically referred to as **Hattie's** by birders, this was the former location of Hattie's Deli, a place that had great muffins and welcomed birders (including a sightings board) until it was sold several years ago. For decades, birders were used to parking here (paying a small fee in summer or patronizing the restaurant) and then scanning **the Pool** and the salt marsh from the edge of the property. Since the ownership change, however, access has become uncertain. If the restaurant reopens, you should ask for permission and see if any rules have changed. A few Saltmarsh and Nelson's Sparrows, along with "Eastern" Willets breed here. Roseate Terns often join feeding Commons at high tide in June and July, while shorebirds can be abundant in migration. This is the best spot in southern Maine to look for Hudsonian Godwit in fall (becoming rarer, while Marbled is becoming more regular), and Red Knots in both spring and fall. Sort through staging "Eastern" Willets for the occasional individual of the "Western" subspecies—a future split, and the subspecies that becomes more likely after early to mid-September. It's also another good spot to look for American Golden-Plovers in the fall. Meanwhile, duck numbers can be very good in spring and fall, and raptor migration is sometimes obvious toward the Pool's west end, especially on northwesterly winds in fall, and Horned Larks and Snow Buntings can often be found.

You can view the west end of the Pool by traveling down Mile Stretch until you come to Bridge Street. On your left is a small parking lot (permit only in summer). Cross the street for a scan of the Pool and take the boardwalk over the dunes for another scan of beach and water, which in summer often has Piping Plovers breeding nearby.

Next, head down Bridge Road, but just before you are back on Route 9, make a right onto Old Pool Road. At the end, in the midst of the campus of the University of New England, make a right onto Hill's Beach Road. After passing the end of the playing fields, take your third left onto Seabreeze Avenue and park just before the end. At high tide, check the **Saco Rivermouth jetties** for roosting shorebirds and terns.

Continue on Hill's Beach Road until you see Bufflehead's Restaurant on the right. On the other side of the road, there are a handful of public parking spaces in the (often soft) sand shoulder. Alternatively, you can grab a bite to eat at the restaurant (and then ask to leave your car in their lot for a short period). Enter **Hill's Beach** *only* via the public access path, which is between the first two houses to the west of the parking area.

I prefer to start here at low tide for shorebirds and roosting gulls and terns, or high tide in winter for waterbirds. Walk the beach, sorting through any groups of shorebirds carefully. Head east to the **Basket Island Sandbar** that connects the island to the mainland at low tide. Beyond the sandbar, the shallow, muddier flats are great at low tide for shorebirds and roosting terns. In July through early August, Arctic Terns occasionally join plentiful Common and Roseate (smaller numbers of Least) loafing or feeding fledglings onshore, and in late summer this is one of the most reliable places for Forster's Tern and the chance of finding other rare southern strays. A pair of American Oystercatchers has been frequenting the beach (and/or the Pool) in the past few years, and a pair or two of Piping Plovers often breed; and check any groups of Bonaparte's Gulls for the rare but fairly regular Little Gull. Lesser Black-backed Gull is occasional spring through fall, and white-winged gulls sometimes stop by in winter. I often spend a couple of hours here, beginning or ending my visit to the area at low tide, allowing the incoming tide to push birds to the sandbar. I then exit the beach via the sandy "road" that allows residents to drive on and off the sandbar. Cross the paved road to access the tiny **Park in the Pines** for another view of the Pool (if you are planning on hitting this at prime time, leave Hill's Beach well before the sandbar is inundated in order to beat the tide here).

Return to your car, and either turn left onto Old Pool Road to follow the tour in reverse, or make a right onto Route 9/208 at the end of Hill's Beach Road to head into Biddeford (and perhaps continuing on to site Y13).

RARITIES

Red-necked Stint, July 1977 (only state record); Variegated Flycatcher, November 1977 (first North American record!); Ruff, May 2004 (the Pool); Ross's Goose, March 2009 (West Street—second state record); Chestnut-collared Longspur, June 2012 (East Point—first or second state record); Kentucky Warbler, September 2013 (East Point); Surfbird, March–April 2015 (first state record)

SITE Y13 Saco "Yacht Club" and Riverwalk

TOWN Saco. DeLorme Map 71: B3. **SEASON** September, October–December, January–May. **VISITATION** 30 min. to 1.5 hrs. No restroom facilities. ♿ **HIGHLIGHTS** Late lingering fall migrants and half hardies; waterfowl including Barrow's Goldeneye (November–March).

A southerly facing hillside in a dense neighborhood along a river has all the makings of a migrant and vagrant trap, especially as winter sets in. This unassuming stretch of hillside, made more accessible by the construction of a path starting in 2007, has yielded remarkable seasonal waifs and genuine vagrants. In 2014, eight species of warblers (including multiple Orange-crowned and exceptionally late American Redstart and Yellow Warbler) were seen between November 1 and early December, while the eight species seen in the same period of 2015 included Yellow, Tennessee, and one of the latest Blackburnian Warblers anywhere in eastern North America.

DIRECTIONS

From I-95 take Exit 36 and follow I-195 east to Exit 2A. Merge onto US Route 1 South. The fast-food joints around here sometimes host Fish Crows from late March to September. Stay straight at the fourth light as Route 1 veers right. Now on Route 9 South, make a left at the second light into Pepperell Square. Immediately bear right at Front Street to pass under a railroad bridge, and proceed to the parking lot for the boat launch. Often referred to by local birders as the Saco Yacht Club, the small, private club is on the right, but the hillside on the left and the river is where our interest lies.

Check the river for waterfowl, which can include Barrow's Goldeneyes when the river upstream freezes, Common Mergansers, and occasionally Iceland Gulls in winter. During migration, check the riparian trees, the scrubby hillside (look for Orange-crowned Warbler and Dickcissel in October and November) and then continue on the path along the road, rounding the sewage treatment facility. Scan the cove, which can be productive for ducks in early spring in particular, and then carefully work the hillside, up the hill, and around the corner. Carolina Wrens are often conspicuous here, and by mid-October expect the unexpected.

From mid-December through the spring thaw, the Saco River upstream from here often hosts a pair of Barrow's Goldeneyes. After leaving the parking lot, make your first right onto Wharf Street, and a left at the stop sign onto Common Street. Go straight at the light, crossing Route 9, onto Water Street. Park along the road in front of the condo on the left and walk into its parking lot and check the river from behind the building. This is the most consistent spot, but they are occasionally found above the dams by checking behind businesses on Route 1 (make a left at the next light).

I often visit here after birding Biddeford Pool (site Y12). To access this spot from there, follow Route 208/9 into Biddeford and make a right at the end of Route 208 to remain on Route 9. Cross the Saco River (the Saco Island Deli, where I usually stop for lunch, is in the second mill building on your left) and then the train tracks, making a right at the next light into Pepperrell Square, then picking up the directions as described above.

RARITIES

Ash-throated Flycatcher, November–December 2006; Western Tanager, December 2015

SITE Y14 Pleasant Point Park

TOWN Buxton. DeLorme Map 3: A1 (denoted as "Salmon Falls Park" on the map). SEASON April–October. VISITATION 45 min. to 2 hrs. Portable toilet in warmer months. HIGHLIGHTS Migrants; common breeders.

This unassuming little park is often pleasantly birdy. While it might not have any "specialty birds," it's a nice place to take a stroll and watch some birds. I discovered this spot while researching this book, but time—and more regular coverage—will tell about how productive it might really be during migration. Early spring, when red maples are blooming along the river, seems to be the best time to visit for migrants.

DIRECTIONS

From I-95 take Exit 36 to head east on I-195. Take Exit 1 (Industrial Park Road) and make a left at the end of the off-ramp. Continue on Industrial Park Road for 0.4 miles to its end, and make a right onto North Street/Buxton Road (Route 112 North).

In 5.2 miles make a left onto Route 117 North (Old Buxton Road, becomes Joy Valley Road). In 1.9 miles make a left onto Simpson Road. After the road makes a hard bend to the left in 0.2 miles, you'll see the parking area for **Pleasant Point Park** (labeled Salmon Falls Park on the DeLorme) on your right.

There are two loops, one on each side of the parking lot. The loop to your right as you enter the lot travels through more mature woods and through eastern hemlock–dominated slopes and gullies along a wide, slow, impounded section of the Saco River (note the trails are a little hard to follow along the riverside), with migrants possible moving through the trees anywhere, and common breeding birds such as Black-throated Green and Blackburnian Warblers throughout. A Louisiana Waterthrush here on April 25 in 2015 seemed out of breeding habitat, but more investigation is likely needed.

The loop on the right side of the parking lot is more interesting, however, as extensive logging in 2008 has resulted in regenerating forest, patches of brambles, and thickets of various fruit-producing native plants. American Redstarts, Chestnut-sided Warblers, and Gray Catbirds are common and conspicuous breeders (at least for now), the ethereal song of the Veery echoes from the brush, and migrants can be anywhere. Regular attention from a local birder or two could prove this spot to be a productive locale. Unfortunately, there are no plans at this time to maintain the ephemeral (and declining) shrub-scrub habitat.

Birding this spot can be combined with a visit to Killock Pond Road (site Y16).

SITE Y15 Waterboro Barrens Preserve

TOWNS Shapleigh and Waterboro. DeLorme Map 3: A3.   SEASON December–March, June–July.   VISITATION 30 min. to 2 hrs. No facilities. HIGHLIGHTS Breeding birds including Prairie Warbler, Eastern Towhee, etc.; crossbills.

A short walk or two at this Nature Conservancy property will offer the opportunity to enjoy some locally common species in fairly impressive numbers, such as Brown Thrashers, Prairie Warblers, Eastern Towhees, and Field Sparrows. Whip-poor-will and Common Nighthawk are reported to breed here as well. Crossbills, especially Red, are possible anytime but are most likely in winter and in good irruption years, and they may breed beginning in February.

DIRECTIONS

From I-95 take Exit 32. At the light after the tollbooth make a right onto Route 111 West. In 11.3 miles make a right at the light onto 4/202 North. In 4.6 miles make a left onto West Road. At the four-way stop in 6.2 miles make a right onto Newfield Road.

There are two options for exploring over two thousand acres of this pitch pine–scrub oak barrens. The first is via the main entrance of the preserve, which can be reached by following Newfield Road for 1 mile. Turn right onto

Round Pond Road. In 0.6 miles the main dirt road curves left and becomes Buff Brook Road. Follow it to the parking area at the end. Follow the two-track straight past the gate, and a short stroll will afford the opportunity to sample the habitat and see most of the breeding birds of note. The more open area on the right, a few hundred yards up, is where I found a territorial Clay-colored Sparrow in June 2015. You can walk trails and two-tracks endlessly here, but note that there are quite a few ATV paths and unmarked trails, so be careful not to get turned around; it is very easy to get lost in here.

Another option is to travel another half mile north on Newfield Road, to a left onto Gray Road. Park in the wide dirt edge of Gray Road and cross Newfield to enter the preserve via the dirt road. A fifteen-to-twenty-minute walk (each way) should yield most of the expected species as well. This area was the most dependable spot for the crossbills in the winter of 2014–15, when my exploration of this area yielded numerous breeding Red Crossbills, from February into spring. Recordings were determined to be Type 10, one of the most expected types in the Northeast. Should Red Crossbills be "split" someday, recordings would likely be critical for separation.

RARITIES

Hoary Redpoll, January 2015; Clay-colored Sparrow, June 2015

More information about the preserve can be found on the Nature Conservancy's website at www.nature.org, with a search for "Waterboro Barrens." Note that the parking areas and access trails may change in the near future, so it would be wise to check the website for any updated information.

SITE Y16 Killock Pond Road, and Maynard Marsh and Little Ossippee River Wildlife Management Areas

TOWNS Hollis and Limington. DeLorme Map 4: E4–5. SEASON May, June–July, August–October. VISITATION 1 hr. to half day. No facilities. ♿ HIGHLIGHTS Breeding Grasshopper, Vesper, and Field Sparrows; Prairie Warbler; Eastern Meadowlark at Killock Pond Road; breeding forest birds at the wildlife management areas.

A friend and I stumbled upon this intriguing site on Killock Pond Road several years ago and were surprised to find breeding Grasshopper Sparrows—a state endangered species. A thorough search also turned up regionally uncommon and declining Vesper Sparrows and Eastern Meadowlarks, among others. Prairie Warblers and Savannah and Song Sparrows are abundant, with numerous Eastern Towhees and Alder Flycatchers (despite the lack of wetlands) sprinkled throughout.

In a "forest restoration project" by Poland Spring to protect the aquifer below for the nearby bottling plant, white and red pines were planted around 2000 to restore what was a degraded potato farm. I could only imagine the numbers of grassland birds (Upland Sandpipers?) that bred here then, but as the trees have matured, these specialists are being replaced by early successional specialists. So bird here soon, as the trees are rapidly maturing. Of course, the next stage of colonizers could be most intriguing, as the area looks ripe for a breeding attempt by Clay-colored Sparrows or perhaps a Blue-winged Warbler, especially in the stands of young birch and aspen. It should also be checked for the possibility of breeding Eastern Whip-poor-will and Common Nighthawk, and likely hosts American Woodcocks.

Although Killock Pond Road is more of a birding destination owing to rare and local species and can be checked in a short amount of time, I usually combine a visit here with two seldom-birded, but often quite birdy, wildlife management areas that are good for a wide range of typical breeding birds and can be fruitful in migration.

DIRECTIONS

Follow the directions to Pleasant Point Park (site Y14, above), but instead of turning onto Simpson Road, continue on Route 117 North to the blinking light at the junction with Route 4/202. Take a left to stay on Route 117 North/4/202 South, and in 1.6 miles bear right to remain on Route 117 North (Cape Road). Continue for 5.3 miles to a right onto Route 35 (Plains Road). Take your first left onto Killock Pond Road. In just over a mile, you'll see the reforested plains on both side of the road. Look for the dirt road on your right and park along it (do not block the road). A quick check entails nothing more than walking up and down this dirt road, and that usually produces most of the target birds.

An ATV trail runs the length of the plains adjacent to the road, which provides access to the edge of the forest restoration area and gets you off the side of Killock Pond Road, which is busy with large truck traffic at all hours. But to reduce disturbance from noisy trucks, you'll want to bird here as early as possible.

You are allowed to walk into the forest restoration area (except where noted—and these signs must be obeyed), but use prudence and common sense when doing so in the breeding season; many of our grassland nesters nest on the ground (and ticks are numerous). Meanwhile, the edges host Indigo Buntings, Brown Thrashers, Chestnut-sided Warblers and many others, and more open patches of grass scattered about host clusters of Grasshopper Sparrows.

The road is probably also worth a quick check in the winter for Northern Shrike and likely holds potential for sparrow migration in April and October. After birding the plains, take a quick look at the detention pond on the north side of the bottling plant, which occasionally hosts migrant shorebirds, and usually has breeding Killdeer.

Then continue on Killock Pond Road until it soon ends at Route 35. Make a left onto Route 35 North. In a half mile turn left onto Sand Pond Road, just before the bridge across the Saco River. Continue straight on Sand Pond Road as it turns to dirt, and just before a bridge over the Little Ossippee River pull off onto either side of the road (Louisiana Waterthrush can sometimes be heard from the bridge mid-April through May). On the north side of the road, a short trail pokes along the river into the **Little Ossippee River WMA**.

However, the more interesting trail is to the south, into the **Maynard F. Marsh WMA**. While following the trail downstream (crossing the power line to stay on the riverside trail), enjoy a variety of woodland birds in the riparian area, and note the impressive stands of ferns. Yellow-throated Vireo might breed here, and both cuckoos are possible. This is often a very birdy area, and it can be especially productive in early spring migration for a variety of warblers. Following the main ATV trail for 1.2 miles, you'll come upon a sphagnum bog that hosts breeding Prairie Warblers, among others, and looks like it deserves some thorough breeding-season attention.

After returning to you car, cross the Little Ossippee River and take an immediate right. Stop now and again to listen for the expected breeding birds as you travel the edge of the Little Ossippee River WMA. In 1.8 miles turn left onto Boothby Road, which will end at Route 117. From there you can make a right to continue on to the Sawyer Mountain Loop (site Y17) for a productive full day of birding, or make a left to return home.

SITE Y17 Sawyer Mountain Loop

TOWNS Limington, Limerick, Cornish. DeLorme Map 4: D–E3–4.
SEASON May–July. **VISITATION** 3 hrs. to half day. Limited restroom facilities (see text). **HIGHLIGHTS** Common breeding birds, Wood Ducks, perhaps Louisiana Waterthrush.

The Sawyer Mountain Highlands Preserve of the Francis Small Heritage Trust is the largest unfragmented block of forest remaining in York or Cumberland Counties. A hike through the woods here provides an excellent way to sample the interior forest birds of the foothills region. The Jagolinzer Preserve is one of those "birdy" places that are worth a visit almost anytime, and the tiny Limerick wastewater treatment plant has loads of potential.

DIRECTIONS

From the Maine Turnpike (I-95) take Exit 32. Make a right at the light onto Route 111 West. In 5.5 miles make a right at the light onto Route 35 North, and in 4.9 miles make a left onto Route 5 North. Follow Route 5 for 15.6 miles to Route 11. Continue straight, and then make a right to stay on Route 11. In 0.8 miles take a left onto Emery Corner Road, just past the town landing in downtown Limerick. In 0.7 miles cross Pickerel Pond Road, and in another 1.2 miles the road will curve to the left, becoming Sawyer Mountain Road. In 0.5 miles the road turns to dirt at Libby & Sons U-Pick (from late fall through early spring it is worth scanning the orchard for frugivores). In another 0.6 miles stay straight onto Sawyer Mountain Road. In 0.2 miles turn right into the trailhead parking lot for the **Sawyer Mountain Highlands Preserve.**

It's a 1.6-mile hike, with only a few fairly steep stretches to the summit of 1,213 feet. Views are obscured, but you can scan across the coastal plain for a good overview of the landscape and note the historical marker for the site of a whale-oil light once used for Portland Harbor navigation. More important, the walk will pass through high-quality mixed forest, with all the expected breeding species. Wood Thrushes sing near the parking lot, while the scrubby summit hosts Dark-eyed Juncos. Ovenbird and Yellow-rumped Warblers are particularly abundant, and note the subtle differences in birdlife as you pass between eastern hemlock glens (Blue-headed Vireo, Hermit Thrush, Winter Wren, Blackburnian Warbler, etc.) and more deciduous-dominated stretches (Red-eyed Vireo, Veery, Scarlet Tanager, etc.). Listen also for Yellow-throated Vireo, especially near the summit.

After summiting, you can return to the car via Sawyer Mountain Road, but note that steep stretches here are loose rubble, often wet or icy, and otherwise less pleasant on the knees than a return trip the way you came.

Following my hike, I usually check a few other places while I am in the neighborhood. First up is the tiny **Limerick wastewater treatment plant**. This unassuming little facility has two uncovered settling ponds, which often host Wood Ducks and Mallards throughout the summer. They are worth a quick check in spring and fall migration as well. Meanwhile, the bubblers keep at least a patch of water open through much of the winter, which—especially when streams are frozen—can attract a variety of passerines in the winter (Eastern Bluebirds seem fond of stopping in for a drink).

To reach the ponds from Sawyer Mountain, backtrack downhill, but make a left onto Pickerel Pond Road. Cross Route 11 (Central Avenue) onto Dole Ridge Road, and in half a mile make a right onto Burnham Road and an immediate right into the horseshoe at the treatment plant. When ducks are present *do not* get out of the car, as ducks—especially the flighty "Wood-ies"—will flush immediately.

Continuing on, make a right back onto Burnham Road and follow it for 1.4 miles to Route 5 (Sokokis Trail South). Make a right and stay on Route 5 North for 1.5 miles to the pull-off on the right into the **Sokokis Lake Scenic Overlook**. This is a good spot to scan for raptors (migration potential?), especially Bald Eagles, but it also has a portable toilet.

Then follow Route 5 for 7.8 miles into Cornish. Turn right to remain on Route 5 North (and 25 East), and in 0.6 miles stay straight/bear right to remain on Route 25 East. In 2.2 miles, shortly after crossing into Limington, make a left onto Olive's Way (the sign for the small dirt road is hard to see). In about a hundred feet, pull off on the left just before a tiny sign marks the entrance trail for the **Jagolinzer Preserve**. A short, easy loop to the banks of the Saco River is always worth a walk at any season, but especially for another sample of common breeding birds. The edge of the river can be good for passerines in migration, and Pease Brook is a great place to *see* Louisiana Waterthrushes by sitting still along its edges. At the mouth of the creek in 2015, I could hear two other "Louies" across the Saco River as well. Breeding locations for the Louies are a bit ephemeral in the foothills, so one year they are at a creek, and the next year they are not. Therefore, throughout this loop—and throughout interior York County—it is always worth stopping at shaded, flowing brooks with emergent rocks from late April through early June to give a listen.

After birding Jagolinzer, you can follow Route 25 East all the way back to I-95 in Westbrook, or, in half a mile after you exit Olive's Way, bear right onto Route 117 South to continue on to bird at the Little Ossippee River and Maynard Marsh WMAS (site Y16). Cross Route 11 in 4.8 miles, and in another 1.7 miles make a left onto Boothby Road. You can now follow the directions for site Y17 in reverse.

RARITIES

Worm-eating Warbler, August 2008 (Sawyer Mountain)

The website for the Francis Small Heritage Trust offers more information about these preserves, and you can click on links in the left-hand toolbar to download trail maps: www.fsht.org/index.html.

2 Cumberland County

DEREK LOVITCH

With over 20 percent of the state's population, Cumberland County is the most densely populated county in the state. The state's largest city, Portland, with its more than sixty-six thousand people and a metro area that contains almost a third of the state's 1.3 million residents, is found here. Portland is known around the world for its restaurants (named America's Foodiest Small City by *Bon Appétit* magazine in 2009) and its craft beer scene, but is known to birders as home to some of the best migrant traps in the state. Dense development, a complex coastline, and the light (and perhaps electromagnetic) pollution of the city combine to concentrate migrants in so-called migrant traps, especially under certain weather conditions during migration.

Outside the urban jungle, Cumberland County also hosts some of the state's premier birding sites, led by Scarborough Marsh (site C1), a year-round birding destination. All year long, various exciting birding opportunities abound, such as breeding specialties from Roseate Tern to Saltmarsh Sparrow, and often the best shorebirding in the state.

In spring, Evergreen Cemetery (C8), Capisic Pond Park (C9), Morgan Meadow WMA (C17), and Florida Lake Park (C20) are top spots to observe migrants, along with hawk watching at Bradbury Mountain (C18). Breeding season visits to Old Town House Park (C16) and Morgan Meadow (C17) are fruitful. But things really heat up again in fall, led by Sandy Point Beach (C14) under the right conditions, the Eastern Promenade (C6), Cape Elizabeth (C2–4), and the south-pointing peninsulas of Harpswell: Harpswell Neck (C22) and Bailey Island (C23). As the season progresses, my attention is turned to the Greater Yarmouth Goose Fields (C15).

It's a great county to bird in winter, and it's no surprise the Greater Portland Christmas Bird Count has the highest tallies in the state. A shoreline tour of Cape Elizabeth (C2–4) is superb, followed by some good gull and duck

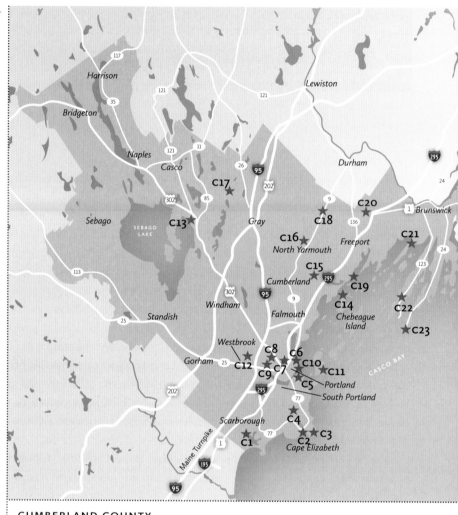

117
Harrison
121
35
Bridgeton
121 11
Naples 26
Casco 95
202
C17★
302 85
Sebago
SEBAGO LAKE
C13★
Gray
113
302
95
Windham
25
Standish
Gorham
25
Westbrook
C12★
202
295

Lewiston

295

Durham

24

9
C20★
1 Brunswick
C18★
136
Freeport
C16★
North Yarmouth
C21★
24
C15★
Cumberland 295
123
C19★
9
C14★
Falmouth
Chebeague
Island
C22★
C23★

CASCO BAY

C8★
C6★
C7★ C10★
C9★ C11
C5★
Portland
South Portland
77

C4★
Scarborough
77 C3★
C1★ C2★
Cape Elizabeth

Maine Turnpike
1
195
95

CUMBERLAND COUNTY

watching in Portland Harbor (c5), and more waterfowl at Winslow Park and South Freeport (c19), or anywhere along the shores of Harpswell.

With such a relatively large population, more birders can be found in this county than anywhere else in the state, from fifty or more a morning at Evergreen Cemetery in May, to dozens of folks fanned out to search for vagrants in late fall. Therefore, we have a lot of data about birding in this county, and a lot of great birds have been discovered—the so-called observer bias: the more birders in the field, the more great birds will be found. —*Derek Lovitch*.

SITE C1 Scarborough Marsh

TOWN Scarborough. DeLorme Map 3: B3–4. SEASON All year.
VISITATION 2 hrs. to all day. Year-round restroom facilities and/or portable toilets at some stops. ♿ ⛴ HIGHLIGHTS Breeding Saltmarsh and Nelson's Sparrows; Least and Roseate Terns; American Oystercatcher; wading birds including Glossy Ibis (and White-faced) and Little Blue Heron in summer; migrant shorebirds; migrant and breeding ducks; winter raptors and waterbirds; Little Gull; rarities.

One of the premier birding destinations in Maine, Scarborough Marsh offers fantastic birding all year long. It is best known for summer birding, however, as the marsh hosts large numbers of breeding Saltmarsh and Nelson's Sparrows (and yes, hybrids thereof, so be careful with your identification; recent genetic work shows that hybrids are common and sometimes a real challenge to ID, so only "textbook" individuals, preferably when heard singing, can be identified with any degree of confidence). The Saltmarsh Sparrows are near their northern breeding limits, and the Nelson's near their southern limits. Other breeders include plentiful "Eastern" Willets, and along the edges everything from Virginia Rails to Marsh Wrens. A territorial Seaside Sparrow or two can be found in most years, and the wading bird diversity is unrivaled in Maine: Glossy Ibis, Little Blue Herons, Great Egrets, and often a Tricolored Heron reach the northern limits of their breeding range on a nearshore island, and they forage in and around the marsh. White-faced Ibis, once a mega-rarity in Maine, occurs annually, with two or three birds each of the past four years—and likely breeding with each other and/or Glossy Ibis.

This is one of the best spots for shorebirding in the state, with the narrow spring migration window running from mid-May through early June. Then,

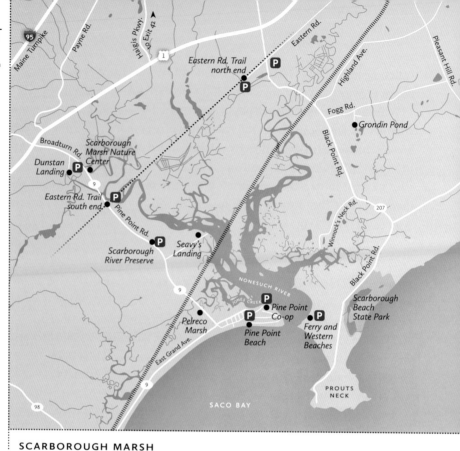

Map labels:
95 / Maine Turnpike / Payne Rd. / Haigis Pkwy. / To Exit #2 / 1 / Eastern Rd. Trail north end / P / P / Eastern Rd. / Highland Ave. / Pleasant Hill Rd. / Fogg Rd. / Grondin Pond / Broadturn Rd. / Scarborough Marsh Nature Center / Dunstan Landing / P / 9 / Black Point Rd. / Eastern Rd. Trail south end / P / Pine Point Rd. / Winnock's Neck Rd. / 207 / P / Seavy's Landing / Scarborough River Preserve / Black Point Rd. / NONESUCH RIVER / 9 / JONES CREEK / Scarborough Beach State Park / Pine Point Co-op / P / P / Pelreco Marsh / Pine Point Beach / Ferry and Western Beaches / East Grand Ave. / 9 / PROUTS NECK / 98 / SACO BAY

SCARBOROUGH MARSH

as the last stragglers are wandering north—or a few immatures, especially either yellowlegs, oversummering right here—the first southbound birds (non- or failed breeders) are arriving by the end of June. Shorebird numbers and diversity have two peaks: adults in late July to early August, and juveniles in mid-to-late August. Spring waterfowl migration is superb (early March in warm springs, otherwise late March through April); but in fall, hunting pressure limits concentrations and viewing opportunities. Landbird migration, both spring and fall, can often be detected along the edges of the marsh as well.

In winter, the frozen marsh can be desolate, but scan for the occasional Snowy Owl and Rough-legged Hawk among the "regulars" including Bald Eagles and Northern Shrikes. Meanwhile, the open waters of the river and bay can be chock-full of waterbirds, including impressive numbers of both loons and a variety of ducks.

54

BIRDWATCHING IN MAINE

Scarborough Marsh offers superb birding at all tides, but some tides are better at some locations than others. A good tide chart is critical to maximize your visit. Below, I include the recommended tide in parentheses after the mention of each location. You will want to skip some sites, return to others, or plan to visit on the recommended tide.

DIRECTIONS

From I-95 take Exit 42 and stay straight at the light after the tollbooth, to head east on the Haigis Parkway until its end in 1.4 miles at US Route 1. I usually begin my tour on the south side of the marsh, and therefore I turn right onto Route 1 South. You'll cross the west edge of the marsh before heading back uphill. At the third light (after crossing the marsh) make a left onto Pine Point Road.

I usually begin my birding at the **Eastern Road Trail** (all tides, but high is best, especially for shorebirds), arriving as early as possible to beat the masses of recreators. After turning onto Pine Point Road, make a left into the dirt parking lot in 1.1 miles, immediately after the lighted pedestrian crossing. Walk the trail to the north (although a walk to the south can be good during migration to sample woodland migrants), scanning the marsh from the bridge, and watching for "sharp-tailed" sparrows, wading birds, and foraging Least Terns throughout (all in summer). Look and listen carefully for Seaside Sparrows, which are found in some years. Especially during flood tides in September and October, walk the edge of the dike carefully, as "sharp-tailed" sparrows (including Nelson's Sparrows of the "interior" or "bay" subspecies) can concentrate on the edges. Shorebirds are often sprinkled about but are in the best numbers and diversity in the large pannes to the east of the trail as you approach the tree line to the north (a scope is important, and high tide is best). This is the best spot in the state for Stilt Sandpiper and Long-billed Dowitcher (rare but regular: adults mostly in August, but usually juveniles September–October, sometimes later), and one of the better places for the occasional Wilson's Phalarope—which sometimes breed somewhere in the marsh. This is also one of the more reliable places in the state for Northern Shoveler, even in midsummer, as one or two pairs breed in the marsh and/or at Stratton Island, and large numbers of Green-winged Teal (migrants and breeders) often contain small numbers of Blue-winged during migration, and rarely "Eurasian" Green-winged (Common) Teal. In late fall through early spring, Lapland Longspur, Snow Bunting, and Horned Lark are occasional on the road or near its edge, and in winter, scan for raptors, especially from the bridge.

Once you reach the tree line you can continue northward, as the woods can be very good during migration. After returning to your car, make a left out of the parking lot and continue for 0.6 miles to the **Scarborough River Preserve** on your left. Here a short loop can be decent during migration and in winter, as the area often hosts frugivores, especially American Robins but rarely also Pine Grosbeaks and Bohemian Waxwings. Otherwise, continue on for another 0.2 miles to a left onto **Seavy's Landing Road** (all tides, but especially mid-tides) and park at the end of the road for another good place to scan the marsh and the river.

Another 0.8 miles east on Pine Point Road, turn right onto Snow Canning Road into the area known to most birders (after the name of one of the companies that occupy the former Snow Canning facility) as **Pelreco Marsh** (all tides, but especially high). Although this is private property, birders are tolerated if they park out of the way and avoid traffic and workers in this busy place. I prefer to park in the dirt on the left, adjacent to the end of the copse of trees, and walk to the edge of the marsh to be sure my car is not in the way—or getting caught in the mud! This is a good spot for Saltmarsh and Nelson's Sparrows, wading birds, roosting shorebirds, and ducks. A few pairs of Gadwall breed, and this is the best spot to see one from April through August. It's also a prime spot to look for White-faced Ibis among the Glossies, especially in April and May while the grass is short and the birds' breeding plumage aspect is bright. Cliff (and Barn) Swallows breed on the building here, and swallow aggregations—led by masses of Tree Swallows—can be impressive here in late summer.

Return to Pine Point Road, make a right, and at its end make a left at the stop sign. An immediate right, then rounding the bend to the left will put you on King Street. In six blocks, turn right onto Avenue 5 Extension and make a right into the parking lot (steep fee in summer) for **Pine Point Beach**. In summer, low and mid-tides are best, when terns roost on the outer sandflats and forage along the shore, especially at the river mouth. Walk the beach north to the jetty and scan the mouth of the Scarborough River. Roseate Terns join the foraging Commons and commuting Leasts from late May through early August, and Arctic is occasional, especially during easterly winds in late July and early August when fledglings are sometimes being fed from land. Search for rarer terns and migrant shorebirds—almost anything is possible here. At high tides, the jetty may host roosting Purple Sandpipers in winter, and at all seasons there are usually plenty of birds feeding in the river mouth. Both loons, Horned (and a few Red-necked) Grebes, Common (and very rarely, a King) Eider, and other sea ducks are abundant in winter in the bay and at the river mouth, with concentrations of Long-tailed Ducks often quite impressive (high tide is best). Check roosting Bonaparte's Gulls for Little (or even-rarer Black-headed) Gulls, and in winter, Iceland and Glaucous Gulls are possible. This is also one of the more reliable places for Lesser Black-backed Gulls, which are possible at any time, but most likely in spring and fall. I like to arrive at dead low and let the incoming waters push birds closer and stir up feeding activity.

Dawn and dusk can be magical here, as the wading birds that breed in the offshore colonies of Stratton Island commute to and from the colony. I can find fewer ways to enjoy a warm summer evening than taking in the "evening rush." Black-crowned Night-Herons can often be seen flying "against traffic," heading into the marsh for the night shift.

You can also access the jetty by walking through the neighborhood from the area known to local birders as the **Pine Point Co-op** (all tides; see below), checking the river as you go, especially at low tide, and checking the rooftops for Snowy Owls (especially at high tide) in winter. Regardless of whether or not you have already checked the beach, your next stop is the large parking area for the co-op, boat launch, etc., at the northwest corner of Pine Point. From the beach parking lot, make a left, and then your second right onto King Street and proceed to its end at a large parking lot. At high tide, check the river for waterbirds, and in summer, feeding terns (Roseate can be common among the abundant Commons). This is also the best low-tide shorebirding in the area. I often plan to arrive at dead low (or on the incoming, after I have spent time at the beach), setting up the scope at the end of the pier on the west side of the building and watching shorebirds concentrate on the incoming tide. While the outgoing to low tides are actually better for American Oystercatcher—one or two of the two to four pairs that breed in the state feed here—they can be seen on the incoming as well; scan the flats across the river to the north in particular. Large numbers of staging "Eastern" Willets occur in August, but as September progresses, stragglers thin out and a few "Western" Willets are found. Over the past decade, Hudsonian Godwits have declined precipitously here (rarely more than one a year now, if at all), but Marbled Godwit has become almost annual. Sunrise at low tide in July or August—or on foggy mornings—can result in impressive numbers of wading birds.

As the tide comes in, shorebirds will begin to head up into the marsh or offshore to Little Stratton Island, depending on where the particular species prefers to roost. The sand along Jones Creek, adjacent to the boat launch next to the harbormaster's shack, will often be the last place to host shorebirds before the high tide crests.

When I am out of sand and shorebirds at Pine Point, I backtrack through the marsh, checking sites as time allows. If I had not checked Eastern Road already, I usually hit it on the high tide for more shorebirds, and then I check the salt pannes around Maine Audubon's **Scarborough Marsh Nature Center** (high tide), which is on the right, 0.4 miles past the Eastern Road Trail parking lot. In early spring, this is a good spot to look for dabbling ducks, and in April through May, White-faced Ibis among the Glossies. Cross the street and check those pannes as well, which is a good spot for longer-legged shorebirds at high tide. Afterward, head west for another half mile and make a left onto Dunstan Landing Road. "**Dunstan Landing**" (high tide) is at the end of the road. Park at the cul-de-sac, check the salt pannes to the north (a reliable spot for White-faced Ibis), and walk the overgrown trail into the marsh, scanning from both sides.

When you are done, return to Pine Point Road, make a left, and head to the light at Route 1. If shorebirds are my focus, I might turn left and head south to Biddeford Pool (site Y12), depending on the tides. Otherwise, to continue birding Scarborough Marsh, make a right and head north on Route 1, crossing the marsh, and making a right at the ninth light onto Black Point Road (Route 207 South) to explore the marsh's less-accessible northern side.

In 0.3 miles you will reach the north end of the **Eastern Road Trail**. From here it is significantly longer to reach the marsh than from the southern end, but you will pass through excellent woodland habitat. This is a good way to start your birding day in April and May, when warblers are moving through en masse and shorebirds are still in short supply. Turn right onto Eastern Road, and in 0.3 miles you'll reach a parking area. Head south on the trail until you reach the salt pannes mentioned above.

Otherwise, continue on Black Point Road. In all but midwinter and midsummer, **Grondin Pond** is worth a check. In fact, from October through freeze-up (which can be anywhere from late November until early January), this is a prime destination on its own. At 1.3 miles east of Route 1, turn left onto Fogg Road and make your second right onto Woodview Drive. Park in the cul-de-sac at the end and scan from the road, respecting private property. Early mornings and afternoons tend to provide the best lighting.

A very deep pond, apparently with some saltwater intrusion, keeps open freshwater well past the freeze-up of almost all other ponds in the area, resulting in impressive concentrations, unseasonable lingering dabblers among the masses of Mallards, and regular rarities. Both scaup are regular through late fall, along with good numbers of Ring-necked (especially in spring) and Ruddy Ducks (more in fall, often some until freeze-up). In midwinter, as long as there is even a patch of open water, gulls will roost here—check for white-winged gulls. Eurasian Wigeon is rare but regular, and fall birds sometimes linger for weeks, usually among the tarrying American Wigeons. Redhead and Canvasback occur every few years.

Return to Black Point Road for another 1.4 miles until the junction with Route 77. Here you can make a left and head into Cape Elizabeth, following Route 77 for 5.1 miles until you make a right onto Kettle Cove Road to reach Kettle Cove (site C2), or another 0.2 miles for a right onto Two Lights Road to reach site C3.

The other option is to continue on Black Point Road/Route 207 south to Prouts Neck, where you can get some culture at the Winslow Homer House, visit **Scarborough Beach State Park** (under-birded, but can be good for winter waterbirds and migrant shorebirds; fee), or in 1.2 miles past the junction with Route 77 make a right onto Ferry Road to reach **Ferry and Western Beaches** (low is best for shorebirds; high for other waterbirds). From the parking lot (steep fee in summer) walk to the water, scanning the river and mudflats opposite Pine Point. Walking to the river, then rounding the corner to the east and onto Western Beach, is a great way to view shorebirds that you were straining to get a look at from Pine Point.

RARITIES

The list of "megas" is impressive, with some of the best including Bar-tailed Godwit, 1978 and 1980 (first and second state records); European Golden-Plover, October 2008 (first state record); Ross's Goose, March 2009; Little Egret, June–July 2001 and July–August 2012 (first and second state records); Presumed Snowy Egret x Tricolored Heron hybrids, July 2012 to present; Black-necked Stilt, June 2013 (Eastern Road); Northern Wheatear, May 2014 (Eastern Road); Clapper Rail, September 2015 (Jones Creek).

Roseate Tern, Pine Point.
© Jeannette Lovitch

SITE C2 Crescent Beach and Kettle Cove State Parks

TOWN Cape Elizabeth. DeLorme Map 3: B5. **SEASON** All year, but especially **September–November.** **VISITATION** 30 min. to 4 hrs. Outhouses open all year; bathhouses in summer. State park fees. **HIGHLIGHTS** Land bird and waterbird migrants; wintering waterbirds; Brant; rarities.

Well worth the visit for the scenery alone, this popular spot is birdy at all seasons. Summertime visitors will enjoy Common Eiders and Common Terns in the water (and often oversummering immature Common Loons) and a variety of the usual breeding birds of the area—plus Willow Flycatcher—in the uplands. Wintertime finds a diversity of waterbirds, including both loons, Purple Sandpipers, and occasionally Harlequin Ducks. It's a great spot during migration, both in the water and the uplands. Late fall in particular can be very productive, especially as falling temperatures push lingering migrants and rarities to coastal microclimates and habitats.

DIRECTIONS

From I-295 in Portland take Exit 6A (Forest Avenue/Route 100 South). At the end of the respective off-ramps bear right onto Forest Avenue. Immediately get into the right lane, and bear right just before the first traffic light onto Route 77 South and follow that through Deering Oaks Park. Stay on Route 77 South (State Street) through six lights and up and over the Casco Bay Bridge into South Portland.

At the second light, turn right to remain on Route 77 South (Ocean Street) and follow for 4.8 miles—through the center of Cape Elizabeth (blinking light)—to a left onto Kettle Cove Road. Bear left slightly to remain on Kettle Cove Road and follow it to its end at the parking lot for **Kettle Cove**.

Begin by birding the lawn (one of the more reliable spots in the state for Brant from late February through April, and good for American Pipit, Horned Lark, and Snow Bunting in early winter), and scan the water of the cove. Be sure to scope Richmond Island, especially in winter (Rough-legged Hawk; rarely Snowy Owl), and check the gulls on exposed rocks (Lesser Black-backed Gull is regular in spring and fall; white-winged gulls are frequent in winter). Follow the trail beyond the pay station at the end of the parking lot, and poke around the various trails through the uplands. This shrub-scrub habitat of mostly invasive species hosts few breeders, and the quality of the habitat is rapidly declining for migrants. However, low-quality food sources such as bush honeysuckle do provide at least some sustenance and can help to concentrate migrants in late fall as other food supplies run out, and the moderated microclimate here helps birds survive longer. You want to be especially thorough here in late October through early December, when most of the rarities have been discovered, with Orange-crowned Warbler regular and White-eyed Vireo and Yellow-breasted Chat almost annual.

The Eastern Road Trail salt pannes in Scarborough Marsh (p. 55). © Derek Lovitch

After birding Kettle Cove, you can return to your car, return to Route 77, and make a left. In 0.8 miles (check the farm fields for the occasional rare goose among the Canadas), turn left into **Crescent Beach State Park**. Proceed through the toll pay booth and follow the entrance road to the parking lot. However, I prefer to skip the drive and walk to the park from my car at Kettle Cove. Usually, I do this by walking down Kettle Cove Road to the trail on the left just past **Fessenden Road** (which itself is worth walking for "scrubby migrants" such as sparrows in fall). Follow this trail through the back of the dunes through more shrub-scrub habitat, including a few pocket wetlands (Willow Flycatcher; Swamp Sparrow) and into the pitch pine grove (check for migrants). Once you are at the bathhouse, you can cross to the beach and return to your car, or continue on to explore the rest of the park. I usually choose the latter, working the edge of the sprawling parking lot, counter-clockwise, and then following the entrance road (winter finches; breeding warblers including Blackburnian). After a sweeping curve, you'll see a wide trail on your left. Follow that through the woods until it opens up into yet more shrub-scrub habitat. It'll curve around and eventually dump you out onto the west end of the beach. Follow the beach back to your car, checking the beach and wrack line for shorebirds, and keeping an eye on the water.

Many birders will combine a visit to these two parks with Dyer Point and/ or Two Lights State Park (site C3), or a site such as Village Crossings (C4) on the way home.

RARITIES

Lark Sparrow, November 2012 and December 2015 (Fessenden Road); Mac-Gillivray's Warbler, November 2015

For a map and trails visit Maine Trail Finder at www.mainetrailfinder.com and use the search feature.

SITE C3 Dyer Point and Two Lights State Park

TOWN Cape Elizabeth. DeLorme Map 3: B5. **SEASON** All year, but especially **October–March**. **VISITATION** 1 hr. to half day. Restroom facilities at Two Lights SP open all year. State park entry fees at Two Lights SP. **HIGHLIGHTS** Harlequin Duck, Purple Sandpiper, and Great Cormorant; sea watching; alcids.

Best known in winter for Harlequin Ducks and the occasional King Eider, Two Lights State Park is worth a visit in any season. A year-round sea-watching destination, Dyer Point was even profiled in the *Peterson Reference Guide to Seawatching: Eastern Waterbirds in Flight* by Ken Behrens and Cameron Cox, featuring my paltry, duration-limited "high" counts. This is *the* spot near Greater Portland for sea watching, especially after strong storms with onshore winds throughout the year. It's also one of the more regular spots for a much sought-after King Eider, and Black Guillemots can be seen year-round.

DIRECTIONS

Follow the directions listed above for Kettle Cove and Crescent Beach State Park (site C2). From the blinking light in Cape Elizabeth Center continue on Route 77 for 1.7 miles, to a left onto Two Lights Road. Scan the open field on your right for geese, gulls, and, especially in winter, Horned Lark and Snow Bunting.

Follow Two Lights Road around the bend at the entrance to the state park until it ends in a dirt parking lot at **Dyer Point**. Check the cove, especially the wrack line, carefully, and then grab your scope and layer up for some wicked good sea watching. I usually stand to the right of the foghorn building, at a slightly higher elevation, or use the building for some shelter in a northerly wind. Or station yourself to the left of the building, near the tip of the point. Check any roosting gulls; Iceland and Glaucous are regular in winter. Scan the rocks for Purple Sandpipers and the surf for Harlequin Ducks from November to early April (occasionally into May). Check the rafts of Common Eiders carefully for the rare King (less regular here than it once was); and Great Cormorants are often on the rocks or fishing offshore.

The onshore winds that are so important for sea watching unfortunately also often bring in fog. However, when visibility is even decent, impressive flights of seabirds can occur. From June through August, easterly winds can produce Sooty, Great, and, exceptionally, Cory's Shearwater, along with plenty of Wilson's Storm-Petrels (which are usually present even without onshore winds). Commuting Common Terns are regular, too, occasionally with a Roseate and Leasts among them. Migrant waterbirds can include big flights of scoters, Common Eiders (check those flocks carefully!), Northern Gannets (usually seen in all but midwinter as well), with the occasional treat of a Pomarine or Parasitic Jaeger. A lobster roll and a cream horn from the adjacent Lobster Shack nicely fuels your summertime sea watching.

In winter, onshore winds (less likely to produce fog) are the time to look for alcids. Razorbill are regular, as are Black-legged Kittiwakes, but search carefully for Thick-billed Murres and Dovekies, especially after strong storms. Most calm mornings also produce Razorbills on the water from November to March, and Black Guillemots are common all year.

After having your fill of sea watching and/or lobster rolls, backtrack on Two Lights Road to **Two Lights State Park**. Various short trails take you to cliff edges and wind through scrubby thickets and red spruce woodlands. This is an alternative/additional place to sea watch (see above), but it's always worth scanning the water here, especially on calm winter mornings. You might be just a little more likely to see Dovekies and Razorbills on the water here than at Dyer Point. Harlequin Ducks and Purple Sandpipers are often on or near the rocks below, and Black Guillemots are common.

Invasive plants (especially black swallowwort) have really taken a toll on the quality of the habitat here, but the scrub is always worth a check in migration and for lingering "half hardies" in winter. In irruption years, White-winged Crossbill can be present. The woodland trails offer a sample of breeding birds in the summer months, including Golden-crowned Kinglets and Black-throated Green Warblers.

RARITIES

"Audubon's" Yellow-rumped Warbler, December 2008 (Dyer Point)

For a map and trails visit Maine Trail Finder at www.mainetrailfinder.com and use the search feature.

SITE C4 Village Crossings and the Cape Elizabeth Greenbelt Trail

TOWN Cape Elizabeth. DeLorme Map 3: A5. **SEASON** October–January, February–May **VISITATION** 1–2 hrs. No restroom facilities. **HIGHLIGHTS** Frugivores; overwintering "half hardies"; Northern Shrike; American Woodcock.

A large freshwater marsh, extensive scrub, and an old orchard combine with a warmer microclimate to offer excellent late-fall and winter birding. Midwinter half-hardies such as Swamp Sparrow are annual. Flocks of American Robins are often joined by Cedar Waxwings and, during irruptions, Bohemian Waxwings and Pine Grosbeaks. Sparrow migration can also be very productive here, and it's a good spot to look for raptors and Northern Shrike in winter. Summertime finds Yellow Warblers and Baltimore Orioles among a variety of others, and Eastern Bluebirds are often seen all year. The trails in and around this area are also a good spot to observe displaying American Woodcocks from mid-March through early to mid-May.

DIRECTIONS

Follow the directions for site C2 above, but at the blinking light in the center of Cape Elizabeth turn right onto Scott Dyer Road. At the stop sign make a left onto Spurwink Avenue, and take your first left onto Starboard Drive. Park off the road at the curve to the left, where you will see the wide mowed trail and the small green Cape Elizabeth Greenbelt trail marker. Work the scrub, and at the four-way trail intersection make a right for the boardwalk across the marsh (Virginia Rail breeds). You can continue straight to link up with an extensive trail network. Or return to the four-way intersection and continue straight through an old orchard that can be loaded with frugivores in winter. This is the area known to birders as Village Crossings, as it is adjacent to the assisted living facility now known as Kindred Assisted Living—Village Crossings. When the apples and crabapples are blooming in spring, migrants can be especially plentiful, including warblers and Baltimore Orioles.

After working this area (the trails are often quite wet), return to the four-way intersection, make a left, and continue along the edge of the marsh to the high school. This is a good spot for sparrows, especially behind the houses (some of which have feeders) and shrikes.

RARITIES

Lark Sparrow, January–February 2013

A map and information about the extensive Greenbelt Trail system can be found at the website of the town of Cape Elizabeth: www.capeelizabeth.com /government/rules_reg/maps/trailmaps/home.html. The Spurwink and Great Pond Trails are also worth a visit.

SITE C5 Portland Harbor Winter Gull Loop

TOWNS Portland and South Portland. DeLorme Map 72–73. SEASON November, **December–February**, March. VISITATION 1 hr. to half day.

Restrooms at local businesses. ♿ **HIGHLIGHTS** White-winged gulls; ducks; Peregrine Falcon.

Although not the thriving fishing port it once was, there is still enough fishery (primarily lobster) activity to attract a number of gulls in winter. It's the most reliable place in southern Maine for Glaucous Gull, and the quantity of Iceland Gulls can be impressive. Almost any rare gull is possible here, and while sorting through the gulls, you may also find a variety of interesting ducks. A couple of hot spots in South Portland are particularly good for unseasonable, lingering, or "pioneering" dabblers, while a good variety of the usual common wintering ducks can often be seen and photographed very well from some of the piers. However, a spotting scope is helpful for most of this tour.

DIRECTIONS

You can either bird the entire loop thoroughly, which could easily take half a day when the going is good, or you can hit the best spots in an efficient hour or so. I'll describe the complete coverage, and you can decide which spots to visit or not. Either way, to start from I-295, take Exit 7 for Franklin Street and head into town. At its end at the eighth traffic light, you hit Commercial Street. Find street parking either to the left or right, or head into the parking deck across the street or one of the many nearby decks.

The **Maine State Pier** is your first stop, which is just beyond the Casco Bay Ferry Terminal (follow the road to the left of the parking deck opposite the end of Franklin Street). Walk to the end of the pier and scan the waters, nearby buildings, and anywhere a gull might be sitting or feeding.

Either return to your car and drive down Commercial Street (see below), or feed your meter and begin your walk (about 1 mile in each direction, not including several pier out-and-backs) by turning left at Commercial Street. Walking (or driving) southwest down Commercial Street, scan any patches of water, rooftops with gulls, and walk to the end of the piers that are not posted as private. See the Portland Harborwalk map at the link below as a guide to what you are able to access, but note that the signage is not often very clear or obvious. Obey no-trespassing signs and watch out for workers and their vehicles. Never drive onto the piers or park illegally; you will be towed. Some piers are off-limits, but most of the best viewing sites are accessible. Be sure to check the lobster docks (and adjacent rooftops) from the alley between Custom House Wharf and Portland Pier, and walk to the end of Portland Pier (part of the Harborwalk Trail), which is a worthwhile spot for scanning the ends of nearby wharves.

The large office building on **Chandler's Wharf** (Pierce-Atwood law building) is a great pier to walk around, as both Iceland and Glaucous Gulls often feed and loaf near here. If you are not on foot, park on the street nearby and walk to the end of the pier. If nets are being worked on, please avoid the area for safety reasons.

The "**Fish Pier**" (or, as the building says, Maine Marine Trade Center) is the best spot on this side of the harbor for gull watching, and if you are doing a quick check, this is the place to hit. There is no public parking on or near the pier, so you'll need to park at Commercial Street if you are not already on foot, and follow the entrance road (signed "Fish Pier" from the light at Commercial and Center Streets).

Walk around the building (clearly posted as "at your own risk"), spending as much time as possible scanning up and down the river—lobster pounds to the north and south are often popular with Iceland Gulls. A dozen or more from this one spot is not uncommon. A scope is helpful but not always required. Scan the bridge, especially the edges of the stanchions and nearby dock cranes, for Peregrine Falcons—the male of the local breeding pair often spends his winter in and around the harbor, returning to the bridge to roost.

Return to your car—wherever it is!—and head west on Commercial Street, passing under the Casco Bay Bridge and taking your first right to go over the bridge and into South Portland. After crossing the bridge, make a left at the third light onto Cottage Road. Turn right into the parking lot for the Hannaford supermarket and park along the edge of **Mill Creek Cove**.

Gulls love to drink and bathe in freshwater, and here, Mill Creek—which remains open through most winters—empties freshwater into the sheltered cove. This is a great spot for studying and photographing roosting gulls, and a reliable spot for both Iceland and Glaucous Gulls. In fact, many birders will make this their only gull stop when birding the area. Gulls come and go with tide and ice conditions, with a lot of turnover, so it's worth spending some time here. Be sure to also sort through the volumes of Mallards and smaller numbers of American Black Ducks (and plenty of hybrids thereof), which in most winters will include at least one unseasonable "pioneering" dabbler that's attempting to overwinter. Between the cove and Mill Creek Park across Cottage Road, Mallard numbers often grow to four or five hundred or more birds by midwinter, so check carefully.

From the parking lot, walk to the road and check Mill Creek from the bridge. Cross into **Mill Creek Park** and walk the paved multipurpose trail on the southern bank of the creek, combing through the Mallard masses. When the creek turns under the path, enter the park to your right and check the pond for ducks (if open) and roosting gulls (sometimes on the ice, too). There's something unusual every winter, with recent winters hosting Green-winged Teal and Northern Pintail, but other finds including Northern Shoveler and even a Wood Duck.

Return to the light at Broadway. If you go straight, follow Cottage Road into Cape Elizabeth and visit Portland Head Light at **Fort Williams Park** to scan for open-ocean waterbirds (sea watching can be decent during a storm) and check the scrubby edges of the park for migrant land birds, especially in late fall.

Alternatively, you can continue to bird Portland Harbor by making a left onto Broadway and checking the mouth of the harbor from **Bug Light Park**. At the end of Broadway, make a left onto Breakwater Drive, followed by a right onto Madison Street, which ends at the park. Scanning the harbor from near the little lighthouse can be productive, and the brush and trees of the park sometimes attract migrants (especially in spring) following a "dawn flight" returning from over Casco Bay; but low-quality habitat rarely holds them for long. In late fall and early spring, check the lawn for Snow Buntings and Horned Larks, however.

After your tour, you can backtrack to Route 77 to head south into Cape Elizabeth (see sites C2, C3, C4) or return to Portland via the Casco Bay Bridge.

RARITIES

Ivory Gull, January–March 1997 (Fish Pier)

A map of the Portland Harborwalk, which will greatly aid in your exploration of the Old Port piers, can be found on the Portland Trails website: http://trails.org/our-trails/harborwalk/.

SITE C6 The Eastern Promenade

TOWN Portland. DeLorme Map 73: E5.   **SEASON** All year, but especially October–December.   **VISITATION** 1 hr. to all day. Washrooms in the summer, portable toilets in the winter at East End Beach. ♿ See map, p. 75.

HIGHLIGHTS Migration fallouts; waterbird concentrations; rarities (especially Dickcissel and Orange-crowned Warbler); Ospreys; general urban birding.

This urban birding oasis sits at the northeast end of the concrete jungle of the Portland Peninsula. Surrounded by water or dense development, "the Prom" offers an island of green—food, shelter, and a place to recover (likely, for many migrants, after being disoriented by the big-city lights while migrating overnight) and has a cumulative list of 208 species as of June 2016.

When I moved to Maine, we lived in Portland's East End, a few blocks off the Prom. Near-daily coverage proved the full potential of this park, and in the past fourteen years I have accumulated a "patch list" of 175 species here! The scrubby hillsides can be rich with migrants, especially in May, and again in late September and October when sparrows are on the move. The stands of goldenrod and other perennials, weedy edges, and mowed grass can hold impressive numbers of common migrants, but also regular rarities. In fact, the Prom may be the most consistent spot in the state for Orange-crowned Warbler and probably the best spot on the mainland to look for Dickcissel (both in October through November).

DIRECTIONS

From I-295 take Exit 7 (Franklin Arterial/Street) and head into town. At the fifth traffic light (including the one immediately at the end of the off-ramp if arriving from the south) make a left onto Congress Street. Follow it up Munjoy Hill to its end, and make a right onto Eastern Promenade. Take your first left—as Eastern Promenade (Road) bends to the right—onto Cutter Street and follow it to its end at the bottom of the hill in the parking lot for East End Beach (if the lot is full, park just uphill in the large parking lot).

Begin your exploration with a scan of the water, first checking the gulls at the little jetty (Iceland is regular in winter) and being sure to check any exposed rocks at lower tides. Afterward, begin to walk the park, choosing how much time you want to spend. At the very least, walk a short distance up and down each side of the paved multipurpose trail to sample the shoreline and scrubby hillside.

I usually bird the park thoroughly by making a lengthy loop that follows the paved path along the shoreline to the west, passing the old rail bridge (roosting gulls; great views into Osprey nests on the railway trestle), up the hill and past the sewage treatment plant. Following the stairway of the Loring Memorial Trail, I head up the hill and then turn left to take the trail through the woods (great for migrants), eventually connecting with the Mid-Slope Trail (see map at link below). I then either return to my car via Cutter Street, or continue on to Fort Allen Park. From there I take the trail back down to the water and return to the car via the paved multipurpose trail.

In summer, breeding birds are limited, but you'll see more Yellow Warblers here than about any other place in the area, and you never know what might show up. Common Eiders and Common Terns are easily observed, with great views of Ospreys in the nest on the old railway trestle to be had from the trail along the edge of the sewage treatment plant. Since Fort Allen Park and the Promenade are a convenient walk from downtown, including the cruise ship terminal, visitors to Portland can sample our local bird life here without getting in a car. Just follow the paved, multipurpose trail along the waterfront, beginning at the corner of Commercial and India Streets (next to the Ocean Gateway Terminal) at the east end of the Old Port.

In winter, Northern Mockingbirds dominate the park, but occasionally large flocks of Cedar and/or Bohemian Waxwings arrive to feast on various native and invasive fruits. A Lark Sparrow overwintered in 2011, so check groups of Song or House Sparrows carefully. Northern Shrikes are also occasional, and in irruption years Snowy Owls appear once in a while (scan rooftops and offshore islets and forts). Meanwhile, waterfowl concentrations can be impressive, especially Common Eider, Buffleheads, Common Goldeneye (now only rarely including a Barrow's Goldeneye), and Long-tailed Ducks. Bald Eagles can often be seen hunting them, and keep an eye out for white-winged gulls and non-Black-Guillemot alcids. Purple Sandpipers are occasional, especially on the offshore rocks at low tide. November through early December, when the Prom remains warmer than the surrounding region owing to the moderating qualities of the water and the heat island of the city, can produce surprises of all sorts.

But in migration, almost anything is possible on any day. Major fallouts can occur when nocturnally migrating songbirds are grounded by weather, such as precipitation from a cold front or a dense bank of fog. But the heavily mowed, invasive-species-rich degraded urban habitat doesn't often hold birds long, so you want to get here early when such conditions are expected. On October 17, 2014, a huge flight of sparrows consisted of eight species, led by an overwhelming and exhilarating two-thousand-plus White-throated Sparrows and more than five hundred Song Sparrows.

Meanwhile, daily turnover of birds can be expected under almost any condition, and the park certainly offers preferred habitat to sparrows and late-season "scrubby migrants." Depending on where city staff have hacked vegetation and gotten overzealous with the mowers, the best places to look for sparrows, Dickcissels, Orange-crowned Warblers, and truant migrants are extensive stands of goldenrod and evening primrose (which often blooms here through October). Be sure to also check patches of orange-spotted jewelweed, especially the extensive stands in the woods to the east of the Loring Memorial.

Shorebirds are occasional, especially at low tide, and sometimes roosts form at high tide, especially along the rocks near the base of Tukey's Bridge (check across the channel, to the left of the B&M factory) and on Pomroy Rock off East End Beach if there is any exposed rock (inundated on flood tides).

But shorebirds are more likely at **Back Cove** (site c7), which I often visit after birding the Prom. For those wanting a long, four-mile walk, you can follow the Eastern Promenade multipurpose trail under Tukey's Bridge (I-295) and circumnavigate Back Cove. This is an excellent trip on a bike, especially with a scope fastened to the bike or on your back. Even without a scope, this easy ride will allow you to sample all the hot corners of the inlet.

RARITIES

Gyrfalcon, March 1992; Lark Sparrow, December 2011–March 2012; Yellow-breasted Chat (almost annual)

A map and more information can be found on the website of the Friends of the Eastern Promenade at www.easternpromenade.org/, while an up-to-date bird list can be viewed at www.easternpromenade.org/protect/birds-of-the-eastern-promenade/.

SITE C7 Back Cove

Entry by Rich Eakin

TOWN Portland. DeLorme Map 73: E4. **SEASON** July, **August–October,** November–April. **VISITATION** 30 min. to 2 hrs. Portable toilets at parking areas in most seasons. See map, p. 75. **HIGHLIGHTS** Migrant shorebirds; winter gulls; waterfowl and other wetland and grassland species.

Established as a wildlife sanctuary in 1915, Back Cove is an accessible and productive year-round birding site in the heart of Portland. This shallow, mile-wide, circular tidal basin, connecting to Casco Bay under Tukey's Bridge and surrounded by major thoroughfares, offers a variety of habitats (open water, mudflats, mussel beds, salt marsh, man-made rocky shore, grassy and weedy areas, ornamental plantings). Adjacent areas along the northwest shore, including Payson Park, feature two tidal brooks flowing into the cove, grassy fields, some trees, and a small pond. With a northwest wind, this spot can be good for fall hawk watching. The cove rarely freezes nowadays, and overwintering flocks of Mallards, American Black Ducks, and Canada Geese sometimes contain unseasonable species, such as Northern Pintail, and an overwintering Greater White-fronted Goose (in 2011–12), along with good numbers of the expected common diving ducks.

I adopted Back Cove and environs as my local patch in 1972 and was a persistent observer and recorder of its bird life until recently departing the state. The current list of 220 species (over half the state's total) attests not only to this site's value as a birding hot spot but also to the rewards of continuous observation. One never knows what to expect. In addition to avian rarities, notable sightings include a mink hunting crabs, the occasional stray moose, a harp seal, and a submerging car from which the startled (and lucky) occupants surfaced and swam safely to shore.

Despite heavy use by pedestrians, joggers, and cyclists, who constantly parade along the 3.5-mile Back Cove Trail encircling it (joining Eastern Promenade Trail under Tukey's Bridge), Back Cove remains a worthy destination for anyone visiting Portland. Although this site is not as productive as it once was, owing to a combination of factors, from increased human presence to natural habitat reduction, the variety of species seen here over the years suggests that continued attention is more than warranted.

DIRECTIONS

From I-295 take Exit 6B and merge onto Forest Avenue (Route 302 West/100 North). At the first light, turn right onto Bedford Street. Turn right at the next light onto Preble Street Extension, where you will see the cove on your left. Park in the lot on your left and scan the cove; a scope is helpful.

Depending on season, tidal stage, and human activity (soccer games, etc.), it is often productive to walk onto the playing field and along the shore where there are paths amid shrubbery and a wet, weedy patch mixed with salt marsh

(Saltmarsh Sparrow has bred in recent years) and a new demonstration garden. This area can be productive, especially during fall migration, for roosting shorebirds and the odd surprise. I have seen everything from Upland and Buff-breasted Sandpipers to Northern Wheatear and Dickcissel here. Small numbers of shorebirds use the cove in spring migration, and numbers don't tend to build until juvenile birds begin to arrive, with numbers and diversity not often peaking here until September. Snowy Owls are occasional in winter, and check the flock of roosting gulls—Lesser Black-backed Gull is fairly regular. It is important to avoid disturbing roosting birds, so use caution and view the area from a distance.

From this lot, you can walk the 3.5-mile trail around the cove. A leisurely stroll along the trail, stopping occasionally to admire the view, provides birders an opportunity to savor the sights of this urban oasis while getting a bit of exercise as well. Or return to your car and drive clockwise around the cove via Baxter Boulevard, checking out Payson Park on the left in the northwest corner of the cove, where birds such as Mew Gull, Western Kingbird, and Northern Hawk Owl have been found. Continue along Baxter Boulevard, then pull into the dirt parking lot on the north side of the cove for another scan of the water.

Many birders will include a visit to Back Cove before or after other seasonable urban hot spots, such as the **Eastern Promenade** (site c6), **Evergreen Cemetery** (c8), or, in winter, the **Portland Harbor gull tour** (c5).

RARITIES

Northern Hawk Owl, December 1981–March 1982; Loggerhead Shrike, April 1982; American Avocet, October 1990; Northern Wheatear, September 1996; Mew Gull, December 2008 (first or second state record), Little Egret, June–July 2015, and May–July, 2016.

A map can be found on Portland Trail's website at www.trails.org/our-trails/back-cove-trail.

SITE c8 Evergreen Cemetery and Other Urban Sites

TOWN Portland. DeLorme Map 73: D–E2. SEASON April, **May–early June**, September–October. VISITATION 1–3 hrs. No facilities. ♿ See map, p. 75. HIGHLIGHTS Migration hot spot.

On a given morning in May you'll find more birders at Evergreen Cemetery than most everywhere else in the state combined! It's a very social atmosphere, with lots of people happy to answer questions. The park is not what it once was, because of invasive plants, sedimentation and/or water quality changes in the ponds, poor maintenance decisions, and increasingly fragmented habitat resulting from an ill-conceived road, a widened power-line corridor, and excessive sewer line access. Nevertheless, it is still one of the prime birding destinations for spring migration in the state and has provided a wealth of rarities over the years; and when conditions align, a May morning can still be absolutely spectacular here.

DIRECTIONS

From I-295 in Portland take Exit 6B and merge onto Forest Avenue (Route 302 West/100 North). After the first traffic light, continue for 1.4 miles, through the chaotic intersection of Woodfords Corner (center lane to continue straight on Forest Avenue), to the eighth light. Make a left onto Walton Street. At the end make a right onto Stevens Avenue and an immediate left into the cemetery. If you arrive early and the gate is still closed, turn around and head south on Stevens Avenue (passing Walton Street) and make your third right onto Brentwood Street. At the end of Brentwood you can park along the road and walk through the gate to head downhill toward the ponds (see below).

If entering the cemetery via the main entrance on Stevens Avenue, continue on the paved entrance road. Stay straight/soft left past the office onto Eastern Avenue. Stay on the pavement as it curves through the cemetery, but as the pavement turns left onto Mulberry at the Whitney mausoleum, turn right onto the dirt and head down the hill to the ponds. Once at the ponds, park along the road (do not block gates or any side roads) and begin your exploration here. The edges of the ponds are often the primary hot spot on many mornings, but don't ignore the surrounding woods. Especially once oaks begin to bud, more warblers and other migrants can often be found in the higher canopy, rather than the convenient scrub around the ponds. Perhaps because of sedimentation, warming water, nutrient overload, or the loss of edge vegetation, the pond edge is not as productive as it once was, and on many days, more migrants are found at other corners of the park.

After rounding the ponds, sometimes more than once, I venture into the woods, first by following trails to the north side of the pond toward and around the "Junk Pond" and working the edges of the playing fields (see map

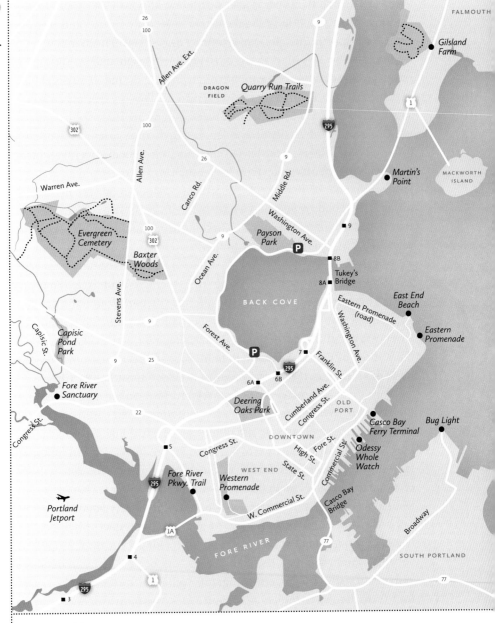

FALMOUTH

Gilsland Farm

DRAGON FIELD

Quarry Run Trails

26
100

100

26

9

295

9

Martin's Point

MACKWORTH ISLAND

1

Allen Ave. Ext.

Allen Ave.

Warren Ave.

302

100

Canco Rd.

Middle Rd.

Washington Ave.

9

302

Evergreen Cemetery

Baxter Woods

Payson Park

P

9

Ocean Ave.

Tukey's Bridge

8B

8A

East End Beach

Eastern Promenade (road)

Eastern Promenade

BACK COVE

Stevens Ave.

Capisic Pond Park

Capisic St.

9

25

Forest Ave.

P

Washington Ave.

Franklin St.

295

7

Fore River Sanctuary

9

22

6A

6B

Deering Oaks Park

Cumberland Ave.

Congress St.

OLD PORT

Casco Bay Ferry Terminal

Bug Light

5

Congress St.

Congress St.

DOWNTOWN

Fore St.

Commercial St.

Odessy Whole Watch

295

Fore River Pkwy. Trail

Western Promenade

WEST END

High St.

State St.

Casco Bay Bridge

Portland Jetport

1A

W. Commercial St.

Broadway

4

FORE RIVER

77

SOUTH PORTLAND

1

295

3

77

PORTLAND

link). The cemetery proper is also worth checking, as Cape May Warblers are most often found in isolated clusters of Norway spruce, and scattered crabapples, hawthorns, etc., can all attract migrants when blooming.

Spring—especially May—is the most heralded time to visit Evergreen. The second and third weeks of the month often produce the best diversity of birds, with the third week usually the most likely to yield twenty species of warblers. The last week of May into the first week of June are undervalued and can yield an excellent diversity of warblers and up to nine species of flycatchers in a single visit. Fall is under-birded, but usually less productive, likely owing to a combination of leading lines for reorienting migrants and less valuable foraging habitat at that season. September visits can be very productive, however, and midsummer and winter before freeze-up can sometimes yield waterbird surprises. It's also worth checking in winter for finches in irruption years, especially in the cemetery proper.

As described above, negative changes to Evergreen—and likely the overall decline in neotropical migrants—are affecting the birding there. Therefore, I encourage you to visit other urban Portland sites. I could not possibly cover every trail and corridor worth checking here, so I shall direct you to the website of Portland Trails (see link). Follow directions from there, and learn about some of the current projects. Besides **Capisic Pond Park** (site C9), the **Fore River Sanctuary** (all year), **Western Promenade area** (migration), **Presumpscot River Preserve** (migration and summer for common breeding birds), **Riverton Trolley Park**, and others can be rewarding in particular. The **Fore River Parkway Trail** used to be extremely productive in both spring and fall, but overzealous clear-cutting by the city has rendered much of it devoid of valuable habitat. Nonetheless, it is worth checking the waters of the Fore River here, especially in winter, and a loop around "Mercy Pond"—as birders call it—on the campus of the Mercy Hospital usually produces Black-crowned Night-Heron in all but winter (including surprisingly late into the fall), and Green Heron in summer. Its scrubby edges can be productive in migration and occasionally host lingering migrants well into November. The **Quarry Run Trails**, known to birders as Dragon Fields, was once a premier sparrowing destination. Unfortunately, invasive plants and poor maintenance have rendered this park of less value to birds. Although good numbers of sparrows are occasionally still found before the mowers cut what's left of the decent perennial growth, few birders visit here anymore.

Always a pleasant walk is Maine Audubon's **Gilsland Farm**, which includes extensive trails through fields, edges that can be good especially during passerine migration, and a view of the mudflats of the Presumpscot River for shorebirds. An impressive array of rarities has been found here over the years, from the state's first MacGillivray's Warbler in December to a Little Egret in June and July of 2015.

Birders often visit nearby **Capisic Pond Park** (site C9) after they bird Evergreen. Return to Stevens Avenue and turn right. At the fifth light, turn right onto Frost/Capisic Street, and in 0.4 miles turn right onto Macy Street.

RARITIES

(Evergreen only) Worm-eating Warbler, May 2004; Hooded Warbler (several occasions)

All the aforementioned trails can be found on this helpful map from Portland Trails at trails.org/our-trails.

SITE C9 Capisic Pond Park

TOWN Portland. DeLorme Map 73: F2. SEASON All year, but especially May–July. VISITATION 30 min. to 2 hrs. No restroom facilities. ♿ See map, p. 75. HIGHLIGHTS Migrants; Orchard Oriole (May–August).

This is simply one of those birdy little places that are worth a walk at any season. While it is most popular in May for migrants, and into June for Orchard Oriole (one or two pairs usually breed in or near the park, the only regular nesting location in the state), good birds can be found at any season, and fall migration is underappreciated, especially when sparrows are on the move in October. A restoration project in 2010–11 increased native plant diversity, especially of fruit sources. Unfortunately in the fall of 2015, misguided and overzealous brush-hogging (a recurring theme in Portland) destroyed much of this. How birds—including the Orchard Orioles—and therefore the birding will be affected by this is unclear at the moment.

DIRECTIONS

From the south, take I-295 into Portland to Exit 5 (Route 22/Congress Street). Bear right on the off-ramp, following signs for Route 22 West. Merge onto

Route 1A (Commercial Street Extension), and at the second light make a left onto Congress Street (Route 22 West).

From the north, take Exit 5B, and at the end of the off-ramp make a right onto Route 22 West/Congress Street.

At the fourth light make a right onto Stevens Avenue (Route 9), and at the next light make a left onto Capisic Street. Proceed for 0.4 miles to a right onto Macy Street and park in the spaces on the right or along the road. Begin your birding by checking the trees along the edge of the pond, which hosts Warbling Vireo, Baltimore Oriole, and Eastern Kingbird in summer. Enter the park and walk the length of it, keeping an eye on the pond for Wood Ducks, Green Herons, and Black-crowned Night-Heron in late spring through early fall, and Ring-necked and other ducks in early spring and fall. The Orchard Orioles are most often found in the southern half of the park but could be anywhere, including surrounding neighborhoods. Yellow Warblers are common breeders, and look and listen for Alder Flycatcher, American Redstart, and others. Late fall brings the chance at lingering warblers and rare-but-regular strays, such as White-eyed Vireo and Orange-crowned Warbler. In most seasons you'll find as many Northern Cardinals here as anywhere in the state. In winter, a healthy crop of fruit, especially various crabapples, attracts frugivores, led by American Robins and, in irruptions years, Bohemian Waxwings and rarely Pine Grosbeaks.

RARITIES

Golden-winged Warbler, May 2006; White-winged Dove, May 2009; Least Bittern, May 2015; Ash-throated Flycatcher, October 2015

A map of the park is available on the website of Portland Trails at www.trails .org/our-trails/capisic-brook-trail.

SITE C10 Odyssey Whalewatch

TOWN Portland. DeLorme Map 73: F5. SEASON June, July–September. VISITATION 3–4 hr. tour. Check web for current schedule. Restrooms and snack bar on board. See map, p. 75. HIGHLIGHTS Pelagic birds and whales.

A popular summertime outing, this whale watch out of Portland is conveniently located for the most densely populated part of the state and is frequented by birders. Excellent birder-naturalists over the years and previous dedicated pelagic birding tours organized by Freeport Wild Bird Supply have resulted in an impressive list of rarities and more data on timing of birds' arrivals than other trips in the area.

Unlike the Kennebunkport trip (York County, site y8), the Portland trip is limited in its range to various smaller ledges north of Jeffrey's Ledge. Over-fishing of herring and the changing water temperatures and food chains of the Gulf of Maine appear to be having an impact on the reliability of both birds and whales in these areas. The resultant inconsistency of trips for either birds or whales has unfortunately reduced the frequency of birders boarding the boat in recent years.

DIRECTIONS

From I-295 in Portland take Exit 7 and head into town on Franklin Street. At its end on Commercial Street, make a right. The whale watch is on Long Wharf on the left in 0.2 miles. Except on Sundays, meters for street parking limit your time, so you'll need to park in one of the many commercial lots or parking garages in the area (including the one straight ahead of you as you reach Commercial Street via Franklin Street).

Ten years ago, Cory's Shearwater was considered rare in Maine, but it is now sometimes the most common tubenose encountered in late summer and early fall trips. June can be slow for birds other than Northern Gannet, but as July moves on and waters warm up, "wintering" tubenoses from the Southern Hemisphere increase, led by Greater and Sooty Shearwaters and Wilson's Storm-Petrels (all common to abundant), while Leach's Storm-Petrels (rare) and Manx Shearwaters (occasional) are breeding here in the Gulf of Maine. Diversity increases in August and September, with the chance at both Red and Red-necked Phalaropes and all three jaegers (Parasitic is by far the most regular). Northern Gannets can be abundant.

While Black Guillemots are common as you sail out of the bay, other alcids, including Atlantic Puffins, are occasionally encountered offshore throughout the summer, and especially in the fall. As evident from the roster of "mega" rarities seen from this boat, you should be looking out for the unexpected.

Minke and fin whales are the most likely whales, while harbor porpoise and harbor seals are common. Common white-sided dolphins and migrant humpback whales are occasional, while *Mola mola* (ocean sunfish), basking sharks, and other fascinating marine life are sometimes seen.

Yellow-billed Loon, October 2010 (first state record); Cave Swallow, October 2010; Brown Booby, August 2011 (first state record), South Polar Skua and Long-tailed Jaeger on multiple occasions

For more information, schedule, and advance tickets (recommended), visit Odyssey's website at www.odysseywhalewatch.com.

SITE C11 Casco Bay Islands (especially Peaks Island) and the Mailboat

TOWNS Portland and Casco Bay environs. DeLorme Map 3: A4–5.
SEASON All year.   **VISITATION** 30 min. to 1 day or more. Restrooms on boats, and seasonal facilities on some islands.   **HIGHLIGHTS** Migrants; waterbirds; rarities; Black Guillemot; Common Eider; Osprey.

The many islands, large and small, of Casco Bay offer a wealth of birding opportunities. The major ones can be reached by ferry from Portland, and most offer plenty of roads to walk or bike. Boaters will find a variety of places to explore, and kayakers can poke around numerous nooks and crannies. The waters of Casco Bay host Common Eiders and Black Guillemots all year, along with often impressive numbers of the common bay ducks from fall through spring. Ospreys are numerous breeders, and Bald Eagles are regular all year long (more in winter). Land birding on any of the islands can be fantastic during migration.

DIRECTIONS

All the trips begin with a ride aboard the Casco Bay Lines ferry, the terminal of which is in Portland's Old Port. From I-295 take Exit 7 for Franklin Street. Head into town, and after eight lights (including the one at the northbound off-ramp) cross Commercial Street and stay straight to access the parking deck adjacent to the ferry terminal (several other parking decks are located nearby, and on Sunday there is no fee or time limit at meters on the street). Be sure to check the schedule in advance (at the link below) and then purchase your respective ticket. Check the dock and nearby piers while you're waiting, especially for white-winged gulls in winter.

All the islands are worth birding, and all the waters are worth exploring, but we'll focus on two "tours": Peaks Island and the Mailboat. The **Mailboat** operates twice a day, all year long, traveling between Portland and five islands, and offers a great way to see the bay and sample its denizens at a relaxing pace from a very steady platform. While true pelagics would be exceptionally rare, I have seen Red Phalarope (once), Razorbills (rare), Wilson's Storm-Petrels, and Northern Gannets from the Mailboat. You can enjoy a sampling of the local waterbirds for each season, including immature Common Loons in summer and white-winged gulls in winter. I think this is a truly underappreciated local birding opportunity; you sure can't beat the price (only $16 for 2.5–3.5 hours on the water as of 2015). It's also a good way to see some birds with a non-birding companion who just wants to take in the sights.

Ferries to and from the various islands, especially the summertime tour to and from Bailey Island, offer similar possibilities, and visits to any of the islands could yield land-bird surprises in migration. My favorite island to visit is **Peaks Island,** which, after a very quick ride, offers a diversity of habitats in a compact loop and has businesses open all year near the dock—including hot coffee for cold winter days.

Once on Peaks, I walk a loop of approximately 3.5 miles that covers the southern third of the island and samples its best habitats. Another option is to rent or carry over a bike, which is a great way to bird the island and efficiently travel between the best habitats. From the dock, walk up the hill to the first intersection and make a right onto Island Avenue (make a left to get to the bike rental shop). Bend left at the end, and take the second right onto Whitehead Street and then Seashore Avenue. Follow the shoreline, scanning offshore, checking the rocks (Purple Sandpipers in late fall through early spring; rarely Snowy Owl) and combing adjacent thickets from the road (please respect private property).

Enter the Battery Steele Conservation Area, a short loop trail (be careful on the makeshift boardwalk; and other sections can often be wet, too) that is birdy at all seasons. I'm convinced I will find a "mega" here some late fall day. Willow Flycatchers and Wood Ducks breed, and Black-crowned Night-Herons are often seen. Check the thickets of both native and, increasingly, invasive vegetation around the old battery, especially in late fall and winter. To reduce the length of the loop, you can exit the conservation area on the backside of the battery, making a left onto Brackett Avenue (the wider dirt road with the telephone poles; see below).

Otherwise, return to Seashore to continue your loop. Make a left onto Whaleback, followed by bearing left onto Brackett Avenue. Passing through woods and wooded yards, expect the common land birds of the season. Follow Brackett back into town, until it ends at Island Street. Making a left will bring you back to the first intersection, just up from the dock. Cyclists may want to circumnavigate the island, checking out any interesting habitats, and always keeping an eye out on the water.

RARITIES

Willow Ptarmigan, May–June 2000 (first and only record, Great Chebeague Island)

The website of the Casco Bay Lines ferry is www.cascobaylines.com, while a map of the trails of Peaks Island from Portland Trails can be seen at trails.org /our-trails/peaks-island-loop.

SITE C12 Riverbank Park and Westbrook Riverwalk

TOWN Westbrook. DeLorme Map 74: Westbrook inset. **SEASON** September–October, **November–March**, April–May. **VISITATION** 15 min. to 1 hr. No facilities. ♿ **HIGHLIGHTS** Migrant and wintering waterfowl, white-winged gulls, regular seasonal waterfowl rarities.

Put on the birding map by the discovery of a Tufted Duck that attempted to overwinter here in 2008–9, this unassuming stretch of the Presumpscot River has become a real winter birding hot spot. Hundreds of bread-fed Mallards congregate here (please, if you are going to feed them, try cracked corn or birdseed for more nutrition, rather than bread, which can lead to a host of problems), and the Saccarappa Falls upstream and narrowing channels keep patches of open water throughout the winter. This combination has attracted an impressive array of rare-for-the-season waterfowl, with at least one "good bird" overwintering each year among the masses of Mallards and smaller numbers of American Black Ducks and hybrids thereof: from one to three Northern Pintails have occurred in each of the last four winters, and Northern Shovelers overwintered for the last three years, including three in 2014–15. Other unseasonable oddities included a drake Wood Duck in January 2009 and a hen American Wigeon in the winter of 2010–11. A strong contingent of Ring-billed Gulls can attract the occasional Iceland Gull in midwinter, and from the winter of 2010–11 to 2013–14 a "mystery" white-winged gull, now simply known as the "Westbrook Gull," overwintered. Yet each year—and plumage cycle—it eluded identification (a runt Glaucous Gull or an Iceland x Glaucous hybrid are the leading candidates). The open water at the base of the falls attracts a variety of gulls, with Iceland regular and rarely Glaucous.

DIRECTIONS

From I-95 (the Maine Turnpike) take Exit 47. After the tollbooth make a left at the light to head west on the Westbrook Arterial (Route 25) toward Westbrook/Gorham. At the second traffic light, in 1.6 miles, make a right and then a left at the next light onto Main Street (Business 25). A tenth of a mile on your right is Riverbank Park (by the way, the hot pastrami on rye at Rosen's Deli across the street is superb); park along the entrance road. First, walk right and check the masses of ducks in the park and/or the river, carefully sorting through the multitudes of Mallards. Walk downriver along the riverwalk to a railroad bridge a few minutes downstream, where a patch of open water is often found when the rest of the river is frozen. Continue farther downstream to the end of the riverwalk at Cumberland Street and check the area above the dam, especially for gulls.

Return to Riverbank Park and either walk the riverwalk west to downtown, checking any open water in between, or return to your car, make a right on Main Street, and in 0.4 miles make a right into the public parking lot (blue sign) just before the Bank of America. Sift through the gulls and ducks that congregate near the base of the falls, especially in midwinter. This is a good spot for rare overwintering diving ducks such as Ring-necked (almost annual) and Common Merganser.

In spring (and again in fall) the riverwalk can host an assortment of the expected passerine migrants in the riparian trees and likely deserves some further exploration. In summer you'll find typical riparian breeders such as Warbling Vireo and Baltimore Oriole.

RARITIES

Tufted Duck, January–February 2009; the "Westbrook Gull," winter 2010 through 2014; Northern Shoveler (several winters; up to three birds)

SITE C13 Sebago Lake State Park and the Sebago Lake Loop

TOWNS Windham, Raymond, Casco, Sebago, Standish. DeLorme Maps 4–5. SEASON All year, but especially April and **October–November**. VISITATION 2 hrs. (state park) up to full day. State park entry fees.

Outhouses at state parks, and seasonal facilities elsewhere. ♿ ⚓

HIGHLIGHTS Waterbird migrants, migrant land birds, breeding birds, Fish Crow.

The second-largest lake in Maine, Sebago Lake is the water source for the city of Portland. From a birding perspective, it is a bit of an enigma. Low phosphorous levels and a sandy bottom limit the growth of algae or emergent vegetation. The lake is up to 380 feet deep, and even diving ducks are restricted to the edges. Waterfowl habitat is limited, as is public access. It takes a while to thoroughly bird the lake by circumnavigating it, and few birders do. Those who do, often find surprisingly few waterbirds. That being said, there's little doubt that the lake deserves more coverage, especially during and after coastal storms, or when migrant waterfowl are likely to be grounded. It is also worthwhile to check the lake as surrounding smaller ponds begin to freeze, and early in spring when the large lake opens up sooner than surrounding shallow bodies of water.

But it is a big body of water, and therefore passerine migrants concentrate around its edges, especially in early spring. I have observed some good "morning flights" around its edges, and pockets of accessible habitat around its edges are always worth a check. The state park is a good place to sample the common breeding birds of mixed pine-oak forest.

DIRECTIONS

I usually begin the loop in North Windham. From I-95 take Exit 48. At the light make a right onto Riverside Street. In 1.4 miles turn left onto Route 302 West. Follow Route 302 for 11 miles, through its intersection with Route 115/35 (stay straight) in North Windham. From April through September there are usually Fish Crows in the area. Be alert for them on wires, poles, and rooftops for the next half mile, especially in and around the dumpsters of the fast-food joints and supermarkets.

We'll make a counterclockwise loop around the lake, taking advantage of the few public overlooks. Horned Grebes are regular in spring and fall, and Common Loons can be seen as long as there is open water. Common Mergansers can sometimes be common, and Bald Eagles are plentiful.

At 4.2 miles past the intersection with Route 115, turn left at the light for Route 85 into the parking lot for the **Raymond Veterans Memorial Park**. This is a good spot for late fall Common Mergansers and tarrying Belted Kingfishers.

Follow Route 302 West for another 0.8 miles to the **Raymond Town Beach** on the left. This is a great place to scan the open water. Walk south along the sidewalk to check the cattail marsh, with Marsh Wrens and Swamp Sparrows—and probably Sora and Virginia Rail—in the breeding season.

In another 4.8 miles turn left onto State Park Road, and turn into **Sebago Lake State Park** in 1.4 miles. Off-season, or prior to the park's opening, make your first right and park near the trailhead signage for the Outer Loop Trail. The entire 4-mile loop can produce up to fifteen species of warblers in the summer (although deerflies can be challenging). The scrub along the Songo River (Blue-gray Gnatcatcher breeds) and the edge of the beach can be good in migration.

Otherwise, drive straight down the road to the parking lot at the end. Scan the water from the beach, and check the lakeside trees in migration. The sandbar at the mouth of the Songo River (walk north from the beach) is worth a check at all seasons. I've seen various shorebirds, including a Buff-breasted Sandpiper, roosting here, and when the water levels are low, a very intriguing mudflat is exposed. The mouth of the river is good for Common Mergansers, and Hooded Mergansers and Wood Ducks can be found upriver.

Return to your car and exit the park. Turn left onto State Park Road, and you'll soon cross the Songo River at the **Songo Locks**. Pull into the parking area on the left, just before the one-lane bridge, and check out the historic locks, the riparian vegetation, and in breeding season listen for Warbling and sometimes Yellow-throated Vireos.

Turn left onto State Park Road, and in 0.1 miles turn left into the west side of Sebago Lake State Park. Follow the road to the campground (no entry outside of posted hours) at the end for another view of the lake, including a sheltered cove.

Leaving the campground, continue on State Park Road for 1.4 miles. Make a left onto Clement Road, and at the end make a left onto Route 11/114 South. In 1.4 miles, make a right into the entrance for the **Trickey Pond Boat Launch**. Scan the pond, and there's a short nature trail loop that is good for a quick sampling of breeding birds.

In another 0.7 miles, turn left into a dirt pull-out just before the bridge at Sebago Cove. Scan the cove to the north from the road, and then take the short trail from the parking spot to scan the lake.

Heading south again, in 3.1 miles, you'll see the lakeshore again on your left in North Sebago. At the campground, scan the lake from the edge of the road. When Route 11 turns away, stay on Route 114 South, and in 0.2 miles make a left onto Shore Road. Take the second left onto Marina Road and park at **Sebago Town Beach.** You need a permit here in the summer, but I usually check the lake only before and after beach season, so I just scan the lake and the beach from the parking lot.

Return to Route 114 and continue south to sample the waters and shoreline of **Sebago Lake.** In 0.8 miles you'll see a series of dead-end side streets to your left. Pick one to scan the lake from its end. A short distance farther south, bear left onto Wards Cove Road and scan the lake again from the road. Continue on Wards Cove Road until it returns to Route 114, and make a left to continue south.

In 3.4 miles make a left onto Harmons Beach Road and follow it to its end for one of the more productive places to scan the middle of the lake. Return to Route 114 and head south for another 1.3 miles, to a left onto Smith Mill Lane. Pull off just before or after the guardrail in 0.4 miles and scan the marsh and lake on both sides. This is one of the better corners for dabbling ducks, thanks to the emergent vegetation.

A half mile farther south on Route 114, pull over into the dirt parking lot on your right and cross the road for another view of the lake. In another 1.2 miles you'll hit the intersection with Route 35. Make a left, and then an immediate left into the **Sebago Lake Station Landing.** This is a good spot to scan the lake, and the scrubby growth along the edges of the parking lot can be productive in migration. This is a corner I like to check immediately following a strong coastal storm, especially one tropical in nature, for the chance at something heading back to the ocean.

Turn left out of the parking lot and continue for 1.5 miles. Opposite the junction with Route 237 pull into a small parking lot at a pumping station for one last look at the lake. From here you can follow Route 35 for 5.2 miles back to its intersection with Route 302 in North Windham.

I always take Route 237 from August through December in order to check the **Colonial Acres Sod Farm** in Gorham. American Golden-Plovers can sometimes be seen in August–September, and "grasspipers" are always possible. Later in fall it's a good spot for Horned Lark and Snow Bunting, occasionally with a Lapland Longspur mixed in. Follow Route 237 for 3.9 miles and make a right onto Wards Hill Road, which affords several safe views of the sod farm. Return to Route 237 and make a right. I usually pull off here on the right, just as you start going downhill and the dirt shoulder is wide, for another scan of both sides of the farm's turf fields. Be sure to carefully check the edges of any standing water.

Route 237 ends at Route 25; make a left and follow Route 25 through Westbrook to return to I-95 at Exit 47, or continuing on into Portland.

SITE C14 Sandy Point Beach, Cousin's Island

TOWN Yarmouth. DeLorme Map 6: D1. SEASON Mid-August–October, November–February. VISITATION 30 min. in winter; up to 4 hrs. in fall. Portable toilet usually present in fall. HIGHLIGHTS Migrants in "morning flight," sometimes in amazing numbers; winter waterfowl.

The "morning flight," or more precisely, "morning redetermined migration," occurs following each night's migration. This phenomenon occurs when migrant passerines reorient come sunrise, likely because of a combination of wind and geography. Whether they were caught over the Gulf of Maine come dawn, or escaping the limited resources and concentrated predators of islands and narrow peninsulas, or reorienting to be in position for the next flight (or, likely, some combination of all these), birds funnel through the Casco Bay Islands as they work their way inland.

In fall, when westerly winds drift migrants offshore and/or to the coast, birds work their way inshore and island-hop through Casco Bay, with many of them concentrating at Sandy Point, a peninsula facing northwest, and the closest point to the mainland of any major Casco Bay Island. While this is a serious oversimplification of the phenomena, it is roughly what produces one of the largest concentrations of migrant land birds in the entire state of Maine in the fall migration.

Using radar and weather (the concepts of both, and a full explanation of the morning flight phenomenon at Sandy Point can be found in my book *How to Be a Better Birder*), we can choose the perfect mornings to visit Sandy Point. Keep in mind that this is a dawn occurrence—after three or four hours at most on the best flight days, you'll find little here, so arrive early! Generally speaking, anytime there are light to moderate northwest (and to a lesser extent, west) winds overnight in August through late October, there will be a morning flight at Sandy Point. Calm air and light northerly winds can also produce smaller flights following a heavy overnight migration.

And finally, in winter, scanning the waters from the point and the bridge can be rewarding: large concentrations of Common Eiders, Common Goldeneyes, and others sometimes include a Barrow's Goldeneye, any of the three scoters, and occasionally Greater or Lesser Scaup.

DIRECTIONS

From I-295 take Exit 15 and head north on US Route 1. At the first light make a right onto Portland Street. At its end, turn right onto Main Street. When that ends, turn right onto Route 88 (Lafayette Street) and follow it for 0.6 miles to a left onto Princes Point Road, and then take your first left onto Gilman Road. Just after the bridge onto Cousins Island make a left into the dirt parking lot of Sandy Point Beach.

If the conditions are right, you'll probably see me at the base of the bridge, which local birders have nicknamed "my office." I'll be desperately trying to count the specks whizzing by overhead, but most people are smarter than I—they'll be in the parking lot enjoying a dazzling array and sometimes-extraordinary numbers and diversity of migrant land birds that are stopping to rest in the brush and trees surrounding the parking lot. Carefully work the edge, always keep one eye open overhead, and be sure to check the trails into the woods and through the power-line corridor.

It usually doesn't take long to see if it's "on" in the morning, but when it is, there may be no better place—at least on the mainland—in Maine to see, photograph, and enjoy long- and short-distance migrants of all kinds.

After extensive cutting, an agreement was reached with Central Maine Power in 2012 that should maintain the park's importance to migrant birds and the birders who enjoy them, by minimizing future cutting and providing oversight.

I'll offer just a brief sample of some of my personal high counts (through 2015) for the morning flight, in order to whet your appetite for a fall visit to Sandy Point—my favorite place to bird in the fall:

1,092 Northern Flickers, 9/21/10
471 Ruby-crowned Kinglets, 10/6/08
1,075 American Robins, 10/17/10
703 Northern Parulas, 9/17/13
758 Yellow-rumped Warblers, 10/12/14
444 Blackpoll Warblers, 9/19/09
408 American Redstarts, 8/24/13
232 Pine Siskins, 10/7/08

MONTHLY HIGH COUNT DAYS
(ALL MIGRANTS):
August: 1,177—8/24/13
September: 4,346—9/21/10
October: 3,069—10/7/08

I have personally recorded a whopping 179 species here since 2006 when I began keeping records at this tiny park, with a litany of rarities including Prothonotary Warbler (9/23/04 and 9/15/14); Connecticut Warbler (almost annual); Western Kingbird (9/24/13); Summer Tanager (8/28/10 and 9/16/12); and Black Skimmer (10/5/13). A Harlequin Duck overwintered in 2007–8, and this is one of the two best spots on the mainland for Dickcissel, with up to eight recorded annually (but mostly as flyovers).

SITE C15 "Greater Yarmouth Goose Fields"

TOWNS North Yarmouth, Cumberland, Falmouth. DeLorme Map 5: D4–5.
SEASON September, **October–November,** December, March–April.
VISITATION 1–3 hrs. No facilities. **HIGHLIGHTS** Rare geese; "grasspipers"; farmland denizens.

Lysle Brinker and I began exploring this route over ten years ago, just about the same time that Arctic geese began expanding in range from both directions. Here, an increasing population of resident, pseudo-migratory Canada Geese has discovered a series of fields where the geese are unharassed and safe from hunting. In August, after the last haying, these local breeders begin to frequent the fields here, and as migration gets going in the fall, large numbers of migratory Canada Geese of multiple subspecies begin to arrive. Vagrant geese can turn up with migrant Canada flocks, and this produces rarities every fall. Small numbers of Cackling Geese (up to six at once have been documented) and one to three Greater White-fronted Geese are almost annual in the fall, and both rarely (especially Cackling) turn up in spring as well—although those stays are always shorter. The flocks, and the vagrants within, move around the area, so you might have to check all the fields, even for previously reported birds. Meanwhile, as the first few geese are arriving, migrant shorebirds, including American Golden-Plover, and rarely, Buff-breasted Sandpiper, can sometimes be seen, especially after rain. Keep an eye out for uncommon gulls, such as Lesser Black-backed, among the throngs of Ring-billed and Herring that seek worms after rains. In winter, check for Rough-legged Hawks and Northern Shrikes. From mid-March through early to mid-May, many of the fields in this loop will host displaying American Woodcocks at their edges.

From I-295 take Exit 15 and follow US Route 1 North into Yarmouth. Shortly after the second light, exit right for Main Street/Route 115. Make a right at the stop sign and follow Main Street/115 West. After 1.9 miles you'll cross into North Yarmouth and you'll see fields on both sides of the road. **Thornhurst Farm** on the right, which is usually the most reliable place for rarities, is the best single field to check if your time is limited.

Route 115 is a busy road with a low, soft, and sometimes treacherous shoulder. Use *extreme caution* if you pull off on the side of the road. Your best bet is to continue west until you reach the farm, and park in the parking lot for Toots Ice Cream (and of course stopping for a snack when still open early in the season; otherwise, please avoid the lot when the stand is open and busy). The landowners have been extremely gracious in allowing parking here to keep (more) birders from ending up in the ditch. Of course, circumstances could change at any time, so if you see anyone here, it's always worth a polite inquiry. Keep in mind that if you are on foot, the geese are more likely to flush, so keep your distance from any feeding flocks—and under no circumstances should you enter the fields.

If you're lucky, the geese will be in the northern field and airstrip, which can easily and safely be viewed from **Prince Wells Road**, the first right after you pass the Thornhurst Farm buildings.

After thoroughly checking the flock, continue west on Route 115 for 0.6 miles to a left onto Pea Lane. At the end make a left onto Route 9 West. Follow for 2.7 miles, to a right onto Winn Road. At the first four-way intersection make a left onto **Cross Road**. This is another great field for geese, and it is one of the better fields on the tour for shorebirds (especially in spring).

Return to **Winn Road** and make a left. In 1.0 miles (passing the Falmouth Country Club on the right—check any geese in the pond from the road) make a left onto Woodville Road. Cross the tracks and check the fields within the next half mile. This is a challenging spot to view—and find a safe place to pull off—as the geese are usually in the fields behind the pond on the eastern side of the road.

Turn around when the fields end, return to Route 9, and make a left. In 2 miles turn right onto **Greely Road**. Shortly, you'll see a golf course on the right (rarely has geese, but check for gulls and shorebirds after rains), and then fields will open up on both sides of the road. The geese can be anywhere, and once again, use extreme caution if you pull over onto the side of the road.

It's best to continue on, noting the pond at the bottom of the rolling hill and passing Spring Brook Farm on the right. Park in the lot for the **Twin Brook Recreation Area** (portable toilets in most seasons). Once again, be careful to not flush the geese—or get hit by a car—as you walk the roadside back.

To extend your tour you can walk the extensive trail system through the woods and around the playing fields of the recreation area. To complete your tour, continue on Greely Road until it ends at Portland Street. Make a left, and that will take you to US Route 1 in Yarmouth.

RARITIES

Barnacle Goose, October 2008 (second state record); Pink-footed Goose (first state record, September–October 2009, followed by the second state record of three different birds later that month through December); Hudsonian Godwit, October 2011 (Thornhurst Farm)

SITE C16 Old Town House Park

TOWN North Yarmouth. DeLorme Map 5: C5.   **SEASON** April–May; June–July, August–November.   **VISITATION** 45 min. to 2 hrs. Portable toilet in warmer months.   **HIGHLIGHTS** Breeding birds, especially Bobolinks and riparian species and both Willow and Alder Flycatchers; migrants, especially in fall.

A lot of habitats are packed into these fifty-five acres, ranging from open fields full of Bobolinks to mature hemlock woods featuring Black-throated Green Warblers and Hermit Thrushes. In between, shrub-scrub habitat can be chock-full of sparrows and riparian woodlands, and brush can hold Warbling Vireos, Baltimore Orioles, and both Alder and Willow Flycatchers.

Spring migration is surprisingly less productive here on most days compared to other nearby sites, for unknown reasons. However, sunny edges and the scrub almost always host some passage migrants. Fall migration is much busier here, however, especially when sparrows get going in late September. Winter is fairly quiet, but the park is good for Northern Shrikes and can host Pine Grosbeaks and Bohemian Waxwings in irruption years.

DIRECTIONS

From I-295 take Exit 17 and head south on US Route 1 into Yarmouth. At the first light make a right onto the ramp, and at the stop sign make a right onto

East Main Street. Make the first left onto North Road. Follow North Road for 4 miles to a blinking light. Turn left onto Route 9 (Memorial Highway). The park entrance is half a mile on the right, next to the park's namesake white Old Town House.

Referencing the trail map, I generally walk the entirety of the park counterclockwise, beginning by walking straight past the gate and curving around through the old Christmas tree plantings. After spinning through the Basin Loop Trail, I walk the Lower Field Loop to the River Loop, following the edge of the Royal River. Bobolinks and a few Savannah Sparrows breed in the hayfields. An agreement reached with the town in 2013 delayed the first haying until at least July 21, providing safety for these grassland nesters.

The willows and alders along the river and in wet spots host both Willow and Alder Flycatchers—this park is a great place to study these two challenging species side by side. Warbling Vireos, Baltimore Orioles, and in the last few years a pair of Blue-gray Gnatcatchers have bred along the river, along with Yellow Warblers, American Redstarts, and more Gray Catbirds and Song Sparrows than you can count.

After the fields, I take the Woods Trail through early successional woodlands that host breeding Veeries, among others, and through the more mature woods, poking in and out of the fields.

RARITIES

Swallow-tailed Kite, August 2007; Sedge Wren, September 2007; Blue-winged Warbler, August 2012 and July 2015

Map and park information can be found on North Yarmouth's website at www.northyarmouth.org and search for "Old Town House Park."

SITE C17 Morgan Meadow Wildlife Management Area

TOWN Raymond. DeLorme Map 5: B3. SEASON April, May–June, July–September. VISITATION 1–3 hrs. No facilities. ♿ HIGHLIGHTS Breeding Yellow-throated Vireo, Blue-gray Gnatcatcher, and sporadically Louisiana Waterthrush; breeding Wood Ducks and Hooded Mergansers; migrants.

This rarely birded WMA hosts a few sought-after "southern" species reaching the northern limits of their breeding range. A wooded swamp hosts breeding

Wood Ducks and Hooded Mergansers, and in early spring in particular, migrant passerines (especially Palm and Yellow-rumped Warblers in late April or early May) can be seen in impressive quantities.

DIRECTIONS

From I-95 take Exit 63. Make a left at the light at the end of the off-ramp to head west on 202/4/115 (West Gray Road) to the first light on the west side of the interstate. Make a right onto 26A North. Route 26A rejoins Route 26 North in 1.1 miles. In another 1.5 miles make a left onto North Raymond Road. In 0.9 miles turn left onto Egypt Road. (Should you continue on North Raymond Road, in another 1.5 miles you'll see the main entrance for the WMA on the left. Trails here lead through typical mixed woods of the area, with lots of Pine Warblers, Hermit Thrushes, and Red-eyed Vireos among other common species.)

Follow Egypt Road for 1.5 miles, to a gated road on the right. You can pull off alongside Egypt Road here or (recommended) proceed for another 0.2 miles and make a right into a dirt parking area. Return to the first gate and follow the often-wet two-track into the WMA, and carefully bird the edge of the pond, where Yellow-throated Vireo and Blue-gray Gnatcatcher can be heard from mid-May through July. At the north end, a running brook has hosted Louisiana Waterthrush, and continuing straight will bring you to a larger, marshier body of water. Note the trails on your left that go up the hill—you can take this loop and work your way to a dirt two-track that returns to the parking area, but be careful—the trails are not well marked.

Return to Egypt Road, and 0.2 miles past the parking area a gully on your right hosts Louisiana Waterthrush as well; they can often be heard singing from the road.

RARITIES

Red-headed Woodpecker, May 2013

SITE C18 Bradbury Mountain State Park and Spring Hawk Watch

TOWN Pownal. DeLorme Map 5: C5. SEASON March–May, June–July. VISITATION 1 hr. to all day. Outhouses open all year. State park entrance fees. HIGHLIGHTS Organized, full-season spring hawk watch staffed daily; mature mixed forest breeding birds.

The Bradbury Mountain Spring Hawkwatch, sponsored by Freeport Wild Bird Supply and partners (currently, Leica Sport Optics), has been conducted from March 15 to May 15 each spring since 2007. With a seasonal average of 4,068 raptors and a cumulative total of nineteen species (including annual rarities), the hawk watch continues to far surpass expectations and is rewriting the book on the status and distribution of many raptor species in Maine (see table, p. 95). Furthermore, Bradbury Mountain State Park (along with nearby Wolfe's Neck Woods State Park) partners with Freeport Wild Bird Supply for the annual "Feathers over Freeport: A Birdwatching Weekend" festival during the last weekend of every April, catering to beginning and intermediate birders.

Extensive trails in the park traverse typical woodland types of the area, including hemlock glens (Black-throated Green and Blackburnian Warblers), stands of white pine (Pine Warblers), thickets of striped maple understory (Black-throated Blue Warblers), and in between, plenty of Wood (declining) and Hermit Thrushes, Red-eyed and Blue-headed Vireos, Winter Wrens, Scarlet Tanagers, and a variety of forest warblers.

DIRECTIONS

From I-295 take Exit 22 and head west on Route 125/136 North (Mallet Road) to an immediate left just after the southbound on-ramp onto Durham Road (follow signs for the state park). Proceed for 4.4 miles (becomes Pownal Road at the ninety-degree curve and Elmwood Road at the Pownal border) to the blinking light at Pownal Center. Make a right onto Route 9 (Hallowell Road), and in half a mile turn left into the park.

From the main parking lot (bear right at the curve past the entrance booth), various trails head in various directions, but I'd skip the east side of Route 9 other than the campground, as mountain bikes dominate the trails. You can head directly to the summit via the short (a quarter mile) but steep Summit Trail, or take a gently climbing 1-mile stroll via the North Loop Trail. For a good hike, and a good sample of the birds in the forest (and passing along some impressive vernal pools, which can be good in migration), follow the North Loop Trail to the Boundary Trail, arriving at the summit in about 2.5 miles. (Note that in early spring, trails—especially the Summit Trail—can be very icy.)

The official counter for the Bradbury Mountain Spring Hawkwatch is stationed at the summit daily from 9 a.m. to 5 p.m., weather permitting, and is

Hawk watch seasonal averages

Species	Season avg. ('08–15)	Season high	High day count
Black Vulture	0.8	3 (2008)	2 (4/26/08)
Turkey Vulture	273	379 (2014)	87 (3/25/10)
Osprey	431	724 (2014)	229 (4/14/14)
Bald Eagle	77	102 (2015)	13 (3/17/12)
Northern Harrier	97	139 (2014)	46 (4/10/13)
Sharp-shinned Hawk	715	1,058 (2014)	254 (4/14/14)
Cooper's Hawk	74	97 (2010)	16 (4/7/10)
Northern Goshawk	8	16 (2013)	3 (3/15/13)
Red-shouldered Hawk	91	190 (2014)	35 (3/23/14)
Broad-winged Hawk	1,545	2,357 (2014)	583 (5/2/14)
Red-tailed Hawk	270	418 (2014)	75 (3/23/14)
Rough-legged Hawk	1	3 (2015)	1 (multiple dates)
American Kestrel	359	431 (2013)	252 (4/7/10)
Merlin	69	91 (2008)	17 (5/3/14)
Peregrine Falcon	5	9 (2013)	2 (5/10/13)
Unidentified	47	66 (2014)	n/a

happy to answer questions and help you spot raptors. Treats (especially hot drinks) are not required, but are always welcome, and if you need a particular species for a particular list, bribes never hurt.

Migration watching, especially for raptors, is at the mercy of the weather. While southwesterly and westerly winds are generally best for good flights, light-to-moderate northwesterly and southerly winds can occasionally produce good numbers. Calm conditions often allow raptors to move by at uncomfortable heights and distances, and an easterly component (especially northeast) will usually mean a very slow day. That being said, almost any day spent hawk watching is a good day in my book, and some of the more intriguing observations (like a migrant Snowy Owl between snow squalls) have occurred in "unproductive" conditions.

Swallow-tailed Kite (5/10/2008, 4/28/09, and 5/7/14); Swainson's Hawk, 4/22/05 and 5/3/09); Summer Tanager (April 2009); Mississippi Kite (5/15/12 [two] and 5/15/14); Golden Eagle (four records in March–April)

For a trail map visit Maine Trail Finder at www.mainetrailfinder.com and use the search feature. More information about the hawk watch, including a link to current and past daily counts, can be found at www.freeportwild birdsupply.com/bradbury-mountain-hawkwatch.

SITE C19 Winslow Park and South Freeport

TOWN Freeport. DeLorme Map 6: D1. SEASON October–November, December–March, April. VISITATION 1–2 hrs. Fee in summer at Winslow Park. Portable toilets at Winslow Park; restrooms at Freeport Wild Bird Supply. & HIGHLIGHTS Barrow's Goldeneye; winter waterbirds; Purple Sandpiper, Dunlin, and Ruddy Turnstone; Bald Eagle.

The Harraseeket River in South Freeport has been home to the southernmost wintering "flock" of Barrow's Goldeneyes on the East Coast. A decade ago, up to two dozen birds were regular, but a good winter now might see four to six birds in all. Whether it is reduced ice to the north, fewer shellfish in the river because of invasive green crabs, or hunting pressure (and quite likely all three and more), these charismatic ducks are declining rapidly in the state, even in their few strongholds such as here. Nonetheless, it is a great spot to still observe this species, and the numbers of more common winter waterfowl, especially Common Eiders, can be truly impressive. Furthermore, it is one of only two spots in the state that regularly host Dunlins and a few Ruddy Turnstones all winter (the other is Biddeford Pool) and one of the few spots in interior Casco Bay that often have Purple Sandpipers.

DIRECTIONS

From I-295 take Exit 17 and head north on US Route 1 toward Freeport. In 1.3 miles turn right at the blinking light onto South Freeport Road. Take your third right onto Staples Point Road and follow it to its end at **Winslow Park**. Park in the large lot on your left, just after the entrance gate (no fee in winter) and begin your visit by scanning the bay to the south, from the boat launch across the street. Dunlin can be here at low tide, and there's a Bald Eagle nest on Lane's Island across the cove. Look for it with a scope; it's in a large stand of oaks, right of the center point in the island.

Enter the park and walk the shoreline on the south side, checking for ducks and watching for land birds in the scrub. When you wrap around the private holdings within the park boundaries at the east end of the campground, return to the dirt entrance road, make a right, and walk through the woods to the end of the point. This is the best spot for Barrow's Goldeneye, Red-throated Loon, and all three shorebirds, especially at mid-tides.

When most of the Harraseeket freezes, there's always some open water right here at the point, and the density of diving ducks, especially Common Eider, can be outstanding.

Return to your car via the main road or the parallel trail on the north side of the peninsula that follows the shoreline through the woods. Head back up to Staples Point Road and make a right onto South Freeport Road. Follow for 1 mile to a four-way stop and make a right onto Main Street. At the end, you will arrive at the **Freeport Town Wharf**.

Barrow's Goldeneyes are often seen within the marina here, feeding on mussels around the pier pilings. It's also a great spot for eider and Common Loon photography. Scan upriver at high tide, and downriver, especially at low tide. Barrow's also sometimes sneak into the nooks and crannies on the opposite side of the river, especially during strong winds, so be sure to scan the far shoreline (of Wolfe's Neck Woods State Park). In the warmer months, Harraseeket Lunch and Lobster offers the best lobster rolls in town.

Head back up the hill on Main Street and stay straight through the four-way intersection at South Freeport Road to continue onto Pine Street. In 1.5 miles you'll be back at Route 1. Turn left, make your first left into the parking lot at the Freeport Plaza and Econolodge, and stop into **Freeport Wild Bird Supply** to say hello. Check the crabapples in front of the store for Bohemian Waxwings or Pine Grosbeaks in winter during irruptions years, and view our often-busy feeding station from the comforts of inside. The feeding station and an extensive native plant garden are worth a visit all year, for the common feeder birds of the area. Lark and Clay-colored Sparrow have each occurred twice as well, as did a Dickcissel in October–November of 2015. Heading back north on Route 1, make a right at the first traffic light to continue on Route 1 into **downtown Freeport**, keeping an eye out for crabapples that can host Pine Grosbeaks and both waxwings in some winters.

Thick-billed Murre, January 2013; Razorbill, March 2013

For a map and information about Winslow Park, visit www.freeportmaine
.gov/department.detail.php?page_id=98 and click on "Park Map Brochure"
in the "Files and Forms" section.

SITE C20 Florida Lake Park

TOWN Freeport. DeLorme Map 6: C1.   SEASON April–May, June–
December.   VISITATION 30 min. to 2 hrs. No facilities.
HIGHLIGHTS Spring warbler migration; twelve species of breeding warblers.

Florida Lake Park is an unassuming town park tucked away in the less-visited
side of this popular town. The park is at its finest in the early stages of spring
warbler migration (late April through the first half of May), when midges
burst from the water and provide ample food before the trees leaf out. The
numbers of Yellow-rumped and Palm Warblers can be breathtaking, and it's
a good place to be during a May "fallout." Summertime features a wonderful
array of breeding species, including a dozen species of warbler (including
Canada Warbler and Northern Waterthrush). Fall migration isn't as exciting
as the spring here, and winter is very quiet, except during finch irruptions
(and rarely, Bohemian Waxwings and Pine Grosbeaks in irruption years
with good winterberry crops). Regardless of the season, it's a perfect place
to stop before, after, or during (for your companions) a visit to the shops of
Freeport.

DIRECTIONS

From I-295 in Freeport take Exit 22. Follow signs for Route 125/136 North
toward Freeport/Durham. At the blinking light in 0.8 miles, make a right to
stay on Route 125 (Wardtown Road). Proceed for 2.35 miles to a small blue
sign on your right (opposite Laughing Stock Farm) and take the narrow dirt
road between the two mobile homes to the parking lot behind the mowed
field. The trailhead begins at the parking lot, and a map is just inside the
tree line at a kiosk.

In the spring the trails are almost always very soft and muddy; waterproof
boots are highly recommended. In the summer you might still need water-

proof shoes for puddles and mud, but you'll definitely need bug repellent, and the trails are rarely maintained, so grass and weeds get waist-high.

Follow the main trail into the park. I usually walk a loop that begins by taking the side trail that goes straight toward the water as the main trail curves left. Check the scrub carefully (there's usually one or two Canada Warbler territories by late May right around the fork), and head toward the water. Especially early on a cold but sunny morning, warblers can be all over the edge of the lake, so slowly work your way through the area. Keep an eye out for Rusty Blackbirds, migrants of which are fairly regular in the park in April and early May. Check the pond and backwaters for breeding Wood Ducks and Hooded Mergansers and migrants such as Ring-necked Ducks. Pied-billed Grebes might breed here, Ospreys are often fishing, and especially in spring the number of feeding swallows (led by Tree, but up to five species are regular) can be impressive.

I usually turn right when I hit the water's edge and follow the trail as it turns into the woods. This is a good trail for breeding Magnolia and Canada Warblers as well. You'll come to a fork, and staying straight will take you to the "Secret Pond," which can be very good on a windy day during migration. Begin to backtrack, and at that last fork you can either return the way you came or take the right and follow the trail for about 2.2 miles around the pond—an often wet and muddy trail, but one that can offer excellent birding.

If you backtrack, turn left when you reach the main pond, and follow the trail through the grass past where you entered and back into the woods, where it merges with the main trail once again. Turn right and follow the trail onto the earthen dike and thoroughly work the woodland edge. At the beginning of the dike, you'll see a trail on your left that heads into the woods. This offers a good loop through excellent mixed wet forest habitat and is always worth birding. At the end of the dike, you'll pick up the opposite end of the trail that circumnavigates the pond.

RARITIES

Black-backed Woodpecker, April 2009; Redhead (five), November 2014; Townsend's Solitaire, November–December 2014

You can find a map of the park (and nearby Hidden Pond, which is worth a visit in migration and has breeding Prairie Warblers) on Freeport's website. Click on the "North Freeport Trail" map at http://www.freeportmaine.com/page.php?page_id=214.

SITE C21 Wharton Point to Simpson Point

TOWN Brunswick. DeLorme Map 6: C3. SEASON All year (except if frozen in midwinter) but especially **May–November.** VISITATION 1–3 hrs. No facilities. ♿ HIGHLIGHTS Migrant shorebirds and waterfowl; oversummering waterbirds; breeding Nelson's Sparrows; Ospreys in summer and Bald Eagles all year; Fish Crows (April–August).

At the north end of two bays on opposite sides of Merepoint Neck, these two public boat launches provide access to a pair of very different bays. Maquoit Bay on the west side is a wide, shallow bay with extensive mudflats at low tide, while the eastern Middle Bay is relatively deep and has open water at all tides, and often well into winter. Shorebirding can be very good at Wharton Point on Maquoit Bay, and Middle Bay often hosts waterbirds that are rare in summer in the state, along with good concentrations of the usual wintering waterfowl until it freezes. Both can be very productive in early spring for ducks.

Tides are critical for birding here, especially for catching shorebirds at Wharton Point. At low tide, birds can be over a mile away, and at high tide they roost in a mostly inaccessible salt marsh. Using a trusted tide chart, I plan to begin at Wharton Point at four hours after daytime high tide in Portland (the usual reporting station on most charts and the local standard). That gives me about one hour of prime viewing time as the shorebirds slowly work their way closer to the boat launch. If you're only visiting Wharton Point, you have another opportunity on the outgoing tide, best viewed between three and four hours before Portland's high. But by arriving on the incoming tide, you'll have the birds coming toward you, and we'll reach Simpson's Point at a prime time as well. In late fall and early spring, waterfowl numbers can be excellent, but these are best viewed at high tide.

DIRECTIONS

To begin at **Wharton Point**, take I-295 to Exit 28 and head east to soon join US (Coastal) Route 1 North. At the third light, stay straight to continue onto Pleasant Street. At its end make a right onto Maine Street. Keep an eye out for Fish Crows on this stretch, with the wires and dumpsters behind the Hannaford supermarket being one of the most reliable places for the birds of this local colony. In 0.2 miles, Route 123/24 bears left, rounding a small church. Instead, stay straight to continue on Maine Street, with the Bowdoin

College campus on your left. In another 1.4 miles bear right onto Maquoit Road. Two miles later, the road makes a hard right, but immediately before that you'll see a dirt parking area on your left. You can also continue straight at the curve into the dirt road to the boat launch, but clammers are often busy here, so I usually stay out of the way by parking at the upper lot and walking down.

Check the surrounding scrub for passerines, and keep an eye overhead for migrant raptors, Ospreys in summer, and Bald Eagles all year. Check any concentrations of gulls for oddities, and a few Nelson's Sparrows breed in the adjacent strip of salt marsh. Shorebirds will be relatively far when you arrive, but be patient, as many birds will take advantage of the last remnants of open mud on either side of the boat launch as the tide rolls in. Snowy Egrets and Great Blue Herons can be surprisingly abundant here in August and September, while good numbers of Bonaparte's and Laughing Gulls are sometimes seen. Common Terns are regular, especially in late summer as well. From ice-out in March or April through early May, check waterfowl flocks carefully. Thousands of American Black Ducks often congregate here, with smaller numbers of uncommon ducks including American Wigeon, sometimes Gadwall and Northern Shoveler, and on several occasions Eurasian Wigeon. Both Lesser and Greater Scaup can build here as well, along with large groups of migrant scoters and Long-tailed Ducks.

After your time here, head back north on Maquoit Road. In 0.7 miles turn right onto Rossmore Road. At the end make a left onto Mere Point Road and then your first (hard) right in 0.5 miles onto Simpson's Point Road. In 1 mile, fields will open up on your left. Pennell Way is a pleasant walk for Bobolinks and Savannah Sparrows in summer and migrant sparrows in spring and fall. Northern Shrike is fairly regular in the area in winter, and this road is a good place to check.

Return to Simpson Point Road and follow it until its terminus at the boat launch. Parking is limited here, and do not park in the cul-de-sac. Instead, turn around and park on the east side of the road, just uphill from the boat launch and beyond the last of the no-parking signs. Scan the bay from the boat launch—a scope is critical here—especially the open water to the southeast. This deeper channel stays open later than most of the upper bays in the immediate vicinity, so it can be good for diving ducks, especially scaup, in early spring and late fall. Also, Simpson Point has recently earned a reputation for being a hot spot for unusual oversummering waterbirds, which in recent years have included Long-tailed Duck, White-winged and Black Scoters, Red-necked Grebe, and Red-throated Loon—all of which are very rare in the state in midsummer. In June–August 2015, for example, a drake Bufflehead, two Red-throated Loons, up to three Long-tailed Ducks, and up to twelve Black Scoters were seen in June, punctuated by the shocking appearance of a breeding-plumaged Pacific Loon.

RARITIES

Canvasback (three, Wharton Point, March 2008, and one December 2011–January 2012); Eared Grebe, September 2012 (Simpson Point); American White Pelican, October 2012 (Wharton Point); Pacific Loon, June 2015 (Simpson Point); Western Grebe, April 2016 (Simpson's Point)

SITE C22 Harpswell Neck

TOWN Harpswell. DeLorme Map 6: C and E2–3.   SEASON All year, but especially **September–November.**   VISITATION Half to full day. Portable toilets at Mitchell Field.   HIGHLIGHTS Migrants, vagrants, waterbirds, diversity of breeding birds.

Thanks to the efforts of the Harpswell Heritage Land Trust, a series of lovely preserves protects some important habitat and offers access to the water in a long peninsula essentially devoid of public space. At all seasons, Harpswell Neck offers a variety of habitats worth exploring, and a pleasant half day can easily be spent in migration hopping between seasonal hot spots. As with all peninsulas, especially here in the Midcoast region, migrants concentrate under certain conditions, and the potential for vagrants increases. While most productive during fall migration, this tour is worthwhile at all seasons.

DIRECTIONS

From I-295 take Exit 28 and head east toward Brunswick, soon joining US Route 1. At the third traffic light, where Route 1 turns left, stay straight on Pleasant Street. At its end make a right onto Maine Street (Business 24). In 0.2 miles make a left at a funky little intersection to stay on Route 24; essentially you are going counterclockwise around the church, keeping the Bowdoin College campus on your right. At the next light make a right onto Route 123 South. Route 123 traverses the spine of Harpswell Neck.

During migration I always begin at the southern tip of the peninsula, at the **Pott's Point Preserve**. Park near the boat launch at the end of the paved road, in 13.5 miles, being careful not to block any access roads, driveways, or the pier (a few more spaces can be found just up the road next to the public pier). Follow the dirt road to the tiny preserve that protects the point. Work the thickets, especially in late fall. On mornings that followed nights with a northerly or northeasterly wind in the fall, and south or southwest in the spring, the morning flight here can be very productive, so keep an eye open overhead. Scan the waters from the point for waterbirds.

Return to your car, check the waters once again, and drive north for 1.4 miles to Stovers Cove Road and make a right. The road makes several turns, but in 0.5 miles, as it curves right, make a left onto a gravel road (be very careful to avoid leaving your oil pan on some exposed ledge protruding into the road), and drive onto the hard gravel beach at **Stovers Point Preserve**. Park, and walk the length of the gravel spit, checking for shorebirds (especially roosting birds at high tide), scanning for waterbirds (duck numbers can be impressive here), and checking the marsh for shorebirds and Nelson's Sparrows (uncommon breeder and migrant). The spit is also a good spot for Horned Lark, American Pipit, and Snow Bunting in late fall through early winter, and again in early spring. This spot also has "mega" rarity written all over it!

Return to your car, backtrack to Route 123, and make a right. In 0.4 miles make a left onto Ash Point Road. Take your second right onto Basin Point Road. There's a small parking lot on your right in half a mile. This is one access point for the new, eighty-six-acre **Curtis Farm Preserve**, the largest undeveloped property in South Harpswell. Check the cove at low tide for shorebirds, and at high tide for ducks, then return to Route 123, make a left, and turn into the main parking lot for the preserve in 0.2 miles. I usually make a quick check of the scrubby edges of the field, especially for sparrows in the fall. But as the forest regenerates from recent logging, it will likely become more productive, and a diversity of habitats and expanded trails completed in 2015 suggest this is a spot worthy of more exploration.

Next, head north on Route 123 for 0.7 miles and turn left into **Mitchell Field**. This is one of the best birding spots in the area and is worth a visit on its own in all seasons. From mid-September through early November, it is at its peak, however, with multitudes of sparrows and often impressive numbers of Palm and especially Yellow-rumped Warblers.

A former US Navy fuel depot, this large property is worth birding thoroughly. Even when the gate is open, I park before the gate and walk in (which you can do when the gate is closed) and walk the entire edge of the property via the paved roads. The scrubby edges and weedy fields are worth checking thoroughly, especially in migration, but in summer you'll find breeding Savannah Sparrows, Bobolinks, and Indigo Buntings, and in winter look for lingering sparrows, the occasional Northern Shrike, and rarely Snowy or even Short-eared Owls. The community garden is always worth a check in particular. Meanwhile, on a clear day, you can often see Mount Washington way out over the western horizon!

After working the uplands, check the water (I often return to my car, then drive down the road with my scope) for the usual waterbirds, and thoroughly check the aggregation of gulls for the occasional white-winged gull in winter. Also, scan the shoreline for shorebirds. Great Cormorants often replace Double-crested Cormorants on the edges at low tide in winter, and this is a good spot to look for hauled-out harbor seals.

For further exploration, there is a series of preserves (see map at link below) as you work your way north on Route 123. Sample these preserves as time, interest, and seasonality allow. The **Widgeon Cove Trail** (3.3 miles north of Mitchell Field) is my favorite of these northern four properties, and the half-mile loop through mixed woods takes you to an overlook of mudflats in a sheltered cove and to a pocket salt marsh. The **Wilson Cove Trail** (diagonally across the road) offers a short, easy walk to an overlook of the productive waters of Middle Bay (a scope is useful).

If you are thirsty for more Harpswell birding, follow Route 123 north for 4.3 miles from Mitchell Field to the blinking light and turn right onto Mountain Road. In 1.2 miles you'll see the Harpswell Town Office on your left. At the far left corner of the parking lot, behind the building, you can pick up the trailhead for the **Cliff Trail**. This is a relatively rugged 2.3-mile hike, passing through diverse habitats, including views from a 150-foot cliff, and its dense red spruce woods are worth checking for finches in winter.

Whether or not you hike the Cliff Trail, continue on Mountain Road until it ends at Route 24. Make a right and pick up the directions for Bailey Island (site C23), or make a left and head back to Brunswick.

RARITIES

Black-backed Woodpecker, November 2009 (Cliff Trail)

For a map and further descriptions of these land trust properties, visit the website of the Harpswell Heritage Land Trust at www.hhltmaine.org.

SITE C23 Bailey Island

TOWN Harpswell. DeLorme Map 6: E2–3. **SEASON** December–April, **May, September–early December.** **VISITATION** 1 hr. to half day. Portable toilets at Land's End. **HIGHLIGHTS** Migrants, vagrants, waterbirds.

At the end of a long, narrow peninsula, Bailey Island provides a concentration point for southbound migrants in the fall and for reorienting nocturnal migrants in both spring and fall. A warmer microclimate in the fall and scrubby edges entice late lingering migrants and the occasional vagrant. Meanwhile, productive waters all around can yield good numbers of all the expected sea ducks and waterbirds in season.

DIRECTIONS

From I-295 take Exit 28 and follow US Route 1 North (eastbound) into Brunswick. At the third light make a left to stay on Route 1 North. Follow Coastal Route 1 North for 3.1 miles to the exit for Cook's Corner/Route 24. Head straight through the light and continue south on Route 24 for 15 miles to its end at **Land's End**.

Park in the dirt parking lot on your right, just before the end of the road. Check the thickets here, the shoreline, and the beach. Shortly after sunrise, reorienting migrants (especially after northerly winds) in the fall, and "onward" migrants in the spring (especially after southerly winds) may be on the move overhead. Scan the waters. Public access is limited, so from here I just walk back up the road, exploring side streets and pishing at thickets where possible (paying particular attention to avoid private roads and staying out of yards). Keep an eye out overhead for migrant raptors in the fall.

After checking the area, return to your car and drive 0.7 miles back north to a right onto Washington Avenue. Park in front of the small Episcopal church on the left (except on Sunday mornings in the summer). Walk to the end of Ocean Street and follow the **Giant's Stairs Trail** to the south and into the **MacIntosh Lot Preserve**. Yellow-rumped Warblers are abundant in fall, and some may linger for much of the winter if bayberry crops are good. Check thickets for migrants. When you reach Washington Avenue, make a right to return to the car.

Back at Route 24, make a right and continue north for 0.3 miles. Make a left onto Abner Point Road, and another left into the gravel parking lot of the **Johnson Field Preserve and Mackerel Cove Lot.** Check the wrack line along the beach for late insectivores, and the field for sparrows. Scan the cove for ducks, and check the piers and wharfs for gulls, including Iceland Gull from late fall through early spring. Walk Abner Point Road around the bend, to the end of the public road, carefully combing thickets and yards (from the road, of course) for migrants and vagrants.

Driving back north on Route 24, check side roads, especially in late fall. At 0.8 miles north of Abner Point Road make a left onto Garrison Cove Road. Drive to its end and park before you get into the lot for the lobster co-op. Check the gravelly beach for roosting shorebirds at high tide, Snow Buntings in winter, and scan the waters. Note the historic Cribstone Bridge that connects Bailey and Orr's Island.

RARITIES

Cattle Egret, October 2010 (Johnson Field); Red-headed Woodpecker, January–March 2012; Bell's Vireo, October 2013 (Abner Point Road); Prothonotary Warbler, September 2015. Yellow-breasted Chat is annual.

For a map and descriptions of additional land trust properties on Orr's Island that are worth exploring, visit the website of the Harpswell Heritage Land Trust at www.hhltmaine.org.

3 Oxford County

KIRK BETTS

From the western edge of the coastal plain to the summit of Old Speck, Maine's third-highest mountain, Oxford County encompasses a wide variety of habitats and therefore hosts an amazing diversity of breeding birds, from species reaching the northern limits of their breeding range, such as Yellow-billed Cuckoo, to some of the southernmost breeding Rusty Blackbirds. Sparsely populated, much of Oxford County is ornithologically unexplored.

Brownfield Bog (site 01) is probably the only truly well-birded destination in the county. Many coastal birders make an annual pilgrimage here during the breeding season for Yellow-billed and Black-billed Cuckoos, Yellow-throated Vireos, and Blue-gray Gnatcatchers, all reliable in one easily accessible place. Meanwhile, Grafton Notch State Park (011) offers excellent roadside birding, including lots of Philadelphia Vireos.

However, most of the rest of the county's breeding "targets" are found via extensive hiking or canoeing. Hiking the Appalachian Trail to Old Speck Mountain in Grafton Notch State Park (011) will yield Bicknell's Thrush and other boreal specialties, for example.

My wife and I spend most of our time in the county hiking places such as Pleasant Mountain (02), one of the closest wonderful mountain hikes to the southern Maine coast and its population. On the other hand, this chapter's author, Kirk Betts, can usually be found on less-visited trails such as at Mount Will (09), or paddling Lake Umbagog National Wildlife Refuge (012) to catch sight of breeding Rusty Blackbirds and other North Woods specialties.

There is no shortage of hikes of all lengths and intensities to enjoy during the busy summer months, but Kirk has done a great job highlighting a variety of hikes of various degrees of difficulty in order to sample the habitats, birds, and scenery of the county. The White Mountain National Forest (08) is a perfect example, with easy birding around campgrounds and challenging hiking deep into wilderness.

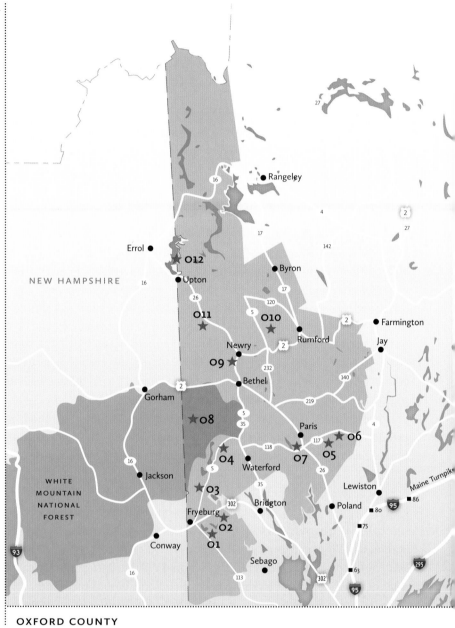

NEW HAMPSHIRE

Rangeley

Errol ●   O12 ★   ● Byron

●Upton

WHITE
MOUNTAIN
NATIONAL
FOREST

O11 ★

Newry

O10 ★   ● Rumford   ● Farmington

● Jay

O9 ★

Gorham ●   ● Bethel

● Paris   O6 ★

O8 ★

O4 ●   O7 ★   O5 ★

Jackson ●   Waterford   ● Lewiston

O3 ★   Poland ●

Fryeburg ●   ● Bridgton

O2 ★

Conway ●   O1 ★   ● Sebago

OXFORD COUNTY

During migration, shorelines of lakes and rivers offer more birding opportunities, such as in the Norway Loop (07). And since most of the county is forested, the agricultural areas in the fertile river valleys, such as around Fryeburg Harbor (03), are often very productive, especially for migrant waterfowl and "grasspipers." —*Derek Lovitch*

SITE 01 Brownfield Bog

TOWNS Brownfield, Fryeburg, Denmark. DeLorme Map 4: B2.
SEASON April–July, September to freeze-up. **VISITATION** 1–4 hrs. No restroom facilities (but see below). ♿ **HIGHLIGHTS** An interesting mix of breeding "southern" songbirds, including Yellow-billed and Black-billed Cuckoos, Yellow-throated Vireo, Blue-gray Gnatcatcher, and Willow Flycatchers; migrant waterfowl and marsh birds; Purple Martin.

Although the Major Gregory Sanborn Wildlife Management Area covers a lot of ground, we're mainly interested in the section accessed from Bog Road.

Brownfield Bog. © Derek Lovitch

Yellow-throated Vireo, Cumberland County. © Jeannette Lovitch

You will either love it or hate it. During warmer parts of the year, bring insect repellent. Wear long sleeves and pants. Bring extra blood. Or bring a friend and ask them to stand still. Seriously, this is often one of the buggiest places in the state, but if you can tolerate it, the birding is great!

Most Maine birders know this as the Brownfield Bog, but the name was changed after the death of Gregory Sanborn, a Maine game warden who passed away in 2013. While not your usual northern bog in the strict ecological sense, it's actually a "leatherleaf bog," characterized by leatherleaf and other shrubs under a meter in height. The Saco River flows through it, and over time the river changes its course, cutting off parts of itself to produce oxbows. In effect you could say it's a bird factory: rich, hardwood forest, meadows, and open water. Over 160 species of birds have been sighted here.

DIRECTIONS

From the center of Fryeburg take Route 5/113 South for 7 miles into East Brownfield. (To scan Lovewell Pond on your way, turn left in 3.2 miles at the blue boat-launch sign and drive to the end.) Turn left onto Route 160/ Denmark Road. In 0.6 miles stop at the dirt parking lot on the left, just before crossing the Saco River, for a quick check of the river and to use the outhouse. At 0.7 miles, after crossing the river, bear left onto Lords Hill Road. And in 0.1 miles turn left onto Bog Road (dirt; between two yards) and into the wildlife management area.

Alternatively, from Bridgton, follow South High Street until it becomes Route 117 South. In 9.2 miles, in the town of Denmark, bear right onto Route 160 West. In about 2.3 miles there is a Purple Martin colony on the north side of the road; look for the gray barn on the left of the curve, with the colony behind the white farmhouse on the right. Pull over very carefully. In 3.8 miles from Route 117, turn right onto Lords Hill Road, and then in 0.3 miles turn left onto the dirt access road of the WMA.

Your best bet is to park adjacent to the small building just before the second gate, about half a mile in, and walk the dirt road through the bog. If the first gate is closed, park on the road and walk all the way. Yellow-throated Vireo can often be heard right here. Continue on the dirt road for as long as your want list dictates, or the bugs allow, scanning the open marsh for Wood Ducks and feeding Purple Martins, checking the scrub for Willow Flycatchers and Blue-gray Gnatcatchers, and keeping your eyes and ears open for both cuckoos, Virginia Rail and Sora, and much more.

SITE 02 Pleasant Mountain

TOWN Denmark. DeLorme Map 4: A2–3.   SEASON April–July, September–November.   VISITATION 3 hrs. to half day. No restroom facilities.
HIGHLIGHTS Hawk watching; spring migrants; typical mixed-forest breeding birds.

With a ridge running north to south and having been burned over in 1860, the 2,006-foot Pleasant Mountain is also one of the highest mountains in southern Maine. The views are wonderful; you have clear views of Mount Washington in New Hampshire and a good portion of southern Maine. It's also one of the closest real hikes to the coast and Portland. You can't go wrong with its view or its birding. Six different trails get to the summit. While they vary in difficulty, they all take about two to four hours to make a round-trip. I would definitely pick up a hiking guide to Maine for more information about them.

It's an isolated mountain, drawing raptors on their northerly and southerly journeys. And as it is one of the first foothills as songbirds move north, spring migration can be very productive here. Each trail will have its own personality, and that will change over the seasons. No matter which trail you take, most of the expected mixed-forest species are there. I don't have a favorite; they're all good, and it's a beautiful place to go for a walk at any season.

DIRECTIONS

From I-95/Maine Turnpike in Portland take Exit 48. At the bottom of the off-ramp, follow the sign for Route 302, turning right onto Riverside Street. Follow Riverside Street north for 1.4 miles to Forest Avenue/Route 302. Turn left and follow Route 302 North through the lovely little town of Bridgton. From the intersection of Route 302 and South High Street, at the war monument near the center of town, continue on Route 302 North for 5.6 miles to a left onto Mountain Road in order to access the trails on the east side of the mountain. Otherwise, in 7.9 miles turn left onto Wilton Warren Road for the trails on the west side of Pleasant Mountain.

The shortest route to the summit is via the steep Ledges Trail, a 3.6-mile round-trip. The trailhead is reached by driving 3.3 miles down Mountain Road. From the summit, you can take the Bald Peak Trail between Big Bald Peak and Pleasant Mountain with scrub-oak habitat that hosts breeding Eastern Towhees and occasionally Yellow-throated Vireo below.

For a map and trails visit Maine Trail Finder at www.mainetrailfinder.com and use the search feature. For more information on the land trust that protects this gem, visit http://www.loonecholandtrust.org/places-we-protect /preserves/pleasant-mountain-preserve/.

SITE 03 Fryeburg Harbor Loop

TOWN Fryeburg. DeLorme Map 4: A1, and Map 10: E1. SEASON March–June, **August–November.** VISITATION 1–4 hrs. Restrooms at businesses in Fryeburg. HIGHLIGHTS Sandhill Crane; Buff-breasted and Baird's Sandpipers and American Golden-Plover; waterfowl migration; winter irruptives.

Draining the White Mountains of New Hampshire, the Saco River winds its way into Maine. Here in Fryeburg it splits into the "Old Course," which flows north, while the main branch flows northeast before turning southeast to the Atlantic. The rich, fertile valley north of the town of Fryeburg is the

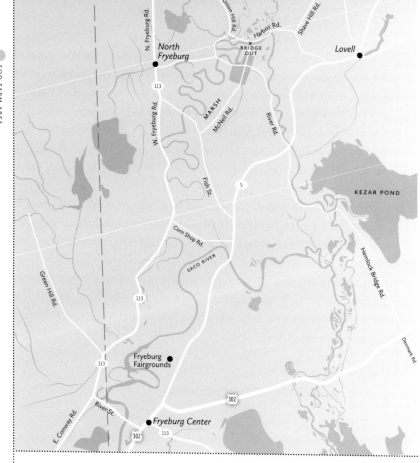

North
Fryeburg

Lovell

KEZAR POND

Fryeburg
Fairgrounds

Fryeburg Center

FRYEBURG HARBOR LOOP

focus of this loop. This is a great area for "grasspipers," especially on one of
the few remaining turf farms in the state. It's also an important spot for migrating (spring and fall) waterfowl, and in winter you can find Snow Buntings,
Horned Larks, Lapland Longspurs, and, if you're lucky, Snowy Owls, even
in non-irruption years. All the roads connect the interior to the loop, giving
you a few options and the ability to shorten or lengthen the route as you
see fit. Keep an eye out in all fields as you travel to and from the highlighted
stretches of the loop tour.

DIRECTIONS

Starting at Fryeburg Center, where Route 5 splits from Route 302, follow
Route 5 North for 4.2 miles and take a left onto Fish Street. In 1.8 miles make

a right onto **McNeil Road**. When you come to a marshy area on both sides of the road, stop and scan carefully for all sorts of goodness. The **sod farms** just beyond here are one of the most reliable places in the state to see American Golden-Plovers each fall, with Baird's and Buff-breasted Sandpipers annually, and they have recently hosted up to eleven Sandhill Cranes in the fall. Wet spots and large puddles can also host almost any other migrant shorebird. At the four-way intersection, turn left onto Old River Road. At its end, make a left onto **Harbor Road**.

Drive until you hit North Fryeburg, and turn left onto Route 113 South. Check fields for the next 3.1 miles, then make a left onto Corn Shop Road, birding these fields until you reach Route 5. Make a left to return to Fryeburg Center to complete your loop.

You can also continue south on Route 113, being careful to follow signs as it goes in and out of New Hampshire. Check more fields (be careful if you pull over on this busy road) until you reach Route 302. A left will take you back to Fryeburg Center.

RARITIES

Greater White-fronted Goose, September 2008

More information on the area can be found on the website of the Mount Washington Valley Chamber of Commerce at http://www.mtwashington valley.org/fryeburg/index.cfm.

SITE 04 Heald and Bradley Ponds

TOWN Lovell. DeLorme Map 10: D2. **SEASON** April–July, September–October. **VISITATION** 1–4 hrs. No restroom facilities.
HIGHLIGHTS Common deciduous forest breeding species plus Yellow-throated Vireo and Louisiana Waterthrush; migration potential.

Whenever I get the chance to spend time in the woods I get a little bit giddy. Sure, I love big views, distant mountains, and ocean, but it is the closeness of the trees that brings me comfort. Here you have 802 acres to look for birds in the quiet woods of Lovell. A few hills, some ponds . . . and a lot of trees. The deciduous-dominated forest here is rich with both flora and fauna.

From the intersection of Routes 5 and 93 in Lovell, turn onto Route 5 North and drive 6.2 miles to a right onto Slab City Road. Drive for another 1.2 miles until you arrive at Heald Pond Road and turn left. Parking is all the way at the end of the road (dirt), on the left at the trailhead.

There are more than ten trails here in the preserve, and all are worthy of exploration. Percky's Path crosses the stream between the two ponds and offers a viewing platform for overlooking the scrubby wetlands. It is very quiet—no traffic noises to compete with the birds, and you will be well rewarded.

RARITIES

Louisiana Waterthrush, May 2015, which may prove to be an annual breeder

For information about the preserve and the trails see the Greater Lovell Land Trust's website at http://www.gllt.org/.

SITE 05 Streaked Mountain

TOWNS South Paris and Buckfield. DeLorme Map 11: D2.
SEASON April–July, September–October. **VISITATION** 1–4 hrs. No restroom facilities. **HIGHLIGHTS** Mixed-forest breeding birds and migrants; migrating raptors in fall.

Rising 1,770 feet above the woods and fields of the foothills, Streaked (pronounced "streak-ed") Mountain offers views of the western mountains in the distance and the coastal plain stretching out before you. The hawk watching is good here in the fall, and in the spring the migrating passerines swarm the mountains. You do share the summit with a collection of radio towers, but the 360-degree views make for a good lookout.

DIRECTIONS

From the intersection of Routes 26, 117, and 119 in South Paris follow Route 117 North toward Buckfield for 4.8 miles and turn right onto Streaked Mountain Road. It's confusing, because part of Route 117 is also called Streaked Mountain Road, but the trailhead is on this side road bearing the same name. In 0.5 miles the trail is on the left, but there is no sign visible from the road marking the trail. Park on the trailhead side of the road.

This moderately difficult trail travels through mixed forest, rich with species such as Red-eyed Vireos, Chestnut-sided Warblers, and lots of Yellow-rumped Warblers. Dark-eyed Juncos breed at the summit. Parts of the trail are bare rock, so use caution if it is wet or icy.

For a map and trails visit Maine Trail Finder at www.mainetrailfinder.com and use the search feature.

SITE 06 Virgil Parris Forest (Packard Trail)

TOWN Buckfield. DeLorme Map 11: C3. SEASON April–early August. VISITATION 1–3 hrs. No restroom facilities. HIGHLIGHTS Spring warbler migration; breeding species typical of deciduous and mixed forest.

The history of the Virgil Parris Forest mirrors that of much of rural Maine: farmland reverting back to forest. What was once a family homestead is now a protected piece of woods. It's quiet, peaceful, and perfect for birds that need mature woods, but just a bit richer with water so close at hand.

DIRECTIONS

From the intersection of Routes 117 and 140 in Buckfield, follow Route 117 South for 1 mile to Sodom Road on the left. Take Sodom Road for 1.4 miles to the Packard trailhead on the left. Part of Sodom Road is dirt, and there are some rocks, but it is passable. Prior to mid-May the roads may be soft, however.

There are a couple of trails here—one going down to South Pond, where you might encounter Hermit Thrushes and Black-throated Blue Warblers. The way is easy, and although it sounds creepy, check the cemetery for your best chance at seeing Chestnut-sided Warblers, Scarlet Tanagers, Great-crested Flycatchers, and others. The edge here can be particularly fruitful during spring migration, as can the edge of the pond.

Trail information and more can be found on the website of the Western Foothills Land Trust at http://wfltmaine.org/virgil-parris-forest.html.

SITE 07 Norway Loop

TOWN Norway. DeLorme Map 11: D1. SEASON April–July, September–November. VISITATION 1 hr. to half day. Restrooms at local businesses.

HIGHLIGHTS Spring warbler migration; breeding species of deciduous and mixed woods, including Canada Warbler.

Originally called Rustfield, after Massachusetts landowner Henry Rust, Norway was a center for manufacturing for most of its history. While that's mostly part of its past, it's still a vibrant town with conservation on its mind. This loop takes you off busy Route 117 and explores the wilder side of the town. It visits a variety of habitats in woods, former farmland, and Pennessewassee Lake that offer a diversity of birdlife in migration and the breeding season. In winter keep an eye out for frugivores in downtown crabapples.

DIRECTIONS

From the intersection of Route 117 and Route 26 follow Route 117 South for 0.9 miles to a right onto Pleasant Street and proceed for 0.2 miles to the **Ordway Grove**, on the left. Park on the street and walk into one of the oldest stands of white pine (the state tree) in Maine.

Back in your car, continue up the road for 0.9 miles to **Witt Swamp Trail** on the left. Park there and walk a very easy mile loop trail through a beautiful section of woods. It's good for woodpeckers, thrushes, and warblers, especially Black-throated Blue, and be on the lookout for Barred and perhaps other owls. It briefly touches a wetland, where Alder Flycatchers and Great Blue and Green Herons can be found.

Turn left back onto Pleasant Street. Follow it as the road curves, and at the stop sign in 2.1 miles make a left onto Crockett Ridge Road. Continue for 1.9 miles to **Shepard's Farm Family Preserve** on the left. Stop here and check out the trails. Follow the Crockett Trail to the Shepard field, skirting the weedy field edge (watch for sparrows in fall) before coming into a stand of autumn olive. The olive is highly invasive, but check it carefully for breeding Cedar Waxwings and migrant thrushes. The trails continue into woods, and side trails go down to **Pennessewassee Lake** (you'll be looking back toward Witt Swamp) for further exploration.

Turn left out of the parking area and follow **Crockett Ridge Road** to the second causeway, where you can park on the left side of the road. Get out and scope for waterfowl (fall) and work the edges for warblers (spring and early summer).

Return to Route 117 and turn right. In 0.6 miles turn left onto Roberts Road. In 0.3 miles turn left into the **Roberts Farm Preserve**. An extensive trail leads through woods (the trail is groomed in winter for Nordic skiing and snowshoeing). If you are looking for birds of more mature forests, this is the place. To complete your loop by returning to Norway, return to Route 117 and turn right.

The Western Foothills Land Trust, which owns the lands here, can be found at http://wfltmaine.org/index.html, and info about the Ordway Grove Trail can be found from Maine Trail Finder at www.mainetrailfinder.com, using the search feature.

SITE 08 White Mountain National Forest

TOWNS Several. DeLorme Map 10.   **SEASON** All year, but especially June–July.   **VISITATION** Several hours to several days. Some trailheads have outhouses, as do the campgrounds.   **HIGHLIGHTS** Spruce Grouse; Boreal Chickadee; Gray Jay; Philadelphia Vireo; breeding forest birds; winter finches.

Moving northward through the northern hardwood forest of the White Mountain National Forest, with the broad valley of Fryeburg and Stow to the south, the WMNF is an important habitat for boreal species. While more easily accessed sites in New Hampshire garner more attention from birders, Maine's lands also offer exceptional hiking into high-elevation boreal habitat, along with a diversity of forest types at lower elevations.

The highest elevations of the Caribou–Speckled Mountain Wilderness offer Blackpoll Warblers, while several peaks offer home to the likes of Gray Jay, Boreal Chickadee, and a few Spruce Grouse. Birding is entirely via hiking here, and there are endless trails to explore. However, for easier birding check campsites and roadside edges throughout the forest.

Winter hikers have had territorial Spruce Grouse accost them on some higher trails, giving them a crazy photo op and stories for years to come. Much of the forest is also worth visiting during winter finch irruptions. There are generally fewer hikers in the Maine section of the WMNF, offering peace and hiking solitude.

You should check with the WMNF for any recreation passes or parking passes and other events here at http://www.fs.usda.gov/main/whitemountain/home.

DIRECTIONS

Most of the trailheads of note are accessed via Route 113, which meanders back and forth between Maine and New Hampshire. Closed from November 1 and reopening late April or early May, this is one of the few remaining seasonal state highways.

From Bethel, follow US Route 2 West. Just outside of town, Routes 5 and 35 split off to the left. Continue on Route 2 for 9.5 miles into Gilead and turn left onto Route 113.

From the center of town in Fryeburg follow Route 113 North for just over 19 miles, passing in and out of New Hampshire, until you reach Stow, Maine, where the road is gated in winter.

A particularly productive stretch of roadside birding is in Evan's Notch, beginning about 2 miles south of Route 2 and continuing for another 8.5 miles until you reach the Brickett House Historical Site. Philadelphia Vireos are sometimes found in this stretch, along with a good cross-section of mixed woodland breeders.

Armed with a good hiking guide, such as the Appalachian Mountain Club's *Maine Mountain Guide,* begin your exploration of the extensive trails through the forest. Caribou Mountain via the Caribou Trail is one of my favorite hikes; it will take you from valley right to krummholz (stunted spruce-fir forest), giving you a good range of birds and beautiful scenery. The trailhead for this route is 4.7 miles south of Route 2.

RARITIES

Mountain Bluebird, November 2011 (first state record; East Royce Mountain)

A trail guide is critical here. For online and downloadable trail maps see Maine Trail Finder. A link to my favorite hike is at http://www.mainetrailfinder.com /trails/trail/white-mountain-national-forest-caribou-mountain.

SITE 09 Mount Will

TOWN Bethel. DeLorme Map 10: A3. SEASON April, May–July, September–October. VISITATION 3 hrs. to half day. HIGHLIGHTS Spring warbler migration; breeding mixed-forest species; fall raptor flights.

Rising 1,726 feet above the Androscoggin River Valley, Mount Will provides hiking along trails through productive mixed forest, with some good vantage points from the cliffs to scan the skies.

From downtown Rumford and Mexico, follow US Route 2 West toward Bethel. At 0.75 miles west of the junction of Route 2 and Route 26 North (Bear River Road), turn into the Mount Will trailhead on the right.

From Bethel, follow US Route 2 East/Route 5 North/Route 26 North. At 4.5 miles past the bridge over the Androscoggin River the trailhead will be on your left, directly across the road from the Bethel Recycling Center; watch for its signs. There is also a diamond-shaped "Tree Farm" sign next to the Mount Will sign. Despite being adjacent to the busy highway, you are immediately surrounded by birdsong if you start your hike early enough. The forest here offers another sample of the region's common breeding forest birds, including up to a dozen species of warblers, while hawk watching from the ridges could be fruitful for finding a migrant Golden Eagle.

At the summit the South Cliffs has the best views, and while the summit is not bare—in fact there are enough trees to block the view—with the red spruces here, it's a good bet for winter finches. It's a moderately strenuous trail, and at the cliff you may need your hands.

For a map and trails visit Maine Trail Finder at www.mainetrailfinder.com and use the search feature.

SITE 010 Rumford Whitecap Mountain

TOWN Rumford. DeLorme Map 18: E5. SEASON May–October.
VISITATION 2–4 hrs. No restroom facilities.   HIGHLIGHTS Breeding species typical of mixed forest; spring passerine migration.

At 2,214 feet elevation, Rumford Whitecap (to distinguish it from another Whitecap Mountain in the state) offers a lot of good birding, from the Ellis River valley below to mountaintop. Portions of the land have been logged, and the summit is open, with patches of trees and shrubs overlying the granite summit dome adding up to a good mix of habitat and therefore a diversity of birds typical of much of Oxford County. However, every mountain offers different scenery and subtle avifauna changes. Rumford Whitecap is also situated along several river valleys, the Androscoggin and the Swift as well as the Ellis, making the chance of seeing raptors a lot better. Take this hike for the birding, but stay for the beautiful scenery and the blueberries.

From the junction of US Route 2 and Route 17 in downtown Mexico, head west on US Route 2 as it winds through Rumford. In 1.2 miles turn left into the J. Eugene Boivin Park, home of a memorial to US Secretary of State and native son Edmund Muskie. A true hero of conservation, Senator Muskie helped author both the Clean Water and Clean Air Acts. There are restrooms and an information center here, and it's a good spot to watch Spotted Sandpipers, Northern Rough-winged Swallows, and Chimney Swifts.

Turn left back onto Route 2 West and in 9.9 miles turn right onto Route 5 North (Ellis River Road) toward Andover. In 2.9 miles turn right onto Andover Road. In 0.3 miles turn left onto East Andover Road. The Rumford Whitecap trailhead parking is on your left in 0.1 miles; the trailhead itself is across the street.

For a map and trails visit Maine Trail Finder at www.mainetrailfinder.com and use the search feature. For more information about the preserve, visit the website of the Mahoosuc Land Trust at www.mahoosuc.org.

SITE 011 Grafton Notch State Park

TOWN Grafton Township. DeLorme Map 18: D–E1. SEASON April, May–July, September–October. VISITATION 30 min. to multiday backpacking trip. Outhouses at several trailheads. No fee. HIGHLIGHTS Roadside Philadelphia Vireos; high-elevation boreal habit with Bicknell's Thrush, Spruce Grouse, Boreal Chickadee, Gray Jay, etc.; Peregrine Falcon.

Cutting through the Mahoosuc Range, Grafton Notch greets you with mountains looming high above. The Appalachian Trail runs over Old Speck, drops down to cross Route 26, and then climbs up Baldpate Mountain, giving you the possibility to catch most of the boreal/mountain species (including Spruce Grouse, Boreal Chickadee, Gray Jay, and Blackpoll Warbler) along with the lower-elevation species via some intensive hiking. From the roadside, however, you can expect many of the typical forest birds, and this is also one of the best places in the state for Philadelphia Vireo.

DIRECTIONS

From Bethel follow US Route 2 East/5 North/26 North. At 5.1 miles past the Androscoggin River bridge, turn left onto Route 26 North. Reset your odometer and drive 8.3 miles into the park. Keep your eyes open for turnouts and trailheads, stopping often to look and listen for Philadelphia Vireos. The stretch of road between the park boundary and Screw Auger Falls (9.3 miles) can be especially fruitful, as is the parking area for the Appalachian Trail (the "AT," at 12 miles) and adjacent roadside. To avoid traffic, bird the roadsides as early as possible, otherwise, for safety, stick to the edges of parking areas. And be aware that the very similar-sounding Red-eyed Vireo is also common here.

Hiking west on the AT up to Old Speck Mountain (4,180 feet; the third-highest mountain in Maine) is a strenuous and very challenging 7.6-mile round-trip and should be attempted only by experienced hikers. Reaching the summit, however, will reward you with Bicknell's Thrush. For a shorter, only moderately steep hike follow the Table Rock Trail (2.4 miles round-trip) to a spectacular rock ledge and an extensive slab-cave system, keeping an eye out for Peregrine Falcons.

For more information about the park and its trails see the state park's website at http://www.maine.gov/cgi-bin/online/doc/parksearch/details.pl?park _id=1.

SITE 012 Umbagog National Wildlife Refuge

TOWN Errol, NH. New Hampshire DeLorme Map 51: F10. See also Maine DeLorme Map 18. **SEASON** Ice-out to July, August–November. **VISITATION** 6 hrs. to a multiday camping trip. No restroom facilities except at some NH state park campsites. ⚓ **HIGHLIGHTS** North country landscape with over 200 species observed; boreal breeders.

Umbagog NWR covers more than 25,650 acres of land and water, with a canoe or kayak being the best way to explore the Maine side (70 percent of the refuge is in New Hampshire), which is almost solely accessible by water. And with a bird list of 233 species, spectacular scenery, and solitude, this is a place that exemplifies that North Woods mystique and ethos.

From an Abenaki word meaning "shallow water," Umbagog averages only 45 feet deep. Ignoring for the moment that this book is about Maine, Umbagog NWR will let you work on your NH list too. Loons, eagles, and Ospreys rule the skies here, while shore areas can be great for Rusty Blackbirds, Swainson's Thrushes, and a variety of warblers.

When I go, I make the most of the Androscoggin River as it leaves Umbagog, watching for river otters and mink and the occasional moose and looking and listening for American Bitterns and Rusty Blackbirds among many other breeding species. Once out into the lake, I head to the northeast to Pine Point over on the Maine side. Bald Eagles often perch in the white pines, especially at the outlet of the Rapid River, and Common Loons are abundant.

To reach this boat launch, which is just north of the New Hampshire town of Errol, from the north (e.g., Rangeley and Oquossoc), follow Route 16 West out of Oquossoc for just over 34 miles into New Hampshire to a well-signed boat launch on your left.

From the south (e.g., Bethel), follow Route 26 North for 38 miles, turning right onto Route 16 North. In 1.6 miles turn right into the boat launch parking area.

For a shorter visit, put in at the Umbagog State Park boat launch (camping available; reservations suggested), which is along Route 26 just over 1.1 miles west of the Maine border, or 8.2 miles southeast of Errol). As you get out to the lake, paddle north or east and look for whatever gets your interest. And since the state line is not readily seen, you could say that the Lincoln Sparrow you just saw was in Maine and not in New Hampshire. Go ahead, I won't tell.

The refuge headquarters is about 5.5 miles north of Errol on Route 16. It's worth stopping there for the latest sightings and a bird list.

American Three-toed Woodpecker, July 2008

More information about the refuge can be found at the refuge's home page at http://www.fws.gov/northeast/lakeumbagog/. For access and camping information for Umbagog Lake State Park (in New Hampshire) see http://www.nhstateparks.com/um.html. For a map and trails, including water trail routes, visit Maine Trail Finder at www.mainetrailfinder.com and use the search feature.

Rangeley Lakes

Although several of the lakes in the Rangeley area are partially, or wholly, within Oxford County, they are covered in the Franklin County chapter, at site F8.

4
133

Jay

Livermore
Falls

17

4

133

Livermore

108

4
Turner

202

Greene

126

Litchfield

Minot

AN7

95

124

119

AN8

Mechanic Falls

Sabattus

26

Auburn

Lewiston

Poland

121

AN6

Maine Turnpike

11

AN5

95

AN3

201

295

AN4

AN2

Lisbon

AN1

Durham

26

202

136

9

1

Brunswick

Freeport

ANDROSCOGGIN COUNTY

4 Androscoggin County

DAN NICKERSON

To most birders, Androscoggin County *is* Sabattus Pond (site AN8). And for one or two months a year in late fall and early winter, it is simply one of the best birding destinations in the state. Because of its shallow water and apparently the presence of an invasive snail, diving ducks congregate here in numbers rarely, if ever, seen anywhere else in the state. Ruddy Duck numbers are unmatched (sometimes close to a thousand!), and it's a great place to study hundreds of Greater and Lesser Scaup side by side. Goodly numbers of many other species, migrant sea ducks rarely encountered inland, American Coots (very local in Maine), and the chance for rarities add to the allure of birding here.

Lake Auburn (AN7) can be very productive for waterbirds as well, especially as the shallow Sabattus freezes over. The flowing Androscoggin River stays open even later and often opens up weeks ahead of the large lakes. In fact, spring waterfowl migration can be particularly fantastic here, with significant concentrations of many early migrant ducks building up in the river and feeding in surrounding farm fields. A trip up and down the river, especially the Durham-to-Lewiston Androscoggin River Tour (AN1), can offer impressive numbers of Ring-necked and Wood Ducks, Green-winged Teal, Canada Geese, and much more.

However, there is much more to the county than ducks. With the twin cities of Lewiston-Auburn (affectionately known as L-A) straddling the Androscoggin River and expansive farmland blanketing the river valley, a wide variety of habitats and birding opportunities exists, even if the county is the second-smallest by area in Maine.

For migrant land birds, the river is once again the focus for concentration. Although "fallouts" are rare, and concentrations here pale in comparison to the coast, spring birding in places such as Lisbon's Miller Park area (AN3) or in one of the urban parks of L-A (AN6) can be particularly fruitful.

Dan Nickerson has single-handedly redrawn the maps for "southern" species such as Yellow-billed Cuckoo, Yellow-throated Vireo, and especially Louisiana Waterthrush, thanks to his extensive exploration of riparian corridors. Whether these are recent colonists marching northward in the face of global warming, or they've simply been overlooked, may never be known, but further exploration of this under-birded county during the breeding season may yield some answers. Traveling the "Louie Loop" (AN4) from late April through early June could yield at least five Louisiana Waterthrush territories—a bird that is clearly not as rare in Maine as conventional wisdom suggests.

Winter birds inland in Maine can be sparse, however, especially in years with few irruptives. Extensive agricultural fields host flocks of Snow Buntings and Horned Larks (sometimes with Lapland Longspurs mixed in), Northern Shrikes (annual, but with many more during irruptions), and raptors. And the ornamental street plantings and yards of L-A can be alive with Bohemian Waxwings and Pine Grosbeaks during irruptions. —*Derek Lovitch*

SITE AN1 Androscoggin River Tour, Durham to Lewiston

TOWN Durham. DeLorme Map 6: B1, Map 5: A5; City Map p. 75.
SEASON All year, but especially **April.** VISITATION 2 hrs. to half day. Portable toilets at Durham Get'N'Go and restrooms at local Lewiston-Auburn businesses. ♿ HIGHLIGHTS Staging of waterfowl in early spring, including Snow Geese, "puddle ducks," and Ring-necked Ducks; birds of the farmlands, forests, and rivers at all seasons; Yellow-throated Vireo.

The major seasonal highlight of this tour is the significant staging of waterfowl in the early spring along the Androscoggin River and adjacent agricultural fields as winter slowly gives way to spring in the state's interior. The timing of this phenomenon greatly depends on weather and ice conditions on the river and farmlands bordering the river. Birds travel between fields, and in some years one field is better than the other, with hydrology, tilling, and predators all variables in dictating where birds will be on a given day. When time allows, it is always worth checking the entire loop, but quick checks of some of the usual hot spots can often be fruitful.

Beginning in mid-to-late March, as the river opens yet lakes remain frozen, large numbers of ducks and geese begin to build. Check flocks of Canada Geese for the occasional Snow Geese, and sort through large numbers of

Mallards, American Black Ducks, Ring-necked Ducks, and some of the best concentrations of Wood Ducks in the state. Green-winged Teal are usually common as well, with solid numbers of American Wigeon and Northern Pintail often punctuated with uncommon species such as Northern Shoveler. In winter, stretches of open water can attract a variety of diving ducks and gulls, especially just after the freezing of lakes and ponds. The farmland adjacent to the river offers winter specialties like Snow Bunting, Horned Lark, and Northern Shrike, and during the breeding season Bobolink, Savannah Sparrow, and Wilson's Snipe. Riparian species during breeding season include Bald Eagle, Osprey, Baltimore Oriole, Northern Rough-winged Swallow, and Spotted Sandpiper. Beaver, river otter, and mink are occasionally seen.

DIRECTIONS

From I-295 take Exit 22 and follow signs for Routes 125/136 North toward Durham. Travel straight through the blinking light in about 0.7 miles to continue on Route 136 North, which travels along the west bank of the Androscoggin River. In 8.1 miles turn right into **Durham Town Park** for your first glimpse of the Androscoggin River.

Walk to the right to the carry-in boat launch and follow the short trail upstream along the water's edge. The small park is home to typical riparian breeders such as Warbling Vireo, Baltimore Oriole, and American Redstart in the summer.

You will note black ash here, a common medium-size tree of the floodplains of Maine's major rivers. The indigenous Wabanaki people use these for making pack baskets, and the trees are now rigorously being monitored for the invasive emerald ash borer. You may see purple bait boxes in the trees along Maine rivers.

Bonaparte's Gull and Snowy and Great Egret have been seen during late-summer post-breeding dispersal, and Spotted and Solitary Sandpiper are common during migration.

Just upstream of the park is the outlet of Gerrish Stream, which can be viewed from the north end of the riverside trail. When everything else is still frozen in early spring this can be a good spot for first-of-year Wood Duck and Hooded Merganser. Bald Eagles nest in this area and may be seen at any season.

Continuing north on Route 136, you'll begin to see farm fields. If the ducks are not in the fields, they may be amassing under the relative safety of trees on the opposite (eastern) shore of the river. Bald Eagles continually reshuffle the deck. If a few hundred ducks take flight, know that there is an eagle somewhere.

Since there is no safe place to view the river or the fields while driving northbound on Route 136, I recommend going north to the **Durham Boat Launch** (2.8 miles north of the Durham River Park) on the right and then reversing direction to view the waterfowl from the wider shoulder of the southbound lane.

Afterward, return to the boat launch. In six years of conducting river bird surveys at this site I have been surprised by the variety of species I have seen. The field just to the north (upstream) of the parking lot can hold hundreds of waterfowl in spring. Bald Eagles nest nearby and are seen frequently. In March or April after ice-out, migrant Great Cormorants are occasional as well. A large colony of Bank Swallows nests nearby and can be seen foraging over the river from May through early August. Continue north and upriver toward Auburn. In half a mile the road takes a strong wiggle as you pass beneath some large power lines. There is a place for just one or two cars to pull off just beyond the guardrail under the power lines, but use extreme caution at all times, especially with cars behind you. Waterfowl sometimes gather here in April, perhaps feeling sheltered from marauding Bald Eagles owing to the presence of the power lines overhead. These birds may be foraging in fields on the east bank in Lewiston (see below).

Just north of where Route 136 passes under the Maine Turnpike you will see the rapids. A cable crosses the river just beyond the guardrail, where there is room to park safely on the shoulder. This cable is a favorite perch of Great Cormorants in early spring—the vision of two courting each other in the big wet flakes of a March snowstorm is forever etched in my memory.

The next stretch of the river is better viewed from the **Lewiston side**. Continue north for 5.8 miles. As Route 136 bears left, stay straight until its end at the stop sign. Turn right onto Broad Street, cross the bridge over the Androscoggin River into Lewiston, as Broad Street becomes Cedar Street and turn right at the light at Lincoln Street. In 0.2 miles there is a riverside parking lot that is excellent for a view upriver to the bridge and downriver nearly to the rapids that you viewed from Route 136. Common Goldeneye gather in numbers here just south of the mouth of the Little Androscoggin River. It is worth checking for a Barrow's Goldeneye. (For more on this area at the mouth of the Little Androscoggin see **Little Andy Park** within site AN6.)

Continue down Lincoln Street, stopping at unimproved turnouts to scan, particularly in early spring, for both scaup, Ring-necked Ducks, and Common and Hooded Mergansers.

In 0.9, just upstream of the water treatment plant, there will be a boat launch on your right. The river here stays open late into the winter and is a good place for concentrations of ducks and gulls. The boat launch is not always plowed and passable, however.

Continue down Lincoln Street, bearing right at Goddard where Lincoln becomes River Road, and stay on River Road (which turns right in 1.1 miles) for a total of about 3.5 miles, at which point you will begin to see agricultural fields that may be flooded in the early spring. The ducks that you saw in the river at the Route 136 power line near the Auburn town line may be foraging in these fields. At Ferry Road (about 4 miles from Cedar Street) there is a large field adjacent to the river that is a good one to check from late March through April or whenever other bodies of water really begin to open up and the ducks and geese disperse.

In the summer breeding season it might be good to check for Louisiana Waterthrush at a couple of the tributaries you crossed. I have heard Yellow-throated Vireo singing over one of them—a bird that is not easy to find in Androscoggin County and would be a good consolation prize if "Louies" are not located.

SITE AN2 Beaver Park, Lisbon

TOWN Lisbon. DeLorme Map 6: A1. **SEASON** April–June; winter during finch irruptions. **VISITATION** 2–3 hrs. Outhouses. Fee $4 nonresident, $2 resident. **HIGHLIGHTS** Red-Shouldered Hawk, Ruffed Grouse, Green Heron, Canada Warbler, Yellow-throated Vireo, Black-billed Cuckoo.

Beaver Park has a surprising feeling of quiet isolation in an otherwise busy commuter corridor between Lewiston and Route 295 in Topsham, as evidenced by breeders such as Ruffed Grouse and Red-shouldered Hawk. The park is a good destination for birding the winter woods by snowshoe or Nordic skis. I recommend printing out a map before you go, as they are not always available at the kiosk.

From I-295 take Exit 31 and follow Route 196 West for 8.9 miles to the traffic light in Lisbon. Turn left onto Village Street, and in 0.4 miles turn right onto Pinewoods Road. In 1.1 miles make a right onto Cotton Road. The entrance to the park is on the right in 0.2 miles.

I like to park by the athletic fields near the entrance and walk the perimeter of the park in a clockwise direction, bearing to the left at the end of the parking lot past the primitive but well-maintained restrooms on the park road. In a short distance on the right is a spur to Middle Pond. The sandy beach can be checked for Spotted or Solitary Sandpiper in migration and ducks or geese. The edges of all the ponds in the park are good for early migrant insectivores.

The Jessup Trail soon bears left from the park road and parallels Salmon Stream. In these wet areas with understory shrubs and trees you will hear Common Yellowthroat and may find White-throated Sparrow and Canada Warbler. Jessup then circles clockwise to drier upland areas where Hermit Thrush and Ruffed Grouse nest. Look for grouse dust baths along the trail. In years of winter finch incursions, the substantial variety of coniferous trees may make it a good place to look for crossbills and other winter finches. A pair of Yellow-throated Vireos have been heard and seen near the wetter margins of some of the upland areas of the Jessup Trail.

After the Jessup Trail, I take the Swamp Hollow Trail around the southern perimeter of the park, although this trail may seasonally be too wet to traverse. There are a few other trail alternatives to explore if this is the case. The wetter areas of the park have a lot of native shrubs with persistent fruit that may provide food in the fall and winter for migrant thrushes and other frugivores.

I find the trail marking confusing. They are all marked with blazes of yellow paint, and placements of trail signs are not always clear to me. I suggest bringing your park map downloaded online and allow time for sorting out the route.

For more information and a trail map (highly recommended), visit Lisbon's website at http://www.lisbonme.org/parks.

Miller Park—Papermill Trail, Ricker Farm, and Androscoggin River Trails

TOWN Lisbon. DeLorme Map 6: A–B1–2. **SEASON** March–May, June–December. **VISITATION** 2–4 hrs. Portable toilets at Miller Park. &

HIGHLIGHTS Migration hot spot, especially in early spring; breeding Louisiana Waterthrush, Blue-gray Gnatcatcher, Red-shouldered Hawk, and Bald Eagle.

Miller Park becomes the prime Androscoggin County hot spot for warblers and other migrant passerines in early spring, particularly along the 1-mile stretch of the paved Papermill Trail that parallels the Sabattus River. It also hosts breeding species such as Louisiana Waterthrush, Indigo Bunting, and Warbling Vireo. The Ricker Farm Trail continues north along Mill Street past open fields that host Bobolink, American Kestrel, and raptors. The Androscoggin River Trail leaves the Miller Park parking lot and parallels the river, affording opportunities for more waterbirds. In early spring before ice has left the lakes this area of the river can be a hot spot for waterfowl, loons, and grebes and has a good variety of summer residents as well.

DIRECTIONS

From I-295 take Exit 31 and turn onto Route 196 West (toward Lisbon and Lewiston). In just over 5.5 miles a stoplight in downtown Lisbon Falls puts you at the epicenter of the July Moxie Festival. This celebration in Mid-July of Maine's unofficial state beverage is down-home Maine at its best. A deep-fried Oreo washed down with a Moxie float with Moxie flavored ice cream will take your mind off a slow day of birding and deerflies.

Continue through the light and take your first left (just past Miller's Variety) onto Davis Street. At the end of Davis Street you will see the **Androscoggin River Trail**, an asphalt path blocked from vehicular traffic by large boulders (you can park alongside the road). The trail makes a steep ascent into a stand of eastern hemlock, where you may find Black-throated Green Warblers and Blue-headed Vireo. One spring I had a Louisiana Waterthrush singing here and Northern Waterthrush in the flooded area down closer to the river.

The trail passes behind the Lisbon High School athletic fields and some weedy wasteland that should be checked for sparrows during migration. The river will soon come into view. In a mile or so you reach **Miller Park**, where the trail intersects Route 196. Continuing along the trail into the park during the breeding season, you will find abundant Baltimore Oriole, Warbling Vireo, Eastern Kingbird, and Veeries in the wetter areas, while the drier banks may have breeding Indigo Bunting or Eastern Towhee. The river should be scanned for waterfowl, Bald Eagle, Osprey, swallow species, and migrant shorebirds, gulls, or waders: Green and Great Blue Heron are regular. In early spring when the lakes are still frozen this stretch of river is a hot spot for migrant waterfowl. Both scaup, other diving ducks, Common Loon, Horned Grebe, and Common Merganser may be seen here. A Bald Eagle nest may be seen on the opposite bank from this end of the trail.

If you return to your car, wishing to drive north to Miller Park, continue on Route 196 West for 1.7 miles. The park is on the right, at the junction of the **Androscoggin River Trail** and the **Papermill Trail**. The portable toilets here may suffer from overuse in the summer months. This is also good place to launch a canoe for an exploration of the river. Be aware of the dangers of paddling a large river like the Androscoggin, and avoid the area above the dam.

From the parking lot scan any exposed mudflats for ducks and shorebirds such as Spotted and Solitary Sandpipers. Blue-gray Gnatcatchers are usually seen near the information kiosk, while Louisiana Waterthrush may be heard midway up the trail. On a cold day in early spring, the warbler hot spot will be near the end of the trail behind the historical interpretive sign. On cloudy days birds may be low to the water's edge, working the shrubs along the old ruins of the mill for emergent aquatic insects.

I bear right just beyond the interpretive sign and walk toward the Lisbon Community School, checking the gully on the left for birds such as Brown Thrasher and the weedy vacant lot on the right for sparrows. Following the paved path bearing right past the school I scan the fields for Bobolinks, foraging swallows, or raptors. One may turn right at the end of the school drive and follow the **Ricker Farm Trail** north along Mill Street for another mile. I generally make a left onto Mill Street, however, checking out a couple of feeders before taking an unimproved return path to the Paper Mill Trail by turning left just before reaching the Sabattus River again.

TOWN Poland. DeLorme Map: B3.   SEASON April–June, July.
VISITATION 3–4 hrs. car birding, plus an additional 1–3 hrs. for Bragdon
Hill Conservation Area. Restrooms at businesses on Route 26 in Poland.
HIGHLIGHTS Breeding Louisiana Waterthrush, Red-shouldered Hawk,
Sandhill Crane, Common Loon, and Virginia Rail; migrant waterfowl.

Before working on this guide I had the *feeling* that Louisiana Waterthrush was
more common in the Androscoggin River valley than was widely known, and
exploration of the area proved this to be the case. This aptly named "Louie's
Loop" will take you by many likely habitats, most of them proven to host
breeding Louisiana Waterthrushes. Try listening in late April through May by
the swift-running, shaded streams. In between, you'll find some good spots
for other species, including warblers, Alder, Least, and Willow Flycatchers,
and other species mentioned above.

DIRECTIONS

I begin my search for Louies at **Outlet Brook** in Poland, which flows out of
Shaker Bog. From I-95 (the Maine Turnpike) take Exit 63. At the end of the
off-ramp, make a left onto Route 115 West. At the next light, make a right
onto Route 26A. In 1.2 miles continue onto Route 26 North for 6.6 miles
(passing the Shaker Village at the crest of a hill). Near the bottom of the hill
you pass into Poland and make a right onto Outlet Road. In 0.2 miles pull off
on the right, just past a stream. Listen by the roadside for the waterthrush.
You can enter the woods on the north side of the road to check out the ruins
of an old mill and canal where the waterthrushes sometimes nest. These are
fascinating structures created by raw human and oxen power.

Outlet Brook is typical Louisiana Waterthrush habitat: look for these sorts
of situations on the rest of the tour. Louies do not appear to be uncommon
but may range for a few hundred yards up and down any such stream, so that
locating one may be a little serendipitous, but most of my tours result in at
least five singing individuals.

Just before returning to Route 26, make a right to reach a small parking
lot to check the pond for migrants and Wood Ducks. Then turn right onto
Route 26 North. In a hundred or so yards there is a pull-off on the left with
room for one or two vehicles, opposite the beginning of the guardrail. There

is a carry of no more than 50 yards to where you can launch a canoe or kayak for an hour or two and paddle around **Shaker Bog**. Sandhill Cranes and Virginia Rail breed in the marsh at the north end near Colbath Road. Common Loons may be seen and heard here. Follow the trail to the right to further bird the shoreline.

Continuing north on Route 26 for 0.4 miles, make a left onto **Range Hill Road** (pronounced "rang"). In half a mile Carpenter Road comes in from the right. The fields at this junction hosted a Northern Lapwing from late April to early May of 2013. This ridge offers a nice view of the bog and hills from which waterfowl, raptors, Bobolinks, and perhaps Sandhill Cranes can be viewed.

Continue 0.3 miles and go left onto **Colbath Road**. The bog is on the left in 0.2 miles. Sandhill Cranes and Virginia Rails may be seen or heard here. Return to Range Hill Road, turn left, and continue for 0.7 miles to the bridge across **Range Pond**. Park at the boat launch at the far end of the bridge: this is a good birdy spot in the spring and summer. The water here tends to stay open in early spring or late fall, when it can be a good spot for Greater and Lesser Scaup, Ring-necked Duck, Hooded and Common Mergansers, Pied-billed Grebe, and other ducks.

From the Range Pond boat launch continue north for another 0.4 miles and go left on Cleve Tripp Road for 1.2 miles to a stop sign. Go right onto North Raymond Road, and in 0.8 miles turn right into the parking lot of **Bragdon Hill Conservation Area**.

The Bragdon Hill Conservation Area is a newly developed spot, formerly the Poland Town Forest, comprising 3.4 miles of trails in mixed woodlands. There is a kiosk at the trailhead with a map and self-guided trail to both natural and historical features of this abandoned farmland. Common birds of these woodlands include Barred Owl, Broad-winged and Red-shouldered Hawk, Hermit Thrush, and up to thirteen species of warblers. Several loops are available, which would take anywhere from one to three hours to bird.

Leaving Bragdon Hill, continue on North Raymond Road for 0.9 miles to the intersection with Route 11 (Bakerstown Road). Continue straight through the intersection to the West Poland Post Office and Megquier Hill Market, which will be on your right in half a mile. Park near the post office and walk right for a few hundred yards to a public right of way to the shore of Tripp Lake, where you can scan for ducks, Common Loon, Osprey, Bald Eagle, and gulls.

Continuing straight across the intersection, walk or drive 0.6 miles up

Megquier Hill Road to Highland Cemetery. There are multiple feeders and birdhouses, which may have finches, House Wrens, or Eastern Bluebirds. Sandhill Cranes regularly forage in the field and even in the cemetery along this ridge.

Return to the Megquier Hill Market and make a right onto Johnson Hill Road. In 0.9 miles you cross **Potash Brook**, and Potash Cove of Thompson Lake will be on your right. Territorial Louisiana Waterthrush have been heard and seen here. The cove may host ducks and loons early in the spring as the ice pulls away from the mouth of the brook.

I now return back to West Poland via Johnson Hill Road, passing the market and post office. In half a mile make a left onto Route 11 North. From here it is a straight shot into Mechanic Falls, crossing Route 26 at 3.1 miles. At this major (and chaotic) intersection there is fast food, gas and a convenience store, or, for a late breakfast, a decent home-style diner.

At 2.4 miles beyond this intersection, the **Little Androscoggin River Boat Launch** intersection is on the left. The large gravel parking lot is anything but scenic, but the 1-mile paddle up the Little Androscoggin is. Common breeding riparian species seen or heard here often include Green Heron, Hooded Merganser, and Black-billed Cuckoo. An ATV/snowmobile trail at the back of the lot allows a bit of a walk along the river.

Taking Route 11 North for another 0.35 miles to the traffic light, I go straight onto Route 124 North. In 2.8 miles, turn left on **Bucknam Bridge Road**. The bridge is about 100 yards down the road; park just beyond the bridge. In April this area routinely floods and is known locally for its gathering of waterfowl. Green-winged and Blue-winged Teal, Northern Pintail, Wood Duck, Hooded Merganser, Ring-necked Duck, and others can be here in numbers. Wilson's Snipe, Killdeer, Greater Yellowlegs, and Solitary or Spotted Sandpipers may forage in the flooded fields. The alders along the brook can be a hot spot for warblers, vireos, and flycatchers. Scan the ridges for raptors at any time of year. Bobolink and Savannah Sparrow breed in the hayfields. In the winter be on the lookout for Snow Bunting and Horned Lark around manure piles stored in the field.

For the last leg of the loop, backtrack on Route 124 South for 0.9 miles and take a left onto Millet Road. In half a mile make a right onto **Pottle Hill Road**. For the next 4.2 miles any stream crossing the road may have breeding Louisiana Waterthrush. Pottle Hill Road rises up over a high ridge with a great view of the surrounding area—a good spot for watching migrating raptors. The corn stubble fields on the ridge are a hot spot for winter Snow Bunting and Horned Lark. The fields opposite Hemond's dairy farm often host a good collection of waterfowl in the spring, including Northern Pintail and American Wigeon. During the last Snowy Owl invasion one was regularly seen in this area.

When Pottle Hill Road ends at Route 119, a right takes you back to Route 11 in 0.4 miles. A left will take you back into Lewiston-Auburn via Route 11 North.

RARITIES

Northern Lapwing, April/May 2013 (Range Hill Road)

For more information about the Bradgon Hill Conservation Area see http://polandme.virtualtownhall.net/Pages/PolandME_Recreation/program%20details/Trails/bragdonhillconservation/bragdonhill.

SITE AN5 Range Pond State Park

TOWN Poland. DeLorme Map 5: A3.   SEASON April–November.
VISITATION 2 hrs. Park open 9 a.m.–sunset, but you may park outside the entrance in early morning or in summer across Empire Road in the bike trail lot. Parking, toilets at beach and boat ramp. State park entrance fee. ♿ ⛴
HIGHLIGHTS Nesting Bald Eagles and Common Loon.

Range Pond State Park is a family-friendly destination for birding, fishing, swimming, and boating, as well as winter sports. The Self-Guided Nature Trail gives information on the geology and natural history of the area. A Bald Eagle nest can be safely viewed across the water, and Common Loons are sometimes close to shore.

DIRECTIONS

From I-95 (the Maine Turnpike) take Exit 75. Follow Routes 202 West/4 South/100 South (Washington Street) for 0.3 miles. Take a right onto Kittyhawk Avenue. As you pass the end of the runway of Auburn Airport in summer you may hear or see Willow Flycatcher, Yellow-billed Cuckoo, and Eastern Towhee.

At 1.9 miles from Route 202 West/4 South/100 South, turn left onto Lewiston Junction Road. In 1.8 miles, at Empire Road, stop to check the fields: Sandhill Cranes have been seen in these cornfields at the junction, and you may want to stop to compare the Alder Flycatcher song with the Willow Flycatcher that you just heard near the airport runway. Turn left onto Empire Road, and the entrance to **Range Pond State Park** (pronounced "rang") is 0.3 miles on the right.

I prefer to park at the bike trail lot on the left across from the Range Pond State Park entrance road. The bike trail lot is designated by a row of boulders. A map of the bike trails is posted on the trail about 100 feet in from the parking lot. The bike trail may be better for warblers and birds such as Scarlet Tanager, Rose-breasted Grosbeak, Yellow-bellied Sapsucker, and Veery. Or you can park outside the main park gate before opening time. After the park opens at 9 a.m., you may drive past the check-in station and park at the beach. This area is wheelchair accessible, including bathrooms, beach access, and boat-ramp access. I would check the beach for shorebirds and the pond for waterfowl and Common Loon. The best area within the park gates for a diversity of passerines, including breeding Swamp Sparrow and migrant warblers, would be to the left facing the beach around the Self-Guided Nature Trail and the trail around the marsh.

As early as February the nesting Bald Eagles will be beginning courtship behavior and freshening up the nest. Facing the lakefront with the parking lot behind you, walk to your right to the end of the beach and continue down a shoreline trail. Continue until you come to a point where you look north across the pond to a small island with some tall pines. If you have not already heard the piping call of the Bald Eagles you may see one perched near a massive nest in the top of one of these pines. Often one or both of the adults will be perched nearby.

Uncommon species recorded from the park include Red-bellied Woodpecker and Carolina Wren. Given the density and diversity of coniferous trees here, this section of the park may be good for crossbills and other goodies in a year of "winter finch" incursions.

For more information on the park see the state park's website at http://www .maine.gov/cgi-bin/online/doc/parksearch/details.pl?park_id=11.

SITE AN6 Lewiston-Auburn Parks and Trails

TOWNS Lewiston and Auburn. DeLorme Map 11: E5. **SEASON** September–October, **November–April**, May–June. **VISITATION** 30 min. to 2 hrs. at each site. Restroom facilities at local businesses. Auburn River Walk is wheelchair accessible from Main Street parking lot. HIGHLIGHTS White-winged gulls, wintering and vagrant waterbirds; nesting Bald Eagles, Peregrine Falcons, and Cliff Swallows.

The Androscoggin River is the centerpiece of birding in the Lewiston-Auburn area at any season, but migrant passerines in spring and fall or waterfowl and gulls during the months when ponds and lake are frozen will turn up the most rarities. Other nearby parks and trails offer microhabitats for resident species, migrant passerines, and half-hardy overwinterers.

DIRECTIONS

From I-95 (the Maine Turnpike) take Exit 80. From the north, turn left at the end of the off-ramp onto the Alfred A. Plourde Parkway. From the south, bear right at the end of the ramp onto the Plourde Parkway.

In 0.4 miles make a right onto Goddard Road. Bear right at the stop sign onto River Road, which becomes Lincoln Street. In 1.6 miles take a left at the first traffic light onto Cedar Street and cross the bridge over the Androscoggin River into Auburn. Take the first right onto Second Street. At the end of the block, Little Andy Park is on the right. The parking lot is immediately beyond the ninety-degree left turn and behind Rolly's Diner at the light on the corner of Mill and South Main Streets.

Little Andy Park, where the Little Androscoggin River meets the larger Androscoggin, is the first stop of the L-A parks tour. The Great Falls of the Androscoggin just upriver was the center of a large fishery for migrating Atlantic salmon and other anadromous fish. This is a hot spot for Common Goldeneye and Hooded and Common Mergansers in the winter.

Walk Second Street back to Broad Street and walk left onto the Bernard Lown Peace Bridge that you just crossed. Scan up and down the river for waterfowl and Peregrine Falcons or other raptors, as well as the ornate steeple of the Franco-American Center.

Nearby **Sherwood Forest** is a nice wooded urban park with a secluded feel and is good for early spring migrants and breeders such as Least Flycatcher, Scarlet Tanager, and Veery. Print a map before you go, since the trail markers may not be clear. I would allow one to two hours, with extra time to check feeders and ornamental plantings in the neighborhood. To get to Sherwood Forest, return to your car and continue on Second Street. At the stop sign next to Rolly's Diner turn right onto Route 136 North/Mill Street. Immediately at the light make a hard left onto South Main Street. Make your second right (in 0.2 miles) onto Cook Street. In 0.6 miles make a right onto Nineteenth Street and follow it until it dead-ends. Park on the side of the road, and the trailhead will be on your left as you enter the trees.

After Sherwood Forest, you can return to the traffic light at Rolly's Diner and make a soft left onto Route 136 North/Main Street, crossing the bridge over the Little Androscoggin River. At 0.6 miles from the light at the diner, the road divides, and you will find the Auburn Hall public parking lot on the left (across from the Roak Block). Park there for the **Auburn Riverwalk Loop**. Cross Main Street on foot and walk through Festival Plaza (look for the huge colorful canopies during the warmer months).

Directly in front of you there are likely to be a hundred or more ducks, or what I like to call the Gene Pool. There are mostly Mallards but also gradations of hybrids of Mallard and American Black Ducks and also domestic species. There will be a few "mutts" to confuse you, but occasionally a Northern Pintail or Green-winged Teal joins the group and even overwinters. Numbers vary according to season and have dropped since feeding has been actively discouraged.

From here I am drawn immediately upriver toward the Great Falls. Particularly in winter this area has concentrations of gulls and waterfowl of all kinds. Glaucous and Iceland Gulls may be seen here, and I once had a "Nelson's" Gull (Glaucous x Herring hybrid).

Continuing above the falls you come to West Pitch Park. Walk uphill past the observation deck over the falls to the railroad bridge. Looking north you can view the Bald Eagle nest in a tall pine on the island above the dam. The brushy areas around here may have migrant sparrows and lingering vagrants in winter.

Retrace your steps to Festival Plaza. On the way, in spring and early summer don't forget to check out the Cliff Swallow colony on the upriver side of the North Bridge. The stretch of river below the falls has Double-crested Cormorant spring, summer, and fall and an occasional Great Cormorant in April. Hooded and Common Mergansers, Common Goldeneye, and Bufflehead may round out your list; a Long-tailed Duck is a recent inland rarity.

Continue downriver to **Bonney Park** at the end of the pedestrian bridge, checking the foliage for resident and migrant passerines.

From Bonney Park cross to Lewiston on the old railroad trestle, which ends

Auburn Riverwalk. © Dan Nickerson

in **Simard-Payne Memorial Park**—the site of numerous festivals and events. An overwintering Gadwall was seen in recent years from the pedestrian bridge. You may walk upriver from here and back across the North Bridge to complete your circuit, checking the river edge and being alert for raptors (always look up when the ducks, gulls, or pigeons flush).

In winter, check the ornamental plantings around the Hilton Garden Hotel on the Auburn end of the bridge and surrounding neighborhoods for Cedar or Bohemian Waxwings or Pine Grosbeaks, which may be feeding on the persistent fruit of the trees and shrubs.

To extend your visit to L-A you can visit the **Thorncrag Bird Sanctuary in Lewiston.** From the Auburn Riverwalk Loop parking lot, turn left onto Main Street. At the light, turn right onto Route 202 East and cross the bridge into Lewiston. In half a mile bear right onto Sabattus Street (Route 126). At the light in another half a mile bear left to continue on Sabattus Street for 1.3 miles. Turn left just before the Hannaford supermarket onto Highland Spring Road. At its end, turn right on Montello Street, and immediately left into the Thorncrag parking lot.

Allow one or two additional hours to explore this sanctuary, maintained by the Stanton Bird Club. It is easily navigated and is best early in the morning, as it gets a great deal of use on weekends and midday. The sanctuary is mostly forested, with some edge habitat, and represents the usual passerines of mixed deciduous/coniferous woodlands, with more variety during migration.

For more information on the Sherwood Forest, visit the website of the Androscoggin Land Trust at http://androscogginlandtrust.org/land-projects /sherwood-forest-conservation-area/. For more information about the Thorncrag Bird Sanctuary, including a checklist of all species recorded there, see www.stantonbirdclub.org/thorncrag-sanctuary/.

SITE AN7 Auburn North Circuit

TOWNS Auburn and Turner. DeLorme Map 6: C1. **SEASON** April, May, July–February. **VISITATION** 2–4 hrs. Restrooms at local businesses. ♿ **HIGHLIGHTS** Bald Eagle nest; early spring and late fall waterbirds, including Snow Goose and Horned Grebe; Snow Bunting, Horned Lark, Northern Shrike, and frugivores in winter; Louisiana Waterthrush possible.

The Auburn North Circuit offers a spectrum of varied birding opportunities from riverfront to lakeside, forest to farmlands, the most exciting being during migration when some of the areas highlighted draw concentrations of migrants to their unique habitat. Several locations for migrant waterfowl, including Lake Auburn and the Androscoggin River, are worth checking regularly; and when open water allows, check for overwintering ducks and roosting gulls.

DIRECTIONS

From I-95 (the Maine Turnpike) take Exit 80. From the north, turn left at the end of the off-ramp onto the Alfred A. Plourde Parkway. From the south, bear right at the end of the ramp onto the Plourde Parkway.

Take your second right in 0.4 miles onto Goddard Road. Bear right at the stop sign onto River Road, which becomes Lincoln Street. In 2 miles Lincoln Street ends at a traffic light at Main Street (Route 202) in downtown Lewiston. Take the left onto Route 202 West, crossing the Androscoggin River North Bridge into Auburn. At the second light turn right on Turner Street. Stay in the right lane, and at the second light continue straight, merging onto Route 4 North (Center Street). At the next light turn right onto **North River Road.**

In a few hundred yards, turn into the **North River Road Boat Launch** on your right. Park here and search the tall pines on the island downriver (to your right) for Bald Eagles that nest on the tiny island with the tall pines.

Ring-necked Ducks and Hooded Mergansers can be seen in good numbers in the spring, with an occasional Greater or Lesser Scaup. Check for shorebirds (including Greater and Lesser Yellowlegs and "peeps," with Spotted and Solitary Sandpipers most regular) during the low water of late summer and for unusual gulls (including Iceland and Glaucous) roosting on the ice in winter. I have seen Horned, Red-necked, and Pied-billed Grebes in this seemingly unlikely place. Check the shrubbery for migrants, and frugivores in winter.

Continue up North River Road, scanning the river as you go, especially the little cove just upriver form the boat launch. One mile north of the boat launch and just beyond Bradman Street you will cross Bobbin Mill Brook, which flows into the Androscoggin. Check this area for migrants and the river for anything unusual in the way of gulls or waterfowl. Louisiana Waterthrush has been heard here in spring. This brook is typical Louisiana Waterthrush habitat. Thanks to research done for this chapter, I now know that "Louies" are regular on nearly any such tributary of a lake or river in the county. Greater Scaup and Barrow's Goldeneye have been reported here in winter as well.

Park here and walk 0.4 miles farther on to Stetson Road, or all the way to the end of North River Road if you have the time. Check fruit-bearing trees and shrubs for frugivores in winter. The slowly rising hill catches the early morning sun and is a great place for migrants and half-hardy overwinterers or "southern" birds such as Carolina Wren and Red-bellied Woodpecker. Bohemian and Cedar Waxwings and Pine Grosbeaks may be numerous here in winter irruptions.

Raptors, Snow Geese, Northern Shrikes, Bobolinks, and Savannah Sparrows all visit the fields in season. Ospreys and Bald Eagles nest nearby.

At the end of the road, retrace your steps and turn onto Stetson Road. Halfway up the hill is a good place to look and listen for birds like Brown Thrasher in the overgrown fields.

After returning to your car, at the light at the end of Stetson Road, turn right onto Center Street (Route 4 North). In 1.2 miles the **Lake Auburn Boat Launch** will be on the left. Scope the lake from the boat launch (closed in winter) or adjacent roadside parking area. Common Loon can be seen spring through fall. During waterbird migration, especially in early spring before smaller bodies of water have opened, and again in fall immediately after

Sabattus Pond freezes (see site AN8), scan carefully for both scaup, Common Mergansers, Ruddy Ducks, and Horned Grebes, occasionally punctuated by a scoter or other migrant sea duck.

I then continue north 0.8 miles to Lakeshore Drive, which follows the northeast shore for 2.7 miles. The parking lot about 0.4 miles on the left is the best place to scan for the waterbird species mentioned above. Check the smaller marshy pond opposite the parking area for species such as Ring-necked Duck and American Wigeon.

Lakeshore Drive ends at a stop sign (there's a well-maintained portable toilet here). Turn left onto North Auburn Road, and in 0.2 miles the **Whitman Spring Trail** is on the left. There is parking here for a few cars, or park across the street. Walk the trail, checking side loops to the lakeshore, for about 1.5 miles until you come to private property and must turn back. This spot can have good numbers of passerine migrants, especially in spring.

From late fall through early spring I extend my birding into Turner for the chance for open-country birds such as a variety of raptors, Northern Shrike, Horned Lark, Snow Bunting, and Lapland Longspur.

Back at Route 4, turn left to head north for 3.5 miles and turn right onto **Upper Street.** For the next 2.8 miles, to the intersection of Pearl Road, there are few places to pull over, and commuter traffic here can be fierce for a country road. Therefore, I turn left onto Pearl Road and pull over. There is little traffic on this side street, so it is a good place to slow down and look. I sometimes walk a loop along Pearl, turning north onto Lower Street and returning to Upper Street by Bryant Street one country block north of Pearl.

Back at your car, continue on to the end of Pearl Road and turn right onto Lower Street, scanning fields along the way. At the end of Lower Street, in 1.9 miles, turn right onto Route 117 North and check out any action at feeders in town.

In 0.4 miles you can turn right and return to Auburn via Upper Street. If I have a little more time, I continue straight at the stop sign onto **Cobb Road** and check out some more agricultural fields and the Nezinscot River. Sometimes large numbers of ducks can be seen in the agricultural fields here.

Or I can go farther on Route 117 North and take the right in 0.5 miles onto **Fish Road,** following the north bank of the Nezinscot. This is good for Eastern Bluebird, Killdeer, Hooded and Common Merganser, and again sometimes huge flocks of ducks in spring—usually at a distance that provides a good challenge for ID of ducks in flight. These fields are rich in raptors at any season.

SITE AN8 Sabattus Pond

TOWNS Sabattus, Greene, Wales. DeLorme Map 12: E1. **SEASON** All year, but especially **October–early December** and, to a lesser extent, April.
VISITATION 1–4 hrs. by car, half-day paddle. Restrooms at businesses on Route 126; portable toilets seasonal at Martin's Point Beach boat launch.
 ♿ ⚓ **HIGHLIGHTS** Impressive concentrations of waterfowl, including both scaup and Ruddy Duck and regular rarities; American Coot; breeding marsh birds.

Sabattus Pond is possibly the best location in the southern part of the state to study diving ducks drawn by the presence of the invasive Chinese mystery snail—an abundant food supply for everything from scaup to the occasional scoters.

Beginning in mid-to-late October and continuing until the pond ices over, large numbers of Greater and Lesser Scaup may be studied at close range—a great learning opportunity for birders who are still trying to master this often challenging identification. Ruddy Ducks amass here by the hundreds, and nearly every species of duck occurring in Maine waters—fresh or salt—can be found on Sabattus Pond during the fall season. The counts of Ruddy Duck are by far the best in the state in most years, and American Coots are regular.

Bald Eagles are regular at every season, with breeding Ospreys active in the area from April through October. Other local breeding birds that can be encountered during the summer include everything from both Willow and Alder Flycatchers to Prairie Warblers.

For those who like to bird by canoe or kayak, the marshes at the north end of the pond are a largely underexplored area that is home to Marsh Wrens and rails in the breeding season and a staging area for swallows, gulls, ducks, and other species during migration.

DIRECTIONS

From I-95 (the Maine Turnpike) take Exit 86. Turn onto Route 9 East. In 1.3 miles make a right at the traffic light onto Route 126 East/9 East. A primitive boat launch with parking on the dirt shoulder is half a mile on the left as you reach the pond.

Particularly in late fall, large rafts of ducks amass at the south end, perhaps owing to the plentiful snails in the shallow, rocky bottom. The location of waterfowl depends on wind direction, drifting ice sheets, and the activity of

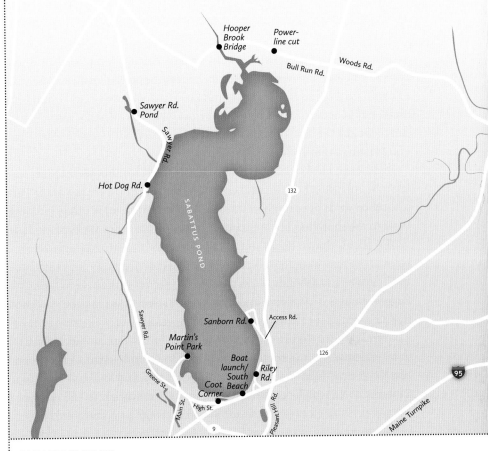

SABATTUS POND

Bald Eagles and hunters. Diving ducks expected include Greater and Lesser Scaup, Ruddy Duck (recent high count of 915 by Derek on October 31, 2014), Ring-necked Duck, Common Merganser, Hooded Merganser, Common Goldeneye, and Bufflehead. Canvasback and Redhead are occasional, as are all three species of scoters. Dabbling ducks, usually hugging the shorelines, can include Mallard, American Black Duck, Wood Duck, Green- and Blue-winged Teal, Northern Pintail, Northern Shoveler, Gadwall, and American Wigeon. Common Loon and Horned Grebe are regular, occasionally punctuated by an inland rarity such as Red-throated Loon or Red-necked Grebe. Shorebirds seen on the beach in spring and especially fall migration, depending on water levels, include Least and Semipalmated Sandpipers, Greater and Lesser Yellowlegs, Spotted and Solitary Sandpipers, Pectoral Sandpiper, and Semipalmated Plover.

Looking toward the northwest you will see Martin's Point Beach and boat launch. You may discover that birds are concentrating in that area and decide to continue west on Routes 126/9 and make a clockwise circuit around the pond, but generally I take the counterclockwise route that I suggest below. But to hit just the best locations, combine the beach with stops at Riley Road and Martin's Point Park.

To make a complete loop follow Route 126/9 East for another 0.2 miles, to a left onto Riley Road. As the road curves to the right, you'll see the water. Park a hundred yards or so up this dirt road, next to a small brick utility building. Walk to the shoreline, but approach carefully—nearshore ducks often flush.

The lake is drawn down in the fall as part of the struggle against algal bloom. You may want to walk the revealed lakebed for closer looks at waterfowl, particularly dabbling ducks that like the shelter of the cove to the north. Large numbers of Mallards and American Black Ducks (and their hybrids) may be scanned for the more uncommon species.

From Riley Road return to Route 126 North/9 East, and at the traffic light in 0.1 miles turn left onto Route 132 North. In 0.7 miles take a left onto Access Road. I park about a hundred yards down this road and walk right onto Sanborn Road, which parallels the east shore. Particularly in the fall, when the water is drawn down, migrant Bonaparte's Gulls or shorebirds may be seen here roosting or foraging on a sandbar, and diving and dabbling ducks can be close to shore, but you must scope the water from the road—do not trespass in yards.

Returning to Route 132, turn left to go north. There is little room to pull over for the next few miles, and traffic moves very fast, but you will find a couple of places where you may scan the flooded fields for Green-winged Teal in early spring or Snow Bunting or Northern Shrike in the winter. At 3.1 miles from Access Road, I turn left on Bull Run Road. This will take you across the northern end of the pond. In 0.8 miles a large power line crosses the road. There is room to park and walk this area. Prairie Warblers nest on the upper end of this power line, and you can enjoy watching several active Osprey nests during breeding season. Willow and Alder Flycatcher can both be heard here. Continue up Bull Run to the bridge over Hooper Brook, where you can put in a canoe or kayak. In the early spring Common and Hooded Mergansers gather in this tributary of Sabattus Pond, sometimes numbering in the hundreds.

Paddling a quarter mile downstream into Sabbatus Pond brings you to a web of marshes that host a healthy population of Marsh Wrens—the largest population that I have found in Androscoggin County. It also is home to Virginia Rail, American Bittern, Wood Duck, and possibly Sora. Great Horned Owls nest on the ridge above the pond. I have seen the downy young in the marsh noisily begging to be fed.

Swallows stage at the north end of the pond during spring and fall migrations in large numbers, perching on the many shrubby islands. Bonaparte's Gull, Common Terns, and shorebirds may gather here to roost on floating vegetation in the late summer and fall.

At 1.4 miles west of the Hooper Brook bridge, make a left onto Ball Brook Road. In 0.2 miles turn left onto Sawyer Road, which will eventually take you into Sabattus Village. One mile down Sawyer Road, the power line crosses the road, and on the right is a small pond that may be good for Pied-Billed Grebe, Hooded Merganser, and painted turtles.

A half-mile walk south from here on Sawyer Road allows a view of Sabattus Pond, where Ruddy Ducks, both scaup, and other waterfowl like to raft up in fall, out of reach of the prevailing winds. Canvasback and Redhead may be found here. Great Black-backed Gulls and Double-crested and an occasional Great Cormorant (in spring) favor roosting on a large boulder just offshore.

There is no shoulder here; use care while viewing the birds. Better yet, continue another 1 mile beyond the pond on Sawyer Road, turning left onto Hot Dog Road, which offers small areas to park while scanning the lake.

Next stop is **Martin's Point Park**. At the end of Hot Dog Road, turn left to continue south on Sawyer Road. In 1.9 miles turn left on Elm Street, and then in 0.3 miles make the left onto Lake Street. Martin's Point Beach and boat launch will be on the right.

When the pond is drawn down in the fall, the cove to the right of the boat launch and above the dam is a hot spot for ducks and shorebirds on the revealed sandbars and mudflats. Pectoral Sandpipers have seemed to favor this area, along with other shorebirds. This area is also reliable for American Coot in the fall. You will see lots of Mallards and some American Black Ducks; scan for more uncommon species. Walking up the shore to the left from the boat launch offers another look at the south end of the lake, and you may spot more waterfowl.

To complete your circuit of the lake, leave Martin's Point via Lake Street, and at the stop sign turn left onto Elm Street, which ends in 0.1 mile at High Street. Make a left and, in 0.2 miles, left again onto Long Beach Road. This is a short spur, which joins Routes 126 and 9 in 0.3 miles. The small cove on

Sabattus Pond is a great place to practice your scaup identification. It's easy when the bird is in flight: note the white secondaries contrasting with the gray primaries on this drake Lesser Scaup.
© Jeannette Lovitch

the left at the south end of the lake, affectionately known as Coot Corner, is a good spot for American Coot, Hooded Merganser, and Wood Duck (spring and early fall) in particular.

After the lake freezes, a good place to check is the Sabattus River, which passes through downtown Sabattus after leaving the pond and remains open longer. From Martin's Point take the left onto Elm Street. At the end of the block go left onto High Street and then an immediate right onto Main Street. In 0.2 miles you again pass over the Sabattus River. Make a right immediately after the bridge onto Island Road.

There are often close looks at lingering ducks from areas near the American Legion parking lot or across Main Street above the dam, where, rather unbelievably, a drake Redhead was seen in the spring of a recent year.

Continuing down Main Street will bring you to Route 126. A right takes you to downtown Lewiston. A mile or so west is the Whole Scoop for those who can't pass up a frozen confection in the warmer months.

RARITIES

Tufted Duck, November 2009 and March–April 2016; Cattle Egret, November 2011. Uncommon to rare but occasional visitors include Iceland Gull, Redhead, Canvasback, Barrow's Goldeneye, and Great Cormorant.

5 Sagadahoc County

JOHN BERRY

Small in size, Sagadahoc County packs in a whole lot of great birding through-out the year. Geographically the first county of the Midcoast Region (where Maine's coast turns to become more east–west than north–south), it is char-acterized by long peninsulas and countless islands that harbor a lot of great birding destinations.

Merrymeeting Bay (site SA10) is a globally significant "inland delta," formed by two major (the Androscoggin and Kennebec) and four minor rivers, com-bining to drain over 40 percent of Maine. Mostly freshwater habitat, but with twice-daily tidal pulses of saltwater, and extensive meadows of wild rice combine to harbor impressive numbers of migrant waterfowl. In early spring, as the bay opens up but rivers and lakes to the north remain frozen, ducks can build in impressive numbers. When conditions (warm southerly winds and plentiful ice to the north) combine in prime time (usually sometime between late March and mid-April in most years), there's no place I would rather be than the "Mouth of the Abby" sifting through a thousand Green-winged Teal for the occasional "Common" Teal.

As the ducks move on, and neotropical migrants begin to return, head over to Green Point WMA (SA11), Morse Mountain (SA1), or Bradley Pond (SA7). During the breeding season, Morse Mountain, Cathance Preserve (SA9), and Green Point offer samples of the area's breeding species.

Fall comes quickly in Maine, and by the middle of July, southbound shorebird numbers are already building. By the end of the month, through early September, shorebirding can be simply outstanding here, especially at Popham Beach State Park (SA2), or, if shifting sands once again cut a chan-nel farther east, Seawall Beach (SA1). As shorebirds move on and land birds become the attraction, Green Point WMA (SA11) heats up, especially when sparrows are on the move in October.

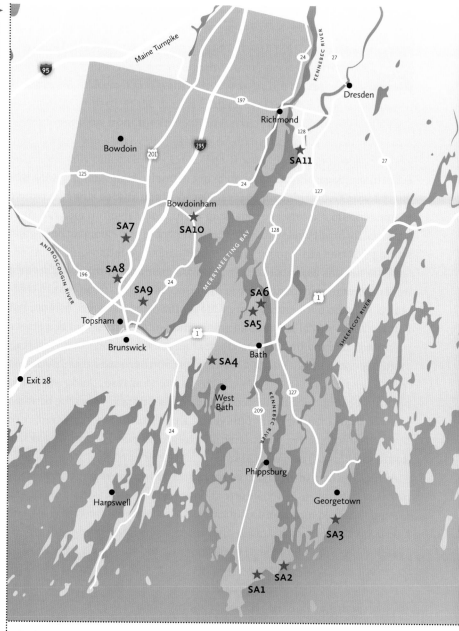

Maine Turnpike

95

197

24 KENNEBEC RIVER 27

Dresden

Richmond

128

Bowdoin

SA11

201 295

125

24

127

Bowdoinham

SA7

SA10

128

SA8

ANDROSCOGGIN RIVER

196

SA9

24

MERRYMEETING BAY

SA6

1

SHEEPSCOT RIVER

Topsham

SA5

Brunswick

1

Bath

SA4

Exit 28

West
Bath

127

KENNEBEC RIVER

209

Harpswell

24

Phippsburg

Georgetown

SA3

SA1

SA2

SAGADAHOC COUNTY

In winter, gull watching at the Bath Landfill and Waterfront (SA5) is a highlight, as is scanning the ocean from Popham Beach (high tide is better).

But when it comes down to it, regardless of all those seasonal highlights at various destinations, Reid State Park (SA3) is my favorite place to bird in the county (which is why John asked me to pen that entry) at any time of the year. If only for a lovely walk, always with some bird(s) of interest—from rafts of Red-necked Grebes in winter to the chance of a rare tern in the summer—it is one of my favorite places in the state. —*Derek Lovitch*

SITE SA1 Morse Mountain and Seawall Beach

TOWN Phippsburg. DeLorme Map 6: E5. **SEASON** All year, but especially April–May and July–August. **VISITATION** 2–4 hrs. No facilities. Stay on the marked trails. If the parking lot is full, you must wait until a spot becomes available. **HIGHLIGHTS** Breeding Least Tern and Piping Plover; migrant passerines and shorebirds; waterbirds throughout the year.

Birders are grateful to the Bates-Morse Mountain Conservation Area Corporation for protection of and access to these six hundred acres of protected salt marsh and coastal upland habitat. The beach does not have the crowds of Popham because of the need to walk in, so it makes an attractive opportunity to observe shorebirds in August. During the spring season, over twenty species of warblers have been reported from the hike as the trail passes through different habitats, with over two hundred species in total recorded from the preserve. The beach area has nesting Piping Plovers and Least Terns in summer, and in fall migration it hosts large flocks of migrating shorebirds. Raptors are also often seen in the fall from the overlook at the top of the mountain, where the open ledges make a convenient spot to watch, with a distant view of Mount Washington on a clear day.

DIRECTIONS

From the south/west, take US Route 1 North into Bath. Take the exit for Route 209 South onto High Street toward Phippsburg/Small Point/Sebasco/Popham Beach. Turn right at the end of the ramp onto High Street.

From the east/north, follow US Route 1 South into Bath to the Bath/Phippsburg/Route 209 exit. Continue straight at the stop sign. At the traffic light, turn left onto Washington Street. Continue for 2.0 miles (two small parks on your left are good places to scan the river) and then turn left onto Route 209 South.

Follow Route 209 South for 11.1 miles (9.2 if you were coming from the east/north). Where Route 209 turns sharply left to Popham Beach, continue straight ahead on Route 216 South for 0.8 miles and turn left onto Morse Mountain Road. Drive 350 feet to the small parking lot on the left. (Do not park on Route 216 or along Morse Mountain Road.) The route is well marked by signs along the way.

There is a 2-mile trail from the parking area through woodlands across a salt marsh and creek, up 180-foot Morse Mountain (in fall, it's worth a scan for migrating raptors) to an overlook of the marsh and beach, and on to Seawall Beach.

When you reach the beach, turn right and walk about a half mile, as far as a red pole at the edge of the dunes where you can scan the mouth of the Sprague River and the sandbar for gulls. Alternatively, turn left when you reach the beach and walk to the mouth of the Morse River, which separates Seawall Beach from Popham Beach State Park (site SA2). Piping Plover nests are found in this area, and there also is the opportunity to see into the marsh along the river. Keep an eye out for a variety of terns, including rarities. Lesser Black-backed Gulls are regularly spotted here in the fall.

Scan the offshore water, especially in winter when scoters, eiders, grebes, and Bufflehead are common. However, oversummering sea ducks are occasional.

RARITIES

Black-backed Woodpecker, November 1980; Curlew Sandpiper, May 2008; White-eyed Vireo, May–September 2014

SITE SA2 Popham Beach State Park

TOWN Phippsburg. DeLorme Map 6: E5. SEASON All year, but especially July–September. VISITATION 1–4 hrs. Open daily 9 a.m.–sunset. State park fees. Year-round restroom facilities (outhouses in winter). HIGHLIGHTS All-around birding, but especially shorebirds and terns in summer; waterbirds and raptors in winter.

Bordering the south side of the mouth of the Kennebec River, Popham Beach State Park is one of Maine's rare geologic landforms: a long stretch of sand beach. Fox and Wood Islands lie offshore, and the Kennebec and Morse Rivers border each end of the beach. Visitors can walk to Fox Island at low tide, but you must pay attention to the rising tides so as not to get marooned. Sand movement and beach dynamics during winter storms have a dramatic effect on Popham Beach, causing extreme shoreline change and dune erosion. The location of the inlet to the Morse River has changed several times in recent years.

This beach is one of the best in Maine and worth visiting all year long. Since it is often crowded with beachgoers on the weekend, weekdays offer better birding. A wide variety of fall shorebird migrants can be seen. In summer, roosting Common and some breeding Least Terns attract the occasional vagrant tern, and several pairs of Piping Plovers nest here as well. Shorebird migration heats up in July. At low and mid-tides, many will be foraging on the beach, especially the inlet to the Morse River at the southwest end where there is a lagoon. At high tide, be careful not to disturb roosting birds as you inspect them. Incoming to high tides are also the best conditions for roosting terns and gulls. The migrating shorebirds regularly attract Merlins and Peregrine Falcons.

DIRECTIONS

From the south/west, take US Route 1 North into Bath. Take the exit for Route 209 South onto High Street toward Phippsburg/Small Point/Sebasco/Popham Beach. Turn right at the end of the ramp onto High Street. The route is well marked by signs along the way.

From the east/north, follow US Route 1 South into Bath to the Bath/Phippsburg/Route 209 exit. Continue straight at the stop sign. At the traffic light, turn left onto Washington Street. Continue for 2.0 miles (two small parks on your left are good places to scan the river) and then turn left onto Route 209 South.

Follow Route 209 South for 14.4 miles (12.5 miles if you came via Washington Street) and enter the park on your right. If you arrive early, you can park along the road, in the turning lane, but you *must* move your vehicle by 8:30 a.m.

From the parking lot, walk past the bathhouse to the beach and concentrate on the area to the right, toward the Morse River. The lagoon, the low dune, and the inlet to the river are the primary concentration points for shorebirds, nesting Piping Plovers and Least Terns, and resting gulls and terns.

Offshore in summer, look for Roseate Terns feeding among the Commons.

Semipalmated Sandpipers take flight along the beach at Popham Beach State Park.
© Jeannette Lovitch

Double-crested Cormorants, Herring, and Great Black-backed Gulls nest on the offshore islands, and Great Cormorants may be spotted there in winter. Also in winter look for Common and Red-throated Loons, Long-tailed Ducks, grebes, and scoters.

Before leaving the park, bird the pitch pine forest and shrubs near the parking lot, especially during spring and fall migration.

As you leave the park, look around the edge of the marsh for Saltmarsh (few), Nelson's, and Savannah Sparrows. Other sparrows are frequently present during migration along the edges of the road as well.

To continue your birding at **Fort Popham**, turn right out of the park and drive 1.2 miles to reach this large granite fort built during the Civil War to command the entrance to the Kennebec River. It is owned and managed by Popham Beach State Park, but there is no admission charge. From here you have an excellent vantage point to scan for terns and gulls during the summer months and seabirds and waterbirds during the winter.

For another view of the mudflats at low tide, exit Fort Popham and take your first right onto Fort Baldwin Road. Follow this for 0.2 miles for the parking area at **Fort Baldwin.** Scan the mudflats, and in spring and fall migration the woodlands accessed from the trail across the street are worth a look.

RARITIES

Gull-billed Tern, June 2006; "Greenland" Dunlin (ssp. *arctica*), August 2015

SITE SA3 Reid State Park

Entry by Derek Lovitch

TOWN Georgetown. DeLorme Map 7: D1. **SEASON** All year.
VISITATION 1–4 hrs. State park fees. Year-round restroom facilities (outhouses in winter). ♿ **HIGHLIGHTS** All-around birding, from migrant land birds and waterbirds, shorebirds and terns in summer, waterbirds (especially Red-necked Grebe) and raptors in winter.

This is one of the real gems of Maine and worth visiting all year long for the scenery, let alone the birding. A wide variety of land birds and waterbird migrants can be seen in both spring and especially fall (south-pointing peninsula). In summer, roosting terns (Common) and sometimes breeding Least attract the occasional vagrant, and several pairs of Piping Plovers nest here as well. Shorebird migration heats up in July, and on quieter weekdays at high tide, large numbers of shorebirds can often be found roosting at the river mouth, while at mid-tides, many will be foraging on the beach and river mudflats (at low, most shorebirds tend to move farther upriver or up into Sheepscot Bay). Baird's and Buff-breasted Sandpipers are sometimes found in late August into September, especially in wrack lines on the two beaches.

Incoming to high tides are also the best conditions for roosting terns and gulls (Lesser Black-backed is regular here in migration, and white-winged gulls are occasional in winter). In winter, high tide is best, drifting waterbirds in closer. Some of the best counts of Red-necked Grebe (often more than two hundred) in the state occur here, along with good numbers of Red-throated and Common Loons, all regular sea ducks, and alcids, especially Black Guillemot and Razorbill. However, after a southerly blow in winter, it's a good spot to look for Dovekies and Black-legged Kittiwakes. In good winter finch years, crossbills—especially White-winged—and Common Redpolls can be numerous.

From US Route 1 in Woolwich follow the signage for Reid State Park/Route 127 South (first exit after the Bath Bridge when traveling eastbound on Route 1 North). Follow Route 127 South for a scenic 10.2 miles. Turn right onto Seguinland Road, following the state park signs. The park entrance is 2 miles ahead, but it is worth pulling over at the two wooded ponds on the right side of the road, which host breeding Wood Ducks, other ducks in migration, and can be decent for warblers in spring migration.

The park gates open at 9 a.m., but I often arrive a couple of hours before that. You are allowed to park in the dirt road/turnaround on the left, just before the gate, and walk in. However, if you do not have a state park pass, you are still obligated to pay the entry fee. I prefer to get here early and walk the entire park (about 5 miles in all). Whether by car or on foot, bear left past the entrance booth and head to Griffith's Head. Scan the marsh and its outlet carefully. Check the thickets around the parking lot, and scan the water—especially with a scope—for waterfowl and alcids, and the rocks for roosting shorebirds and, in winter, Snowy Owl and Purple Sandpiper (regular).

You can either walk Mile Beach to Todd's Head—check for shorebirds, especially Piping Plover (May–August) and Sanderlings (late fall through early spring), and scan the water—or if you drove into the park, you can return to your car, head back up the road, and make a left before the entrance booth, to drive down to Todd's Head. (The road is closed for most of the winter; when it is, it is best to walk Mile Beach.) The beach is also good for "Ipswich" Savannah Sparrow in October and November.

At Todd's Head, thoroughly bird the edge of the parking lot and headlands, which can be very good in migration, especially in late fall. Sparrows are often plentiful, and Snow Buntings and Horned Larks are regular in late fall/early winter in the parking lot. Scan the water—often the largest number of Red-necked Grebes are seen from here.

Continue walking west on Half-Mile Beach to the mouth of the Little River. Be very careful not to flush roosting shorebirds, gulls, or terns at the point; sort through them from a comfortable distance. Check any groups of Bonaparte's Gulls carefully for the rare Black-headed, and check the usual terns for vagrants.

Walk around the corner, following the shore of the Little River, and take the well-worn (but often wet) trail across the small pocket salt marsh. A few

Reid State Park. © Kristen Lindquist

Saltmarsh Sparrows breed here, but are outnumbered by Nelson's Sparrows. Willets breed in the open marsh across the river as well. Take the trail up the short hill and return to the parking lot.

When on foot, make a left to follow the Todd's Head Road back to your car at the entrance booth, or take the road all the way back to your car at Griffith's Head to complete the loop. The road is often very birdy in migration and good for winter finches when they are around. In summer, Winter Wrens and Dark-eyed Juncos are among the breeders, along with numerous Yellow-rumped and Black-throated Green Warblers. A handful of Yellow-rumped Warblers still overwinter in what is left of the hedgerow of northern bayberry along one side of the road through the marsh (the cutting of wide holes in this productive hedgerow defies explanation). Scan the marsh for shorebirds in season, and in winter keep an eye out for Snowy Owl, Northern Harrier, and Rough-legged Hawk, along with Northern Shrike along the edges.

This is one of those places worth birding daily—especially in migration—and if I lived closer, I would probably do that. Therefore, when I do visit, I almost always walk the entire loop to sample all the habitats. Meanwhile, in snowy winters, I might do the loop by cross-country ski, or bird and then take advantage of the long, groomed loop through the woods (good for winter finches).

RARITIES

Hooded Warbler, October 2004; Wilson's Plover, May 2010; White-eyed Vireo, October 2012; "Oregon" Dark-eyed Junco, December 2015

SITE SA4 New Meadows River

TOWN West Bath. DeLorme Map 6: C4. **SEASON** October to ice-up **VISITATION** 30 min. No restroom facilities. **HIGHLIGHTS** Barrow's Goldeneye.

This "quick hit" spot is reliable for Barrow's Goldeneye and can often feature migrant and odd lingering waterfowl.

DIRECTIONS

From US Route 1 in West Bath take the West Bath/New Meadows exit and head south on New Meadows Road. Proceed through the stop sign at Old Bath Road and onto Fosters Point Road. Take the first right onto Bullrock Road. At the stop sign, a boat launch is straight ahead and a parking lot is on your left. From the boat launch scan both right and left for Barrow's Goldeneyes among the Commons, Hooded Mergansers, and others.

SITE SA5 Bath Landfill and Waterfront

Entry by Derek Lovitch

TOWN Bath. DeLorme Map 6: B5. **SEASON** October–November, **December–March**, April. **VISITATION** 1–2 hrs. Open Monday–Friday, 7:30 a.m.–4 p.m. No restroom facilities. ♿ **HIGHLIGHTS** White-winged gulls; vagrant gull potential; Bald Eagles; ducks, especially Common Mergansers.

Birders are indebted to the staff at this municipal landfill for welcoming us to the facility. Abiding by a few simple rules and protocols allows us to enjoy access to some great gull-watching and a good concentration of Bald Eagles, with up to twenty sometimes present. Herring Gulls dominate—often 95 percent or more of the birds present, with smaller numbers of Great Black-backed Gulls and sometimes a few Ring-billed Gulls. Iceland and Glaucous Gulls are regular in winter in small numbers. More spring and fall visitation would probably yield Lesser Black-backed Gulls fairly regularly (they used to be regular when the sardine cannery near the boat launch was still in operation). While the Bath landfill has not had the "mega" gull rarities that Hatch Hill in Augusta (see site KE5) has attracted, it did host two Golden Eagles throughout the winter of 2013–14.

Several sites along the Kennebec River offer more opportunities to study gulls, as well as looking for ducks, especially sometimes-impressive numbers of Common Mergansers, especially as ice on the river begins to go out in late March or early April. A few are present throughout most winters as well.

DIRECTIONS

From US Route 1 North (eastbound from Brunswick) take the right-hand exit for Route 209/Phippsburg as the two-lane highway splits. At the stop sign turn left onto High Street. In 2.0 miles, make a left onto Detritus Drive.

From US Route 1 South (westbound from Woolwich), bear right at the end of the Bath Bridge for the exit for Downtown Bath. At the immediate stop sign, go straight onto Vine Street. At the traffic light, turn right onto Washington Street, and at the next light turn left onto Centre Street. At the top of the hill turn right onto High Street and turn left onto Detritus Drive in 2.0 miles.

Detritus Drive ends at the landfill entrance. Proceed toward the entrance booth, parking to the right of it. Walk around the office, knock on the door, and ask for permission to look at birds. Ask about the current best place to park. Usually, you would simply pull your car forward and make a right, parking immediately to the side of the large blue barn. Do not block any vehicles, and do not block access to anything. Set up a scope near your car, and scan the gulls as they commute overhead to and from various water sources, and as they circle over the landfill.

Usually, the area of actual dumping is not visible—you are *not* permitted to drive into the landfill itself—so feeding gulls are often mostly out of sight. However, it won't be long before an eagle or equipment flushes them, so with a little patience you can usually sift through every gull.

I usually spend at least an hour here, watching the turnover of gulls as they come to and from the landfill. Gulls feeding at dumps need to bathe and drink regularly, and you'll see many birds "commuting" to the west until

Mill Cove freezes up. If they are heading in that direction, you can check the gulls there via the Whiskeag Trail (See site sa6). Otherwise, gulls head east to the Kennebec River near downtown Bath.

After departing the landfill, make a right at the end of Detritus Drive. Take your second left on Harward Street. At its end at Washington Street, make a right. You can scan the river from a dirt parking area immediately on your left, or park at the edge of the road. Current ice conditions and the tide will dictate where most of the gulls are bathing and roosting on the river and/or ice, but the best spot is usually from the North End Boat Launch.

Continue south on Washington Street for half a mile, then bear left onto Bowery Street (a hard left takes you down a dead-end street), following the small blue **boat launch** sign. Make your first left, pass the sewage treatment plant, and park at the end of the road in the boat launch area. If you saw gulls around the sewage facility—usually all Ring-billed—scan that group; a Black-headed Gull was here in March 2010. Otherwise, scan the river, especially to the north, for loafing and bathing gulls, and ducks, especially Common Mergansers, and keep an eye overhead for more eagles. Gull watching is best here when large chunks of ice are floating with the incoming and outgoing tide, providing a convenient "conveyor belt" of gulls going one way or the other. When they drift too far upriver, or too close to the bridge, they will fly back the other way and start the trip again, offering a second chance to comb through the masses.

Head back uphill and make a left onto Bowery Street. Bear left at the next fork onto Front Street. Keep an eye on the river for concentrations of ducks or gulls. Then make a left onto **Commercial Street**, just before the hotel. In 0.2 miles there's a small park on your left. Park here and walk to the river. Scan for ducks and gulls, and check the bridge for Peregrine Falcons. Afterward, head toward the bridge on Commercial Street and follow the signs to return to your desired direction.

Downtown Bath, especially the waterfront (including the streets south of Route 1), has a good number of crabapples planted, so check these carefully in winter for irruptive Bohemian Waxwings and Pine Grosbeaks.

RARITIES

One to two Golden Eagles, December 2013 through February 2014

SITE SA6 Whiskeag Creek Trail (Sewall Woods and Thorne Head)

TOWN Bath. DeLorme Map 6: B5. SEASON April–June, September–
March. VISITATION 3–4 hrs. No restroom facilities. Please stay on marked
trails. HIGHLIGHTS Bald Eagles; white-winged gulls; ducks; shorebirds.

This trail connects two properties of the Kennebec Estuary Land Trust. The
first, Sewall Woods, protects ninety-one acres of primarily mixed species forest with over 2,300 feet of shore frontage on the Whiskeag Creek, a brackish
tidal marsh. The trail also provides a limited view of the Bath landfill (especially for days when the landfill is closed). Thorne Head is a ninety-six-acre
property that includes a half mile of shoreline along the east side of Whiskeag
Creek and the Kennebec River, a freshwater marsh, old pine and hemlock
trees, vernal pools, and tidal wetlands. This preserve provides an additional
opportunity to search for rare gulls that may be frequenting the Bath landfill.

DIRECTIONS

Follow the directions for the Bath landfill (See site SA5) to reach High Street.
In 1.4 miles turn left onto Whiskeag Road. Proceed past the field on the right
and turn right through the stone gateposts to the parking, kiosk, and trail
guide.

Walk the Whiskeag Trail through the woods along the bank of the creek,
checking for shorebirds in the fall, ducks in the spring and fall, and gulls
in the fall and winter. There is an active Bald Eagle nest on the west bank
of the creek in a large pine. The woods themselves are a good opportunity
for warblers, vireos, and woodpeckers. There are several small streams and
pocket ponds and lowland marsh areas. When you reach the open area at
the back of the landfill, it is worth checking the surrounding trees for eagles
and other raptors and vultures. At this point you may retrace your steps to
the parking area or continue on the Whiskeag Trail all the way to Thorne
Head, crossing several parcels of private property. I prefer to return to my
car and drive to Thorne Head by turning left on Whiskeag Road and left on
High Street and following it to the parking lot at the end.

From this end, walk the Whiskeag Trail through the woods along the bank
of the creek, checking for shorebirds in the fall, ducks in the spring and fall,
and gulls in the fall and winter. The woods themselves are a good opportunity
for canopy warblers, vireos, thrushes, and woodpeckers. There are several

lowland marsh areas and vernal pools. When you reach the Narrows Trail, turn right and follow it to the northern portion for views into both Whiskeag Creek and the Kennebec River. When it intersects with the Overlook Trail, turn left to return to the parking area.

SITE SA7 Bradley Pond

TOWN Topsham. DeLorme Map 6 B3. SEASON April, **May**, June. VISITATION 1–2 hrs. No restroom facilities. No dogs. Please stay on the marked trails. HIGHLIGHTS Migrant and breeding passerines, including Northern Waterthrush and Bobolink.

Thanks to the Brunswick-Topsham Land Trust and the Call family, birders have access to this wonderful site. Since it is a working farm with a private residence, you must stay on the trails and out of the fields. The perimeter trail starts at the second parking kiosk and extends about a mile and a half around the farm fields and the edges of the wooded areas. The Upper Loop Trail starts at the first parking area and proceeds for about a half mile through a softwood forested area.

DIRECTIONS

Southbound on I-295 take Exit 31B (Route 196). At the end of the off-ramp, turn right onto Route 196 East.

Northbound on I-295 take Exit 31A (Route 196) and make a right at the end of the off-ramp.

At the fourth traffic light, turn left (north) onto Route 201 and follow it for 3.9 miles and then turn left on Bradley Pond Road. The road will become dirt and turn to the left at the property entrance. There are two small parking areas marked by kiosks on the left side of the drive.

Walk the Perimeter Trail along the drive, and it will turn into the field on the left. Proceed through the field and along a row of pine trees before entering a wooded area that is behind the farmhouse and above and along the flooded edge of Bradley Pond. Northern Waterthrush is often heard from your left as you proceed through the field and may be heard or seen along the edge of the pond. Warblers, flycatchers, and vireos, along with other forest birds, are often found on this portion of the trail. Emerging from the woods, the trail follows the edge of the fields with excellent transition habitat. Bobolinks breed in the fields. The trail goes behind a flooded gravel pit, which should not be entered, then reenters the wooded habitat along the edge, until it exits through a field back to the drive and the parking area.

The Upper Loop Trail is a shorter walk through a more mature softwood forest. It starts at the first parking kiosk near a small pond and a power-line cut that frequently produces a Winter Wren.

SITE SA8 Bisson's Farm

TOWN Topsham. DeLorme Map 6: B3.   SEASON March–April, November. VISITATION 30 min. to 1 hr. No restroom facilities.   HIGHLIGHTS Migrant waterfowl; gulls.

The farm is private property, with farm fields that extend from Meadow Road down to the Cathance River. The river often floods the lower portions of the fields, attracting large numbers of ducks, geese, and gulls from ice-out on the river in mid-March until late April. Nineteen species of waterfowl have been recorded here, including a Eurasian Wigeon that was present for a week in 2014. As many as fifty Snow Geese have been reported, and Canada Goose numbers are often in the hundreds.

DIRECTIONS

From I-295 take Exit 31A. At the end of the respective off-ramps, bear right onto Route 196 East. At the fourth traffic light, turn left onto Route 201 North. In 1.2 miles turn left onto Meadow Road. The farm fields extend for approximately 1 mile on the right side. There is no designated parking place, so you must park carefully on the side of the road. Do not park in front of Bisson's Market, but if it is open, it is always worth a visit.

Because of the rolling nature of the fields, I usually make several stops, scanning from each location. A spotting scope is helpful for identification of ducks in the river. Green-winged Teal are often present in large numbers, with an occasional Blue-winged Teal. Both scaup species have been seen, along with Common Goldeneyes, Buffleheads, and Ring-necked Ducks. The fields also may have Eastern Meadowlark, Wilson's Snipe, Killdeer, and both yellowlegs. Various raptors also frequent the area, along with early Turkey Vultures. Hundreds of Herring and Ring-billed Gulls should be sorted through for the occasional white-winged or Lesser Black-backed.

This area does not get a significant fall migration of waterfowl, but it can be worth checking.

RARITIES

Cattle Egret, November 2012; Eurasian Wigeon, April 2014

SITE SA9 Cathance Preserve

TOWN Topsham. DeLorme Map 6: B3.   **SEASON** April–June.
VISITATION 1–2 hrs. No restroom facilities.   **HIGHLIGHTS** Breeding Louisiana Waterthrush and Canada Warbler; spring migrant passerines.

The Brunswick Topsham Land Trust, Highland Green, and the Cathance River Education Alliance worked together to preserve these two areas with several hiking trails. The Heath Sanctuary is 30 acres, and the Cathance River Nature Preserve is 230 acres with about 5 miles of trails. Both areas offer a variety of breeding species of note and good birding in spring migration.

DIRECTIONS

From US Route 1 just east of downtown Brunswick take the exit for Route 196/Topsham. At the second traffic light turn right onto Village Drive. In 0.7 miles turn right at the Cathance Preserve sign. The road will turn to dirt; follow the signs to the kiosk and hiker parking.

The Heath Trail starts at the parking area and proceeds for about a mile around the heath sanctuary, with small quarries, vernal pools, and wetlands through a mixed forest. Take the short overlook trails to observe the heath; Canada Geese and Mallards nest in the area, and Alder and Least Flycatchers can often be spotted. Red-tailed Hawks have been nesting in this area as well.

Access to the Cathance River Trail system is via the Old Quarry Road trail located across the road from the parking area. This system can be described as a crooked ladder that parallels the river for approximately a mile and a half. The Cathance River Trail follows the river, and the Highlands Trail parallels it at a higher elevation. The rungs of the metaphorical ladder are the Barnes Leap, Beaver, and Rapids Trails, which connect the two longer trails and can be used to shorten the hike. My preference is to walk the Highlands Trail first at the higher elevation, and then when it joins the river at the top of the ladder proceed back downstream on the Cathance River Trail. In early spring there are class-four rapids that have a lot of water noise. This is an excellent area for Rose-breasted Grosbeaks, various thrushes, warblers, vireos, and Wood Ducks. Twenty-two species of warblers have been reported, along with four vireos and six thrushes. Louisiana Waterthrush has nested about 100 yards downriver from Barnes Leap under some overhanging ledges where Eastern Phoebes also nest. The Canada Warbler has been located at the lower end of the trail system near the river.

SITE SA10 Merrymeeting Bay
(including the Mouth of the Abagadasset River)

Entry by John Berry and Derek Lovitch

TOWNS Bowdoinham, Richmond, Dresden. DeLorme Map 6: A4–5.
SEASON March–April, September–December.   VISITATION 2 hrs. to all day. Open dawn to dusk every day. Restrooms at Mailley Park. ♿ ⚲
HIGHLIGHTS Waterfowl; Bald Eagle; Northern Harrier; migrant shorebirds; migrant passerines.

Merrymeeting Bay is a huge tidal, mostly freshwater estuary often referred to as an inland delta. The bay is formed at the joining of the Kennebec and Andoscoggin Rivers as well as four smaller rivers, which together drain nearly 40 percent of Maine. According to the Friends of Merrymeeting Bay, this is the largest waterfowl staging area in the Northeast. The bay is also home to a large population of Bald Eagles.

The mouths of these smaller rivers provide excellent feeding habitat for waterfowl, especially where wild rice still dominates. This is the best place in Maine to see large numbers and great variety of waterfowl, as well as Bald Eagles and other raptors. The birding is best from mid-March when the ice goes out into April, and again in early September and October when teal are on the move. Many sites are tide dependent, but for the most part birding is best at mid-tide when some flats are exposed. The tides in the bay are about an hour and a half later than Bath, so refer to a tide chart before going.

DIRECTIONS

A total loop of the bay can be made starting in Topsham and ending in Woolwich, scanning the fields and the bay wherever the opportunity exists, but we prefer to concentrate on these areas, starting at the Bowdoinham Town Landing.

From I-295 take Exit 37. Follow Route 125 North (Main Street) to the junc-

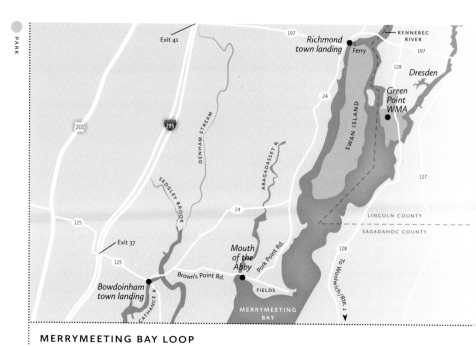

MERRYMEETING BAY LOOP

tion with Route 24 in the center of Bowdoinham. Stay straight, cross the railroad tracks, and enter the dirt parking lot of Mailley Park and the **Bowdoinham Town Landing** (restrooms). At this point scan the Cathance River for Common Mergansers in the spring; they can often be found in large numbers just after ice-out. Other ducks, especially goldeneyes, may also be present.

Return to Route 24 at the blinking light and make a right. In 0.6 miles make a right onto Browns Point Road. In 1.7 miles you will cross the Abagadasset River at the area known to birders affectionately as the Mouth of the Abby, where you should stop under the power line and scan the river and emerging mudflats for waterfowl. There will be enough room to pull over on your right, near the first power-line transmission tower on the east side of the bridge. Approach the shoreline slowly and carefully so as not to flush any close birds.

When conditions are right there may be thousands of ducks visible at this point. Among the large flocks of Mallards, American Black Ducks, and Green-winged Teal ("Eurasian Green-winged" or "Common" Teal are annual) may be Northern Shovelers, American Wigeon, Northern Pintails, Gadwall, and Blue-winged Teal. Ring-necked Ducks and Common Mergansers can be abundant. In 2013 there were two Canvasbacks and a Eurasian Wigeon present here, and American Coots are seen in some years. Derek birds here often in spring and recommends arriving as the tide begins to inundate the extensive flats, pushing birds closer, and staying put for an hour or two, allowing the birds to work their way into the close coves. On most days, pending Bald Eagle activity, prime time is three to four hours after Portland's low (the region's tide standard).

As you continue along the road, in another quarter mile the paved road makes a sharp bend to the left, and Browns Point Road continues straight and becomes dirt. Drive or walk this dirt road for about 1 mile, scanning the fields, especially when flooded, and checking the wet woods for Rusty Blackbirds in April and May and migrant warblers. Just before the road becomes private, a path on your left leads to a tree-obscured overlook of the bay that can be very good for waterfowl and shorebirds. This road can also be good for migrant sparrows in spring and fall.

Return to the curve, make a right, and follow Pork Point Road for 2.3 miles to rejoin Route 24, keeping an eye out in the fields, especially when they are flooded. Make a right and follow Route 24 North into Richmond. A quick stop at the **Richmond Town Landing** in 3.9 miles on your right, in the center of town, will likely yield Bald Eagles and more Common Mergansers.

For further exploration from May through mid-September you may take the ferry to **Swan Island**, a state-owned wildlife management area administered by the Maine Department of Inland Fisheries and Wildlife. The island, in the Kennebec River, is about 4 miles long and a mile wide. It is open daily for day or overnight visits by reservation only and is reached by a ferry from downtown Richmond, just north of the town landing. A fee (currently $8) is charged for access to the island. The island has a combination of hayfields (breeding Bobolinks) and mixed woods and 7 miles of hiking trails. For detailed directions and information on making reservations on Swan Island, visit the State of Maine website, www.maine.gov/ifw/education/swanisland/index.htm.

Continuing north, at the intersection with Route 197 turn right and cross the Kennebec River. In 1 mile, turn right onto **Route 128 South** and travel down the east side of the bay. This road passes through farm fields that in the spring may attract Canada Geese in large numbers (check for Snow Geese and rarities), Horned Larks, American Pipits, Snow Buntings, and an occasional shorebird. In 1.9 miles, **Green Point Wildlife Management Area** (site SA11) is on your right, which is worth a stop in spring and fall on its own account. In another 0.2 miles Route 128 crosses the Eastern River, where you can briefly stop at a parking area just before the river for a quick check.

In another 9.0 miles turn right onto Route 127 South and continue 1.8 miles to its junction with US Route 1 in Woolwich, just across the river from Bath. Turning right toward Bath will take you to I-295 and the completion of the loop.

Although most birders bird the bay in early spring for waterfowl, the fall is also exceptionally productive. However, duck hunters are sometimes as abundant as well, so Sundays are best. In recent years, flocks of around a thousand each of Blue-winged and Green-winged Teal have been seen, primarily feeding on the wild rice that grows in the bay.

RARITIES

"Eurasian" Green-winged (Common) Teal, annual; Black Vulture, April 2010; Canvasback, March 2013; Eurasian Wigeon, several records, most recently March 2013

SITE SA11 Green Point Wildlife Management Area

TOWN Dresden (Lincoln County). DeLorme Map 6: A5. SEASON April, May–June, August, September–November. VISITATION 2–4 hrs. No restroom facilities. HIGHLIGHTS Migrant and breeding warblers and sparrows; migrant waterfowl.

Green Point WMA consists of two apple orchards, two large grassy meadows, a freshwater pond and stream, a wooded wetland, shorefront on the Eastern River and the Kennebec River, a mature evergreen stand, and hardwood and shrub edge habitat. In the spring it provides excellent opportunities to observe warblers, with twenty-five species being seen here. Alder, Willow, and Least Flycatchers breed, as do Baltimore Orioles and Warbling Vireos. Wilson's Snipe are common in migration. Although this site is in Lincoln County, it is included here, as it is often combined with other stops in and around Merrymeeting Bay, almost all of which fall within Sagadahoc County.

DIRECTIONS

From US Route 1 in Woolwich take Route 127 North for 1.8 miles. Turn left on Route 128 North, and in 9.0 miles you will cross the Eastern River. After another 0.2 miles turn left into a driveway by a large green storage shed.

When including Green Point within your tour of Merrymeeting Bay, follow the directions as described in site SA10 above to reach the WMA from the north.

To bird the area, walk the roadway from the shed straight ahead past a large sugar maple. Cross a chain gate and proceed down to the pond and brook for the first major stop, where you should find breeding Yellow Warblers and Common Yellowthroats. Wood Ducks may also be found here, and occasionally Rusty Blackbirds in migration.

After checking this, go back up the hill and follow the dirt roadway to the right at the back edge of the field, checking both the field and the trees on your right. This is an excellent spot for breeding Warbling Vireos and Baltimore Orioles, and migrant warblers. At the end of the field continue into the orchard, which is especially productive when the apple trees are blooming in the spring. After exploring the orchard, follow the road down to the right, crossing the stream again, and then turn left. The road will cross a tidal marsh and pond on the right, with views on the left of the Eastern River, and then will pass through a wooded wetland until it reaches the Kennebec River with views of Swan Island.

After checking the river and marsh area for waterfowl and shorebirds, proceed to the left up the incline to the evergreen wooded area and continue to the tip of the point, with views of Merrymeeting Bay and its wild rice meadows that are so attractive to waterfowl. Then retrace your steps back to the pond on your left and turn left to walk through an old orchard and blueberry bushes to an old meadow. The path crosses the meadow and then turns right around a point of trees dividing the two meadows. Following the path back through the second meadow to a left turn will take you to the first pond and brook where you started. In the spring the walks through the meadow may be less productive than retracing your steps through the orchard.

In the fall the first field by the green shed and the two meadows are excellent habitat for sparrows, with ten species recorded. Large flocks of waterfowl are seen both in the spring and fall, but you should be aware that hunting is allowed in Merrymeeting Bay in the fall, so use caution, and wear blaze orange in season—and Sundays are the most productive and peaceful time for birding.

RARITIES

Bell's Vireo, October 2012; Cackling Goose, April 2012

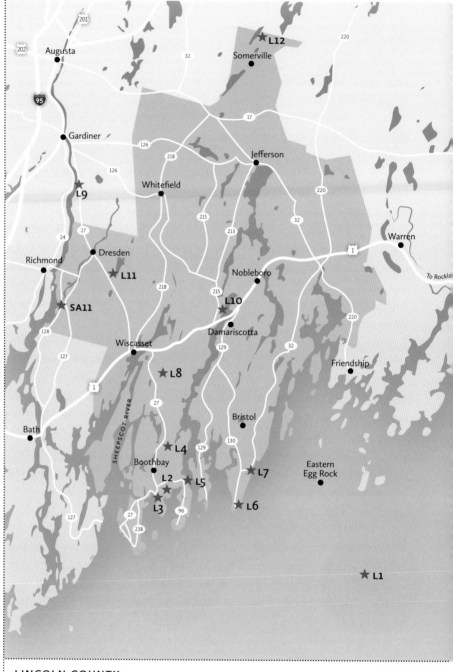

201
202 Augusta
95
Gardiner
126
126
L9
27
24
Richmond
Dresden
L11
SA11
128
127
Wiscasset
1
Bath
SHEEPSCOT RIVER
27
218
Whitefield
215
218
215
L10
Nobleboro
Damariscotta
129
32
L12
Somerville
17
Jefferson
220
213
32
220
1
Warren
To Rockla
Friendship
220

L8
27
129
L4
Boothbay
L2
L5
L3
96
130
Bristol
L7
Eastern
Egg Rock
L6
27
238

L1

LINCOLN COUNTY

6 | Lincoln County

ALLISON CHILDS WELLS & JEFFREY V. WELLS

A lot of birders probably don't even know how much they love birding Lincoln County! But Monhegan Island (site L1) is a world-class birding destination, and the density of birds in late May and September is unrivaled in Northern New England. In fact, it's one of my favorite places in the world, and not just for birding. Many birders in Maine and New England—including Jeff and Allison Wells, me, and hundreds of others—make regular pilgrimages to this birdwatcher's paradise. And the Monhegan Island Brewing Company and pizza at the Novelty only makes a visit even better! Over 330 species, almost three-fourths of Maine's checklist, have been recorded here, and the mind-boggling list of rarities from almost every direction shows that anything is possible here.

While I make annual spring and fall trips to Monhegan, I can't imagine a summer going by without a visit or two to Eastern Egg Rock (L7). Although it is in Knox County, the best way to access Eastern Egg Rock is via the Hardy Boat out of New Harbor in Lincoln County. The southernmost Atlantic Puffins in the western Atlantic breed here, where recovery efforts by Dr. Steven Kress and his Project Puffin revolutionized seabird restoration and reintroduction. Arctic, Common, and Roseate Terns, countless Black Guillemots, and the chance for other seabirds on a short, easy, and cheap evening trip make this a must-visit destination for all, birders and non-birders alike.

An extensive coastline, with miles upon miles of shoreline and innumerable points and islands, makes for a lot of geography to explore. Spruce-dominated peninsulas mesh into thick, deciduous woods, remnants of farmland, and extensive mudflats and wetlands, all combining to offer a wide variety of breeding birds.

Boothbay Harbor and surrounding towns are a major tourist destination, and active land trusts in the area have done a wonderful job at protecting unique properties within easy access of visitors. Check out the Boothbay

Harbor Loop (L2) or the Boothbay Center Loop (L4) for a sample of the area's breeding birds and passage migrants, in between lobster rolls and browsing artwork.

But saltwater is the star of the show in Lincoln County. The more open waters of the Gulf of Maine, such as from the Ocean Point—Linekin Preserve Loop (L5) and the Pemaquid Point Loop (L6) are rich with sea ducks in winter and offer year-round sea-watching opportunities. Meanwhile, the bays and inland waterways host migrant waterbirds, shorebirds . . . and migrating fish. The Great Salt Bay Loop (L10) is a fantastic year-round birding tour, but in late May through June, when the alewives are running, the fish ladder at Damariscotta Mills should not be missed! *—Derek Lovitch*

SITE L1 Monhegan Island

TOWN Monhegan Plantation. DeLorme Map 8: D1. SEASON April–May; August–October. VISITATION 5-plus hrs. or overnight. Facilities at local businesses; public pay toilet behind the Novelty (behind the Monhegan House). HIGHLIGHTS Migrant songbirds, hawks, waterbirds, seabirds; vagrants.

A trip to Monhegan Island, a place of dark, spruce-clad forests, rocky shores, high cliffs, dirt roads, and sleepy village feels a bit like going back in time. As you step off the boat from your ride across the Atlantic onto the old, traditional wharf, there may be a lobster boat loading along one side and an artist painting at an easel on the other.

At the height of spring or fall migration, Monhegan can host an astounding abundance and diversity of birds. During migration periods, birds that have flown out over the ocean during their nocturnal migration are often searching for a place to land at dawn. Under some conditions, Monhegan is the closest land that large numbers of these birds encounter. For birders, this means that there are sometimes thousands of birds in a small area. The number of rarities on the island is higher than it would be on an area of comparable size on the mainland, and they are also generally easier to detect, owing to limited habitats on the island. Over 330 species have been recorded on this tiny island.

Monhegan is 12 nautical miles from the closest point on the mainland. Roughly egg-shaped, it's about a mile and a half long and a half mile wide. A small, year-round community is nestled on one side, and undeveloped, pro-

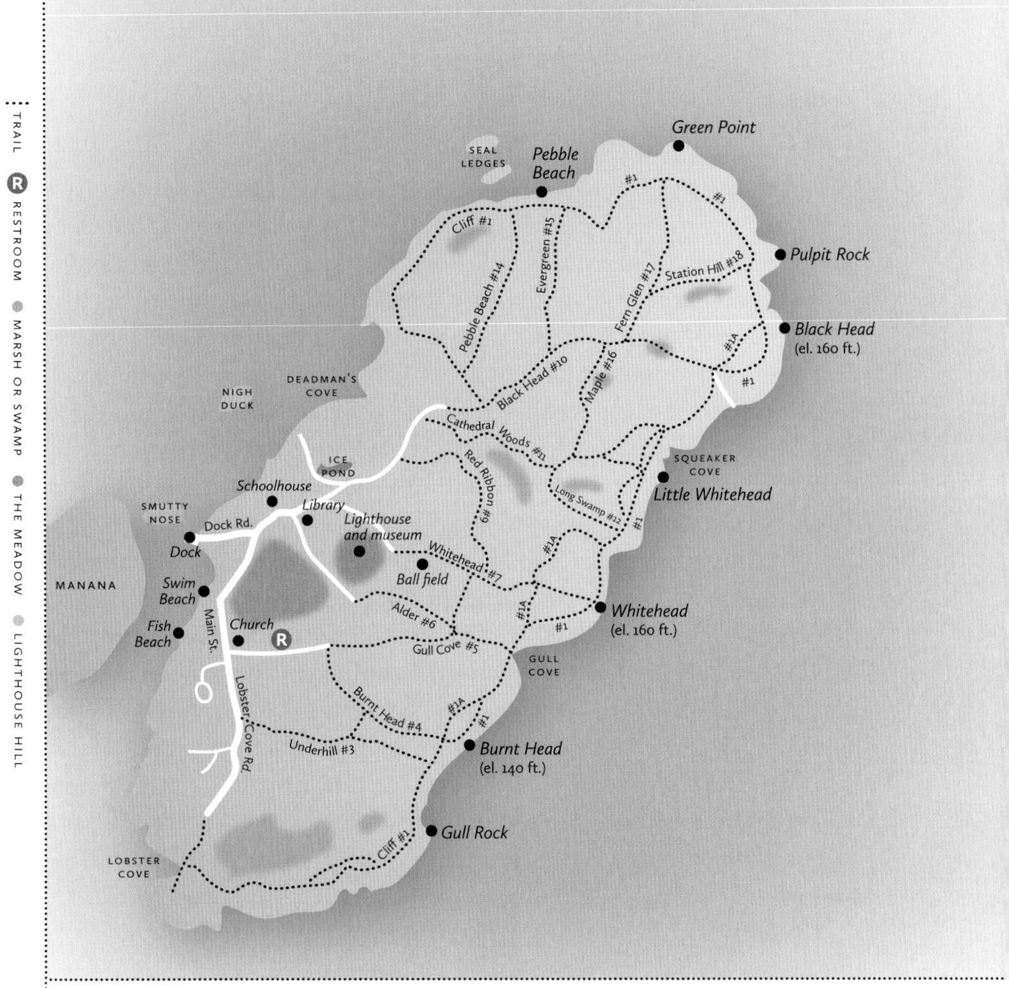

MONHEGAN ISLAND

Map labels:

TRAIL · RESTROOM · MARSH OR SWAMP · THE MEADOW · LIGHTHOUSE HILL

Green Point
SEAL LEDGES
Pebble Beach
#1
Cliff #1
#1
Pulpit Rock
Evergreen #15
Pebble Beach #14
Station Hill #18
Fern Glen #17
Black Head (el. 160 ft.)
#1A
Maple #16
Black Head #10
#1
DEADMAN'S COVE
NIGH DUCK
Cathedral Woods #8
Red Ribbon #9
Long Swamp #12
SQUEAKER COVE
Little Whitehead
ICE POND
Schoolhouse
SMUTTY NOSE
Library
Dock Rd.
Lighthouse and museum
Whitehead #7
#1A
MANANA
Dock
Swim Beach
Main St.
Church
Ball field
Alder #6
#1A
Whitehead (el. 160 ft.)
#1
Fish Beach
Gull Cove #5
GULL COVE
Lobster Cove Rd.
Burnt Head #4
#1A
#1
Underhill #3
Burnt Head (el. 140 ft.)
Cliff #2
Gull Rock
LOBSTER COVE

tected lands, mostly spruce forest, make up about two-thirds of the island. Monhegan is traversed by foot; there are a few dirt roads in the village and many miles of footpaths throughout the island. There are three primary inns, which are open from late May/early June through early October, and also many small apartments or houses available to rent, mostly in the same period but a few year-round. There is, at the time of this writing, a single small general store that is open year-round and serves soups and sandwiches. Each of the three seasonal inns on the island also has a restaurant that is open to the public. There is also currently a small seasonal coffee shop and a seasonal pizza and ice cream shop.

LINCOLN COUNTY

173

Although a trip to Monhegan is always a walking tour, the island does have a few working trucks to carry luggage and freight for visitors. The ferries do not offer transport of vehicles, only walk-on passengers. During part of the season, boat schedules allow a day visit to Monhegan that provides about four to five hours on the island. For those who want a more extended visit, the three inns and various rental units are available. All require reservations well in advance, as the island is popular not only with birders but with tourists as well. There are three boats that offer trips to Monhegan; two are seasonal only (May–October), and one is year-round. The Monhegan Boat Line out of Port Clyde (see site KX3) operates year-round, with multiple daily departures from late May through October, and Monday, Wednesday, and Friday departures from November through April. The Hardy Boat departs from New Harbor (L7), with twice-daily trips to Monhegan from mid-June through September and a limited schedule from mid-May through early June and from late September through early October. The Balmy Days boat leaves from Boothbay Harbor (see site L2) and offers single daily trips to Monhegan from early June through late September, with some weekend departures before and after this period. Check the websites for all three boats for up-to-date schedules and prices, and we recommend always getting reservations well ahead of time. Some of the websites also have great information about Monhegan and what to expect.

The boat rides are all about an hour to ninety minutes long and, depending on the weather, can vary from being flat calm to decidedly bouncy and rough. (Those prone to seasickness are advised to take the ferry out of Port Clyde—bigger, heavier boats, with less time spent in open water often make for a smoother ride.) Birding can often be very good on the boat rides to and from the island, with opportunities to view seabirds like Northern Gannet, Wilson's Storm-Petrel, Great Shearwater, Sooty Shearwater, Atlantic Puffin (they nest at nearby Eastern Egg Rock), Red-necked Phalarope, and other pelagic species. Harbor porpoises are commonly seen, and sometimes so are larger cetaceans like minke whales. Migrating Common and Red-throated Loons, scoter species, and other waterbirds are often seen during boat crossings. As the boat nears Monhegan, scan the outer ledges for Great Cormorants (along with gray seals among the more common harbor seals) and Bald Eagles.

Once you are on the island, the best birding opportunities are generally found at sites within the community on the mainland side. Birders typi-

Town from Lighthouse Hill, Monhegan Island. © Derek Lovitch

cally walk the dirt roads watching for birds just about anywhere. There are favorite spots to visit, like the Ice Pond and the path between there and the schoolhouse. Other hot spots include the Meadow and the road that leads to the back side of the Meadow (to the water pumping station), the road to the lighthouse and the top of Lighthouse Hill, Swim Beach, Lobster Cove, and others. There are typically other birders around to share information about the latest bird sightings and to let you know where some of the active bird feeders are located. We remember the Cerulean Warbler that spent several days feeding on the ground one spring at Swim Beach and the Swallow-tailed Kite that glided back and forth over the Meadow that same spring. On Monhegan, birds can show up anywhere and everywhere!

The opposite side of the island faces open ocean and has high headlands and cliffs so is visually quite spectacular. Accessing that side of the island requires walking narrow paths through spruce woods where the numbers and diversity of birds are typically much lower than on the mainland side. However, certain species are more regularly found in this part of the island, including Winter Wren, Golden-crowned Kinglet, White-winged Crossbill (during irruptions), and Red-breasted Nuthatch. The headlands (Black Head,

Monhegan is known for vagrants. The Brewer's Sparrow that appeared in May 2014 was one of the more unexpected birds in recent years. © Jeannette Lovitch

White Head, and Burnt Head) offer great places to scan for seabirds and to watch migrating Peregrine Falcons and Merlins in fall, although during fall hawk migration both these and other raptors are regularly seen throughout the island. With limited time during a day trip, the best option for doing a little sea scanning from the island is to walk down to Lobster Cove and watch from there. While the trails to the headlands are well defined, be sure to have a trail map (which can be purchased on your ferry or from a little box on a tree opposite the Island Inn on Dock Road) for navigation on the sometimes poorly marked trails throughout the deeper woods.

RARITIES

Black-throated Sparrow, April 1983 (first state record); Band-tailed Pigeon (two records); Shiny Cowbird, May 1991 (first state record); Townsend's Warbler, September 1993 (first state record); Bell's Vireo, May 2003, October 2012, and May 2015; Calliope Hummingbird, October 2005 (first state record); Hermit Warbler, September–October 2008 (first state record); Harris's Sparrow, March–May 2012; LeConte's Sparrow, October 2012; Brewer's Sparrow, May 2014 (first state record); four records of Virginia's Warbler (most recently May 2014); Say's Phoebe (five of seven state records)

The three boat lines listed here offer ferry service to Monhegan but also have information about the island and how to find accommodations and rentals.

Hardy Boat Cruises: http://www.hardyboat.com
Monhegan Boat Line: http://www.monheganboat.com
Balmy Days: http:/www.balmydayscruises.com

SITE L2 Boothbay Harbor Loop

TOWN Boothbay Harbor. DeLorme Map 7: C2. **SEASON** March–April, May–July, August–November. **VISITATION** 1–4 hrs. Public restrooms and facilities at local businesses. **HIGHLIGHTS** Waterbirds, shorebirds, and migrant songbirds.

Boothbay Harbor is a popular tourist destination in Maine's Midcoast region, about an hour north of Portland. For those spending time in the area, perhaps vacationing with family or on the way to or from an event or a whale or puffin watch trip, there are a number of excellent and easy-to-access Boothbay Region Land Trust Preserves that offer excellent land birding opportunities, especially during migration. To add some ocean viewing, you can make a longer day by including the Ocean Point Loop (site L5).

DIRECTIONS

From US Route 1 in Edgecomb, take Route 27 South 10.5 miles to where you'll see, on the right, the Flagship Inn and then the Carousel Music Theater. Turn right into the Carousel Music Theater parking lot and follow the dirt road to the right of the theater. The road goes behind the theater and leads you to the kiosk and parking area for the Boothbay Region Land Trust's **Penny Lake Preserve**. A mile and half of easy trails traverse the property, winding through former orchards, brushy areas, and woodland. A bridge in the middle of the preserve provides great views of a freshwater cattail marsh and stream. The area is a great spot for migrant land birds in spring and fall and is a nice spot to check when you have limited time.

From here, continue the few hundred yards south on Route 27 to the traffic light near a small strip mall and beside a Hannaford supermarket. Turn left onto Route 96 (Ocean Point Road) toward East Boothbay. Follow this for 0.4 miles and then turn right onto Eastern Avenue. Follow Eastern Avenue for about 100 yards to where you'll see a small convenience store on your left.

Just beyond the store, there's a small, dirt driveway to a house—before you get to the house you'll see a kiosk and small parking area for the Boothbay Region Land Trust's **Lobster Cove Meadows Preserve**. Park here and follow the wide and easy-to-see path down through the woods. The path takes you through a variety of habitats, from mixed woodland to open meadow to brushy edges, and to several openings where you can view an extensive open wetland. The mix of habitats, including wetlands, makes the preserve a hot spot for migrants in spring and fall. More than 140 species have been documented from the property. American Bitterns can sometimes be heard "galumphing" from the marsh, and Wood Ducks are a common sight in the open water. In cool days in early spring, the edges can be hopping with Palm Warblers, Yellow-rumped Warblers, Northern Parula, Ruby-crowned Kinglets, and a host of other species.

Descriptions and maps of the Boothbay Region Land Trust's Lobster Cove Meadow and Penny Lake Preserves are available at the organization's website at http://www.bbrlt.org/.

SITE L3 Cap'n Fish's Whale Watch

TOWN Boothbay Harbor. DeLorme Map 7: C2. **SEASON** May–October. **VISITATION** See website (next page) for current trip times and parking details. Restrooms on the boat. **HIGHLIGHTS** Pelagic birds, including Northern Gannet, Great, Sooty, and Cory's Shearwater, Wilson's Storm-Petrel, etc.; rarely Leach's Storm-Petrel and Manx Shearwater; humpback, minke, and finback whales, harbor porpoise, other whales more rarely.

An easy Midcoast departure point for whale watching in Maine, the trip from Boothbay Harbor usually lasts about three hours (check website for current schedule), motoring about 15–20 miles offshore. The trip is not regularly taken by birders, so there are few specific reports, but the trips should offer sightings of all regularly occurring pelagic species and occasional more uncommon species.

DIRECTIONS

From US Route 1 in Edgecomb take Route 27 South for 11.5 miles straight into downtown Boothbay Harbor (the road splits and becomes one way a quarter mile after the traffic light near the Hannaford supermarket). There are a number of pay parking options, which can range in price from about $5 to $30, but parking near the fire station and municipal offices, if available, is typically more affordable. There is limited and more expensive parking right at the waterfront where the ticket booth is located and where the whale-watching boat departs.

For more information and reservations (recommended) visit the website for Cap'n Fish's Whale Watch at http://www.mainewhales.com/.

SITE L4 Boothbay Center Loop

TOWN Boothbay. DeLorme Map 7: C2. **SEASON** March–April, **May–July**, August–November. **VISITATION** 1–4 hrs. Restroom facilities at local businesses. **HIGHLIGHTS** Migrant and nesting forest songbirds, migrant ducks, shorebirds, and waterbirds.

Ovens Mouth in Boothbay is an unusual tidal estuary with a very narrow opening through which a vast amount of water flows when the tide changes. Swift currents and whirlpools abound in the narrow channel during these times. The channel opens into a wider, shallow estuary known variously as Back River, Cross River, or Ovens Mouth River, which at low tide features large areas of mudflats that provide great habitat for shorebirds (where you'll also see many commercial marine worm diggers). From fall through early spring the area can also host lots of American Black Ducks, Buffleheads, Common Goldeneyes, Common Eiders, and sometimes scoters, Horned and Red-necked Grebes, and Common and occasionally Red-throated Loons. Ospreys, Bald Eagles, Common Terns, Laughing Gulls, and Bonaparte's Gulls are often seen feeding here from spring through early fall.

The trails through the preserves offer good land birding from spring through fall. Nearby Adams Pond flows into the Ovens Mouth Estuary. This pond is the major water supply for Boothbay and is off limits to most uses in order to maintain its purity and safety. Some spots on the south end of Adams Pond are easy to check for waterfowl; in spring and early summer they can be good for songbirds of open and brushy habitats.

DIRECTIONS

From US Route 1 in Edgecomb take Route 27 South for 6.3 miles. Watch on the right for a small, gravel parking area and kiosk for the Boothbay Region

Land Trust's **Cross River Preserve** (if you come to the intersection with River Road, you've just missed it). It's a quick ten-minute walk through the woods to the shore of the tidal estuary, where you can scan for shorebirds, terns, ducks, and other waterbirds.

From here, continue south on Route 27 for 1.5 miles, watching carefully for a sharp right-hand turn on Adams Pond Road. In a couple hundred yards turn right onto Dover Road. There are two different access points to the trails at the Boothbay Region Land Trust's **Ovens Mouth Preserve**. To reach the eastern parking area, which is easier walking and probably a bit better for birding, stay straight on Dover Road. At about 2 miles, what appears to be the main road takes a sharp left and becomes Dover Cross Road—don't take this road, but instead bear right. The road turns to dirt, and near the end of the road (about half a mile) look for the parking area and kiosk on the left. From here you can either do a mile-long loop through mixed oak-maple and spruce-fir-hemlock woods with views of the narrows and the tidal estuary, or walk out to a beautiful overlook about a third of a mile from the parking area. The preserve can have a variety of songbirds during migration; during spring and summer look and listen for mixed-woods species such as Winter Wren and Blackburnian Warbler. On the walk out to the point you'll pass a footbridge leading over a small inlet and salt marsh—this connects the eastern peninsula of the preserve with the western peninsula. You can cross here and connect to another mile or so of somewhat steeper and rougher trails on the other side. At the tip of either peninsula, scan for feeding terns and Bonaparte's Gulls in late summer and fall. The trail loop around the east side of the eastern peninsula of the preserve provides overviews of the larger tidal estuary, where in late fall and early spring you may see hundreds of American Black Ducks and smaller numbers of Common Loons and other waterbirds. When the tidal flats are exposed here during May and August, small numbers of feeding shorebirds, sometimes are found here.

To access the trailhead for the **preserve's western peninsula**, go back to the intersection with Dover Cross Road and continue another few hundred yards, where you'll see the parking lot and kiosk on your right. To reach Adams Pond, retrace the route back on Dover Road to the intersection with Adams Pond Road. Turn right onto Adams Pond Road, following it as it skirts the shore of Adams Pond, and continue three-quarters of a mile to the Boothbay Region Water District office. Park here and walk the short distance to overviews of the pond to scan for ducks. Across the street along the edge of a wet, brushy field you may hear Alder Flycatchers, Bobolinks, Chestnut-sided Warblers, and Indigo Buntings in spring and early summer.

Descriptions and maps of the Boothbay Region Land Trust's preserves are available at the organization's website, http://www.bbrlt.org/.

SITE L5 Ocean Point—Linekin Preserve Loop

TOWN Boothbay. DeLorme Map 7: D2–3.   **SEASON** All year.
VISITATION 1–4 hrs. Restroom facilities at local businesses.
HIGHLIGHTS Waterbirds; migrant and breeding passerines; rarities.

Ocean Point is at the tip of the East Boothbay peninsula also known as Linekin Neck, a spruce-clad finger of land that extends out to sea toward historic Damariscove Island, one of the islands first colonized by Europeans in North America. From the loop road that encircles the outer edges of the point there are expansive views of open ocean across rockweed-covered ledges and small, gravel beaches. Ocean Point has been a vacation community since the 1800s, and now, along with many seasonally inhabited homes and cottages, also includes many year-round residences and a small hotel. Farther north up the peninsula from the point are evergreen forests where several preserves offer hiking trails that lead you into mossy groves that give the feel of being in a remote wilderness. The loop offers great birding at any time of year, with sea ducks, grebes, and loons in winter and a variety of sea and land birds from spring through fall. Feeders at year-round homes at the point often attract interesting and sometimes rare birds, including a Painted Bunting in 2013.

DIRECTIONS

From US Route 1 in Edgecomb take Route 27 South 10.5 miles to the traffic light near a small strip mall in Boothbay Harbor. Turn left here onto Route 96 South, following signs toward East Boothbay. In about 2 miles the road will wind toward the right around a salt pond, where you may see a small parking area for the **Mill Pond Overlook** (a Boothbay Region Land Trust Preserve) on the right—if you have time, it may be worth a short stop to scan the pond for ducks.

A few hundred yards farther, you'll come to the little village of East Boothbay. Continue onward through the twist and turns in town and past the East Boothbay General Store (restrooms and wonderful food) for 1.2 miles. Look carefully on the left (across from McKown Road) for a narrow dirt road and a small parking area with a sign for the **Linekin Preserve**. In spring and summer the woods along the trails here resound with the songs of Blackburnian Warblers, Hermit Thrushes, and many other species. The trails are rocky and steep in places; if you walk all the way to the ocean on the east side use caution, as parts of the preserve fall rather steeply down to the shore.

Continuing on from the Linekin Preserve, follow Route 96 South for 2 miles, where you'll arrive at a striking ocean overlook above a small, gravel beach officially called Grimes Cove. The Town of Boothbay provides access and a few parking spaces along the road here, as well as a larger parking lot a hundred yards back from the beach near the junction with Grimes Road. From October through March this is great spot to scan for scoters and other ducks, and for grebes and loons. From here you can follow the road that skirts the shore (appropriately named **Shore Road**) around the entire tip of the peninsula, watching for the relatively few parking spaces and walking and scanning the ocean. Please be careful to respect landowner privacy and pay attention to signs. Like all locations with great views of the ocean, there are always possibilities for finding interesting birds virtually year-round. Watch for Common Eiders and Black Guillemots any time of year, and Northern Gannets throughout much of the year. Look for the occasional King Eider or Barrow's Goldeneye in winter.

About 1.25 miles from Grimes Cove the road will make an abrupt right-hand turn onto Van Horn Road. Follow for about 0.3 miles, where you'll see little Tibbets Pond on your right and then the parking lot for the Boothbay Region Land Trust's **Ocean Point Preserve**. This preserve's short (0.9-mile loop) trail is a delight, with breeding Winter Wren, Hermit Thrush, Red-breasted Nuthatch, Blackburnian Warbler, Magnolia Warbler, White-throated Sparrow, and many other species; in spring and fall migration it can be full of migrant songbirds. From here it's just a few hundred yards back to Route 96, where you can trace your route back to Boothbay Harbor and Route 1.

RARITIES

King Eider (about every two to three years); Painted Bunting, January–February, 2013

Descriptions and maps of the Boothbay Region Land Trust's Ocean Point Preserve and Linekin Preserve are available at the organization's website, http://www.bbrlt.org/.

SITE L6 Pemaquid Point Loop

TOWNS Bristol and New Harbor. DeLorme Map 7: C3–4. **SEASON** All year. **VISITATION** 1–4 hrs. Seasonal restroom facilities at Pemaquid Point and Pemaquid Harbor. Many stores and restaurants with bathrooms in Damariscotta, and a few in Bristol and New Harbor, but many are seasonal. Fee at Pemaquid Point from spring through fall. **HIGHLIGHTS** Sea watching; winter waterfowl, grebes, and loons; migrant and nesting land birds, terns, and shorebirds.

Perched on a series of high, dramatic granite ledges, Pemaquid Point lighthouse is one of the most famous and most photographed lighthouses on the Maine coast, with expansive views of the open ocean and of birding mecca Monhegan Island, 10 miles offshore. But the point and nearby areas also feature some exceptional birding opportunities. As one of the most exposed and accessible peninsulas on the central coast, Pemaquid Point is a fabulous place for seabird watching at virtually any time of year. Nearby Pemaquid Harbor often hosts feeding terns, including Roseate Terns, especially in midsummer. It also often hosts a variety of shorebirds during migration periods, and bay and sea ducks during winter. The small village of New Harbor is located nearby. Here, in season, bird enthusiasts can take the Hardy Boat to Monhegan or out to Eastern Egg Rock to get close-up views of Atlantic Puffins, Roseate Terns, Common Terns, and sometimes Razorbills and Arctic Terns. Several preserves in this part of the peninsula provide excellent land birding from spring through fall and are perfect for a visit before you board the boat to Monhegan Island (site L1) or Eastern Egg Rock (L7).

DIRECTIONS

From US Route 1, heading eastbound in Newcastle, exit right for downtown Damariscotta and Business Route 1. Bear right just before the blinking light to travel through downtown. At the stoplight at the south end of the downtown turn right onto Route 129 South (Bristol Road; you should see signs for Pemaquid Point).

Heading westbound on US Route 1, make a left onto Business Route 1 (Main Street) as the road temporarily becomes divided. At the second light make a left onto Route 129 South (Bristol Road).

Follow Route 129 South (Bristol Road) for 2.8 miles to an intersection near a convenience store (Hanley's Market), where Route 129 branches off to the right. Stay straight as Bristol Road becomes Route 130 South and follow it for 11.5 miles to **Pemaquid Point**.

The point is now a park managed by the Town of Bristol; from late May through early fall, a small fee is charged for access during regular hours. The large parking lot is open even when the parking attendant booth is not being manned. Park here and walk out to the edge of the lawn to scan for birds. Often Northern Gannets can be seen feeding very close to shore here, and Common Eiders and Black Guillemots are almost always present. In summer, terns often pass back and forth; although most will be Common Terns, occasionally Roseate and, very rarely, Arctic terns (check during strong south and easterly winds) are seen here. Atlantic Puffins are a possibility as they make feeding runs to and from Eastern Egg Rock just off to the east. In winter, Purple Sandpipers can sometimes be seen feeding on the wave-dashed ledges at the point, and scoters as well as Red-necked and Horned Grebes are regular. King Eider, Razorbill, and other alcids are a possibility. On cold, windy days it is often possible to find a sheltered spot, behind one of the small buildings associated with the lighthouse, from where you can scan.

To reach Pemaquid Harbor from the point, follow Route 130 North (Bristol Road) back for 2.5 miles to the village. Take a left here onto Snowball Hill Road; three-quarters of a mile down this road you'll come to the town-owned and managed **Pemaquid Beach** on your left. During the non-summer seasons this can be a great spot for looking for land birds around the edges. The beach itself can have a few shorebirds when it's not too busy and can host winter sea ducks, loons, and grebes offshore.

Continuing on Snowball Hill Road for another 0.1 miles, you'll come to a spot where the main road takes a sharp right. Continue straight here onto the grounds of **Fort Pemaquid State Park**. There are a number of parking areas for access to the fort, archaeological sites, and museum (restrooms here), but for the best birding continue the 0.3 miles to the end of the road where there is a boat landing and parking area that overlooks the harbor. From fall through spring, Common Eiders, Buffleheads, Common Goldeneyes, Common Loons, Horned Grebes, and sometimes scoters and Red-necked Grebes can be found here. When the tide has exposed some mudflats and shoreline during late spring and early fall, you may see shorebirds feeding here; in summer, Common and Roseate Terns often feed in the harbor.

After exiting the park, retrace your route on Snowball Hill Road back to the village and Route 130 and turn left (north). In about 0.1 mile turn right (east) onto Route 32, following the signs for New Harbor. The road takes a sharp right in about 0.3 miles, where you'll see the parking lot for passengers of the Hardy Boat's Monhegan Island and puffin trips (site L7). The wharf from which the boat departs is a few hundred yards farther on after another couple of sharp curves. It is also the parking lot for the locally well-known Shaw's Fish & Lobster Wharf restaurant. Continue on Route 32 through New Harbor for another half mile; this will bring you to the **Rachel Carson Salt Pond Preserve**, owned by the Nature Conservancy. Parking is limited to some spaces along the roadside on the right. The preserve offers great views of outer Muscongus Bay and is worth scanning for terns in summer and for sea ducks, grebes, loons, Northern Gannets, and other birds from fall through spring. Retrace your route back on Route 32 through New Harbor to Route 130 and turn right (north). Follow Route 130 North for 2.2 miles and turn left onto Harrington Road. Make an immediate left onto the dirt Town Landing Road. This short and sometimes rutted road takes you to a parking area at the head of Pemaquid Harbor where the Pemaquid River flows into the harbor. In late spring and summer, if the alewives (a native Maine fish) are running, the area can be packed with Great Blue Herons, Osprey, Bald Eagles, Double-crested Cormorants, and other birds.

To venture into the woods to look for more land birds, a couple of options exist nearby. The Pemaquid Watershed Association's **Crooked Farm Preserve** can be reached by getting back onto Route 130 and traveling south for 0.2 miles and turning left onto Old County Road near the Bristol Library. Travel 0.8 miles and look for preserve parking on your left. Another enjoyable spot for land birding can be reached by getting back onto Route 130 and traveling north for 2.8 miles and turning right (east) onto Sproul Hill Road. Travel 0.2 miles and turn right on Austin Road, then proceed to a parking area for the Pemaquid Watershed Association's **Bearce Allen Preserve**, which adjoins the Damariscotta River Association's NORGAL preserve.

RARITIES

Northern Hawk-Owl, January–March 2009 (Route 130, Bristol)

Descriptions and maps of Pemaquid Lighthouse and Pemaquid Beach can be found at the Bristol Parks and Recreation website, http://www.bristolparks .org/.

Descriptions of Pemaquid Watershed Association preserves can be found at http://www.pemaquidwatershed.org/.

Descriptions of Damariscotta River Association Preserves can be found at http://www.damariscottariver.org/.

SITE L7 Eastern Egg Rock via the Hardy Boat

Entry by Derek Lovitch

TOWNS New Harbor and St. George (Knox County). DeLorme Map 7: C4–5. **SEASON** June–August. **VISITATION** 1.5 hrs. round-trip for evening puffin watch. Restroom facilities and small snack bar on boat. **HIGHLIGHTS** Atlantic Puffin, Razorbill (few), and Black Guillemot; Arctic, Roseate, and Common Terns; other seabirds.

The most convenient, cost-effective, and easy way to see Atlantic Puffins is to take an evening tour to Eastern Egg Rock with New Harbor's Hardy Boat Cruises. It's a mere thirty minutes or so in most conditions to the island, and thirty minutes or more around the island offers ample opportunity to see and enjoy this charismatic bird for everyone, especially non-birders. A naturalist from the Puffin Project offers information and narration throughout. Arctic and Roseate Terns are common among the abundant Common Terns, and Black Guillemots are in very high density. While you won't be as close to the birds as within the blinds of Machias Seal Island (see site WN7), many evenings find birds sitting on the water close enough to be easily photographed. This is a relaxing evening, especially when coupled with dinner on the waterfront or a good day's birding, and a great way to get your lifer puffins!

DIRECTIONS

Follow directions as described above in the Pemaquid Point Loop (L6) to reach the intersection of Routes 129 and 130 in Bristol. Continue south on Route 130 for 8.7 miles to a left onto Route 32 North. The parking lot for the Hardy Boat is about 0.3 miles on your right. You can drop off luggage (for Monhegan) or passengers at the dock near Shaw's Lobster 0.3 miles farther down the road. However, you must then move your car; otherwise you will be towed.

I recommend arriving at least thirty minutes before your departure time, to get a seat on the upper deck of the boat, as close to the front as possible to assure a good view of birds on either side as you are in transit. Ospreys, Common Eiders, and Black Guillemots are usually in the harbor and along with Laughing Gulls and Common Terns will be a constant companion throughout the trip. Be alert for Wilson's and (in fog, rarely) Leach's Storm-Petrels, and any shearwater. Watch for terns and Red and Red-necked Phalaropes around seaweed mats in late summer.

At the island, an often-bewildering abundance of terns is dominated by Common, but with about 10 percent Arctic and, recently, over a hundred pairs of federally threatened Roseate Terns (watch for their quicker wingbeats, long tails, and more "glowing white" overall appearance). Atlantic Puffins, a few Razorbills in recent years, and Black Guillemots will be seen on the island, loafing on the water, and in transit. Watch for shorebirds (Spotted Sandpipers breed, but migrants are regular, especially Ruddy Turnstone) along the tide line of the rocks, and search the Double-crested Cormorants for the occasional oversummering Great. And be on the lookout for rarities!

RARITIES

Brown Booby, July 2013

For trip information and reservations (highly recommended) see the website for Hardy Boat Cruises at www.hardyboat.com, or call 207–677–2026.

SITE L8 Schmid Preserve–Zak Preserve Loop

TOWNS Edgecomb and Boothbay. DeLorme Map 7: B2.   SEASON March–April, May–July, August–November.   VISITATION 1–4 hrs. Restroom facilities at local businesses in Boothbay Center and Boothbay Harbor. HIGHLIGHTS Migrant and nesting forest songbirds; American Woodcock; Barred Owl; migrant shorebirds; wading birds.

Together, these two preserves protect one of the largest blocks of intact habitat in the Midcoast area—over nine hundred acres! The size of these two preserves allows species (including moose) that require large territories relatively free of disturbance to survive even in this busy region. The preserves also provide abundant and varied habitat for a great diversity of bird species, with more than a dozen regularly breeding warblers (and many more during migration), and most of the typical breeding bird species of central Maine. The woods here seem to be loaded with Barred Owls year-round and with

Broad-winged Hawks during summer. The Schmid Preserve encompasses the highest point of land on the peninsula, called Mount Hunger, where there was once a thriving community including a store, dance hall, school, and homes, as well as a mica mine. Most of these disappeared by the early 1900s, and the area has now regrown into mixed spruce-fir-hemlock-pine and oak-maple forest patches. Zak Preserve also includes some tidal salt marsh that sometimes hosts Snowy Egrets and small numbers of migratory shorebirds, especially in fall migration.

DIRECTIONS

There are three access points to the Schmid Preserve, described below from north to south. With limited time, we recommend the third one through the Boothbay Region Land Trust's Church Property. To reach the **Schmid Preserve** from US Route 1 in Edgecomb (a half mile east of the Wiscasset bridge) take Route 27 South for 2.5 miles and turn left onto Middle Road. In just under 1 mile look for a parking lot and trailhead on your right. Another access point is about a half mile farther south on Route 27—take a left onto Old County Road. Follow this for about a half mile to a parking area, but beware that the last few hundred yards is sometimes heavily rutted, so use caution. From here, a short walk of about a quarter mile up the old road leads to several small open fields and old apple trees, which can be good for migrants, especially in spring.

Perhaps the most productive and easiest access is available through the Boothbay Region Land Trust's **Church Property**, which can be reached by driving about half a mile farther south from Old County Road and turning left onto McKay Road. The well-maintained parking lot and trailhead are about a half mile down McKay Road on the left overlooking overgrown field habitat. More than 5 miles of trails traverse the Schmid Preserve, including the River-Link Trail, by which you can hike all the way to the Dodge Point Preserve and the Damariscotta River.

To reach **Zak Preserve**, go back to Route 27 from McKay Road and travel south on Route 27 for 1.7 miles. Turn left into the preserve's spacious parking lot. A loop trail starts at the edge of a large field adjoining the parking lot. In early spring (March–April) this is a great area to listen and look for displaying American Woodcock at dusk. If you follow the path closer to Wildcat Creek, it will take you back to the salt marsh, where you can scan for egrets, shorebirds, and ducks during migration. The mixed woods throughout the preserve are great for land bird migrants and host an abundance of breeding warblers and other songbirds. If you're lucky you may find some moose tracks and droppings, or, if really lucky, sight a moose itself!

Descriptions and maps of the Boothbay Region Land Trust's Zak Preserve are available at the organization's website, http://www.bbrlt.org/.

The Damariscotta River Association provides a map and description of the Schmid Preserve as part of the River Link Trail system, http://www .damariscottariver.org/trail/riverlink-trail-schmid-preserve/.

SITE L9 Old Cedar Grove Road and Pownalborough Court House Trails

TOWN Dresden. DeLorme Map 12: E5.   SEASON April–May, June–October.   VISITATION 1–4 hrs. In summer, restrooms at historic Pownalborough Court House, otherwise facilities at local businesses. HIGHLIGHTS Migrant and breeding warblers (including Black-throated Blue, Blackburnian, and Prairie) and other songbirds; Virginia Rail, nesting Bald Eagles, Bobolink.

Located only about fifteen minutes from Augusta, this loop in the northwestern corner of Lincoln County is a little-known gem that is at its best during spring migration. Old Cedar Grove Road is a mostly unpaved road that parallels the Kennebec River on the east side starting just over the Lincoln County line in the Kennebec County town of Pittston; somewhere along the way, the name of the road changes to Everson Road. There are a number of productive spots to stop and bird along the several miles of road that cross through mixed and deciduous forest, open wet meadows, marshes, and shrubby fields with views of the river. In spring and early summer, stops along the generally quiet road here can yield fifteen or more warbler species, including (occasionally) Prairie Warbler, plus Brown Thrasher, Bobolink, Rose-breasted Grosbeak, Baltimore Oriole, Virginia Rail, Swamp and White-crowned Sparrows, and many others. A pair of Bald Eagles nest along this route along the shore of the river.

A few miles south of Old Cedar Grove Road/Everson Road sits the historic Pownalborough Court House. Built in 1761, the building has been preserved by the Lincoln County Historic Society, whose volunteers provide tours of the building during summer. Across the road from the courthouse are seventy-five acres that are part of the property. Two miles of well-marked trails traverse beautiful forested habitats of oak, pine, and some larger old hemlock groves. Along with a variety of migrant land birds in spring and fall, look and listen for nesting species typical of deciduous woods. These locations can be easily combined with a stop at Green Point Wildlife Management Area (five to ten minutes south of Pownalborough Court House; see site SAII) or Dresden Bog (ten to fifteen minutes southeast; see site LII).

DIRECTIONS

From US Route 1 just west of downtown Wiscasset take Route 27 North (Wiscasset Road) for 11.8 miles. Watch for **Old Cedar Grove Road** on the left. (This is well past Cedar Grove Road/Route 128 South, where you should not turn.) Old Cedar Grove Road is about 2.5 miles long and ends at its junction with Route 128.

Traveling slowly along Old Cedar Grove Road with the windows down is a great way to find birds, but there are a number of particularly good spots to stop at. The first is a small stream-crossing at 1 mile in that is frequented by migrating warblers early in the season and a variety of breeding songbirds in May and June. One of our favorite and most productive stops along the road is where this road meets Crocker Road (also unpaved) at about 2 miles. Here there is a wonderful mix of habitats, including a small marsh, meadow, shrubby field, and nearby deciduous woods. An apple tree right along the road explodes into a sea of white blossoms in late May and draws in Baltimore Orioles, warblers, and other birds. Several very large oak trees along the field edge also attract birds during leaf-out in mid-May, Rose-breasted Grosbeaks among the most consistent. Bobolinks bubble up from the fields nearby, and some years one can hear the buzzing chromatic-scale song of the Prairie Warbler from the overgrown field upslope. A small marsh hosts Swamp Sparrows, Virginia Rails, and even occasionally some shorebirds. Listen along the remaining piece of road for other birds. The farm near where the road intersects with Route 128 is, thankfully, protected with an easement purchased some years ago with Land for Maine's Future funds, so will never be subdivided. Although the road is unpaved for most of its length, there are a few people who live on the road, and they and others travel on it, sometimes probably a bit faster than they should. Make sure that you pull safely to the side of the road, and when out of the car listen for approaching vehicles and stay out of their way.

From the intersection of Old Cedar Grove Road/Everson Road with Route 128 turn right onto Route 128 South. In 1.8 miles you will see the signs for the Pownalborough Court House on your right (west—toward the river). You can park along the entrance road here and walk across the road for one access point to the trails along the edge of a small meadow. You can also drive into the driveway and follow the signs for the parking area as the dirt driveway curves around to the left. Trail maps are available at the kiosk here. You can also walk a section of the trail that runs between the courthouse and the Kennebec River and then bends inland past a historic cemetery and across the road to another trailhead. The trails are generally very easy and walkable, but in the farther reaches of the trail system you may encounter some muddy spots. From mid-May through mid-June the woods here ring with the songs of Ovenbirds, Blue-headed Vireos, Scarlet Tanagers, Black-throated Blue Warblers, Blackburnian Warblers, and Pine Warblers. Broad-winged Hawks nest here and may be heard or seen flashing through the trees. During migration, expect to find any number of other songbird species.

For a map and trails visit Maine Trail Finder at www.mainetrailfinder.com and use the search feature. Lincoln County Historical Society has more detail about the history of the Pownalborough Court House and the trails; see http://www.lincolncountyhistory.org/PCHAboutTrail.html.

SITE L10 Great Salt Bay Loop

TOWNS Newcastle and Damariscotta. DeLorme Map 7: A3. SEASON All year. VISITATION 1 hr. to half day. Portable toilets during most of the year at Damariscotta Mills and at the parking lot for Great Salt Bay Farm and Heritage Center; restroom at the Great Salt Bay Farm and Heritage Center when it is open. HIGHLIGHTS Migrant waterbirds, including shorebirds and waterfowl; breeding grassland birds.

Great Salt Bay is a unique, virtually enclosed tidal bay that has been designated as a state Marine Protected Area to protect and maintain its special ecological value. At the north end of the bay lies the outlet of Damariscotta Lake, providing freshwater into the bay and access for an impressively healthy seasonal run of anadromous alewives (also called river herring) that make their way back from the ocean to spawn in Damariscotta Lake. The southern end drains through a narrow passageway into Damariscotta Harbor so that at low tide a strong current flows under the bridge into the harbor; at high tide the water flows back up into the bay. The bay itself and its tidal wetlands and mudflats provide rich habitat for shorebirds during spring and fall and for waterfowl from fall through spring. At Damariscotta Mills, the spring alewife run, and to a lesser degree the fall return of young alewives to the sea, attracts large numbers of gulls, Double-crested Cormorants, Great Blue Herons, Osprey, Bald Eagles, and other birds and provides a fascinating scene to watch as the thousands of fish move upstream.

Trails at the Salt Bay Preserve pass along the edge of a salt marsh and into mixed oak/maple woods and spruce/fir woods. They provide dozens of excellent vantage points of the bay. Great Salt Bay Farm is a gorgeous, old-fashioned restored saltwater farm with magnificent fields for grassland birds, a freshwater pond and marsh, and incredible views of Great Salt Bay. One winter a Pink-footed Goose spent time here with a flock of Canada Geese that frequented the fields surrounding the bay.

DIRECTIONS

Traveling north on US Route 1 in Newcastle, take the exit for Damariscotta ("To 129/130/215"). In 0.4 miles, the road takes a sharp right-hand turn toward downtown Damariscotta. Instead, bear left to pass straight through the blinking light near the Newcastle Publick House restaurant and stay straight through onto Route 215 (Mills Road). In 0.3 miles you'll pass under US Route 1, and Great Salt Bay will be on your right. In another hundred yards or so you'll see the Newcastle Post Office and Lincoln County Publishing offices on your left. Parking is permitted in the Lincoln County Publishing offices as long as you park away from business operations.

The trailhead for the **Salt Bay Preserve** is directly across the street from the parking lot. The preserve has a 3-mile loop trail, but those with limited time can enjoy walking out to several of the vantage points for the bay or can scope the salt marsh and mudflats for shorebirds and waterfowl. 0.1 miles farther up the road on the left is the Faith Baptist Church, where, if there are no functions happening, a large parking lot provides open views of the bay and mudflats perfect for scoping.

From here continue for 1.1 miles to the **Damariscotta Mills fishladder**. When alewives are running from late May to mid-June, this stop is a must, and not just for the piscivorous birds. Just before the bridge you'll see a small, dirt parking area on the left. Park here and walk across the bridge and into the fish ladder entrance on your left. You'll see a small, low barn. There are various places here to watch the birds preying on the fish; if you walk upstream you'll find boardwalks that afford close-up views of the schools of migrating alewives. In winter it is possible to view parts of the bay from near the bridge and parking lot where there are often wintering Hooded Mergansers.

About 100 yards past the Damariscotta Mills bridge, Route 215 North makes a sharp left. Here, stay straight onto Bayview Road, and in 0.75 miles turn right onto **Belvedere Road**. In winter, check the fields here for flocks of Canada Geese and for rarities, such as the Pink-footed Goose in the winter of 2014–15.

On Belvedere Road just over a mile from the intersection with Bayview Road you'll see the **Great Salt Bay Farm and Heritage Center** on your right. There is ample parking here and easy-to-follow paths through the fields to the pond and eventually to the shoreline. During spring and summer watch for Bobolinks and occasionally Eastern Meadowlark in the fields. The freshwater pond has hosted American Bittern, Virginia Rail, and Sora, as well as a variety of freshwater ducks and breeding Willow and Alder Flycatchers. An Osprey nest down near the water affords easy views, but don't get too close if the nest is still active. One summer, a Clay-colored Sparrow set up a breeding territory in the shrubs down by the old Native American replica village that is a highlight for kids.

Continue on Belvedere Road for a 0.3 miles to its intersection with US Route 1. Here you can cross US Route 1 and then take a right onto Business Route 1 to get back into downtown Damariscotta. About half a mile south on Business Route 1 on the right is the locally famous Roundtop Ice Cream shop and the Damariscotta River Association's Roundtop Farm Center, which is another good place to stop in spring or early summer to enjoy an ice cream while listening to the Bobolinks and other birds in the fields out back.

RARITIES

Pink-footed Goose, May 2013 and winter 2014–15; Clay-colored Sparrow, June 2011

Descriptions and maps of the Damariscotta River Association's Great Salt Bay Farm and Heritage Center and Salt Bay Preserve are available at the organization's website, http://www.damariscottariver.org/. Information about the Damariscotta Mills Fish Ladder can be found at https://damariscottamills .org/.

SITE L11 Dresden Bog Loop

TOWNS Dresden and Alna. DeLorme Map 13: E1.   **SEASON** March–April, **May–June**, July–November.   **VISITATION** 1 hr. to half day. Restroom facilities at local businesses.   **HIGHLIGHTS** Migrant and breeding warblers (including Blackburnian and Prairie) and other songbirds; Bald Eagles; Ruffed Grouse; Winter Wren; Bobolink.

About thirty minutes southeast of Augusta or ten minutes north of Wiscasset, this easily accessible loop along the eastern edge of Lincoln County provides diverse birding opportunities within close proximity of one another.

The Dresden Bog is eight-hundred-plus acres, a state-owned preserve of mixed woods, beech-dominated woodlands, and shrubby edges that offers incredible birding opportunities. During spring and fall migration the area can be dripping with songbirds, with up to fifteen species of warbler routine. On the other side of a small ridge lies the Sheepscot River watershed, where several properties of the Sheepscot Valley Conservation Association offer additional birding access. Along the way, a shrubby power-line cut supports Prairie Warblers and others.

The Trout Brook Preserve is a 126-acre delight with 2 miles of trails passing through meadows, shrubby semiopen areas, second-growth woodland, tall pines, and a shaded, cool hemlock grove. Migrants can abound in spring and fall, especially in the shrubby areas near the parking lots and along the old railroad right-of-way and trails into good breeding habitat.

Finish this birding route at the Bass Falls Preserve, a 216-acre preserve with about 2 miles of trails that pass along field edges and through a variety of forest types as they meander to the shores of the Sheepscot River.

DIRECTIONS

Begin at **Dresden Bog (Erle R. Kelley WMA)**. From US Route 1 in Wiscasset take Route 27 North for 7.7 miles to its intersection with Blinn Hill Road in Dresden and turn right. In 1.2 miles bear right at the intersection with Bog Road. The road turns to dirt in 0.3 miles, and in another 0.2 miles you'll see a dirt road on the right with a chain across it (if you see a large, brown state sign for the Erle R. Kelley State Wildlife Management Area, you've gone about 100 feet too far. Don't be dissuaded; this is the official entry to this state-owned parcel.

For a sample of the eight-hundred-plus acres, this easy, mile-long road winds through a variety of habitats. Four hundred yards or so in lies a small meadow bordered by a brushy area where Alder Flycatchers breed. About halfway in, the main road branches off to a few camps on the small lake; listen for Canada Warbler, Winter Wren, and Yellow-bellied Sapsucker here. (Please stay away from the camps.) A short, public woods road leads off to a view of the Dresden Bog Reservoir and a great little migrant stop. The last half mile passes through beech woods and mixed forest, where you will find Black-throated Blue and Magnolia Warblers, Scarlet Tanagers, and lots more. When you get back to Blinn Road you may want to walk down the road a few hundred yards to a shrubby, wet area on the left where Canada Warblers are sometimes found.

From Dresden Bog continue east on **Bog Road** for 2.7 miles (it becomes Rabbit Path Road) to the power-line corridor. During the breeding season pull off here into the dirt access road and listen for Prairie Warbler and other shrub-loving species. Continue another half mile to the intersection with Route 218 (Alna Road). Turn right. In 0.1 miles turn left onto Head Tide Road and watch for the parking area a few hundred yards down on the left at the **Head Tide Dam.** A quick stop here often yields migrants in spring and a chance to read about the efforts to save the endangered Atlantic salmon that still breed in the Sheepscot River.

To reach the **Trout Brook Preserve** return to Route 218/Alna Road and turn left to go south. Follow Route 218 for 0.75 miles, where you will find the short, dirt road entrance and kiosk for the parking area on the right. Check the scrub around the parking area for migrants and head down the trail for breeding species typical of mixed forest.

The old railroad right-of-way crosses the road about 100 yards north of the entrance to the preserve and is open to the public for hiking. Be careful, as the entrance to the right-of-way on the opposite side of the road from the Trout Brook Preserve is loaded with poison ivy. The right-of-way parallels the road here, and if you walk north about 100 yards you will see a small parking area and a gate. Watch for Bald Eagles that nest in the area. This is also another great spot for migrants, and you may see or hear Spotted Sandpipers feeding on the rocks in the river, Baltimore Orioles in the apple trees nearby, or hear Bobolinks singing from the fields across the river.

To reach the **Bass Falls Preserve**, travel south on Route 218 for 0.7 miles, to the small gravel parking area and kiosk on your left (just a quarter mile past the locally well-known Alna General Store, where you can stop for food and a restroom break). In May and early June the meadows near the parking lot can be Bobolink heaven, with males bubbling into song from all around as you walk down the path. Nest boxes have been placed all around the meadow (stay on the path, as the field area is privately owned), with most of them taken up by enterprising Tree Swallows and a few by Eastern Bluebirds. After passing along the edge of the meadow, the trail plunges into the woods and passes over a small ridge before descending to the peaceful shores of the Sheepscot River. In spring the areas near the river can be particularly good for migrants.

From here it is about 7 miles south to US Route 1 in Wiscasset to complete your loop.

The Maine Department of Inland Fisheries and Wildlife has background about the Erle R. Kelley Wildlife Management Area at http://www.maine .gov/ifw/wildlife/land/department/region_b/earlekelley.htm. The Sheepscot Valley Conservation Association gives specific directions to and background information about its preserves at http://www.sheepscot.org/.

SITE L12 North Lincoln County Loop

TOWNS Palermo, Windsor, Whitefield. DeLorme Map 13: B–C2–4.
SEASON March–November. **VISITATION** 1 hr. to half day. Restroom facilities at local businesses. **HIGHLIGHTS** Migrant and breeding warblers (including Black-throated Blue, Blackburnian, and Prairie) and other songbirds; Bald Eagles, Broad-winged Hawk, Ruffed Grouse, Winter Wren, Rose-breasted Grosbeak, Scarlet Tanager, Indigo Bunting, Bobolink.

This loop is about thirty minutes east of Augusta and runs along the northern edge of Lincoln County, moving back and forth across the Lincoln County–Kennebec County line, connecting good birding spots located conveniently near one another, offering a wide range of habitats and a variety of migrant and breeding species.

DIRECTIONS

The loop begins at **Palermo Preserve** at the boundary between Kennebec and Lincoln Counties. To reach it from I-95 take Exit 113 and drive east on Route 3 for 20.5 miles to Turner Ridge Road. Turn right (south) on Turner Ridge Road and travel just under 3 miles. Watch for a small SVCA sign on the east side for a short dirt road that leads to the small parking lot and kiosk. This Sheepscot

Valley Conservation Association (SVCA) preserve is nestled into a curve in the upper reaches of the Sheepscot River, where 1 mile of trails passes through mixed white pine and red oak near the parking lot and leads down to a shaded hemlock and yellow birch forest along the mossy riverbank. In spring and fall migration watch for a variety of songbirds; during late spring and summer the preserve hosts breeding Black-throated Blue Warblers loudly singing their buzzy "I'm so lazee" along with Magnolia, Pine, and other warblers. Winter Wrens breed in the tangled brush in damp areas near the river, and listen for Yellow-bellied Sapsuckers giving their scolding *keear* calls.

To reach the **Maxcy's Mill Road cemetery**, drive 2.5 miles south on Turner Ridge Road from the Palermo Preserve to the intersection with Route 105. Travel west for 4.7 miles on Route 105 from Somerville to the intersection with Route 32 (Ridge Road), where the locally famous Hussey's General Store is located. Take a left to go south on Route 32 and follow it for 1 mile to the intersection with Maxcy's Mill Road, where you will see the cemetery. There are a number of small access roads where visitors can park. Across from the cemetery is a large hayfield where breeding Bobolinks display; you can observe them from the edge of the cemetery. The areas surrounding the cemetery are often great for spring migrant warblers, and Indigo Buntings nest in the vicinity. Bald Eagles are often spotted flying overhead here.

The **Windsor Fair Grounds** are about a half mile south of here, and when the fair is not under way you should be able to enter the parking area across the street to search for Prairie Warblers in the northeast corner of the ball fields.

To reach the **Whitefield Salmon Preserve** continue south to the intersection of Routes 32 and 17. Take a left here to go east on Route 17. Use caution at this intersection, as traffic moves faster than you expect on this route. Travel 2.5 miles and turn right onto Howe Road. Follow Howe Road south for 1.3 miles to the parking lot and kiosk for the Whitefield Salmon Preserve on your left, a fifty-six-acre SVCA preserve where two branches of the Sheepscot River come together. A walk along the 2 miles of trails can be fruitful throughout the year, with breeding Scarlet Tanagers among the many species to be found. Watch the river carefully in late May and early June and you may also bear witness to the migration of sea lamprey returning to spawn as they wiggle up the fast-moving waters

Just a few hundred yards beyond here on Howe Road is a one-lane bridge (closed for repairs in 2016) over the Sheepscot River where there is a wonderful view of the river, and migrants can be plentiful. There is a small pull-out parking area here, but sometimes it can be rutted and muddy, and poison ivy is abundant nearby. To get back to I-95 take Route 17 West back about 14 miles to Augusta.

The Sheepscot Valley Conservation Association gives specific directions to and background information about its preserves at http://www.sheepscot .org/.

7 Kennebec County

HERB WILSON

In the heart of Central Maine, two of the state's four largest cities are found, straddling the most important geographical, economic, and historical feature of the county: the Kennebec River. Former mill towns powered by dams on the river, these two population centers host a growing cadre of loyal birders.

In the breeding season, many of Maine's birders make at least an annual pilgrimage to Messalonskee Lake (site KE6), where Sandhill Cranes (breeding here for over a decade), Black Terns (near the eastern edge of their breeding range), and Purple Martins (at the northeastern edge of their breeding range) all overlap and can be easily observed.

Likewise, Vaughan Woods (KE2) hosts one of the northernmost pairs of Louisiana Waterthrushes, while other breeding-season hot spots include the Augusta State Airport (KE3), with species such as Prairie Warbler approaching their northern limits. In contrast, Palm Warblers reach their southern limits at the Sidney Bog (KE7).

Come fall, the lakes of the county host numerous migrant waterfowl, with Cobbosseecontee Lake (KE1) often hosting impressive numbers and regular rarities, as can China Lake (KE8). As lakes and ponds begin to freeze, action on the river heats up, and a variety of access sites in Waterville and Winslow (KE10, Kennebec River) can be very fruitful from late fall through the winter, especially for Barrow's Goldeneyes.

Meanwhile, in the depths of winter, dedicated larophiles head to Hatch Hill Landfill (KE5), where white-winged gulls, large numbers of eagles, and a history of "mega" rarities attract birders. Herb Wilson asked me to pen this entry since I spent more time than most rational birders studying gulls here. More gulls, along with raptors and open-country specialists, can often be found in the River Road Farmlands (KE12).

After a long and often cold winter, birders anxiously await the arrival of the first waves of spring migrants. Augusta's birders flock to Viles Arboretum

Pittsfield

Skowhegan

2

201

95

River Rd.

Smithfield

139

100

KE12 ★

Unity

Rome

23

137

Fairfield

KE11 ★

8

KE9 ●

Waterville

Albion

Chesterville

Vienna

Mount Vernon

27

KE10 ★

202

9

China

Livermore
Falls

41

23

KE8

★

Belgrade

Palermo

17

KE6 ★

KE7 ★

100

201

3

Fayette

Readfield

Maine Turnpike

9

Wayne

3

32

Somerville

KE3 ★

202

KE5 ★

Winthrop

KE1 ★

Augusta

105

Hallowell ●

KE4

202

KE2 ★

17

West
Gardiner

32

135

Gardiner

126

Litchfield

95

295

Dresden

32

1

Sabattus

201

KENNEBEC COUNTY

(KE4), while birders in Waterville have a variety of productive sites to choose from (KE9). —*Derek Lovitch*

SITE KE1 Cobbosseecontee Lake

TOWNS Winthrop and Monmouth. DeLorme Map 12: C3–4.
SEASON April–September, **October to freeze-up.** **VISITATION** 2–4 hrs.
No restroom facilities. & **HIGHLIGHTS** Migrating waterfowl (especially inland rarities) and shorebirds.

Western Kennebec County has a series of lakes (Cobbosseecontee Lake, Little Cobbosseecontee Lake, Lake Annabessacook) that offer excellent birding potential. The shores of these lakes are heavily populated, with limited access to the waterfront, but several viewpoints can produce excellent numbers of birds, especially in the productive south end of Cobboseecontee.

DIRECTIONS

From I-95 take Exit 109 and follow Route 11 South/17 West/100 South/202 West toward Manchester. In the center of Manchester remain on 11/100/202 West as Route 17 branches to the northwest. In 3.2 miles, passing the north shore of Cobbosseecontee Lake, turn left onto Route 135 South, which travels along the western shore of the lake. In 6.2 miles turn left onto Launch Road and follow it to its end at the boat launch for a view of the open lake. Return to Route 135 and make a left. In 0.1 miles the road crosses Jug Stream, which connects Cobbosseecontee Lake and Lake Anabessacook.

Turn left on Sanborn Road and pull into the parking area on the left to check the stream for ducks. In 1.7 miles turn left on Cobbossee Road. In 0.8 miles you will pass along a causeway. Park on the right side of the road, just beyond the guardrail. You can scan the southern portion of the lake here.

The marshes may harbor Marsh Wrens, Soras, and Virginia Rails. But the real attraction is waterfowl and shorebirds during the spring and particularly the fall migration. Depending on the water levels, this region may be attractive to shorebirds like Pectoral Sandpipers, Wilson's Snipe, both yellowlegs, Black-bellied Plovers, and American Golden-Plovers. When the water is higher, waterfowl congregate here. Common species include American Black Ducks, Mallards, Green-winged Teal, Blue-winged Teal, American Wigeon, Ring-necked Ducks, both species of scaup, Common Goldeneyes, and Hooded Mergansers. Over the years, many rarities have been detected on several occasions, including Canvasback and Redhead, along with "inland rarities" such as Surf Scoters; scanning the lake after strong late-fall storms can be especially fruitful.

Many birders will combine a trip to "Cobbosee" with a visit to Sabattus Pond in Androscoggin County (site AN8) by taking Route 9/126 West into Sabattus.

RARITIES

Brant, November 1982

SITE KE2 Vaughan Woods

TOWN Hallowell. DeLorme Map 12: C5. SEASON April–August, September–October. VISITATION 1–2 hrs. No facilities. HIGHLIGHTS Breeding Louisiana Waterthrush; migrants.

Vaughan Woods is a gem located in the midst of densely populated Hallowell. Maintained since 1988 by the Kennebec Land Trust, Vaughan Woods offers a series of trails through woods and an expansive meadow. Vaughan Brook passes through the property, and the trails parallel the stream for part of the way. Winter melt may cause the stream to flow quickly, interfering with hearing birdsong in the vicinity of the babbling water. The trail is very popular for local residents, so I recommend visiting earlier in the morning.

DIRECTIONS

From I-95 take Exit 109 (the southern Augusta exit) and head east on Western Avenue (Routes 11 North/100 North/17 East/202 East) to the rotary. Take the first exit off the rotary and head south on State Street (Route 201/27 South). You will enter the town of Hallowell in a couple of miles as State Street changes to Water Street. Look for Central Street in the heart of downtown and turn right. Proceed for three blocks and turn left onto Middle Street. Follow Middle Street to its end, and as the road curves right, park in the small parking lot ahead.

From the parking lot a trail leads through a small meadow that can be good for Savannah Sparrows and Song Sparrows. The trail leads into the woods, and you will see and hear Vaughan Brook below. Listen for the Louisiana

Waterthrush's piercing song. This site is the most reliable spot in Kennebec County at this time for this species, although we expect its distribution to extend farther northward, as has occurred with other species such as Prairie Warbler, Eastern Towhee, and Field Sparrow. Listen for Eastern Wood-Pewees, Brown Creepers, Winter Wrens, and Black-throated Green Warblers in the trees. Follow the trail to the right. The trail descends to a bridge across the brook. Walk to the west and scan Cascade Pond for waterfowl. The trail continues to a field that may hold Bobolinks and Eastern Meadowlarks. Additional trails traverse the property. I recommend that you take a map with you (available from the website) if you decide to walk other trails. Usually, the walk down to the stream and to the field will sample most of the birds in the area.

For more information and to download a trail map see the Vaughan Homestead website at http://vaughanhomestead.org/.

SITE KE3 Mill Park and Augusta State Airport (West Augusta)

TOWN Augusta. DeLorme Map 12: C5.   SEASON March, April–May, June–October.   VISITATION 1–2 hrs. No facilities.
HIGHLIGHTS Lesser Black-backed and white-winged gulls; Prairie Warbler, Field Sparrow, Eastern Towhee.

Mill Park offers opportunities for river birding, and the Augusta State Airport provides excellent chances for some passerines that are near the northern limit of their ranges in Maine.

DIRECTIONS

From I-95 take Exit 112A (Exit 112 if traveling southbound) and follow Route 8/11/27 South for just over 2 miles. Turn left at the blinking light onto Route 104 East. At the stop sign turn left to remain on Route 104 (Water Street). In 0.2 miles bear right onto Canal Street and enter **Mill Park** for excellent scoping opportunities for waterbirds. Gull numbers sometimes approach one thousand individuals, with the possibility of Lesser Black-backed, Iceland, and Glaucous Gulls.

Return to Water Street and make a left. Turn right at the traffic light onto Bridge Street. At the top of the hill, turn left onto State Street (Route 27) and then right onto Winthrop Street at the next light. Follow Winthrop Street for 0.6 miles (to the top of the hill) and you will see **Mount Hope Cemetery** on your right (look for the sign, as there are three other cemeteries along Winthrop Street). Take one of the several entrances into the cemetery and walk or drive to the northwest corner, keeping an eye out for Northern Mockingbirds on the way in. Park in the small parking lot and walk down the trail to the northwest into a bowl, adjacent to the airport. This area is excellent for Prairie Warblers, Eastern Towhees, and Field Sparrows, all of which are difficult to find farther north.

RARITIES

Blue-winged Warbler, May 2013

SITE KE4 Viles Arboretum

TOWN Augusta. DeLorme Map 12: C5. **SEASON** All year, but especially **April–May.** **VISITATION** 1–4 hrs. Restrooms in visitor center open weekdays 8 a.m.–5 p.m. **HIGHLIGHTS** Migrant passerines; Sora and Virginia Rail; Eastern Meadowlark; winter irruptives.

This arboretum is one of the best birding areas in Kennebec County. The 224-acre property has great habitat diversity: planted stands of trees, second-growth forest, fields, several marshes, and several small ponds. An extensive trail system makes it easy to sample all these habitats. April and May mornings, following nights of strong migration, can be fantastic here.

DIRECTIONS

From I-95 take Exit 109 (the southern Augusta exit) and head east on Western Avenue (Routes 11 North/100 North/17 East/202 East) to the rotary. Take the second exit to continue on Routes 201/100/202/17 and cross the Kennebec River. At the next rotary take the first exit onto Route 9 West/17 East. Follow Route 9 West for 1.1 miles to the Viles Arboretum entrance on the left.

The extensive trail system gives you many options for a birding trip here. I recommend stopping at the arboretum office to pick up a map (or download a copy from the arboretum website). Behind the arboretum building follow the trail through the meadow, keeping an eye out for Eastern Bluebirds and House Wrens among the many Tree Swallows using the abundant nest boxes provided. Listen and look here for Eastern Meadowlarks, a species that is not easy to find in Kennebec County.

The trail continues through the Hosta Garden. Keep an eye out for migrant thrushes in the woods adjacent to the trail. Swainson's Thrushes are regular, and be on the lookout for a rarely detected Bicknell's Thrush/Gray-cheeked Thrush, especially in late May.

At the end of the Hosta Garden Trail, walk to your right to the amphitheater. You can walk around the rim of the amphitheater and have eye-level views of the canopy of some trees below. This area can be excellent for migrant warblers, vireos, and flycatchers.

From the amphitheater, walk to the north on the Viles Pond Trail. Head east at the remnants of the piggery (once a three-story heated barn) to reach Viles Pond. The vegetation around the pond can be hopping with warblers in migration, and the adjacent upland shrubs can be good for migrant sparrows.

East of the pond you have the choice of many trails to explore the forested part of the arboretum. Continuing due east from Viles Pond, you will skirt the forested area, often getting good views of migrants in the treetops.

To the north you will see a pond and marsh with a boardwalk across it. Work your way along the well-marked paths to the boardwalk. In late spring and summer the area will be hopping with Yellow Warblers. Bobolinks will be common in the grasses. The marsh has both Virginia Rails and Soras, both of which, with patience, may be seen from the boardwalk, lurking through the marsh. A Willow Flycatcher is often heard in the area.

Coming off the boardwalk you can either work your way back to the arboretum parking lot or detour slightly to take the grassy road to the north to Piggery Road. Adjacent to some of the baseball fields is a marsh that has Soras and Virginia Rails and a dense population of Red-winged Blackbirds.

RARITIES

Sedge Wren, June 2010; Orchard Orioles nested here 2008 through 2010 but have not been present since; Townsend's Solitaire, November 2015

For more information and to download a trail map visit Viles Arboretum's website at http://www.vilesarboretum.org/.

SITE KE5 Hatch Hill Landfill

Entry by Derek Lovitch

TOWN Augusta. DeLorme Map 13: C1. **SEASON** September–November, December–March, April. **VISITATION** 1–2 hrs. Closed Sunday and Monday. No restroom facilities. ♿ **HIGHLIGHTS** "White-winged" gulls; vagrant gulls; Bald Eagles.

Birders are indebted to the staff at this municipal landfill for welcoming us to the facility. By abiding by a few simple rules and protocols, we can enjoy access to some great gull watching and one of the best concentrations of Bald Eagles in the state. In fact, at least a dozen eagles of various ages are usually present, with high counts approaching forty birds on occasion. Herring Gulls dominate—often 98 percent or more of gulls present. Handfuls of Great Black-backed Gulls are usually present, Ring-billed Gulls are few, and Iceland and Glaucous Gulls are regular in winter. More spring and fall visitation would probably yield Lesser Black-backed Gulls fairly regularly. Several "mega" rarities have been discovered here over the years as well. Common Ravens join abundant American Crows, and the occasional Rough-legged Hawk is spotted in addition to a Red-tailed Hawk or two.

DIRECTIONS

From 1-95 take Exit 113 and follow Route 3 East. At the fourth light in just over 3 miles, turn right onto Church Hill Road (Note that gulls often roost in the fields and on the rooftop of the lumberyard at this intersection, so take a moment to scan any flocks). At the next light make a left onto Route 105 (South Belfast Avenue). In 1.1 miles turn left into the entrance for the landfill.

Proceed toward the Scale House booth, stopping at the traffic light until it turns green. Pull up to the booth, let them know you are here to bird, and sign in. Check to see if any visitation rules have changed. Follow the road as it curves right. On your right, you'll see various piles of recyclables. Park at the far edge of this paved area in front of the junked appliances, being careful not to block any access to any pile or equipment. Stay away from the piles themselves to avoid flat tires.

Where trash is being dumped at a given time will determine where gulls are feeding and roosting. Regardless, I prefer to spend most of my time near the car, scanning the sides of the hills, the active landfill dumping area, and the surrounding trees. At the very least you can study the gulls in flight as they take off following a loud noise or another pass by a Bald Eagle. In fact, the tall trees behind you are a favored perching spot for Bald Eagles, and this is a great place for eagle photography—especially of birds in flight as they commute to and from these trees.

Most of the time, you are permitted to walk up the large capped landfill to the *right* of the active landfill. Carefully cross the road and walk up the hill on the *outside* of the fence to the summit. There is *absolutely no smoking* when doing this, owing to the presence of active methane vents. While you can often study gulls and eagles feeding and roosting in the landfill site this way, gulls often roost on the hills behind you, and disturbing them can greatly reduce the number of gulls you will get to enjoy and/or stress over identifying, hence my preference just to watch from near the car.

Please remember that safety of all users, from workers to visitors, is the top priority, and therefore rules and accessibility are subject to change. This is a very busy municipally run landfill, and if our behavior jeopardizes the safety of anyone, access would be restricted. Please use care and common sense in order for us all to continue to enjoy the birding opportunities here.

I usually spend at least an hour, watching the turnover of gulls as they come to and from the landfill. Gulls feeding at landfills need to bathe and drink regularly, and you'll see many birds "commuting" to the west to the river in downtown Augusta. In fact, when the Kennebec River freezes completely during prolonged cold spells, gull numbers are reduced markedly at the landfill.

After having your fill here, recheck the fields at the intersection of Route 3 and Church Hill Road, and/or head into downtown to check the riverfront by backtracking on Route 3 from Church Hill Road. Make a left at the next light to stay on North Belfast Avenue (Route 9), and at its end make a left onto Route 201/100 South (Bangor Street). At the rotary, take the first exit to cross over the bridge to downtown. At the first light, make a right onto Water Street—gulls often congregate on the river behind the buildings on your right—or continue straight until you reach Mill Park (Site KE3), where you can scan more of the river.

RARITIES

Thayer's Gull, January 2010 (second state record); Slaty-backed Gull, January 2013 (first state record)

Black Tern,
Messalonskee Lake.
© Jeannette Lovitch

SITE KE6 Messalonskee Lake

TOWN Belgrade. DeLorme Map 12: A5. **SEASON** March, **April–July,**
August–October. **VISITATION** 1–2 hrs. No facilities. ♿ ⚓
HIGHLIGHTS Sandhill Crane, Black Tern, Purple Martin.

Like the other Belgrade Lakes, Messalonskee Lake (Snow Pond) is ringed with
cottages and therefore has limited access for birding. The southwestern end of
the lake is sparsely developed, however, and extensive marshes there make for
excellent and accessible birding opportunities. This area is the most reliable
place in the state for Sandhill Cranes and one of the few breeding locations
for Black Terns and Purple Martins. An easy-to-view Bank Swallow colony,
breeding Ring-necked Ducks and Pied-billed Grebes, and many others add
to the allure of this fantastic destination.

DIRECTIONS

From I-95 take Exit 112B and follow Route 8/11/27 North for just over 7 miles
to the **boat launch** parking area on your right. Kayakers and canoeists launch
boats here, but trailered boats no longer have access. A short pier leads onto
the lake during the boating season.

The marsh around the pier has a diversity of waterbirds, including Pied-
billed Grebes, American Bitterns, Great Blue Herons, Virginia Rails, Soras,

Swamp Sparrows, and Red-winged Blackbirds. The trees are magnets for warblers during spring migration. Scanning from the pier may produce a Sandhill Crane. Scoping the boating channel east from the pier will yield Black Terns; they frequently perch on the navigational buoys.

Paddling a kayak on the waterways through the marsh is a marvelous way to experience the area, but please avoid approaching the tern colonies; they are sensitive to disturbance. Marsh Wrens are more abundant away from the boat landing, and Common Gallinules and Least Bitterns have been found occasionally.

Retrace your drive by walking or driving 0.1 miles to the south to a small building that serves as a seasonal **tourist information center.** Walk behind the building to find a small baitfish pond. The trees around the pond are usually bedecked with Palm Warblers and Yellow-rumped Warblers in the second part of April and with a broad diversity of migrant warblers in May.

Sandhill Crane, Messalonskee Lake. © Jeannette Lovitch

You can walk beyond the pond to the edge of the marsh. You will have a less obstructed view of the marsh than you get from the boat landing. Sometimes Sandhill Cranes will be foraging within 100 yards.

At 0.2 miles north of the boat launch, bear left onto Depot Road at **Hammond Lumber,** and immediately turn right into a dirt parking area with a large, white electrical box on the ground. Park at the box and scan the marsh across the road. A little scoping will usually lead to a Sandhill Crane or two, as well as dabbling ducks, Great Blue Herons, and Canada Geese. Ospreys and Bald Eagles are frequently seen soaring.

Continue on **Depot Street.** In 0.5 miles notice the chained entrance road for Hallowell Pit. Pull over and scan the edges of the sand embankment to check out the breeding Bank Swallows. In late June and early July many of the holes will be bursting with fledglings thinking about taking their first leap. A few pairs of Northern Rough-winged Swallows also breed here, as do a pair of Belted Kingfishers—look for their larger holes often near the top of the sand bank. In another 1.1 miles a white house on the right with a large lawn and fields behind it hosts many Purple Martin houses. Continuously occupied since 1909, this colony is currently being renovated in a joint project of Freeport Wild Bird Supply, local birders, Hammond Lumber, and private donors. Tree Swallows and Eastern Bluebirds nest here as well.

RARITIES

Garganey, June 1994 (first state record); Common Gallinule, June 2010 and June 2013; Willet, June 2015

SITE KE7 Sidney Bog

TOWN Sidney. DeLorme Map 12: B5.   **SEASON** April, **May–June,** July–October.   **VISITATION** 1–3 hrs. No restroom facilities.
HIGHLIGHTS Nesting Palm, Canada, and Prairie Warblers; Eastern Towhees.

Sidney Bog is a vast bog extending for about 4 miles along the western side of Bog Road in Sidney. The bog is over a mile wide, so the amount of habitat is large. Sidney Bog is not a "kettlehole bog" (a glacially gouged pond that has filled in by peat accumulation over the past ten thousand years), so it offers firmer footing than a typical quaking kettlehole bog. The area may be profitably birded without entering the bog.

From I-95 take Exit 112B and follow Route 8/11/27 North. A 0.3 miles beyond the third traffic light (second light if arriving from the north) turn right onto Bog Road. Follow Bog Road for I mile to the beginning of the bog on the left. The road has fairly heavy traffic and narrow shoulders, so the best place to stop is the school bus turnaround at the Sidney/Augusta town line at 1.2 miles. Do not leave you car unattended if you park here, as buses use this turnaround quite frequently.

In the forest ringing the bog, Least Flycatchers, Canada Warblers, Nashville Warblers, and Northern Waterthrushes are abundant, with Wilson's Warblers possible. You will be able to hear Hermit Thrushes, Palm Warblers, Common Yellowthroats, Song Sparrows, and White-throated Sparrows on the bog proper. Over the past twenty years, two species have expanded into the bog: Prairie Warbler and Eastern Towhee as shrubs have filled in and/or these species' range has expanded.

If you want to get onto the bog, a trail is available 0.2 miles north of the school bus turnaround. Look for the trail heading off to the northwest adjacent to a tall bigtooth aspen on the west side of the road. You will need to negotiate the lagg (moat) to get into the bog, so a pair of waders or shoes that you don't mind getting wet will be needed. Once on the bog, footing is fairly firm, and tennis shoes or even sandals will be fine.

The bog is spectacular in late May when the abundant *Rhodora* on the bog are blooming, making a sea of pink. Palm Warblers usually sing from tall trees, and listen for Lincoln's Sparrows: males have occasionally set up a territory, but I know of no successful breeding.

SITE KE8 China Lake

TOWN China. DeLorme Map 13: A–B2–3. **SEASON** March, **April–May**, June–October. **VISITATION** 1–2 hrs. No restroom facilities. ⛵
HIGHLIGHTS Migrant and nesting waterfowl.

This large Y-shaped lake offers excellent waterfowl and waterbird diversity, despite its eutrophic nature. Birding trips by canoe, kayak, or motorized boats can be rewarding, although birding from shore can be equally productive.

From I-95 take Exit 113 and follow Route 3 East for about 12 miles to the intersection with Route 32 North. Turn left onto Route 32 and proceed 4.5 miles to the East Vassalboro Boat Landing on your right. Park in the parking lot and scan the western portion of China Lake. This area is reliable in November and December for American Coot, a difficult species to find in Kennebec County, and Redheads have been seen here as well. Continue north on Route 32, keeping an eye on the outlet stream on the east side of the road. This area usually remains unfrozen in the winter and can harbor several hundred ducks, including American Wigeon, Ring-necked Duck, Greater Scaup, and mergansers.

In 1.4 miles from the boat launch, turn right onto Lombard Dam Road. At the stop sign in 0.8 miles go straight ahead onto Stanley Hill Road. Keep an eye out for raptors along the road. At its end in 3.1 miles turn left onto Neck Road. In 1.6 miles turn right onto Causeway Road. Just beyond the Baptist Church on the left, pull into the parking area. You can scan the north end of China Lake as well as the marsh to the north of the causeway. Long-tailed Ducks occur here occasionally on the lake. In the marsh, Wood Ducks are regular, along with dabbling ducks and American Bitterns. At the east end of the marsh a road leads into a cemetery. Walk the short loop, which offers vantage points for the marsh. Swamp Sparrows are common in the marsh in spring and summer.

Return to your car and continue driving along Causeway Road. At the stop sign turn left onto Route 202. In 0.2 miles stop along the shoulder of the road and scan the beaver pond area (called a flowage in Maine) north of the highway. This wetland is excellent for Ring-necked Ducks, Pied-billed Grebes, and Osprey.

If you have time, a woodland trail begins on the east side of the marsh at the intersection of Causeway Road and Route 202 and continues all the way to Albion. The first half mile passes along the marsh and through some mixed forest.

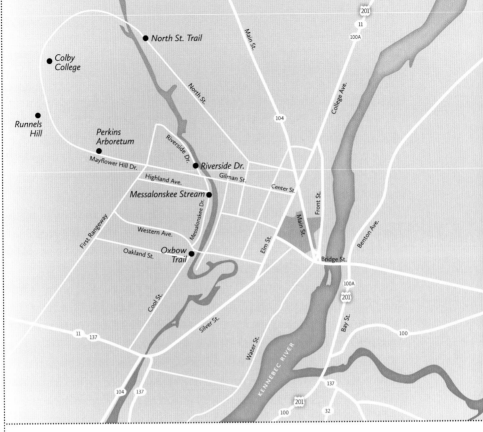

WATERVILLE AREA

SITE KE9 Waterville Loop

TOWN Waterville. DeLorme Map 20: E2; Detail Map 76. **SEASON** March–June, July–December. **VISITATION** 1–4 hrs. Portable toilets available on North Street beyond the covered picnic area, adjacent to the tennis courts. & **HIGHLIGHTS** Waterfowl; spring warbler migration.

This area is centered on the Messalonskee Stream that bisects the town of Waterville. The stream is one of the first bodies of water to open up in the spring and so provides a magnet for waterfowl. In April and May, migrant passerines may be abundant in the area. The three-hundred-acre Perkins Arboretum at Colby College has an extensive trail system and is open to the public.

213

From I-95 take Exit 130 and head south on Route 104 South (Main Street). You will pass Elm Plaza on your right and then a McDonald's. At the next light turn right on Eustis Parkway. At its end, turn right onto North Street. In 100 yards, turn left into a small parking lot on the left adjacent to Messalonskee Stream. If the few spots are taken, parking is available in marked spaces along North Street.

The **North Street Trail** extends for about half a mile to the east along the stream. The trail is paved and wheelchair accessible. The trail is tree lined, but the stream is easily seen along the length of the trail. At the east end of the trail, a small field can be good for migrant sparrows.

During spring migration the trail will produce a nice list of migrant warblers, including Wilson's and Canada Warblers. Occasional overshoots like Blue-gray Gnatcatchers appear. Yellow Warblers, Northern Waterthrushes, Warbling Vireos, and Baltimore Orioles are often abundant.

In March and April expect Wood Ducks, Common Goldeneyes, and the occasional Northern Pintail. A pair of Merlins have nested in the vicinity over the past few years. The nest has moved in recent years from behind the Alfond Youth Center along the North Street Trail to an area adjacent to Thayer Hospital along Quarry Road and most recently to the Colby College campus.

Continue the exploration of Messalonskee Stream by backtracking east along North Street and turning right on West Street in 0.8 miles. At the first stop sign turn right onto Mayflower Hill Drive. Drive over the Messalonskee Stream bridge and turn right onto **North Riverside Drive**. This area is excellent in March and April for waterfowl.

Turn around and make a left onto Mayflower Hill Drive, followed by an immediate right onto Messalonskee Drive. A pair of Bald Eagles have nested along this stretch of the stream. The road will come out at Waterville High School and becomes one-way there. Turn right onto Brooklyn Avenue and then take the first left onto Morrison Street. In one block turn left on Western Drive, and then take a right onto Cool Street. In 200 yards turn into the parking lot for the Lutheran Church on the left (Matthews Street enters on the right). From the north edge of the parking lot follow the **Oxbow Trail**, a loop of less than a mile that follows the edge of an oxbow of Messalonskee Stream. The beginning of the trail is below a dam, and the running water keeps this section of the stream open even in the middle of winter, so it is always worth checking for waterfowl.

The trail passes through second-growth forest, with a small cattail marsh at the east end of the trail. The expected breeding passerines are present.

From the church parking lot turn right onto Western Avenue. At the stop sign turn left. At the next stop sign (and blinking light) turn right onto First Rangeway. Turn left at the next stop sign onto Mayflower Hill Drive. At the top of the hill you will see a stone Colby College sign. Park along the road here and follow the trail adjacent to the stone sign into **Perkins Arboretum**.

The Perkins Arboretum has a color-coded system of trails. My recommendation is to start out on the Yellow Trail, which passes through a dense stand of eastern hemlocks that is good for Black-throated Green Warblers and Brown Creepers; a pair of Barred Owls have nested here for years. The trail approaches Perkins Stream and diverges to become the Red Trail on the left and the Yellow Trail on the right. Take the Red Trail as it passes through some second-growth forest that is good for Chestnut-sided Warblers and Yellow-bellied Sapsuckers. Listen for Broad-winged Hawks overhead. The Red Trail then ascends through some older forest to end at the railroad track. Walk left along the railroad track. This area can be spectacular during spring migration as birds perch in the trees to warm in the morning sun. The Messalonskee Stream and the North Street Trail beyond will be visible through the trees.

An extensive marsh along Perkins Stream will be seen just south of the railroad track. Solitary Sandpipers and Spotted Sandpipers can be found here in migration, along with breeding Red-winged Blackbirds and Swamp Sparrows.

Continue walking along the railroad track. Just beyond the limits of the marsh, scramble down the railroad embankment to the Blue Trail. Follow this trail through deciduous forest to a stand of white pines. Pine Warblers can be found here, along with Northern Parulas and Scarlet Tanagers. The Blue Trail will veer off to the right and proceed down the hill. Rather than following the Blue Trail here, continue straight on the trail, now the White Trail, through deciduous forest. Continue for about half a mile. The trail ends on Mayflower Hill Drive, and your car will be about 50 yards to the left.

Instead of returning directly to your car, you may wish to walk across Mayflower Hill Drive and walk up **Runnels Hill** on the left. This extensive meadow with scattered apple trees is great for Savannah Sparrows, Eastern

Bluebirds, and Indigo Buntings, and has had nesting Field Sparrows, unusual for this part of the county.

RARITIES

Cerulean Warbler, May 2001

SITE KE10 Kennebec River

TOWNS Waterville and Winslow. DeLorme Map 76. **SEASON** October–April. **VISITATION** 1–2 hrs. Restroom facilities at local businesses. &
HIGHLIGHTS Waterbirds including Barrow's Goldeneye.

The stretch of the Kennebec River between the two Waterville-Winslow bridges can be a highly productive and accessible habitat for waterfowl in the fall through the spring. The dam beside the north bridge and the confluence with the Sebasticook River keep this section of the Kennebec free of ice for much of the winter.

DIRECTIONS

From I-95 take Exit 130 and follow Route 104 South into downtown Waterville. At the junction of Route 11/104/201, proceed straight to remain on Main Street. Proceed through the next two lights and turn left into the parking lot of the Hathaway Creative Center. Drive to the **overlook area** adjacent to the chain-link fence. This observation point is just below the dam, and a small island (which may be inundated when water levels are high) usually has Ring-billed Herring and Great Black-backed Gulls. Check carefully for white-winged and Lesser Black-backed Gulls. Double-crested Cormorant and Great Cormorant (rare) may be seen here as well.

Return to Water Street and turn left. In 0.4 miles you will see a small parking lot adjacent to a metal stairway. The long stairway provides access to the river, although viewing the river from the parking lot can be productive as well.

Retrace your route north on Water Street to the traffic light and turn right. Cross the bridge, turn right at the light, and drive south on Route 20/100 South. Just beyond the next light turn right into the parking lot for **Fort Halifax.** If you cross the bridge over the Sebasticook River, you have gone too far. Cross the railroad track into the parking lot and walk to the shore of the Kennebec River for excellent, expansive views. Over two hundred Common

Goldeneyes may occur here from fall to spring. This site is one of the two most reliable spots for Barrow's Goldeneye in Kennebec County, and hybrid Barrows x Common have been seen on a couple of occasions. Wood Ducks, Common Mergansers, Hooded Mergansers, and various dabbling ducks can be common as well.

From the parking lot turn right onto Route 20/100 South, then turn right at the next light onto **Eutaw Street**. This street parallels the Kennebec and offers several convenient vantage points to survey the river south of the confluence with the Sebasticook River.

RARITIES

Canvasback, February 2007; Harlequin Duck, December 2006

For information about Fort Halifax see http://www.maine.gov/dacf/parks/discover_history_explore_nature/history:/fort_halifax/index.shtml.

SITE KE11 Kennebec Highlands Trails

TOWN Rome. DeLorme Map 20: E3–4. **SEASON** April–October.
VISITATION 3–4 hrs. No restroom facilities. **HIGHLIGHTS** Pristine forest with great overlooks of the Belgrade Lakes region and a variety of breeding species and migrants.

The Belgrade Region Conservation Alliance (BRCA) maintains a series of trails in the Kennebec Highlands west of Long Pond and Great Pond. The forests are mostly coniferous. The trails involve some elevational gain, and some scrambling on rocks is required. I would describe the difficulty of the trails as moderate. The conserved land here does not offer any regional specialties but does provide beautiful habitat, with some spectacular vistas of the Belgrade Lakes region.

DIRECTIONS

From I-95 take Exit 112B for Route 27 West into the village of Belgrade. There, I recommend stopping at Day's Store to purchase an inexpensive trail guide and map to the Kennebec Highlands Trails. Before leaving, take the opportunity to scan Long Pond to the west and Great Pond to the east for Common Loons, mergansers, and other waterfowl. You can also find some trail information on the BRCA website, given below.

The Round Top Trail is a good introduction to this area. From Belgrade village continue north on Route 27 for 4 miles beyond the Rome town line to Watson Pond Road. Turn left, and in 3.7 miles park in the small lot (the second of two) for the Kennebec Highlands Public Reserve Land. The Round Top Trail ascends to the summit of Round Top Mountain, at 1,133 feet elevation. The trail is marked with blue blazes. Crossing the Kennebec Highlands Trail after a mile, stay on Round Top Trail and begin a steady climb in a northerly direction. As you approach the summit, nice views will open up to the east and south. Near the summit, at 1.7 miles, take the Round Top Spur Trail (0.3 miles) for spectacular views. Return to the Round Top Trail, admiring the view of Belgrade village, Long Pond, and Great Pond. The trail will then descend steeply, intersecting the Kennebec Highlands Trail again at 2.1 miles. Walk to the right (south) onto the gravel trail. Keep to the right at a three-way junction at the 2.9-mile mark. Snowmobile signs will mark the spot. About 100 yards past this junction, a rock cairn on the east side of the logging trail marks the first junction with the Kennebec Highlands Trail. Turn left (east) and return to the parking lot.

During the breeding season, expect to see and hear Red-eyed Vireos, Brown Creepers, Winter Wrens, Hermit Thrushes, Black-throated Green Warblers, Magnolia Warblers, Ovenbirds, and White-throated Sparrows. During the spring and particularly the fall, the vantage points near the summit can be productive for migrating raptors.

For more information and to download a trail map visit the website of the Belgrade Region Conservation Alliance at http://www.belgradelakes.org/.

SITE KE12 River Road Farmlands

TOWN Clinton. DeLorme Map 21: D2–3. **SEASON** All year, but especially **October–March**. **VISITATION** 1–4 hrs. No restroom facilities. **HIGHLIGHTS** Raptors; white-winged gulls; Horned Lark; American Pipit; Lapland Longspur.

An extensive series of farms lines the eastern bank of the Kennebec River north of Winslow. The open terrain attracts American Pipits, Horned Larks, and Lapland Longspurs, as well as a diversity of raptors. Wetland areas can have a variety of migratory shorebirds in spring and fall migration.

Please note that the farms in this region are working farms, with some employing tens of workers. Do not drive onto the farms without permission of the farmers. Most of the birds can be seen from the roadside.

DIRECTIONS

From I-95 take Exit 132 and follow Route 139 East (Western Avenue) to Fairfield. Turn right as Route 201 joins Route 139 and enters the downtown. In 0.1 miles turn left on Route 100 North/139 East and cross the Kennebec River. At the top of the hill turn left at the stoplight onto River Road.

Proceed north for 4 miles (but see the recommendation below). Along the way in season you may see large flocks of Canada Geese. Check them carefully, as Snow Geese will sometimes be among them, and vagrants should be looked for.

After you pass under I-95 the Shawmut Dam will come into view on your left. For the next 2 miles you will be in prime birding habitat for longspurs, larks, and pipits.

You will see a pullout on the left where there is a path to the Shawmut Dam. Excellent views of the region below the dam are possible here. You can have similar views from Shawmut on the opposite side of the river with a minimum of walking (see the Somerset County chapter, site S02).

In the winter, gulls commute between the Shawmut Dam and the agricultural farms. Iceland, Glaucous, and Lesser Black-backed (rare in midwinter) Gulls can all usually be found with a little effort. The gulls often roost on the roofs of the many barns along the road.

During the winter this area can be spectacular for diurnal raptors, particularly Red-tailed Hawks, Rough-legged Hawks, Merlins, and Peregrine Falcons. A Golden Eagle spent a couple of weeks in the area in 2013.

My recommendation is to turn right onto Wyman Road, your first paved right after passing under I-95. This safe and quiet dead-end road offers excellent visibility for raptors and ground-dwelling birds. Retrace your steps and turn right onto River Road. Keep your eyes peeled along the next 2 miles and turn right onto Tardiff Road. Turn right onto Booker Lane. At the stop sign, turn left (a 135-degree turn) onto Hinckley Road and follow it until you reach forest on both sides of the road. Then retrace your route to return to Winslow.

RARITIES

Gyrfalcon, December 1991; Ross's Goose, April 2002; Golden Eagle, January–February 2013; Glossy Ibis, July 2015

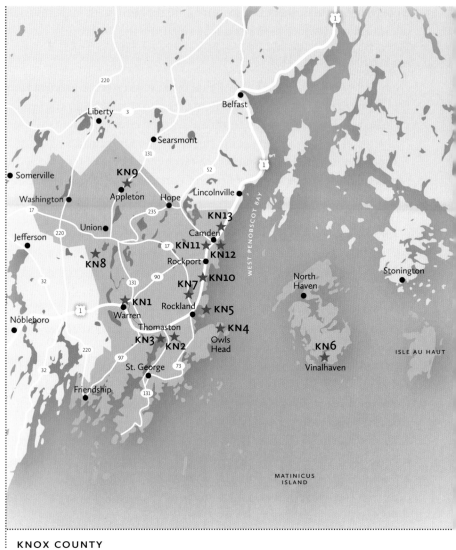

KNOX COUNTY

8 Knox County
KRISTEN LINDQUIST

It's hard to imagine a more quintessential Maine town than Camden, with its beautiful but busy harbor, array of shops and restaurants, and access to some of the best hiking in the Midcoast in the Camden Hills State Park (site KX13). The growing city of Rockland has a more industrial waterfront, complete with a surviving fishing industry and its attendant gulls. Bucolic and forested, the rural interior of Knox County contrasts with the development and wealth of the immediate coast.

For year-round birding look no further than Weskeag Marsh (KX2), which offers something at all seasons. Saltmarsh Sparrows reach the northern (and eastern) limits of their breeding range here, and herons and egrets become much rarer farther up the coast. Shorebird and waterfowl migrations are probably favorite times to visit for most local birders.

While spring migrant traps are few (try Merryspring Nature Center, KX11), the spring show of alewives running up the St. George River (KX1) in Warren (with its attendant piscivorous birds) is not to be missed! Breeding birds abound in the fields and forests of the Beech Hill Preserve (KX10) and a variety of other wonderful little land-trust jewels.

Come fall, Weskeag shines, and hawk watching from Clarry Hill (KX8) can be outstanding. Vinalhaven Island (KX6), off the southern shore of the county, is a major migrant (and vagrant) trap, and including the productive ferry crossing, it really should be a major birding destination. As fall progresses and changes into winter, it's time to start checking the waters, with late-freezing Chickawaukie Lake (KX7) a worthy destination.

Once winter has fully arrived, there are few tours in Maine I personally enjoy more than the Owls Head Area Loop (KX4). Ideally, my wife, Jeannette, and I join Kristen Lindquist and her husband, Paul Doiron, for this loop on New Year's Day, followed by brunch at the award-winning Primo restaurant in Rockland. —*Derek Lovitch*

St. George River in Warren

TOWN Warren. DeLorme Map 14: E1–2. SEASON November–February, May–June. VISITATION 30 min. to 4 hrs. Payson Park is open 7 a.m.–8 p.m. Seasonal restroom, picnic tables, playground. The gate is closed in winter, but you can walk in if there is roadside parking. Woolen Mill Park in Warren is open year-round, but parking can also be a challenge in winter. HIGHLIGHTS Bald Eagle; Osprey; winter waterfowl; spring warbler migration.

Merrill Payson Park is perhaps better known to fishermen than birders, but this small town park teems with avian activity in late May when alewives (also called shad or river herring) are running up the St. George River. Bald Eagles, Ospreys, Double-crested Cormorants, and Herring, Ring-billed, and Great Black-backed Gulls crowd the river for an easy meal within full view of the riverbanks. A footbridge over the river leads to a small network of paths through the woods along the eroding remnants of a historic canal. This walk through history and spring trout lilies offers the opportunity to spot warblers and other migrating passerines. Flycatchers such as Eastern Phoebe, Eastern Wood-pewee, Great Crested Flycatcher, and Eastern Kingbird are often feeding along the river's edge. Belted Kingfisher and Spotted Sandpiper frequent the river corridor. This park is also worth a stop in late fall/winter when ducks congregate in pockets along the river.

When the alewives are running in spring, the tiny Woolen Mill Park perched on the bank of the St. George River in Warren Village can be teeming with photographers poised to get the perfect shot of a Bald Eagle or Osprey nabbing a fish. Large fishnets can affect the viewing as well as the fish flow. This park is worth a stop in late fall and through the winter into early spring when ducks congregate in pockets of open water along the river, as viewed up- and downriver from the bridge at the center of town. Common Goldeneye, Bufflehead, Common and Hooded Mergansers, Wood Duck, and Ring-necked Duck are regulars most years and have been joined on occasion by such species as American Wigeon, Northern Pintail, Barrow's Goldeneye, Northern Shoveler, and Lesser Scaup, all well into winter.

DIRECTIONS

From US Route 1 in Warren turn left onto Route 90 and follow it for 1 mile. The well-marked entrance to **Payson Park** is on your left, just south of the river. From the north the park itself is visible on the right from the road overpass, just before the entrance. The unmarked but well-traveled trails on the other side of the very sturdy bridge meander upriver within sight or sound of the water. Insect repellent is a must in spring.

After enjoying Payson Park, turn left onto Route 90 and cross the St. George River. As you cross, look to your right and you'll see the bridge mentioned above. Take your first right onto Union Street immediately after you cross the river and follow it into the center of town, taking a right onto Main Street to cross the bridge. Woolen Mill Park is to your left, with parking off adjacent Four Rod Road.

After visiting these two sites, I usually visit Beth's Farm Market, a local fresh produce and food mecca (featuring the area's earliest and latest strawberries, summer blueberries, and a corn maze in fall) that is well worth the short detour. The farm stand is on Western Road and well-signed from Routes 1 and 90.

SITE KX2 Weskeag Marsh

TOWN South Thomaston. DeLorme Map 8: A3. SEASON All year, but especially **April–October.** VISITATION 30 min. to 4 hrs. Open year-round. No restroom facilities. The marsh is actively hunted during waterfowl season. ⚓ HIGHLIGHTS More than twenty species of shorebird during migration, including American Golden-Plover, Pectoral and Western Sandpipers (very rare), and Long-billed Dowitcher (very rare); breeding and migrant waterfowl; wading birds, including Snowy and Great Egrets, Green Heron, and Glossy Ibis; Northern Harrier; Virginia Rail; Sora; Nelson's Sparrow (breeding); Saltmarsh Sparrow (at the northernmost edge of their breeding range); and Rough-legged Hawk and Snowy Owl in winter.

The R. Waldo Tyler Wildlife Management Area, known to birders as Weskeag Marsh, is a thirteen-hundred-acre tidal salt marsh, the largest in the Midcoast. This highly productive area is critical to migrating shorebirds, which feed on the mudflats along the St. George River at low tide and then move to the salt pannes of the marsh as the tide rises.

Although most productive during spring and fall migration, Weskeag Marsh is worth a stop any time of year, even if that stop merely consists of pulling over in the parking lot and scanning the pannes or watching the

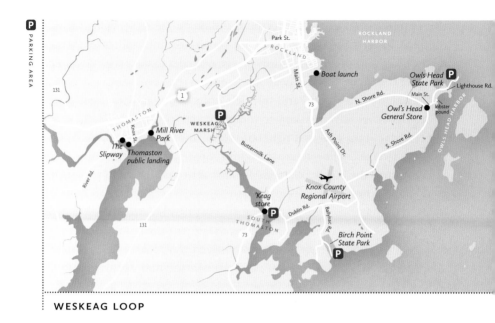

WESKEAG LOOP

sky for a few minutes. This is one of my favorite stops in spring when early arriving wading birds such as Great Blue Heron and Snowy Egret can be seen above the marsh grasses, dabbling ducks feed in the pannes, Killdeer call from the marsh, and the first flocks of inbound American Robins fill the uplands. In summer, the "hot frying pan being dipped in cold water" song of the Nelson's Sparrow can be heard out in the marsh, while Virginia Rails skulk around the edges. In fall, clouds of shorebirds move between the pannes, followed by hunting Peregrine Falcons and Merlins, while Northern Harriers hover and drift nearby. In winter, a Rough-legged Hawk often kites above the marsh, and Hooded Mergansers display on the river. Deer, coyotes, and otters are also regular inhabitants of the marsh. This is an area teeming with life, but it requires patience, as well, to wait for the watery pockets of the marsh to reveal their secrets as the tides rise and fall.

DIRECTIONS

Follow us Route 1 for 2 miles north from the traffic light in downtown Thomaston to Buttermilk Drive on your right after you pass the hulking Dragon Cement Plant. Follow Buttermilk Drive to the stop sign and make a right onto Buttermilk Lane. In 0.6 miles is a parking area on the right that overlooks the marsh. Informational kiosks recount the significance of the marsh habitat and detail some key bird species found here.

This site has seen increased visitation in recent years to the detriment of the sensitive habitat, and walking into the marsh itself is highly discouraged. While scoping from the parking area usually provides the most rewarding birding experience, I also enjoy walking the short nature trail. This path, built by Maine Department of Inland Fisheries and Wildlife volunteers, heads into the woods from the road just north of the parking area to a small observation deck at the back of the marsh. On the walk out to the deck, be alert for warblers and other migrant and breeding songbirds, especially in the tangle of alders as the path crosses a wetland. The deck itself is a good place to set up a scope to scan the salt pannes that are just beyond the view from the parking area, and which often host large numbers of "peeps," yellowlegs, and other shorebirds, as well as wading egrets and herons. This perspective can also help in observing ducks and wading birds downriver and "around the corner" from the parking area. Hunting raptors often perch in snags along this edge of the marsh to plot their next moves or to pluck their hapless prey, and can be close enough that you can tell which species of peep they are dining on.

The pannes are best birded on a rising tide, when birds are moving off the tidal flats. An important consideration when birding Weskeag, however, is that the parking area faces west—meaning that as the sun sets, you're looking right into it from that vantage point. So plan accordingly. Fortuitously, the pannes immediately in front of the parking area can be the most productive, but the larger wading birds are often at the back of the marsh. When scanning the back of the marsh, don't overlook the fence posts that border the edge of the woods, or the duck blind(s)—these structures are common perches for raptors and Belted Kingfishers.

The alder thickets and the overgrown (occasionally mown) areas around the parking area can also be quite birdy, hosting sparrows, Chestnut-sided Warblers, Eastern Bluebirds, and Alder Flycatchers.

Across the street from the nature trail is a tiny, cattail-lined pond that can be scanned from the roadside in just a few minutes. This little pocket of water has hosted Sora and Virginia Rail, as well as the occasional Wood Duck.

The Weskeag River flows under the road just south of the parking area, making that spot an easy put-in point for canoes or kayaks. Birding by boat can be a low-impact way to access the marsh, but you'll want to be mindful of tides. As you're driving, keep an eye on nearby power lines and fences, as American Kestrels regularly hunt the marsh's uplands.

An option to birding from the dangerous roadside edges (the shoulder is narrow, and traffic moves through here at a fast clip) is to walk or drive 0.1–0.2 miles farther south (from the parking area) along Buttermilk Lane to where you can walk out into one of the fields that overlook the marsh. Please be mindful of crops; these fields are occasionally leased to local farmers. Eastern Meadowlarks have been seen in the fields, and Bobolinks may nest here. In the right winter, the fields that surround the marsh are likely places to find a Snowy Owl.

RARITIES

Garganey, April 1999; Ruff, May 2016

SITE KX3 Thomaston Waterfront

TOWN Thomaston. DeLorme Map 8: A2. **SEASON** November–February, August–September. **VISITATION** 30 min. to 1 hr. No restroom facilities. ♿ **HIGHLIGHTS** Shorebirds and wading birds, including Snowy Egret and breeding Black-crowned Night-Heron; wintering waterfowl, including all three mergansers.

Whether you are scanning for feeding shorebirds or wintering waterbirds, this convenient loop offers a chance at a nice diversity of species. Although the clouds of shorebirds that used to frequent this area have diminished in recent years, numbers of Black-bellied and Semipalmated Plovers, Least and Semipalmated Sandpipers, and Greater and Lesser Yellowlegs are all common, and the occasional locally unusual species such as Hudsonian Godwit might appear.

DIRECTIONS

From the traffic light on US Route 1 in the center of downtown Thomaston turn left/south onto Knox Street and drive 0.4 miles to its intersection with Water Street. Make a left onto Water Street and then turn right in 0.2 miles at the sign for the **Thomaston Public Landing.** Park if you can for a good view of the St. George River. In cold weather, viewing of the river is possible without leaving the warmth of your car, although a scope is helpful for lower stretches of the river. You'll definitely want a scope for scanning this spot at low tide during fall migration to have any chance of identifying flocks of peeps that may land on the opposite shore. If the Slipway Restaurant adjacent to the public landing is open, I recommend a visit to this excellent seafood restaurant. In warm weather, bring your binoculars and sit out on the deck or pier and watch for ducks, herons, and Ospreys overhead and scan the trees carefully for the Black-crowned Night-Herons that nest nearby.

Leaving the Public Landing, turn right onto Water Street, pass the Lyman-Morse shipyard on your right, and bear left onto Knox Street. Take your first right onto Thatcher Street. Follow Thatcher Street, which becomes Fish Street, to **Mill River Park** on your right, just before a stop sign. This town-owned park, which borders Mill River where it joins the St. George, offers good space for parking and a path down to the water's edge for scanning the flats during migration in late summer into fall. This is probably the best publicly accessible place from which to adequately view the flats, which can be quite extensive at low tide. In May when the alewives are running, Double-crested Cormorants, Ospreys, gulls, and the occasional Bald Eagle frequent the waterways here, although the fishing is better—and thus the birds are more concentrated—farther up the St. George River (site KX1). The weedy thickets along the park's edges look like they might one fall day yield an Orange-crowned Warbler or a Dickcissel, so are worth a scan before you go, as well.

Upon leaving the park turn right onto Fish Street and follow it along the river back to US Route 1. If you turn right here and then take an almost immediate right onto Route 131, you're about 14 miles from the village of **Port Clyde**. Port Clyde features one of the three ferry services to Monhegan Island (see site L1), a premier birding destination described in the Lincoln County chapter. Whether or not you're headed to Monhegan, be sure to leave yourself some time to stop at **Marshall Point Light** (when you reach Port Clyde, follow signs from Route 131), a highly picturesque spot from which to check for seabirds, as well as migrants reorienting from Monhegan and other offshore islands first thing in the morning. In the summer, Common Eider, Black Guillemot, Laughing Gull, and the occasional Common Tern are expected, along with limited sea-watching. In the winter, scan for rafts of sea ducks, Common and Red-throated Loon, Horned and Red-necked Grebes, and Great Cormorant.

Mew Gull, August 2013

SITE KX4 Owls Head Area Loop

TOWN Owls Head. DeLorme Map 14 E4, and Map 8: A3–4.
SEASON November–March, May–June.   **VISITATION** 1–4 hrs. Owls Head State Park open 9 a.m.–sunset, outhouses available year-round. Birch Point State Park open 9 a.m.–sunset, restrooms available Memorial Day–Labor Day; may be accessed year-round or in off-hours by walking in from the gate.   **HIGHLIGHTS** Winter gulls (including Iceland, Glaucous, Bonaparte's, and the occasional Black-headed); Snowy Owl; Horned Lark; Snow Bunting; White-winged Crossbill; spring warblers and other songbird migrants.

This driving loop can be combined with a stop at Weskeag Marsh (site K2) for a good day's outing, especially in winter, when raptors may include Rough-legged Hawk and Snowy Owl; Northern Shrikes, white-winged gulls, a diversity of waterbirds, and, during irruptions, notable numbers of winter finches and frugivores can often be found. It's also incredibly scenic, adding pleasure to the loop at any season.

DIRECTIONS

Starting in downtown Rockland at the intersection of US Route 1/Main Street and Park Street (just past the Rite Aid), follow Route 73 south out of town for 1.9 miles. Turn left and follow signs to **Owls Head State Park** along North Shore Drive for 2.6 miles. At the town "center" you'll see the post office and Owls Head General Store. Turn left onto Main Street and then take your next left onto Lighthouse Road. Continue for half a mile to where the road ends at the state park.

From the parking lot follow the easy wooded path to the beach. Listen for crossbills in the spruces, especially in winter, as well as breeding birds typical of mixed woodlands in the summer, including Yellow-bellied Sapsucker and Swainson's Thrush. The beach itself is a great vantage point for sea watching year-round. In winter months it's also worth scanning the rocks for Purple Sandpiper.

When you head up to the scenic lighthouse from the parking lot, be sure to scan the inlet to the right. A variety of winter sea ducks can congregate here, including all three scoters, Common Eider, Long-tailed Duck, and Common Goldeneye; we once spotted a Harlequin Duck here. From the height of the lighthouse itself, looking out into more open waters, you may spot alcids such as Black Guillemot and Razorbill, along with Black-legged Kittiwake.

As you work your way back to the village, a left turn on Main Street (instead of a right to take you back to North Shore Road) will take you to **Owls Head Harbor**. The beaches and buildings here are worth a careful scan in the winter, as a variety of gulls congregate here, attracted by the lobster pound visible beyond the northernmost stretch of beach. The lobster pound and surrounding wharves are private property, but you can scan them well enough from the beach just north of the public parking area. One Christmas Day we were fortunate enough to find seven gull species here: Herring, Ring-billed, Great Black-backed, Bonaparte's, Iceland, Glaucous, and Black-headed. Numbers of white-winged gulls (Iceland and Glaucous) found here in the winter are greater than in any other location in the Midcoast.

On your way back to North Shore Road, a stop at the locally popular Owls Head General Store is highly recommended. From there turn left onto South Shore Drive and follow it 2.4 miles to the intersection with Ash Point Drive. The **Knox County Regional Airport** will be directly in front of you. In winter the airport is a good place to look for Snowy and occasional Short-eared Owls, Snow Bunting, and Horned Lark.

Over the course of this loop, scan the runways and open space from all angles. Begin by making a left onto Ash Point Drive. In 0.4 miles make a right onto Dublin Road. Follow Dublin Road for 0.8 miles to Ballyhac Road on the left. Look for the sign to **Birch Point State Park**. Follow Ballyhac Road for 0.7 miles to the park entrance. If the gate is closed you can park outside and walk in, about 0.4 miles through mixed spruce forest to the parking lot and beach. Scanning from the beach for sea ducks has turned up species similar to those seen from Owls Head State Park, and during the 1997 Christmas Bird Count we even turned up a drake King Eider among the rafts of Common Eiders.

Return to Dublin Road, make a left, and continue for 1.3 miles to Route 73. Make a left into the parking lot for the boat launch, opposite the 'Keag Store. Make a quick stop to scan the waters on both sides of the road at the mouth of the Weskeag River, which, depending on the tide, can yield a surprising number of ducks.

Afterward, follow Route 73 North for 2 miles (scanning the fields and scrub as you go) to its intersection with North Shore Road to complete your loop. To continue birding, I often backtrack on Route 73 for 1.3 miles to a right onto Buttermilk Lane. In 1.6 miles you'll cross the Weskeag River again (much narrower at this point), and you'll see the parking area from which to scan the marsh on your left, as described in site KX2.

RARITIES

King Eider, December 1997 (Birch Point State Park); Clark's Grebe, March 2005 (Owls Head State Park—first state record); Mew Gull, January–March 2016 (Owls Head Harbor); Western Grebe, February 2016 (Owls Head Harbor)

SITE KX5 Rockland Breakwater

TOWN Rockland. DeLorme Map 14: E4. SEASON All year, but especially December–February. VISITATION 1–2 hrs. Round-trip walk to the lighthouse at the end of the breakwater and back is 2 miles. Parking for the breakwater at Lighthouse Park at the end of Samoset Road is open during daylight hours year-round. No restroom facilities. HIGHLIGHTS Sea ducks, including all three scoters, Long-tailed Duck, Common Goldeneye; Horned and Red-necked Grebes; Purple Sandpiper; gulls including Bonaparte's, Laughing, Lesser Black-backed and Black-legged Kittiwake; alcid potential; Snowy Owl.

Walking the Rockland breakwater, especially if you bring along a spotting scope, provides the unique opportunity to observe birds way out in Rockland's outer harbor without leaving land. While relatively flat, the breakwater is composed of granite blocks with uneven, often wet surfaces and large gaps, and is extremely exposed to the elements, including wind and high surf (people have died from being struck by lightning here). So depending on the weather and other conditions, this may not be an easy walk. During high tides and storms, parts of the breakwater may be entirely underwater, and in frigid stretches may be fully encased in treacherous ice. In the summer the breakwater can be quite crowded with sightseers and fishermen, as well. So my favorite time of year to bird here is late fall into early winter, when small flocks of Purple Sandpipers may be found foraging at surf's edge on the rocks along the breakwater's length, loons have returned to ocean waters, and sea ducks have begun to show up from their northern breeding grounds. But walking the length of this stone jetty is an invigorating, scenic outing in any season, and you never know what you might turn up.

DIRECTIONS

From the intersection of US Route 1 and Route 17 (Maverick Street) in Rockland (the "McDonald's intersection" just north of downtown), travel north on Route 1 for 0.4 miles to the traffic light. Turn right at the light onto Waldo Avenue. Make a quick stop at **Littlefield Baptist Church** on this corner. On a falling tide, gulls congregate on the exposed shore behind the church and have included Lesser Black-backed, Bonaparte's, and Black-headed. (On one memorable Christmas count, we spotted a Snowy Owl on the church roof!) Continue on Waldo Avenue for 0.4 miles and take the first right onto Samoset Road, just before the entrance to the Samoset Resort.

Samoset Road dead-ends at the end of Jameson Point, at Lighthouse Park and a small parking area. The path out to the base of the breakwater skirts the top of a small beach; the path may be completely buried in a snowy winter, in which case you can get there via the beach itself.

Start scanning the water from the benches in Lighthouse Park, and if the small beach is free of human activity, be sure to give it a close look, too: American Pipits sometimes stop over during fall migration, as well as the occasional shorebird. If the tide is low, the rocks on the far side of the breakwater often host a lounging harbor seal or two, as well. Ducks may also be sheltering in the "cove" between the beach and the breakwater.

The breakwater is narrow enough that you can bird both sides without much effort. Be looking ahead for birds perched on the breakwater itself—in winter, this may include a Great Cormorant or an unusual gull—and for Purple Sandpipers, typically present from November through March, flushing along the edges. While Black Guillemots may frequently be observed feeding at very close range, scanning out to sea with a scope from late summer through the winter may also bring Razorbills and Black-legged Kittiwakes into view. Rarely, single Thick-billed Murres have been seen from the breakwater. Horned and Red-necked Grebes are expected in winter, along with a wide variety of ducks: from the Mallards and American Black Ducks that hug the shore, to diving Common Eider, Bufflehead, Common Goldeneye, Red-breasted Merganser, and talkative Long-tailed Duck. Bonaparte's Gulls may fly by; other winter visitor gulls seen in Rockland Harbor include Iceland,

Lesser Black-backed (rare), and Black-headed (very rare). In summer, watch for Laughing Gulls and Common Terns.

The Samoset Resort, which borders the breakwater, features an eighteen-hole golf course, which should not be overlooked for its birding potential. Hundreds of Canada Geese linger on the greens through the winter, and the occasional Snow Goose can be found among them (and once, a Ross's Goose!). One Christmas Bird Count even turned up a Lapland Longspur in a sand trap. Another year, a Lesser Scaup and some Wood Ducks were hanging out in the unfrozen golf course ponds. In irruption years, one or more Snowy Owls have visited the tundra-like space of the golf course and have been observed on the breakwater itself. And on one lucky occasion while I was trying to track down a reported Snowy Owl, I was fortunate enough to catch sight of a Short-eared Owl instead as it flew in over the water to land on the breakwater.

Leaving the breakwater, turn right from Samoset Road onto Warrenton Road. In a mile you'll see **Clam Cove** on your right, worth a quick stop in winter to scan the gulls and ducks. Black-headed Gull has been seen here more than once, along with a good variety of winter ducks. Just beyond this point you will reconnect with Route 1 in Rockport.

RARITIES

Ross's Goose, February 2013; Yellow-throated Warbler, December 2015

SITE KX6 Vinalhaven Island (and Ferry)

TOWN Vinalhaven. DeLorme Map 9: A1–2. **SEASON** All year.
VISITATION Several hours, as perhaps dictated by the ferry schedule. There's a grocery store in the downtown area and other options for food, depending on the season. Public restrooms are available in the ferry terminal and downtown in the town parking lot on Main Street. Check at the Tidewater Motel at 15 Main Street for bicycle rentals. **HIGHLIGHTS** Harlequin Duck, Great Cormorant, Purple Sandpiper, white-winged gulls and alcids in winter; owls including Long-eared; migrating songbirds spring and fall; crossbills in irruption years. Red-billed Tropicbird at Seal Island NWR.

Seven miles out in the heart of Penobscot Bay, scenic Vinalhaven Island is one of the most populous of Maine's inhabited offshore islands and features a lively year-round community with an active fishing fleet. A state-run ferry makes the trip between Rockland and Vinalhaven six times a day all year, and that eighty minutes can in itself provide an entertaining birding experience. A birder friend who was lured to move to the island by reports of Dovekies being seen regularly from the ferry has told me that while that never happens, what he *has* seen from the ferry and on the island more than makes up for it.

The island can be a great migrant and vagrant trap. Varied Thrush and Townsend's Solitaire have both been spotted there in late fall, and unusual Maine visitors such as Greater White-fronted Goose, Cackling Goose, Cattle Egret, Red-headed Woodpecker, and Hooded Warbler have turned up on occasion during migration.

DIRECTIONS

The Maine State Ferry Terminal is just off US Route 1/North Main Street in Rockland, on the harbor just north of downtown. Check the ferry schedule for times and prices. If you are thinking of bringing a car, plan on arriving at least one hour before desired departure time (even earlier in summer) to get your vehicle in line. Because bringing a car to the island can be a serious challenge and is not necessary to enjoy a good day's birding there, the following directions will assume you are on foot or on a bicycle.

BIRDING FROM THE FERRY

The two trips earliest in the day tend to be the most productive, bird-wise. Because the ferry is heading toward the rising sun, cloudy, overcast days make for better observation conditions as well. The ferry ride can be very productive for seabirds, ducks, and raptors, especially in winter.

In Rockland Harbor in late fall through early spring an observer can see good numbers of Common Eider and Long-tailed Duck, as well as other sea ducks, Common Loon, Horned and Red-necked Grebes, and Black Guillemot. Beyond the breakwater (made of Vinalhaven granite) and lighthouse to the north (described in KX5), the ride enters the open waters of western Penobscot Bay. In winter there can be impressive numbers of Common Eider, Long-tailed Duck, Common Loon, Black-legged Kittiwake, Bonaparte's Gull, and Black Guillemot, with lesser numbers of Northern Gannet and Razorbill. In summer Common Terns are indeed common. Wilson's Storm-Petrels are abundant some years, and the occasional Parasitic Jaeger or group of Red-necked Phalaropes may also be spotted.

After crossing the bay the ferry ride works its way through several islands and ledges before cutting between Leadbetter and Lawry's Islands, an area called the Narrows. In winter, check the ledges leading up to the Narrows for Great Cormorants, Purple Sandpipers, Bald Eagles, and Snowy Owls. In spring scan for harbor seals with pups. Common Terns linger on the ledges with young in the summer.

Once past the Narrows the ferry enters Hurricane Sound, which can be productive for Surf Scoter, Red-necked Grebe, Northern Gannet, Osprey, Bald Eagle, Purple Sandpiper, and Parasitic Jaeger.

The last stretch from Hurricane Sound into Carver's Harbor is good for Surf Scoter, Long-tailed Duck, Bufflehead, and Purple Sandpiper in the winter, Common Eider year-round, and Common Tern in the summer. In the harbor check the boats and piers for Glaucous and Iceland Gulls.

LANE'S ISLAND PRESERVE

From the ferry terminal follow Main Street to the right and through town for half a mile. Turn right onto Water Street, which soon merges into Atlantic Avenue, and continue 0.3 miles to the Lane's Island Bridge. On your way to the bridge, as you walk through town, check buildings and piers for white-winged gulls and scan the harbor for seabirds. In winter, sea ducks, Iceland and Glaucous Gulls, and Thick-billed Murre are seen regularly in the harbor.

The bridges in town provide views of Carver's Pond, a brackish tidal pond connected to Carver's Harbor that is worth a good scan any time of year. Good numbers of Hooded Merganser, Bufflehead, Red-breasted Merganser, and Common Goldeneye spend much of the late fall and winter in the pond. Greater White-fronted Goose and Cackling Goose have both been seen in the pond, and a Barrow's Goldeneye or two turn up most winters.

As you follow Water Street, watch for **Armbrust Hill Town Park** on the hill to your left, a good place to swing by during migration to look for warblers, including rarities.

When you reach the Lane's Island Bridge, scan both sides for seabirds. Continue 0.2 miles to the Lane's Island Preserve entrance on the left. The forty-five-acre preserve is owned by the Nature Conservancy. While walking in on the preserve driveway, also check the marsh on either side for American Bittern, Great Blue Heron, Solitary Sandpiper, Greater and Lesser Yellowlegs, and Marsh Wren. Check the trees around the parking area as well: Long-eared Owls roost in the area most falls/winters.

From the parking area, bird your way to the field. American Woodcock use this area to do their wonderful aerial displays, with several male woodcocks sometimes displaying on a given night (late March/April). From the field scan the water for sea ducks, shorebirds (along the wrack line), and seabirds. Ospreys nest nearby, and Harlequin Ducks have been seen in this cove after big storms. Scan tree and shrub tops in the winter for Northern Shrike.

The *Rosa rugosa* bushes along the beach are good for sparrows—all the regulars, plus Nelson's and "Ipswich" Savannah. Alder Flycatchers, Eastern Phoebes, and Yellow-rumped Warblers sally and snag bugs from low perches over the washed-up seaweed.

Lane's Island has a network of trails well worth exploring. Past the beach the trail splits. Bear right here, away from the water, and follow the trail up a small hill—scanning the bayberry bushes and the trees for birds—to the set of trees at the highest point of the preserve: the best spot on Vinalhaven for sea watching. With a scope scan the ledges for Great Cormorant, Purple Sandpiper, and Peregrine Falcon, and scan the water for seabirds. Dovekie, Thick-billed Murre, and Razorbill have all been seen from this spot in winter, and Black Guillemot is resident, as well as Northern Gannet, Sooty Shearwater, and Great Shearwater. In early spring significant numbers of migrating waterfowl pass Lane's, including all three scoters, Red-breasted Merganser, Harlequin Duck, and Brant.

From this high point continue on the trail to where it joins with the shoreline loop. Follow the shoreline loop back to the main field.

If you're staying on Vinalhaven overnight, Lane's Island can be a great place to visit at dusk. Short-eared, Long-eared, Great Horned, Saw-whet, and Snowy Owls have all been seen here.

STATE BEACH

If you've brought along a bike or car and a spotting scope, State Beach is always worth a visit. From the ferry terminal bear right onto Main Street and travel 2.7 miles to a fork (Main Street becomes Pequot Road after 0.9 miles). Take the right fork, Poole's Hill Road, follow 0.1 miles, then turn right onto State Beach Road. After 0.3 miles the road splits into three: the right and middle options are two ends of a small (0.1 mile) loop, and the left option continues to State Beach.

We'll begin with the small loop. Follow the right option (Breakers Road) to a causeway, which is a private road that breaks off to the right. Park before the causeway, leaving enough space for cars to pass. Low-tide mudflats to the right of the causeway can be very productive for shorebirds in July–August; Marbled Godwit has made a rare appearance. Osprey and Merlin have nested nearby. Scan the waters for sea ducks and seabirds.

Continue around the loop and turn right to continue to State Beach. The road can be good for warblers in migration: Tennessee and Mourning Warblers are standouts from this area.

From the parking lot head toward the water, scanning the shoreline for shorebirds and waders during fall migration. All the shorebirds mentioned above may also be seen here. Buff-breasted Sandpiper, Long-billed Dowitcher, and Sanderling have been seen along this shoreline as well. Scan the waters in winter.

Scope the islands and ledges. The closest island with a small shack on it, Greer Island, is worth checking for raptors in migration and Rough-legged Hawks in winter. At low tide a sandbar and ledge are exposed and can be good for shorebirds. Ruddy Turnstone and Whimbrel have both been seen there. Farther in the distance is Sheep Island, with a large house on top. With a scope scan the few boulders and treetops on that island for Rough-legged Hawks (yearly) and Snowy Owls in winter.

From here walk the dirt road between the edge of the beach and the marsh on the left. The marsh and the road itself can be good for sparrows in fall. The dirt road ends at a turnaround with grasses and Fish House Cove to your left, and a thin isthmus to your right (underwater at high tide) that connects to a small forested island. Nelson's Sparrows nest in the grasses and marsh by the turnaround, and Horned Lark, Snow Bunting, and Lapland Longspur are seen among the rocks and grasses along the isthmus in winter. White-rumped Sandpipers are sighted here yearly during fall migration.

In fall/winter Fish House Cove to the left can host many grebes, with more than a hundred Red-necked Grebes and small numbers of Horned Grebes not uncommon in November. At high tide the ledge in Fish House Cove can host roosting shorebirds in migration, including American Golden-Plover in fall.

If the tide permits, cross the isthmus and follow the trail across the forested island to a viewing area that faces Isle au Haut to the east. The small tidal pond at the island's edge can be good for Solitary Sandpipers, and the grasses along the shore can host sparrows, including annual Ipswich Sparrows. With a scope scan the waters of eastern Penobscot Bay for scoters and other common sea ducks and Harlequin Ducks in winter, Common and Red-throated Loons,

"Troppy" the famous Red-billed Tropicbird of Seal Island. © Derek Lovitch

Red-necked Grebe, Northern Gannet, Black-legged Kittiwake, Parasitic Jaeger, and Razorbill. Nearby ledges host Purple Sandpiper and Great Cormorant from late fall through early spring.

For a current ferry schedule and fares see http://maine.gov/mdot/ferry /vinalhaven/.

RARITIES

Red-billed Tropicbird (an annual summer visitor to nearby Seal Island NWR since 2005); Townsend's Solitaire, November 2007; Black-browed Albatross, July 2009 (offshore); Hooded Warbler, April 2010; Varied Thrush, March 2015

Note: For those interested in seeing the Red-billed Tropicbird that has been spending its summers within the tern colony at Seal Island NWR, there is no easy or cheap way to do it. While a few organized tours are arranged (such as Freeport Wild Bird Supply's "Birding by Schooner" tour), the best way to look for the bird is to hire John Drury for a private charter, which leaves from Vinalhaven Island. See www.maineseabirdtours.com for more information and to make arrangements. It's also a good way to see Great Cormorants, alcids, terns, and sometimes Manx Shearwaters.

KNOX COUNTY

237

SITE KX7 Chickawaukie Lake and Maces Pond

TOWNS Rockland/Rockport. DeLorme Map 14: E3. **SEASON** October to freeze-up. **VISITATION** 30 min. to 1 hr. Restroom facilities open only in summer. & **HIGHLIGHTS** Variety of ducks; American Coot; resident Bald Eagles.

Bounded on one side by busy Route 17, Chickawaukie Lake might seem like an unprepossessing spot for finding birds. But between the season of water skiers and that of ice-fishing shacks, until it freezes over, this little water body can host some interesting ducks and other waterfowl and is always worth a careful look in fall. Just north of "Chickie," also bounded on one side by Route 17, tiny, undeveloped Maces Pond can also offer up some surprises in the right season.

DIRECTIONS

From the intersection of US Route 1 and Route 17 (Maverick Street) in Rockland (the "McDonald's intersection" just north of downtown) follow Route 17 North for 1.75 miles to the parking lot for this city-owned park on the southwest shore of the lake. (Try to scan the Rockland Golf Course on your right as you pass; gulls hanging out on the greens have more than once included Lesser Black-backed.) In fall and winter, dozens of resident Mallards crowd near an inlet stream beyond the park facilities building (not open after Labor Day), and the flock sometimes includes other species such as American Wigeon or American Black Duck.

You'll have the best luck, though, scoping from the shore. For reasons that probably have something to do with water flow, ducks tend to group loosely in the same general area at this end of the lake—usually you can see them by looking directly out from this spot all the way to the opposite shore. It's worth taking your time here, as some waterfowl may at first be hidden from view in a small cove to your right. Regularly occurring ducks here include Common Goldeneye, Bufflehead, Ruddy Duck, Lesser and Greater Scaup, and Ring-necked Duck. Gulls, too, occasionally including Bonaparte's Gull, also congregate in this spot. Pied-billed Grebe is a late fall regular. And congregations of American Coots can approach the dramatic: one Christmas Bird Count yielded a high count of over 630 birds.

As you'd expect, all these waterbirds bobbing around a small lake bring out the predators, too. Bald Eagles and Red-tailed Hawks, year-round neighborhood residents, often perch lakeside to keep a close eye on the coots (or can be seen plucking their freshly caught lunch onshore). And when the lake freezes over and ice fishermen scatter across its surface, you might see up to a dozen eagles at once out on the ice scavenging unwanted fish.

The wet, scrubby habitat bordering the park and across the street should be scanned before you leave. Common Redpoll and American Tree Sparrow can turn up here, and we've observed on occasion a teed-up Northern Shrike with its own interest in the songbirds.

The shoulder along the lakeshore is very narrow, so don't be tempted to pull over along Route 17 north of the public park until you reach the pull-out near the lake's north end. This is the only other safe public spot for observation of the lake by scope.

From the park, drive 2.25 miles north on Route 17 to **Maces Pond**, on your left. There is space for several cars to park here, either in front of the wooded entrance to the Sides Preserve or along the very wide shoulder adjacent to the guardrail. In spring, this is a popular fishing spot, as evidenced by the well-worn, usually trash-strewn path leading from the guardrail to an ideal spot at the water's edge on which to set up a scope. The same species of ducks found on "Chickie" can often be found here, although they are usually easier to see here because the pond is so much smaller.

The wooded property to the left of this spot is the eight-acre **Sides Preserve** owned by Coastal Mountains Land Trust. The preserve features a short trail that follows the edge of the pond and loops back around near a small, historic cemetery. In spring I have been surprised more than once to find myself surrounded by pockets of warblers here. Both Maces Pond and Chickawaukie also see regular Osprey activity in the summer and host nesting Common Loons.

RARITIES

Tufted Duck, December 1996 and December 1998 (Chickawaukie), November 1999 (Maces Pond)

SITE KX8 Clarry Hill

TOWN Union. DeLorme Map 1: D1. **SEASON** September–October, November–June. **VISITATION** 1–3 hrs. No restroom facilities. Visiting is not recommended during blueberry harvest season (July–August) or during times of field management (field burning and spraying, etc.).

HIGHLIGHTS Fall raptor migration; Snowy Owl; Northern Shrike; Horned Lark; breeding Vesper Sparrow.

With its open fields offering panoramic views to the north and east, Clarry Hill is a great location for watching hawks during fall raptor migration (primarily September into October). In recent years an average of almost twelve thousand raptors have been seen each season by a local hawk watcher, predominately Broad-winged Hawks, but also good numbers of Sharp-shinned Hawk, Turkey Vulture, Red-tailed Hawk, Osprey, Bald Eagle, American Kestrel, as well as Cooper's Hawk, Northern Harrier, Red-shouldered Hawk, Merlin, and Peregrine Falcon. Rough-legged Hawk and Golden Eagle have also been spotted.

Breeding birds in the open fields formerly included Upland Sandpiper but are now limited to Vesper and Savannah Sparrow and, potentially, American Kestrel. Local Bald Eagles may be seen year-round. In the winter, fields may host flocks of Snow Buntings and Horned Larks, in addition to the occasional Snowy Owl, and sometimes attract hunting Rough-legged Hawks or lingering Northern Harriers, so keep your eyes open for hovering hawks. Check the treetops along the road for a Northern Shrike looking for its next meal in the fields below.

Captive game birds such as Ring-necked Pheasant are often released on the hill for hunting, so don't be surprised if one struts across your path. Unfortunately, you'll have to head to Monhegan to "count" one!

DIRECTIONS

From the intersection of us Route 1 and Route 17 (Maverick Street) in Rockland (the "McDonald's intersection") head north on Route 1A/17. Follow Route 17 for 15 miles to Clarry Hill Road, on the left north of Union village. Follow Clarry Hill Road for 2 miles to Elmer Hart Lane, a dirt road on your right. Proceed up the dirt road to the small parking area in front of the Medomak Valley Land Trust kiosk and park only here; do not drive up the road past this point. Much of Clarry Hill is privately owned, and the blueberry fields on either side of the dirt road are managed commercially.

From this point proceed on foot to the summit, scanning the fields on both sides of the road as you go. If you're visiting during fall migration, you will want to periodically scan the sky as well, especially from the summit, which offers a 360-degree view of the surrounding countryside, the perfect vantage point to watch hawks progress along the ridgelines on their way south. Please stay out of the fields and respect the landowner's signs, which make it very clear where to go no farther at the summit and elsewhere.

After lunch at the Badger Café in Union village, a visit to nearby Sweetgrass Winery and Distillery for a tasting is highly recommended.

RARITIES

Golden Eagle has been consistently reported in recent years during fall migration.

For a trail map, visit the website of the Medomak Valley Land Trust and look under "Protected" on the toolbar.

SITE KX9 Appleton Ridge to the Gibson Preserve

TOWNS Appleton and Searsmont. DeLorme Map 14: B–C1–2.
SEASON April–June, September–October.   **VISITATION** 1–2 hrs., depending on stops. No restroom facilities. Appleton Ridge Road is a public road, the paved portion of which is open year-round. One dirt section is closed in winter. Be mindful of private property, including commercial blueberry fields, when stopping to observe birds from the road.
HIGHLIGHTS Northern Harrier; Upland Sandpiper; American Woodcock; American Kestrel; Vesper Sparrow; migrant passerines.

The 124-acre Gibson Preserve was donated to Georges River Land Trust in 1999 by Charles Dana Gibson and Elizabeth Gibson. This forested property, which is managed for its wildlife habitat, boasts 1.25 miles of very scenic frontage on the St. George River, along with several miles of trail on either side of the river. The directions below guide you to the more visited and easily accessed of the two trailheads, on the east side of the river. (The two sets of trails do not as yet cross the river or connect.)

DIRECTIONS

From the intersection of US Route 1 and Route 90 in Rockport, head west on Route 90 for 2.7 miles to its intersection with Route 17 in West Rockport. Follow Route 17 for 8.7 miles, then turn right onto to Route 131 East. In 3.25 miles turn left onto Route 105 and follow it for just over a mile to Appleton

Ridge Road. Turn right to follow the ridge for almost 7 miles before it reconnects with Route 131. A portion of the dirt road between Town Hill Road and West Appleton Road is closed November 1 through May 1.

On your way up to the ridge in early spring be sure to check the St. George River where it flows close to Route 131 at the outflow of Sennebec Pond. After ice-out, Wood Ducks and other waterfowl may be found congregating in this area, which is also a noted local fly-fishing spot. American Woodcocks can be seen displaying here at dusk, especially from late March through early May.

Approaching the Gibson Preserve via **Appleton Ridge Road** is worth the detour, especially in spring, for the opportunity to scan the blueberry fields on both sides of the road. Raptors, especially Northern Harrier and American Kestrel, are commonly seen, as well as Killdeer, Eastern Bluebird, and Bobolink (more typically in the non-blueberry fields).

In winter, watch fields for flocks of Snow Buntings and Horned Larks. Upland Sandpipers and Vesper Sparrows have historically bred in nearby blueberry fields, but lack of good public access into these fields beyond the road have prevented similar observations here. And even when bird sightings are few, the road offers spectacular views east of the river valley and the Camden Hills beyond.

From the intersection of Appleton Ridge Road and Route 131 follow Route 131 North (left) about 0.5 miles to its intersection with Route 173 just outside Searsmont village. Turn left onto Route 173/Woodmans Mill Road and head west for about 3 miles to the **Gibson Preserve.** You'll see the preserve sign just before the parking area at the edge of a field on the left.

Follow the trail on a mown path across the field and into the woods. The trail makes two loops that skirt a private residence. Please stay on the trail in the vicinity of this private property.

Much of this very scenic and easygoing trail follows the river (Alder Flycatchers). In late spring the trail wends through big patches of flowering bunchberry and other wildflowers, as well as a very pretty stretch of more open woods appropriately called the Fern Garden. Various butterflies and clouds of ebony jewelwing damselflies flit about brightly in season. Even when birds are scarce, the preserve is worth a visit to simply enjoy the natural beauty of its riparian forest.

Along with typical species you would expect to find in a mixed forest like this, such as Blue-headed and Red-eyed Vireos, Hermit Thrush, and Veery, warblers you might typically see or hear along the length of the trail include Ovenbird, Chestnut-sided, Magnolia, Black-throated Blue, Blackburnian, and Nashville. Listen also for Winter Wren and, in spring, the thrumming wing beats of Ruffed Grouse. Holes in many of the trees bear evidence of the diversity of woodpeckers on the preserve, including Pileated and Yellow-bellied Sapsucker.

Additional trails that explore the woods on the other side of the river are accessible off Ripley Corner Road (the sign says Ripley Road), off Route 173 about 1.2 miles east of the trailhead described above. Directions to this trailhead and additional information about the preserve, including a link to a downloadable trail map, can be found at the website of the Georges River Land Trust at www.georgesriver.org/gibson-preserve/.

SITE KX10 Beech Hill Preserve

TOWN Rockport. DeLorme Map 14: E3.   SEASON All year.
VISITATION 1–3 hrs. No restroom facilities (although sometimes in summer there's a portable toilet at the summit). Please follow preserve guidelines posted at the trailhead. Hunting is allowed in the preserve's forested areas, so wearing orange is encouraged during hunting season.
HIGHLIGHTS Northern Harrier; American Woodcock; American Kestrel; Eastern Bluebird; spring and fall warblers; Field Sparrow; Eastern Towhee.

This 295-acre preserve, owned by Coastal Mountains Land Trust, features almost seventy acres of open fields, about twenty acres of which are managed as a commercial, organic blueberry farm. Maintaining the fields for the farm serves the dual purpose of also ensuring their continuity as increasingly rare bird habitat for such species as Savannah Sparrow, Northern Harrier, and American Kestrel. While they don't breed there, Upland Sandpipers have been regularly observed stopping over in the fields during spring migration. Tree Swallows and Eastern Bluebirds inhabit nest boxes on the field edges.

The shrubby and wooded edges of the fields teem with Eastern Towhees, which can be heard singing from every corner of the preserve in season, and also host a growing population of Field Sparrows. Moist alder thickets serve as the breeding grounds of American Woodcock, which can be heard displaying each spring. Wild Turkeys abound. The deciduous forest surrounding the fields is home to Black-billed Cuckoo, Barred Owl, Wood Thrush, Veery, and Scarlet Tanager, among many others.

More than twenty species of warbler have been observed on the hill, many as breeding birds, including some species that are uncommon in the area, including Prairie and Tennessee Warblers, and rarely, Yellow-breasted Chat. The winter fields see flocks of Eastern Bluebirds, Horned Larks, Snow Buntings, and the occasional Northern Shrike and Snowy Owl. The land trust has tallied more than 130 species on the preserve; a detailed checklist is available via its website.

DIRECTIONS

From US Route 1 in Rockport, 0.3 miles south of the intersection of Routes 1 and 90 (directly across from the Hoboken Gardens nursery), turn right onto Beech Hill Road. (Grab a sweet treat or a sandwich for the trail at nearby Three Dogs Café.) Follow Beech Hill Road for 1.6 miles to the parking area on the left. If you reach South Street, you've just missed it.

You can begin actively birding the preserve as soon as you get out of your car, as the woods around the parking area can be quite lively with birds, including Pileated Woodpecker and American Redstart. Eastern Towhees and Gray Catbirds abound in the stand of young trees crossed by the trail before it emerges into open field. At this point the trail joins the old farm road to the summit, with regenerating woods to your left and fields to your right. Be listening also for Alder Flycatcher, Tree Swallow, Eastern Bluebird, Prairie Warbler (which has attempted to breed on the preserve in the past), and Field Sparrow. This is a good spot to stand at dusk in spring to listen for displaying American Woodcocks. In winter, start scanning the treetops from here on for potential Northern Shrikes. As the view opens up on either side of the trail, watch for a Northern Harrier or an American Kestrel hovering over the fields; harriers visit the hill almost year-round. Rarely, Short-eared Owls have also been seen here.

The trail is an easy climb of about three-quarters of a mile to the summit. It can be very wet and muddy in spring; you will want waterproof footwear. Be respectful of the farm by staying on the trail and out of the blueberry fields, which are commercially harvested by the land trust to support stewardship of the preserve. During the harvest, fresh, organic berries are available for purchase at the land trust's farm stand located right in the parking lot, so

Snowy Owl and Indian Island Light from Beech Hill Preserve. © Brian Willson

you'll want to time summer visits for late July–mid-August to take advantage of this delicious bounty.

Savannah Sparrows rule the fields as you climb the hill. In spring and summer you can hear dozens of them on all sides, in addition to several Field Sparrows. At the top of the hill, a spectacular vista of Penobscot Bay and beyond, all the way to Mount Desert Island, opens before you. The summit also features a sod-roofed stone hut that is over a hundred years old. During summer months the hut is open to the public two days each month. Savannah Sparrows also like the hut, perching to sing from its stone walls, and Eastern Phoebe and Mourning Dove have nested in its eaves and stonework.

At the summit, especially during migration in September–October, watch for hawks. In addition to harriers and kestrels, other raptors in the neighborhood include Northern Goshawk and Bald Eagle. The open summit and the panoramic views enable good looks at birds passing over the hill. Rough-legged Hawk may be seen in late fall to winter. Other unusual flyovers have included Glossy Ibis and Black Vulture.

From here another trail continues for about a mile, down the backside of the hill along the forested edge of the fields and through the woods to another parking area on Rockville Street. This parking area is several miles from the Beech Hill Road parking area, so a loop by road is not recommended. This trail does, however, make a loop just before it reaches the second parking area, so you can hike down and back and then return via the original trail to your car. This is my preference, as the woods on the other side of the hill can produce species you didn't see in the more open habitat on the way up, including Ruffed Grouse, Veery, Wood Thrush, Black-throated Blue Warbler, Scarlet Tanager, and Rose-breasted Grosbeak.

Detailed information on the preserve can be found on the Coastal Mountains Land Trust's website, www.coastalmountains.org/conserved_lands /preserves/beech_hill.html. A bird checklist can be found at http://www .coastalmountains.org/downloads/Beech%20Hill%20Bird%20Brochure.pdf.

SITE KX11 Merryspring Nature Center

TOWN Camden. DeLorme Map 14: D3–4. SEASON Year-round, but especially **April–June**. VISITATION 1–3 hrs. Open during daylight hours. Restrooms in nature center when open. HIGHLIGHTS American Woodcock; spring warbler migration.

This sixty-six-acre nature park and garden education center, tucked away just outside downtown Camden, offers a variety of habitats in a relatively small space: lawn, gardens, open field, mixed deciduous forest including an overgrown arboretum, pine groves, wetlands, a vernal pool, and a brushy power-line corridor. Charismatic species such as Barred Owl, Pileated Woodpecker, and Wild Turkey are resident. Spring kicks off with drumming Ruffed Grouse and displaying American Woodcock. Warbler waves may bring great numbers and diversity, including such unusual species for the area as Cape May and Prairie Warblers, as well as more expected species that may breed here: Chestnut-sided, Blackburnian, Nashville, Yellow, Black-throated Blue, and dozens of Black-throated Greens and Ovenbirds in the woods. Bobolinks have been seen in the central field in the past, although in recent years this area was overrun by off-leash dogs. Now that dogs have been banned, birding is more enjoyable and productive.

DIRECTIONS

From the traffic light on the Rockport/Camden town line (at the Hannaford supermarket), travel north on US Route 1 and take your first left onto Conway Road, just in front of the Subway restaurant. Follow it to the parking lot at the end of the cul-de-sac and start listening for birds as soon as you get out of your car; sometimes the parking area can be the busiest spot of the day.

In season the gardens and trees around the education center commonly host Great-crested Flycatcher, White-throated Sparrow, and Purple Finch, among others. The surrounding woods resound with birdsong on a typical spring morning—up to eighteen or more species of warbler and three or four species of thrushes.

The center's trail system enables access to just about anywhere you want to explore. Trail 1, for example, circumnavigates the park perimeter, mostly through forest and across the power-line corridor. Other trails circle the fields, passing old apple trees, wooded borders, and an experimental American chestnut grove; lead to the park's boundary along a young pine grove and wet agricultural field bottomlands; and wind through the arboretum past a vernal pool. The power-line corridor can be hiked as well, with a trail on the south side dipping down through juniper thickets and into wet patches of alders where woodcocks sky-dance in early spring.

Now that the center is no longer a dog park, the Merryspring staff plan to restore the arboretum and fields to their former productivity as wildlife habitat. This will only improve future birding potential for this pretty little park.

RARITIES

Golden-winged Warbler, May 2005

Download a park trail map at the Merryspring Nature Center's website at http://www.merryspring.org.

SITE KX12 Camden Harbor

TOWN Camden. DeLorme Map 14: D4. **SEASON** November–May.
VISITATION 30 min. to 1 hr. Public restrooms are nearby at the Camden
Public Landing. **HIGHLIGHTS** Winter waterfowl.

DIRECTIONS

Camden Harbor can be best observed from **Harbor Park** at the head of the
harbor. This town-owned park, which includes the grounds surrounding the
Camden Public Library, can be easily accessed by foot from most places in
downtown Camden. Public parking (most of which is two-hour parking) is
available at the public landing and throughout town. The park itself borders
Main Street/Route 1 and Atlantic Avenue and can be accessed by paved paths
from either street. The paths traversing this little park can be quite slippery
in winter, especially those along the seawall where the Megunticook River
flows over human-made and natural waterfalls to join the harbor.

Resident Mallards and domestic mixed-breed ducks frequent this area at all
times of year, where they are often fed bread and other unhealthy treats. In
late fall and winter months they are regularly joined by American Black Ducks
and at random by other species, making the group always worth a close look; a
Northern Pintail and an American Wigeon joined the flock one recent winter,
for example, and an American Coot was consistently seen nearby. Bufflehead,
Common Goldeneye, and Common Eider, as well as Common Loon, Black
Guillemot, and Horned Grebe, are frequently spotted in the harbor in late fall
and throughout the winter, along with the occasional Great Cormorant. In
spring, Laughing Gulls rejoin the year-round species for the summer.

In spring and fall months, the thick hedges along the harbor's edge, clumps
of arbor vitae, and dense trees along the edges of the adjoining amphitheater
can attract pockets of migrants, in addition to a resident Northern Mockingbird or two. At any time of year you should keep an eye to the sky: a pair
of Peregrine Falcons nests in nearby Camden Hills State Park, and one is
frequently seen perched on the steeple of the Chestnut Street Baptist Church.
Bald Eagles also nest on nearby Megunticook Lake (and used to nest on
Curtis Island, the small island with the lighthouse at the head of Camden
Harbor) and can be seen in the vicinity of the harbor year-round. Cooper's
Hawks are regulars throughout the winter. Ospreys nest in the harbor and
are commonly seen and heard during summer months.

Harbor Park and the amphitheater are often occupied for community events such as craft shows, concerts, and theatrical performances or rented out for weddings. Being in the center of a popular vacation destination town, the park is within easy access of amenities such as restrooms, shops, and good restaurants, but this also means that in summer and fall months the park (and the harbor itself) can be quite crowded with visitors (and boats). An attractive option for harbor viewing, then, might be to bring your binoculars along for a meal on the deck of Peter Ott's or the Waterfront Restaurant, which offer front-row seats to the harbor and a great view of scenic Mount Battie above the town.

Additional vantage points from which to scan inner and outer Camden Harbor include the public-landing boardwalk, the Camden Yacht Club, and Laite Beach, another town-owned park off Chestnut Street. The west side of the harbor can be viewed from a public right-of-way near Wayfarer Marine on Sea Street, which can be accessed via Atlantic Avenue.

RARITIES

Dickcissel, January 2016

SITE KX13 Camden Hills State Park

TOWNS Camden and Lincolnville (Knox and Waldo Counties). DeLorme Map 14: C–D3–4. **SEASON** May–June, September–October. **VISITATION** 30 min. to an entire day, depending on the structure of your visit. Open 9 a.m.–sunset. Facilities, including parking, restrooms, and camping, are available at the main park headquarters off US Route 1. Restrooms are available at the summit of Mount Battie and in the campgrounds on both sides of Route 1. Day-use fee required to enter the park trails from the main entrance, to access the Mount Battie Auto Road to the summit of Mount Battie, or to access trails from the Youngtown Road trailhead (described below). Hunting is allowed in many parts of the park, so wear blaze orange when appropriate. **HIGHLIGHTS** Spring songbird migration and breeding warblers; breeding Peregrine Falcon and Northern Goshawk; migrating raptors in fall; sea watching possible from section of park south of Route 1.

Camden Hills State Park is a very popular hiking mecca and thus offers birders a wide selection of trails to access its forests and rocky open ledges. While

I don't recommend a visit to the park for any special quality of the birding there, birds are among the many rewards you may find while spending time on the park trails, many of which offer ocean vistas and other breathtaking views of this highly scenic area.

The park primarily comprises mixed deciduous forest, with conifers predominant along the upper ridges of Megunticook, some open ledges on the mountaintops, and blueberry fields on and near Cameron Mountain. During breeding season, typical species found in the woods along most trails can include Broad-winged Hawk, Yellow-bellied Sapsucker, Winter Wren, Wood Thrush, Black-throated Blue Warbler, Ovenbird, and Scarlet Tanager. Common Raven and Dark-eyed Junco can be found at higher elevations. Around the blueberry barrens on Cameron Mountain you can find Eastern Towhee. The open summits of Bald Rock, Mount Battie, and Mount Megunticook offer especially good vantage points for watching hawks soar past during fall migration. A Peregrine Falcon pair found nesting in the park beginning in 2006 were the first to nest in the Midcoast area since the 1950s, and they can often be seen over the hills and downtown Camden.

DIRECTIONS

Comprising over five thousand acres, the park has many access points. From the junction of us Route 1 and Route 52 just north of downtown Camden, follow Route 1 north for 1.5 miles to the main park entrance. To the left is the Mount Battie Auto Road and the main campground, as well as access to hiking trails up Mount Battie and Mount Megunticook. To the right is a picnic area that offers viewing access to Penobscot Bay and a small group camping area.

Other trailheads offering excellent hikes that birders may want to try:

- The Carriage Trail off Route 52 in Camden offers limited parking along the roadside. From this trail one can access the Mount Megunticook ridgeline via the Tablelands Trail or the Mount Battie Auto Road near the summit of Mount Battie via the Carriage Road Trail.
- The parking area near the intersections of Youngtown Road and Route 173 in Lincolnville offers access to many trails, including those to Bald Rock and its vistas (3.5-mile round-trip) and the blueberry fields of Cameron Mountain (4.5-mile round-trip).
- A parking area off Route 52 near Megunticook Lake accesses a trail to Maidens Cliff (technically not part of the state park) that also intersects,

via the Jack Williams Trail, the park's spruce-lined Ridge Trail that traverses Mount Megunticook to Ocean Lookout just below the mountain's 1,385-foot summit.

To download a park trail map via the state park website on Maine.gov see http://www.maine.gov/dacf/parks/docs/fpl/camdentrails.pdf.

Bangor

Orrington

Bucksport

Pittsfield

Burnham

Troy

Monroe

Unity

Thorndike

WO13

Brooks

Prospect

WO14

Waterville

Swanville

Knox

Waldo

Stockton Springs

WO12

WO8

WO9

WO7

Searsport

WO11

WO10

Belfast

Palermo

WO4

WO5

wo6

Castine

Liberty

Belmont

Searsmont

Northport

WO2

Washington

Hope

WO1

Lincolnville

WO3

Islesboro

Camden

Rockland

North Haven

WEST PENOBSCOT BAY

EAST PENOBSCOT BAY

WALDO COUNTY

9 Waldo County

SETH BENZ

For birding, Waldo County might be one of the least explored and appreciated counties in the state, according to Seth Benz. With the southern end close to Rockland-Camden, the western reaches of the county a short drive from Waterville, and the northern hot spots just south of Bangor-Brewer, it's hardly remote. And with the lovely, vibrant town of Belfast growing as a destination for Mainers and visitors alike, more eyes in the field could yield surprising results.

In spring, and especially in fall, following a night of strong migration (preferably on northwesterly winds that continue through sunrise), there may be no better place in all of the Midcoast of Maine to be than Sears Island (site wo10) to observe migration. Many species pause near the end of the island before continuing their "morning flight" (aka "morning redetermined migration") back to the mainland. Whether it's to compensate for overnight drift, find better habitats, avoid the shoreline competition and concentration of predators, or some other unknown instinct, the morning flight can offer diversity and numbers that are extraordinary.

In the breeding season, birding the Unity Area (wo13) will yield rare species such as Black Tern, Purple Martin, and perhaps Sandhill Crane. Meanwhile, several wonderful preserves protect habitat for a variety of common, uncommon, and locally rare species. Local species such as American Bittern and Eastern Whip-poor-will can be sought at Bog Brook Sanctuary (wo8), while a visit to the Sandy Point WMA (wo12) can yield American Bitterns and Ring-necked Ducks. Furthermore, the Mendall WMA (wo14) hosts Nelson's Sparrows and other wetland denizens. Strolls at places such as Fernald's Neck Preserve (wo1) or the Head of Tide and Stover Preserves (wo7) will provide a sample of the region's woodland species.

During the colder months, the waterfront is the place to be, although during irruption years, the Unity Area can be very fruitful (excuse the pun).

Belfast Harbor (Belfast Tour, w06) is a hot spot, although what was the largest wintering flock of Barrow's Goldeneyes in the state is now a thing of the past. For me, a morning birding the local preserves and Belfast Harbor (including a check of the waterfront hillside and neighborhoods in late fall for vagrant potential), followed by lunch at the acclaimed Chase's Daily and topped off with a pint at Marshall Wharf Brewing in town, makes for a perfect day—and is a testament to the burgeoning food and beverage scene of Belfast.

Back over at Sears Island (w010), Ruddy Ducks sometimes join the other more common waterbird species, but Cape Jellison (w011) harbors the best overwintering concentrations of this cute little stiff-tail. But don't forget about tiny Ducktrap Harbor (w02), which even provides good waterbird watching from the cozy confines of your vehicle. —*Derek Lovitch*

SITE W01 Fernald's Neck Preserve

Entry by Kristen Lindquist

TOWN Lincolnville. DeLorme Map 14: C–D3. **SEASON** April–October. **VISITATION** 1–3 hrs. No restroom facilities. The preserve gate is open 7:30 a.m.–7:30 p.m. No dogs. If the parking area is full, please return another day; do not park anywhere along the road. **HIGHLIGHTS** Breeding Common Loon, Osprey, and Bald Eagles; Winter Wren; variety of warblers including Blackburnian and Black-throated Blue; Bobolink; fall migrant sparrows.

This approximately three-hundred-acre property, which comprises most of a large peninsula jutting into the northern end of Megunticook Lake, was first put into conservation by the Nature Conservancy, thanks to the efforts of neighboring landowners in 1969, and is now owned by the Coastal Mountains Land Trust. The preserve protects almost 3 miles of lake shoreline, and the calls of Common Loons and Ospreys can be heard from deep within the woods. It also features an old farm field maintained for its stands of milkweed, a small bog, patches of mixed hardwood forest, and, predominantly, stands of old pines with sparse understory vegetation. A color-coded network of trails winds throughout these habitats and also offers access to the waterfront and to Balance Rock, a large glacial erratic that has been a sightseeing destination since the late 1800s.

The pine-needle-covered trails are least visited on spring mornings. In the summer the preserve is a popular enough spot for hikers and picnickers that visitation is monitored by a seasonal preserve steward. The preserve is well populated by white-tailed deer. I often startle them along the trail on early morning hikes.

A portion of Camden Hills State Park is visible across the lake from areas of the preserve, and in fall you may spot migrating raptors passing overhead as they follow the ridgeline southward.

DIRECTIONS

As US Route 1 heads out of Camden just north of downtown, bear left onto Route 52. Follow Route 52 North for 17.8 miles out of town and along the shore of Megunticook Lake into Lincolnville. Just after the Youngtown Inn you will spot Fernalds Neck Road on your left. The road soon turns to dirt. Bear left at the fork and continue to the preserve parking area at the very end.

Before you hit the trail it's worth a short walk back up the road to scan the fields, which often host nesting Bobolinks in summer, while the sky above can be full of feeding Tree and Barn Swallows. The fields around the trailhead—those on the preserve itself are not mowed every year and not until late summer—may also host swallows and Bobolinks, as well as various sparrows. In late summer the dense patches of milkweed attract monarch butterflies.

From the trailhead kiosk you have two trail options: the White Trail bears left across the field and into the woods, emerging quickly onto the lakeshore. The Blue Trail heads across the field and into the pine woods, where it intersects at various points with the Red, Orange, and Yellow Trails. My favorite hike follows the Blue Trail on a loop that bears left through the pines, passes over rocky outcrops and ledges that offer a view of the lake from some height, then dips back into the woods to loop around the Great Bog, which lies off the right side of the trail, before reconnecting to the starting point. The woods along this stretch regularly host numbers of Blackburnian, Black-throated Green, and Pine Warblers, and others during spring migration. You can hear Winter Wren, Veery, and Hermit Thrush singing here as well. Patches of more mixed deciduous trees can hold Warbling, Blue-headed, and Red-eyed Vireos, Black-throated Blue Warbler, Northern Parula, and Scarlet Tanager. The bog can be an interesting spot to pause if you can tolerate the insect swarms. Alder Flycatchers probably breed there, and the berry bushes are an attractive food source for birds in fall and winter—I've come upon a flock of hundreds of American Robins flitting about the bog in late fall.

From the various lakeshore access points, including the end of the White Trail, as well as the quiet cove just beyond Balance Rock, you can scan the lake for Common Loons in summer—several nest on the lake—in addition to migrating waterfowl, including Wood Duck, Bufflehead, Mallard, and American Black Duck. Spotted Sandpiper and Belted Kingfisher are also summer lake residents.

The forested field edges can be hopping with sparrows, and although I've only come across more expected species, I'd like to spend more time here during September and October to see what other sparrows might be passing through to feed in the seed-filled fields.

RARITIES

Red-necked Grebe, November 2013

A detailed preserve brochure with trail map can be downloaded from the Coastal Mountains Land Trust at http://www.coastalmountains.org/down loads/preserves/fernaldsneck.pdf.

SITE WO2 Ducktrap Harbor

TOWN Lincolnville. DeLorme Map 14: C4–5. **SEASON** October–April. **VISITATION** 15–45 min. No restroom facilities. **HIGHLIGHTS** Wintering and fall and spring migrant waterbirds including Red-throated Loon, Red-necked Grebe, Red-breasted Merganser, and Bufflehead.

A picturesque yet somewhat secretive and sizable rocky spit constricts the channel of the Ducktrap River before the river flows out into its delta-like mouth. It offers very accessible nearshore waterfowl watching, which is best in winter. Using a window-mounted scope allows for birding from the warmth of your car. However, it is also a popular local spot for anglers, respite seekers, and rock hounds at any time of year. The Ducktrap River is one of eight rivers along the Maine coast with a small population of wild Atlantic salmon, a federally endangered species.

DIRECTIONS

This spot is situated between Belfast and Camden on US Route 1. Proceed 0.9 miles north of the junction of Routes 1 and 173 in Lincolnville Beach and turn right onto Howe Point Road. The road at first seems like you've turned into a residential driveway but continues a few hundred yards downhill to a rocky berm on the left where there is plenty of room to park. There is also a two-car-size slot on the right, which is protected by trees.

Whether watching from your car or stepping out on the rocks, you'll need a scope to achieve satisfactory birding. Across the water of West Penobscot Bay, the land you see is Islesboro Island, Warren Island, and Seven Hundred Acre Island, an archipelago that dictates the boundary of this portion of the bay and your view. With the Ducktrap River on your left and the river mouth's great pool slightly behind you, be sure to scan the water in all directions, especially out on the larger bay. It is best to scan this relatively shallow fan-shaped area before the channel on a rising tide (from mid- to high tide) as birds move from the distant channel toward the flooding shallows. Be sure to scan carefully, and pay attention to the waters around the private dock well off to the right as well as the nearby wooded shoreline.

Be advised that birding here on a sunny morning can be a challenge, as the angle of the sun produces a glare that can reduce target species to mere silhouettes. Nevertheless, a variety of species, often in surprising numbers, congregate in this area from late fall through winter and into early spring.

After birding, especially on a cold, must-have-mittens day, Dot's café on the southern outskirts of Lincolnville Beach, backtracking toward Camden, is a great place to warm up with hot chocolate or freshly brewed coffee, not to mention delicious baked goods and gourmet sandwiches.

RARITIES

Barrow's Goldeneye, March 2013

SITE WO3 Islesboro (Island)

TOWN Islesboro via Linconville Beach (Maine State Ferry). DeLorme Map 14: C5, and Map 15: B1. **SEASON** May–August, December. **VISITATION** 3 hrs. to 1 day; includes round-trip ferry from mainland. Public restrooms at the ferry terminals and aboard the ferry itself. **HIGHLIGHTS** Warbler and shorebird diversity during spring migration; wintering waterbirds.

Islesboro, a well-established island historically tied to shipbuilding in Penobscot Bay, is 14 miles long and varies from several yards wide at the mid-island Narrows to 3 miles wide toward the northern end. Birding on the island is divided into two general sections: "north of the Narrows" and "south of the Narrows." The whole island can be somewhat cursorily summed up as a patchwork of (mostly) well-to-do summer residences and hardy year-round homesteads placed among fragmented woodlands, occasional fields, tidal lowlands and marsh grasses, and outcroppings of geologically significant shoreline with limited access and beautiful vistas. Getting to Islesboro requires an easy ferry ride from Lincolnville Beach on the mainland to the island's Grindel Point. Birding while waiting to board the ferry on either side can be rewarded by species like Common Eider, Black Guillemot, Red-breasted Merganser, and Double-crested Cormorant, as well as Herring, Great Black-backed, and Ring-billed Gulls. Once you are on island, the variety of birds quickly increases according to the habitats you have time to explore.

DIRECTIONS

The mainland Lincolnville Beach Ferry terminal is located at the junction of US Route 1 and Route 173, 10 miles north of Camden. Turn right onto McKay Road and proceed to the ferry terminal a few hundred yards ahead on the left. Signage for entering the correct auto ferry lane is evident. Purchase a ticket after placing your car in line. Expect to pay a round-trip fare of $27.50 for a car plus $10 per adult passenger (as of 2015). The crossing is just twenty minutes each way. Check the website (listed below for ferry schedule) and plan on getting there, to get in line, about thirty minutes ahead of time (and even earlier in summer).

While Islesboro is not a common birding destination, it has been getting more attention over the past five years, and access to key locations is improving. The Islesboro Island Trust (ITT) maintains some thirteen preserves, seven of which have walking trails. Here I suggest three destinations: **Pendleton Point (Town Beach)** south of the Narrows, and **Hutchins Island** and **Marsh Preserve** (accessed from the same trailhead) north of the Narrows. To reach any of these destinations from the island's ferry terminal at Grindel Point follow Ferry Road for 1.1 miles and turn left onto West Bay Road. After 2.1 miles you arrive at an intersection with Main Road. The Islesboro Historical Society will be on your left. Turning left onto Main Road takes you toward the Narrows and points northward. Going right onto Main Road takes you south for 8.2 miles to Pendleton Point.

Along the way south, Main Road turns into Pendleton Point Road and takes you to a recreation area at the road's end. Bird the trees leading to and bordering the beach and shoreline. I made a loop from the parking area by walking down to the beach and then scampering left along the rock outcropping and following along the shore a quarter mile to another gravelly pocket beach with a path leading back up to the road and parking area.

To go north from the junction at the Historical Society turn left onto Main Road and follow it for 3.4 miles—making sure to bear right to stay on Main Road where it intersects with Meadow Pond Road—and turn right onto a dirt road labeled as both Hutchins Island and Bluff Road. Follow it for 0.8 miles to a three-way intersection. Park along the road here on the left just before the intersection. Walk left down Hutchins Island Lane for a quarter mile to a small trail information kiosk. Just beyond the kiosk the trail splits and is well signed, pointing the way to circumnavigate the woodland surrounding the marsh via Elaine's Trail or access Hutchins Island via a tidal sandbar for shoreline exploration. According to ITT publications, the combined length of the two trails is 2.5 miles, and birding here has generated a checklist of 139 species. I found the longer woodland section of Elaine's Trail, with fine vantage points for observing the ponds and marsh edge, to be more interesting and far more active than the thick conifer woods and shoreline of Hutchins Island. Timing your visit to coincide with low tide is highly advisable to cover both trails. Winter Wren, White-throated Sparrow, Golden-crowned Kinglet, and Hermit Thrush were easily seen along Elaine's Trail. Check the sandbar and surrounding tidal flats carefully for foraging shorebirds and gulls. When coming ashore via the ferry or while awaiting departure, it is advised to take some time to scan the waters and shoreline of Grindel Point. Look for Bald Eagle perched high along the various tree lines and Great Blue Heron wading the shallows.

RARITIES

Boreal Chickadee, September 1978 (north of the Narrows)

For a ferry schedule, current fares, and more information see the Maine Department of Transportation's ferry website at www.maine.gov/mdot/ferry /islesboro. For preserve and trail information visit the website of the Islesboro Island Land Trust at www.islesboroislandtrust.org.

SITE W04 Lake St. George State Park

TOWN Liberty. DeLorme Map 13 B5 and Map 14: B1. **SEASON** May–
October. **VISITATION** 20 min. to 2 hrs. Open all year with outhouses.
State park entrance fees apply. **HIGHLIGHTS** Breeding Common Loon;
Bald Eagle; migratory waterfowl and songbirds.

Lake St. George State Park's birding focal point is the lake itself, which covers
some twelve hundred acres. Common Loons nest on undeveloped islands,
and the woods surrounding the lake often resonate with a variety of birdsong,
including White-throated Sparrow, Winter Wren, Hermit Thrush, and Rose-
breasted Grosbeak throughout the summer. Waterfowl, which can be found
in hidden pockets of the lake, especially during migration periods, include
Hooded Merganser, American Black Duck, and Red-breasted Merganser. Bald
Eagles are sometimes easily seen from shore in winter when ice fishermen
leave behind discarded fish entrails.

DIRECTIONS

From the junction of US Route 1 and Route 3 in Belfast (Reny's Plaza) follow Route 3 West for 17 miles. The state park entrance is well marked and
becomes visible on the left about 1 mile after the lake starts on the left (or
south side) of Route 3. The park can also be reached by driving 25 miles east
along Route 3 from Augusta.

Birding the lake thoroughly is best accomplished by boat (motor or paddle
craft). One can also scan from shore; however, access is limited to the most
heavily used areas of the lake. A canoe or kayak can be put in at the main
entrance, while motorboat access is restricted to a public boat launch, half
a mile west of the main entrance. A locally known second access point can
be found by turning left onto Marshall Shore Road, half a mile farther west
along Route 3 beyond the public boat launch. Follow for 0.8 miles to an
obvious but limited parking area on the right and a makeshift boat launch
area with portable toilet.

The lake's shoreline here is dotted with well-spaced camps. It is much
quieter than the bustle of the main entrance area. This is a worthwhile
spot to check, especially if you don't have a boat. The roadside woods for a
short distance in the vicinity of the parking area is heavily wooded, with a
mix of deciduous trees and a small stand of eastern hemlock. Black-capped

Chickadee, Red-breasted Nuthatch, Brown Creeper, Ovenbird, and Red-eyed Vireo were all present during a brief stop in mid-July. Blue-headed Vireo and Yellow-rumped Warbler frequent this stretch during fall migration.

SITE WO5 James Dorso (Ruffingham Meadow) Wildlife Management Area

TOWN Searsmont. DeLorme Map 14: B2. **SEASON** April, **May–June**, July–August, **September**, October–November. **VISITATION** 15 min. to 2-plus hrs. No restroom facilities. **HIGHLIGHTS** Breeding Pied-billed Grebe, Common Goldeneye, and Marsh Wren; Osprey; Ring-necked Duck.

This is a Maine Department of Inland Fisheries and Wildlife managed impoundment, encompassing 675 acres. A substantive, shallow, roadside pond bounded by mixed woods on two sides leads north away from a Route 3 pull-off parking area to submerged wetlands where wild rice and other aquatic plants attract waterfowl for hunting (and birders). This can be a quick stop at the pull-off to scan the open water and pond edges, or alternatively, the pond and wetland are better explored by canoe or kayak.

DIRECTIONS

From the junction of US Route 1 and Route 3 in Belfast follow Route 3 West for 13 miles (toward Augusta). Thompson Ridge Road is an approaching landmark to watch for on the right, 0.1 miles before the targeted pull-off, also on the right. There is no official boat launch; however, locals launch their boats from this roadside pull-off. There is no other road access to the entire area.

As ice loses its grip in spring, the immediate roadside pond section, scanned from the parking area, can be teeming with Ring-necked Duck and Wood Duck. American Black Duck are usually found as well, while Blue-winged Teal, Green-winged Teal, and Hooded Merganser are harder to find. Exploration by boat can be much more rewarding, especially to get to the far edges of the pond and distant wetlands. When no ducks are apparent upon first stopping, methodically searching the shorelines usually turns up Hooded Merganser, Pied-billed Grebe, Common Merganser, American Bittern, Belted Kingfisher, and Canada Goose. To have a chance to find Sora, Marsh Wren, and get closer to Red-winged Blackbird communities, a boat and a paddle of at least a quarter mile are necessary. Upland areas bordering the wetlands host

American Woodcock, Ruffed Grouse, and Wild Turkey. Birdsong often rings from the extensive deciduous woods bordering the pond. Scarlet Tanager, Great-crested Flycatcher, and Eastern Wood-Pewee have been fairly common.

SITE W06 Belfast Tour

TOWN Belfast. DeLorme Map 14: A4. SEASON All year, but especially November–March. VISITATION 30 min. to 2 hrs. Public restroom at town landing. HIGHLIGHTS Barrow's Goldeneye and other wintering waterfowl (diminishing in certainty) and Bohemian Waxwings; breeding Cliff Swallow, Bobolink, and Wilson's Snipe.

Belfast is located at the junction of US Route 1 and Route 3, about 45 minutes away when traveling either north from Rockland or east from Augusta. The convergence of highways brings you to a well-known and recently transformed small city that slopes toward a tidal river and extensive bay that eventually contribute to the much greater Penobscot Bay. Two to three decades ago Belfast was known as a poultry-processing center with unkempt warehouselike buildings and a deteriorating waterfront. Offal from a fish processing plant at the time brought throngs of gulls to Belfast Harbor. Additionally, extensive mussel shoals and tidal currents combined to make the northern end of the harbor a gathering spot for wintering ducks, formerly attracting from ten to thirty Barrow's Goldeneyes annually.

Today, the waterfront has been transformed in many ways. The fish processing plant has been removed, replaced by a busy shipyard, and there is an 0.9-mile-long harbor walk, one section of which features a world-class pedestrian bridge that spans the Passagassawaukeag River upstream from the town landing and Belfast Bay. The city also has fine land birding, and many of Belfast's residential streets are planted with fruit-bearing crabapples, mountain ash, and shadbush (serviceberry) trees. In addition to birding, there is a well-known community food co-op, many chic eateries, a microbrewery, art galleries, and owner-friendly tchotchke shops, and a plaza on the top edge of the town aptly named for the iconic Reny's department store that routinely shares its many parking spaces with an assortment of gull species throughout the year.

While the downtown harbor area remains waterfowl-centric at any time of year, the former number of winter-visiting Barrow's Goldeneyes has dwindled

137
7
141
3
1

Pedestrian
bridge
● Town landing
● Heritage Park

Waldo Ave.
Bridge St.

Grove
Cemetery

Main St.

● Belfast Boathouse

3

Belmont Ave.

Lincolnville Ave.

Cedar St.

Church St.

Pearl St.

Park St.

High St.

Union St.

Bayview St.

Kirby
Lake ●

Miller St.

Salmond St.

Race St.

BELFAST BAY

52

Congress St.

Wight St.

Northport Ave.

✈

Belfast
Municipal
Airport

Lower Congress St.

1

Perkins Rd.
fields
●

Perkins Rd.

Mouth of
Little River

Woods Rd.

Herrick Rd.

BELFAST

to fewer than five birds. However, Common Goldeneye, Bufflehead, American Black Duck, and Common Loon can be found in surprising numbers. South of the harbor, Belfast Bay annually attracts Bonaparte's Gull, Red-necked Grebe, Long-tailed Duck, and occasional Red-throated Loon.

DIRECTIONS

To bird Belfast in an efficient, survey-like manner, I recommend starting at the **Mouth of the Little River** at the southern end of Belfast along us Route 1, some 16.3 miles north of the entrance to Camden Hills State Park (or about 3 miles south of the junction with Route 3). There is a one-car narrow pull-off on the right (bay) side just before a small cement bridge, under which the Little River runs into Belfast Bay. It is best at low tide when this part of the bay is reduced to a series of shallow pools and the river is little more than a

WALDO COUNTY

263

Belfast Harbor. © Dan Avener

trickle. Gulls and dabbling ducks gather in this area. You can scan from the road edge at any tide. Look for other species among the masses of Mallards and American Black Ducks. A scope will greatly enhance this experience.

Next, travel half a mile farther north and turn left onto **Perkins Road**. In short order you will see grasslands/agricultural fields on your right. These fields are home to Bobolink and Savannah Sparrow, while Barn, Tree, and Cliff Swallows are a constant presence on sunny summer days. The tree line that bounds the fields often harbors Red-tailed Hawk, and Northern Harrier can be seen coursing over the fields about half the time. As you continue along the road, a barbed-wire fence defines a barnyard where llama and sheep are often grazing. Look for Wilson's Snipe along the wet corner where the fence comes closest to the road and water pools in a small natural depression. This specific spot is especially good for snipe after a soaking rain. Beyond the farmhouse, a rectangular fenced pasture parallel to the road is worth a scan.

To reach the third destination along this Belfast tour route turn right onto Lower Congress Street and continue 0.9 miles to the intersection with US

Route 1. Turn left onto US Route 1 North and go 0.8 miles to a stoplight. Turn right onto Lincolnville Avenue. In 0.2 miles you'll arrive at a dirt parking area on the right by a small pond known as **Kirby Lake or "the Muck."** A wood-chip trail 50 feet north of the parking lot begins at the wood edge and leads you on a dogleg around the backside of the pond. The wet woods teem with warblers during spring and fall migration, and Great Blue Heron find a way to blend in along the open pond edge. Black-crowned Night Heron has also been found here. The woods trail hugs the water and leads you around the pond and back to pavement. Bearing right, you can easily follow the way to return to your car.

From the parking area at the Muck continue straight ahead on Lincolnville Avenue for 0.3 miles where it intersects with Main Street. Turn right and continue downhill into the heart of the downtown. From the stoplight at the intersection of Main Street and High Street continue straight for another 0.2 miles to the town landing area parking lot. Allow time to walk all or a portion of the newly constructed **Harbor Walk.** Heading north takes you through the impressive shipyard toward the pedestrian bridge. Going south takes you from the town landing toward the **Belfast Boathouse.** Either way parallels Front Street.

If you don't have time to walk and bird the entire length of the Harbor Walk, you can instead drive along Front Street, stopping at obvious vantage points such as the Boathouse, the **town landing,** and the **pedestrian bridge.** With more than ten years as a resident of Belfast, I have found this section along the river (now the recently completed Harbor Walk) to be the most productive and surprising. Osprey perch on sailboat masts, Bald Eagles throw the loafing gulls into skyward frenzy, Common Nighthawks migrate through in late August, Great Blue Heron fish the tidal shallows, Common Loon search for Green Crab, and wintering ducks come and go from the river out into the bay.

RARITIES

Sandhill Crane, October 2007 (mouth of Little River); Lesser Black-backed Gull, September 2015 (harbor); Little Gull, September 2015 (harbor)

The Belfast Bay Watershed Coalition website provides printable maps of various trails (www.belfastbaywatershed.org), including an in-town nature trail that features street-side birding places. The citizens of Belfast have supported the development of an annual birding festival in mid-May (information at the link above). The Waldo County YMCA sponsors the "Bird Bus," which visits local hot spots. For more information visit http://www.waldocountyymca.org.

SITE W07 Head of Tide and Stover Preserves

Entry by Kristen Lindquist

TOWN Belfast. DeLorme Map 14: A4. **SEASON** May, June.
VISITATION 1–2 hrs. No restroom facilities. Please follow preserve guidelines posted at trailhead. **HIGHLIGHTS** Spring warbler migration; nesting Osprey and (nearby) Bald Eagle.

The ninety-two-acre Head of Tide Preserve, put in conservation by Coastal Mountains Land Trust in 2009 as part of its Passagassawakeag Greenway along the Passagassawakeag River, features old farm fields, forest, and almost 2,500 feet of river frontage. The recently expanded trail system offers easy access to this variety of habitats, as well as a power-line corridor that divides the property. As the name indicates, the tidal part of the river reaches its upper limit here. The forty-five-acre Stover Preserve across the street offers another mile of trail that also follows the upper river along a much narrower stretch shaded by a hemlock grove.

DIRECTIONS

From the main entrance to Camden Hills State Park on US Route 1 in Camden, take Route 1 North for 17.7 miles to the Route 7/137 exit in Belfast (the last one before the bridge over the Passagassawakeag River). At the stop sign turn left onto Waldo Avenue. In 1 mile make a right onto Doak Road and proceed for 0.75 miles. You can access both preserves from the parking area on the right just after Doak's Machine Shop.

The trail leads from the parking area along an experimental permaculture garden onto an old farm road. Following the trail to the left around three old farm fields offers access to lush edge habitat that is frequented by Alder Flycatcher, Great Crested Flycatcher, Eastern Bluebird, Chestnut-sided Warbler, Rose-breasted Grosbeak, and Indigo Bunting. Beyond the fields the trail enters mixed deciduous woods along the upper riverbank. Pine Warblers can be heard singing from a stand of white pines just upriver. Yellow-bellied

Sapsucker, Eastern Wood-Pewee, Blue-headed and Red-eyed Vireos, Hermit Thrush, and Ovenbird are regular denizens of this pretty wooded stretch. A visit to the river shore may turn up a Red-breasted Merganser with chicks, a fishing Great Blue Heron, Spotted Sandpiper, or Belted Kingfisher.

Emerging from the wooded riverside section of trail, you reconnect with the old farm road and the start of another trail loop. If you choose to bear right and follow the farm road straight back to the parking lot, then you've walked about a mile total. The old farm road can be quite wet and muddy in spring. Listen for Ruffed Grouse drumming in the woods to your left in spring, and keep your eyes open—I have surprised a hen grouse with chicks along the path in early summer.

If you choose to bear left and continue exploring, the trail passes through a strip of dense woods and emerges on a power-line corridor. Magnolia and Canada Warblers have been seen regularly in this strip of woods during spring migration, and Prairie Warbler has been found more than once singing along the power line. Look down the power line toward the river and you will easily spot one or more Osprey nests on either side of the river, which may be active in spring through summer. A pair of Bald Eagles nest annually a short distance downriver from this point, and the birds are often seen patrolling the river. The trail crosses the power-line cut and makes a big loop through mixed deciduous woods on the other side. Listen for drumming Ruffed Grouse, Pileated Woodpecker, Wood Thrush, Winter Wren, and Black-throated Blue Warbler here. The trail brings you back to the power-line corridor uphill from where you first crossed, then back through another stretch of woods to reconnect with the old farm road. Turn left on the road to return to the parking area from here. The Woods Loop done by itself is also about a mile in length.

The entrance to the Stover Preserve is across the street and up the road (to the left) a few hundred yards from the Head of Tide Preserve parking area. Birding the now blocked-off driveway in and the open area around the trailhead kiosk can be very productive during spring migration, turning up similar warblers as found along the deciduous edges of the Head of Tide Preserve. This trail makes a 1.5-mile loop that begins and ends at the trailhead kiosk area, meandering through wet deciduous forest, a riparian stand of eastern hemlock, and a grove of dense white pine. (As you follow the trail, you will also see evidence of a years-long effort to eradicate invasive honeysuckle on this preserve.) The woods are punctuated with old apple trees as well—evidence of the property's agricultural past.

Blackburnian Warblers are common in Waldo County. Look for them especially in mature stands of eastern hemlock and mixed woods with some spruce and fir, or in spring, at your favorite migrant trap. © Jeannette Lovitch

Bearing right on the trail will get you to the river more quickly. Listen for similar species as in the wooded sections of the Head of Tide Preserve. Pileated Woodpeckers frequent these woods and are regularly heard and seen. The river frontage is shorter and less dramatic than at Head of Tide but is equally serene, shaded by big old hemlocks that may harbor Blackburnian Warblers in spring.

Continuing along the trail takes you away from the river but through habitat that may host additional songbirds, including Yellow-bellied Sapsuckers and potentially Ruby-throated Hummingbird on the apple trees, and Pine Warblers trilling at the tops of the white pines. You emerge back at the trailhead kiosk.

You can download preserve brochures, which include trail maps for the Head of Tide Preserve and the Stover Preserve at the Coastal Mountains Land Trust website, at http://www.coastalmountains.org.

SITE W08 Bog Brook Sanctuary/Sheepscot-Wellspring Land Alliance Properties

TOWN Montville. DeLorme Map 14: A1. **SEASON** May–June, September–November. **VISITATION** 20 min. to several hrs. No restroom facilities. **HIGHLIGHTS** Spring and fall migration; breeding American Bittern, Red-shouldered Hawk, and Whip-poor-will, a variety of warblers, thrushes, other songbirds.

While Bog Brook (loop) Trail, whose blue-blazed length is 2.5 miles and which includes a stand of old-growth eastern hemlock, is the most noteworthy of the SWLA lands, the Alliance also maintains some 20 miles of trails in Freedom, Knox, Liberty, and Montville called the Sheepscot Headwaters Trail Network. This trail complex is tightly linked with eight loop hikes of varying lengths that pass through twelve hundred acres of contiguous protected land. Habitats include hemlock forest, mixed forest, marsh, streams, wetlands, and several old fields. The entire area is rich with bird life. Red-shouldered Hawks are known to breed here, Whip-poor-wills can still be heard, and Pileated Woodpeckers are heard or seen on most visits.

DIRECTIONS

From the junction of US Route 1 and Route 3 in Belfast go west on Route 3 (toward Augusta) for 16 miles and turn right onto Route 220. Continue for 3.2 miles and turn left onto Halldale Road. Keep straight on Halldale Road for 0.6 miles and look for a small wooden post with signage marking the Bog Brook trailhead on your right. There is barely enough room on the right side of the road to pull off just beyond the trailhead and before a narrow water view to your right.

   The trail starts out uphill through thick, mostly coniferous woods, then levels out and follows a minor ridgeline overlooking Bog Brook, a backed-up beaver flowage that creates a pond with flooded margins. After 0.3 miles the trail drops down to stream level, where the understory opens up and a stretch of mixed forest borders a small woodland stream, leading you from the pond to the main part of the Bog Brook Loop Trail. The trail is set back from the marsh for ease of walking and continues through mostly mixed woods with occasional pockets of conifers. A short spur on the west side of the loop trail leads to the best spot for studying the marsh. Ovenbird and Hermit Thrush are found in the woods, while Green Heron and Eastern Kingbird hunt the marsh. American Bittern have been found, as have occasional Olive-sided Flycatcher (in migration). This trail has a dark, deep-woods feel yet leads to a marshy oasis where sunlight pours in to illuminate the wood edges, where activity seems always to be best. I have found birding to be good here at any time of day, especially if you are patient. Continue around the far end of the marsh, passing by Whitten Hill Trail, the Hogback Connector Trail, and the Halldale Spur, to return to the Bog Brook trailhead.

Before or after your search for birds along the Bog Brook Trail, I encourage you to visit John's Ice Cream, located 3 miles west of the junction of Routes 3 and 220. Purchasing any of the fantastic homemade flavors at John's will certainly enhance your experience!

For more information see the website of the Sheepscot Wellspring Land Alliance at http://swlamaine.org/trails/.

SITE W09 Frye Mountain State Wildlife Management Area

TOWN Knox. DeLorme Map 14: A2. **SEASON** April–October.
VISITATION 30 min. to 2 hrs. Restroom at western entrance maintenance shed. **HIGHLIGHTS** Ruffed Grouse; breeding American Woodcock and a variety of songbirds; migratory raptors.

The Frye Mountain Wildlife Management Area, administered by the Maine Department of Inland Fisheries and Wildlife, features over five thousand somewhat mysterious but publicly accessible acres comprising mixed upland forests, old homestead remnants, and abandoned fields. It is managed for grouse and woodcock hunting. An orange safety vest and hat are advisable when birding during any hunting season. While various patches of habitat are accessible via a rough road network or by walking an arduous hiking trail, I instead recommend a specific section of trail to bird and a car route that bisects the area, allowing you to drive from one side to the other. The summit of Frye Mountain is 1,122 feet. A visit to the site of an old fire tower near the summit, an 0.6-mile trail from the road, has been a popular spot for watching hawks during spring and fall migration. Red-tailed Hawk, Osprey, and Turkey Vulture can be seen migrating in April and again in September/October.

Frye Mountain is located between Knox, Montville, and Freedom. The quickest route to the better birding is via Route 220. From the junction of US Route 1 and Route 3 in Belfast follow Route 3 West for 16 miles to Liberty. Turn right onto Route 220 (South Mountain Valley Road) and follow it for 6.5 miles to a right onto Walker Ridge Road. A maintenance shed and outhouse facility will be visible on your left in a very short distance. Park here and bird the adjacent alder-and-willow-dominated wetland. Alder Flycatcher, Yellow Warbler, and Common Yellowthroat should be easy to find in spring. Fall mornings can yield a variety of migrants.

A couple of alternative routes allow you to advance deeper into the management area. One is to walk from the maintenance shed on Walker Ridge Road for 0.3 miles and turn right onto the Walker Ridge Trail, a 7.5-mile ascending loop trek around the flanks of Frye Mountain, mostly through mixed forest. However, the best birding is within the first 1.5 miles, where the trail follows along Bartlett Stream. Listen for Broad-winged Hawk overhead, the burst of Ruffed Grouse flight from the forest floor, and the melodic calls of Hermit and Wood Thrushes. If you prefer walking, this little stretch of the management area is where I would recommend investing most of your time.

To bird the management area by auto—not advisable for autos with low ground clearance—continue beyond the maintenance shed for 1.4 miles and turn right onto High Ridge Road, follow it for 1 mile, then turn left onto Getchell Road. Stretches of this road are rough, rutted dirt track, better suited for snowmobiles in winter. It winds through thick stands of reestablished younger forest as well as tracks of older forest, passes occasional fields, and eventually goes the length of the management area, 4.9 miles to the east side, and brings you out to Route 137. Along the way, Getchell Road changes to Frye Mountain Road. Stop to bird at places with noticeable habitat changes, such as evidence of past timber harvesting, wet areas, field breaks, and stream crossings. Any of these places can be productive for common birds of the management area. Visits in September and October, on days with winds from the north or northwest, can produce a preponderance of Sharp-shinned Hawks along with an occasional Cooper's Hawk or the even less frequently seen Northern Goshawk.

271

Connecticut Warbler, October 1998

SITE WO10 Sears Island

TOWN Searsport. DeLorme Map 15 A1.   **SEASON** All year, but especially **May** and **September–October.**   **VISITATION** 30 min. to 3-plus hrs. Portable toilet at entrance to island.   **HIGHLIGHTS** Abundance and diversity of birds migrant warblers, sparrows, flycatchers, and finches; wintering waterbirds including Ruddy Duck.

Connected to the mainland by a short auto causeway, Sears Island, despite proximity to the mainland, is by far the shining gem of Maine coastal bird-ing from Rockland to Mount Desert Island. Once known as Wasumkeag—currently translated by the Penobscot nation as "darkly covered island"—the island, following European exploration in the seventeenth century, be-came known as Sears Island after four generations of ownership by the David Sears family. Now a local conservation group, Friends of Sears Island, oversees trail maintenance and other visitor amenities, such as an information kiosk and an oversize wooden bench near the gateway to the island. The island's trail system is a popular destination for people out for a stroll, dog walkers, beachcombers, photographers, and natural history enthusiasts of all kinds. The forested interior, stone walls and old homestead sites, vernal pools, tidal shoreline, grassy dunes, patchy wetlands, and surrounding waters combine to create a true birding hot spot, producing an impressive annual list of avian diversity. The island is rich with fruiting shrub and tree species such as chokecherry, shadbush, apple, and elderberry. Canopy trees include red oak, balsam fir, red spruce, and white pine. Alder, birch, and maple trees make up a good portion of the understory. Birding here is rewarding any time of year, with songbird abundance and diversity being best during spring and fall migration. Raptor numbers, shorebird variety, fall and winter waterfowl abundance, and sparrow phenology produce seasonal surprises each year. If there is a slow time, it is during the height of summer. But even then, Scarlet Tanager, Rose-breasted Grosbeak, Veery, and Winter Wren are among the findable breeding species.

From the junction of US Route 1 and Route 3 in Belfast follow US Route 1 North/Route 3 East for 8.2 miles. Turn right onto Sears Island Road. The causeway begins about a half mile from the turn. However, birding the stretch from US Route 1 to the beginning of the causeway is often overlooked, unless throngs of migratory sparrows steal one's attention as they feed along the grassy road edge. For maximum yield, just after turning onto Sears Island Road, make a quick stop at an immediate dead-end road that goes off to the right. Pull into the dirt parking lot. Walk down the shrub-lined road. You'll know in a minute if this section is worth your investment. Some mornings, especially during fallout conditions, birds saturate this area. Palm Warbler and Yellow-rumped Warbler are often most numerous when this phenomenon takes place.

Continue back on Sears Island Road and proceed toward the causeway. Drive slowly and keep an eye out for roadside birds. In early to mid-October, during most years, hundreds of sparrows occur along this stretch before the road crosses the railroad tracks. After crossing the tracks, it is worthwhile to pull over, if only briefly, to check the woods on both sides of the road. Again, bird activity will be the barometer. I've had a few mornings over the past ten years or so when I was unable to make it to the causeway because of the volume of birds in these scrubby woods.

The trees finally peter out just before the short causeway crossing begins. The causeway to the island was built in the 1980s in anticipation of constructing a shipping port. Happily, that plan has faded. Scan the open waters on both sides. The Mac Point gas and oil freighter depot and storage facility is on the west side, and the 0.4-mile distance of water between the causeway and that industrial spit of land can be teeming with waterbirds, such as Common Eider and Bonaparte's Gull. The view to the east side of the causeway looks 1.25 miles across the water to secluded Stockton Harbor. This section of the bay is excellent for finding Surf Scoter, Long-tailed Duck, and Ruddy Duck, albeit the latter in relatively small numbers. If you are in a hurry to bird the island, some visits may warrant using blinders along the road to get from Route 1 to the end of the causeway! Finally, park as close to the island toward the southern end of the causeway as the painted road lines allow.

Sears Island is 2 miles long north to south by a mile wide east to west, 940 total acres in area, 600 of which are under special land-protection designation. Development of the remaining island acreage, such as the proposed shipping port, is no longer a short-term threat.

Beyond the barricade, a paved road starts at the north end of the island and center-cuts the island as a walking boulevard most of the way before the pavement ends where an old dirt road bends off to a jetty along the western shore. A sparse grass, weed, and shrub area on the east side of the road begins at the barricade and runs for a couple of hundred feet. This vegetation gives way to an embankment with small trees. This area often has a variety of sparrows, and I have found Snow Bunting and Horned Lark here. On the west side a few tall trees form a narrow northern terminus to the island forest. These last few deciduous trees, some 40–50 feet high, are the northern hopping-off point before the quarter-mile flight to the mainland. Often warblers and vireos will hesitate in these treetops just long enough for ease of identification. Below the trees, the ground cover, thick alder, and assorted vegetative understory can be loaded with migrant songbirds in spring and fall.

It is not unusual to spend a good hour or more right here because the birding can be that good and busy. Lately, during fall migration, I have been observing and monitoring the "morning flight" of passerines as they come to the island's north end after sunrise. During the first couple of hours of daylight, "morning redetermined migration," when birds head inland to forage, avoid predators, and/or compensate for drift, many will pause here before heading north to the mainland. Several hundred birds can be seen on mornings when conditions are perfect (northwesterly winds overnight continuing into dawn, especially following the passage of a cold front).

Continue uphill (south) on the pavement, a gradual stroll, birding both edges and forest on each side of the road. The volume of birds in the first quarter mile of the north end is a telltale indicator of general bird activity for the entire island. Thrushes and sparrows forage at ground level, sometimes coming out on the pavement (in numbers); understory trees hum with warbler chip notes; Black-capped Chickadees lead one's eye into the trees back from the road edge where vireos, waxwings, finches, and warblers seek insects or ripened fruit during the early fall. During spring this same area is often alive with American Redstart and Chestnut-sided Warbler, even on days with less bird variety and abundance. Annual spring bird walks (mid-May to early June), sponsored by local conservation groups, report thirty to fifty species in just two to three hours of effort when birding conditions are prime. Among these, fifteen to twenty species of warblers can occur.

A couple of excellent side trails—Homestead Trail and Green Trail—on the east and west sides of the pavement, respectively, allow roughly equidistant deeper-forest birding leading downhill to the shore. Both cross small streams and feature a diversity of habitat including alder thickets, mature mixed woods, scattered fruit trees, and views out to water. Access to the shoreline, which leads back to the island's north end, albeit on opposite sides of the island, completes the loop for each trail. Moving slowly along these trails can reward you with exceptional views of species such as Ruby-crowned Kinglet, Yellow-bellied Sapsucker, White-throated Sparrow, Yellow-breasted Chat (rare), and other low-foraging birds.

The island's southern interior is best reached via a dirt road beginning a quarter mile beyond the barricade, on the left side of the paved road in the vicinity of where the two aforementioned trails leave the pavement. It tracks beneath a power line leading nearly 2 miles to a cell tower. From an initial shrubby clearing, the dirt road leads through mature mixed forest with a few towering red oak trees overhead, then passes by an open field with a bayberry copse and scattered young pine trees, through a long stretch of older conifers, and finally to a patch of wind-thrown younger mixed forest and alder-dominated shrubbery upon reaching the cell tower. A blue-blazed trail a quarter mile from the tower leads east from the dirt road steeply downhill to the southeastern shore. From here one can walk at low tide along the southern shoreline. Given the distance involved and the relative low number and variety of birds encountered on a typical visit, walking the entire length of the dirt road is a lower priority. However, the field area along the dirt road is the most consistent location on the island to find American Woodcock during spring or early fall migration. Along the southeastern shoreline, a tidal sandbar sometimes attracts shorebirds such as Semipalmated Plover and Black-bellied Plover.

The first hundred yards to half mile of Sears Island beyond the causeway barrier is where it is most advisable to invest the bulk of your time. It is not unusual to experience impressive waves of land birds here during spring or fall migration. Likewise, the water within scoping distance of either side of the causeway is of equal importance. Charismatic birds such as Common Loon, Osprey, or Bald Eagle always seem to make an appearance. And vagrants are also a possibility at any time of year. For a premier birding opportunity, Sears Island is not to be missed.

Forster's Tern, September 2011; Red Phalarope, May 2014; Gray Jay, April–May 2016

For more information and a trail map, visit the website of the Friends of Sears Island at http://friendsofsearsisland.org/explore-the-island/.

SITE W011 Cape Jellison Loop

TOWN Stockton Springs. DeLorme Map 15: A1.   **SEASON** October–November, **December–March**, April.   **VISITATION** 45 min. to 3 hrs. No restroom facilities. State park entry fees at Fort Point.
HIGHLIGHTS Wintering waterbirds including Ruddy Duck, Red-throated Loon, and Red-necked Grebe.

The Cape Jellison Loop is a 7-mile circular route that allows limited but adequate access to outstanding birding vantage points around the perimeter of a relatively small, boot-shaped forested peninsula of approximately sixteen hundred acres. It is accessed from downtown Stockton Springs. The peninsula once supported a fort overlooking the Penobscot River, the premises of which have now become a state park; later, Cape Jellison became an important shipping port with a railroad connection to Bangor. Coincidentally, both fort and shipping port met their demise by fire, separately. The birding route can be done quickly, simply focusing on waterfowl, or, if interested in a more leisurely approach, by incorporating walks of varying lengths investigating pockets of changing habitats, especially at the old fort, now Fort Point State Park.

DIRECTIONS

Beginning from the junction of US Route 1 and Route 3 in Belfast, follow US Route 1 North/Route 3 East for 10 miles and turn right onto East Main Street in Stockton Springs. In 0.7 miles turn right onto Cape Jellison Road. Proceed for 0.8 miles to a split in the road where the loop begins.

Go left at the road split to first reach a privately owned, user-friendly parking area a half mile on the left by the side of a brown garage with green doors. Greater **Fort Point Cove** is viewable from this vantage point, which is best for scoping the entirety of the cove. American Black Duck sometimes huddle along the shoreline to the left of the parking area, while Common

Goldeneye and Bufflehead are seen out on open water. Small groups as well as larger rafts of Ruddy Duck can usually be spotted here, especially by looking out in the direction of where cove waters mingle with the river current.

Continuing on for an additional mile brings you to the entrance road to **Fort Point State Park.** This 0.9-mile road leads to an unmanned fee station and a parking area near the grass-covered foundation of old, historical Fort Pownal, a British post built circa 1758, during the French and Indian War. The state park is open from 9 a.m. to sunset from Memorial Day to Labor Day. It features 120 mostly spruce-fir wooded acres and includes a mile of rocky shore, a tidal sandbar, a squat lighthouse on a bluff overlooking the river, secluded picnic sites, and a two-hundred-foot wooden pier jutting out into a portion of the southern reaches of Fort Point Cove. In the off season you can walk the 1-mile gated entrance road or drive beyond it a few hundred feet and turn left onto an alternative entrance road, aptly named Lighthouse Road. Drive down this road 1 mile to a dead end at a secondary entrance to the state park. From here, a short walk (0.1 mile) leads to an outstanding overarching view of the Penobscot River channel and an expansive view looking south from the lighthouse bluff. A list of potential birds and wildlife from the bluff includes terns, gulls, diving ducks, loons, an occasional Black Guillemot, harbor seals, and harbor porpoise.

You can also walk a winding path that leads to the shore just beyond the lighthouse bluff. This path (an additional 0.4 miles) takes you to the aforementioned yet somewhat secretive elevated pier for an extra-special, water-level perspective for scoping the cove and river. Look for Red-throated Loon, Red-necked Grebe, Horned Grebe, and Ruddy Duck, among others.

Back in your vehicle, continue approximately 3 miles along the Cape Jellison Road loop, where you come to a left turn for **Stockton Harbor.** This is the **town dock** area where local fishermen and summer sailors alike moor their boats. It is the best place to scan the inner protected waters of the peninsula and provides a perfect view toward the westerly located Sears Island causeway. This vantage point often affords closer inspection of assorted waterfowl, using a scope, of course. A small town pier and an adjacent longer private pier are situated a few hundred feet apart, and both often support resting Herring Gulls, but sort through them for the possibility of other gull species.

The various habitats of Cape Jellison include river/bay/cove waters; spruce-fir forest, mixed forest; developed house lots, some with bird feeders, some with natural landscaping; and promising-looking dirt lanes with private property signs. Looking down these side roads, I've often found Ruffed Grouse dust bathing or foraging along the (unpaved) lane edges, or feeding in old apple trees.

A spotting scope is a must to get the most out of this route. I often combine the Cape Jellison Loop with a Sears Island causeway excursion, especially when seeking winter waterfowl, easily completing the combined route within two to three hours. Cape Jellison and Fort Point State Park are also good places to check during years with finch irruptions.

SITE WO12 Sandy Point Beach and Sandy Point Wildlife Management Area

TOWN Stockton Springs. DeLorme Map 23 E2. SEASON April–October.
VISITATION 30 min. to 1.5 hrs. for Sandy Point Beach (SPB); ♿ and restroom at SPB; 1–2 hrs. for SPWMA; no restroom facilities. HIGHLIGHTS Breeding Osprey and Double-crested Cormorant; warblers during spring migration (SPB); breeding Ring-necked Duck and American Bittern (SPWMA).

Sandy Point Beach is a one-hundred-acre pocket park that combines mixed woodland with a narrow strip of sandy beach along the Penobscot River. It is a popular spot for sunbathing and swimming in summer. During the nineteenth century, several schooner shipyards were active on Sandy Point Beach, and a sawmill bordered the north end. Today, remnants of an old pier support nesting Double-crested Cormorant and Osprey in plain view a short distance from shore. Sandy Point Wildlife Management Area, also known as Stowers Meadow, is 2 miles northeast of Sandy Point Beach. American Bittern, Ring-necked Duck, and Hooded Merganser are found at the southern end of this 564-acre freshwater wetland that drains into the Penobscot River at Sandy Point. To bird this patch adequately you'll want to do so by canoe.

DIRECTIONS

From the junction of US Route 1 and Route 3 in Belfast follow US Route 1 North/Route 3 East for 13.3 miles and turn right onto Steamboat Wharf Road. Drive 0.3 miles to the intersection of Steamboat Wharf Road and Hersey Retreat Road (French's Point Road). To go to Sandy Point Beach continue straight downhill (on Steamboat Wharf Road) to a gravel parking lot, where several paths lead through low, weedy vegetation to the beach. To explore the woodland, instead of going directly to the beach, turn right onto Hersey Retreat Road and immediately left into a small parking lot with trail signs and a restroom. This lot is the trailhead for two good birding trails. Sandy Point Beach Trail is an 0.3-mile-long wheelchair-accessible path that connects the upper woods to the beach. A spur leads to an exceptional overlook of the beach and river.

A quick walk to the overlook will give you a good indication of bird activity in the area.

The Amazon Trail is a 1.1-mile blue-blazed trail, with over 1,000 feet of bog bridging through a lowland forest of cedar and tamarack. This trail takes more effort and time, as the tighter habitat makes for slower birding. Birds are usually detected by ear, and then the visual search can commence.

Both these trails offer forest birding, including all the expected residents. During spring migration expect to see a variety of warblers and other perching birds. Northern Waterthrush and Canada Warbler are among those, especially along the Amazon Trail. Where Sandy Point Beach Trail overlooks the beach and river, look for waterbirds. To get to the Sandy Point Wildlife Management Area, located off Muskrat Farm Road, start at the intersection of Steamboat Wharf Road and Hersey Retreat Road. Follow Hersey Retreat Road east for 0.6 miles and turn right onto Sandy Point Road. In 0.2 miles turn left onto Muskrat Farm Road, and in another 0.2 miles, at the stop sign, continue straight across Route 1/3. In yet another 0.2 miles turn right onto a poorly marked rough dirt track (Game Reserve Road). Drive the last 0.1 mile carefully to a parking area by a small dam breast. Scan the open water, wetland edges, and surrounding forested uplands from this vantage point. It is best if you put in a canoe here and go upstream to enjoy much better birding and access to some of the farther and fingered reaches of this surprising wetland. Pied-billed Grebe and Least Bittern are reportedly breeding here, though I could find no confirmation of the latter.

RARITIES

Black Skimmer, September 2010 (SPB); Tundra Swan, November 2014 (SPWMA)

SITE WO13 Unity Area

TOWNS Unity, Thorndike, Troy. DeLorme Maps 21 and 22: C, D, and E.
SEASON All year, but especially **April–October.**   **VISITATION** 2-plus hrs.

Seasonal facilities located at Field of Dreams.   HIGHLIGHTS   Black Tern, Purple Martin, and sixteen species of breeding warblers; spring and especially fall migration.

The Unity area is best known as the home of the Common Ground Fair, an annual regional rural life and agricultural harvest celebration, and Unity College, a small liberal arts college that specializes in experiential learning and sustainability science. Additionally, the area boasts a variety of habitats that support an intriguing array of bird life from spring through fall. Area breeding birds include little-known colonies of Black Tern, Purple Martin, and, more recently, Sandhill Crane. Farmlands surrounding Unity support American Kestrel, Eastern Meadowlark, Northern Harrier, and Bobolink. Fall migration can be impressive for the diversity of birds found at the sunny edges of agricultural habitats during early morning hours. During winter, diversity dwindles; however, concentrations of Bohemian Waxwings and other irruptives make an investigative trip to this area worthwhile anytime.

DIRECTIONS

To get to Unity from I-95 take Exit 132 and head east on Route 139 for about 15 miles to the junction of School Street and Main Street (Route 202/9) in the town center. The directions to prime birding destinations in this section can be reached by going relatively short distances in various directions from this central intersection.

The Sebasticook Regional Land Trust (SRLT), headquartered across the street from the intersection of School and Main Streets in "downtown" Unity, has conserved almost four thousand acres, primarily concentrated in the Unity area. One example of SRLT holdings is the Kanokolus Bog Preserve 3 miles south of town. This bog's unique plant community, dominated by dwarf sheep laurel, black spruce, and larch, is similar to habitats in northern Maine. Palm Warblers seen late in spring may indicate that they may breed at this site. Access to the bog itself is quite difficult but possible from the SRLT trail system. Pick up a map at the office or check the website for a full list of properties, directions, and events. Better yet, SRLT folks are your best source to get the skinny or at least an orientation to the destinations that follow.

Two bodies of water, Unity Pond and Carlton Pond, situated less than 5 miles apart, are the focal points around which the other area birding locations mentioned can easily be incorporated during a visit. To start, head for **Unity**

Pond's southern end, which gets the most birding attention, by turning left at the intersection of School and Main Streets. Follow Main Street for 0.2 miles and make a left onto **Kanokolus Road**, which leads to a public boat launch. Be sure to bird this road all along the way. If you have time, walk it (1.2 miles) and bird from the cemetery through the forested wetlands, searching from forest floor to treetops, before reaching the lake. Continue on Kanokolus Road to a parking lot and public boat launch area separated by railroad tracks. The road becomes private beyond the parking lot.

Take time to carefully scope the lake. Mergansers in spring and diving ducks in autumn often occur here. Black Scoter visit every year in October, while Common Eider and Harlequin Duck have been onetime finds.

Opposite the lake, across the railroad tracks, scan the extensive willow-dominated wetlands for American Bittern, Pied-billed Grebe, and Eastern Kingbird. This expanse, thickly vegetated and bordered by deciduous woods, is also a great place to hone your birding-by-ear skills, as a cacophony of birdsong seems always to precede visual detection of any one species.

A great way to see more of Unity Pond is by boat from this launch. In particular, paddle or motor northwest about a quarter of a mile and go under the railroad trestle. Keep to the left to explore a stream outlet area to look for Sora, Virginia Rail, shorebirds, and breeding waterfowl. Boating progress will eventually become blocked by low water or deadfalls. However, Northern Waterthrush, both cuckoos, and other lowland species occur along this waterway. Return by backtracking to the boat launch.

Field of Dreams is another place to gain access to Unity Pond and is the easiest location in the area to find Purple Martin. This public recreation complex is located 0.6 miles north of the intersection of School Street on Route 202/9 East (Main Street).

Carlton Pond, a human-made wetland and waterfowl production area of over one thousand acres, shaped like an emaciated dragon with an outstretched wing, is best known for its Black Tern colony. They are best observed by canoe launched at Bog Road in Troy. Head north from the central intersection in Unity, follow Main Street (Route 202/9 East) for 3.8 miles until Route 220 North splits. Continue on Route 220 North for 3.1 miles and take a right onto the dirt Bog Road. In 0.4 miles you'll reach a pull-off area on the left. Put in your paddle craft here and head upstream into the large yet narrow and somewhat mysterious Carlton Pond, with plenty of shoreline and open water to investigate. It is a spectacular, isolated spot that also holds Marsh

Wren, American Bittern, Pied-billed Grebe, and other interesting species, including recently confirmed breeding Sandhill Crane.

The agricultural fields of **Ward Hill Road** can be reached by following Route 202/9 East from the central intersection for 0.2 miles. Make a right to continue on Route 139 East, which joins Route 220 South in 0.7 miles. Make a right and continue on Route 139 East/220 South for 1.3 miles. Make a left onto Ward Hill Road. Scan the fields for the next 0.3 miles and turn left on Fisher Road. The short stretch of Ward Hill Road leading to and including farms along Fisher Road, especially the scrubby habitat in early fall, is where rare species in recent years have included Blue Grosbeak, Western Kingbird, and Clay-colored Sparrow. Later in the season an orchard just beyond Fisher Road attracts Purple Finch, waxwings, and wintering robins.

The **Unity College campus trail system** also offers easy access to fine birding. At 0.3 miles south of the blinking light at the central intersection on Route 202/9 West, turn left onto Quaker Hill Road. In 0.3 miles turn right to enter the campus on Loop Road. In 0.3 miles make a right into the parking lot adjacent to the athletic fields. Walk across the field to the trail marker; a trail map is a short distance beyond. The trails support an array of mature forest species, and the Hemlock Trail has hosted Black-backed Woodpecker in the past.

Across Quaker Hill Road from the main campus, old-field habitat and overgrown multiflora rose often yield surprises. Brown Thrasher is a probable breeding bird here, and migrating warblers linger in the thickets and hedgerows longer than in surrounding areas. During winter this area provides food and shelter for robins and both species of waxwing, which are sometimes joined by Eastern Bluebird, Gray Catbird, or Hermit Thrush.

RARITIES

Wilson's Phalarope, May 2014 (Unity Pond); Crested Caracara, August 2014 (Freedom)

Learn more about the "Field of Dreams" at Unity College's website, http://www.unity.edu/, and about the other sites at the Sebasticook Regional Land Trust's website, http://www.sebasticookrlt.org/.

SITE WO14 Howard L. Mendall (Marsh Stream) Wildlife Management Area

TOWN Frankfort. DeLorme Map 23: E1. **SEASON** May–October.
VISITATION 30 min. to 1 hr. Portable toilet at public boat launch.
HIGHLIGHTS Breeding Nelson's Sparrow, Virginia Rail, and Bald Eagle.

This is one of the most significant tidal salt marsh areas in the greater Penobscot Bay estuary. It appears promising upon first glance and can often yield good birding rewards. However, some sought-after species are relatively small and skulking and can be quite hard to hear over the din of constant traffic along Route 1A. Expanses of mudflats at low tide are worthy of careful scanning for peeps and larger shorebirds foraging for invertebrates. Access is via two parking areas along the South Branch of Marsh Stream, a tributary of the Penobscot River.

DIRECTIONS

From the junction of US Route 1 and Route 3 in Belfast follow US Route 1 North/Route 3 East for 10.7 miles. Bear left to follow Route 1A. The marsh will come into view on the right in 5 miles, a striking contrast to the otherwise rural scenery along the highway until this point. The first parking area, which is somewhat hidden by a stand of aspen trees, is a short, tricky downhill pull-off at 6.4 miles from the where you turned onto Route 1A from Route 1/3. The main access point and public boat launch is another 0.6 miles north of the first opportunity to park.

Start at the first parking area and walk an 0.1-mile dirt lane leading to a skeleton of an old jetty. Emerging from the woods, you will have marsh on both sides and the river's edge directly ahead. Look and listen for Nelson's Sparrow on both sides, as well as nesting Spotted Sandpiper. The key is to scan carefully time and again while listening between the passing traffic for the gentle sneeze of the Nelson's Sparrow. There is considerable marsh acreage across the river, which is bounded by a wooded hillside. Bald Eagle often perch on hillside snags, while low-lying marsh snags, between river and hillside, support predaceous birds such as Belted Kingfisher and Peregrine Falcon.

Turning into the main parking and boat launch area allows you to drive directly to the river's edge. Inspect the parking area for sparrows, Horned Lark, and Snow Bunting from fall through early spring. Use a spotting scope to scan the larger upstream expanse of marsh and river for Common Merganser (fall through spring) and Northern Harrier. This section of the Penobscot River watershed, in addition to a variety of common birds, can turn up occasional oddities such as Common Tern in early fall and Rough-legged Hawk and Snowy Owl in winter.

10 Hancock County

RICH MACDONALD

Hancock County is the home of Mount Desert Island and Acadia National Park. Acadia is magnificent and should be on everyone's list of places to visit, birders and non-birders alike. Great hiking, breathtaking scenery, and easy access combine to make this a prime destination for all. The lovely town of Bar Harbor is the gateway to this national park, and although it can be crowded and a bit overwhelming for residents in the summer, it doesn't rival the abominations that have sprung up at the entrances to many of America's other national treasures. It also offers some good birding nearby and great places to eat and drink.

Mount Desert Island—"MDI"—is a big island, the second largest on the US East Coast (only New York's Long Island is bigger). You'll want several days to do it justice, especially to combine the other pleasures of the national park and Bar Harbor with your birding.

When I visit, I will often spend one morning at Sieur de Monts Spring (within site H4), or in fall, following a north or northwest wind, try the "morning flight" from the island's north end at Thompson Island (H4). With northwesterly winds in the fall, I will then head up Cadillac Mountain (H4) for some hawk watching, or I'll check out some of the hot spots such as Bass Harbor Marsh (H4), Sewall Picnic Area (H4), and the MDI High School water treatment ponds (H6). Afternoon hiking or sightseeing is always added to the mix, with a break for popovers at the park's Jordan Pond House.

On the next day, a visit to the island's "Quiet Side" (H5) can be rewarding, for both relative tranquillity and the birding. I also work in a trip with the Bar Harbor Whale Watch Company (H7), which in summer offers a combined "Whales and Puffins" tour that will produce Atlantic Puffin, Razorbills, and Arctic Terns at Petit Manan Island, followed by a trip to deeper waters to look for whales (especially humpbacks) and the chance at a variety of pelagic species. From the end of May through mid-October, the regular whale watch trip offers the most consistently productive pelagic birding in Maine.

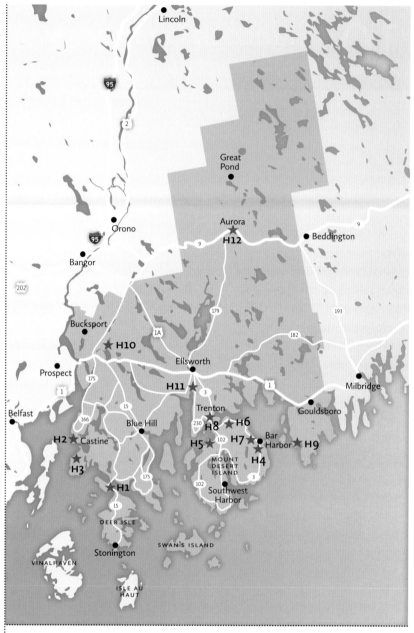

Lincoln

95

2

Great
Pond

Aurora
H12

9

Beddington

95

Orono

Bangor

202

Bucksport

H10

179

9

193

Prospect

175

1A

Ellsworth

182

1

Milbridge

Belfast

1

15

166

Blue Hill

H11

3

Trenton

230

Gouldsboro

H2 Castine

H8 H6

H5 H7 Bar H9
Harbor

H3

102

H4

MOUNT
DESERT
ISLAND

175

102

3

H1

Southwest
Harbor

15

DEER ISLE

SWAN'S ISLAND

Stonington

VINALHAVEN

ISLE AU
HAUT

HANCOCK COUNTY

Like most people, birders tend to head straight to MDI, but Hancock County offers a whole lot more. In fact, for most species of interest, and even for a lot of general birding, the birding off of MDI is often quite a bit better.

During migration, especially in fall, try Deer Isle (H1). Following a northerly wind, the morning flight from Causeway Beach or Scott's Landing can be fantastic. Meanwhile, the diverse habitats encountered on the Blue Hill Peninsula Tour (H2) can produce over twenty species of warblers in the breeding season and has amassed an impressive list of rarities over the years.

Although it's not covered specifically in Rich MacDonald's chapter, I am drawn to the town of Stonington at the south end of Deer Isle. It gives me a serious case of "rarity fever," and the village center and waterfront look prime for a "mega" rarity, especially in late fall. One early November visit with some friends resulted in an unidentified warbler flying over, giving an unfamiliar call note—the one that got away?

During the breeding season, many of the sought-after "boreal specialists," especially Black-backed Woodpecker and Spruce Grouse, are more likely off of MDI, such as in Acadia National Park's mainland section on the Schoodic Peninsula (H9). Even better, venture farther inland and explore the Stud Mill Road (H12), which can yield Boreal Chickadees, Gray Jays, and more of the spruce-loving warblers. —*Derek Lovitch*

SITE H1 Deer Isle Tour

TOWNS Deer Isle and Stonington. DeLorme Map 15: C–E3–4.
SEASON All year, but especially **May–September.** VISITATION An entire day for thorough coverage; 15–30 min. for Causeway Beach; otherwise, a couple of hours for each of the hot spots mentioned below. Restrooms at local businesses. HIGHLIGHTS Spring and fall warbler migration; spring and fall shorebird migration (more than sixteen species of shorebird can be found in numbers on the abundant mudflats nestled in coves).

Deer Isle is actually two towns, each on its own island—Deer Isle on Little Deer Isle to the north, and Stonington on Deer Isle to the south—connected by a causeway, Route 15. With 112 miles of shoreline, there are seemingly countless places to explore for birds. Public lands are few on Deer Isle, so birding is largely focused on the preserves of Island Heritage Trust.

From May to early August, Old Quarry Ocean Adventures offers boat tours

If you're anywhere along the Maine coast and you're looking at saltwater, you'll probably see Common Eiders. © Jeannette Lovitch

to Seal Island to see Atlantic Puffins and a massive Common and Arctic Tern nesting colony (with smaller numbers of Razorbill, Common Murre, and Great Cormorant) and the possibility of arranging to chase the Red-billed Tropicbird that has returned to the island annually since 2005.

DIRECTIONS

From us Route 1 drive 4.4 miles east of the traffic light at the main intersection in downtown Bucksport, turn right onto Route 15 South, and travel for 23.8 miles to the Deer Isle Bridge, a historic suspension bridge over Eggemoggin Reach at the head of Deer Isle.

Alternatively, westbound on us Route 1 South from Ellsworth, just on the west side of the Union River, turn left onto Route 172 South and continue for 13.5 miles to Blue Hill. In Blue Hill, head south on Routes 15/176. In 11.2 miles, Route 15 will bring you to the Deer Isle Bridge.

Cross the bridge. Continuing south, Route 15 quickly makes a ninety-degree left turn onto a causeway (do not stop on the causeway, as there is no shoulder). Just after the south end of the causeway, on the left, is **Scott's Landing**

Preserve, twenty-two acres of mixed upland habitat, fields, and oceanfront shoreline owned and managed by the Island Heritage Trust (IHT). Breeding warblers such as American Redstart and Yellow Warbler predominate in the second-growth habitat, while many species can often be found in migration. The fields are good for Savannah Sparrow and Eastern Towhee. Along the shore, look for sea ducks—Common Eider year-round; scoters, mergansers, goldeneye, and Bufflehead in the winter—Black Guillemot, and Bald Eagle. Plan on a minimum of one hour, but you can easily spend several more.

Across the street is IHT's **Causeway Beach** (there is parking here, too; or just walk across the road from Scott's Landing, but beware of traffic zooming by). On a rising tide in the spring and fall, look for shorebirds; a good day can yield more than ten species. A quick scan can be done in minutes from the comfort of your car, but spending more time can bring nice results. Ospreys nest nearby. Bald Eagles are common year-round. This is an excellent place to look for sparrows, especially in late October. In winter, look for Red-throated and Common Loons, Horned and Red-necked Grebes, Red-breasted Mergansers, and gulls (including Bonaparte's and sometimes Black-headed, Iceland, Lesser Black-backed, and Glaucous).

Continue south on Route 15 for another 8.1 miles. Turn left onto Oceanville Road. In 0.8 miles turn right onto Settlement Road. Drive to the end to **Old Quarry Ocean Adventures.** There is camping here, restrooms, and a modest general store. The staff are experts in local information. They offer nature tours of various lengths through the surrounding islands on a converted lobster boat, with visits including Isle au Haut (home to a portion of Acadia National Park) and Seal Island National Wildlife Refuge, the site where Dr. Stephen Kress successfully reintroduced puffins to the Maine coast in 1973 following his revolutionary project on Eastern Egg Island to the southwest. For the more adventurous, kayak tours are available, led by registered Maine sea kayak guides.

Our last stop on Deer Isle is **Barred Island Preserve,** owned by the Nature Conservancy and managed by IHT. Head back to Route 15 and turn right and head north for 0.6 miles. Turn left onto Airport Road. In 2.1 miles turn right onto Burnt Cove Road/Route 15A. In 2 miles turn left onto Goose Cove Road. In 1.2 miles there will be parking for several cars on the right. A 1-mile trail of moderate difficulty takes you to the water, where you can walk at low tide to Barred Island (plan your trip for the low-tide cycle from mid-tide to mid-tide). The variety of habitat means a variety of birds—sea ducks, loons, cormorants, raptors, shorebirds, gulls, woodpeckers, flycatchers, warblers, thrushes, and sparrows—but this preserve is best appreciated in spring and fall.

RARITIES

Lesser Frigatebird, July 1960 (only state record! exact location uncertain)

For more information about Island Heritage Trust and links to its preserve guides visit www.islandheritagetrust.org/visit.html. Old Quarry Ocean Adventures can be reached by visiting www.oldquarry.com or calling 207–367–8977.

SITE H2 Blue Hill Peninsula Tour

TOWNS Brooklin, Sedgwick, Brooksville, Castine, Blue Hill, Penobscot, Surry. DeLorme Map 15: A–C2–5.   SEASON All year, but especially **November–February** and **May–June**.   VISITATION 2 hrs. to half day. Restrooms at local businesses.   HIGHLIGHTS Spring warbler migration; more than twenty species of breeding warblers; spring and fall shorebird migration; fall raptor migration; winter sea ducks. During spring migration, Olive-sided and Yellow-bellied Flycatchers, as well as Rusty Blackbird, are observed with regularity.

The Blue Hill Peninsula has a rich history that spans boatbuilding, fishing, rusticating, and academia. Today, the peninsula is stippled with magnificent colonial homes and quaint villages, with a variety of excellent birding sites in between.

DIRECTIONS

Witherle Woods, an eighty-five-acre property of the Maine Coast Heritage Trust (MCHT), offers a variety of easy trails for walking and birding. From the traffic light at the main intersection in downtown Bucksport head east on US Route 1 for 1.7 miles. Turn right onto Routes 166/175 South.

From Ellsworth to the east, from the intersection of Routes 1, 1A, and 3, follow US Route 1 South (westward) for 15.9 miles. Turn left onto School House Road. In half a mile, School House Road merges into Routes 166/175.

Continue on Routes 166/175 South for 9.9 miles to the intersection of Routes 166 and 166A, just north of Castine. Head another 0.9 miles on Route 166 South, then turn right onto Battle Avenue. In 0.8 miles the parking area will be on the right; park along the fence, but be sure not to block the gate.

Birding is at its best here May through July. Plan on spending one to three hours to hike some or all of the 4.2 miles of trails. In recent years, MCHT has employed logging as a management tool to restore the vigor of the forest after tree mortality resulting from age, insects, and major blowdowns. Today, this mixed forest of hardwoods and softwoods offers excellent birding in the spring for a wide variety of warblers.

After birding Witherle Woods, backtrack on Battle Avenue for a half mile, then turn left onto Wadsworth Cove Road. In another half mile, **Backshore Beach** parking will be on the right, and the beach will be on the left. In spring and summer, walk the road north and then east, looking for common birds such as Common Yellowthroat, Yellow Warbler, and Song Sparrow. Wadsworth Cove Road generally gets little traffic, so walk the 0.3 miles to **Hatch Cove**. If you have a spotting scope, it is worth scanning both coves, especially in winter, for sea ducks, loons, and grebes. Head back to Backshore Beach, which could prove an excellent place to look for sparrows in late fall.

Blue Hill Mountain is a preserve of Blue Hill Heritage Trust and the Town of Blue Hill. Beginning in downtown Blue Hill, at the intersection of Routes 176 and 172, follow Route 172 North for 1.2 miles, then turn left onto Mountain Road. In 0.4 miles there will be a parking area on the left. From the parking lot early on a spring morning you can find Eastern Bluebirds working the fields for insects, courting, and staking out nest boxes. Cross the road to begin hiking up Blue Hill Mountain. An 0.3-mile-long swath, perhaps 200 feet wide, is maintained most of the way up the mountain (good blueberry picking in late summer). Eastern Bluebirds nest along this trail in boxes maintained by Downeast Audubon. Continue your explorations on the six trails encompassing the open area, surrounding forests (Winter Wren and Hermit Thrush), and the summit to find more birds.

RARITIES

Calliope Hummingbird, October–November 2008, and Painted Bunting, February 2010 (amazingly, both in the same Blue Hill yard!); Northern Wheatear, May 2008 (Sedgwick)

Additional information can be found online for several of the sites listed here:

- Witherle Woods: www.mcht.org/preserves/witherle-woods.shtml
- Blue Hill Mountain: www.bluehillheritagetrust.org/blue-hill-mountain

SITE H3 Holbrook Island Sanctuary

TOWN Brooksville. DeLorme Map 15: B2. SEASON All year, but especially May–June and August–September. VISITATION A half day for thorough coverage. A couple of hours should take in most hot spots mentioned below. Restrooms at park headquarters and elsewhere as indicated on the sanctuary trail map. HIGHLIGHTS Spring passerine migration; breeding species including six species of flycatchers; six species of thrushes, at least fourteen species of warblers, Wilson's Snipe, Great Horned Owl, Yellow-bellied and Least Flycatchers, Boreal Chickadee.

Located on Cape Rosier, the 1,230-acre **Holbrook Island Sanctuary** borders Penobscot Bay and Goose Pond and includes Holbrook Island just offshore. The variety of ecosystems range from beach and mudflat coastal communities through upland habitats of spruce-fir and mixed hardwood forests to boreal wetlands to rocky hillside. The nine trails, totaling 7.5 miles, range from easy to moderate (trails can be wet, so wear appropriate footwear). Walking along the Cape Rosier Road can be just as good as hiking the trails. If doing the former, pay particular attention to areas where the road crosses wetlands. Visit the sanctuary headquarters to request a bird list.

DIRECTIONS

From the traffic light at the main intersection in downtown Bucksport head eastbound on US Route 1 North for 4.3 miles. Turn right onto Route 15, then head south for 0.7 miles. Turn right onto Route 199 South, and in 5 miles turn left onto Route 175 South. In 4.8 miles bear right on Routes 175/176 South. Turn right to remain on Route 176 South, then take a quick left onto Varnum Road. In 2.6 miles turn left onto Route 176 South again. Another 1.7 miles brings you to Cape Rosier Road.

From Ellsworth and points east, just on the west side of the Union River, turn left onto Route 172 South. Continue for 13.5 miles to Blue Hill. From the traffic circle west of Blue Hill where Routes 175 and 176 intersect, head west on Route 176 South. Pay close attention to road signs, as Route 176 twists and turns, sometimes not when you would expect it. In approximately 12 miles turn right onto Cape Rosier Road.

In 1.6 miles you will enter Holbrook Island Sanctuary, which is well signed. At this point, let your explorations begin.

All trails are worth exploring, but a few are of particular note. From the preceding intersection, turn left on Cape Rosier Road. In 0.9 miles turn right onto Otis Gray Road. Parking for the 1.4-mile **Fresh Pond Trail** begins a short distance down this dead-end road. The trail takes you through a mixed forest composed largely of conifers (a goodly portion of warbler reports come from this trail). The trail circles Fresh Pond, a kettle-hole pond with boggy fringes (look for breeding Palm Warblers) and standing spruce snags that offer perches to flycatchers (on a good day, you may find four or more species, including Yellow-bellied). Plan two hours for a casual-paced birding walk on this flat hike.

Alternatively, take the **Iceworks Trail** for 1 mile to Fresh Pond Trail. From the intersection of Cape Rosier Road and Back Road bear right onto Back Road. The trailhead will be on the left in approximately 0.6 miles. Iceworks Trail passes in and out of mixed forests, hardwood forests, and spruce-fir forests.

Continue another half mile along **Back Road** to where an unnamed wetland is plainly visible to the left. Park on the shoulder and scan the area for Wood Ducks, flycatchers, and blackbirds, including Common Grackles and possibly Rusty Blackbirds in migration. While here, walk a short distance along the road in either direction to add to your day list.

In another 0.3 miles down Back Road, turn right onto the **unnamed road** and drive to the parking at the end, where there are views of Penobscot Bay, the sanctuary's namesake Holbrook Island, and restrooms. Scan the bay for typical seabirds.

Maps and information may be found at the website for the Friends of Holbrook Island Sanctuary at www.friendsofholbrook.org/p/park-map.html.

MOUNT DESERT ISLAND

The following four sites—Acadia National Park Tour (H4); Mount Desert Island (West) Tour (H5); East Mount Desert Island Tour (H6); and Bar Harbor Whale Watch (H7)—cover a lot of ground (and a good deal of ocean), but only one island. At more than 50 miles in circumference, "MDI" is the second-largest island on the US East Coast. The Great Fire of 1947 burned a significant portion of its eastern half. As a result, MDI now has a high percentage of hardwood forest, while the western half retains a majority of boreal natural communities. The resultant admixture has yielded an impressive 352 species

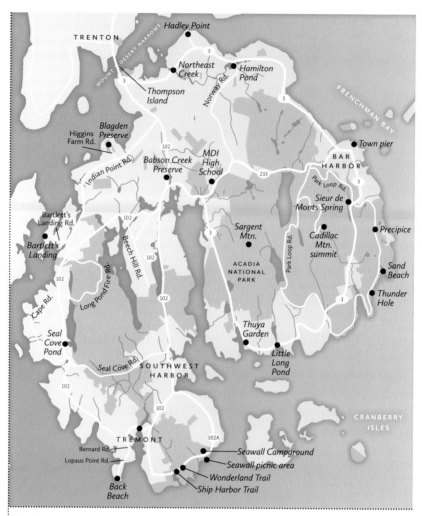

MOUNT DESERT ISLAND

documented for MDI. The island is nearly cleaved in two by Somes Sound, a fjord-like body of water. To simplify here, MDI is treated in three sections: Acadia National Park (ANP), MDI West, and MDI East. It is worth noting that, despite ANP literature claiming otherwise, Gray Jay, Boreal Chickadee, and Three-toed Woodpecker are now absent from MDI (excepting the very rare vagrant), and Spruce Grouse is a rarely observed resident. However, a wealth of birding opportunities await. I have divided the island up into three birding tours. The waterproof map of Acadia National Park by Map Adventures offers by far the best coverage of the region and is available online from the Natural History Center at www.TheNaturalHistoryCenter.com.

SITE H4 Acadia National Park Tour (including Park Loop Road)

TOWNS Tremont, Southwest Harbor, Mount Desert, Bar Harbor, Trenton. DeLorme Map 16: A–D2–4. **SEASON** All year, but especially **May–June** and **September–October.** **VISITATION** 2 hrs. to half day. Restrooms and out-houses are scattered around Acadia National Park, often at trailheads and parking lots; otherwise, visit local businesses. Fee required (see ANP website for current prices). Passes may be purchased at the ANP visitor centers on Thompson Island and in Hulls Cove, and the Park Loop Road entrance station in Bar Harbor (all open seasonally); at ANP headquarters on Route 233; or at the Bar Harbor Chamber of Commerce information center on the corner of Cottage and Main Streets in downtown Bar Harbor. **HIGHLIGHTS** Spring and fall passerine migration; at least eighteen species of breeding warblers; fall hawk watching, with ten species regularly reported and seasonal counts tallying in the thousands; spring and late fall sea watching.

Most of **Acadia National Park** is on Mount Desert Island, but there are also sections of ANP on Isle au Haut (Knox County) and the Schoodic Peninsula (treated under Schoodic Peninsula Tour, site H10 below). The entire park consists of more than forty-seven thousand acres. The Great Fire of 1947 consumed nearly nine thousand acres of ANP forest and a comparable area of the town of Bar Harbor, resulting in a greater diversity of natural communities in the eastern half of the island, which directly translates into an equally diverse bird population. Meanwhile, the western half of the island is dominated by conifers, especially spruce (as are those eastern portions of ANP that did not burn). It is in these boreal portions where there has been past evidence of breeding Cape May, Bay-breasted, and Blackpoll Warblers.

DIRECTIONS

From the intersection of US Routes 1 and 1A and Route 3 in Ellsworth, Acadia National Park can be reached by driving south on Route 3. At Trenton, cross the causeway onto **Thompson Island**. A visitor center is on the right; across the road, **Thompson Island Picnic Area** is good for gulls, winter ducks, and shorebirds (albeit in low numbers on a rising tide); you'll be thankful for a spotting scope to scan the mudflats. This is also a potential migrant trap and has been a good place for both warblers in the spring and sparrows in the fall. Walk the perimeter of the grassy area, especially the south end. Restrooms are open seasonally.

From Thompson Island make your way to **Beech Mountain** by continuing south (keep one eye peeled for herons and egrets in the wetland on the left side of the road at the south end of Thompson Island in late summer). In 0.4 miles bear right at the fork onto Routes 102/198. Continue south 5.2 miles, through Somesville—the oldest village on MDI—to the flashing light by the Somesville Fire Department and turn right onto Pretty Marsh Road/Route 102. Drive 0.2 miles on Pretty Marsh Road and turn left onto Beech Hill Road. Drive 3.1 miles and park in the lot at the end of Beech Hill Road. Take the trail at the north end of the parking lot. In just a few hundred feet, bear left at the first intersection. At approximately 0.3 miles is a vantage point offering views to the north and east. College of the Atlantic studies suggest this is the best fall hawk-watching locale in the region. Look for raptors from mid-August to mid-October on a northerly blow. Continue the remaining 0.1 mile to the summit, where an abandoned fire tower and the largely barren surroundings offer excellent views. The summit may be a good place to look for migrating raptors in the spring. On occasion, Spruce Grouse have been observed from the summit, sometimes walking between picnicking parties. While the moderate round-trip hike to the summit is less than 1 mile, plan on a minimum of two hours to have plenty of time for birding.

Backtrack down Beech Hill Road to Pretty Marsh Road and turn left. There are a number of dirt roads on the left, open seasonally to automobile traffic, that offer easy walking in very mature boreal habitat. Head 3.8 miles to Hodgdon Road on the left; within a few hundred feet turn right onto **Long Pond Fire Road**. Alternatively, continuing south another 2.4 miles on Pretty Marsh Road brings you to **Seal Cove Road** on the left. For either of these dirt roads, drive to likely birding spots—particularly dense stands of spruce and fir, and alder-laced stream crossings, which can be migrant traps—and pause to look and listen for birds (remember to walk away from your car to escape the noises of a cooling engine). These roads have a history of revealing good boreal birds, including Northern Goshawk, Olive-sided Flycatcher, Black-throated Blue Warbler (as well as a variety of other wood warblers), and White-throated Sparrow. Get an early start; the more time spent here, the better (plan thirty minutes to three hours). Take a map, as not all roads are adequately marked and can be confusing.

From Seal Cove Road continue south on Pretty Marsh Road/Route 102. In 4.6 miles Route 102 crosses a small bridge just past the Tremont Consolidated School. On the left is a small but adequate shoulder for several cars to park, within sight of **Bass Harbor Marsh.** Walk a short distance to the marsh (beware of deer ticks). Also be sure to check the vantage of Bass Harbor Marsh from Adam's Bridge (locally known as Abner's Bridge) in 0.3 miles. Parking at Abner's Bridge is on the widened shoulders on either side of the bridge. Beware, as this is a busy road, traffic is heavy, and there are not adequate shoulders to walk. Birds can be found year-round at either location as long as there is open water. A wide variety of ducks use Bass Harbor Marsh in migration, although generally in low numbers. Late summer, post-nesting-dispersal Great Egret and Snowy Egret are often found. Small numbers of shorebirds are found through much of the year, with Greater Yellowlegs being among the most common in spring and fall. The highlight species, though, is Nelson's Sparrow: this is an easy bird to hear (if you can overcome the sound of traffic) but not so easy to see. *Please note it is illegal to use audio playback to attract birds in the national park.*

Backtracking to the Tremont Consolidated School, take Route 102 toward Abner's Bridge for 0.2 miles to the gas station and turn right onto Route 102A. Parking for the **Ship Harbor Trail** is 2.3 miles on the right (there is an outhouse here). Another 0.3 miles finds the **Wonderland Trail,** also on the right. Ship Harbor is a 1.2-mile loop; Wonderland is 1.4 miles out and back. Both are nice walks in the woods with a lower, more open coniferous canopy predominated by spruce and pitch pine. The more common warblers are, well, common, but Cape May Warbler has been documented breeding here. Both trails are mostly easy, and they can be particularly good for birding during fall migration when warblers can "stack up," waiting for suitable weather to continue their migration. A nearby inaccessible patterned peatland bog offers nesting Palm Warbler and Lincoln's Sparrow, so listen carefully. Shorebirds can be found in small numbers during migration. Plan a minimum of two hours for each trail.

Another 1 mile farther along 102A is the **Seawall Picnic Area.** Turn right to enter the picnic area and park anywhere. Explore the surrounding vegetation, including the vegetation "islands" within the loops of the two parking areas, for migrating and breeding songbirds. Scan the shoreline and surrounding waters for seabirds. In winter, birds such as Red-throated Loon, Horned and Red-necked Grebe, and Great Cormorant are relatively common. Closely view the wrack line for shorebirds during migration. You will appreciate having a spotting scope here. Alcids—primarily murres and Razorbills; infrequently Dovekies—are sometimes seen. It will help to be able to identify the whirli-gig-like rapid wing-beats of alcids at a distance. This is certainly a good place to conduct a sea watch. In winter, park on the cobble verge and bird from the comfort of your heated car. Purple Sandpiper are routinely found here, often in good numbers. Northern Shrike can also appear in winter, looking for prey. A nearby former University of Maine fall banding station caught a surprising number of interesting birds, including Warbling and Philadelphia Vireo (both of which were far more abundant than previously thought), an-nual Blue-winged Warbler and Yellow-breasted Chat. The picnic area is open year-round. During the tourist season, facilities are available.

During winter, walk back to Route 102A, cross the road, and walk the var-ious loops of the **Seawall Campground** to look for winter finches, especially Purple Finch, but also White-winged and sometimes Red Crossbills. Plan thirty minutes to two hours for any of the Seawall locations.

Follow Route 102 North until it ends at Route 3 just before the bridges back to Thompson Island. Turn right to follow Route 3 South for 12.9 miles, continuing through Bar Harbor, past the Jackson Laboratory, and then turn right into **Wild Gardens of Acadia** and **Sieur de Monts Spring**. If you were to bird just one place on MDI in the spring, this would be it! An excellent network of easy, flat trails takes you through a variety of habitats, including hemlock forest, alder thickets, red maple swamp, and a scenic white birch hedgerow. Raptors, especially Turkey Vulture, Bald Eagle, and Peregrine Fal-con, regularly cruise the eastern face of Dorr Mountain, readily visible from the parking lot (MDI's two Black Vultures were seen here). As expected, the variety of birds can be tremendous. A small nature center, the Abbe Museum (featuring Native American artifacts), and good restroom facilities are all here.

From the Sieur de Monts Spring parking lot, walk out the **Hemlock Road** (more a trail, actually) 0.7 miles to the Park Loop Road. Turn left and walk 0.1 mile until you come to the **Jesup Path**, then return on that (the last 0.4 miles is a handicap-accessible boardwalk through a red maple swamp). For years, Barred Owl have nested in the vicinity of the Hemlock Trail. At least thirteen breeding warbler species can be found here, including Ovenbird, Northern

Waterthrush, Nashville, American Redstart, Northern Parula, Magnolia, Chestnut-sided, and Black-throated Blue. Up to eight species of flycatchers also breed in the area. Brown Creeper and Winter Wren can regularly be heard singing. A good morning can easily yield upward of forty species. Easily plan two to four hours, and be sure to spend some time birding and checking out the native plant collection in the Wild Gardens.

Next up is the **Precipice**, an east-facing cliff rising more than 800 feet. It is also one of four sites in ANP where Peregrine Falcons nest. To get there from Sieur de Monts Spring, make your way to the Park Loop Road (most of the road is one-way, so pay attention to the signs). Precipice will be on the right in 1.8 miles. A spring Peregrine Falcon watch is staffed by ANP rangers, and volunteers often have spotting scopes trained on the resident raptors. Peregrines were reintroduced to ANP through a hacking program beginning in 1984. Other raptors occasionally fly by, especially in spring, including Red-shouldered Hawks. The shrubby copses across the road have been known to shelter the secretive Yellow-billed and Black-billed Cuckoos. Warblers, sparrows, and finches can all be found during the spring. Plan fifteen minutes to two hours.

From Precipice, continue for another 1.4 miles along the Park Loop Road, through the entrance station (you will need a park pass, which can be purchased here if you haven't already acquired one), to Sand Beach. The next 4.8 miles of the Park Loop Road are known as **Ocean Drive**, closely paralleling the rocky shoreline. The first 2 miles are open year-round. There are numerous parking areas, several with seasonal facilities (heated, year-round facilities can be found at the Fabbri Picnic Area at 2.4 miles).

Most any seabird can be observed along this stretch, depending on the season: sea ducks, loons, grebes, gannets, cormorants, and gulls (including Black-legged Kittiwake). Alcids are known to turn up on occasion during the winter, especially Razorbill and Atlantic Puffin. A good southerly blow during summer and fall will sometimes even push in pelagic seabirds such as storm-petrels and shearwaters, especially on foggy days. The shore margin can be good for warblers, especially in the fall. **Otter Cliffs** offers an excellent place for sea watching (the Natural History Center and Schoodic Institute conduct a weekly sea watch in the fall). During winter, Purple Sandpipers can usually be found along the rocky shoreline, especially on a rising tide. In summer, check any offshore rocks or outcroppings for the occasional immature Great Cormorant that attempts to oversummer.

The view of Bar Harbor from the summit of Cadillac Mountain. © Rich MacDonald

While all the park's mountains offer spectacular hiking opportunities, and each is worth exploring, **Cadillac Mountain** can be driven. At 1,530 feet, it is the tallest mountain in Acadia (and the tallest mountain rising from the ocean on the East Coast of the United States). Continue along the Park Loop Road for another 7.5 miles and turn right onto Cadillac Summit Road. It is a 3.4-mile drive to the summit (be sure to put your car in low gear for the descent). In addition to the spectacular views, Eastern Towhee, White-throated Sparrow, and Dark-eyed Junco all nest in the krummholz forest, tucked in wind-protected pockets around the summit. Horned Lark is frequently found in spring and fall. From mid-August to the middle of October ANP operates a hawk watch at the summit where all are welcome to visit. For the intrepid (and cold tolerant), those hawk watchers putting in long hours into November are rewarded most years with a single Golden Eagle sighting.

Every winter since at least 1994, ANP has hosted a number of Snowy Owls, seen atop each of the barren summits. To have a good chance of finding them, though, means going up a mountain. Cadillac Mountain is certainly the easiest, as the road can be walked or skied or snowshoed, but **Sargent Mountain** is another place to look. In recent years, as many as six have been seen above tree line on a single hike! This is a more challenging adventure requiring the right equipment, clothing, and experience (or a guided tour with the Natural History Center). Make your way to Jordan Pond House and park. From there follow the Around Mountain Carriage Road for 1.4 miles along the west shore of Jordan Pond to the Deer Brook Trail. Climb the Deer Brook Trail 0.6 miles to the Sargent South Ridge Trail. Another 0.7 miles up that trail brings you to the summit. Snowy Owls are generally found above tree line in habitat simulating their Arctic tundra environment.

RARITIES

Lark Sparrow, September 2004 (Fabbri Picnic Area); Black Vulture, July 2005 (Sieur de Monts Spring) and October 2005 (Cadillac Mountain Hawk Watch); Magnificent Frigatebird, August 2007 (Sieur de Monts); Townsend's Solitaire, March 2009 (Huguenot Head); Western Kingbird, November 2014 (Stanley Brook, Seal Harbor); Swainson's Hawk, October 2015 (Cadillac Mountain); Eurasian Wigeon, December 2015 (Bass Harbor Marsh)

For visitation information, fees, and maps, visit the park's home page at www.nps.gov/acad.

SITE H5 Mount Desert Island (West) Tour

TOWNS Tremont, Southwest Harbor, Mount Desert, Bar Harbor, Trenton. DeLorme Map 16: A–D1–3. **SEASON** December–March, April, **May–June**, July–August, **September**, October–November. **VISITATION** Many sites can be covered in half an hour; otherwise, up to a half day to cover a good representation of the "hot spots" mentioned below. Restrooms at local businesses. **HIGHLIGHTS** Spring and fall passerine migration; at least fifteen species of breeding warbler; early spring and late fall sea watching.

The west side of Mount Desert Island—that is, everything west of the fjord-like Somes Sound—is locally known as the Quiet Side. Spared the ravages of the Great Fire of '47, the overall landscape more resembles that of forests farther north. As a result, there is a higher concentration of boreal species; for example, a 1970s Acadia National Park study found that the only Spruce Grouse nesting on MDI were in the vicinity of Hall Quarry, along the north-west shore of Somes Sound. Today, the Quiet Side offers superb birding. For those rainy days when you just cannot rally to go birding, check out the Wendell Gilley Museum in Southwest Harbor, a museum dedicated to the bird carvings of Wendell Gilley (1904–83).

From the intersection of US Routes 1 and 1A and Route 3 in Ellsworth, drive south on Route 3. At Trenton, cross the causeway onto tiny Thompson Island at the head of MDI, then continue south 0.4 miles, bearing right at the fork onto Route 102 South. Continue south for 1.9 miles, then turn right onto Indian Point Road. In another 1.9 miles, Higgins Farm Road will be on the right. At the intersection is a red barn with a parking lot and a small sign indicating the Nature Conservancy's **Indian Point Blagden Preserve.** This 110-acre preserve is largely forested in spruce-fir with frontage on Western Bay. A checklist of birds and a trail map can be found in the alcove in the side of the barn near the Big Wood trailhead.

While birding is generally quiet, it's a fine spot to sample the local resident species. Along the shoreline, sea ducks, loons, and grebes are common, especially in winter. The lure that continues to attract birders is the hope of seeing a Black-backed Woodpecker—Blagden Preserve contributes many of the island's infrequent sightings. Plan on spending two to four hours.

In the winter, continue south on Indian Point Road for another 3.8 miles, then turn right onto Bartletts Landing Road. Drive to **Bartletts Landing** at the end (1 mile) and scan the water for sea ducks (Common Eider, all three scoters, Long-tailed Duck, Bufflehead, Common Goldeneye, and Red-breasted Merganser), Red-throated and Common Loons, Horned and Red-necked Grebes, Great Cormorant, and Bald Eagle. Alcids, especially Thick-billed Murre and Razorbill, can be seen surprisingly often as you look west toward Bartlett Island. On the way out, park near the cemetery and quickly check out Pretty Marsh during the breeding season.

Backtrack to Indian Point Road and turn right. Drive the 0.3 miles to the end, then turn right onto Pretty Marsh Road (Route 102). In 1.6 miles turn right onto **Cape Road.** Park on the shoulder as soon as you turn and can find a suitable spot. The wetland in the southwest corner of Cape Road and Route 102 has been known to yield Sora and Virginia Rail, as well as Yellow-bellied Flycatcher. Walk across Route 102 and up Hodgdon Road. This is one of the few places where House Wren is found on MDI. Return to your vehicle.

The more ambitious may choose to walk the entirety of the Cape Road; others may choose to drive it, reaching the waters of Seal Cove in 2.7 miles. The alder swales that are bisected by Cape Road often have nesting Canada

Warbler. Black-billed Cuckoo and Blue-gray Gnatcatcher are sometimes found in the hedgerows closer to Seal Cove. Walk along the Cape Road to the boat launch (0.4 mile). The scrubby alders lining the inland side of the road produce a good variety of breeding and migrant songbirds. During the winter, Seal Cove offers yet another look for sea ducks, loons, grebes, and Black Guillemot. Plan on spending as little as a half hour and as much as two to three hours, depending on how much walking you do. There is an outhouse near the boat launch.

Continue on the remaining half mile of Cape Road, making a big loop, back to Route 102. Turn left onto Route 102 and head 0.3 miles to a pull-off on the right at **Seal Cove Pond.** You can scan it from the road, but it is a good place to launch a canoe or kayak. It is likely that Pied-billed Grebe and American Bittern nest in this area, as they are sometimes seen during breeding season.

Turning around, continue south on Route 102, driving 4.4 miles toward Bass Harbor, then turn right onto Bernard Road. Drive down Bernard Road for half a mile, then turn right onto **Lopaus Point Road.** On the left at 0.4 miles are a school bus turnaround and a dirt lane heading a few hundred feet to **Back Beach.** This is a good year-round birding hot spot. Scan the waters of Bass Harbor, walk the cobble seawall of Back Beach, and walk up and down Lopaus Point Road. Sea ducks, loons, grebes, cormorants, herons, shorebirds, gulls, flycatchers, warblers, sparrows, and more all turn up in appropriate seasons. Breeding Nelson's Sparrow can be found here, too. Plan on twenty minutes to an hour. There is an outhouse here.

Backtrack to Route 102 and turn right. Drive 10 miles north, passing through Southwest Harbor and Somesville. On the north edge of Somesville, look for the offices of Maine Coast Heritage Trust on the right (0.2 miles north of the Foster's Somesville On the Run convenience store). As you pull into their drive, it bends ninety degrees to the left, where there is parking on the right for the trailhead to **Babson Creek Preserve.** After signing the register, walk down the hill and follow the mown path. There is a mixture of field, deciduous forest edge, and estuarine wetland. From spring through fall this is a good birding locale. Highlights include nesting Canada Goose (which have been nesting on MDI only since 2010), American Black Duck, Osprey, Belted Kingfisher, and Nelson's Sparrow, as well as a variety of other passerines. Greater Yellowlegs can be found here for much of that time, perhaps nonbreeding individuals that did not continue their migration north. Plan on spending thirty minutes to two hours.

Lark Sparrow, November 2014 (Manset); Lark Bunting, May 2015 (Seal Cove)

SITE H6 East Mount Desert Island Tour

TOWNS Mount Desert and Bar Harbor. DeLorme Map 16: A–C3–4.
SEASON December–March, April, **May–June**, July–August, **September,**
October–November.   **VISITATION** An entire day for thorough coverage.
A half hour each for the highlight sites; otherwise, a couple of hours for
each of the hot spots mentioned below. Restrooms at local businesses.
HIGHLIGHTS Spring and fall passerine migration; at least fifteen species
of breeding warbler; early spring and late fall sea watching.

If the west side of MDI is the Quiet Side, then the east side (everything east
of the fjord-like Somes Sound) must be "the Noisy Side." It certainly gets the
vast majority of the tourists. It is also home to the MDI's largest village, Bar
Harbor, as well as the villages of Northeast Harbor and Seal Harbor, where
many of the most expensive homes on the island are found. A good variety
of forest and habitat types yields a diversity of birdlife in all seasons.

DIRECTIONS

From the intersection of US Routes 1 and 1A and Route 3 in Ellsworth, drive
south on Route 3. At Trenton, cross the causeway onto tiny Thompson Island
at the head of MDI, then continue south for another 2.3 miles on Route 3 to
Northeast Creek, where there is good parking on the right, just beyond the
guardrail. Scout the pool across the road (beware of traffic, as this is a busy
road) for ducks and shorebirds (especially Greater and Lesser Yellowlegs)
during spring and fall migration and Belted Kingfisher anytime, so long as
it is not frozen.

Continue along Route 3 the 1 mile to **Hadley Point** on the left. Drive 0.7
miles to the glacial outwash plain at the end. Park anywhere except in the
way of the boat launch. This is a particularly good place in winter to look
for sea ducks, loons, grebes, and cormorants. Bald Eagles nest nearby on the
Twinnies (two small islands to the west; they blend in with the far shore) and
frequently fly by. During spring, check the forest edge for songbirds. And in
spring and fall migration this is a good spot for shorebirds and Bonaparte's
Gull. Here you can bird from the comfort of your vehicle. A spotting scope

is particularly helpful. Plan on a minimum of fifteen minutes, but on a good day be prepared to spend one or more hours.

Backtrack to Route 3 and turn left. Continue 1.6 miles to Norway Drive and turn right. The fifty-one-acre **Hamilton Pond** is nestled in the corner of Route 3 and Norway Drive. Park as you can and scour the pond, especially in late fall before it freezes over and in the early spring after ice-out for ducks, when Ring-necked Duck and Greater Scaup are regularly found.

Continue down Norway Drive for 0.8 miles to a red-roofed barn on the right. These agricultural fields are part of the College of the Atlantic's **Peggy Rockefeller Farm.** Park in the first lot before the barn and at a slightly higher elevation. The fields are prime breeding habitat for Tree Swallow, Eastern Bluebird (albeit in very small numbers), Savannah Sparrow, and Bobolink. Walk along Norway Drive and count the abundant Bobolink or listen for the soft and gentle *see-say* of the Savannah Sparrow.

Drive to the end of Norway Drive, through the Crooked Road intersection, for a total of 3.2 miles to Eagle Lake Road/Route 233 and turn right. In 1.2 miles you will approach the **MDI High School** on the right. Pull into the high school and park in the first parking lot on the left, all the way to the far edge near the baseball backstop. Walk the dirt lane behind the school and around the water treatment ponds (a total of a quarter mile). The ponds and surrounding mixed habitat (including a tamarack forest) are excellent for birding all year long except when they are frozen. Along with Sieur de Monts Spring in Acadia National Park, this is one of the two best places on MDI for spring warbler migration. That said, you need to be here early; sunrise is best. Wood Duck nest here, and the Tamarack forest yields singing Winter Wren. Shorebirds, especially Solitary Sandpiper, are routine in migration. This can be birded as quickly as twenty minutes and can take up to four hours, all depending on the birds.

Take Route 233 East toward Bar Harbor, where in 5.7 miles there is a stop sign. Turn left onto Main Street. In 0.3 miles turn right onto West Street. The **town pier**, with plenty of parking, will be on your left. During the winter, browse the harbor for sea ducks, Great Cormorants, Black Guillemots, and, on rare occasion, Thick-billed Murres and Razorbills.

From there, walk the half-mile **Shore Path** that hugs the rocky harbor behind downtown Bar Harbor. This is an easy out-and-back walk. Sea ducks, especially Common Eider, are common, as are Red-breasted Merganser in all but summer. Red-throated Loon can often be seen from October to April, and the rare Pacific Loon also has been observed from here on several occasions. Bald Eagle and Black Guillemot are year-round regulars. Plan on a minimum of thirty minutes for this walk.

From Bar Harbor take Route 3 South for 9.2 miles through Seal Harbor to **Little Long Pond**. Check the pond for ducks, and the 4-mile Carriage Road loop around the preserve is a lovely walk through a mature forest of spruce and fir. Of most interest are the spruces at the north end of the property, which often host White-winged Crossbills year-round. Plan on a minimum of half an hour, or two hours or more to walk the entire 3.9-mile loop.

Continuing along Route 3, in 1.8 miles on the left is a parking lot for the **Thuya Garden** (open seasonally). Cross the road and follow the easy-to-moderate 0.2-mile path (handicapped parking at the top) uphill to Thuya Garden. The garden itself is in the old English style, replete with vast beds of flowers. Ruby-throated Hummingbirds are abundant in late summer. Plan a minimum of thirty minutes.

RARITIES

Ivory Gull, February 1940 (one collected in Southwest Harbor); Black Vulture, summer 2004 and September 2006 (both Bar Harbor); Magnificent Frigatebird, August 2005 (Bar Harbor Town Pier); Green Violetear, August 2007 (Northeast Harbor; first state record); White-winged Dove, July 2010 (head of MDI); Black-bellied Whistling-Duck (six), May–June 2013 (MDI High School ponds); Yellow-throated Warbler, April 2016 (Southwest Harbor)

SITE H7 Bar Harbor Whale Watch

TOWN Bar Harbor. DeLorme Map 16: B4.   SEASON End of May to mid-October.   VISITATION 4 hrs. Restrooms at the Bar Harbor Whale Watch building ashore; "heads" are available on the ship, as is a snack bar. See website for schedule, prices, and reservations.   HIGHLIGHTS Breeding Atlantic Puffin, Razorbill, and a few Common Murres, along with Arctic and Common Terns; pelagic seabirds including Great, Sooty, Manx (uncommon), and Cory's (rare) Shearwaters, Northern Fulmar, Wilson's and Leach's Storm-Petrels, Northern Gannet, Red and Red-necked Phalaropes, Great and South Polar Skua, Pomarine and Parasitic Jaeger, and Black-legged Kittiwake.

Perhaps the best way to see true pelagic birds in Maine is to go on a tour with Bar Harbor Whale Watch. From the end of May through mid-August, their morning tour takes in Petit Manan Island, one of the islands in the Maine Coastal Islands National Wildlife Refuge, where there is a vibrant nesting colony of seabirds. The boat spends twenty to forty minutes there, then heads farther offshore to look for whales. And where there are whales there are seabirds. The afternoon tour, as well as all tours from mid-August through the end of their season, only heads offshore to look for whales and seabirds. Other whale watch outings bypass Petit Manan but spend more time in deeper water looking for whales and hopefully spotting a variety of pelagics.

DIRECTIONS

From the intersection of US Routes 1 and 1A and Route 3 in Ellsworth, head south on Route 3 to Bar Harbor. In 17.7 miles, as you enter the Bar Harbor village limits, turn left onto West Street. The Bar Harbor Whale Watch is 0.6 miles on the left. Parking is along West Street or on the Town Pier, just beyond Bar Harbor Whale Watch. Note that as you approach the downtown business district, parking is timed, and scofflaws will receive a fine. Plan to arrive at least an hour early to park, get your tickets, and get on line for the boat. Arrive even earlier to get near the front of the line to be assured of your desired spot—I prefer the bow (especially for photography), but others prefer the top deck for visibility and/or proximity to the naturalist, some of whom are particularly knowledgeable about birds.

RARITIES

Chuck-will's-Widow, October 2014 (first state record; landed on the boat!); White-chinned Petrel, August 2010 (first state and first East Coast record; well offshore, in the vicinity of "the Ballpark"). An Ancient Murrelet was photographed from Petit Manan in May 2016 as part of a string of sightings of this first state record along the coast.

For schedules, tickets, and additional information visit the website of the Bar Harbor Whale Watch Company at www.barharborwhales.com.

site h8 Trenton

TOWN Trenton. DeLorme Map 16: B2.   **SEASON** All year, but especially
November–March and **May–June**.   **VISITATION** 15 min. to 2 hrs. Restrooms
at local businesses.   **HIGHLIGHTS** Snowy Owl (winter), spring warbler
migration; more than fifteen species of breeding warbler; Lincoln's Sparrow.

On your way to and from Bar Harbor and MDI, Route 3 passes through Trenton, and a couple of hot spots are always worth a check. Check the airport from late fall through early spring for Snowy Owls, and throughout the year for other grassland denizens. Meanwhile, the Trenton Community Trail can offer a nice variety of migrants and breeding species.

DIRECTIONS

The **Bar Harbor Airport** can be an excellent place to look for Snowy Owls with little effort in the winter. From the intersection of US Routes 1 and 1A and Route 3 in Ellsworth, the airport is 7.9 miles south of Ellsworth on Route 3. Turn left onto Caruso Drive. Airport personnel are accustomed to cars parked on the shoulder of the road looking for Snowy Owls. Slowly work the road all the way to the airport terminal, looking atop any post, pole, structure, or snowbank where a Snowy Owl might get a vantage point to espy potential prey. While looking for Snowy Owls, look for Snow Buntings, too. In recent years airport personnel have done some clearing of the swale at the south end of the runway. Before this clearing, it was a favored haunt of Short-eared Owls in spring and fall.

The **Trenton Community Trail,** located at the Acadia Gateway Center, is 2.1 miles north of Caruso Drive on Route 3. Turn left into Gateway Center Drive and head to the end (0.6 miles). Look for the kiosk indicating the trailhead for the 1.8-mile trail. This is a local secret, in that it gets very little use. A former Acadia National Park interpretive ranger who once lived nearby regularly found Gray Jay in the vicinity through 2013, when he moved away. A spur trail offers a boardwalk overlooking a dwarf shrub bog where Lincoln's Sparrow may be found.

A map and trail information are available from the Friends of Acadia at www.friendsofacadia.org/wp-content/uploads/2013/05/TrentonTrailInformation.pdf.

SITE H9 Schoodic Peninsula Tour

TOWN Gouldsboro. DeLorme Map 16: A–B5, Map 17: A–C1–2.
SEASON All year. **VISITATION** 2 hrs. to full day. Restrooms at local businesses and in Acadia National Park. Fee required for Acadia National Park (see Acadia National Park Tour above for details). **HIGHLIGHTS** Spring and fall warbler migration; more than thirteen species of breeding warbler; early spring and late fall sea watching; wintering Harlequin Duck and alcids.

While the Schoodic Peninsula sees far fewer visitors than Mount Desert Island, it is every bit as beautiful. Spruce Grouse and Black-backed Woodpecker breed; unfortunately, they are not easily found; still, keep your eyes peeled. In winter, small numbers of Harlequin Duck are regularly observed from Schoodic Point. Razorbills and murres are seen with enough frequency to warrant careful observation. In fact, winter birding is particularly good for the ease of access and diversity of habitats (and this is the time to look for Thick-billed Murre).

DIRECTIONS

From the intersection of US Routes 1 and 1A and Route 3 in Ellsworth, head east on US Route 1 for 18.2 miles to Route 186 in Gouldsboro. Turn right onto Route 186 South (South Goldsboro Road). Drive for 6.6 miles to the stop sign in Winter Harbor. Across the street from the stop sign is a **boat launch and small park.** During the winter, gulls often roost in the vicinity, and Iceland and Glaucous Gulls can often be found mingling with the Herring and Great Black-backed Gulls.

Continue along Route 186 for another half mile, then turn right onto Schoodic Loop Road. At 0.9 miles is the entrance to the new (opened 2015) **Schoodic Woods,** a combination campground and mixed-use recreation area spread over fifteen hundred acres in the **Schoodic Section of Acadia National Park.** This area is largely forested in dense spruce-fir, with an understory of mosses and ferns, perfect habitat for boreal birds. During the 2014 and 2015 construction of the campground, workers reported frequent encounters with Spruce Grouse! Ruby-crowned Kinglets are a common breeding bird, as are American Redstarts and Black-throated Green Warblers. During migration, birds such as Tennessee and Bay-breasted Warblers can also be found.

From the entrance to Schoodic Woods, turn left and continue on the Park Loop Road for 0.4 miles to a causeway. Look in both directions for shorebirds in spring and fall, and for Sandhill Crane (reported 2013). Both Common and Thick-billed Murres seem to make an appearance one at a time in winter, where they sometimes fall prey to Bald Eagles.

Just across the causeway, turn right into **Fraser Point,** which has plenty of parking and seasonal facilities. Explore the area for spring and fall migrants, and in winter this is a good place to search for sea ducks.

Back on Schoodic Loop Road—which now becomes one-way—continue 2.2 miles to a road on the left: **Schoodic Head Trail.** Walk up this gravel road and look and listen for birds. Among the thrushes and warblers and sparrows, Black-backed Woodpecker has been found here over the years.

Continue on the Schoodic Loop Road for another 0.8 miles and bear right onto **Arey Cove Road.** This road takes you in half a mile to the southern tip of **Schoodic Point.** Birding along the road can be quite good any time of year. Near the mouth of Arey Cove on your left and from the parking lot at the tip of Schoodic Point are good places to look for Harlequin Duck and alcids during the winter. During the breeding season, the woods along the road can be alive with songbird activity. It is an easy walk, with little traffic most times. The Schoodic Institute conducts a sea watch here from September to November each year.

Make your way back to Schoodic Loop Road and bear right at the intersection. In half a mile is the **Blueberry Hill** overlook, offering another vantage of the ocean. Across the road is the Alder Trail trailhead. In spring and summer this is an easy out-and-back walk to look for songbirds.

RARITIES

Scissor-tailed Flycatcher, May 2003 (Prospect); Lark Sparrow, September 2012 (Schoodic Section of Acadia National Park); Townsend's Solitaire, November 2015 (Schoodic Point)

A number of online resources cover this area:

- www.frenchmanbay.org covers the preserves of the Frenchman Bay Conservancy.
- www.schoodicwoods.com/project.html (see map 9) lays out the plans for this new recreational area (in the future, look to the ANP website for more current maps).

- www.nps.gov/acad/planyourvisit/upload/schoodic.pdf includes a map of the Schoodic Section of ANP.
- www.schoodicinstitute.org/about/map-directions offers additional information about the Schoodic Section of ANP.

SITE H10 Great Pond Mountain Wildlands

TOWN Orland. DeLorme Map 123: D–E3–4. **SEASON** All year, but especially May–June and August–October. **VISITATION** An entire day for thorough coverage, although the road can be birded in 1–2 hrs. Minimal facilities are available, and those are in the middle of the Valley Road. **HIGHLIGHTS** Spring and fall passerine migration; at least sixteen species of breeding warbler and more than eight species of breeding flycatcher.

The forty-seven-hundred-acre Great Pond Mountain Wildlands offers a wide range of year-round recreational opportunities, including birding, and it's particularly good for warblers. The Wildlands are available for day use and camping, walking, biking, cross-country skiing, and driving; the diversity of habitat ranges from freshwater wetlands to mountaintops, with seemingly everything in between.

DIRECTIONS

From the traffic light at the main intersection in downtown Bucksport, head east for 8.4 miles on US Route 1 North to the Wildlands south entrance on the left.

Alternatively, from the intersection of US Routes 1 and 1A and Route 3 in Ellsworth, head west on US Route 1 for 10.9 miles to the Wildlands south entrance on the right—as a landmark, look for Route 176 on the left: the Wildlands are just beyond it on the right.

Valley Road transits the property south to north and is open for car traffic weekends mid-June through September. If you are birding in May or on weekdays, it may mean a long walk to reach some of the trails, so a bicycle could make some of the trails more accessible; otherwise, park at the entrance and walk.

On the right, just a few hundred feet from the south gate, is the Esker Path following an ancient glacial streambed, where Canada Warblers are regularly found.

Another 2.8 miles down Valley Road on the left is the Hothole Brook Trail. For the first 0.9 miles the trail winds through a variety of habitats, much of it heavily modified by beaver activity. A short 0.3-mile spur leads down the Bump Hill Path.

As an alternative to the south entrance try the Wildlands north entrance. From the intersection of US Routes 1 and 1A and Route 3 in Ellsworth, head west 6.6 miles on US Route 1 to Happytown Road on the right. Follow Happytown Road for 6.8 miles (take care at intersections, as road signs in this area have a habit of disappearing; GPS, or a good map, would be particularly helpful here) to Winkumpaugh Road. Turn left and drive 0.8 miles on Winkumpaugh Road, then turn left onto Bald Mountain Road. The north gate to the Wildlands is 0.3 miles on the left. When the gate is closed, it is a much shorter walk to good birding.

Head south 0.9 miles to the Hothole Pond Trail. The 1.2-mile trail goes through a variety of forest types, culminating at Hothole Pond. Walking from the north entrance to Hothole Pond Trail and back is just over 4 miles. A good spring birding day will likely be rewarded with Northern Waterthush, Magnolia Warbler, Black-throated Blue Warbler, Rose-breasted Grosbeak, and Indigo Bunting, to name a few. The **Birding Path**, an 0.4-mile offshoot along Hothole Brook, is worth the extra effort.

From the Wildlands south entrance, follow US Route 1 west for 2.5 miles to Hatchery Road on the right (you will pass the Craig Brook National Fish Hatchery; the forests around the hatchery are older and a good place to look for Blackburnian Warbler and Black-throated Blue Warbler). At 1.9 miles up Hatchery Road is Dead River Gate. The **Dead River Trail** roughly parallels the Dead River for 1.8 miles. In addition to forest cover, there are many fields where Whip-poor-will and Common Nighthawk can be found in the evening.

Browse the Great Pond Mountain Conservation Trust website, www.great pondtrust.org, for maps and information.

SITE H11 Ellsworth Tour

TOWN Ellsworth. DeLorme Map 23: D5, and Map 24: D–E1.
SEASON April, **May–June**, July. **VISITATION** 3–4 hrs. to entire day for thorough coverage; 15–30 min. per site. Restrooms at local businesses.
HIGHLIGHTS Spring warbler migration; at least fifteen species of breeding warbler; Upland Sandpiper, Vesper Sparrow.

Drive through Ellsworth and it is the box and chain stores that stand out, making it look like anywhere America. However, there is another side of Ellsworth, a natural beauty that is more than House Sparrows and Ring-billed Gulls looking for scraps at restaurants and dumpsters; it just takes a little digging. And dig away you should, as there is some surprisingly good birding, especially in the spring.

DIRECTIONS

Our first stop is Frenchman Bay Conservancy's **Indian Point Preserve.** From the intersection of US Routes 1 and 1A and Route 3 in Ellsworth, head south-west on Route 3 for 0.2 miles to the traffic light, then turn left onto Water Street/Route 230. Head down Water Street (which eventually becomes Bay-side Drive/Route 230) 1 mile to Tinker Farm Way on the right. Take Tinker Farm Way for 0.1 mile, then turn right into the marked trailhead parking area. The out-and-back trail is a fairly easy three-quarter-mile round-trip. This mixed forest is on a small peninsula in the tidal section of the Union River. Eiders make their way up this far. It is one of the first places in the spring to find Double-crested Cormorants. Warbler song abounds in the woods in the spring.

Return to Bayside Drive/Route 230 and turn left. Head 0.3 miles on Route 230, then turn right onto Foster Street. Drive 0.4 miles to the end of Foster Street, then turn right onto Route 3. Head southeast on Route 3 for 0.5 miles; **Stanwood Wildlife Sanctuary** will be on the right. Better known as **Birdsacre,** Standwood Wildlife Sanctuary honors the legacy of Cordelia Stanwood, an inveterate observer and chronicler of the natural world, especially birds. A variety of activities for bird enthusiasts can be found here. First, please register at the parking lot kiosk. There is the wildlife rehabilitation center with educational birds—birds whose injuries precluded them from being released—on display. Sometimes the educational birds are used in nature programs. A modest nature center, open from late May into October, offers a variety of natural history exhibits, and a network of trails crisscrosses the two-hundred-acre property. The property, largely forested, offers a nature oasis amid the hubbub of Ellsworth.

Back to the intersection of Routes 1, 1A, and 3, head north 7.4 miles on Route 1A and turn left onto **Branch Pond Road.** Slowly drive through fields (beginning at 0.5 miles), blueberry barrens (1 to 1.4 miles), and orchards to look for Upland Sandpiper (particularly in the blueberry barrens) and Vesper Sparrow. Turn around where the road makes a ninety-degree bend to the left.

Instead of turning left on Branch Pond Road, turn right onto **Nicolin Road** and drive 0.7 miles to a gravel lot on the right. Park and walk either direction along the railroad tracks (this is a particularly good spring birding walk). Paralleling the railroad tracks is Boggy Brook. The mixed habitat—edge along the tracks, wetlands along Boggy Brook, mature forests of spruce, fir, pine, and oak, as well as transitional scrubby habitat—lend to the diversity of birds. Walking south (the same side as the gravel parking) tends to offer the best birding opportunities. Osprey and Great Horned Owls nest along here, as does a diversity of flycatchers, warblers, sparrows, blackbirds, and finches. Rose-breasted Grosbeak and Indigo Bunting are among the regulars.

On the east edge of Ellsworth, technically in the town of Hancock, is a network of **blueberry barrens** that can be good for Upland Sandpiper and, to a lesser degree, other grassland birds. From the intersection of Routes 1, 1A, and 3, follow Route 1 North/3 East for 1 mile, then continue on Route 1 as the roads split. In 2.1 miles turn left onto Old County Road, immediately past a trailer park. Head north on Old County Road 0.3 miles to an intersection; park here. This is blueberry country. Walk left and right along the dirt roads, but be sure to respect all posted signs. Birding early in the morning on a spring day is best.

Additional information can be found online for several of the sites listed here:

- Stanwood Wildlife Sanctuary, aka Birdsacre: www.birdsacre.com/trails .html
- Branch Lake Public Forest: www.frenchmanbay.org/images/stories /preserves/TrailMaps/branch_lake_trails.pdf

SITE H12 Route 9, Airline Road ("the Airline") and Stud Mill Road Tour

TOWNS Multiple towns over three counties. See DeLorme Maps 23–26 and 33–36. **SEASON** All year, but especially **May–July** for breeding species; winter for irruptives, especially finches **VISITATION** This tour encompasses a large area. While you could visit a few sites in an hour or two, given the time to drive there, it is better to plan at least a long morning, if not an entire day. Restrooms are scarce, but certainly at the local businesses along the Airline; of particular note is the Airline Snack Bar, which has facilities at the west end of the parking lot.

HIGHLIGHTS Boreal specialties (Spruce Grouse, Black-backed Woodpecker, Olive-sided Flycatcher, Gray Jay, and Boreal Chickadee); more than twenty species of breeding warbler, including Palm and Blackpoll Warbler; spring passerine migration.

The northern part of Hancock County is certainly under-birded, as it is difficult to get to. Receiving fewer visitors than coastal hot spots, the area is not nearly as well known or thoroughly explored. Furthermore, there are few clearly defined places to go birding. The area in and around the Airline and Stud Mill Road are worth a day's exploration, as is Sunkhaze Meadows National Wildlife Refuge, if for no other reason than to see some beautiful country. Locally, Route 9, or Airline Road, is referred to simply as the Airline, and stretches from Calais on the Maine–New Brunswick border west through Bangor. Much of this road between Bangor and Calais is good black bear and moose country. The Stud Mill Road is a dirt logging road stretching from the Penobscot River well into Washington County. Use these directions as a starting point, but get out of your car frequently to look and listen; use a DeLorme atlas to guide your explorations.

DIRECTIONS

From the Ellsworth intersection of us Routes 1, 1A, and Route 3, head north on Route 1A for 1.6 miles to Ellsworth Falls. Turn right onto Route 179/180 North. In 1.6 miles Route 179 bears right and Route 180 bears left. Bear right on Route 179—look out over Graham Lake for Black Tern—and continue north 20.7 miles. The road ends at a T intersection with Route 9, "**the Airline.**" There are numerous opportunities to pull over and look and listen for birds. Where the vista is more open and looks out over wetlands, a spotting scope will be helpful. For instance, from where Route 179 ends at the Airline, take a right and drive 4 miles east to a pull-off on the left overlooking the Middle Branch of the Union River. This wetland complex is good for birds such as Yellow-bellied Flycatcher.

Continue another 4 miles to Alligator Lake Road on the left. Follow this road for 10.3 miles north to **Stud Mill Road.** Stud Mill Road goes in both directions—23 miles west to Costigan on the Penobscot River and 33.7 miles east to Birch Hill Road, just west of Crawford Lake in No. 21 Township. It's a wide and well-maintained dirt road used by logging companies to haul timber and pulp to market, so be sure to yield to the big trucks and park well off the road. Birding Stud Mill Road is particularly rewarding in the spring and early summer for breeding birds, but it is worth exploring anytime during the rest of the year for nonmigratory boreal specialties. Birding it entails frequent stops to look and listen for birds, and be sure to explore side roads. For more extensive coverage of the Stud Mill Road and the **Sunkhaze Meadows National Wildlife Refuge** at its western end, see their respective entries in Penobscot County (PE10 and PE9).

As an alternative to going up Alligator Lake Road to Stud Mill Road, continue on the Airline for 4.9 miles. The **Airline Snack Bar** is on the left, nearly on the Hancock/Washington County boundary. There are public toilets here in a separate building at the west end of the parking lot. Birding from the parking lot can turn up a variety of flycatchers and warblers. Shortly after this, the Airline crosses into Washington County.

Continue 14.9 miles from the Airline Snack Bar, turn left onto Machias River Road (in Washington County), also known as CCC Road. Drive north 8.8 miles on Machias River Road, making occasional stops, especially near wetlands and the Machias River (the Machias River corridor is part of the Maine Public Reserve Lands system), to look for boreal birds. This will also bring you to Stud Mill Road.

Franklin County

KIRK BETTS

Franklin County is home to some of the best boreal birding in the state, and the closest prime habitat to the population of Greater Portland for the entire suite of specialty species (Spruce Grouse, Black-backed Woodpeckers, Olive-sided and Yellow-bellied Flycatchers, Gray Jay, Boreal Chickadee, and up to twenty species of warblers). It therefore receives a lot of birding attention, and deservedly so.

This is also the home range of the county contributor, Kirk Betts, and he knows the trails and lakes of this area better than anyone, and offers insight into some of the most popular locales, such as the famous Boy Scout Road (site F10).

Franklin County also hosts Bicknell's Thrushes at higher elevations, and there are several hikes that vary in intensity to bring you into their realm. Saddleback Mountain (F6) is well known as a thrush destination, but Burnt Mountain (F13) also offers only a moderately strenuous trek into their krummholz (dense, stunted spruce-fir forest) habitat.

The Rangeley Loop (F8) offers a variety of habitats in proximity to this popular town, which has plenty of visitor amenities and is a great way to expand your birding beyond the famous destinations. And unassuming little Quill Hill (F11) not only hosts accessible Mourning Warblers, but may turn out to be the best fall hawk-watching site in the area.

But Kirk has also proven that the southern half of the county is not just a wasteland to pass through on your way to the higher hills. Patches such as White Granite Park in North Jay (F1) and the Foothills Land Conservancy in Wilton (F2) offer some exceptional birding in migration and deserve thorough attention. Parks around Farmington, such as the Whistlestop Trail (F3), are great for local birders and for travelers looking to break up their drive. Although winter birding, especially after lakes and rivers freeze, can be sparse, the allure of irruptives—from owls to finches—can provide loads

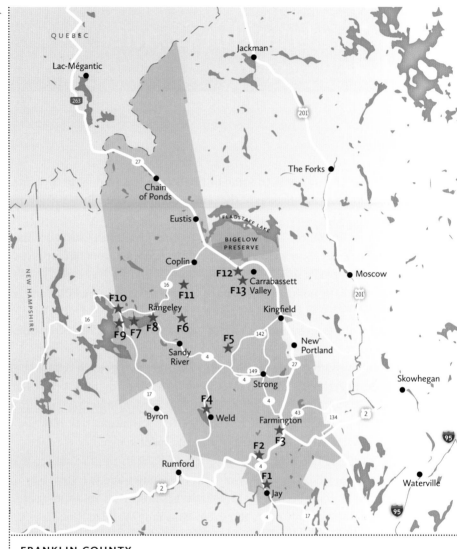

QUEBEC

Jackman

Lac-Mégantic

263

The Forks

27

Chain
of Ponds

Eustis

FLAGSTAFF LAKE

BIGELOW
PRESERVE

Moscow

Coplin

F12 Carrabassett
F13 Valley

201

16   **F11**

NEW HAMPSHIRE

F10
Rangeley

Kingfield

16   **F8**   **F6**

F9 **F7**

New
Portland

Sandy
River

142

F5

Skowhegan

4   149   27

4   Strong

17

Byron

F4

4

Weld   Farmington

43

134   2

95

F2
F3

Rumford

4

2   **F1**
Jay

Waterville

95

G   9   4   17

FRANKLIN COUNTY

of excitement. The diverse habitats of the Rangeley area offer your best bets, but frugivores can be numerous in and around towns such as Farmington.
—*Derek Lovitch*

SITE F1 White Granite Park

TOWN North Jay. DeLorme Map 19: E5. SEASON April–July, September–October. VISITATION 1–2 hrs. No restroom facilities. HIGHLIGHTS Spring migrants; breeding Bobolinks.

Driving on Route 4 through North Jay it's easy to just keep going, thinking there is nothing of interest until you reach the mountains. However, turn off the main road, drive up a hill, and you'll find yourself at an old apple orchard. While I am certain it's a shadow of its former self, it's still worth a walk for spring migrants (especially when the trees are blooming) and the common breeding species associated with second growth.

DIRECTIONS

From Lewiston-Auburn follow US Route 4 North into Jay. At 0.9 miles north of the Hannaford supermarket, at the top of a hill, bear right onto Old Jay Hill Road. Follow it for 1.2 miles to Woodman Hill Road and turn right. A quarter mile up the road, turn into the dirt parking area on the left.

From the north, at the junction of Routes 4 and 17, turn left onto Old Jay Hill Road and drive 1 mile to Woodman Hill Road, then turn left. The park is a quarter mile up the road on the left.

The trail goes over a little bridge and starts up the center of the field, passing a few apple trees (Macintosh, in case you're curious). In late spring through summer, Bobolinks are abundant. Follow the mowed trail counterclockwise, skirting the wood's edge (Hermit Thrush, Chestnut-sided Warbler, etc.) before entering the woods via the gravel "Hiking Trail" at the top of the field. Tall northern red oaks tower overhead. Follow the trail up the hill and soon you'll pass through a clearing that's worth a check. Turn right at the dirt road and walk a short distance to a gate. Just before it are picnic tables and a gazebo; listen for Indigo Bunting. The view overlooks a granite quarry that is still working; you can see a lot of the white granite that Maine is famous for.

Backtrack to the field edge, continuing to round the field to return to your car. Wild turkeys will stare at you from the woods, and in the grass Bobolinks will sing. Late May is prime time for the apple trees to be in bloom, which is extremely attractive to migrants. A Prairie Warbler in May 2016 may prove to be an annual breeder of this range-expanding species.

For more information about the park see the Town of Jay's website: http:// www.jay-maine.org/granite-park.html. For a map and trails visit Maine Trail Finder at www.mainetrailfinder.com and use the search feature.

SITE F2 Foothills Land Conservancy

TOWN Wilton. DeLorme Map 19: D4.   SEASON April–July, September– November.   VISITATION 1–2 hrs. No restroom facilities. Most of the trails are flat, but the ground is often rough.   HIGHLIGHTS A variety of grassland (Bobolink, Savannah Sparrow, etc.) and wetland breeders (including American Woodcock); migrant sparrows; rarity potential.

Maine is the most forested state in the country, and open fields can be at a premium. That wasn't the case less than a hundred years ago, however, when farms covered a good portion of the state. While agriculture is again on the rise in Maine, much of the land has reforested, making grasslands one of the rarest habitats in New England. The Foothills Land Conservancy protected a parcel of farmland at the head of Wilson Lake, a mix of fields, woods, and wetlands. While the land is managed for American Woodcock, other birds like Bobolinks and Eastern Kingbirds benefit. Abundant breeding birds include Warbling Vireo, Baltimore Oriole, and several species of warblers.

DIRECTIONS

From US Route 4/Route 2 in Wilton head north on Route 156 (Weld Road) toward Weld. Travel for 3.4 miles, through Wilton Center, to Pond Road and make a left (it's the first left after the Wilson Lake Country Club; the street sign may be hidden by branches). Turn onto Pond Road, and in 0.1 miles turn into the parking lot for the trail on the right, at a kiosk. Cross the road and enter the trails by passing through the metal gate.

Calm evenings, shortly after sunset from early April until at least the middle of May, can be great for observing woodcock, as the males perform their impressive flight display overhead. The trails ring the fields, with bridges crossing the small streams. The fields are not mowed every year, and especially when they are not, it's worth checking in the spring and in the fall for migrating sparrows, Northern Harrier, American Kestrel, and possibly Short-eared Owl. This site has the potential for harboring some rarities during fall and therefore deserves more attention.

For a map and trails visit Maine Trail Finder at www.mainetrailfinder.com and use the search feature.

SITE F3 Whistlestop Trail

TOWNS Farmington, Wilton, Jay. DeLorme Map 20: C–D1, and Map 19: D–E5. **SEASON** April–June, September–November. **VISITATION** 30 min. to full day. No restroom facilities. ♿ **HIGHLIGHTS** Spring migration; variety of breeding species.

One hundred years ago this was a major freight railroad. Today it is 14 miles of multiuse, level dirt trail between Farmington and Jay. Mostly passing through hardwoods, it crosses over and runs along streams, back roads, and old fields. With a map in hand, and using some ingenuity, you can explore off the trails to widen the variety of habitats. Bring your bike or walk for exercise, and the birding will keep you coming back. Just about every mile, every foot, can produce another bird, and although they may be mostly expected common species, it just makes the trail more enjoyable.

DIRECTIONS

I like the section from Farmington to Wilton the best, mostly because between Wilton and Jay you are alongside a major highway. That does tend to diminish the experience for me, even though you are following a stream for part of the way, with its attendant riparian species. Although the trail goes through Wilton and ends in Jay, there aren't any really convenient parking places at the other points.

Starting in Farmington on US Route 4 West, drive toward Wilton. Cross over Center Bridge (where Route 2 East and Route 27 turn to the left) and take the first right onto Bridge Street (Route 43). At the stop sign turn left onto Oakes Street. In 250 feet there will be a sign for the Whistlestop Trail on the right (at Farmer Lane). Drive about 500 feet on this dirt road until you come to a large parking area.

Near the parking lot in Farmington, Veeries and a variety of warblers can be seen. Farther along, as you follow the trail west toward Wilton, look and listen for Indigo Buntings at the edge, Scarlet Tanagers in the woods, and Alder Flycatchers in wetlands.

RARITIES

Cattle Egret, June 2014; Carolina Wren, October 2014

For a map of the entire trail (which is recommended for further exploration) visit Maine Trail Finder at www.mainetrailfinder.com and use the search feature.

SITE F4 Mount Blue State Park

TOWN Weld. DeLorme Map 19: C2–3.   **SEASON** May–July, September–October.   **VISITATION** 1 hr. to full day. Outhouses at trailheads. State park entry fees.   **HIGHLIGHTS** Typical northern hardwood species; waterfowl on Webb Lake.

Camping at Webb Lake and hiking Mount Blue make a quintessential Maine vacation. While the hiking around the state park is excellent, and the campground is a good spot for close-to-your-tent birding, it's the Center Hill Nature Trail that should be your first stop for great birding. In the parking lot you can see Eastern Bluebirds, Tree Swallows, and Chipping Sparrows, and on the trails Chestnut-sided and Black-throated Blue Warblers, Swainson's and Hermit Thrushes, and much more. Down at Webb Lake are a nature center and trail (about an hour's worth of walking) that passes through the woods as it heads down to the lake.

DIRECTIONS

From the junction of Routes 142 and 156 in Weld (accessible from several directions), follow Route 142 North for 2.3 miles to a fork; bear left toward Mount Blue State Park/Webb Beach. Follow the signage, and in 3.9 miles turn left to enter the **Webb Beach section** of the park. Birding around the campground in the early morning can be productive, and scan the lake from the beach area in spring and fall for migrant waterfowl and for Common Loons all summer. On the way out, stop by the nature center and walk the nearby trail for woodland birding and another view of the lake.

To hike the mountain, return to Weld. At the junction of Routes 142 and 156 make a left onto Center Hill Road. In 1.3 miles you will reach the park headquarters. Continue on Center Hill Road for 1.2 miles to the **Center Hill area.** The nature trail here is an easy and birdy walk.

One of the quickest trails to the summit is the 1.6-mile **Mount Blue Trail,** which passes through mixed woods. To reach this trailhead, return to Center Hill Road and make a right. In 0.8 miles bear right onto Mount Blue Road. Follow it for 2.4 miles to the trailhead; this is a good road for car birding as well. The open vistas of the summit host breeding Blackpoll Warblers and Swainson's Thrush, but also a massive complex of towers and antennas that make you wonder why you just put in all that effort.

For a map and trails visit Maine Trail Finder at www.mainetrailfinder.com and use the search feature.

SITE F5 Perham Stream Birding Trail

TOWN Madrid. DeLorme Map 19: A3. **SEASON** April–July, September–October. **VISITATION** Minimum 2–4 hrs. No restroom facilities. **HIGHLIGHTS** Typical northern forest birds and old farm fields and migration rarities; American Woodcock.

The history of East Madrid goes back two hundred years, when farming was hard and the country was harder. The old fields are far off the main track, and when you look north and west, a crescent of high peaks rises before you. The fields and woods here are rich in birdlife, and it's a great place for what western Maine offers: White-throated Sparrows, a wide variety of warblers, Ruffed Grouse, and raptors. With trails going into the woods and edging the fields, it's a quiet, wild spot. The fields are worth working for breeding Savannah Sparrow and, in early spring, American Woodcock at dusk.

DIRECTIONS

From Route 4 in Phillips: Take Route 142 North toward Kingfield for 2.5 miles to East Madrid Road on the left (look for a sign for the Bruce Manzer gravel pit on the left). Follow East Madrid Road for 4.5 miles until you cross a small bridge. Just beyond the bridge is a wooden rail fence on the left with the trailhead kiosk for the Perham Stream Birding Trail; park here.

Explore the trails at your leisure. The diversity of habitats can provide a diversity of breeding species in a small area; it's a great place to sample the species of the foothills.

Snowy Owl, winter 2014–15.

For a map and trails visit Maine Trail Finder at www.mainetrailfinder.com and use the search feature.

SITE F6 Saddleback Mountain

TOWN Sandy River Plantation. DeLorme Map 29: E1. **SEASON** May–July, September–October. **VISITATION** 3 hrs. to full day. No restroom facilities at the AT parking lot, but outhouses at Piazza Rock lean-to. There are also restrooms at Saddleback Mountain base lodge (check for times when they are open). **HIGHLIGHTS** Bicknell's Thrush; Fox Sparrow; boreal specialties including Boreal Chickadee and Spruce Grouse; American Pipits (in migration) and hawk watching with killer views.

Please stay on the trails. With one of the longest alpine ridge hikes in Maine, the 4,120-foot Saddleback Mountain (the eighth-highest mountain in Maine) offers extensive alpine tundra habitat, which is very rare in the Northeast. The stunted trees just below the summit host breeding Fox Sparrows, Bicknell's Thrush, Blackpoll Warblers, and Dark-eyed Juncos. And during the fall migration this is a prime hawk-watching spot, though you probably will be the only one there doing so.

There are two ways to get to the summit. The first is from the base lodge at Saddleback, which is also the shortest, most direct way; but it is a very strenuous, 1.3-mile hike *straight* up. And the second way is from the Appalachian Trail, a longer, more gradual, and wooded trail that passes through more great habitat for Spruce Grouse, Black-backed Woodpecker, and Boreal Chickadee.

Via the AT it is a moderate-to-difficult 5.7 miles, with a short, challenging stretch just up to the summit. As far as hikes at these altitudes in Maine go, this hike is not that difficult, but allow all day, and combine that with an early start. I highly recommend downloading the Saddleback Trail map for the best trail to take.

DIRECTIONS

To reach the **ski area** from Rangeley, drive south on Route 4, and just past the IGA grocery store on your left turn left onto Dallas Hill Road. In 2.5 miles

Perhaps the most sought-after bird in all Maine, the Bicknell's Thrush is challenging even to glimpse in its dense krummholz habitat. © Derek Lovitch

turn right onto Saddleback Mountain Road. In 4.5 miles you'll come to the base lodge, where you can park and follow the trails through the ski slopes to the summit.

To reach the trailhead for the **Appalachian Trail** from Rangeley, follow Route 4 South 8.6 miles past the IGA grocery store, and just past the turn for Dallas Hill Road you'll arrive at the AT trail as it crosses Route 4. Turn right into the lot and park.

From Farmington, where US Route 2 splits from Route 4 just south of downtown, follow Route 4 for 30.6 miles to the AT parking lot, on your left. Cross Route 4 and begin your ascent.

You'll pass through some quality boreal-transition forest; keep your eyes and ears open for Boreal Chickadees, Gray Jays, etc. As you approach the summit, and the spruce forest becomes stunted into krummholz, you will enter the dark and dense realm of the Bicknell's Thrush. From just below the summit of Saddleback across the ridge to the Horn, multiple dozens of Bicknell's Thrushes may be heard on a good day, with activity centered mostly on dusk and dawn.

Saddleback Mountain has maps of is trails available at http://www.saddle backmaine.com/trail-map-maine and http://www.saddlebackmaine.com /downloads/Hiking-Map-Summer-2010.pdf. With rumors of a pending ownership change of the ski resort, it is worth checking the website to see if there are any changes in access via the ski area in the future.

SITE F7 Rangeley Lakes

TOWN Rangeley. DeLorme Map 28: E3–5, and Map 18: A1–3. SEASON Ice-out (April–May) to November. VISITATION 2 hrs. to all day. Restroom facilities are available at public boat launches and businesses in Rangeley and Oquossoc. ⚲ HIGHLIGHTS Common Loons throughout the ice-free months; migrant waterbirds.

About 1,500 feet above the rest of Maine are the Rangeley Lakes. Since the late 1800s they have been renowned for their fishing and scenery. It used to be that the only way you could get to the area was by train, but that is a lifetime ago. The names Rangeley, Mooselookmeguntic, Cupsuptic, Aziscohos, and Parmachenee speak of the Native Americans that had called this area home. This is Big Lake country, and do not discount the dangers that boating on these lakes can present. You can pretty much scrap the idea of going out on a windy day, because you won't see much. Otherwise, while you can see a fair amount from the shore, you can see a lot more out in a boat. Loons are plentiful, and in the wilder spots of the lakes Great Blue Heron, Bald Eagle, Osprey, ducks (mostly mergansers, Mallard, Black, and Common Goldeneyes) are fairly common, but less common are wigeon, teal, scaup, Ring-necked Ducks, and grebes. Anytime I have seen any of them it has always been in small groups, during migration, and they usually are here today, gone tomorrow. For the best chance at birds try looking in any outlets, inlets, or coves on the big lakes. Don't be surprised to be sitting on the shore with a Swainson's Thrush. There is also some good Lincoln Sparrow habitat around here. All the lakes have public boat launches, marked by signs, and marked in the *Maine Atlas and Gazetteer*. The lakes are also part of the Northern Forest Canoe Trail. You can't say "go to this lake for X bird, and this one for Y." Part of the allure and fun of the lakes is picking one and getting out on it. Mornings are best, the earlier the better.

DIRECTIONS

Each lake has its own appeal, and all should be explored to find your favorite; I certainly have mine! Also, many of the region's smaller ponds are worth a look. Here I give a sample of the access points to some of the major lakes that offer the best birding. A good map is critical.

1. **Rangeley Lake** has public boat launches at Lakeside Park in the center of downtown, in Oquossoc at the bridge before town, and at Rangeley Lake State Park on the south shore.

2. **Mooselookmeguntic Lake** has boat launches at Haines Landing (the end of Route 4 in Oquossoc) and on the west shore off Shelton Trail (go down to Bemis, which is off Route 17, about 3 miles from Oquossoc; turn right onto Bemis Road, and in 7 miles you will come to a causeway; go over the causeway and at the other end turn right).

3. **Cupsuptic Lake** has a boat launch off Route 16 in Lower Cupsuptic Township.

4. **Upper Richardson Lake** has a boat launch at Mill Brook as it crosses Route 16 in Richardson Township as you are heading toward New Hampshire.

Rangeley Lakes. © Kirk Betts

5. **Lower Richardson Lake** is accessed by way of South Arm Road in Andover.

6. **Aziscohos Lake** has a public boat launch at Black Brook Cove Campground, which is off Route 16 West. You'll have to pay for parking.

7. **Kennebago Lake** is harder to get to, unless you are a guest of Grant's Kennebago Camps, have friends there, or you are renting a camp. However, if you have meal reservations at Grant's Camps, they may allow you to spend a day there.

RARITIES

Golden Eagle, July 2014 (Mooselookmeguntic Lake); Great Egret, September 2014 (Cupsuptic Lake); Brant, November 2014 (Rangeley Lake)

The Rangeley Lakes Region has several websites where you can get information:

- http://www.rangeleymaine.com/ (for tourist information on the Rangeley area)
- http://www.rangeley-maine.com/rangeley-lakes-region-map/ (for a map of the area)
- http://www.northernforestcanoetrail.org/ (the Northern Forest Canoe Trail, which passes through the area; with information and a map of the lakes)
- http://www.rlht.org/ (the Rangeley Lakes Heritage Trust has maps and info on the trust's land in the area)

SITE F8 Rangeley Loop Drive

TOWN Rangeley. DeLorme Map 28: E4–5. **SEASON** May–July, September–November. **VISITATION** 1 hr. to full day. Restroom facilities are available at Lakeside Park, Orgonon, and Hunter Cove. **HIGHLIGHTS** Waterfowl and gulls; fields of flowers; a variety of the breeding birds of the northern forest.

It's hard to write about home, a place I love so much; the problem is there are so many great places and only so much room to cover them all. Therefore, I offer a sample of my favorite sites for a taste of what Rangeley has to offer.

Lakeside Park is good for gulls and the surprises that can hang out with

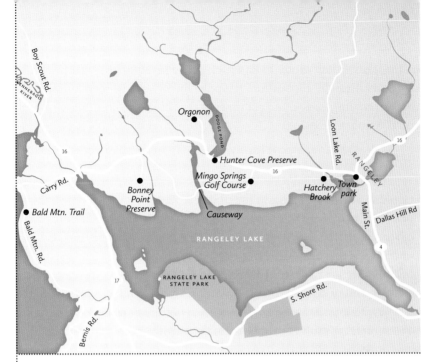

**RANGELEY LAKE LOOP PLUS
THE BOY SCOUT ROAD**

them. Hatchery Brook combines brushy, waterside habitat close to town that is excellent for warblers. Mingo Springs Golf Course has a great trail system of over 3 miles that is open to the public. A visit in June when the lupines are in bloom makes watching the Eastern Bluebird incomparable, and you can see deciduous forest species such as Baltimore Oriole and Scarlet Tanager. It's also worth noting that throughout the summer and fall, gulls and geese make use of the golf course. You never know what will be in the mix here, so check them carefully.

Bonney Point is good for some wading birds and waterfowl at the end of the trail, and a mix of other passerines. The woods here are also good for a variety of birds, such as Swainson's and Hermit Thrushes. Orgonon, the Wilhelm Reich Museum, is a fascinating museum of the late Austrian psychoanalyst, and features a great trail system. Go back on Sunday afternoons during the summer for a free nature program.

Up the road at the Hunter Cove Preserve there is an extensive trail system that has been a pretty reliable place for Cape May Warblers, or even a bobcat. It's a rich spot that usually will give you something good, but it can be wet on the trails. While winter in Rangeley can be bereft of birds, during irruption years it can be a lot of fun. Irruptive finches can be seen in town and the surrounding forests, and plantings in the village can host Pine Grosbeak and Bohemian Waxwing.

DIRECTIONS

These directions, including mileage, are for the entirety of the Rangeley Loop beginning at **Lakeside Park** in the center of Rangeley. Check the gulls and ducks that hang out there. You may have a surprise such as a Bonaparte's Gull or a tern. Derek swears a "mega" rarity will show up here someday, and I once watched a Great Blue Heron escape an onslaught by a Bald Eagle. And in September 1982 a flamingo (yes, a presumed escapee) was sighted on a lawn just west of here, so you really never know what might show up! Based on time and interest, you can stop by each of the following locations for a short sample, or explore each of them thoroughly. Reset your odometer as you exit the park.

From the park, go to Main Street, turn left, and drive 0.8 miles to Manor Drive, across the street from the cemetery. Turn left and go 0.1 miles to **Hatchery Brook Preserve** and explore the trails for species including Blackburnian Warbler and Northern Parula.

Back in your car, return to Main Street and reset your odometer. Turn left, and at 2.5 miles make a left onto Mingo Loop Road. At 2.9 miles you will come to the **Mingo Springs Golf Course Bird Trail**; parking is on your left just a few feet up Alpine Way. Here at Mingo Springs you have two trails. The Back Nine Trail goes around the woods (hardwoods, then spruce, then mixed forest) following the edge of the course. The Front Nine Trail starts directly across the street from where the Back Nine ends and travels through woods and out into the lupine patch. Although lupine is often considered an invasive, it does provide habitat for Savannah Sparrows and Common Yellowthroat—and photography. (See frontispiece!)

Back in your car again, turn left on Mingo Loop and drive down to the causeway (at 4.0 miles) that crosses **Hunter Cove**. Stop here for waterbirds, especially migrant and breeding Common Mergansers and Common Loons. Continuing on, at the end of Mingo Loop turn left on Main Street and then make the next left at 5.9 miles onto Bonney Point Road. At 6.5 miles, turn left into the **Bonney Point Conservation Area** parking lot. Once finished here, backtrack on Bonney Point Road and turn right on Main Street to head back to Rangeley. At 8.5 miles turn left onto Dodge Pond Road and drive up to **Orgonon** (at 8.9 miles), the Wilhelm Reich Museum (open 9–5). Enter the property and follow the road up the hill to reach the nature trails that are good for Black-backed Woodpeckers and warblers.

Return to Main Street, turn left, and drive for another half a mile to the **Hunter Cove Sanctuary** on your right. Although the trails are often very wet here, this small preserve of the Rangeley Lakes Land Trust offers some great birding close to town. Check the spruce grove near the trailhead for Bay-breasted and Cape May Warblers, and along the scrubby edge of the lake I sometimes find Bald Eagles and Hooded Mergansers, especially in early spring.

To finish up the loop, turn right and drive back to town.

RARITIES

Great Gray Owl, November 2009 (Hunter Cove Sanctuary); Snow Geese, November 2014

You can find out area details by visiting the website of Rangeley Lakes Maine at http://www.rangeley-maine.com/.

SITE F9 Bald Mountain

TOWN Oquossoc. DeLorme Map 28: E3. **SEASON** May–July, September–October. **VISITATION** 1 hr. to several hrs. Restroom facilities at the trailhead. **HIGHLIGHTS** Boreal species in a short, relatively easy hike; spring and fall hawk watching; spring migrant passerines.

At 2,443 feet, rising above the valley between Rangeley and Mooselookmeguntic Lakes, Bald Mountain acts like a rock in a stream. The wind spills over and eddies around it, and birds, especially raptors not wanting to fly over water, will use the updrafts to help them on their way. The summit has spectacular views, from Mount Washington in New Hampshire all the way to Mont Mégantic in Quebec, and all of the local land and lakes, including Saddleback Mountain. It's a good trail for Ovenbird and Hermit Thrush, among other forest species. There is an observation tower at the summit, and many times I have watched Osprey, Bald Eagles, and other raptors flying by.

From Rangeley, drive west on Main Street toward Oquossoc (Abenaki for a blueback trout). At the intersection where Route 16 turns to the north (toward New Hampshire), continue on Route 4 North for 1.4 miles and turn left onto Bald Mountain Road. In 0.8 miles make a left at the "Public Reserved Land—Bald Mountain" sign and park at the trailhead. The 1.3-mile (each way) trail starts out easy enough, with a steady climb through beech-maple woods (look and listen for Yellow-bellied Sapsuckers and many others). After about twenty minutes, the trail gets steeper, with bare rock in places. Use caution if the trail is wet or icy; if it is, you might want to consider turning around, rather than attempting going over slick rock. From the trailhead to the summit you will pass through enough of a habitat change where you should see and hear many of the birds of the western mountain forest, from Ovenbirds down low to Boreal Chickadee and Yellow-bellied Flycatcher near the summit. The summit, although wooded, has a tower well worth climbing for an awe-inspiring view.

If you want a longer (2.2-mile) hike, stop at the public parking on Carry Road before Bald Mountain Road on the left. There is a second trail there at the far side of the parking. You'll spend more time on the lower portion of Bald Mountain, still with some good birding.

For a map and trails visit Maine Trail Finder at www.mainetrailfinder.com and use the search feature.

SITE F10 Boy Scout Road and the Kennebago River

TOWN Rangeley Township (Oquossoc). DeLorme Map 28: E3.
SEASON April, **May–July**, September–October. **VISITATION** 1 hr. to half day. There is an outhouse about 2 miles up the road, just past Steep Bank Pool. Look for the signs. ♿⚲ **HIGHLIGHTS** Boreal species including Spruce Grouse, Black-backed Woodpecker, Olive-sided and Yellow-bellied Flycatchers, Gray Jay, Boreal Chickadee, and warblers, including occasional Bay-breasted and, rarely, Cape May.

The Kennebago River Valley is a northern hardwood forest at its finest in Maine. A lower-elevation spruce-fir forest with riverine habitat makes this a very rich area full of much sought-after species. What was once a narrow-gauge railroad track, built for hauling logs out of the mountains, now is a road with easy walking. I could even be so bold as to say that this is one of the best wildlife roads in the state.

If it nests in the Rangeley Lakes region, then it probably can be found here. In the spruce-fir patches you can look for Spruce Grouse, Black-backed Woodpecker, Gray Jay, and Boreal Chickadee; in the other areas, thrushes, kinglets, flycatchers (Olive-sided, Alder, and Yellow-bellied)—the list goes on. May is very busy birdwise along the road. It's not unheard of to have Spruce Grouse displaying alongside the road; I've seen them many times. One of my favorite ways to spend a day is to combine a walk on the Boy Scout Road with a float trip down the Kennebago River to rapidly expand your list, and possibly see some moose.

DIRECTIONS

From downtown Rangeley follow Route 4 West (joined by Route 16 from the north) toward Oquossoc. Take Route 16 West as it leaves Route 4 once again on your right. In 1.3 miles turn right at the dirt **Boy Scout Road.** While you can park at the beginning of the road, I recommend parking at least a half mile in, but be sure not to block side roads or gates.

Wherever you park, walk up and down the road (it runs for a total length of 2 miles) and explore side roads and trails, such as Koob's Pit Road (first right off Boy Scout Road) for as long as you want.

Boy Scout Road is very popular with fisherman, and it may also be used by logging trucks, so be careful. It's also the only spot in Franklin County where you are likely to run into other birders!

Whether by foot or by car, you'll arrive at the end of the road adjacent to the fishing hot spot of Steep Bank Pool on the **Kennebago River.** To continue your birding, pass the gate and continue up the road—a stretch that is a little more reliable for Bay-breasted Warbler these days.

This is also the spot to put in for your canoe or kayak to head down the river to Rangeley Lake.

On the river are Wilson's Warbler, Veery, Black-billed Cuckoo, and Osprey. It's an easy float, with some rocky spots. Allow at least two hours for it. The Kennebago River winds through spruce and fir when you start off, then transitions over to a floodplain covered in alders (with Alder Flycatchers). I pay attention to the sandbars on bends (or wherever they show up) for gritting crossbills, especially in July when the river drops. In the oxbows—those cutoff,

U-shaped narrow lakes off the main channel of the river—look for American Bitterns, moose, and ducks. The river is a popular float, and the crowds, such as they are, start after 9 a.m. The bugs can be bad in the morning, so some sort of repellent might be nice. If you have two cars, that can make a shuttle easy.

RARITIES

American Three-toed Woodpecker, September 2014

SITE F11 Quill Hill

TOWN Dallas Plantation. DeLorme Map 29: D1.   **SEASON** May–November (road may be impassable or closed before mid-May and by November owing to snow or mud, and may be closed at times for timber harvesting). **VISITATION** 30 min. to half day. No restroom facilities. Fee. ♿ **HIGHLIGHTS** Breeding Mourning Warblers; fall hawk watching.

Across the broad valley between Saddleback, Bigelow, Crocker, Sugarloaf, and East Kennebago Mountain to the west, Quill Hill (2,830 feet) stands as an island for birds, both nesting and migrants. Having been logged over and now in the process of regrowth, it's an early successional forest and a great feeding, resting, and nesting spot for birds on the move. The area is privately owned, but the landowner has graciously built this 4.1-mile road and observation area for all to enjoy.

The views are outstanding, with Flagstaff Lake to the north and Rangeley Lake to the southwest, and the wide vistas make for great hawk watching in the fall. The scrubby summit is excellent for Mourning Warblers and has one of the denser concentrations of their territories in the area. Although the summit is below what Bicknell's Thrush prefers, it's worth looking for them, for a few may be around, especially in June and in the fall. It's best for songbirds in early mornings before wind and visitation pick up. But of course, that's when the hawks take to the air.

DIRECTIONS

From downtown Rangeley drive on Route 16 North toward Stratton for 7.2 miles. You will see signs for Quill Hill as you near the turn (the signs are not up prior to mid-May). Turn right onto Oddy's Road.

From Stratton, take Route 16 South for 11.1 miles to Oddy's Road on the left.

Route 16 is also a well-known road for moose, so use caution in early morning and late in the day. There are also good places to stop and bird all along the road, especially Redington Road.

At 4.6 miles from Rangeley turn right onto Redington Road. Park as the row of boulders begins on the right; from here a diffuse trail takes you to the bridge over the South Branch Dead River, which is worth a check for Wilson's Warbler. From the wide parking area on the left in about 100 yards walk to a large beaver swamp, which sometimes hosts Olive-sided Flycatcher and moose.

Once at Oddy's Road follow the well-maintained dirt road for 4.1 miles to the summit. You can stop and bird at places along the way, so don't just race to the top. Ruffed Grouse, Rose-breasted Grosbeaks, Common Yellowthroats, and Chestnut-sided Warblers are seen at lower elevations.

Park at the summit, where thickets of raspberry are popular with the Mourning Warblers, and where a growing cadre of local hawk watchers might be found during favorable conditions (mostly northwest winds) in the fall.

RARITIES

Bicknell's Thrush, June 2014

SITE F12 Sugarloaf Area

Entry by Derek Lovitch

TOWN Carrabassett Valley. DeLorme Map 29: C–D4–5.
SEASON April, **May–June,** July, **August–September,** October.
VISITATION 4 hrs. to full day. Outhouse at eastern end of Narrow Gauge Pathway. **HIGHLIGHTS** Northern mixed-forest species; high-elevation boreal breeders such as Bicknell's Thrush and Boreal Chickadee; migrant shorebirds; Wood Duck.

Extensive multipurpose trails in the area, increasing year-round recreation opportunities, and the Sugarloaf ski resort combine to offer a variety of options for birding. The Carrabassett River runs through the village of Carrabassett Valley, with lots of opportunities for riparian and woodland birding, especially via the flat Narrow Gauge Pathway that runs for over 4 miles along the river. Sugarloaf Mountain hosts breeding Bicknell's Thrush just below the summit, along with Boreal Chickadees, Blackpoll Warblers, and others.

And finally, the Carrabassett Valley Snowfluent Ponds that hold the waste-water from the ski resort and spring snowmelt offer a rare opportunity for mountain-region shorebirding.

DIRECTIONS

The best way to easily sample most of the species of the mixed woods in the valley is via the **Narrow Gauge Pathway,** a former narrow-gauge railway that runs along the river from Sugarloaf toward town. Numerous trails in the area offer days of birding opportunities, but the four main miles of the pathway are level and often quite birdy. While you can walk or bike this (and even continue east for another 2 miles to **Riverside Park** and Carriage Road in town), short walks from each end can often be just as fruitful.

To start at the **Sugarloaf end,** turn into the parking area marked by a small Maine Huts and Trails "Trailhead Parking" sign, 0.1 miles west of the blinking light on Route 27 North/16 West at the entrance to Sugarloaf, on the right.

To start at the **eastern end,** from the blinking light at Sugarloaf, follow Route 27 South/16 East for 5 miles. Turn left into a poorly signed dirt road, just past the Sugarbowl bowling alley, to reach the trailhead parking. Take the trail across the field, into the woods, over the bridge, and make a left at the T onto the Narrow Gauge Pathway.

To reach this trailhead from Kingfield and points south, follow Route 27 North/16 West for 10 miles beyond the junction with Route 142 in the center of Kingfield, and make a right just before the Sugarbowl bowling alley.

At roughly the midway point, a wet, grassy meadow is particularly good for Alder Flycatchers, and especially in spring the riparian vegetation can be very good for migrants.

While in the area, it's always worth a quick check of the Carrabassett Valley Sanitary District's **Snowfluent Ponds.** From the blinking light at Sugarloaf, take Route 27 North/16 West for 1.3 miles. Make a right onto the dirt road and travel around the curve to the building. If anyone is present, please check in.

Then walk the dirt road to the left of the building and check the series of four ponds by carefully and slowly approaching each one. Wood Ducks and Spotted Sandpipers breed, and good numbers of both can be seen in late summer. In late May and especially in August to early September, migrant shorebirds often drop in, especially Solitary and Least Sandpipers, but almost anything is possible. Regular checks would likely yield some very rare birds for Maine's interior.

Sugarloaf Mountain itself can offer great birding, but it's a bear of a mountain to climb. However, from the Fourth of July through Columbus Day, one of the ski lifts runs on the weekends, whisking birders into higher elevations with little effort. Unfortunately, Bicknell's Thrushes are usually a little higher up than the top of the lift, and it's a steep climb. Worse, they are often really hard to detect after early July when the chairlift starts running again. While other mountains nearby offer better access for this enigmatic bird, the ride is worth it for the view alone, along with a good chance for Boreal Chickadee and Blackpoll Warbler.

RARITIES

Whimbrel, August 2015 (summit of Sugarloaf!)

Download a map of the Narrow Gauge Pathway (owing to poor signage to the trailheads, this is highly recommended) from the Town of Carrabassett at http://www.carrabassettvalley.org/assets/Narrow-gauge-pathway.

SITE F13 Burnt Mountain (aka Burnt Hill)

TOWN Carrabassett Valley. DeLorme Map 29: D4. SEASON May–July and September–November. VISITATION About 2.5 hrs. for the trip up, 5 hrs. for the round-trip. Sugarloaf has restaurants and restroom facilities at the base lodge. HIGHLIGHTS Bicknell's Thrush near the summit; spring warbler migration lower down; fall migrant American Pipits and Horned Larks near the summit

A wildfire burned the summit in 1909, leaving it bare—an event the fragile habitat is still recovering from. The topography of Sugarloaf Mountain forms a cirque facing to the north, funneling southbound birds through a notch between the summit of Sugarloaf and Burnt Hill. I once watched twenty Ravens playing in the wind from here, chased by a Red-tailed Hawk. A moderately strenuous hike uphill brings you to the 3,600-foot summit, with spectacular views and a spruce-fir zone that hosts breeding Bicknell's Thrush, Boreal Chickadee, and Blackpoll Warblers.

DIRECTIONS

From Stratton to the north or Carrabassett Valley to the south, follow Route 16/27 to the base lodge of Sugarloaf. Park near the base lodge (Lot C) and walk between the Sugarloaf Mountain Hotel and the base lodge. Follow the road as it curves to the left of the base lodge entrance, under the next set of chairlifts, and over the stream. Follow the road between condos, cross Mountainside Road, and continue straight onto Bigelow Mountain Road. At its end, enter the woods, following signs for the trail. Make a right just beyond the bridge and begin your climb. The hike to the summit is "moderately strenuous" and has a couple of stream crossings. You should be able to cross without getting your feet wet (but use caution after heavy rains and in the spring). The trail itself is good birding, with Blue-headed and Red-eyed Vireos at the base and Dark-eyed Juncos and White-throated Sparrows in the upper stretches. Right before you get into the spruce-fir zone below the summit (in about 1.5 miles) you'll cross through paper birch glades, part of Sugarloaf's Brackett Basin, which can host Pine Grosbeaks and lots of redpolls in irruption years. As you enter the stunted spruce-fir forest near the summit, be vigilant for Bicknell's Thrush.

For a map and trails visit Maine Trail Finder at www.mainetrailfinder.com and use the search feature. A map of the Sugarloaf Mountain Resort can be found at http://www.sugarloaf.com/the-mountain/resort-maps.

12 Somerset County

RON JOSEPH

Perhaps the most birder-neglected county in the state, Somerset County actually offers some of the best boreal birding closest to the population centers of central Maine. While the county may be lacking in public land, open access to private timberlands offers numerous opportunities for birding.

Somerset County is most visited during the breeding season. Long Falls Dam Road (site s06), Moore Pond (s07), and their environs host some of the state's most sought-after "boreal breeders," including Spruce Grouse, Olive-sided and Yellow-bellied Flycatchers, Gray Jay, Boreal Chickadee, and a wealth of warblers, including Cape May, Bay-breasted, Blackpoll, Palm, and Wilson's—all of which are near the southeastern limits of their breeding range.

Further south in the county, the trails of Goodwill-Hinckley (s03) offer a good opportunity to sample the species of fields and deciduous forests, contrasting nicely with the boreal-transition forests this county is better known for. The Madawaska Bog WMA (s04) is home to a number of sought-after wetland birds, but a canoe or kayak is called for.

While Ron Joseph has highlighted some of the best and most-explored birding areas of the county, further exploration of countless logging roads, bogs, and spruce-fir woods would undoubtedly turn up many additional birding hot spots.

Migration watchers head to wetlands and riparian corridors to find concentrations and search for uncommon species. As waters begin to freeze in late fall, attention is turned to the rivers, and the action heats up along the Kennebec River, especially at Mill Island Town Park and the Shawmut Dam (sites s01 and s02), where the rapidly declining Barrow's Goldeneyes can be found. *—Derek Lovitch*

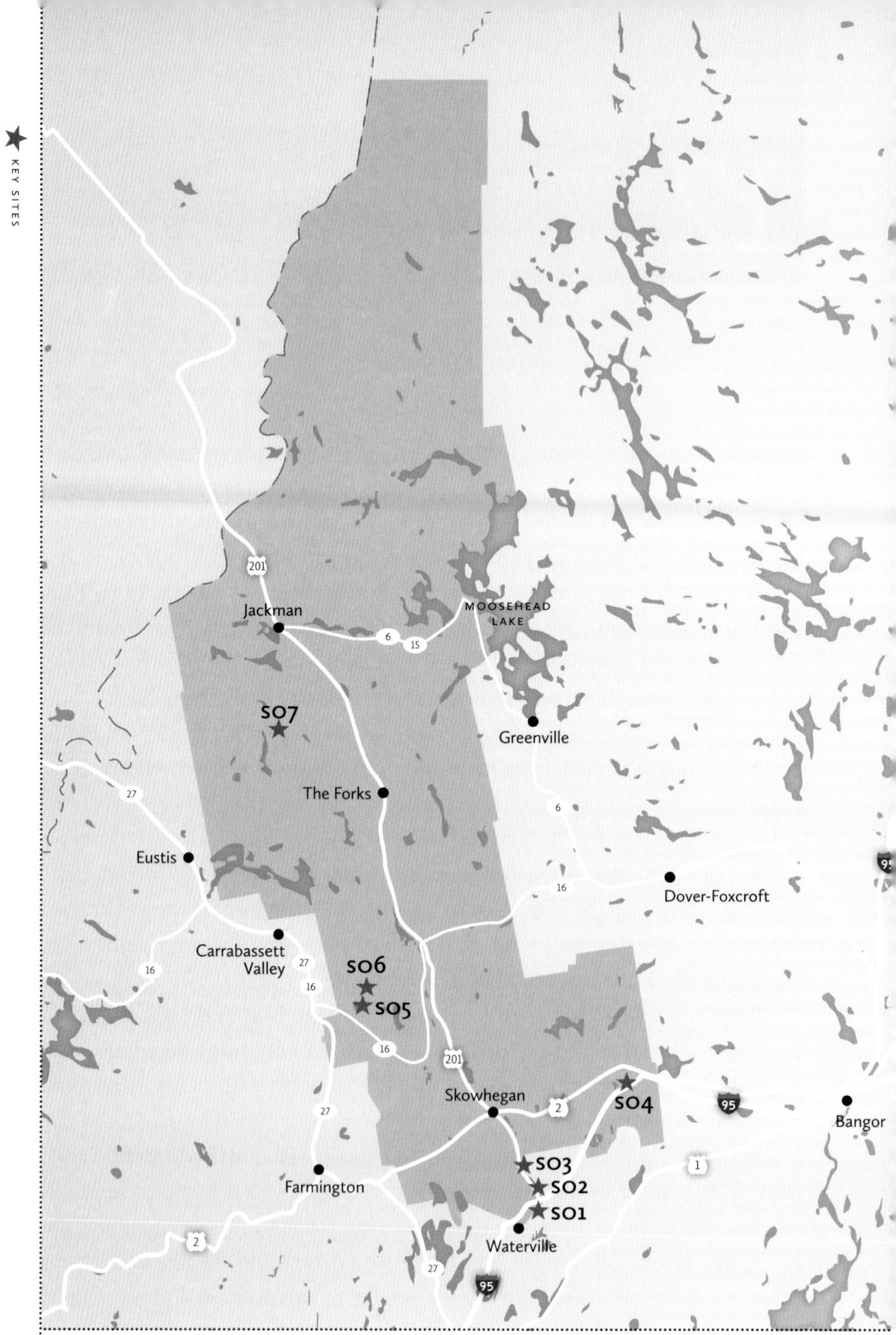
KEY SITES
MOOSEHEAD LAKE
Jackman
Greenville
The Forks
Eustis
Dover-Foxcroft
Carrabassett Valley
Skowhegan
Bangor
Farmington
Waterville
SO1
SO2
SO3
SO4
SO5
SO6
SO7
201
6
15
27
16
2
95
1

SOMERSET COUNTY

SITE SO1 Mill Island Town Park

TOWN Fairfield. DeLorme Map 21: D–E2–3. **SEASON** December–March, May–September. **VISITATION** 1–2 hrs. Restrooms open in summer. ♿ **HIGHLIGHTS** Barrow's Goldeneye and Iceland Gulls in winter; spring and fall passerine migration.

Mill Island Town Park is off the beaten path, tucked away on an island on the Kennebec River between Fairfield and Benton. The park is best for birding in midwinter when wintering waterfowl—dabblers and divers—forage in the rapids and flat waters of the river. During May and September migration the park attracts a surprising number of warblers and vireos. Summer finds the park pleasantly birdy, offering great opportunities to study and enjoy the common riparian breeders.

DIRECTIONS

From I-95 take Exit 132. Turn onto Route 139 East toward downtown Fairfield. On the left side of 139, in about three-quarters of a mile, is Hillman's Bakery. Bear claws, raspberry tarts, and the half-price rack are not to be missed! Continue on Route 139 East, which makes a sharp right and then a left turn at a light in downtown. Immediately after crossing the first bridge, turn left onto Island Avenue. In 0.2 miles you'll reach the Mill Island Park parking lot. A trail map can be found in the kiosk. For history buffs, be sure to read the "River Driving Ballad" by Jed Calder. Logs were floated down the Kennebec River past Mill Island for over a hundred years, until 1976, when the colorful log-driving era came to an end in Maine.

I usually make a counterclockwise walk on the small island by first walking to the edge of the island to scope the river for eagles and waterfowl. Among the waterfowl I've seen from the island are Barrow's and Common Goldeneyes, American Wigeon, American Black Duck, Mallard, Canada Geese, Bufflehead, Common Merganser, and Wood Duck.

In the trees near the parking lot, during spring and fall migration I've encountered a dozen warblers, including Tennessee and Cape May. Philadelphia Vireos are also regularly seen here during migration. Come June, breeding birds take over, and Mill Island is busy with Warbling Vireo, American Redstart, Veery, Gray Catbird, and other common breeders typical of woodlands along rivers in Central Maine. Watch for Osprey (spring through fall) and Bald Eagles (all year) fishing over the river.

Orange-crowned warbler, September 2010 and 2011; Canvasback, February 2013

You can learn more about Mill Island Park at http://www.fairfieldme.com/town/pages/mill-island-park.

SITE S02 Shawmut Dam

TOWN Shawmut. DeLorme Map 21: D2–3. **SEASON** December–March, May–September. **VISITATION** 30 min. to 1 hr. No restroom facilities. **HIGHLIGHTS** Winter waterfowl including Barrow's Goldeneye; gulls (Iceland Gull, Glaucous Gull in winter); raptors; spring and fall migrant songbirds foraging in the riparian zone.

Much of the river north of Shawmut Dam remains frozen throughout winter. However, the open waters below Shawmut Dam (a few miles upriver of Mill Island Park, site S01), and immediately above the dam, attract one of Maine's largest inland concentrations of wintering Iceland and Glaucous Gulls. Be sure to check the calm waters above the dam for bathing gulls that forage in the fields of Maine's largest dairy farm on the east side of Shawmut Dam. Large wintering concentrations of waterfowl (Common Goldeneyes, usually including one or more Barrow's, plus Mallards and American Black Ducks) attract Bald Eagles and waterfowl hunters.

During the fall I've seen migrant Long-billed Dowitcher, Pectoral Sandpiper, American Golden Plover, and other shorebirds roosting on boulders below the dam. Look for "peeps" and American Pipit foraging in the short grass growing on the shore of the Kennebec. Concentrations of shorebirds and waterfowl attract Peregrine Falcons and an occasional Northern Goshawk.

DIRECTIONS

From I-95 take Exit 133. Follow Route 201 North for 1.8 miles (1.9 if arriving via I-95 North) and turn right onto Kennebec Street. Park in the gravel lot at its end. Follow the dirt road to the right of the building to the public boat launch site to scan the river or launch your boat (there's parking here as well). Back at your car, walk to the left of the building to the grassy area and view the river above the dam.

From Mill Island Town Park (site S01), backtrack to I-95 and continue north on the interstate to the next exit (133). Then follow directions in the above paragraph.

Gyrfalcon, winter 1992; Golden Eagle, winter 2012

SITE S03 Goodwill-Hinckley School Nature Trail, L. C. Bates Museum, and Kennebec Valley Community College Farm Fields

TOWN Hinckley. DeLorme Map 21: C–D2. **SEASON** May–September. **VISITATION** 3–4 hrs. Restroom facilities at the L. C. Bates Museum; $3 museum entrance fee for adults, $1 for children. No fee for trail use. **HIGHLIGHTS** Variety of breeding birds of fields and woods.

The L. C. Bates Museum is home to Maine's largest collection of mounted birds. The museum, open year-round, offers birding activities for children. The staff is bird knowledgeable and friendly. I recommend timing your visit to coincide with the museum's open business hours (see link below). Not everyday are visitors able to observe full mounts of extinct species, once common in Maine, such as Passenger Pigeon and woodland caribou. The staff can also assist you in finding the latest "most birdy" trails.

DIRECTIONS

From I-95 take Exit 133 and drive 5 miles on Route 201 North. As you approach the Goodwill-Hinckley School, turn left at the L. C. Bates Museum sign.

I recommend parking at the museum, where you can pick up a trail map to use as a guide to hike the 5 miles of trails that bisect/skirt farm fields and woodlands. From there, walk north on the paved road to Uncle Ed's Trail. Be sure to scan the frog pond on your left. It often holds Wood Duck and Green Heron. During the spring, the willows along its edge can be very active with migrating warblers. Uncle Ed's Trail bisects a stately stand of white pine, red pine, and eastern hemlock, along with an assortment of deciduous trees. Watch and listen for Hermit and Wood Thrushes, Black-throated Blue Warbler, Barred Owl, and many others.

Return to your vehicle or walk to the Farm Road (labeled on trail map). Proceed down the Farm Road, which is now the property of Kennebec Valley

Community College. This is an active farm, so be mindful of tractors and other farm machinery. Please check with the farm manager, who will advise you on parking your vehicle. Check out the farm pond for Sora and Virginia Rail. Both have nested in the cattails on the west shore. The large cattail stand in the wet field east of the pond is a fall staging area of mixed flocks of blackbirds. The hayfields are home to nesting Bobolink and Savannah Sparrow. Kestrels can also be found hovering over the fields in search of grasshoppers and field mice.

After exiting the Goodwill-Hinkley School and Kennebec Valley Community College grounds, continue north on Route 201 and turn right onto Route 23 North. Make a right into the boat launch site next to the Kennebec River. Pan the cement bridge over the river for nesting Cliff Swallows. The swallows often collect mud for their nests from the parking lot's puddles. Listen for hard-to-see Warbling Vireos in the trees lining the river. Common Loons are also occasionally seen here during open-water seasons.

RARITIES

Yellow-headed Blackbird (three), September 2005

A descriptions of the trails can be found at Healthy Maine Walks, http://www .healthymainewalks.com/walks/good-will-hinckley-arboretum-and-nature -trail. For information about the L. C. Bates Museum visit http://www.gwh .org/lcbates/LCBatesMuseum.aspx.

SITE S04 Madawaska Bog Wildlife Management Area

TOWN West Palmyra. DeLorme Map 21: A–B5. SEASON May, June– July, August–September. VISITATION 2–3 hrs. No restroom facilities. ⛵ HIGHLIGHTS Breeding and migrant wetland birds, including Black Tern, Common Gallinule, and Least Bittern.

Madawaska Bog is a 291-acre wetland owned and managed by the Maine Department of Inland Fisheries and Wildlife. It's best accessed by canoe or kayak from a boat-launching site 100 feet left of the dam. In June, the emergent wetland is one of the better places in central Maine to see Black Tern, Green Heron, American Bittern, Wood Duck, Pied-billed Grebe, Wilson's Snipe, Common Gallinule, and Least Bittern.

From 1-95 take Exit 150. Follow signs for Routes 11 and 100 toward Pittsfield. Drive 1 mile to a light in Pittsfield and turn left. In 0.3 miles bear left onto Madawaska Avenue. Drive 2.9 miles to the Madawaska Bog sign on the right. Turn right into the gravel parking lot.

I launch my kayak at the dam and paddle upstream, which is bordered by tall hardwoods. Watch and listen for foraging and nesting birds, including Warbling Vireos. Northern Waterthrush, Swamp Sparrow, Osprey, and Sora will greet you at the marsh, a short paddle from the parking lot.

SITE S05 Gilman Pond Farm and Stream Inlet

TOWN New Portland. DeLorme Map 30: E2. SEASON May–October. VISITATION 2–3 hrs. No restroom facilities. ♿ HIGHLIGHTS Grassland birds; Wilson's Snipe; five species of swallows.

This is one of the best places in Somerset County to see and hear numerous courting Wilson's Snipe high above the fields, especially from mid-May until mid-July. In June, the hayfields abound with Bobolinks, Savannah Sparrows, and several American Bitterns. All five of Maine's small swallow species can be seen here in summer, and other breeding birds include Black-billed Cuckoo and Warbling Vireo in the riparian areas. Pioneering Sandhill Cranes, whose population is increasing in Maine, are occasionally seen foraging in the fields, especially in April. As of 2015, cranes have not been documented as nesters here, but that might change, since their breeding habitat requirements are met by this remarkable ranch and neighboring emergent wetland.

DIRECTIONS

From 1-95 take Exit 133. Follow Route 201 North for 15 miles to Skowhegan. Continue on 201 through the downtown, where you loop around to remain on 201 North. Approximately 4 miles north of Skowhegan's Main Street, turn left onto Route 148 West. Drive 6 miles into downtown Madison. After crossing the Kennebec River, turn right onto Routes 201A/8 North and reset your odometer. Continue for 4.7 miles into North Anson and turn left onto Route 16 West. When Route 16 West makes a hard left in the village of North New Portland (Chase Memorial Building on your left), continue on 16 West for another 1.1 miles to a right onto Gilman Pond Road. In 1.6 miles park near the large culvert and stream that winds through Cold Stream Ranch, one of the most picturesque farms in Maine. The owners of the ranch are birder friendly. However, please bird along the public dirt road and not in their driveway.

For the best birding, walk the dirt road in both directions to where the fields give way to forests. I've seen American Pipit in May and September foraging in the cattle-grazed pastures bordering the road. Check the telephone wires for swallows: it's not uncommon to encounter five of Maine's nesting species here (Northern Rough-winged, Tree, Barn, Cliff, and Bank), and I've even observed them in my scope all side by side as they preen and rest. Black-billed Cuckoo, Warbling Vireo, Brown Thrasher, and Alder Flycatcher are among the nesters in the riparian zone that stretches from the culvert to Gilman Pond.

Continue north on Gilman Pond Road for 0.4 miles. Turn right at the boat-launch sign. Proceed about 200 yards to Gilman Pond. Park here and scan the pond for Pied-billed Grebe, Common Loon, and other wetland-dependent species. In September and October, particularly when water levels are low, scan the exposed muddy shoreline for migrant shorebirds. I've also seen fair numbers of fall migrant American Pipits foraging in the grasses along the pond edge. Canoe/kayak paddling is a productive way to bird the pond, especially in mid-May and again in late September. (To inquire about canoe rentals, call Claybrook Mountain Lodge, 207–628–4681.) The botanically rich silver maple floodplain at the north end of the pond is a good place to see small flocks of Rusty Blackbird and an occasional Olive-sided Flycatcher, especially during migration. Even if the birding is relatively quiet, boating is a very enjoyable way to experience this mostly underdeveloped, picturesque body of water. The boat launch parking lot is especially good for viewing spring and fall migrating songbirds.

RARITIES

Sandhill Crane, April 2015; Yellow-throated Vireo, May 2015

SITE S06 Long Falls Dam Road

TOWN New Portland. DeLorme Map 30: E2.   SEASON All year, but especially **May–July.**   VISITATION half to full day. No restroom facilities.

HIGHLIGHTS Rusty Blackbird; Spruce Grouse; Black-backed Woodpecker,

Olive-sided and Yellow-bellied Flycatchers, Gray Jay, Boreal Chickadee; Evening Grosbeak; breeding warblers including Cape May, Bay-breasted, Wilson's, and Palm.

A sparsely populated public road bisects forested wetlands, streams, numerous beaver ponds, sandy hayfields, and forested uplands habitat. As such, the birding here from May to September can produce many of Maine's boreal specialties, and winter can be good during finch irruptions and when road conditions permit.

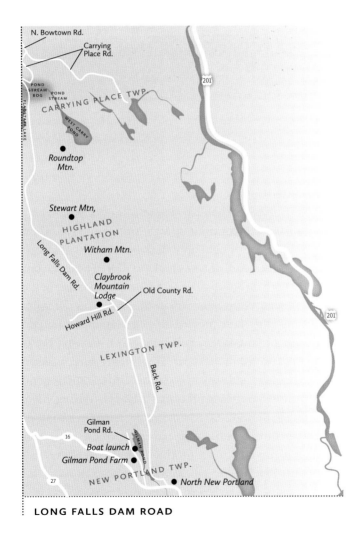

SOMERSET COUNTY

Boreal Chickadee. © Luke Seitz

DIRECTIONS

Follow directions to North New Portland as described in site S05. Where Route 16 West makes a hard left, continue straight onto Long Falls Dam Road. Proceed for 3.7 miles and turn right onto Back Road.

From the beginning of **Back Road**, drive 1.5 miles to a large field on your left. Walk the dirt road in both directions. I've seen Upland Sandpiper in the sandy field, and heard singing Whip-poor-will in the woods on the right, especially at dusk. The tall pines here provide an excellent opportunity to compare the trilling songs of Pine Warbler, Chipping Sparrow, and Dark-eyed Junco. Continue 1 mile and stop next to a large beaver pond (called a flowage) on your right. Park here and walk in both directions. Scan the pond and its wetlands for American Bittern and other marsh birds. Warbling Vireo, Brown Thrasher, and Indigo Bunting are reliable in the upland pond edges.

Continue on Back Road until it ends at the pavement of the Long Falls Dam Road. Turn right and drive 2.8 miles north on Long Falls Dam Road. Turn left onto Old County Road. In 0.3 miles turn right onto Howard Hill Road and continue 0.2 miles to **Claybrook Mountain Lodge**. Check the lodge's bird feeders for Evening Grosbeaks, especially during fall through spring. Pat and Greg Drummond, owners of the lodge, have hosted numerous weekend birding trips since 1990. Their yard is very birdy, especially in May when the apple trees are flowering. On Memorial Day weekend, Tennessee Warbler, Blackpoll, Magnolia Warbler, and many other migrants visit these trees like clockwork, foraging for insects in the flowering apple trees. In May and June, courting male Ruffed Grouse can be regularly heard drumming in the woods across the dirt road from the lodge. Keep your eyes and ears open for Red-shouldered Hawk, which have nested nearby since 2010. As with most raptors, Red-shouldered Hawks are most visible (and vocal) during early spring courtship (March–April) and again in late June/early July after the young have fledged. Each spring, American Woodcock use the field in front of the lodge as evening displaying grounds. Eastern Bluebird and Tree Swallow often nest in the lodge's nest boxes.

From the lodge, return to the Long Falls Dam Road. Turn left (north) on Long Falls Dam Road and drive 12 miles to a large wetland on your right, known locally as **Pond Stream Bog.** Park your vehicle near the culvert that drains the forested and scrub/shrub wetland. In spring/summer, scan the wetland's dead trees for Rusty Blackbirds (now very rare as a breeder in the state), Bald Eagles, and perched Wilson's Snipes. Listen and watch for nesting Wilson's, Palm, and Canada Warblers, Lincoln's Sparrows, Olive-sided and Yellow-bellied Flycatchers, Ruby-crowned Kinglets, and many others. It's best to walk north along the road for a mile to absorb all the bird life here. Watch and listen for uncommon Gray Jays and Black-backed Woodpeckers.

Words of caution: Moose are prevalent on Long Falls Dam Road. Driving the road, especially at night and early morning, can be very dangerous. Please slow down and be mindful of Maine's largest land mammal. Some bulls weigh a thousand pounds or more. Logging trucks frequent these roads, too. If you encounter one of these trucks, pull far to the right and let it pass.

Return to your vehicle and drive 0.7 miles north to **Carrying Place Road** (also labeled Capital Road on some maps). Turn right onto this logging road and drive 2.5 miles to a T intersection. Turn left onto North Bowtown Road and drive 0.8 miles to a gravel parking area on the right. Park here and walk northwest along the spruce-fir lined road. Watch and listen for Gray Jay, Boreal Chickadee, and Bay-breasted Warbler. This boreal forest is the closest, most reliable spot for Cape May Warblers for central Maine's birders. Spruce Grouse and Black-backed Woodpeckers are also occasionally encountered here.

Migrant Golden Eagles are seen in this area every few years; Louisiana Waterthrush, May 2009 and 2010 (Claybrook Mountain Lodge)

SITE S07 Moore Pond

TOWN Bradstreet Township. DeLorme Map 39: C–D4–5.   SEASON All year, but especially **May–July.**   VISITATION 2–4 hrs. No restroom facilities. HIGHLIGHTS Gray Jay; Spruce Grouse; Boreal Chickadee; Olive-sided and Yellow-bellied Flycatchers; Cape May and Bay-breasted Warblers.

Maine's largest jack pine stand (a state-designated "S1 Critically Imperiled Natural Community" because of its extreme rarity), this remarkably beautiful closed canopy forest *feels* primeval. Birding aside for a moment, in June the jack pine forest floor is carpeted with red-stemmed moss, twinflower, pink lady's slippers, bluebead lily (clintonia), starflower, creeping snowberry, Canada mayflower, and acres of bunchberry with its white blossoms. In short, the spring ephemerals are a sight to behold and savor. You would be remiss by not pausing to smell the hanging trumpetlike blossoms of twinflower, reportedly the favorite plant of the famous botanist Carl Linnaeus. The plant's Latin name bears his name: *Linnaea borealis*. Born in Sweden in 1707, Linnaeus is widely known as the father of modern taxonomy.

For birders, jack pines provide nesting habitat for many highly prized coniferous forest specialists. This rare plant community is also one of the best places in Maine to encounter federally threatened Canada lynx. I've seen two here—several years apart—during birding trips to Moore Pond. Look for their "salad plate"–size roundish footprints in the mud along the trail.

DIRECTIONS

From 1-95 take Exit 133. Follow Route 201 North toward Jackman. Drive approximately 56 miles on Route 201 North through Skowhegan, Bingham, and West Forks. At Berrys General Store in West Forks reset your trip odometer and drive 13.6 miles to Parlin Pond (Lake) rest area on the right-hand side of Route 201. Shortly after the rest area, turn left onto Spencer Road (some DeLorme maps label it as Hardscrabble Road).

Drive 8.5 miles to a grassy parking area on the right. There's parking for only one or two vehicles. A log laid across the trail prevents vehicular access.

Linnea or "twinflower" carpets the boreal forest floor.
© Ron Joseph

Park here and walk the half-mile forested trail to **Moore Pond.** Look and listen for Bay-breasted and Cape May Warblers, Gray Jay, Spruce Grouse, Swainson's Thrush, Black-backed Woodpecker, Boreal Chickadee, and Yellow-bellied Flycatcher. Other nesters here include Blackburnian, Northern Parula, Yellow-rumped, and Magnolia Warblers.

From the Moore Pond parking area continue west on Spencer Road about 1 mile to a four-way intersection of two logging roads. Turn right onto Spencer Rips Road. Go 0.2 miles to the left-hand spur road to a camping area next to **Whipple Stream.** Park here and walk to the edge of the stream and listen and watch for Olive-sided, Yellow-bellied, and Alder Flycatchers.

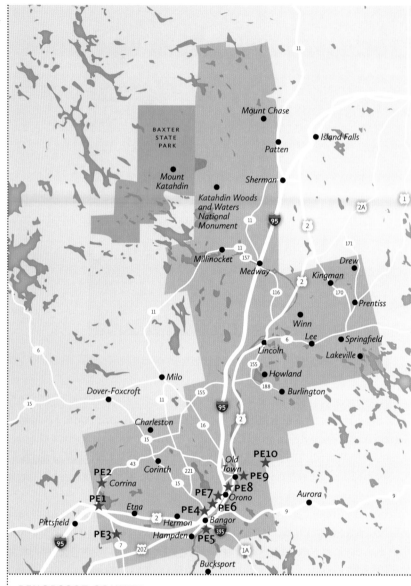

Mount Chase

Island Falls

Patten

BAXTER
STATE
PARK

Sherman

Mount
Katahdin

Katahdin Woods
and Waters
National
Monument

Drew

Kingman

Millinocket

Medway

Prentiss

Winn

Lee

Springfield

Lincoln

Lakeville

Milo

Howland

Dover-Foxcroft

Burlington

Charleston

PE10

Old
Town

PE2

Corinth

PE9

Corrina

PE8

PE7

PE1

Etna

Orono

Aurora

PE4

PE6

Pittsfield

Hermon

Bangor

PE3

Hampden

PE5

Bucksport

PENOBSCOT COUNTY

13 Penobscot County

LUKE SEITZ

Stretching from the tidal waters of the lower Penobscot River in Orrington all the way to the new Woods & Waters National Monument, next to Baxter State Park, Penobscot County covers a lot of land and a lot of very diverse habitats. From the city of Bangor (the second-largest city in Maine) to the unincorporated territories in the northern reaches, Penobscot hosts everything from an increasingly vibrant downtown Bangor to seclusion and isolation of unbroken forests. The Penobscot River, beginning near Millinocket, is the county's spine, but Interstate 95 is the county's artery and vein—bringing people north and natural resources (primarily timber) south. Much of the northern two-thirds of the county has been virtually unexplored by birders, but the southern half has some prime birding destinations.

Bangor-Brewer hosts a series of excellent parks that provide year-round birding. Spring and fall migration, wetland breeders, and winter irruptives can all be enjoyed at places including Essex Woods (site PE4), and the Bangor City Forest and Orono Bog (PE7) lie just minutes from most of the city's residents. I'm also convinced that someday a "stretch break" at the Bangor Waterfront Park (within PE5) on my way to or from Mount Desert Island or Washington County will result in some "mega" rarity.

Extensive marsh systems in the region host sought-after breeders, which Luke Seitz works to find on his "Big Day" adventures, such as Least Bitterns at Corinna Marsh (PE2) and sometimes at Sebasticook Lake (PE1), and Common Gallinule at Corinna Marsh and Penjajawoc Marsh (PE6), along with American Bitterns, Marsh Wrens, and Sora and Virginia Rails. While Willow Flycatchers approach the northern limits of their breeding range in Penjajawoc, nearby Orono Bog (PE7) hosts some of the southeasternmost (and very accessible) Lincoln's Sparrows and Palm Warblers. Meanwhile, for a true taste of boreal birding—including most of the charismatic species such as Spruce Grouse, Gray Jay, Boreal Chickadee, and a variety of warblers, be sure to visit Sunkhaze Meadows NWR (PE9) and Stud Mill Road (PE10).

And despite the distance here from the coast, waterfowl migration can be fantastic in the county, especially at its southwestern corner, starting with Sebasticook Lake (PE1), which is one of the state's premier duck-watching locations.

Winters are usually cold and harsh, as they are throughout interior Maine, but birding in Penobscot County can really heat up. White-winged gulls and Barrow's Goldeneyes inhabit open stretches of the river from Bangor south (PE5), while irruptive frugivores—Pine Grosbeaks and Bohemian Waxwings—can be seen almost every winter on the campus of the University of Maine at Orono (PE8). Sunkhaze Meadows and Stud Mill Road can be great during finch years, while every few winters a Northern Hawk-Owl turns up in some random field somewhere off the beaten track. —*Derek Lovitch*

SITE PE1 Sebasticook Lake

TOWN Newport. DeLorme Map 22: A1–2. SEASON **March–May**, June–September, **October–December**. VISITATION 1–3 hrs. Restroom facilities at businesses in Newport. ⚓ HIGHLIGHTS High diversity of migrant waterfowl including several species of *Aythya* and Ruddy Duck; shorebirds in fall; marsh birds sometimes, including Least Bittern.

Sebasticook Lake can hold great numbers and diversity of waterfowl in the spring and fall and is one of the few reliable spots in the state for Ruddy Duck. Additionally, shorebirds frequent the mudflats when water levels are low. The marshy fringes of the lake, especially on the northern side, hold chattering Marsh Wrens, grunting Virginia Rails, and sometimes even Least Bittern.

DIRECTIONS

From I-95 take Exit 157. From the south, make a left at the end of the off-ramp onto Route 100/11 toward Newport, and from the north, make a right. Continue straight through the intersection with Route 2, and in 0.3 miles turn right onto High Street. In 0.2 miles turn left onto North Street. This road makes a ninety-degree turn to the right in a quarter mile; at the bend, look for a park on your left with a boat launch. The tour begins here.

The small park gives you a view of the southwestern arm of Sebasticook. Migrant waterfowl are most numerous here in October and November; look especially for Ring-necked Duck, Greater and Lesser Scaup, and Ruddy Duck.

You might even get lucky with a Redhead or Canvasback mixed in with the other diving ducks. Dabblers are also a frequent sight, especially along the edges of the lake. These can include Blue- and Green-winged Teal, American Wigeon, and Northern Shoveler. Also keep an eye out for shorebirds when there is exposed mud. The most common species include Greater and Lesser Yellowlegs, Killdeer, and Least and Pectoral Sandpipers. Rarer species that have been found here include American Golden-Plover, Hudsonian Godwit, and Long-billed Dowitcher. As the fall progresses, especially in November, shorebirds on the mud might be replaced with open-country passerines. Scan carefully for American Pipit, Lapland Longspur, Horned Lark, and Snow Bunting.

From the park turn left onto Elm Street and head into Newport. Bear left when Elm Street hits Route 100 and continue for another 2.8 miles. Turn left onto Stetson Road and continue for 2.3 miles until you hit a four-way intersection. Turn left here onto Dunham Bridge Road, and in 1.5 miles you'll reach a causeway. Cross the causeway, pull off on the left, and walk back to scan the water for the species as described above.

Continue north along Dunham Bridge Road for 2.2 miles to a four-way intersection with Route 222. Turn left. In 0.2 miles fork left onto County Woods Road and continue for 2.2 miles. Along the way you'll cross a relatively narrow branch of the lake that you can scan for waterfowl. However, your destination is the marsh at the northwestern corner of the lake. Carefully pull over and scan the open water on your left and the edges of the cattails. In spring and summer look and listen for Virginia Rail, Sora, and Marsh Wren here—the latter are quite conspicuous. Least Bittern has been seen flying over the cattails, but they are very secretive, and you'd be lucky to even hear one.

County Woods Road comes back out to Route 7/11 South shortly beyond the marsh. A left turn here will bring you back to Newport and I-95.

RARITIES

Sabine's Gull, September 1993; American White Pelican, November 2012; Franklin's Gull, November 2015

SITE PE2 Corinna Marsh

TOWN Corinna. DeLorme Map 22: E1. **SEASON** April–July, August–December. **VISITATION** 15 min. to 3 hrs. No restroom facilities. ⚓

HIGHLIGHTS Excellent marsh with Common Gallinule, American and Least Bitterns, rails, and many ducks.

This extensive marsh is close to Sebasticook Lake but makes for a great birding location in its own right. In spring and fall it's worth a check for migrant waterfowl, but the real highlights here are the breeding marsh birds. This is one of the better spots in the state for breeding Common Gallinule and Least Bittern, along with more common species such as Virginia Rail, Sora, Pied-billed Grebe, and American Bittern.

DIRECTIONS

From I-95 take Exit 157. From the south, make a left at the end of the off-ramp onto Route 100/11 toward Newport, and from the north, make a right. Go straight through the intersection with Route 2 onto Route 7/11 North. Continue north for 6 miles into the town of Corinna. Turn left onto Route 43. Take the first right onto Main Street and then the first right onto Hill Street. Continue to the end of the pavement, where you'll see a dam on the right. It's easiest to park here and walk to the end of the dirt road, where you have a view of the extensive wetlands to the north. The boardwalk that begins over the dam can be very good for passerines, especially during migration.

Least Bittern. © Luke Seitz

A scope is recommended to scan the open water for ducks. Wood Duck, Ring-necked Duck, Common Goldeneye, and Hooded Merganser have all been noted breeding here, and Common Loons are often present. With luck, you might spot a distant Common Gallinule slinking around the edges of the reeds, or even a bittern (American or Least) flying over the marsh.

The best way to enjoy this spot, however, is to launch a canoe or kayak and paddle north to the marsh. This gets you much closer to the variety of marsh birds found here and increases your chances at rare breeders like Least Bittern and Common Gallinule. More common breeders here include Virginia Rail, Sora, American Bittern, and Pied-billed Grebe. Keep an ear out for both Willow and Alder Flycatchers, which nest side by side and provide excellent comparisons. Marsh Wrens and Swamp Sparrows chatter loudly from the reeds.

In spring and fall you can expect a wider variety of ducks on the water. Look for Blue- and Green-winged Teal, American Wigeon, Northern Shoveler, Gadwall, and both scaup in addition to the species mentioned above. Adding a quick check here to your loop around Sebasticook Lake (site PE1) is easy and often worthwhile.

SITE PE3 Plymouth Pond

TOWN Plymouth. DeLorme Map 22: B2. SEASON March–
December. VISITATION 15 min. to 2 hrs. No restroom facilities. ⚲
HIGHLIGHTS Breeding birds include Pied-billed Grebe, American Bittern, and Common Loon; migrant waterfowl.

Plymouth Pond used to be known as one of Maine's few breeding colonies of Black Tern. This colony has since disappeared, but the marsh and lake still hold exciting marsh birds in the breeding season, and they are worthy of a check during waterfowl migration.

DIRECTIONS

From I-95 take Exit 161. At the end of the respective ramps turn right onto Route 7 South. Continue for 2.4 miles into the village of Plymouth and turn left to stay on Route 7. You'll soon be on the causeway over Plymouth Pond. At the far end of the causeway is a boat launch on the left, where you can park and scan the lake.

The marsh to your west is typically the most interesting (this is where the Black Terns used to nest), but it is worth scanning both sides of the causeway. Common Loons are always present in the summer. Keep a sharp eye out for Pied-billed Grebes in the emergent vegetation, although you're probably more likely to see waterfowl like Wood and Ring-necked Ducks and Hooded Merganser. I'd recommend using a scope to scan the back edge. If you have a canoe or kayak, this is an excellent place for a paddle—birding by boat is definitely the best way to explore the marsh. You might hear a Virginia Rail grunting from the reeds or come across an American Bittern standing still along the edge.

There is also excellent habitat at the far southeastern tip of the lake, but this is a longer paddle from the boat launch. For a less strenuous activity, walk south along the road from the parking area (but be careful, as there can be fast traffic). The lakeside woods here are usually packed with birds in the breeding season.

Outside the breeding season, Plymouth Pond is significantly quieter. However, if you're in the area, such as to or from your ducking on Sebasticook Lake (PE1), it is worth a quick check in spring and fall. Migrant waterfowl, sometimes including scoters or Long-tailed Ducks, can appear on inland bodies of water like this after heavy rain.

SITE PE4 Essex Woods

TOWN Bangor. DeLorme Map 77: B3. SEASON All year, but especially **April–May.** VISITATION 1–2 hrs. No restroom facilities. HIGHLIGHTS Migrant ducks, Pied-billed Grebe, Green Heron, rails, migrant warblers, and sparrows

Essex Woods is a small complex of varied habitats right next to I-95. The woods can be productive for migrant warblers in spring and fall, and the wetland holds an excellent selection of breeding marsh birds (including Virginia Rail and Sora). The trail is short and easy, so this site makes for a pleasant birding outing at any time of year.

DIRECTIONS

From I-95 in Bangor take Exit 185. At the traffic lights at the end of the respective off-ramps turn right onto Broadway. If arriving via I-95 North, make a right at the sixth light (arriving via I-95 South, make a right at the fifth light) onto Grandview Avenue. At its end, turn right onto Essex Street. Take your first left onto Watchmaker Street and drive to its end at the park.

From the parking area, take the main path straight ahead. This path heads down through the woods, where you should keep an eye out for mixed flocks of migrants in the spring and fall. Up to twenty species of warblers, plus uncommon migrants like Philadelphia Vireo and Yellow-bellied Flycatcher, have occurred here. At the end of this path, you'll come to a T intersection. Turn right. You'll pass through more woods, but in a couple hundred yards the wetland will open up on your left. This area rarely fails to disappoint. In spring and fall, nearly all of Maine's regularly occurring dabbling ducks have been seen here, including Gadwall, American Wigeon, Blue- and Green-winged Teal, Northern Shoveler, and Northern Pintail. Ring-necked Duck and Hooded Merganser are regular. Breeding waterbirds include Pied-billed Grebe, American Bittern, Green Heron, Sora, and Virginia Rail. The scrubby habitat surrounding the wetland should be searched for sparrows in the fall (including Lincoln's) but also holds a variety of more common breeding birds. Warbling Vireos and Baltimore Orioles are particularly noisy and conspicuous. Look and listen for both cuckoos (Black-billed is more likely) and search the muddy margins of the pond for shorebirds, especially Solitary Sandpiper and Wilson's Snipe.

The trail hooks around the southeast corner of the wetland and continues toward a small neighborhood off Stillwater Avenue. If you've reached the end, turn around and retrace your steps to the parking lot. If you have time, there are some other smaller trails through the woods that are worth exploring for migrants.

SITE PE5 Bangor Waterfront Tour

Entry by Luke Seitz and Derek Lovitch

TOWNS Bangor and Brewer. DeLorme Map 77: C–D2–3.
SEASON November–April. VISITATION 1–2 hrs. Restroom facilities at local businesses throughout, portable toilets at Waterfront Park.
HIGHLIGHTS Gulls including Iceland and Glaucous; Barrow's Goldeneye; potential for migrant songbirds.

The Penobscot River in Bangor is well known as a reliable wintering area for Barrow's Goldeneye and Iceland and Glaucous Gulls, among the more common species. Several other species of ducks can also be found, including good

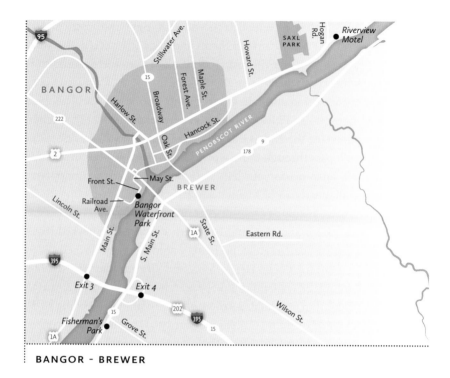

BANGOR - BREWER

numbers of Common Mergansers. The recently expanded Bangor Waterfront Park on the banks of the river holds potential for migration, especially under fallout conditions, and especially as recently planted vegetation matures (although future development plans may affect this).

DIRECTIONS

From I-395 just east of the bridge over the Penobscot River take Exit 4. Turn left at the end of the respective off-ramps onto Route 15 south. In just under a half mile, turn into **Fishermen's Park** on your right. Barrow's Goldeneye is often seen here, along with Common Merganser. Turn left onto Route 15 North and continue north for 1.2 miles and turn left onto Route 1A. Cross the river and take your first right to stay on 1A. Turn right again to remain on 1A, and then take your first left onto May Street. At the end of May Street turn right onto Front Street, which parallels the river. In 0.1 miles turn into the parking lot on your left.

This is the **Bangor Waterfront Park**. Check the river in front of you, and check the riparian vegetation and hillside by following the trails to the south.

Barrow's Goldeneye are sometimes present, and concentrations of Common Mergansers can be impressive in late fall and early spring. Iceland (uncommon) and Glaucous gulls (rare) sometimes join Herring and Ring-bills at the edge of the ice. This park is essentially unvisited in migration, but the riparian vegetation and new landscaping could hold migrants, especially as plantings fill in. After the river freezes, few birds are around, except for a Northern Mockingbird or two—actually a fairly rare bird in winter in interior Maine—but keep an eye out for Bohemian Waxwings and Pine Grosbeaks in irruptions years, as long as the European Starlings haven't already cleaned out the fruit resources.

Continue south along Front Street, which bends to the right and becomes Railroad Street. At the end, turn right onto Main Street. In 0.5 miles, in the heart of downtown, turn right onto Route 2 East. Follow Route 2 East for 1.9 miles, cautiously searching for patches of open water along the river when you have a chance. Keep right at the fork with Hogan Road to stay on Route 2, and look for the **Riverview Motel** on your left. This is also a good place to scan the river for Barrow's Goldeneye and other ducks. Once you're finished, the quickest way back to I-95 is to backtrack slightly and turn right onto Hogan Road, which leads you to the interstate.

SITE PE6 Penjajawoc Marsh

TOWN Bangor. DeLorme Map 77: A3.   SEASON April, **May–July**, August–September.   VISITATION 15 min. to 1 hr. Restroom facilities at local businesses nearby.   HIGHLIGHTS Marsh birds including Virginia Rail and Sora, both bitterns, and Common Gallinule.

The southern outflow of this productive marsh is visible from the edge of the Home Depot parking lot. The diversity of marsh birds here can be excellent; this is one of the best-known spots in the state for Common Gallinule. Much of the marsh is frustratingly inaccessible, but even a quick scan often turns up something worthwhile.

DIRECTIONS

From I-95 in Bangor take Exit 186. At the end of the off-ramp turn right onto Stillwater Avenue. In 0.2 miles turn left toward Home Depot. Looking toward the building, continue to the far right (northern) end of the parking lot, from which you can scan the marsh.

There is a shrubby field between the edge of the parking lot and the out-flow of Penjajawoc Marsh, which once hosted a singing male Clay-colored Sparrow in the late spring! More regular birds around here include Willow Flycatcher (approaching the northern limits of its regular breeding range in interior Maine), Warbling Vireo, and Brown Thrasher. Scan from the parking lot toward the marsh and look closely along the edges for Common Gallinule and American Bittern tucked in at the edge of the reeds. Least Bittern has been seen here infrequently; it might still occur, but much of the farthest section of the marsh is distant and inaccessible, so detection is unlikely. More regular species include Sora and Virginia Rail, Wood Duck, Blue-winged Teal, and Ring-necked Duck. In early spring (April) and fall (September through November), check the marsh for a wider variety of ducks, including rarely Northern Shoveler.

RARITIES

Clay-colored Sparrow, May 2012

SITE PE7 Bangor City Forest and Orono Bog

TOWNS Bangor and Orono. DeLorme Map 23: A3. SEASON All year, especially May–July. VISITATION 1–3 hrs. ♿ Restrooms.
HIGHLIGHTS Spruce Grouse, Palm Warbler, Lincoln's Sparrow, and an excellent diversity of other breeding songbirds.

The Orono Bog might be the closest location to I-95 where you have a chance at seeing Spruce Grouse. In addition to this gem, the flat, easy trail through the forest and bog is excellent for birding in spring and summer. This area harbors many enticing species, such as Lincoln's Sparrow and Palm, Black-burnian, and Canada Warblers. It's much quieter in winter but might give you a chance at finding winter finches, including Common Redpoll and White-winged Crossbill.

DIRECTIONS

From I-95 North take Exit 186. At the end of the off-ramp turn right onto Stillwater Avenue. Continue for 2.6 miles and turn left onto Tripp Drive. Take this to the end, where you can park and begin your hike.

From the start of the trail at the parking lot, turn right. A short way down the trail you'll see the Orono Bog boardwalk heading off to the right. The boardwalk is popular and well-signed and is an excellent area for birding. It heads through a short stretch of forest, where you should keep a close eye out for Spruce Grouse—they are sometimes seen right on the boardwalk itself! Be careful, though, because Ruffed Grouse are also in the area, and females of the two species can be difficult to tell apart.

Listen for a variety of warblers singing in the surrounding woods. As you approach the bog itself, look and listen for Northern Waterthrush and Canada Warbler in the low shrubby vegetation. You'll come out into the open peat bog, where Palm Warbler and Lincoln's Sparrow breed and you can scan the sky for raptors such as Broad-winged Hawk.

After completing the boardwalk loop, you can backtrack to the parking lot, but I prefer to continue along the main trail. This loops through the Bangor City Forest (with a few side trails, too), all of which is excellent habitat. Ruffed and Spruce Grouse are both possible (although Ruffed is more likely), and you'll be serenaded by many talented songsters: Veery, Swainson's and Hermit Thrushes, and Winter Wren are all fairly common, along with at least seventeen species of warblers.

Outside the breeding season the trails through the forest are much quieter, but they can produce good numbers of migrant songbirds in May and September. Winter is unlikely to produce a long list, but such a patch of woods could easily hold either species of crossbill or a flock of Common Redpolls.

SITE PE8 University of Maine Campus

TOWN Orono. DeLorme Map 23: A3–4.   SEASON December–March.
VISITATION 15 min. to 1 hr. Restroom facilities at businesses in Orono.
HIGHLIGHTS Bohemian Waxwing and Pine Grosbeak.

The University of Maine's Orono campus is one of the most reliable locations in Maine to find Bohemian Waxwings and Pine Grosbeaks, even in non-irruption years. There are plenty of fruiting trees around campus, but the best place is the Littlefield Ornamental Garden with its two-hundred-plus varieties of crabapples!

DIRECTIONS

From I-95 take Exit 191. From the south, at the end of the ramp, turn right onto Kelley Road. From the north, turn left onto Kelley. Continue for about a mile to Route 2 and turn left. Continue on Route 2 East for 1.9 miles. After

Few things brighten up a gray winter day like a male Pine Grosbeak. © Luke Seitz

crossing the Stillwater River (check for Barrow's Goldeneye by turning right onto North Main Avenue and walking through the park to the river) turn left onto Rangeley Road. Continue on Rangeley Road for 0.8 miles and turn right just before the Emera Astronomy Center. Park in the lot behind the center and walk south into the Littlefield Ornamental Garden.

This garden is certainly the most reliable place on campus (and one of the better spots in the state) to find Bohemian Waxwings and Pine Grosbeaks in the winter. Their numbers fluctuate from year to year, but there are almost always at least a few around. Bohemian Waxwings tend to travel in tighter flocks, sometimes mixed with Cedar Waxwings or even European Starlings, while Pine Grosbeaks are more likely to be found in small, looser flocks. Check all the fruiting trees in the garden, and with a little luck you'll stumble upon some of these exciting northern birds.

If the Ornamental Garden doesn't produce, try driving around campus to the west and south. There are fruiting trees scattered around, or you might chance upon a flock of waxwings just flying over. After a loop around, it might be worth checking the garden again in case something new dropped in. When you do come across Bohemians or Pine Grosbeaks, they can often be absurdly tame as they gobble down crabapples or mountain-ash fruit.

SITE PE9 Sunkhaze Meadows National Wildlife Refuge

TOWN Milford. DeLorme Map 33: D–E4–5.   **SEASON** April–May, June–July, August–September.   **VISITATION** 1–3 hrs. No restroom facilities.
HIGHLIGHTS Boreal specialties including Yellow-bellied Flycatcher, Gray Jay, Boreal Chickadee, and Cape May Warbler.

Sunkhaze Meadows National Wildlife Refuge is a complex of marsh and forest that can be very productive for birding. This is the closest spot to Bangor that regularly holds Boreal Chickadee and Gray Jay, along with many breeding songbirds, including Cape May Warbler. There are historical records of Yellow Rail and Sedge Wren from within the bog, which is mainly inaccessible except by canoe or kayak. Several trails weave through the forest and give you a chance to see and hear many of Maine's common breeding species. Coupled with nearby Stud Mill Road, Sunkhaze makes for an excellent outing from nearby Bangor for those yearning for a touch of boreal forest.

DIRECTIONS

From I-95 take Exit 193. From the south, turn right onto Stillwater Avenue at the end of the off-ramp. From the north, make a left onto Stillwater.

In 2.6/2.7 miles respectively, keep right onto Center Street. Stay straight through Old Town. After crossing the second bridge over the Penobscot River, make your second right, onto County Road. Continue on County Road for 6.2 miles to a small parking area on your left for the Carter Meadow Trail.

A variety of trails run through Sunkhaze Meadows National Wildlife Refuge, but this is as good a place as any to start. The **Carter Meadow Trail** begins about a hundred yards south of the parking area and leads through productive forest to an overlook of the bog. This trail should give you an excellent overview of the species in the area. Winter Wren and Hermit Thrush can be heard singing, Least Flycatchers give their loud *che-BEK* song, and Northern Waterthrushes chip from the edge of the wetland. You might even hear the wheezy call of a Boreal Chickadee. At the end of the trail is an observation platform from which you can scan the marsh for American Bittern, Hooded Merganser, and moose.

There are several other good trail options in the vicinity. Just 0.3 miles beyond the parking area for the Carter Meadow Trail is another small parking area on the left for the **Oak Point Trail**, which ends in about 1.5 miles at a bog with Palm Warbler and Lincoln's Sparrow. At 0.7 miles beyond that is the parking lot for the **Johnson Brook Trail.** This is a slightly longer loop (around 3.5 miles) that makes for a very pleasant walk through excellent habitat.

If you aren't feeling up for a hike, keep in mind that birding anywhere along County Road in this area can be productive for many forest species, including upward of twenty breeding warblers, Boreal Chickadee and Gray Jay, Yellow-bellied Flycatcher, and rarely even a Black-backed Woodpecker. Continue driving along County Road, and shortly past the Johnson Brook Trail you'll come to a four-way intersection. Turn left onto Stud Mill Road (see PE10) to keep skirting the national wildlife refuge. Continue birding along this road, which eventually takes you back to Route 2 along the Penobscot River in Costigan. Or turn right and continue on Stud Mill Road into Hancock County.

RARITIES

Historical breeding records of Yellow Rail and Sedge Wren

Additional information about the refuge can be found at the website of the Friends of Sunkhaze Meadows at www.sunkhaze.org.

SITE PE10 Stud Mill Road

TOWN Milford. DeLorme Map 33: D4–5. SEASON All year, but especially **May–July.** VISITATION 1–3 hrs. No restroom facilities. HIGHLIGHTS Boreal specialties including Boreal Chickadee, Gray Jay, and Spruce Grouse; more than twenty species of breeding warblers, including Cape May; Yellow-bellied Flycatcher; winter finches.

The Stud Mill Road is wide and offers easy birding. The species here are much the same as at site PE9, but with even more of a boreal flavor. Boreal Chickadee and Gray Jay are the most regular boreal specialties, but keep an eye out for Spruce Grouse in the road, especially in early morning. Black-backed Woodpecker is rare but should be looked for in every bog with lots of dead trees

DIRECTIONS

Follow directions in site PE9 above to reach the intersection of County Road and Stud Mill Road. Turn right onto Stud Mill Road.

Much like other locations in northern and central Maine, here the fun is all about birding by habitat, instead of searching out specific species at specific locations. I recommend getting here in the early morning and driving slowly with your windows down. Look for areas of forest dominated by spruce; these increase after a few miles of driving. In the sprucier patches, look especially for Cape May Warbler, which is irregular but often present somewhere along the road. Stop at all the little bogs and stream crossings, particularly at 4.0 and 7.0 miles east of the four-way intersection. These boggy areas can hold Palm Warbler and Lincoln's Sparrow, and you should keep an ear out for Yellow-bellied Flycatcher singing from the periphery. Alder Flycatchers are abundant. One particularly good spot to look for Boreal Chickadee is just about 11 miles east of the four-way intersection with County Road, when the small Brandy Pond Road forks off to the left; but really, you could luck into them anywhere!

Although the wide clear cut that parallels Stud Mill Road might seem to hinder forest birding, it is good for American Woodcock and Whip-poor-will—even more incentive to arrive here super early in the morning, or stay until dusk. Indigo Buntings and Chestnut-sided Warblers also breed along the edges, and you might even luck into a Mourning Warbler.

Stud Mill Road is also worth a check in the winter. Northern Shrike often patrol the open roadsides, and one winter, two different Great Gray Owls were present within a couple miles of each other. The boreal specialties, especially Boreal Chickadee and Gray Jay, can still be conspicuous in the colder months, and both Ruffed and Spruce Grouse are possible on the roadside or perched up in trees. All the winter finches (Pine and Evening Grosbeak, White-winged and Red Crossbill, Common and Hoary Redpoll, and Pine Siskin) should be searched for.

I typically drive for around 15 miles before turning around and retracing my steps back to Milford. For more coverage of the Stud Mill Road as it passes into Hancock County see site H12.

RARITIES

Great Gray Owl, winter 2006

Weston

Danforth

Kingman

Brookton

McAdam

Vanceboro

WN15 ★

NEW BRUNSWICK

Topsfield

Lakeville

Waite

Princeton

Baileyville

Calais

Grand
Lake
Stream

St. Andrews

WN14 ★

Charlotte

Cooper

WN13 ★ ★ Eastport

Wesley

"the Airline"

Beddington

WN12 ★

WN9 ★ ★ **WN11**

WN10

WN8 ★

Machias

WN6 ★

Cutler

GRAND
MANAN
ISLAND
(CANADA)

WN2 ★

WN3 ★

Harrington

WN5 ★

Milbridge

Beals

Gouldsboro ●

WN1 ★

WN4

WN7 ★

WASHINGTON COUNTY

14 Washington County

HERB WILSON

I'll admit my bias—I absolutely love Washington County and its birding. In fact, this was the hardest county for me to turn over to one of my esteemed contributors; I wanted an excuse to bird it even more. But Herb Wilson, a summertime resident of Lubec, was up to the task, and I was excited to learn of a few more sites, beyond the beaten path, for my own visits to the area—between visits to Monica's Chocolates in Lubec and Helen's Restaurant in Machias, that is!

Washington County is a large county with a sparse human population. With a tidal range in excess of 20 feet, Cobscook Bay is a highly productive embayment because of the great nutrient fluxes into the bay. The algal, invertebrate, and fish diversity of Cobscook Bay is greater here than in any other embayment in Maine, and the bird diversity follows suit. The Cobscook Bay region also has an abundance of land that is accessible to the public (a national wildlife refuge, state parks, and land trust holdings).

Boreal-type forest reaches the coast here, providing easy access to many popular species within a short drive from the boat to the important birding and photography destination of Machias Seal Island (site WN7). There are few words to describe this magical place; it is a must-see destination for all birders, and the only chance in the United States to get off a boat and into blinds among a bustling colony of Atlantic Puffins, Common Murres, Razorbills, and Arctic Terns.

Machias Seal Island is often the excuse to visit this lovely region, with many birders then staying for the boreal habitats of places such as the Burn Road (WN15), Great Wass Island (WN4), Boot Head Preserve (WN8), and Quoddy Head State Park (WN10), with species such as Boreal Chickadee, Spruce Grouse, Lincoln's Sparrow, and up to fifteen species of warblers. Heading farther inland, the two units of the Moosehorn National Wildlife Refuge (WN12 and WN14) offer a wealth of breeding bird diversity, from

American Woodcock and Spruce Grouse to Bay-breasted and Cape May Warblers.

In spring and fall shorebird migration, the Lubec Bar and Flats (WN9) is a great spot—more birders at this season would likely result in an even more impressive array of rarities. But don't ignore other good shorebird spots such as Addison Marsh (WN3) and Pleasant Island–Eastport (WN13).

All year long, but especially from fall through early spring, the productive nearshore waters offer tremendous sea-watching opportunities, especially at Quoddy Head, but also at Roque Bluffs (WN5) and East Quoddy Head off Campobello Island (WN11).

In winter, the coast is fantastic, and the Machias River (WN6) is a great spot, and when irruptions of finches or frugivores occur, birding the county can be most rewarding. —*Derek Lovitch*

SITE WN1 Petit Manan National Wildlife Refuge

TOWN Steuben. DeLorme Map 17: A1. **SEASON** May–July.
VISITATION 2–4 hrs. No restroom facilities. **HIGHLIGHTS** Coastal seabirds; breeding warblers.

The Petit Manan NWR comprises this mainland site as well as Petit Manan Island offshore (see separate account, site H7). The mainland portion of the refuge includes a diversity of habitat, offering a summer birder the chance to see a variety of breeding birds.

DIRECTIONS

The refuge is reached via Pigeon Hill Road off US Route 1. If you are coming from the south on Route 1, Pigeon Hill Road intersects 2.9 miles north of Steuben on the right; if you are coming from the north, Pigeon Hill Road is a left turn, 2.2 miles south of Milbridge. Follow Pigeon Hill Road south to the refuge. A kiosk along the road has maps and other information.

Two trails traverse the refuge. If you only have time for one trail, I recommend the Hollingsworth Loop. This trail is 1.5 miles long and offers good boreal forest birding as well as visibility to the waters beyond the rocky shore. In the forest, expect plenty of Winter Wrens, Hermit Thrushes, Magnolia Warblers, Black-throated Green Warblers, Black-and-white Warblers, Yellow-rumped Warblers, and American Redstarts. Common Eiders and Black Guillemots nest along the rocky shore.

A second trail, the Birch Point Trail, offers easier walking and more habitat diversity. The trail begins at an old field and then passes through some spruce-fir stands, some deciduous forest, and parallels a blueberry barren. The trail is a 4-mile loop, but you may prefer to walk partway in and turn around. Boreal Chickadees are possible. Nashville Warblers, Magnolia Warblers, and Black-throated Green Warblers will be the most common warblers. The blueberry barren offers a chance for Vesper Sparrows.

For a trail map see the website for the Maine Coastal Islands NWR at http://www.fws.gov/refuge/maine_coastal_islands/. Site WN2 Southern Washington County Blueberry Barrens

SITE WN2 Southern Washington County Blueberry Barrens

TOWNS Cherryfield, Deblois, Columbia. DeLorme Map 25.
SEASON May–July. **VISITATION** 2–3 hrs. No restroom facilities. ⚓
HIGHLIGHTS Breeding Upland Sandpiper and Vesper Sparrow.

The blueberry industry in Washington County is a staple of the local economy. Large tracts of land are devoted to the culture of low-bush blueberries, particularly in the area of Cherryfield, Deblois, and Columbia. (A look at the area with Google Earth gives you an appreciation for the size of these barrens.) The diversity of birds in this habitat is relatively poor, but these barrens do provide habitat for two otherwise hard-to-find birds in the state: Upland Sandpipers and Vesper Sparrows. The barrens are privately owned, but excellent views are possible from state and county roads that traverse the fields.

DIRECTIONS

Birding mostly by car (barrens are private and should not be accessed except via defined roads) and stopping frequently at fields, edges, and any wet areas, you can often find the target species. This loop begins and ends at US Route 1, from where you can then head farther east into the county.

From US Route 1 in Cherryfield take Route 193 North. In 1.3 miles turn right onto Ridge Road. In about 2.5 miles, excellent views of the barrens will open up on either side of the road. Continue on Ridge Road for 2.2 miles and turn right onto Cherryfield Road/Schoodic Road. Continue for 2 miles and turn right onto Georgetown Woods Road. Drive south for about 4 miles to the intersection with US Route 1 in Harrington. You may find that you see your target birds early in the trip and may wish to backtrack rather than following the mostly unpaved roads to get to Harrington.

SITE WN3 Addison Marsh

TOWN Addison. DeLorme Map 25: D5.   **SEASON** May–June, **July–August.** **VISITATION** 1 hr. No restroom facilities. ⚓ **HIGHLIGHTS** Migratory shorebirds; Nelson's Sparrow.

This small marsh is a gem. Wading birds (especially in late summer, when post-breeding dispersal brings a few egrets to the area), migratory shorebirds, and breeding Nelson's Sparrows are the highlights, but this marsh is always worth at least a quick stop at any season, and especially during "fall" shorebird migration from late June through early September.

DIRECTIONS

Just east of Columbia on US Route 1, turn south onto Route 187 at Wild Blueberry Land. When Route 187 makes a 90-degree turn, bear right onto Wescogus Road. At its end, turn right onto Water Street. Cross the bridge and carefully pull over. Check both sides of the road, especially the salt pannes and the edge of the river.

Great Blue Herons and Snowy Egrets are the most likely long-legged waders here, although Great Egrets are possible in late summer and fall. The typical migratory shorebirds will be here in May and July to September (Semipalmated Plovers, Black-bellied Plovers, Least and Semipalmated Sandpipers, both yellowlegs, etc.). Sorting through birds may yield White-rumped and Baird's Sandpipers, and even Hudsonian Godwits (although this bird is declining and becoming rare throughout the state). In the summer, listen for Nelson's Sparrows in the marsh. Next, continue into the village of Addison. Make a left at the post office onto Ridge Road, and pull into the boat launch on your left. Scan the marshes and, at mid- to low tides, the muddy edges of the river.

SITE WN4 Great Wass Island

TOWN Beals. DeLorme Map 25: D5.   **SEASON** All year, but especially May–July.   **VISITATION** 1 hr. to half day. No facilities. **HIGHLIGHTS** Spruce Grouse; Boreal Chickadee; Yellow-bellied Flycatcher,

Palm Warbler, and Lincoln's Sparrow in the summer; Migratory shorebirds; breeding Nelson's Sparrow.

This pristine island, much of which is owned by the Nature Conservancy, is accessible via bridge from Jonesport. The 5-mile-long island has a rich mix of habitats: coniferous forests, bogs, and rocky outcrops, and considerable topographic relief. The plant and bird diversity of the island remarkable.

DIRECTIONS

From US Route 1 take Route 187 South to Jonesport. Turn south (at the Coast Guard station) onto Bridge Street and cross the bridge over Moosabec Reach to Beals. Turn left at the end of the bridge onto Barney's Cove Road (which turns into Bay View Drive, also known as Great Wass Island Road). Continue approximately 1.1 miles to the causeway to Great Wass Island. Just beyond the causeway, at the T intersection, turn right onto Black Duck Cove Road and continue 2 miles to a parking area on the left to access the trail. *Please do not drive down the road beyond the parking lot, and if the parking lot is full, please return at another time.*

A trail leads from the parking lot and splits into two trails about 100 yards into the forest. The Mud Hole Trail to the left is 1.5 miles long. This trail follows the northern coastline of the island until the trail ends. The other trail, the Little Cape Point Trail, is 2 miles long and goes through the interior of the island, mainly through spruce-fir forest. The trail also passes through a stand of jack pine (uncommon in Maine), as well as skirting some bog habitats. The Mud Hole Trail offers ocean birding, while the Cape Point Trail is better for land birds. The diversity of birds encountered will likely be higher on the Cape Point Trail. By hiking along the shoreline between the two trails, birders can complete a 5.5-mile loop.

Spruce Grouse and Boreal Chickadees are possible at any time of year on the island, on either trail. During the summer, Yellow-bellied Flycatchers, Palm Warblers, Lincoln's Sparrows, and a number of nesting warblers will all be present at the bogs along the Little Cape Point Trail.

RARITIES

Yellow-headed Blackbird, August 2014

For a trail map and more information from the Nature Conservancy, use the search feature on its website at www.nature.org.

SITE WN5 Roque Bluffs State Park

TOWN Roque Bluffs. DeLorme Map 26: D3. **SEASON** All year.
VISITATION 1–2 hrs. Outhouses. State park fee. ♿
HIGHLIGHTS Grebes, sea ducks, dabbling ducks.

This state park is a tract of nearly three hundred acres of forest, wetlands, and shoreline on Englishman Bay south of Machias. The area can be birded with a minimum of walking and offers both headland views of the Gulf of Maine and freshwater views.

DIRECTIONS

From US Route 1 in Jonesboro, just east of the Chandler River, look for Roque Bluffs Road to the south. Follow it for 5.5 miles until it ends in a T intersection. Turn right and follow the road for 1.7 miles into the park.

On the left you will see a cobble beach extending for half a mile. On the opposite side of the road, scan the freshwater lake for dabbling ducks and Hooded and Common Mergansers during spring and fall migration. Views of Englishman Bay will produce Common Eiders and Black Guillemots all year, and in spring and fall migration and throughout the winter a diverse assemblage of sea ducks, both Common and Red-throated Loons, and Horned and Red-necked Grebes can often be seen. Extended periods of sea watching can be fruitful, especially in spring and fall—be on the lookout for Black-legged Kittiwakes, alcids, and jaegers.

For further exploration of the park, walk the trails for breeding species such as Winter Wrens, Hermit Thrushes, Magnolia Warblers, and Black-throated Green Warblers, and in winter be on the lookout for irruptives including Pine Grosbeak and both crossbills.

For more information visit StateParks.com at http://www.stateparks.com /roque_bluffs_state_park_in_maine.html.

SITE WN Machias Loop

TOWNS Machias and East Machias. DeLorme Map 26: C3–4.
SEASON All year, but especially **May** and **July–August** (shorebirds); and December–February (ducks). **VISITATION** 1–3 hrs. Restroom facilities at nearby businesses. ♿ **HIGHLIGHTS** Barrow's Goldeneye; dabbling ducks, sea ducks; Bald Eagles; shorebirds.

The Machias River between Machias and East Machias offers excellent birding for waterfowl. Intertidal flats in the vicinity of the causeway provide good shorebirding as well.

DIRECTIONS

Entering Machias from the south via US Route 1, descend into the downtown section of Machias past the University of Maine–Machias and the Irving gas station (both on the right). Look for a small road on the right between buildings that will take you to a public parking lot. This lot provides great views of waterfowl on the Machias River at most times of the year, and in summer look for Northern Rough-winged Swallows. But in winter the waterfall just upriver and the tidal movements below keep this section of the river ice-free. All three mergansers are often present, and Bufflehead are usually abundant. Check the numerous Common Goldeneyes for a Barrow's Goldeneye or two.

Return to US 1 and turn right to head north for 0.4 miles to the causeway just beyond Helen's Restaurant (stopping for pie). You can park along the causeway and scan the area for ducks and shorebirds at low tide, fishing Ospreys in the summer, and Bald Eagles all year.

You'll see the Down East Sunrise Trail at the end of the causeway, with a parking area on the right. This trail, open to walkers, bicyclists, and ORVs, provides viewing access to the Machias River. The Sunrise Trail extends from Ellsworth to Dennysville and can offer excellent birding anywhere along its length. On the west side of the road, the trail passes through second-growth and alder wetlands, with abundant Veeries and Alder Flycatchers, among others.

Continue north on US Route 1 about 4 miles to East Machias. Just beyond the Riverside Inn and Restaurant on your right look for Willow Street on your right. Cross the river and park your car. The area just south of the bridge has been reliable for Barrow's Goldeneye in recent years. You can either scan from the bridge or walk south along the section of the Down East Sunrise Trail here as well.

Return to Route US 1 and turn right. Just beyond the junction of Route 191, make a left onto Bridge Street. Pull over to check the river; this is a reliable spot for Barrow's in midwinter. Return to Route 1, turn left, and after crossing the river look for an expansive area of the river called Gaddis Pool, which is worth checking for waterfowl. Also check the body of water on the east side of US Route 1, opposite Gaddis Pool, for ducks and other waterbirds.

Greater White-fronted Goose, March 2012 (Gaddis Pool)

SITE WN7 Machias Seal Island

TOWN Disputed—New Brunswick or Maine, depending on whom you ask. DeLorme Map not shown. **SEASON** early June–early August. **VISITATION** 4–5 hrs., including transit and time at and around the island. Restrooms on tour boats, and outhouses on island. **HIGHLIGHTS** Nesting Arctic Tern, Atlantic Puffin, Razorbill, and Common Murre.

New Brunswick and Maine both claim sovereignty of this island 10 miles southeast of Cutler, Maine. From a birder's perspective, this twenty-acre island is a paradise. The island is accessible for Canadians and US citizens without having to clear customs. Unlike at other seabird colonies on the Maine coast, visitors here can land on the island (only via limited-permit tours) and visit viewing blinds. Photography opportunities are unmatched.

DIRECTIONS

Two tour companies offer cruises to Machias Seal Island: Bold Coast Charters out of Cutler, Maine, and Seawatch Tours out of Grand Manan Island, New Brunswick. Demand for these tours is high, so plan in advance—often at least one year for reservations in July. Passengers are allowed to go ashore on the island, alternating days between the Cutler and Grand Manan tours. Try to book the "landing" tours in order to have the chance to go ashore for the opportunity to use the spacious photographic blinds. You will be able to photograph puffins, Razorbills, murres, and terns from 10 feet or less. In fact, puffins often walk on the roof of the blind above your head!

The cruise to the island takes about forty-five minutes each way. In Cutler Harbor and nearshore waters, keep an eye out for Black Guillemots and Bald Eagles. Look for Northern Gannets, Wilson's Storm-Petrels, Northern Fulmars, Sooty Manx, and Great Shearwaters, phalaropes and jaegers on the open water, but most trips encounter few pelagics en route. However, as you near the island, Atlantic Puffins, Razorbills, and Common Murres will become abundant. Keep an eye peeled for the bridled morph of Common Murres. Arctic Terns usually nest on the island, but their numbers are tied to the abundance of their major fish prey, capelin, which varies greatly from

Atlantic Puffins, Razorbills, and Common Murres from the blinds on Machias Seal Island.
© Herb Wilson

year to year. After several years without nesting, Arctic Terns have begun attempting to nest again in the last few years. Land birds are limited to Savannah Sparrows and a few Common Yellowthroats, plus Spotted Sandpipers, but migration fallouts in spring and fall (unfortunately, no public visitation) are legendary, and vagrants can show up at any time.

RARITIES

Tufted Puffin, June–July 2014; Ancient Murrelet, May 2016 (part of a string of coastal sightings of this first state record)

Bold Coast Charters in Cutler can be reached at www.boldcoast.com or at 207–259–4484.

SITE WN8 Hamilton Cove and Boot Head Preserves

TOWN Lubec. DeLorme Map 27: B3. **SEASON** April, **May–July**, August–October. **VISITATION** 1–6 hrs. No restroom facilities. Hamilton Cove is &.

HIGHLIGHTS Spruce Grouse and Boreal Chickadee; nesting passerines in coastal spruce-fir forest and bogs, including Lincoln's Sparrow, Palm Warbler (Boot Head), and Yellow-bellied Flycatcher; Wilson's Warbler and Alder Flycatcher (Hamilton Cove); sea ducks; alcids.

The Maine Coast Heritage Trust maintains these two properties, each traversed by well-maintained trails. Both offer opportunities to sample the most interesting habitats of the Bold Coast, as this area is called, and combining the two gives you a nice cross-section of habitat types and their avifauna. Boot Cove used to be one of the most reliable places in the state for Spruce Grouse, but in recent years they have become much less frequent—likely due at least in part to overuse of playback.

DIRECTIONS

From US Route 1 in Whiting turn right onto Route 189 toward Lubec. In 10.5 miles turn right onto South Lubec Road. In 2.7 miles bear right onto Boot Cove Road. In 2.4 miles turn left into the parking lot of Hamilton Cove.

Hamilton Cove is a 1,225-acre property with a diversity of vegetation types. A trail with ample boardwalks through wet areas passes through a large stand of speckled alder. Alder Flycatchers are fittingly here, along with Common Yellowthroats, American Redstarts, and occasionally a Mourning Warbler. The trail ascends to the coast, and the habitat changes to coniferous forest, with the expected species of this habitat. Viewing areas allow you to scan the water for seabirds. Check along the roadside, especially from the bridge over the creek, for Wilson's Warblers.

Boot Cove is a seven-hundred-acre property, reached by turning left on Boot Cove Road out of the Hamilton Cove parking lot and driving for another 1.3 miles to a small dirt parking lot on the left (opposite a telephone pole with "52" on it; it's easy to miss).

Warbling Vireos and Rose-breasted Grosbeaks are possible around the parking lot and roadside, but the trail leads through thick coniferous woods where Blue-headed Vireos, Golden-crowned and Ruby-crowned Kinglets, Winter Wrens, and Magnolia, Yellow-rumped, and Black-throated Green Warblers are common. In about 0.2 miles you will reach an information sign where the trail splits. Spruce Grouse can be encountered anywhere along the trail, and be sure to keep an eye out for droppings on the boardwalk in spring. Just before a fork in the trail, you will see a small spur trail off to the right leading to a boardwalk and a view of a large bog. In the summer you should hear Yellow-bellied Flycatchers, Hermit Thrushes, Nashville Warblers, Palm Warblers, White-throated Sparrows, and sometimes Lincoln's Sparrow.

Return to the main trail, and at the fork bear right toward Broad Cove. From the bog boardwalk the next quarter of a mile is the best place for Boreal Chickadees and Swainson's Thrushes, and look carefully for Spruce Grouse: I once walked right under one on the trail!

Once the forest starts to get stunted as you near the Broad Cove overlook, listen for Blackpoll Warblers. They are a tough find, but this stunted headland forest is the place they like. Meanwhile, the promontory offers spectacular views; a spur trail to the right provides even better views of the Bold Coast's cliffs and waters.

Here you have a choice. You can either retrace your path back to the parking lot or take a circular route involving a cliff walk back to your car. If you prefer the latter, walk left along the coastal trail. This trail involves significant elevational changes, but the trail is good, with stairs provided in steep portions. Seabirding is usually pretty slow, with a few Black Guillemots, Common Eiders, and Herring Gulls. Skeins of migrating scoters and cormorants may be offshore, however. A pair of Merlins has nested on the cliffs in recent years; you will not miss them if they are there; they are very noisy.

In about half a mile the coastal trail descends to the shore. Take the spur trail to the right to Boot Cove. From the steps leading down to the shore you should be able to see a Bald Eagle's nest, about two-thirds the way up in a conifer, about midway along the headland to the right. It can be seen with the naked eye once you know where to look. Finding it through binoculars should be easy enough.

The trail from the beach back to the main trail goes through some shrubs as well as some forest adjacent to a meadow. This area is great for warblers on a sunny morning as they congregate on the trees on the eastern side of the forest. Gray Jays are found here occasionally.

The trail back passes through a lot of deciduous forest. Red-eyed Vireos should be common, along with Least Flycatchers and Black-throated Green Warblers. Hermit Thrushes will be heard all along the trail. Black-backed Woodpecker is possible, with a little luck.

The length of Boot Cove Road, like many of the roads in this area, is rich with American mountain ash, the fruit of which is the favored food of Bohemian Waxwings and Pine Grosbeaks during irruption winters.

For more information and trail maps visit the website of the Maine Coast Heritage Trust at http://www.mcht.org.

SITE WN9 Lubec and the Lubec Bar and Flats

TOWN Lubec. DeLorme Map 27: A–B4.   SEASON All year, but especially **May** and **August–October**.   VISITATION 2 hrs. to half day. Restrooms at Lubec businesses.   HIGHLIGHTS Shorebirds; gulls (late fall–early spring for white-winged and Lesser Black-backed Gulls; late summer for Bonaparte's Gulls and rarity potential); migrant and breeding warblers; Nelson's Sparrow.

DIRECTIONS

From US Route 1 in Whiting begin this tour by turning right onto Route 189 (County Road) toward Lubec. Look for the **Eastland Motel** on the left in 9 miles. A pond in a field on the right can have dabbling ducks and shorebirds; Willow Flycatcher has been reported in June, well east of usual breeding range. Bald Eagles often gather here outside the breeding season.

Continue on Route 189 for 3 more miles into the village of Lubec. Just before the bridge, turn left at the post office onto **Water Street**. Turn right between Frank's Restaurant and the Water Street Tavern into a public parking lot. The channel here can be excellent for cormorants, sea ducks, and other piscivorous birds. Diversity will be best at mid-tide, when the currents are at their strongest. Seals are usually abundant when the tidal currents are near their peak. Harbor seals and gray seals are the most common, but there is a chance for harp seals and hooded seals. Gulls often roost on the roofs of buildings. In season, check for white-winged gulls and Lesser Black-backed Gulls. Return to Water Street and turn right to reach the public docks, where there is abundant parking. **Sentinel Island** just offshore often has a Bald Eagle or two roosting in the top of one of the tall conifers, but the nest has not been used in the last few years. Scan the water for waterbirds all year.

Walking the **neighborhood** during spring and fall migration can be fruitful. Otherwise, turn around and retrace your route down Water Street. Cross Washington Street (Route 189) and bear slightly right to Pleasant Street. Continue to the end of Pleasant Street to the parking lot for the **Mowry Beach boardwalk**. The boardwalk (wheelchair accessible) is about 0.4 miles long and passes through wetland vegetation (an interesting mix of bog and

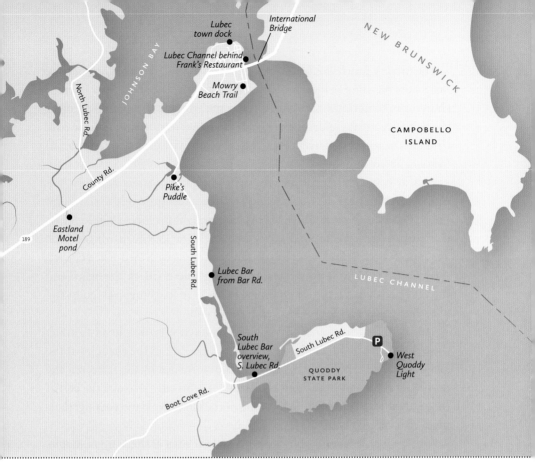

LUBEC TO QUODDY HEAD STATE PARK

marsh plants). Yellow Warblers, Common Yellowthroats, and Song Sparrows nest, but in migration a diversity of passerines may be found, especially in fall. Northern Cardinals are regular here, an uncommon species in the county. Near the beginning of the trail, a side trail to the left will take you to Mowry Beach, a gravel-and-sand beach that can be productive for shorebirds in July through September. You'll need to pick your time carefully here. At low tide, the amount of real estate left uncovered is huge, so wait until the tide is coming in when the birds will be concentrated near the high-tide level. Semipalmated Plovers, Black-bellied Plovers, Semipalmated Sandpiper, and Least Sandpipers are the most common species here, but other shorebirds can be present. In late fall be sure to check piles of rotting seaweed for lingering migrants feeding on seaweed flies.

The Mowry Beach Trail ends at the Lubec School. The lawns and playing fields host breeding Killdeer, but in inclement weather or high tides migrant shorebirds sometimes roost here. From mid-August through September check for American Golden-Plovers. You can either retrace your steps or walk through the residential neighborhoods in a clockwise direction to return to Pleasant Street and the parking lot.

Back at your car, retrace your route to Washington Street and turn left. At the stop sign near the IGA turn left and head west for 1 mile to the South Lubec Road. In about half a mile look on the right for **Pikes Puddle**, a lily-pad-covered freshwater pond. American Black Ducks, Green-winged Teal, and Blue-winged Teal should be expected here, along with Pied-billed Grebes. Alder Flycatchers sing from the surrounding alders. Check the beach and the water offshore on the opposite side of the road for shorebirds, gulls, and waterbirds; Nelson's Sparrows nest in the marsh.

Continue for about another mile and turn left onto Bar Road to reach the **South Lubec Sand Bar** and the **Lubec Flats.** Park in the small lot at the end of the road. The tip of the sandbar is now owned by the state, but the portion of the bar adjacent to the parking lot is private. To reach the end of the sandbar you will need to walk along the beach to avoid trespassing; signs must be respected here.

The sandbar is one of the premier shorebird sites in the state of Maine. The numbers of shorebirds using this area have declined over the past thirty years, but the diversity of shorebirds is still high. While spring migration of shorebirds through the area is relatively light, fall migration can be fantastic. Expect to see southbound shorebirds in the area beginning in early July, peaking in August and continuing into October.

Shorebirds disperse broadly across the expansive tidal flats at low tide. The birds are concentrated as the tide comes in. Once the best foraging areas are covered, the shorebirds fly to local fields or other roosting sites during the high tide phase of the cycle. The best way to bird the area is to arrive four hours before the predicted high tide. Hike 1 mile to the tip of the bar. By the time you reach the tip, the shorebirds will be moving toward the high-tide level. Over the next hour, the shorebirds will be concentrated close enough for excellent viewing. About two hours before high tide, the birds will depart for upland roosting areas. Some shorebirds will be present along the beach as you walk back to your car.

In July expect Semipalmated Plovers, Least and Semipalmated Sandpipers, Sanderlings, and both yellowlegs. Diversity increases in August with

Black-bellied Plovers, White-rumped Sandpipers, Red Knots, and Willets arriving. September into October is the best time for American Golden-Plovers and Dunlin. Be sure to check the highest parts of the beach for Baird's and Buff-breasted Sandpiper. They typically occur higher along the beach than other sandpipers, in late August through mid-September.

These high densities of shorebirds usually attract Merlins and Peregrine Falcons. Parasitic Jaegers can sometimes be found here as well, doing their best falcon impersonations.

In the winter this habitat can be good for Horned Larks, Snow Buntings, and Lapland Longspurs. Snowy Owls are occasional, and a Gyrfalcon was reported in 2014. Returning to your car, you can head back to town for lunch or a visit to the famous Monica's Chocolates, or continue east to Quoddy Head State Park (site WN10). If the latter, continue east on South Lubec Road. Curving to the left, you'll see a small turnout just big enough for a few cars on the left. You can scan the flats for shorebirds here, especially as high tide approaches. Shorebirding is usually not as productive as walking down the South Lubec Sand Bar but is an effective way to get a quick view of the shorebirds in the area on a particular day without a long hike.

RARITIES

Whooper Swan, November 1997 (Pikes Puddle); Common Ringed Plover, August–September 2003 (Lubec Flats); Orchard Oriole, May 2008 (Lubec village); Gyrfalcon, December 2014; Yellow-headed Blackbird, August 2015 (Bar Road)

SITE WN10 Quoddy Head State Park

TOWN Lubec. DeLorme Map 27: A–B4. SEASON All year. VISITATION 2 hrs. to half day. Outhouses open all year. HIGHLIGHTS Sea watching (including jaegers, Black-legged Kittiwakes, and alcids); Great Cormorant and Black-legged Kittiwake in summer; Harlequin Duck, Great Cormorant, kittiwake, and Purple Sandpiper in winter; Spruce Grouse; Boreal Chickadee; breeding warblers including Palm; Lincoln's Sparrow.

Following the directions to the parking lot for the Lubec Bar in site WN9, continue east on South Lubec Road. In about 2 miles bear left at the intersection with Boot Cove Road.

Continue along South Lubec Road to its end at Quoddy Head State Park.

Rather than bearing right into the park, go straight and park in the lot just above the lighthouse. Walk down the hill to the lighthouse. (Handicapped parking is available at the lighthouse with a permit.) This area is the eastern-most point of the United States (unless you are technical, as the westernmost Aleutian Islands are on the other side of the 180th meridian, making them more east than west!). The birding can be great here at any time of year. During the summer, Common Eiders will be abundant, and scan for Razor-bills and plenty of Black Guillemots. In late summer, Sail Rock just offshore reliably has Black-legged Kittiwakes. Double-crested Cormorants, sometimes including an immature Great, perch on Sail Rock during the summer, but Great Cormorants dominate from mid-fall through early spring. The rocky intertidal has Purple Sandpipers from October into May. This area is the most reliable place in the county for Harlequin Ducks (October–May). In the win-ter, massive number of Razorbills may be present, along with Red-throated Loons, Red-necked Grebes, Horned Grebes, and a variety of sea ducks.

Scanning the water can be productive for Northern Gannets, Great Shear-waters, Sooty Shearwaters, Parasitic Jaegers, and Pomarine Jaegers. Minke whales are possible here as well.

From the lighthouse, walk south along a well-marked trail that hugs the coastline (keep an eye out for Purple Sandpipers in season along the rocks) until you come to a large parking lot on your right. Continue to follow the trail right along the coast. The trail will intersect with an inland trail in about 0.1 miles. Walk left, taking the left-most trail when a choice is possible. You will climb up the spectacular cliff you see before you (keep right at the last fork to avoid the climb, which includes some short stretches of stairs). Several vantage points along the trail afford excellent views of the water and Grand Manan Island in the distance.

Once you have reached the high point of the trail, look for a smaller trail off to the right. Take this spur trail. If you start to descend sharply on a set of stairs along the coastal trail, you have gone too far and missed the spur trail. This spur trail will intersect with an inland trail in about 100 feet. Turn left and you will see a sign marked Arctic Bog, indicating a trail to your right. This quarter-mile trail leads to a coastal raised bog. Along the way, listen for Boreal Chickadees and watch carefully for Spruce Grouse—a dust bath in the trail is often a sign that you just missed one. In the summer, Yellow-rumped Warblers and Black-throated Green Warblers will be common. Listen for Swainson's Thrushes and Winter Wrens.

There's a reason this is called the Bold Coast. © Derek Lovitch

The trail ends at the bog, where a circular boardwalk allows you to bird different parts of the bog. The vegetation here (marked by helpful signs) is quite diverse. During the summer, Palm and Nashville Warblers and Common Yellowthroats will be obvious, and a couple of pairs of Lincoln's Sparrows breed here. At any time of the year, White-winged Crossbills or Red Crossbills may be present, especially during irruption winters.

Retrace your steps to the end of the bog trail and turn left. This time, stay on the inland trail by keeping left at any trail junction, staying alert for Boreal Chickadees. To extend your visit, you can turn right and take a long and sometimes rugged loop trail for 3 miles. Back at the large parking lot (bathroom facilities available), either walk out on the road leading into the park or walk along the coast back to the lighthouse (the museum is worth a look, and a photo at the lighthouse is mandatory) to reach your car.

For more information and for a trail map visit State Parks.com at http://www .stateparks.com/quoddy_head_state_park_in_maine.html.

SITE WN11 Campobello Island

TOWN The island is part of the Canadian province of New Brunswick. DeLorme Map 27: A4. **SEASON** All year, but especially **May–July** for breeders and **August–October** for sea watching. **VISITATION** 2 hrs. to full day. Restroom facilities at various locations. Passport required for crossing border. Some locations ♿. **HIGHLIGHTS** Sea watching, included shearwaters, alcids, and whales; Black-legged Kittiwake; sea ducks; nesting passerines including Gray Jay and a variety of warblers.

For a little international birding, a trip to Campobello Island is just the ticket. A bridge connects this Canadian island to Lubec. You will need your passport to cross the border. Gray Jays are often easier to find here than in Washington County, and the sea watching can be fantastic.

DIRECTIONS

From the border crossing, drive north and look for a tourist information center on the right. You can get a map of the island here. Continue northward and turn right onto Glensevern Road (just opposite the entrance to the Roosevelt Cottage, a popular tourist stop and a perfect place to spend a rainy afternoon). You are in the **Roosevelt Campobello Provincial Park,** a large tract of forested land. In 2.4 miles you will come to the parking lot for Eagle Hill Bog. This bog is traversed by an excellent boardwalk (wheelchair accessible). In the summer, Palm Warblers and Nashville Warblers are common.

Using the map you picked up at the tourist center, drive any of the roads through the park, stopping frequently to look and listen for breeding warblers and Gray Jays, among many others. Traffic through the park is surprisingly light, especially since the passport requirement was mandated at the border, and birding via a bicycle can be very productive.

Return to the main road and head north to the T intersection. Turn right and drive about 10 miles to the end of the road at the **Head Harbor Light** (East Quoddy Head). This area can be spectacular for seabirds and whales feeding in Head Harbor Passage, with Sabine's, Little, and Black-headed Gulls often spotted among the thousands of Bonaparte's Gulls in late summer. Parasitic Jaeger is regular, and Razorbills (rarely, puffin and Common Murre) are often seen. Looking across the bay, notice a cliff in the distance—this is the southernmost breeding location for Black-legged Kittiwake in the Western Atlantic, and its residents can sometime be seen feeding from the lighthouse in summer, with post-breeding birds frequent by the end of August. You can walk to the lighthouse when the tide is low enough (and for a small fee), but watch the tide so you don't spend time on the island waiting for the tide to fall again.

RARITIES

Sabine's Gulls are annual from Head Harbor Light.

For more information about the International Park, the Roosevelt Cottage, and trails on the island see www.fdr.net.

SITE WN12 Moosehorn National Wildlife Refuge: Edmunds Division

TOWN Edmunds. DeLorme Map 27: A1.   SEASON April, **May–July,** August–October   VISITATION 1–3 hrs. No restroom facilities. HIGHLIGHTS Spruce Grouse; Boreal Chickadee; diversity of nesting warblers including Bay-breasted and Cape May; American Woodcock.

There are two large sections of this refuge, mostly managed for the production of American Woodcocks. Second-growth areas that the birds breed in, and open fields that the birds display from, are home to a wide range of species. Pockets of spruce woods offer shelter for boreal specialties, and abundant wetlands host a diversity of breeding birds. The Edmunds Division of the refuge is the southern "half," with convenient access from Lubec and Machias.

DIRECTIONS

From the intersection of US Route 1 and Route 189 in Whiting continue north on US Route 1 for 4 miles. Just beyond Old US 1 (a sign for Cobscook Bay State Park is on the right) look for a dirt road to the left marked South Trail. Stop your car about every 0.2 miles or so to listen and look for birds. The habitat changes from cutover areas to second-growth forest to older stands of trees. In addition to the more common warblers, look for Mourning Warblers in young scrubby areas, along with Lincoln's Sparrows. In 0.9 miles Crane Hill Road intersects on the right. Continue a short distance ahead on South Trail to a parking area on your left. Walk westward along the path to a small lake where Wood Ducks, Northern Waterthrushes, and Canada Warblers breed.
   Turn around and then turn left onto Crane Hill Road, continuing to stop

frequently to listen and look. In 1.2 miles the road ends in a T intersection. At the intersection, an old field may have Mourning Warblers. Turn left onto the North Trail. In 0.2 miles a swampy, black-water area on the right provides excellent habitat for migrating Rusty Blackbirds in April and May, as well as nesting Alder Flycatchers, Northern Parulas, and Swamp Sparrows in the summer. Continue on the North Trail until its end in 0.9 miles along Hobart Stream. A trail parallels the stream to the south and may be productive. Turn around and drive along the North Trail for 2.7 miles back to US Route 1. The habitats will be quite varied along this stretch. Keep an eye out for Spruce Grouse, and this section is the best stretch for Bay-breasted and Cape May Warblers. Check scrubby stream crossings for Canada Warbler as well, and be on the lookout for Gray Jays, Boreal Chickadees, and finches during irruptions.

If you have time, another excellent road is **Bell Mountain Road** (labeled Camp Road in the DeLorme atlas) about 2 miles south of the South Trail. Use the same strategy of driving a short distance and getting out of your car in promising habitat. The road is narrow, but good places to turn around can be found at 2.8 miles and 3.8 miles in. The road ends 5.5 miles from US Route 1.

In April and May, most open areas, in and out of the refuge, will be productive for American Woodcock. The refuge is closed thirty minutes after sunset, so you may wish to find habitats outside the refuge for timberdoodle observations. The fields along Old US 1 north of Cobscook Bay State Park are excellent. Arrive about thirty minutes before dusk and listen for the *peent* calls of displaying males. You should be able to see the males displaying in the air before darkness sets in.

For more information about the refuge see the refuge's home page from the USFWS at http://www.fws.gov/northeast/gis/refuge1/moosehorn/bnd /edm_statmap.pdf.

SITE WN13 Pleasant Island–Eastport Loop

TOWNS Eastport and Perry. DeLorme Map 37: E3, and Map 27: A3–4. **SEASON** April–October. **VISITATION** 1 hr. to half day. Portable toilets at Sipayik Trail. **HIGHLIGHTS** Waterbirds; shorebirds including Red and Red-necked Phalaropes; "hooded" and white-winged gulls; American Pipits and Lapland Longspurs.

This loop is centered on Eastport, a town at the northeastern terminus of Cobscook Bay. Although only 4 miles separate Eastport and Lubec via water, the drive from one to the other is nearly 50 miles. This loop offers varied habitats without requiring a lot of automobile travel. In late summer through early fall, tens of thousands of Bonaparte's Gulls amass in Passamaquoddy Bay and Head Hard Passage, especially around the Old Sow Whirlpool off Eastport. Little and Black-headed Gulls are regular in the masses, and Sabine's Gulls are rare but regular. Lesser Black-backed Gulls are seen from fall through spring in many years as well, and both Iceland and Glaucous Gulls can be common.

DIRECTIONS

From the intersection of US Route 1 and Route 189 in Whiting, follow Route 1 North through the town of Pembroke and in 6 miles turn right onto Route 190 South. When you reach the Passamaquoddy Reservation on Pleasant Island, look for a park with some baseball diamonds on the left. This area has a trail (wheelchair accessible), the **Sipayik Trail** (also called the Passamaquoddy Walking Trail), which parallels Gleason Cove. The trail passes adjacent to a tract of sweetgrass marsh and a small pond. From fall through spring, sea duck watching is excellent here. The fields offer a great chance to see American Pipits, Snow Buntings, and Lapland Longspurs in the fall. Shorebirds can be common around high tide; look for Baird's and Buff-breasted Sandpipers in late August and September. The trail also passes through some coniferous forest, affording good warbler diversity in the breeding season.

Continue south on Route 190 toward Eastport. Along the causeway to Moose Island/Eastport, a pullout on the right provides a chance to scan for waterfowl and gulls, particularly at high tide.

Follow Route 190 into the **town of Eastport** to a T intersection with Water Street. Just north of the town, the Old Sow, reputedly the largest whirlpool in North America, can be seen and heard. The intensity of the whirlpool depends on the stage of the tide, and it is maximally evident at the middle of a tidal cycle. The tremendous upwelling in the area is a magnet for seabirds and gulls, especially the "hooded gulls," led by thousands of Bonaparte's. You can find several vantage points to scan the Old Sow along Water Street. Alternatively, you can ride the short ferry between Eastport and Deer Island or between Eastport and Campobello Island (you will need a passport for both ferries, but the small fee is worth it, especially for photography) and ride right through the whirlpool. Possibilities include Little, Black-headed, and Sabine's

Gull, along with Red-necked and Red Phalaropes (August–September), and Atlantic Puffins and Razorbills (August–October).

Retrace your route out Route 190 until you see Deep Cove Road on the left, just south of the Eastport Airport. Turn left and proceed 1.2 miles to the parking lot for **Shackford Head State Park**. This park has a series of interconnected trails through coniferous forest with excellent vistas from the Shackford Head overlook (173 feet in elevation). The area can be productive in the summer for warblers and other nesting passerines. **Deep Cove Road** in the vicinity of the airport is worth checking in the winter for Short-eared Owls.

RARITIES

Little and Black-headed Gulls are annual; Sabine's Gull is rare but regular.

SITE WN14 Moosehorn National Wildlife Refuge: Baring Division

TOWNS Meddybemps, Baring Plantation, Calais. DeLorme Map 36: C–D5.
SEASON April, **May–July**, August–October.   **VISITATION** 1 hr. to half day.
Restroom facilities at refuge headquarters. & **HIGHLIGHTS** American Woodcock; Eastern Whip-poor-will; breeding warblers.

The Baring Division of the Moosehorn NWR is over twice the size of the southern Edmunds Division (see site W12). While the refuge is managed for American Woodcock, other species that rely on scrubby, bush-dominated habitats benefit. This large tract of land is accessible via car by the Charlotte Road, extending from Route 214 to US Route 1 in Calais. Many dirt roads branch off the Charlotte Road, but most are gated. Birders are welcome to walk down these roads.

DIRECTIONS

From US Route 1 in Pembroke turn left onto Route 214 North. Drive for about 6 miles and turn right onto the Charlotte Road (labeled as "Station Road" in the DeLorme atlas). **Round Lake** (not a part of Moosehorn) will appear on your left and is worth checking for waterfowl and breeding Common Loons. Continue driving north on the Charlotte Road. Once you enter the refuge, it is worth exploring some of the side roads on foot for nesting passerines.

As you continue north, look for a road on the left leading to the **Moosehead NWR Headquarters**. Some informational material is available here, and the rangers can offer suggestions for good birding sites.

As you reach the northern end of Charlotte Road, look for a parking lot on the right leading to a small pond in the midst of **Magurrewock Marsh**. This site is worth checking in the summer for Marsh Wrens, Nashville Warblers, and Swamp Sparrows as well as breeding waterfowl. Just beyond the parking lot, you will see a nesting platform that has been used by Bald Eagles. You can scan other portions of Magurrewock Marsh from US Route 1 (turn right at the T intersection of Charlotte Road and US Route 1).

Eastern Whip-poor-wills are uncommon birds in Washington County, but the Baring Division of Moosehorn NWR is one of the best places to listen for these birds at dusk. The management practices for American Woodcock favor Whip-poor-wills as well. **Ice House Road** is particularly good; it can be reached directly from US Route 1. At the intersection of the Charlotte Road with US Route 1, turn right and look for Ice House Road on the right in half a mile. A May or June visit here starting half an hour before dusk will usually produce both American Woodcocks and Whip-poor-wills.

For more information about the refuge see USFWS's website at http://www .fws.gov/refuge/Moosehorn/.

SITE WN15 The Burn Road

TOWN Topsfield. DeLorme Map 45: D4.   **SEASON** May–July, August–September.   **VISITATION** 2 hrs. to all day. No restroom facilities.
HIGHLIGHTS Spruce Grouse, Black-backed Woodpecker, Yellow-bellied Flycatcher, Gray Jay, Boreal Chickadee, twenty-two species of nesting warblers, White-winged Crossbill.

The Burn Road is an active logging road offering access to a diversity of habitats in northern Washington County. It offers a better chance at species like Black-backed Woodpecker, Gray Jay, and White-winged Crossbill, which are harder to find in southern parts of Washington County.

This site is remote. Be sure to have plenty of gasoline in your car, and a four-wheel-drive vehicle is recommended. Logging trucks travel the Burn Road at fairly high speeds, and they have the right of way. Baskahegan Timber recommends visiting on weekends, when logging trucks are not usually working. Regardless, the best way to bird the Burn Road is to find areas near promising habitat where you can pull safely off the road. Exploring side roads can be productive as well. Be sure to pack some insect repellent—mosquitoes, blackflies, and deerflies can be abundant.

From Calais follow US Route 1 North for 36 miles to Topsfield. As you head north, you will pass through Woodland and Princeton (the last place to get gasoline and other provisions). In Topsfield, Route 6 intersects with US Route 1. Continue northward on US Route 1 for 4.8 miles from this intersection. Look for a Burn Road sign on the left.

Because of the logging in the area, any suggested stops will likely be outdated. Instead, simply drive the road and look for the proper habitat for the species you are seeking. Spruce Grouse are most likely to be along the road in coniferous habitat. Older stands of spruce and fir will be the place to look for Black-backed Woodpecker, Gray Jays, Boreal Chickadee, and White-winged Crossbills. Make sure you can identify Boreal Chickadees and White-winged Crossbills by vocalization, as location by sound is more likely than sight. Regenerating clear cuts may harbor Mourning Warblers and Lincoln's Sparrows. Boggy areas may have Yellow-bellied Flycatchers, Northern Waterthrushes, Palm Warblers, and Cape May Warblers.

I generally go no farther than 4 miles west along the Burn Road. Looking at the DeLorme map, you will see there are a number of side roads off the Burn Road. I encourage you to stick to the main road; it is easy to get lost, and the dense forest interferes with GPS reception.

15 | Piscataquis County

LUKE SEITZ

Maine's least populous county, Piscataquis County is home to only seventeen thousand people. With a total area of over 4,377 square miles, that calculates to just under four people per square mile (and falling), one of the lowest densities in the Eastern United States. Mostly timberlands owned by a handful of large companies, the county also includes some prized public open space.

Of course, the biggest gem is Baxter State Park (sites PS7 to PS9). Adjectives and superlatives fail to do this place justice, so I won't even try. You just need to go, whether for birding, hiking, or just to have your breath taken away. Over two hundred thousand acres, hundreds of miles of hiking trails, and untouched wilderness await. Luckily, a well-maintained dirt road, the Park Tote Road, runs the length of the park, affording access (but note vehicle size restrictions) to many of the best birding spots. Luke Seitz has done a fine job of focusing our birding effort on three prime areas for a chance at all the boreal specialties the region has to offer: Spruce Grouse, American Three-toed and Black-backed Woodpeckers, Yellow-bellied and Olive-sided Flycatchers, Gray Jay, Boreal Chickadee, twenty species of warblers, Fox Sparrow, and finches. Mount Katahdin also hosts Bicknell's Thrushes and American Pipits. And few places offer a better chance of seeing moose.

But there's a lot of other great birding in the region. Especially with Greenville or Millinocket as a base, birding opportunities are endless. After your fill of Baxter State Park, be sure to explore other areas in the breeding season for boreal specialties, especially the Golden Road (PS5) and the Harvester Road (PS6). Other destinations for many of the specialties birders seek in the region include Big Moose Mountain (PS2), especially for Bicknell's Thrush, and the Kokadjo Area (PS4).

Moosehead Lake, the largest lake in Maine, has untapped birding potential during migration. Try Lily Bay State Park (PS3), or perhaps even the yards and edges in and around downtown Greenville. Waterfowl undoubtedly rest

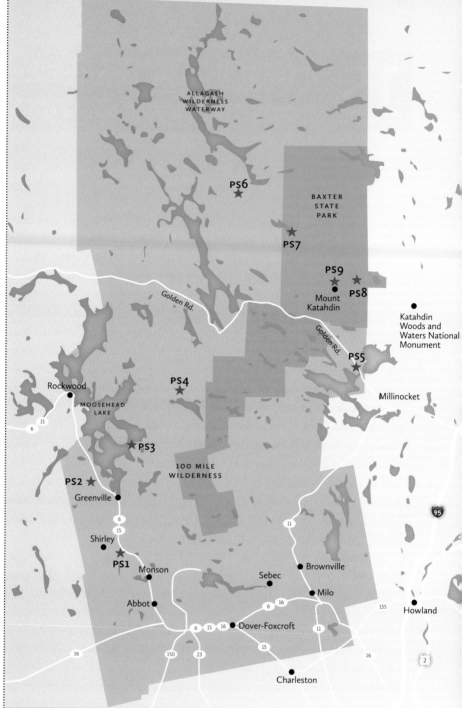

ALLAGASH
WILDERNESS
WATERWAY

PS6

BAXTER
STATE
PARK

PS7

PS9

PS8

Mount
Katahdin

Golden Rd.

Golden Rd.

Katahdin
Woods and
Waters National
Monument

PS5

Rockwood

PS4

Millinocket

MOOSEHEAD
LAKE

6 15

PS3

100 MILE
WILDERNESS

PS2

Greenville

6
15

Shirley

11

PS1

Monson

Sebec

Brownville

95

Abbot

Milo

6 16

155

Howland

6 15 16

Dover-Foxcroft

11

150 23

16

2

16

150 23

16

Charleston

PISCATAQUIS COUNTY

here, perhaps in sizable numbers during inclement weather, but access to the countless coves and inlets without a boat is severely limited.

In winter, seasonal road closures and heavy snows reduce visitation, but during finch and owl irruption many of the sites should be checked, even along the main thoroughfares. —*Derek Lovitch*

SITE PS1 Shirley Bog Railroad Bed

TOWN Shirley. DeLorme Map 41: E2. **SEASON** April–August.
VISITATION 1–3 hrs. No restroom facilities. **HIGHLIGHTS** Boreal specialties including Spruce Grouse, Gray Jay, and Boreal Chickadee; breeding songbirds including Olive-sided Flycatcher and Canada Warbler; marsh birds including American Bittern.

This dirt road south of Greenville holds a good variety of habitats and is a pleasant place for a morning of birding. You can check it pretty quickly, or spend a good amount of time walking any portion of its 6-mile length. The bogs along the road are good places to watch for ducks and marsh birds while keeping an eye out for warblers in the bordering trees. There are even some spruce forests on the north end of the road that have produced boreal birds like Spruce Grouse.

DIRECTIONS

From the center of Greenville where Routes 6 and 15 make a hard turn to the west, head south on Route 6 for 5.9 miles. Turn right onto Upper Shirley Corner Road. Continue for 1.3 miles and you'll see a dirt road on your right. Take this road, roll your windows down, and start birding.

This former railroad bed is now a rough dirt road full of potholes. From the southern end, it continues north for about 6 miles before connecting with Dyer Road and heading into Greenville Junction. Those 6 miles are laced with excellent bogs and boreal forest. I'd recommend stopping every few hundred yards to look and listen; you can also find somewhere to pull off and walk a good stretch of the road.

The shrubby boggy areas hold plentiful Alder Flycatchers, Northern Waterthrushes, and Canada Warblers. Keep an eye out on snags for Olive-sided Flycatchers. Ring-necked and Wood Ducks are often seen in the open water. Although secretive, American Bitterns can often be heard thunder-pumping

Spruce Grouse, Aroostook County. © Luke Seitz

in the wetter spots. Even Sedge Wren, now a very rare breeder in Maine, has been recorded here in recent years.

Beginning about 3 miles north of the turnoff in Shirley, you'll be mostly out of the main bogs and into some more spruce-filled forests. For the next 3 miles before you hit Dyer Road be on the lookout for boreal breeders such as Boreal Chickadee, Gray Jay, and even Spruce Grouse (they can occasionally be seen gathering grit from the roadside—but beware, Ruffed Grouse occurs here too). The diversity of warblers is usually excellent: Nashville, Northern Parula, Black-throated Green, and Blackburnian are all common. Cape May and Bay-breasted Warblers are rare but possible. A few other roads and snowmobile tracks branch out from the main road; these can be worth exploring for some of the less-common species.

RARITIES

Sedge Wren, June 2008

SITE PS2 Big Moose Mountain

TOWN Greenville Junction. DeLorme Map 41: C–D1.
SEASON May–July, August.   **VISITATION** 3–4 hrs. No restroom facilities.
HIGHLIGHTS Bicknell's Thrush, Boreal Chickadee, Gray Jay, and other woodland breeders.

This is a fairly strenuous but rewarding hike through varied habitats, starting in hardwoods and ending in stunted spruce at the summit of 3,196 feet. It is known as a good place to look for Bicknell's Thrush during the breeding season, and also holds many other interesting boreal species as a supporting cast. Beautiful views from the overlook make the hike worthwhile even without the birds.

DIRECTIONS

From the center of Greenville, where Routes 6 and 15 make a hard turn to the left, follow Route 6/15 North for 5 miles. Turn left onto North Road. In 1.4 miles you'll see the parking area for Big Moose Mountain on the right.

From the parking area the trail heads west through mostly deciduous forest. Here you will probably hear Scarlet Tanager and Red-eyed Vireo singing and might even luck upon a Philadelphia Vireo (be careful, as their song is exceptionally similar to Red-eyed). This first section of the trail is not too strenuous, but after about 1.5 miles it starts climbing more steeply. After an old cabin you can take the spur to the left for a scenic view, or continue to the summit.

The most interesting birding is between the old cabin and the summit. This is where spruce and fir dominate the forest, and Boreal Chickadees, Gray Jays, and Yellow-bellied Flycatchers are frequently seen and heard. You might even luck upon a Spruce Grouse on the trail. As you climb higher, the spruces start to appear stunted, and you'll hear Blackpoll Warbler singing its high-pitched song. This is the realm of the Bicknell's Thrush. These shy thrushes are highly sought after in Maine, and this is a pretty reliable spot for them. However, they are most vocal at dawn and dusk, so you'll need to start your hike very early (or late) for the best chance. Bring a flashlight just in case. Listen for their wiry song and piercing call note.

This hike is just over 4 miles round-trip, so expect it to take several hours if you want to reach the summit. June is the best time for Bicknell's Thrush, but birding can be good any time from May through August, and quieter in the fall.

SITE PS3 Lily Bay State Park

TOWNS Beaver Cove and Lily Bay Townships. DeLorme Map 41: C3.
SEASON April–September.   VISITATION 1 hr. Restrooms at the
campground. State park entry fees. ♿ HIGHLIGHTS Common mixed-
woodland breeders.

This peaceful state park offers a good base to explore the Moosehead Lake
area. The birding here is typical of Maine's woods, and you should enjoy a
pleasant variety of birdsong in the spring and summer.

DIRECTIONS

From the center of Greenville, where Routes 6 and 15 make a hard turn to
the west, head north on Lily Bay Road. Continue for 8.7 miles to the state
park entrance on your left.

Lily Bay State Park does not usually hold any particularly sought-after birds
(although Black-backed Woodpecker has been seen here), but it is a pleasant
spot to camp and enjoy the woods with friends and family. There are two
main camping areas, one to the north and one to the west, and some short
hiking trails that head along the lakeshore. For birding purposes, I'd recommend walking the entrance road. You'll likely find many species typical of
Maine's woodlands, including Hermit and Swainson's Thrush, Winter Wren,
Blackburnian and Black-throated Green Warblers, and Dark-eyed Junco. Pine
Warblers start to thin out in this area of Maine, but they occur here. You might
luck upon a Ruffed Grouse crossing the road, especially early in the morning.

Camping at Lily Bay State Park makes for an excellent base to explore other
nearby areas, including Kokadjo (site PS4) and Big Moose Mountain (PS2).

SITE PS4 Kokadjo Area

TOWNS Lily Bay, Spencer Bay, Frenchtown Township, and T1 R13. DeLorme
Map 41: A–B4–5.   SEASON April, **May–July**, August.   VISITATION 1–4 hrs.
Restrooms at businesses in Greenville.   HIGHLIGHTS Boreal specialties
including Spruce Grouse and Boreal Chickadee, Yellow-bellied Flycatcher,
Bay-breasted and Mourning Warblers.

The Kokadjo area north of Greenville is a famous moose-watching destination. The extensive forest and logging roads also make for excellent birding.

I mention a few particularly nice roads, but it is possible to explore more thoroughly. Sought-after warblers, including Bay-breasted and Mourning, and boreal specialties like Gray Jay and Spruce Grouse are all possible in this area. The diversity of birdsong on a June morning is usually wonderful!

DIRECTIONS

From the center of Greenville where Routes 6 and 15 make a hard turn to the west, head north on Lily Bay Road. This heads north for 18.5 miles to the town of Kokadjo, where Cliff Swallows breed and are often seen flying around town. Continue for 1.9 miles past Kokadjo and bear right onto a dirt logging road. This is one particularly good place to begin birding, but the entire area north of Kokadjo is full of productive habitat and excellent birding. There is significant potential for exploring.

From the start of the logging road (called Medaw Island Road on Google Maps), slowly bird your way east. You're immediately in a regenerating clear cut that often has Mourning Warbler. The next stretch of road goes through various stages of forest. About 3.7 miles from the start you'll see a side road heading off to the left. Park here (make sure you're well off the road) and walk up this road, which is less than a mile long and is particularly good for Bay-breasted Warbler and Yellow-bellied Flycatcher. You'll probably hear Canada Warbler and Northern Waterthrush around the wetter areas. The road ends at a clear cut that could hold Mourning Warbler or Lincoln's Sparrow.

Make your way back to your car and backtrack to the main road. Turn right and continue north, stopping at any good patch of spruces or a clear cut. There are Bay-breasted and Mourning Warblers along this stretch, Olive-sided Flycatchers sing from snags in the open areas, and Gray Jays can sometimes be seen near the side of the road. In just over 3.5 miles you'll come to a bog with a small parking area on the right. This is an enjoyable stop; there are often moose in the bog, and Alder Flycatchers sing loudly from the shrubs.

Although I mention these couple of particular locations as productive, you could easily spend days weaving around all the logging roads in this area. There is a lot of potential to turn up desirable boreal birds, so don't hesitate to stop frequently wherever you see interesting habitat. A GPS and especially a good map as a backup are recommended if you want to spend a lot of time exploring more remote logging roads.

SITE PS5 Golden Road

TOWNS Millinocket and beyond. DeLorme Map 43: B–3 to start, and on to maps 51–47. **SEASON** April–September. **VISITATION** 1–3 hrs. No restroom facilities. **HIGHLIGHTS** Boreal specialties including American Three-toed Woodpecker; breeding songbirds.

The Golden Road is a famous Maine logging route that heads west from Millinocket and continues all the way to the Canadian border. The road passes along several productive bogs and great pockets of boreal habitat. American Three-toed Woodpecker has occurred along the Golden Road fairly close to Millinocket, but you're more likely to see a wide variety of regular woodland species.

DIRECTIONS

From I-95 take Exit 244 and head west on Route 157 into East Millinocket. Continue on Route 157 as Route 11 joins it from the north, and into downtown Millinocket. Where Route 157 ends at Katahdin Avenue (Route 11 continues on), turn right and continue north on Katahdin Avenue. In .02 mile, turn left onto Bates Street. Continue for 8.1 miles, where you can turn left onto a small cutover that brings you to the Golden Road, immediately before the North Woods Trading Post. Turn right onto the Golden Road.

Much like the North Maine Woods (site AR13), birding along the Golden Road is exploratory. I'd recommend setting out from Millinocket and birding the road by car, stopping wherever you see interesting habitat. Once you've cut over to the Golden Road as described above, the next several miles of road are adjacent to a power-line cut that holds Chestnut-sided and sometimes Mourning Warblers. There are several bogs along this stretch, where you'll likely hear Alder Flycatcher and American Bittern vocalizing. Look for Ring-necked Duck, Common Goldeneye, and Hooded Merganser in the patches of open water. Keep an eye out in dead trees surrounding bogs, which have rarely held American Three-toed Woodpecker.

As you head farther west on the Golden Road you'll pass through a long stretch of fairly monotonous hardwood forest. The birds here are wonderful but not particularly noteworthy. You'll likely hear Ovenbird, Scarlet Tanager, Eastern Wood-Pewee, and American Redstart. Note that in 19.2 miles after turning onto the Golden Road you'll pass the Telos Road, which brings you to some great birding areas described in site PS6. However, continuing straight on the Golden Road past Telos Road is also an adventurous and productive way to spend a day birding. You'll notice more logging roads branching out on either side; these are always worth a check, although a GPS and a good map for backup are recommended if you are in a particularly adventurous mood.

Refer to site AR13 for some notes on birding by habitat in the woods here. I would use this as a guide to bird the Golden Road. This entire area, especially past Telos Road, is seldom explored by birders. You have a great chance to see all the boreal specialties (Spruce Grouse, Black-backed and American Three-toed Woodpeckers, Gray Jay, and Boreal Chickadee), as well as up to twenty species of breeding warblers. Olive-sided and Yellow-bellied Flycatchers, Fox Sparrows, and both species of crossbill occur throughout the region. With an early start from Millinocket, you're sure to turn up some exciting birds!

SITE PS6 Harvester Road

TOWN N/A. DeLorme Map 50: A1–2. SEASON April–September.
VISITATION 1–4 hrs. No restroom facilities. HIGHLIGHTS American Three-toed and Black-backed Woodpeckers, Spruce Grouse, Fox Sparrow, finches, breeding warblers including Wilson's and Cape May.

Harvester Road was made famous several years ago when American Three-toed Woodpeckers were discovered in a stand of spruces. In addition to this rare breeder, the road is excellent for a variety of breeding warblers, finches, and all other boreal specialties including Spruce Grouse. Birding is easy from the roadside, and you can also explore the wet tracks that head into the forest. May and June are best for vociferous breeding birds, but the boreal specialties and finches can be found year-round (weather permitting; check with the North Maine Woods at www.northmainwoods.org to determine the latest access situation).

DIRECTIONS

Follow the directions in PS5, and turn right onto Telos Road from Golden Road. Be careful along this stretch—moose are common, especially in the early morning. Continue on Telos Road for 14.2 miles to the North Maine Woods checkpoint. Check in here, and then continue past the gate for another 2.5 miles. Turn left onto Harvester Road (there is a sign). Drive down

Harvester Road for about 2.9 miles, when it heads downhill and a bog opens up on both sides of the road (more extensive on the right). Find a place to pull off; this is the best area for birding.

As the road heads slightly downhill toward the bog, it gradually bends to the right. Listen for Wilson's Warbler singing its chipping song from the shrubby alders. This can be a good spot to scan for an Olive-sided Flycatcher perched atop a snag. Yellow-bellied and Alder Flycatchers also breed here. Just 100 yards farther, you'll notice a stand of tall spruce trees on the left with several wide overgrown tracks heading into them. This is the spot for American Three-toed Woodpecker, which has been reliable here for several years. In the past, they have nested very close to the road, but sometimes they retreat farther into the stand. Also note that Black-backed Woodpeckers nest here too, and are usually more conspicuous than the Three-toeds.

Walking up and down the road along the spruce stand, or taking one of the tracks into the trees (beware, this is often a wet and treacherous undertaking), can be a productive way to spend an hour or more. You'll likely also run across Gray Jay and Boreal Chickadee. Spruce Grouse are around, and sometimes seen in the road. A variety of warblers can be found in this general area, and the stands of spruces can hold sought-after species like Cape May and Bay-breasted. The regenerating area across the road from the spruce stand has Palm Warbler and Lincoln's Sparrow. Finches such as White-winged and Red Crossbill and Evening Grosbeak are always possible.

One mile past the end of the spruce stand is another logging road that heads off to the right. This is also a great area—it is drivable for at least three-quarters of a mile before becoming rather sketchy, but I'd recommend parking at the beginning and walking. The regenerating area on your left holds breeding Fox Sparrow and Wilson's and Palm Warblers. The taller spruces on the right have Black-backed Woodpecker and Bay-breasted Warbler. Also keep an eye out here for American Three-toed Woodpecker—I've never seen them at this exact spot, but it's close enough to the aforementioned location that I'm sure they could occur here.

If you have the time, other nearby areas are worth exploring for a similar mix of species. From the start of the side logging road mentioned above, continue farther north on Harvester Road for 1.2 miles to a four-way intersection. Turn right. This road goes through more excellent boreal habitat, with potential for Spruce and Ruffed Grouse, Boreal Chickadee, Bay-breasted Warbler, and Fox Sparrow. It ends at a T intersection with Umbazookus Road. Turn left. The next 3 miles or so are productive for birding. This stretch has a few nice bogs, with Olive-sided Flycatcher and Wilson's Warbler, and stands of tall spruces similar to those on Harvester Road. Keep an eye out for both "sprucey" woodpeckers (Black-backed and American Three-toed) and Bay-breasted and Cape May Warblers. Fox Sparrows breed in areas of regenerating spruce along this stretch.

Continuing on this road leads you into forested areas and clear cuts with similar possibilities. See site AR13, the North Maine Woods section in the Aroostook County chapter, for some more information about birding the logging roads in this zone. However, I'd recommend retracing your steps back down Harvester Road at this point.

BAXTER STATE PARK

A gift to the people of Maine from former Governor Percival P. Baxter in 1931, Baxter State Park has grown in size to almost 210,000 acres. Over forty peaks and ridges are protected, including the magnificent Mount Katahdin, Maine's highest peak. And thanks to the vision of Governor Baxter, who established a trust fund to maintain the park, entry into the park remains free to Maine residents.

I have divided this crown jewel of Maine public land into three birding sites. A couple of nights in one of the campgrounds or based at an inn in Millinocket is the best way to thoroughly explore all the productive birding areas in and around the park. For more information about the park, including out-of-state fees, reservations, hiking and campground maps, and more, visit www.baxterstateparkauthority.com.

DIRECTIONS

Here are the directions **to the park entrance** (then see sites listed below). From I-95 take Exit 244 and head west on Route 157 toward East Millinocket. Stay on Route 157 as Route 11 joins it from the north, and continue through East Millinocket and into downtown Millinocket. Where Route 157 ends at Katahdin Avenue (Route 11 continues on), turn right and continue north on Katahdin Avenue. In less than a quarter mile, turn left onto Bates Street. Continue on this road, which turns into Millinocket Road. You'll pass the Northwoods Trading Post on your right. About 8 miles past the trading post, you'll come to the Togue Pond Gatehouse for Baxter State Park. Follow directions as described in each site entry.

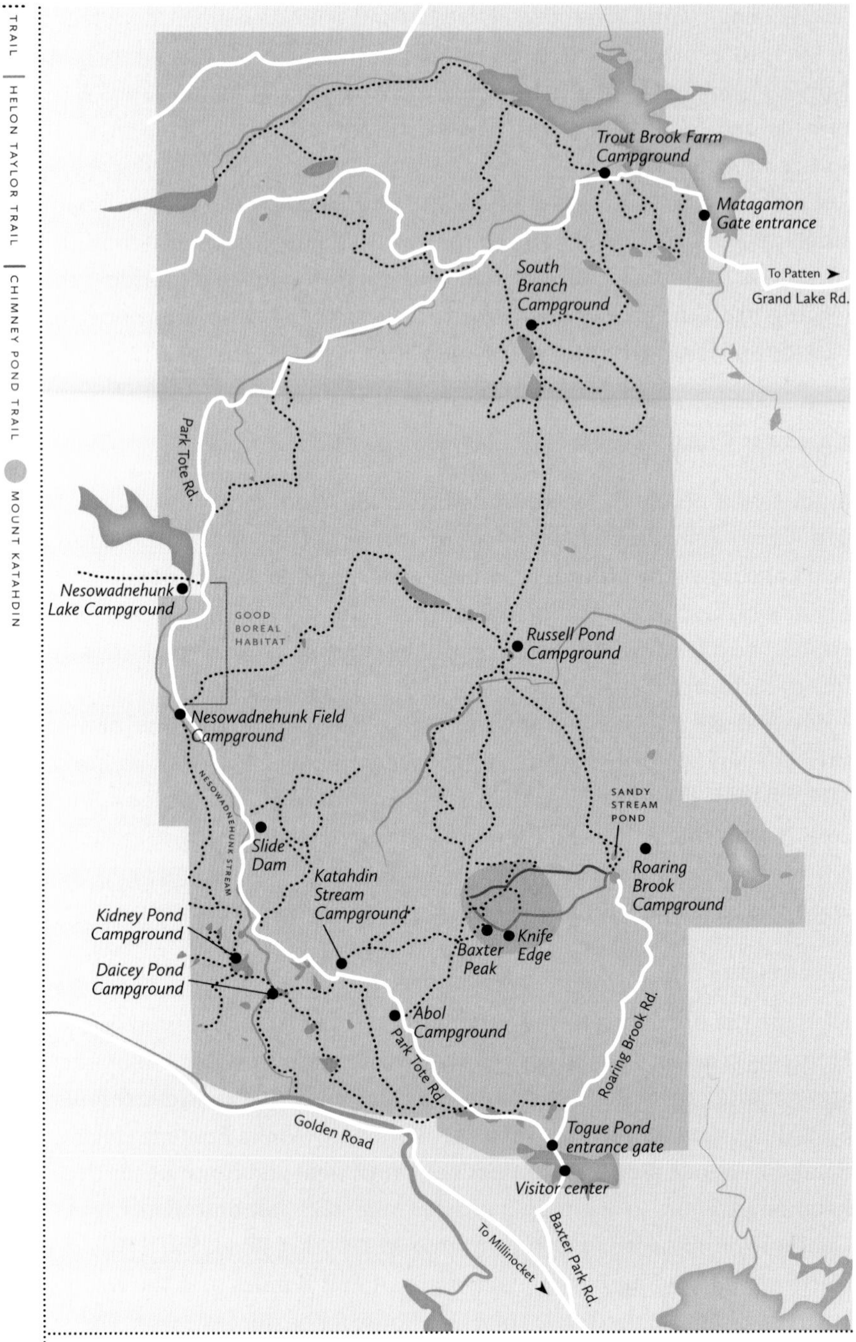

TRAIL
HELON TAYLOR TRAIL
CHIMNEY POND TRAIL
MOUNT KATAHDIN
Trout Brook Farm Campground
Matagamon Gate entrance
To Patten
Grand Lake Rd.
South Branch Campground
Park Tote Rd.
Nesowadnehunk Lake Campground
GOOD BOREAL HABITAT
Russell Pond Campground
Nesowadnehunk Field Campground
NESOWADNEHUNK STREAM
SANDY STREAM POND
Slide Dam
Roaring Brook Campground
Katahdin Stream Campground
Kidney Pond Campground
Knife Edge
Baxter Peak
Daicey Pond Campground
Abol Campground
Park Tote Rd.
Roaring Brook Rd.
Golden Road
Togue Pond entrance gate
Visitor center
To Millinocket
Baxter Park Rd.

BAXTER STATE PARK

Mount Katahdin looms large over Maine in all seasons. © Serena Doose

SITE PS7 Baxter State Park: Nesowadnehunk Campground

TOWN Nesourdnahunk Township. DeLorme Map 50: C4. **SEASON** April–September. **VISITATION** 2–4 hrs. Restroom at the campground. See park introduction for more information. **HIGHLIGHTS** Boreal species including Spruce Grouse, American Three-toed and Black-backed Woodpeckers, Cape May and Bay-breasted Warblers, Merlin, and finches.

The stretch of road around and beyond the Nesowadnehunk Campground is one of the most popular birding destinations within Baxter State Park. This area holds all boreal specialties: Black-backed and American Three-toed Woodpeckers, Spruce Grouse, Gray Jay, and Boreal Chickadee. Additionally, the area is well known for producing sought-after warblers, including Tennessee, Cape May, Bay-breasted, and Blackpoll, among others. This spot should be one of the top priorities for a birder visiting Baxter State Park.

DIRECTIONS

Once in the park (see directions in introduction), the road splits just beyond the gatehouse. The right split heads toward the Roaring Brook Campground; you want to stay to the left. From the split, the Nesowadnehunk Field Campground will be on your left in 16.6 miles.

PISCATAQUIS COUNTY

Park at the campground and start walking to enjoy the best boreal habitat. You can often find Boreal Chickadee and Gray Jay right around the campground. Head back out to the main park road and continue north. The next 4 miles are excellent—walk for as long as you want! More common warblers include Magnolia, Nashville, and Northern Parula. Keep an eye and ear out for less common species as well. I remember one particularly exciting day when I was birding here with a group, and we came across Bay-breasted, Cape May, Blackpoll, and Blackburnian Warblers in about five minutes—almost in view at the same time! And that's not to mention the numerous other breeding birds in the area: Yellow-bellied Flycatchers, Blue-headed Vireos, Winter Wrens . . . the birding here in the spring and summer is truly wonderful!

In addition to warblers, Black-backed and even American Three-toed Woodpeckers have been seen along this stretch, and Spruce and Ruffed Grouse can occur in the road (especially very early). Boreal Chickadee and Gray Jay are fairly common. 3.7 miles beyond the campground entrance, a diffuse trail on the left leads to an old road. Pass the lake, go through the developed campground, and bird for the next mile or so (before the road doglegs to the right). There are spruce stands and regenerating areas along this stretch, and it has been reliable for American Three-toed and Black-backed Woodpeckers in recent years. Many of the same species previously mentioned, including Spruce Grouse, have been seen along this road.

Return to the Park Tote Road and continue north, which gets into more mixed forests, or head back south toward the park entrance.

SITE PS8 Baxter State Park: Roaring Brook Campground and Sandy Stream Pond

TOWN Mount Katahdin Township. DeLorme Map 50–51.
SEASON May–August. VISITATION 1–3 hrs. Outhouses at campground.
HIGHLIGHTS Philadelphia Vireo, Boreal Chickadee, breeding songbirds, and moose.

The parking lot at Roaring Brook Campground is well known as a spot to see breeding Philadelphia Vireos. The hike to Sandy Stream Pond is pleasant and not very strenuous, and you're likely to see moose around the pond. Some boreal species such as Boreal Chickadee are present around here, but this hike takes advantage of a wider assortment of more common forest species as well.

Once in the park (see directions p. 403), the road splits just beyond the gatehouse. Take the right fork toward Roaring Brook Campground.

Bird along the road for American Bittern, Wilson's Warbler, and ducks (including Ring-necked and Common Goldeneye) in the bog. The mixed woodlands hold a variety of typical species, including Black-throated Blue and Green Warblers and Winter Wrens. Once you reach the parking lot for the Roaring Brook Campground, start peering into the treetops in search of Philadelphia Vireos. Keep in mind that their song is nearly identical to that of the Red-eyed Vireo; even with extensive experience, birders may find the two impossible to distinguish. Look for the Philadelphia Vireo's shorter bill and yellow underparts.

Take the trail to Sandy Stream Pond, which leaves from the north end of the parking lot. The trail starts through deciduous woodland, which holds species such as Yellow-bellied Sapsucker, Least Flycatcher, and Eastern Wood-Pewee. As you start entering more coniferous forest, listen for Winter Wren, Magnolia Warbler, and Swainson's Thrush. Boreal Chickadee can often be heard wheezing in the stands of thick spruce. Once you reach the pond, you have a great chance at seeing moose and a variety of ducks, including Ring-necked Duck, Common Goldeneye, and Common Merganser. The view from the edge of the pond is beautiful, and moose are usually present.

You can backtrack from here, or make a longer loop around the pond and return on the Russell Pond Trail. For this longer loop you'll need to turn left after the pond and take another left to head back south (see trail map in Baxter State Park introduction above).

SITE PS9 Baxter State Park: Mount Katahdin

TOWN Mount Katahdin Township. DeLorme Map 51: D1.
SEASON May, June–July, August–September. **VISITATION** 2 hrs. to full day (or overnight). Outhouses at campgrounds and some trailheads.
HIGHLIGHTS Breeding Bicknell's Thrush and American Pipit; other breeding songbirds including boreal specialties.

Mount Katahdin is one of Maine's most famous landmarks, and at 5,267 feet it is the tallest mountain in the state. The scenery all around it is simply stunning, and there are several hikes of varying difficulty to take in this magnificent area. Two particularly special birds can be seen around Mount Katahdin: American Pipit, which nests in the alpine habitat above tree line, and Bicknell's Thrush, which is found in stunted spruces on the mountain's slopes. In fact, this is one of only two locations in the Eastern United States (the other is Mount Washington in New Hampshire) that host breeding pipits. In addition, the spruce forests hold a variety of boreal breeders, including many species of warblers, Spruce Grouse, Gray Jay, and Boreal Chickadee.

DIRECTIONS

Once in the park (see directions, p. 403), the road splits just beyond the gatehouse. Take the right fork toward Roaring Brook Campground.

From the parking lot for Roaring Brook Campground, two trails head up toward Mount Katahdin: Chimney Pond Trail and Helon Taylor Trail. You can reach Chimney Pond Campground from either trail, which is a great base for more extensive exploring of this area. It is very popular, however, so make a reservation in advance. If you're not up for an overnight stay, you can hike for any shorter amount of time and still have enjoyable birding.

The two trails offer similar birdlife. You start out in deciduous-dominated woodland, which holds species like Veery, Wood Thrush (uncommon and near the northernmost limits of its range), Ruffed Grouse, Ovenbird, and Scarlet Tanager. As you climb in elevation, you enter more spruce-fir forest, and the birds change accordingly. Blackpoll Warblers are quite common in the spruces, and Bay-breasted and Cape May Warblers are possible as well. Always keep an eye out for Boreal Chickadees and Gray Jays. Both species of crossbill and even Pine Grosbeaks sometimes breed in the conifers.

One of the star birds of Maine's higher elevations is the Bicknell's Thrush. This shy bird breeds in the stunted spruce trees close to tree line and is most vocal near dawn and dusk. This species can be encountered just above the Chimney Pond Campground or on the Helon Taylor Trail. It tends to be found at higher elevations than other thrushes but overlaps with Swainson's Thrush.

Additionally, Mount Katahdin is the only place in Maine where American Pipits breed. They can be found in the alpine habitat above tree line, especially in the area west of Baxter Peak around the Hunt and Abol Trails. Don't expect to see many other species up here, although the spruces near tree line hold plentiful Blackpoll Warblers. Reaching the area where pipits breed would be a very long day hike from Roaring Brook Campground, so unless you're staying overnight at Chimney Pond, I'd recommend hiking from the Abol Campground or Katahdin Stream Campground (both are along the Park Tote Road).

Of course, these few trails barely scratch the surface of Mount Katahdin and the wider Baxter State Park area. The areas that I've mentioned are great, but that's not to say that the rest of the park should be ignored. For birders with more time to explore, I would highly recommend camping in any of the other campgrounds in the park, and trying some more of the 200-plus miles of trails that weave through the wilderness. To help you plan a longer trip, check the maps on the park website, listed in the Baxter State Park introduction above. You are likely to see many of the same birds that I've listed for the above locations, and maybe you'll even luck into a less common species like American Three-toed Woodpecker. Even Boreal Owl might be a possibility in some of the higher spruce forest!

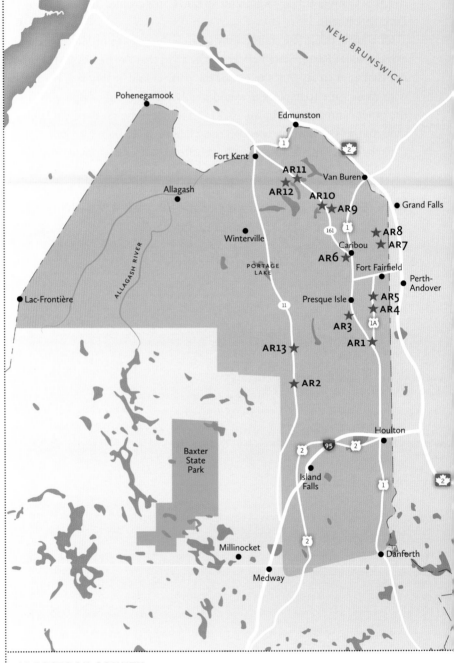

Pohenegamook

Edmunston

NEW BRUNSWICK

Fort Kent

AR11

Van Buren

AR12

Allagash

AR10

AR9

Grand Falls

Winterville

161

AR8

Caribou

AR7

PORTAGE LAKE

AR6

Fort Fairfield

Perth-Andover

ALLAGASH RIVER

Lac-Frontière

11

Presque Isle

AR5

AR4

AR3

1A

AR13

AR1

AR2

Baxter State Park

Houlton

95

Island Falls

Millinocket

Danforth

Medway

AROOSTOOK COUNTY

16 Aroostook County

LUKE SEITZ

Known to most Mainers simply as "the County," Aroostook, the largest county by land area in the United States east of the Rocky Mountains, is larger than the states of Rhode Island and Connecticut combined, with a total area of over sixty-eight hundred square miles.

There are a lot of potato fields, a lot of woods, and a lot of birds. And with a population of a mere sixty-nine thousand, there are not many people exploring it. Countless lakes, ponds, and rivers and endless miles of remote logging roads, some of which have probably never been searched by a birder, await the adventurous explorer. Meanwhile, the scattered towns offer a mosaic of interesting habitats that can be a magnet for birds. Much of the county is inaccessible, especially by motor vehicle, but two major north-south routes, US Route 1 and State Route 11, offer easy access to some of the best birding the county has to offer.

Most birders head to Aroostook in search of boreal specialties, such as Spruce Grouse, American Three-toed and Black-backed Woodpeckers, Gray Jays, Boreal Chickadees, and up to twenty species of breeding warblers, including Bay-breasted and Cape May. There are many areas to search, but Luke Seitz has outlined some of the most productive here, including the Masardis Area (site AR2), the Stockholm–Van Buren Path (AR9), the Muscovic Road (AR10), and Square Lake Road (AR12). Of course, the North Maine Woods (AR13) offer even more of these sought-after species, but a little more effort and exploration is usually called for. However, such effort can be rewarding on so many different levels. You might even discover something like a breeding Boreal or Great Gray Owl, or see a lynx, or maybe find a new hot spot for American Three-toed Woodpecker. A birder with a sense for the thrill of discovery is automatically smitten with the area.

Aroostook County is also a major hot spot for waterfowl watchers. Spring and fall concentrations of migrant ducks and especially geese (with vagrant geese seen on an annual basis) can be astounding. As long as there is open water, Lake Josephine (AR4) and Christina Reservoir (AR5) should be on every birder's must-see list. "Lake Jo" is also the only known breeding area for Redhead and Ruddy Duck in Maine, and other wetland birds, such as Common Gallinule and American Bittern, are sometimes found.

Later in the fall, and often throughout much of the winter, tiny Collins Pond (AR6) hosts large numbers of Canada Geese that feed in the surrounding fields, and many of the area's rare geese have been found here. It is also one of the county's few good spots for migrant shorebirds. It's best to combine your rare goose searching with early mornings and late afternoons sifting through the flock here, with daytime searching via the Limestone/Fort Fairfield Goose Tour (AR7). —*Derek Lovitch*

SITE AR1 Mars Hill Pond

TOWN Mars Hill. DeLorme Map 59: A3. SEASON April–November.
VISITATION 15 min. No restroom facilities. ♿ HIGHLIGHTS Waterfowl.

This tiny pond (really just a wide bulge in the river) is worthy of a quick check on your way to or from the more productive sites farther north in Aroostook County. It is easily accessible from Route 1 and can provide close views of many waterfowl species in spring, summer, and fall.

DIRECTIONS

From I-95 take Exit 302 and follow US Route 1 North for 26.5 miles into the town of Mars Hill. As Route 1 peels off to the left, you want to continue straight onto Route 1A. Look for the next road on the left, which is Silver Street. Just beyond where it turns off, pull into the parking lot behind the small building, where you can overlook the pond.

This pond might not look like much, but it is an easy, quick check and can hold good numbers of waterfowl whenever there is open water. Look for Wood Duck, American Wigeon, Blue- and Green-winged Teal, Northern Shoveler, Northern Pintail, Ring-necked Duck, and both Hooded and Common Mergansers. A careful scan of the pond edge might reveal a few shorebirds (Solitary and Spotted Sandpipers are most common).

RARITIES

Pink-footed Goose, October 2015

SITE AR2 Masardis Area

TOWN Masardis. DeLorme Map 58: A–B2. **SEASON** All year, but
especially **May–August.** **VISITATION** 1–3 hrs. No restroom facilities.
HIGHLIGHTS Boreal specialties (especially Boreal Chickadee); breeding
songbirds (especially spruce-loving warblers and Yellow-bellied Flycatcher).

The Route 11 corridor on either side of the town of Masardis has an excellent amount of boreal habitat. The spruce-dominated forests and bogs are
home to all the resident boreal species that can be expected in Maine, and a
wonderful diversity of breeding warblers and other passerines. If you have a
little extra time, taking this route to Aroostook County instead of US Route
1 puts you in a better position for some fun exploratory birding.

DIRECTIONS

From I-95 take Exit 286. Head north on Smyrna Road, cross straight over
Route 2, and continue for 10.3 miles to the intersection with Route 11. Turn
right on Route 11 and continue north for 11.5 miles, where you'll see a small
logging road heading off to the left. This is where I recommend starting to
pay particular attention to the habitat and to start looking for birds. For the
next several miles of Route 11 you'll notice many logging roads branching out
in both directions. Like the rest of the North Maine Woods, this area does
not have particular stakeouts for the most sought-after species. Instead, it is
most fun to explore. Choose a logging road and drive or walk along it for as
far as you want, looking for areas dominated by spruce, fir, and larch. Boggy
areas can also be exciting to check out.

This whole area is home to Spruce Grouse, Black-backed Woodpecker, Gray
Jay, and Boreal Chickadee. Breeding warblers can include the boreal specialties such as Tennessee, Cape May, and Bay-breasted. May and June are the
best times for lots of singing activity; near dawn is always most productive.
However, other times of year can still produce the resident boreal species
as well as finches, including both crossbills and Pine (winter) and Evening
Grosbeaks (sporadically at any time of year).

As you continue north you'll reach the small town of Masardis, situated
along the Aroostook River. This area is dominated by farm fields, which are
often patrolled by American Kestrels and can be worth a scan for Horned
Larks, American Pipits, or Snow Buntings in the fall or early spring. The next
town to the north is Ashland, where you should turn right onto Route 163.
This road passes several productive bogs (listen for Yellow-bellied Flycatcher)

and spruce-dominated forest. Again, there is so much habitat to check out, and it is best to explore wherever you see interesting habitat. You'll surely find something fun! Continuing straight on Route 163 will take you right into Presque Isle.

Please be aware that Route 11 and Route 163 are both heavily traveled, especially by logging trucks, and you should be very cautious when pulling over. Early mornings are best for avoiding traffic.

SITE AR3 Aroostook State Park

TOWN Presque Isle. DeLorme Map 65: E1.   SEASON All year, especially April–September.   VISITATION 1–3 hrs. Usually open 9 a.m.–dusk. Camping, picnic area, restrooms. State park entry fee.
HIGHLIGHTS Breeding and migrant songbirds (including breeding Blackburnian and Canada Warblers and Scarlet Tanager), waterfowl (especially mergansers and Ring-necked Ducks) in spring and fall.

Maine's first state park is home to a small lake and a network of hiking trails. The birding is typical of mixed forest in the region and quite enjoyable in the spring and summer. In particular, it makes for a nice casual outing with friends or family.

DIRECTIONS

From the intersection of Route 10 and US Route 1 in Presque Isle, head south on US Route 1. Continue for 3.7 miles. Turn right onto Spragueville Road. In 1 mile turn left onto the State Park Road. Pay the small fee at the gate and continue to the parking lot on the shore of Echo Lake. I recommend that you pick up a trail map at the gate, or use the online map at the link listed below.

From the parking area, several miles of trails branch out in all directions. For birding purposes, there isn't one trail that is particularly good, but I enjoy the hike up to South and North Peaks (west of the parking area). However, these trails have some steep sections (particularly South Peak), and less strenuous options can be found south of the lake.

The birds here are typical of northern Maine's mixed forests. Look and listen for several species of breeding warblers (including Blackburnian, Magnolia, and Black-throated Green), Scarlet Tanager, Veery, Swainson's, Hermit, and Wood Thrushes, Winter Wrens, and Ruffed Grouse. Northern Goshawk has been seen in summer and might nest nearby—but if it does, don't get too close, unless you want to lose your scalp! In early spring when Echo Lake opens up, large numbers of Hooded Mergansers sometimes congregate. Also keep an eye out for Common Loons, Bald Eagles, and Ring-necked Ducks. Winter is much quieter at this park, but the trails provide a pleasant place to cross-country ski or snowshoe, and you might luck upon a few Pine Grosbeaks or Pine Siskins flying over.

For more information on the park from Maine.gov see http://www.maine.gov/dacf/parks/docs/fpl/aroostookbrochure.pdf.

SITE AR4 Lake Josephine

TOWN Easton. DeLorme Map 65: D3.   SEASON April–November.
VISITATION 15 min. to over 1 hr. No restroom facilities.
HIGHLIGHTS Waterfowl migration; breeding ducks (including Redhead and Ruddy Duck); Common Gallinule, American and (rarely) Least Bitterns.

Lake Josephine is one of the highlights of birding Aroostook County, especially from spring through fall. The diversity of breeding ducks in its marshy margins is unmatched by any other location in the state; indeed, it is the only spot in Maine that hosts nesting Redhead and Ruddy Duck. The lake can also hold a variety of sea ducks during migration, and shorebirds are often seen on the muddy edges in fall (less so in spring). Migrant songbirds are sometimes in the surrounding shrubs and woods as well. Lake Josephine and the surrounding land are owned by McCain Foods, which allows access to birders. Please be aware and respectful of any farming operations or vehicles traveling on the narrow dirt roads.

DIRECTIONS

Heading north on US Route 1 in Presque Isle, turn right (east) onto Academy Street (just north of Rite Aid). In about 1.5 miles turn left onto Conant Road in front of the church. Continue for 3.7 miles and turn right onto Station Road. In just under a mile turn left onto Johnson Road, which quickly becomes rather rough and full of potholes (usually navigable without a high-clearance vehicle, or park off to a safe side and walk in). You'll quickly see the lake on your left. At the far edge of the lake the road bends ninety degrees to the left, and an ATV trail heads downhill to the right. Pull off anywhere around here, making sure you are as far off the road as possible—but be careful of the steep roadsides!

Most of the waterfowl action takes place on the edges of the main lake—scan carefully, as birds can often be tucked among the floating logs and can be difficult to find. A spotting scope is very useful. Breeding ducks here include Wood, Gadwall, American Wigeon, American Black, Mallard, Blue-winged Teal, Northern Shoveler, Green-winged Teal, Redhead, Ring-necked, Common Goldeneye, Hooded Merganser, and Ruddy. Common Mergansers nest nearby and often visit the lake. As the summer progresses, numbers can build greatly as broods of youngsters join the adult birds—it is possible to see over a thousand ducks here in August and September. In spring and fall the list of breeders can be augmented by Northern Pintail, both scaup, all three scoters, Long-tailed Duck, Bufflehead, Red-breasted Merganser, and even rarely a Canvasback or small flock of Common Eider.

Of course, the impressive variety of waterfowl is not all that Lake Josephine has to offer. While scanning the lake from the suggested parking area at the first ninety-degree bend, don't forget to turn around and check over the marshy ponds on the lower side of the dike. Marsh birds such as American Bittern, Pied-billed Grebe, Virginia Rail, and Sora all regularly occur here and can be quite vocal. Occasionally you may spot a Common Gallinule slinking among the reeds. Listen for a sneezy *fitz-bew* coming from the shrubs; this is sometimes the location of Maine's northernmost Willow Flycatcher.

It is also well worth keeping an eye out for shorebirds on the edge of the lake, especially in May and from August to October. Killdeer, Spotted and Solitary Sandpipers, both yellowlegs, and Semipalmated and Least Sandpipers are among the most common species, but sorting through them might yield less common species such as Pectoral, White-rumped, or even Baird's Sandpipers. Congregations of gulls in late fall have produced Iceland, Lesser Black-backed, and Glaucous in the past.

Continuing from the first bend, the road heads north along the east side of Lake Josephine. Keep scanning for ducks on your left side; you never know what might pop out of the lakeside logs and emergent vegetation. Before hitting pavement again you will pass through some fields where Savannah Sparrows often sing in spring and summer. These fields can be worth a scan for Horned Larks, American Pipits, and Snow Buntings in the fall and winter. Once you have returned to Conant Road, a left will bring you back to Presque Isle; a right turn will get you to another productive birding spot, Christiana Reservoir (this is recommended), site AR5.

Eurasian Wigeon, May 2010 and July 2014; American White Pelican, July–September 2013

SITE AR5 Christiana Reservoir

TOWN Easton. DeLorme Map 65: D3.   SEASON April–November.
VISITATION 1–2 hrs. No restroom facilities.   HIGHLIGHTS Waterfowl (breeding ducks and migrating geese); marsh birds including Common Gallinule and both bitterns; migrant songbirds.

Larger than nearby Lake Josephine, Christiana Reservoir is an excellent location to look for waterfowl as well as a good variety of passerines in the nearby shrubbery. Although it has not been as productive for breeding waterfowl in recent years, it can still hold excellent numbers of birds in spring and fall. The dike on the south side is a pleasant place for a walk, giving excellent vantages of the water as well as productive patches of marsh.

DIRECTIONS

Follow the directions to Lake Josephine (site AR4), but instead of turning right onto Station Road, continue east on Conant Road for another mile. You'll pass a small marshy pond on your left, and in 0.2 more miles look for a small dirt track leading off to the left. There is a large no-trespassing sign here, but the land is owned by McCain Foods, which graciously allows access for birders. Park at the start of this track (careful not to block it with your vehicle) and walk up to the dike that runs along the south end of the reservoir. Your birding begins here.

Christiana Reservoir holds many of the same birds as nearby Lake Josephine, although it hasn't been quite as productive for breeding waterfowl in recent years. However, it is still very much worth a check from spring through fall. All of Maine's regular dabbling ducks have occurred here, with noteworthy high counts of Gadwall, American Wigeon, both Blue- and Green-winged Teal, Northern Shoveler, and Northern Pintail occurring in the fall. Large congregations of post-breeding Ring-necked Ducks stage here in the late summer, with numbers sometimes exceeding five hundred. Especially in April and October, look for less common diving ducks, including all three scoter species, Long-tailed Duck, and even Common Eider, which occasionally drop in. Especially in fall, look for large flocks of Canada Geese, which can sometimes hold Snow Geese or even something rarer, like the Barnacle Goose that showed up here in 2014!

You can walk either direction on the dike to scan the reservoir from multiple vantage points, but take a left for the most productive stretch. You'll be able to look down on marshy vegetation below the dike, which can produce American Bittern, Pied-billed Grebe, Virginia Rail, Sora, and Common Gallinule. Least Bittern has been reported here in the past and is probably a regular breeder, but much of the best habitat is inaccessible on the north side of the reservoir. Don't ignore the shrubby woodland along the dike during migration, which can sometimes hold flocks of migrant warblers. When water levels are lower, scan any muddy areas for shorebirds: yellowlegs, Spotted and Solitary Sandpipers, Killdeer, and Least and Semipalmated Sandpipers are most common, but Pectoral and White-rumped Sandpipers have occurred.

Breeding songbirds are normally typical for such open secondary habitat and include Yellow Warbler, Alder Flycatcher, and Swamp Sparrow. Keep an ear out for Willow Flycatcher, which can occur here alongside the more common Alder.

RARITIES

American White Pelican, July–September 2013; Barnacle Goose, October 2014

SITE AR6 Collins Pond

TOWN Caribou. DeLorme Map 65: B1.   **SEASON** August–May.
VISITATION 15 min. to 1 hr. Restrooms are sometimes locked. ♿
HIGHLIGHTS Migrant and overwintering geese (including vagrants); gulls; waterfowl.

Despite its small size and downtown location, Collins Pond is remarkably productive. Over 130 species have been recorded here, with the main highlight being rarities mixed in with large flocks of Canada Geese. However, the pond is always worth a check for a diverse assortment of ducks, shorebirds, and gulls, and the surrounding shrubs and trees can sometimes hold migrant songbirds.

DIRECTIONS

From Presque Isle take US Route 1 North to the split with Route 164. From this split, continue on US Route 1 for 3 miles and turn left onto Lyndon Street.

After 0.2 miles, Lyndon Street connects with Route 164. Turn right and take your immediate left onto Grove Street. Grove Street bends to the left; take your first right onto Caribou Street and drive to the end. You'll see a small park on the right with a paved pathway; this is your vantage for the pond.

Collins Pond is most notable for its impressive haul of rare geese. Large flocks of Canada Geese, sometimes several thousand, can be found on this small body of water where they don't have to worry about hunters. Mid-October is the best time for rarities, which can include Greater White-fronted, Snow, Cackling, and even Pink-footed or Barnacle Geese.

Rare geese notwithstanding, Collins Pond is productive for other water-fowl, gulls, and shorebirds. April and September tend to be best for ducks; large numbers of Northern Shoveler, Blue- and Green-winged Teal, and Hooded and Common Mergansers have been recorded, among other species. Large congregations of gulls from late fall through early spring are fun to sort through (for some people, at least) and can produce uncommon species like Iceland (sometimes over a dozen), Lesser Black-backed, and Glaucous.

When water levels are low, mudflats are revealed that provide habitat for migrant shorebirds. August through October is best. Killdeer, Greater and Lesser Yellowlegs, and Solitary, Spotted, and Least Sandpipers are usually most numerous, but Collins Pond has attracted its fair share of more uncommon species. Careful sorting could pay off with an American Golden-Plover or Pectoral Sandpiper. And don't ignore the trees and shrubbery along the paved path and the surrounding neighborhood: these can hold migrant warblers and other songbirds in spring and fall.

RARITIES

Barnacle Goose, October 2011; Pink-footed Goose, October 2013

SITE AR7 Limestone/Fort Fairfield Goose Tour

TOWN Limestone. DeLorme Map 65: B–C2–3. SEASON April, October–November, December. VISITATION 2–3 hrs. Restroom facilities at local businesses in towns along the route. & HIGHLIGHTS Migrant waterfowl; open-country passerines.

The fields and ponds of Aroostook County are home to thousands of Canada Geese and a large diversity of waterfowl in spring and fall. They move around a lot, but this loop highlights some of the most consistently productive spots.

October is typically the best month for large numbers of geese, and the sorting through the flocks can often produce a rarity or two. Duck watching is best when the ice starts to melt in early to mid-April.

DIRECTIONS

I'd recommend that you start your waterfowl excursion from **Collins Pond** in Caribou (site AR6), which can be very productive for ducks and geese itself. From the park at the end of Caribou Street, backtrack to Route 161 and turn north. Cross the river and take your second left onto Route 89 East. Turn left onto US Route 1 North and follow this for a half mile, turning left again to stay on US Route 1. In 0.2 miles stay to the right to follow Route 89 East for another 9.7 miles to Limestone.

Along the way, you'll pass by several fields that could have flocks of geese. However, one of the best spots is right in Limestone itself. When you come to the junction with Route 1A, turn left. Very shortly you'll see a small dirt pull-off on the right, at the edge of a pond. Park here and scan the pond, which often holds flocks of loafing geese. Cackling and Greater White-fronted Geese have been seen mixed with the Canada Geese here.

From here, turn around and head south on Route 1A for 0.9 miles. Turn right onto Bog Road and continue for 1.3 miles and turn left onto Ward Road. Follow this for 0.8 miles and turn left onto Lake Road, which ends at a parking lot and boat launch. This is **Trafton Lake,** which is a popular spot for geese and ducks. Greater White-fronted and Cackling Geese have been seen here, along with several species of diving ducks.

From the parking area head back out to Ward Road and turn left. In 0.7 miles turn left onto Route 223. This brings you back to Route 1A in 1.5 miles; turn right to follow Route 1A South. Continue for 8 miles. Just before crossing the river, you can turn left onto Riverside Avenue, which turns into Russell Road. This follows the Aroostook River and gives you some vantages to scan for ducks and geese. Alternatively, follow Route 1A across the Aroostook River and take your first right onto High Street (Route 161). This also passes along the river and nearby fields and eventually brings you right back to US Route 1 in Caribou. Keep in mind that geese can be found in any field along this route, so it's worth keeping an eye out as you drive. Additionally, dirt fields (especially recently plowed) can be productive for open-country passerines such as Horned Lark, American Pipit, Snow Bunting, and even Lapland Longspur in the fall and spring, and you might even luck upon a Rough-legged Hawk or Snowy Owl.

Black-legged Kittiwake, November–December 2011

SITE AR8 Aroostook National Wildlife Refuge

TOWN Presque Isle. DeLorme Map 65: E1. **SEASON** All year, but especially May–July. **VISITATION** 1–3 hrs. Open half hour before sunrise to half hour after sunset. Visitor center (with restrooms) has limited hours (see website). **HIGHLIGHTS** Breeding and migrant songbirds including Bay-breasted and Cape May Warblers, Boreal Chickadee and Gray Jay, and Upland Sandpiper.

Aroostook National Wildlife Refuge is home to 13 miles of hiking trails that weave through some excellent habitats. The woodlands here are mixed with some nice patches of spruce and small boggy areas, giving the area a boreal feel. Adding to the diversity, the nearby airfield can hold grassland birds.

DIRECTIONS

From US Route 1 North in Caribou bear right onto Route 89 toward Limestone. Continue for 7.4 miles and turn left onto Loring Commerce Road (also called Commerce Center Road). In 1.3 miles bear right at the fork onto Refuge Road, and the visitor center for Aroostook NWR will be on your right.

You can park here and take one of the hiking trails, or continue driving on Refuge Road to other parking areas. My favorite area is around East Loring Lake, around 2 miles beyond the visitor center, and the East Loring Trail, which is a longer (3.5-mile) hike that starts at the visitor center and heads north. The Don Lima Trail is a nice shorter loop that starts and ends from the visitor center parking area. However, several other trails are worth exploring—pick up a map at the visitor center or use the link below.

Mixed woodland along the trails makes for good habitat for breeding warblers and other passerines. At least fifteen species of warblers breed here, possibly upward of twenty if you include some separate chunks of national wildlife refuge property. More sought-after species like Tennessee, Mourning, Bay-breasted, and Cape May are possible. Boreal Chickadees and Gray Jays are uncommon to rare. Make sure to check the airfield on your drive in (near where you bear right toward the visitor center)—this can produce breeding Upland Sandpipers, Savannah Sparrows, and American Kestrels. East Loring Lake (next to the northernmost parking lot) and the nearby smaller wetlands can hold ducks, including Blue- and Green-winged Teal, Ring-necked Duck, and Hooded Merganser.

For a trail map go to USFWS's website at http://www.fws.gov and search for "Moosehorn Complex."

SITE AR9 Stockholm–Van Buren Path

TOWN Stockholm. DeLorme Map 69: E5. SEASON All year, but especially **May–August**. VISITATION 1–3 hrs. No restroom facilities. HIGHLIGHTS Boreal specialties (especially Boreal Chickadee, Gray Jay, and Black-backed Woodpecker); breeding songbirds including spruce-loving warblers and Yellow-bellied and Olive-sided Flycatchers.

This path has similar habitat and birds to what you'll find at the Muscovic Road (it's very nearby) and Square Lake Road but offers some quieter walking away from the potential of logging trucks.

DIRECTIONS

Coming from Presque Isle on US Route 1 North (toward Caribou), reset your odometer as you cross the Aroostook River just outside downtown Presque Isle. In 7.7 miles turn left onto Route 164. Continue on Route 164 into downtown Caribou and prepare for a confusing little jog. You're looking for Route 161 North. This involves taking a left onto Herschel Street, about 0.2 miles past the crossing over the Collins Pond outflow, then taking a left at the end of Herschel Street (which turns into Prospect Street), and quickly taking a right onto Sweden Road/Route 161. Once on Route 161, it's a straight shot north for 13.6 miles. Then turn right onto Stockholm Road. Continue on Stockholm Road for 2.2 miles until you cross the Little Madawaska River. From this crossing, drive another 0.2 miles until you see the path cross the road (it's obvious—if you see School Street on your right, you've gone a few feet too far). Turn left onto the path, which takes you to a baseball field, where you can park.

From the ball field, continue walking northwest along the path. After a few tenths of a mile you'll come to an obvious split. Either way can be productive, but I like to turn right here. For the next 2 miles you'll be walking through some nice spruce forest, open areas, and bogs. The birding can be excellent. Boreal Chickadees and Gray Jays are both regular here year-round,

Black-backed Woodpecker,
Aroostook County. © Luke Seitz

and Black-backed Woodpeckers are occasionally seen. Warbler diversity is high. Northern Waterthrush, Nashville, Magnolia, Blackburnian, and Yellow-rumped Warblers are particularly common, but also keep an eye out for scarcer species like Cape May, Bay-breasted, and Tennessee. Yellow-bellied Flycatcher is fairly common. In shrubbier, more cut-over areas, Olive-sided Flycatcher, Lincoln's Sparrow, and Palm Warbler occur. Although it has never been reported here, American Three-toed Woodpecker has been seen nearby and should always be considered a possibility.

About 2 miles from the split, the path intersects with the upper end of the Muscovic Road (see site AR10). I usually turn around here, but for those who fancy a longer walk, you can turn left onto Muscovic Road and make it all the way back down to Route 161. From there, you can head south and turn left on Lake Street, which cuts back into the village of Stockholm.

If you haven't undertaken this approximately 8-mile loop but still have some time, return to the split and take the other option, which heads southwest. This has the same types of habitat and birds as the northern split and is certainly worth some time. From there, retrace your steps back to the parking area at the ball field.

It's worth mentioning that, as at all other forested sites in northern Maine, fall and winter here can be very quiet. However, all the resident boreal specialties and finches are still around and can actually be easier to find in winter. The Stockholm–Van Buren Path is a great place for a hike or snowshoe at any time of year, even when there aren't colorful warblers for special entertainment.

SITE AR10 Muscovic Road

TOWN Stockholm. DeLorme Map 65: E5. **SEASON** Year-round, but especially **May–August.** **VISITATION** 1–2 hrs. No restroom facilities. **HIGHLIGHTS** Boreal specialties (Boreal Chickadee, Black-backed and, rarely, American Three-toed Woodpeckers); breeding songbirds including Rusty Blackbird, and Blackpoll and Wilson's Warblers.

This dirt road holds some excellent boreal habitat close to Route 161. It is not heavily trafficked (except for the occasional logging truck) and offers a pleasant roadside stroll with productive birding. The mosaic of bog and spruce forest can hold Black-backed and American Three-toed Woodpeckers, many breeding warblers, and finches year-round.

DIRECTIONS

Follow the directions under site AR9 to get onto Route 161 North from Caribou. From the same starting point of Route 161, continue north for 15.5 miles. Cross the slow-moving Madawaska River and take the next dirt road on the right. This is the Muscovic Road.

Shortly down the road, you'll see a wide dirt pull-off on the left. I recommend parking here and continuing on foot, although birding by vehicle is possible (just watch for logging trucks). You're already in great habitat at the pull-off—Boreal Chickadees and Gray Jays are often around. Continuing north, you will soon enter a mixture of open bog and conifer forest. In the breeding season, diversity is excellent: warblers, vireos, thrushes, and flycatchers sing loudly from the roadside forest. Listen for Wilson's Warblers in the shrubby alder thickets, and keep an eye out for Olive-sided Flycatchers perched upon the snags in the bog. Rusty Blackbirds are irregular breeders. This stretch has held American Three-toed Woodpecker, although Black-backed Woodpecker is more regular. Some of the more common species from May through August include Yellow-bellied and Alder Flycatchers, both species of kinglet, Swainson's and Hermit Thrush, Nashville, Magnolia, and Yellow-rumped Warblers, Northern Parula, Northern Waterthrush, White-throated Sparrow, and Dark-eyed Junco.

Outside the breeding season, the forest is much quieter. However, even in winter this road can be worth a walk for boreal specialties and finches. Both White-winged and Red Crossbills, Pine Siskins, and Evening Grosbeaks occur year-round, although numbers fluctuate greatly. Pine Grosbeaks and Common Redpolls can sometimes be found in winter, and the wheezy calls of Boreal Chickadees still resonate from the cold spruces.

In exactly a mile the road starts heading uphill and another dirt road splits off to the left. This is the end of the best boggy boreal habitat, but it is always fun to explore the logging roads further. If you choose to do this, keep in mind that logging trucks are still active in the area, so be aware and get far off the road if one is approaching.

RARITIES

Acadian Flycatcher, June 2012

SITE AR11 Sinclair Area

TOWN Sinclair. DeLorme Map 70: D4.   **SEASON** April, **May–July,** August–December.   **VISITATION** 1–2 hrs. No restroom facilities.
HIGHLIGHTS Breeding songbirds and Cliff Swallow; storm-grounded waterbirds.

The small town of Sinclair lies at the southeastern tip of Long Lake. Although not a major birding destination, the lake is worth a check in spring and fall for migrant waterfowl, and the drive in passes through productive boreal forest. The longer drive up to Saint Agatha is productive for scenic views as much as birding.

DIRECTIONS

Follow the directions under site AR9 to get onto Route 161 North out of Caribou. From the same starting point of Route 161, continue north for 26.2 miles and turn right onto Route 162 toward Sinclair/Saint Agatha.

Route 162 runs through productive woodland, with many breeding song-birds. The best place to stop is 3.2 miles along the road, where you'll see a gated road heading off to the left. This road leads to a wastewater treatment facility and is a great place for a short walk. Park at the start of the road (don't block the gate) and walk up—it's less than a mile long. The spruce forest can be loud with the voices of songbirds in May and June and has produced Black-backed Woodpecker, Boreal Chickadee, and Cape May and Bay-breasted Warblers in the past.

Continue farther along Route 162 to the town of Sinclair. Turn right at the T intersection in town and cross over the lake outflow (which often holds Common Mergansers). Immediately on your left is a boat launch where you can view the lake. Especially after stormy weather in spring and fall, ducks such as scoters (all three species are possible) and Long-tailed Duck can occur, and Red-necked and Horned Grebes rarely drop in. Cliff Swallows nest in town and can often be seen coursing over the water.

From here you can turn around and continue north up Route 162 toward the town of Saint Agatha, looking for ducks and breeding Common Terns along the way, or backtrack to Route 161.

SITE AR12 Square Lake Road

TOWN Sinclair. DeLorme Map 68: D2. SEASON May–August.
VISITATION 2–3 hrs. No restroom facilities. HIGHLIGHTS Boreal specialties; breeding songbirds (especially warblers, including Blackpoll).

This road was put on the birding map when American Three-toed Woodpeckers were discovered here with some regularity. Although they have not been seen for several years, Square Lake Road is still an excellent and accessible area of boreal habitat. It holds all the boreal specialties (Spruce Grouse, Black-backed Woodpecker, Gray Jay, and Boreal Chickadee), along with at least twenty species of breeding warblers, Olive-sided Flycatcher, and Lincoln's Sparrow, among others. This is mostly roadside birding, although it is possible to explore off-road if you are feeling adventurous.

DIRECTIONS

Follow the directions under site AR9 to get onto Route 161 just outside downtown Caribou. Once on Route 161 it's a straight shot north for 28.4 more miles. Be very aware of moose on this drive, especially at dawn and dusk—they are plentiful and can be very difficult to spot. Just after crossing over a stream (and

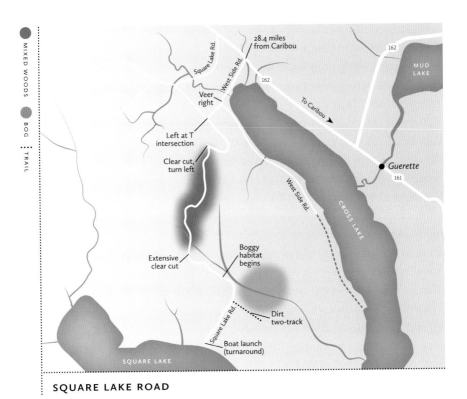

SQUARE LAKE ROAD

where the power-line cut crosses the road) look for a road heading left. This is West Side Road, which leads to Square Lake Road. Your birding starts here.

You can sometimes find Bay-breasted Warbler right at the turnoff from Route 161 (listen on either side of the bridge), but the best birding is farther down the road. Continue straight (heading southwest), crossing a small bridge, and take your first right. This will lead to a T intersection. The area around the T often holds Bay-breasted Warbler and Boreal Chickadee. Turn left and continue through mixed woods, veering right at the next intersection (near a brush dump). The road then curves to the right, and you'll quickly notice an extensive clear cut on your right. Pull over here, as it can be an excellent spot for Mourning Warbler, Lincoln's Sparrow, and Olive-sided Flycatcher. American Woodcocks and Wilson's Snipe are often audible at dawn and dusk.

Continue by taking the next left turn about midway along the clear cut. You're now entering a longer stretch of mixed woodland that holds more common species, including Magnolia Warbler, Swainson's and Hermit Thrush, and Ruffed Grouse. You'll pass a small clear cut and dirt road heading off to the right, then more woods, and then another small clear cut on the left. Just beyond this clear cut is a bog on the right that hosts breeding Yellow-bellied Flycatcher.

Just past the small bog, you'll enter the most extensive clear cut on Square Lake Road. It's worth getting out here and walking for a bit, enjoying the vociferous Lincoln's Sparrows and sometimes an Olive-sided Flycatcher or two. Broad-winged and Sharp-shinned Hawks can be seen soaring overhead, and Northern Harriers have been documented breeding here. The road heading off to the right goes through more mixed woods and small cuts and can be fun to explore, but continue straight for the best boreal habitat. You'll pass through another stretch of more deciduous-dominated forest and soon come upon a patch of alders on your left. Pull over around here. Off to the east is an extensive system of bogs, and the habitat along the road for the next half mile or so is an excellent mix of spruce forest and boggy alder swales. Wilson's and Palm Warblers breed here; it's fun to learn how to distinguish their trilled songs from the more common Dark-eyed Juncos and Swamp Sparrows. Black-backed Woodpeckers are regularly seen. In the taller larches and spruces, listen for the exceptionally loud song of Tennessee Warbler, which can be remarkably common on this road in some years (although Nashville is almost always more common and widespread). Cape May and Bay-breasted Warblers are often present as well, and Gray Jays and Boreal Chickadees are fairly common. Spruce Grouse is rare.

As you walk south you'll notice an overgrown track heading off to the left and a more open view of the bog. Walk along this track (it is often quite wet and muddy) for as long as your footwear allows. Many of the aforementioned boreal specialties occur here, and moose are often seen in morning and evening. American Three-toed Woodpeckers, a highly sought-after bird in Maine, used to occur here regularly, but they haven't been seen in several years. However, the habitat is excellent, and a sighting is always a remote possibility (although Black-backed Woodpecker is always more regular).

Returning from the track to Square Lake Road, continuing south will bring you through some more productive boreal habitat that can be excellent for general birding (especially breeding warblers). At the end of the road is a boat launch that overlooks Square Lake (this isn't usually very productive for birding, although there are usually several Blackburnian Warblers singing within earshot). It is recommended that you turn around and work your way back up Square Lake Road, with windows open and ears alert for any singing birds you might have missed on the way down.

SITE AR13 The North Maine Woods

TOWN N/A. SEASON April–September, but especially **May–July.**
VISITATION At least one full day, preferably more. Daily fee of $7 for Maine residents, $12 for nonresidents. Rustic campsites; see website for more details. No restroom facilities, other than outhouses at some campsites.
HIGHLIGHTS Boreal specialties (Spruce Grouse, American Three-toed and Black-backed Woodpeckers, Gray Jay, and Boreal Chickadee); breeding songbirds (over twenty species of breeding warblers including Tennessee, Cape May, Bay-breasted, and Mourning); winter finches, including both crossbills and Pine Grosbeak.

The entirety of northwestern Maine—generally north of Baxter State Park and west of Route 11—is collectively called the North Maine Woods. Most of the land is owned by several private industrial logging corporations and state agencies, which allow public access to the woods through a variety of different checkpoints. Snaking through the vast forests are hundreds of miles of logging roads, some of which are heavily traveled by large trucks, while others are abandoned for years at a time. Within the North Maine Woods is the Allagash Wilderness Waterway, a popular outdoor destination, and many rustic campsites managed by the North Maine Woods organization.

Exploring the North Maine Woods is one of the most adventurous activities for a Maine birder. Highly sought-after boreal species can be delightfully common, and you could literally spend days without seeing another human being. In addition to birds, mammals such as moose and black bear are more common here than anywhere else in the state, and you might even get lucky enough to glimpse an endangered Canada lynx. The sense of remoteness is fun but also overwhelming—where does one even start when looking for birds here? It would hardly do the area justice to mention only a couple of sites, and logging activities often change the habitat and render certain hot spots moot from year to year. Therefore, instead of a set of places to provide specific birds, the North Maine Woods should be thought of as a lesson in birding by habitat. The 3.5 million acres include lakes and rivers, bogs and

Boreal habitat in the timberlands of northern Maine. © Derek Lovitch

clear cuts, thick spruce and tall hardwoods. Simply driving or walking along the endless roads will certainly be productive, especially when breeding birds are most active in May and June (but bring insect repellent).

Some of Maine's most sought-after species are the "boreal specialties": Spruce Grouse, Black-backed and American Three-toed Woodpeckers, Gray Jay, and Boreal Chickadee. All these species occur in the North Maine Woods. The woodpeckers are usually toughest, but look for them especially in areas with plenty of spruce and dead trees with loose bark to flake off in their search of grubs. Especially Black-backed Woodpecker can be quite vocal and conspicuous when feeding youngsters in June; American Three-toed is much less common and quieter and tends to be found in denser, wetter areas. Spruce Grouse is difficult to predict but can often be seen picking gravel from the roadside. If you're lucky, you might even catch the flurry of wingbeats as a male displays in spring. Gray Jays and Boreal Chickadees are the most common of the boreal specialties and can be found anywhere with conifers.

Of course, the woods hold more than just those boreal species. Clear cuts and bogs provide interesting habitats that hold many breeding species. Alder Flycatchers and Nashville Warblers are abundant. Fox Sparrows, with their clear whistled song, are often found in regenerating clear cuts with dense ten- to twenty-year-old spruce trees. Palm Warblers, Olive-sided Flycatchers (look for them on snags), Lincoln's Sparrows, and Wilson's Warblers (alder thickets) are other species that prefer these more open regenerating habitats. Mourning Warblers like similar open areas but with denser thickets of undergrowth and some taller trees, and show a special preference for raspberry. Cape May and Bay-breasted Warblers can be found in any place with lots of spruce and fir . . . and the list goes on and on.

That is really just the tip of the iceberg. Who knows what else will turn up in this vast forest? Are Boreal Owls regular breeders? Might Yellow Rails or Sedge Wrens occur in one of the bogs? Only more birder exploration will tell!

DIRECTIONS

Visit the North Maine Woods website to plan your trip carefully. I usually enter from the Oxbow Checkpoint (DeLorme Map 58: B2), along Route 11 just south of Masardis, or the Telos Checkpoint west of Baxter State Park (covered in Piscataquis County). There are many other options, and rustic campsites allow you to stay for a longer period of time; but you must register at a checkpoint before deciding to stay overnight. Also note that there are no facilities, so be sure you have plenty of fuel, food, and water. Outside of spring and summer, maintenance of the logging roads is variable. Winter finches and boreal specialties are still around, but check with the North Maine Woods to find out which roads are passable.

For more information and to plan your visit, look for a variety of resources at http://www.northmainewoods.org/.

17 | Species Accounts

The following bar graphs cover 286 species that occur annually in Maine, not including rarities that occur in very small numbers (e.g., Pacific Loon, Western Kingbird, Connecticut Warbler, etc.) on an annual or near-annual basis. A few exceptions are made for sought-after species such as northern owls, but for the most part, if you can count the number of annual reports on one hand, I did not include them here.

The bar graphs include four levels of abundance: Rare, Very Uncommon, Uncommon to Fairly Common, and Common to Abundant. These abundances are generalizations, used only as a suggestion about what to consider at a given time of year, and not designed to be used for identification purposes. These are not scientific analyses, either, as they are less a quantification of actual abundances than the perception of abundance based on detection probabilities when the observer is in the right place at the right time. For example, owls are rarely detected, even though some, such as Barred and Great Horned, are fairly common and are found throughout much of the state. Furthermore, statuses change from year to year, and in the face of climate change, such statuses (especially arrival and departure dates) are fluctuating dramatically. Keep in mind, also, that Maine's avifauna can be the "tale of two states," with marked difference in status between the north and south, or inland versus coastal.

The right-hand margin on each right-hand page offers a key for a few additional resources that are included in each species account. Arrows for increasing or decreasing populations are noted. Unfortunately, the lack of a comprehensive survey or modern resource for population changes in Maine precludes a comprehensive analysis or listing of trends. An egg symbol denotes species that breed in the state, and a wave symbol denotes pelagic species.

Maine hosts a number of species that are much sought-after by visiting and resident birders alike, from "boreal specialties" that reach the southern and eastern limits of their breeding range in Maine to breeding seabirds on offshore islands. For these "most wanted" species, a brief synopsis of the species occurrence, status, and suggested sites to target is included after the bar graph. This takes the place of the extra appendix included in most bird-finding guides for the "target." While this is by no means a complete list of all the species you may want to see in Maine and is not an exhaustive compilation of every single site where a species is possible, it should help narrow your search. The most important sites (where you have the best chance of finding the species) are listed in roughly descending order, sometimes ranked arbitrarily. For additional species, please refer to the index.

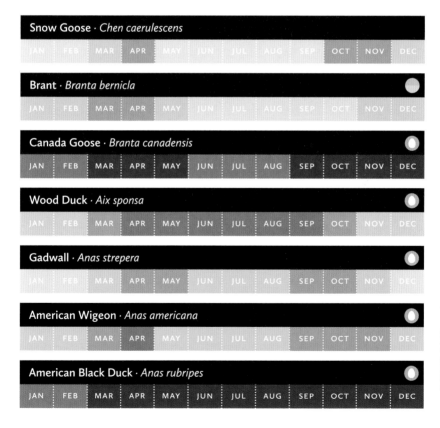

Mallard · *Anas platyrhynchos*

JAN	FEB	MAR	APR	MAY	JUN	JUL	AUG	SEP	OCT	NOV	DEC

Blue-winged Teal · *Anas discors*

JAN	FEB	MAR	APR	MAY	JUN	JUL	AUG	SEP	OCT	NOV	DEC

Northern Shoveler · *Anas clypeata*

JAN	FEB	MAR	APR	MAY	JUN	JUL	AUG	SEP	OCT	NOV	DEC

Northern Pintail · *Anas acuta*

JAN	FEB	MAR	APR	MAY	JUN	JUL	AUG	SEP	OCT	NOV	DEC

Green-winged Teal · *Anas crecca*

JAN	FEB	MAR	APR	MAY	JUN	JUL	AUG	SEP	OCT	NOV	DEC

Redhead · *Aythya americana*

JAN	FEB	MAR	APR	MAY	JUN	JUL	AUG	SEP	OCT	NOV	DEC

Ring-necked Duck · *Aythya collaris*

JAN	FEB	MAR	APR	MAY	JUN	JUL	AUG	SEP	OCT	NOV	DEC

Greater Scaup · *Aythya marila*

JAN	FEB	MAR	APR	MAY	JUN	JUL	AUG	SEP	OCT	NOV	DEC

Lesser Scaup · *Aythya affinis*

JAN	FEB	MAR	APR	MAY	JUN	JUL	AUG	SEP	OCT	NOV	DEC

King Eider · *Somateria spectabilis*

JAN	FEB	MAR	APR	MAY	JUN	JUL	AUG	SEP	OCT	NOV	DEC

Rare in winter, often with only 1–2 reported each season. Likely more regular Downeast, but most reports come from more heavily birded south coast, and mostly distinctive drakes. Site list: Y4, C3, WN10.

Common Eider · *Somateria mollissima*

JAN	FEB	MAR	APR	MAY	JUN	JUL	AUG	SEP	OCT	NOV	DEC

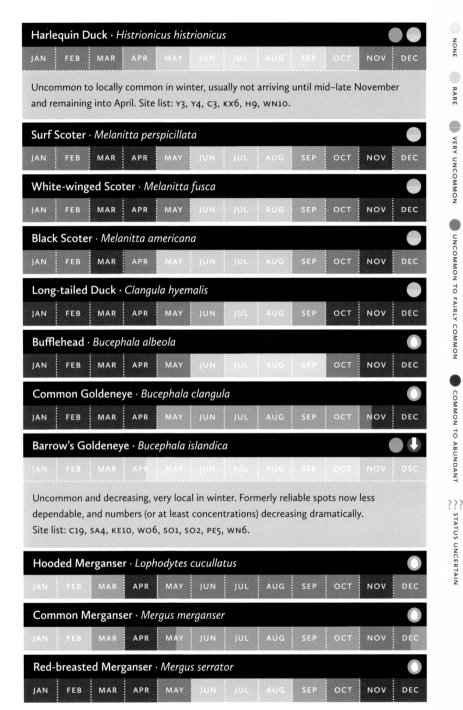

Harlequin Duck · *Histrionicus histrionicus*

JAN	FEB	MAR	APR	MAY	JUN	JUL	AUG	SEP	OCT	NOV	DEC

Uncommon to locally common in winter, usually not arriving until mid–late November and remaining into April. Site list: Y3, Y4, C3, KX6, H9, WN10.

Surf Scoter · *Melanitta perspicillata*

JAN	FEB	MAR	APR	MAY	JUN	JUL	AUG	SEP	OCT	NOV	DEC

White-winged Scoter · *Melanitta fusca*

JAN	FEB	MAR	APR	MAY	JUN	JUL	AUG	SEP	OCT	NOV	DEC

Black Scoter · *Melanitta americana*

JAN	FEB	MAR	APR	MAY	JUN	JUL	AUG	SEP	OCT	NOV	DEC

Long-tailed Duck · *Clangula hyemalis*

JAN	FEB	MAR	APR	MAY	JUN	JUL	AUG	SEP	OCT	NOV	DEC

Bufflehead · *Bucephala albeola*

JAN	FEB	MAR	APR	MAY	JUN	JUL	AUG	SEP	OCT	NOV	DEC

Common Goldeneye · *Bucephala clangula*

JAN	FEB	MAR	APR	MAY	JUN	JUL	AUG	SEP	OCT	NOV	DEC

Barrow's Goldeneye · *Bucephala islandica*

JAN	FEB	MAR	APR	MAY	JUN	JUL	AUG	SEP	OCT	NOV	DEC

Uncommon and decreasing, very local in winter. Formerly reliable spots now less dependable, and numbers (or at least concentrations) decreasing dramatically. Site list: C19, SA4, KE10, WO6, SO1, SO2, PE5, WN6.

Hooded Merganser · *Lophodytes cucullatus*

JAN	FEB	MAR	APR	MAY	JUN	JUL	AUG	SEP	OCT	NOV	DEC

Common Merganser · *Mergus merganser*

JAN	FEB	MAR	APR	MAY	JUN	JUL	AUG	SEP	OCT	NOV	DEC

Red-breasted Merganser · *Mergus serrator*

JAN	FEB	MAR	APR	MAY	JUN	JUL	AUG	SEP	OCT	NOV	DEC

NONE

RARE

VERY UNCOMMON

UNCOMMON TO FAIRLY COMMON

COMMON TO ABUNDANT

??? STATUS UNCERTAIN

INCREASING

DECREASING

IRRUPTIVE

THREATENED OR ENDANGERED IN MAINE

BREEDS IN MAINE

PRIMARILY COASTAL

PRIMARILY PELAGIC

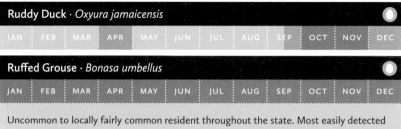

Ruddy Duck · *Oxyura jamaicensis*

JAN	FEB	MAR	APR	MAY	JUN	JUL	AUG	SEP	OCT	NOV	DEC

Ruffed Grouse · *Bonasa umbellus*

JAN	FEB	MAR	APR	MAY	JUN	JUL	AUG	SEP	OCT	NOV	DEC

Uncommon to locally fairly common resident throughout the state. Most easily detected when males are drumming in early spring, but possible almost anywhere in mixed forest habitats. Site list: C20, O8, O9, L11, L12, KX10, KX13, WO9, F8, F10, SO6, PE9, PE10, WN12, WN 15, PS3, PS4, PS5, PS7, AR3, AR11, AR13.

Spruce Grouse · *Dendragapus fuliginosus*

JAN	FEB	MAR	APR	MAY	JUN	JUL	AUG	SEP	OCT	NOV	DEC

Uncommon and usually secretive resident of boreal forest. Most readily found when males are displaying in early spring, when females are leading young around in early summer, and mostly when you are not looking for them! Site list: O8, O9, H9, H12, F6, F10, SO6, SO7, PE7, PE10, WN4, WN8, WN10, WN12, WN15, PS1, PS4, PS5, PS6, PS7, AR2, AR9, AR12, AR13.

Wild Turkey · *Meleagris gallopavo*

JAN	FEB	MAR	APR	MAY	JUN	JUL	AUG	SEP	OCT	NOV	DEC

Red-throated Loon · *Gavia stellata*

JAN	FEB	MAR	APR	MAY	JUN	JUL	AUG	SEP	OCT	NOV	DEC

Common Loon · *Gavia immer*

JAN	FEB	MAR	APR	MAY	JUN	JUL	AUG	SEP	OCT	NOV	DEC

Widespread breeder in small numbers of inland lakes. Locally common on saltwater in winter throughout the coast, with immatures and nonbreeding adults regular along the coast year-round. Site list (breeding): O12, AN5, KE6, WO1, WO4, F7, F8, PE3.

Pied-billed Grebe · *Podilymbus podiceps*

JAN	FEB	MAR	APR	MAY	JUN	JUL	AUG	SEP	OCT	NOV	DEC

Horned Grebe · *Podiceps auritus*

JAN	FEB	MAR	APR	MAY	JUN	JUL	AUG	SEP	OCT	NOV	DEC

Red-necked Grebe · *Podiceps grisegena*

JAN	FEB	MAR	APR	MAY	JUN	JUL	AUG	SEP	OCT	NOV	DEC

Northern Fulmar · *Fulmaris glacialis*

JAN	FEB	MAR	APR	MAY	JUN	JUL	AUG	SEP	OCT	NOV	DEC

Cory's Shearwater · *Calonectris diomedea*

JAN	FEB	MAR	APR	MAY	JUN	JUL	AUG	SEP	OCT	NOV	DEC

Great Shearwater · *Puffinus gravis*

JAN	FEB	MAR	APR	MAY	JUN	JUL	AUG	SEP	OCT	NOV	DEC

Sooty Shearwater · *Puffinus griseus*

JAN	FEB	MAR	APR	MAY	JUN	JUL	AUG	SEP	OCT	NOV	DEC

Manx Shearwater · *Puffinus puffinus*

JAN	FEB	MAR	APR	MAY	JUN	JUL	AUG	SEP	OCT	NOV	DEC

Very local, but perhaps expanding, breeding visitor to offshore islands. Rarely seen from land; boat trips are your best option. Site list: Y8, Y12, C3, C10, L3, H7.

Wilson's Storm-Petrel · *Oceanites oceanicus*

JAN	FEB	MAR	APR	MAY	JUN	JUL	AUG	SEP	OCT	NOV	DEC

Leach's Storm-Petrel · *Oceanodroma leucorhoa*

JAN	FEB	MAR	APR	MAY	JUN	JUL	AUG	SEP	OCT	NOV	DEC

Common to abundant breeder on inaccessible, offshore islands. Rarely seen from land; boat trips are your best option. Site list: Y8, C10, L3, H7.

Northern Gannet · *Morus bassanus*

JAN	FEB	MAR	APR	MAY	JUN	JUL	AUG	SEP	OCT	NOV	DEC

Double-crested Cormorant · *Phalacrocorax auritus*

JAN	FEB	MAR	APR	MAY	JUN	JUL	AUG	SEP	OCT	NOV	DEC

Great Cormorant · *Phalacrocorax carbo*

JAN	FEB	MAR	APR	MAY	JUN	JUL	AUG	SEP	OCT	NOV	DEC

Very local and declining breeder, with immature birds rare but regular along the coast in summer. Locally common in winter throughout the coast and rare inland, especially along large rivers. Site list (breeding): H1. Site list (nonbreeding): Y3, Y4, Y12, C2, C3, L1, KX6, H4, H6, H7, W10.

American Bittern · *Botaurus lentiginosus*

JAN	FEB	MAR	APR	MAY	JUN	JUL	AUG	SEP	OCT	NOV	DEC

Least Bittern · *Ixobrychus exilis*

JAN	FEB	MAR	APR	MAY	JUN	JUL	AUG	SEP	OCT	NOV	DEC

Great Blue Heron · *Ardea herodias*

JAN	FEB	MAR	APR	MAY	JUN	JUL	AUG	SEP	OCT	NOV	DEC

Great Egret · *Ardea alba*

JAN	FEB	MAR	APR	MAY	JUN	JUL	AUG	SEP	OCT	NOV	DEC

Snowy Egret · *Egretta thula*

JAN	FEB	MAR	APR	MAY	JUN	JUL	AUG	SEP	OCT	NOV	DEC

Little Blue Heron · *Egretta caerulea*

JAN	FEB	MAR	APR	MAY	JUN	JUL	AUG	SEP	OCT	NOV	DEC

Green Heron · *Butorides virescens*

JAN	FEB	MAR	APR	MAY	JUN	JUL	AUG	SEP	OCT	NOV	DEC

Black-crowned Night-Heron · *Nycticorax nycticorax*

JAN	FEB	MAR	APR	MAY	JUN	JUL	AUG	SEP	OCT	NOV	DEC

Glossy Ibis · *Plegadis falcinellus*

JAN	FEB	MAR	APR	MAY	JUN	JUL	AUG	SEP	OCT	NOV	DEC

Turkey Vulture · *Cathartes aura*

JAN	FEB	MAR	APR	MAY	JUN	JUL	AUG	SEP	OCT	NOV	DEC

Osprey · *Pandion haliaetus*

JAN	FEB	MAR	APR	MAY	JUN	JUL	AUG	SEP	OCT	NOV	DEC

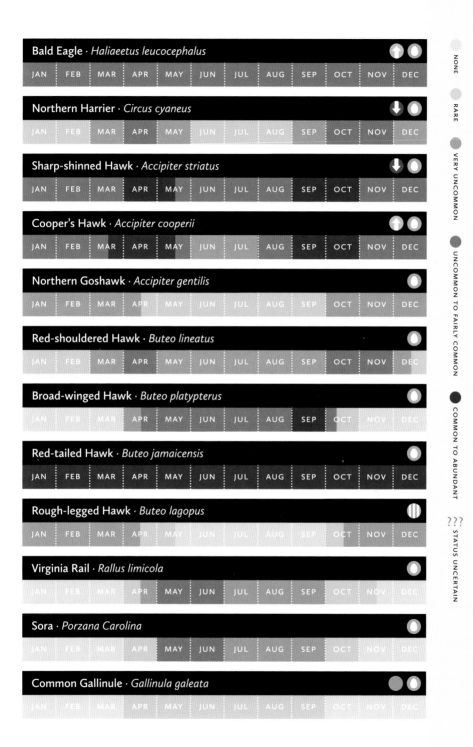

Bald Eagle · *Haliaeetus leucocephalus*

JAN | FEB | MAR | APR | MAY | JUN | JUL | AUG | SEP | OCT | NOV | DEC

Northern Harrier · *Circus cyaneus*

JAN | FEB | MAR | APR | MAY | JUN | JUL | AUG | SEP | OCT | NOV | DEC

Sharp-shinned Hawk · *Accipiter striatus*

JAN | FEB | MAR | APR | MAY | JUN | JUL | AUG | SEP | OCT | NOV | DEC

Cooper's Hawk · *Accipiter cooperii*

JAN | FEB | MAR | APR | MAY | JUN | JUL | AUG | SEP | OCT | NOV | DEC

Northern Goshawk · *Accipiter gentilis*

JAN | FEB | MAR | APR | MAY | JUN | JUL | AUG | SEP | OCT | NOV | DEC

Red-shouldered Hawk · *Buteo lineatus*

JAN | FEB | MAR | APR | MAY | JUN | JUL | AUG | SEP | OCT | NOV | DEC

Broad-winged Hawk · *Buteo platypterus*

JAN | FEB | MAR | APR | MAY | JUN | JUL | AUG | SEP | OCT | NOV | DEC

Red-tailed Hawk · *Buteo jamaicensis*

JAN | FEB | MAR | APR | MAY | JUN | JUL | AUG | SEP | OCT | NOV | DEC

Rough-legged Hawk · *Buteo lagopus*

JAN | FEB | MAR | APR | MAY | JUN | JUL | AUG | SEP | OCT | NOV | DEC

Virginia Rail · *Rallus limicola*

JAN | FEB | MAR | APR | MAY | JUN | JUL | AUG | SEP | OCT | NOV | DEC

Sora · *Porzana Carolina*

JAN | FEB | MAR | APR | MAY | JUN | JUL | AUG | SEP | OCT | NOV | DEC

Common Gallinule · *Gallinula galeata*

JAN | FEB | MAR | APR | MAY | JUN | JUL | AUG | SEP | OCT | NOV | DEC

NONE
RARE
VERY UNCOMMON
UNCOMMON TO FAIRLY COMMON
COMMON TO ABUNDANT
??? STATUS UNCERTAIN

INCREASING
DECREASING
IRRUPTIVE
THREATENED OR ENDANGERED IN MAINE
BREEDS IN MAINE
PRIMARILY COASTAL
PRIMARILY PELAGIC

BIRDWATCHING IN MAINE

American Coot · *Fulica Americana*

| JAN | FEB | MAR | APR | MAY | JUN | JUL | AUG | SEP | OCT | NOV | DEC |

Sandhill Crane · *Grus canadensis*

| JAN | FEB | MAR | APR | MAY | JUN | JUL | AUG | SEP | OCT | NOV | DEC |

Increasing, local breeder and now-regular migrant. Site list: O3, AN4, KE6, WO13, SO5.

American Oystercatcher · *Haematopus palliatus*

| JAN | FEB | MAR | APR | MAY | JUN | JUL | AUG | SEP | OCT | NOV | DEC |

Rare, but slowly increasing breeder, but still very local. Site list: Y12, C1.

Black-bellied Plover · *Pluvialis squatarola*

| JAN | FEB | MAR | APR | MAY | JUN | JUL | AUG | SEP | OCT | NOV | DEC |

American Golden-Plover · *Pluvialis dominica*

| JAN | FEB | MAR | APR | MAY | JUN | JUL | AUG | SEP | OCT | NOV | DEC |

Semipalmated Plover · *Charadrius semipalmatus*

| JAN | FEB | MAR | APR | MAY | JUN | JUL | AUG | SEP | OCT | NOV | DEC |

Piping Plover · *Charadrius melodus*

| JAN | FEB | MAR | APR | MAY | JUN | JUL | AUG | SEP | OCT | NOV | DEC |

Endangered breeder only on sandy beaches. Actively managed to protect nests from predators and minimize disturbance, critical for their continued success. Site list: Y7, Y12, C1, SA1, SA2, SA3.

Killdeer · *Charadrius vociferus*

| JAN | FEB | MAR | APR | MAY | JUN | JUL | AUG | SEP | OCT | NOV | DEC |

Spotted Sandpiper · *Actitis macularius*

| JAN | FEB | MAR | APR | MAY | JUN | JUL | AUG | SEP | OCT | NOV | DEC |

Solitary Sandpiper · *Tringa solitaria*

| JAN | FEB | MAR | APR | MAY | JUN | JUL | AUG | SEP | OCT | NOV | DEC |

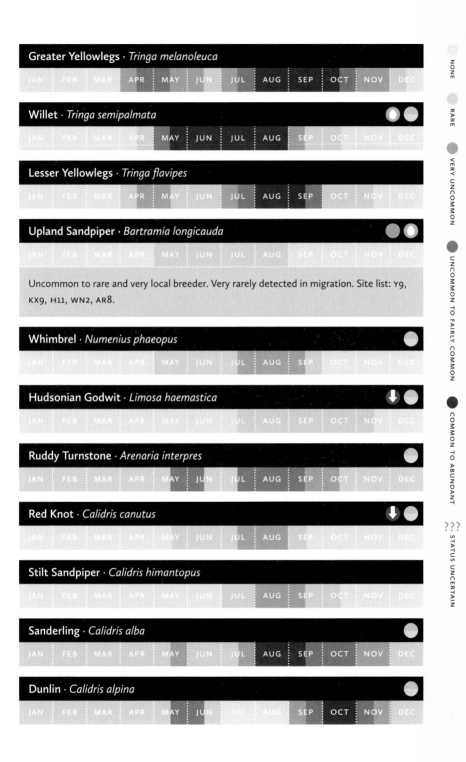

Greater Yellowlegs · *Tringa melanoleuca*

JAN | FEB | MAR | APR | MAY | JUN | JUL | AUG | SEP | OCT | NOV | DEC

Willet · *Tringa semipalmata*

JAN | FEB | MAR | APR | MAY | JUN | JUL | AUG | SEP | OCT | NOV | DEC

Lesser Yellowlegs · *Tringa flavipes*

JAN | FEB | MAR | APR | MAY | JUN | JUL | AUG | SEP | OCT | NOV | DEC

Upland Sandpiper · *Bartramia longicauda*

JAN | FEB | MAR | APR | MAY | JUN | JUL | AUG | SEP | OCT | NOV | DEC

Uncommon to rare and very local breeder. Very rarely detected in migration. Site list: Y9, KX9, H11, WN2, AR8.

Whimbrel · *Numenius phaeopus*

JAN | FEB | MAR | APR | MAY | JUN | JUL | AUG | SEP | OCT | NOV | DEC

Hudsonian Godwit · *Limosa haemastica*

JAN | FEB | MAR | APR | MAY | JUN | JUL | AUG | SEP | OCT | NOV | DEC

Ruddy Turnstone · *Arenaria interpres*

JAN | FEB | MAR | APR | MAY | JUN | JUL | AUG | SEP | OCT | NOV | DEC

Red Knot · *Calidris canutus*

JAN | FEB | MAR | APR | MAY | JUN | JUL | AUG | SEP | OCT | NOV | DEC

Stilt Sandpiper · *Calidris himantopus*

JAN | FEB | MAR | APR | MAY | JUN | JUL | AUG | SEP | OCT | NOV | DEC

Sanderling · *Calidris alba*

JAN | FEB | MAR | APR | MAY | JUN | JUL | AUG | SEP | OCT | NOV | DEC

Dunlin · *Calidris alpina*

JAN | FEB | MAR | APR | MAY | JUN | JUL | AUG | SEP | OCT | NOV | DEC

NONE
RARE
VERY UNCOMMON
UNCOMMON TO FAIRLY COMMON
COMMON TO ABUNDANT
??? STATUS UNCERTAIN

INCREASING
DECREASING
IRRUPTIVE
THREATENED OR ENDANGERED IN MAINE
BREEDS IN MAINE
PRIMARILY COASTAL
PRIMARILY PELAGIC

Purple Sandpiper · *Calidris maritima*

JAN	FEB	MAR	APR	MAY	JUN	JUL	AUG	SEP	OCT	NOV	DEC

Common winter visitor to rocky shorelines throughout the length of the coast. Site list: Y4, Y12, C2, C3, L5, KX5, KX6, H4, H7, H9, WN10.

Baird's Sandpiper · *Calidris bairdii*

JAN	FEB	MAR	APR	MAY	JUN	JUL	AUG	SEP	OCT	NOV	DEC

Fairly rare but regular FALL migrants. One of the "grasspipers" that are often found away from water, they are most regularly seen in Maine on sod farms and a few coastal beaches, especially those that have buildups of seaweed at the high-tide lines. Site list: Y12, C1, O3, SA2, SA3, WN9.

Least Sandpiper · *Calidris minutilla*

JAN	FEB	MAR	APR	MAY	JUN	JUL	AUG	SEP	OCT	NOV	DEC

White-rumped Sandpiper · *Calidris fuscicollis*

JAN	FEB	MAR	APR	MAY	JUN	JUL	AUG	SEP	OCT	NOV	DEC

Uncommon to locally common FALL migrant. Fairly rare spring migrant. Site list: Y1, Y7, Y10, Y12, C1, C2, SA1, SA2, SA3, KX2, WN9.

Buff-breasted Sandpiper · *Trymgites subruficollis*

JAN	FEB	MAR	APR	MAY	JUN	JUL	AUG	SEP	OCT	NOV	DEC

Fairly rare but regular FALL migrants. One of the "grasspipers" that are often found away from water, they are most regularly seen in Maine on sod farms and a few coastal beaches, especially those that have buildups of seaweed at the high-tide lines. Site list: Y12, C1, O3, SA2, SA3, WN9.

Pectoral Sandpiper · *Calidris melanotos*

JAN	FEB	MAR	APR	MAY	JUN	JUL	AUG	SEP	OCT	NOV	DEC

Semipalmated Sandpiper · *Calidris pusilla*

JAN	FEB	MAR	APR	MAY	JUN	JUL	AUG	SEP	OCT	NOV	DEC

Western Sandpiper · *Calidris mauri*

JAN	FEB	MAR	APR	MAY	JUN	JUL	AUG	SEP	OCT	NOV	DEC

Short-billed Dowitcher · *Limnodromus griseus*

JAN	FEB	MAR	APR	MAY	JUN	JUL	AUG	SEP	OCT	NOV	DEC

Long-billed Dowitcher · *Limnodromus scolopaceus*

JAN	FEB	MAR	APR	MAY	JUN	JUL	AUG	SEP	OCT	NOV	DEC

Wilson's Snipe · *Gallinago delicata*

JAN	FEB	MAR	APR	MAY	JUN	JUL	AUG	SEP	OCT	NOV	DEC

American Woodcock · *Scolopax minor*

JAN	FEB	MAR	APR	MAY	JUN	JUL	AUG	SEP	OCT	NOV	DEC

Wilson's Phalarope · *Phalaropus tricolor*

JAN	FEB	MAR	APR	MAY	JUN	JUL	AUG	SEP	OCT	NOV	DEC

Red-necked Phalarope · *Phalaropus lobatus*

JAN	FEB	MAR	APR	MAY	JUN	JUL	AUG	SEP	OCT	NOV	DEC

Red Phalarope · *Phalaropus fulicarius*

JAN	FEB	MAR	APR	MAY	JUN	JUL	AUG	SEP	OCT	NOV	DEC

Great Skua/South Polar Skua · *Stercorarius skua/Stercorarius maccormicki*

JAN	FEB	MAR	APR	MAY	JUN	JUL	AUG	SEP	OCT	NOV	DEC

An identification challenge; the actual status of each species is unclear, as few reports are documented well. Great is probably uncommon offshore in winter, but without any birder access it's hard to know for sure. Seen irregularly in summer—but sometimes for periods they can be somewhat dependable, and they seem to be more frequent in some years than others—and more spring and fall pelagic or whale-watching options could prove this bird to be more regular than current reports suggest. South Polar Skua is seen in summer and fall and is likely the more "regular" warmer-month skua but is still rather rarely detected. Site list: C10, H7.

Pomarine Jaeger · *Stercorarius pomarinus*

JAN	FEB	MAR	APR	MAY	JUN	JUL	AUG	SEP	OCT	NOV	DEC

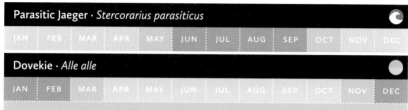

Parasitic Jaeger · *Stercorarius parasiticus*

JAN	FEB	MAR	APR	MAY	JUN	JUL	AUG	SEP	OCT	NOV	DEC

Dovekie · *Alle alle*

JAN	FEB	MAR	APR	MAY	JUN	JUL	AUG	SEP	OCT	NOV	DEC

Rare winter visitor to the immediate coast, most often after strong winter storms, especially "nor'easters" with raging onshore winds. Weakened birds may linger for days but are often predated. Your best bet is to comb favored shoreline locations during or immediately after conducive storms. Site list: Y3,Y4, C3, SA3, H4, H9.

Common Murre · *Uria aalge*

JAN	FEB	MAR	APR	MAY	JUN	JUL	AUG	SEP	OCT	NOV	DEC

Uncommon to locally fairly common breeder on a few offshore islands. The rarest alcid from land in Maine. Site list (breeding/summer): H4, H7, WN7, WN10, WN11. Site list (nonbreeding): Y4, C3.

Thick-billed Murre · *Uria lomvia*

JAN	FEB	MAR	APR	MAY	JUN	JUL	AUG	SEP	OCT	NOV	DEC

Rare winter visitor to the immediate coast, most often after strong winter storms, especially "nor'easters" with raging onshore winds. Weakened birds may linger for days but are often predated. Your best bet is to comb favored shoreline locations during or immediately after conducive storms. Site list: Y4, C3, SA3, H4, H9.

Razorbill · *Alca torda*

JAN	FEB	MAR	APR	MAY	JUN	JUL	AUG	SEP	OCT	NOV	DEC

Uncommon to locally common breeder on a few offshore islands. The most common non-guillemot alcid from land, especially from late fall through early spring. While most common during or after onshore winds, almost any calm day in midwinter should produce a few birds from favored promontories. Site list (breeding): L7, H7, WN7, WN10. Site list (nonbreeding): Y3, Y4, Y12, C3, SA3, L1, L6, KX5, KX6, H4, H9, WN10, WN11.

Black Guillemot · *Cepphus grylle*

JAN	FEB	MAR	APR	MAY	JUN	JUL	AUG	SEP	OCT	NOV	DEC

Uncommon to locally common, widespread resident of the rocky coast. Can be found throughout the year at many locations but is usually most common in winter. Site list: Y3, Y4, Y12, C1, C3, C6, C10, C23, SA3, L1, L5, L6, L7, KX4, KX5, KX6, H6, H7, H9, WN1, WN5, WN7, WN10.

Atlantic Puffin · *Fratercula arctica*

JAN	FEB	MAR	APR	MAY	JUN	JUL	AUG	SEP	OCT	NOV	DEC

Locally common to abundant breeder on a few offshore islands. An organized boat tour is by far your best way to see this species, as they are very rarely detected from land, mostly in late summer and fall. Site list: C10, L1, L7, H7, WN7, WN10.

Black-legged Kittiwake · *Rissa tridactyla*

JAN	FEB	MAR	APR	MAY	JUN	JUL	AUG	SEP	OCT	NOV	DEC

Uncommon to fairly common winter visitor to nearshore waters, regularly seen from coastal promontories, especially during or after onshore winds. While most whale watches end before kittiwakes arrive, a few can often be seen throughout the summer in Downeast Maine. Site list (summer): WN10, WN11. Site list (winter): Y3, Y4, Y12, C3, SA3, L1, L16, KX4, KX5, KX6, H4, H7, H9, WN5, WN10, WN11.

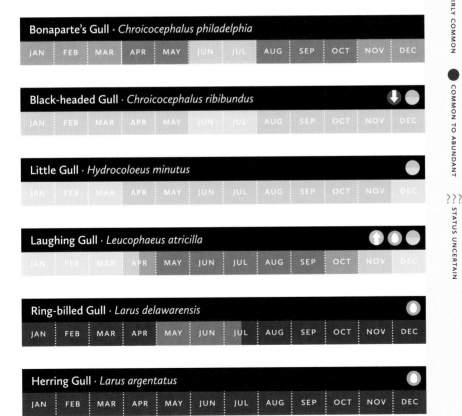

Bonaparte's Gull · *Chroicocephalus philadelphia*

JAN	FEB	MAR	APR	MAY	JUN	JUL	AUG	SEP	OCT	NOV	DEC

Black-headed Gull · *Chroicocephalus ribibundus*

JAN	FEB	MAR	APR	MAY	JUN	JUL	AUG	SEP	OCT	NOV	DEC

Little Gull · *Hydrocoloeus minutus*

JAN	FEB	MAR	APR	MAY	JUN	JUL	AUG	SEP	OCT	NOV	DEC

Laughing Gull · *Leucophaeus atricilla*

JAN	FEB	MAR	APR	MAY	JUN	JUL	AUG	SEP	OCT	NOV	DEC

Ring-billed Gull · *Larus delawarensis*

JAN	FEB	MAR	APR	MAY	JUN	JUL	AUG	SEP	OCT	NOV	DEC

Herring Gull · *Larus argentatus*

JAN	FEB	MAR	APR	MAY	JUN	JUL	AUG	SEP	OCT	NOV	DEC

NONE
RARE
VERY UNCOMMON
UNCOMMON TO FAIRLY COMMON
COMMON TO ABUNDANT
??? STATUS UNCERTAIN

INCREASING
DECREASING
IRRUPTIVE
THREATENED OR ENDANGERED IN MAINE
BREEDS IN MAINE
PRIMARILY COASTAL
PRIMARILY PELAGIC

Iceland Gull · *Larus glaucoides*

JAN	FEB	MAR	APR	MAY	JUN	JUL	AUG	SEP	OCT	NOV	DEC

Uncommon to locally common visitor from late fall through early spring. Very rare in warmer months. Site list: C2, C3, C5, C12, AN6, SA3, SA5, SA6, KE3, KE5, KE12, KX4, KX6, SO1, SO2, PE5, WN10, WN13.

Lesser Black-backed Gull · *Larus fuscus*

JAN	FEB	MAR	APR	MAY	JUN	JUL	AUG	SEP	OCT	NOV	DEC

Glaucous Gull · *Larus hyperboreus*

JAN	FEB	MAR	APR	MAY	JUN	JUL	AUG	SEP	OCT	NOV	DEC

Uncommon to locally common visitor from late fall through early spring. Very rare in warmer months. Site list: C1, C3, C5, C12, SA5, SA6, KE3, KE5, KE12, KX4, KX6, SO2, PE5, WN10, WN13.

Great Black-backed Gull · *Larus marinus*

JAN	FEB	MAR	APR	MAY	JUN	JUL	AUG	SEP	OCT	NOV	DEC

Least Tern · *Sternula antillarum*

JAN	FEB	MAR	APR	MAY	JUN	JUL	AUG	SEP	OCT	NOV	DEC

Caspian Tern · *Hydroprogne caspia*

JAN	FEB	MAR	APR	MAY	JUN	JUL	AUG	SEP	OCT	NOV	DEC

Black Tern · *Chlidonias niger*

JAN	FEB	MAR	APR	MAY	JUN	JUL	AUG	SEP	OCT	NOV	DEC

Locally common, colonial breeder at a few inland locations. Very rarely detected in migration. Site list: KE6, WO13, SO4.

Roseate Tern · *Sterna dougallii*

JAN	FEB	MAR	APR	MAY	JUN	JUL	AUG	SEP	OCT	NOV	DEC

Uncommon to common at very few sites in breeding season. Breeding on a few offshore islands, foraging birds are regular into inshore waters, especially in the second half of summer when they are feeding young. Site list: Y1, Y12, C1, L6, L7.

Common Tern · *Sterna hirundo*

JAN	FEB	MAR	APR	MAY	JUN	JUL	AUG	SEP	OCT	NOV	DEC

Arctic Tern · *Sterna paradisea*

JAN	FEB	MAR	APR	MAY	JUN	JUL	AUG	SEP	OCT	NOV	DEC

Locally abundant breeder on offshore islands, fairly rare from land. A few sites on the mainland can be checked, especially after onshore winds in midsummer. Site list: Y12, C1, L7, H7, WN7.

Rock Pigeon · *Columba livia*

JAN	FEB	MAR	APR	MAY	JUN	JUL	AUG	SEP	OCT	NOV	DEC

Mourning Dove · *Zenaida macroura*

JAN	FEB	MAR	APR	MAY	JUN	JUL	AUG	SEP	OCT	NOV	DEC

Yellow-billed Cuckoo · *Coccyzus americanus*

JAN	FEB	MAR	APR	MAY	JUN	JUL	AUG	SEP	OCT	NOV	DEC

Black-billed Cuckoo · *Coccyzus erythropthalmus*

JAN	FEB	MAR	APR	MAY	JUN	JUL	AUG	SEP	OCT	NOV	DEC

Eastern Screech-Owl · *Megascops asio*

? ?

Likely rare but regular and resident in southernmost York County, with vagrants occasionally reported elsewhere. Owling effort in winter and early spring would likely yield more sightings and help to determine extent of range.

Great Horned Owl · *Bubo virginianus*

JAN	FEB	MAR	APR	MAY	JUN	JUL	AUG	SEP	OCT	NOV	DEC

Snowy Owl · *Bubo scandiacus*

JAN	FEB	MAR	APR	MAY	JUN	JUL	AUG	SEP	OCT	NOV	DEC

Irruptive. Some are seen in almost every winter at favored locations, but during irruption years can be widespread and even locally fairly common. Farmlands, dunes, airports, barren mountaintops, and other open locations are favored. Site list: Y4, Y6, Y12, C1, C6, O3, SA2, SA3, KX2, KX4, KX5, KX8, KX10, H4, H8, AR7.

NONE
RARE
VERY UNCOMMON
UNCOMMON TO FAIRLY COMMON
COMMON TO ABUNDANT
??? STATUS UNCERTAIN

INCREASING
DECREASING
IRRUPTIVE
THREATENED OR ENDANGERED IN MAINE
BREEDS IN MAINE
PRIMARILY COASTAL
PRIMARILY PELAGIC

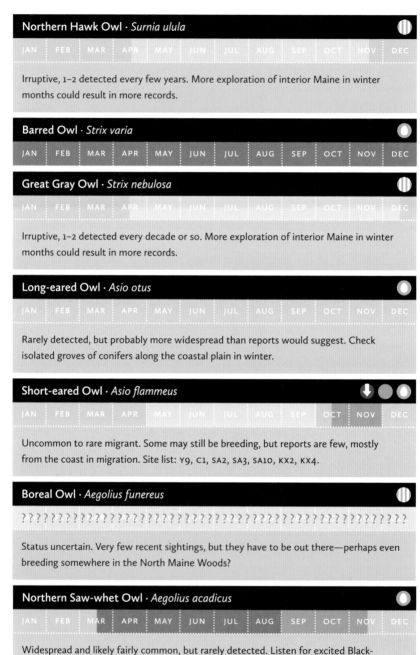

Northern Hawk Owl · *Surnia ulula*

JAN	FEB	MAR	APR	MAY	JUN	JUL	AUG	SEP	OCT	NOV	DEC

Irruptive, 1–2 detected every few years. More exploration of interior Maine in winter months could result in more records.

Barred Owl · *Strix varia*

JAN	FEB	MAR	APR	MAY	JUN	JUL	AUG	SEP	OCT	NOV	DEC

Great Gray Owl · *Strix nebulosa*

JAN	FEB	MAR	APR	MAY	JUN	JUL	AUG	SEP	OCT	NOV	DEC

Irruptive, 1–2 detected every decade or so. More exploration of interior Maine in winter months could result in more records.

Long-eared Owl · *Asio otus*

JAN	FEB	MAR	APR	MAY	JUN	JUL	AUG	SEP	OCT	NOV	DEC

Rarely detected, but probably more widespread than reports would suggest. Check isolated groves of conifers along the coastal plain in winter.

Short-eared Owl · *Asio flammeus*

JAN	FEB	MAR	APR	MAY	JUN	JUL	AUG	SEP	OCT	NOV	DEC

Uncommon to rare migrant. Some may still be breeding, but reports are few, mostly from the coast in migration. Site list: Y9, C1, SA2, SA3, SA10, KX2, KX4.

Boreal Owl · *Aegolius funereus*

? ?

Status uncertain. Very few recent sightings, but they have to be out there—perhaps even breeding somewhere in the North Maine Woods?

Northern Saw-whet Owl · *Aegolius acadicus*

JAN	FEB	MAR	APR	MAY	JUN	JUL	AUG	SEP	OCT	NOV	DEC

Widespread and likely fairly common, but rarely detected. Listen for excited Black-capped Chickadees and especially Golden-crowned Kinglets in deep woods or coastal migrant traps.

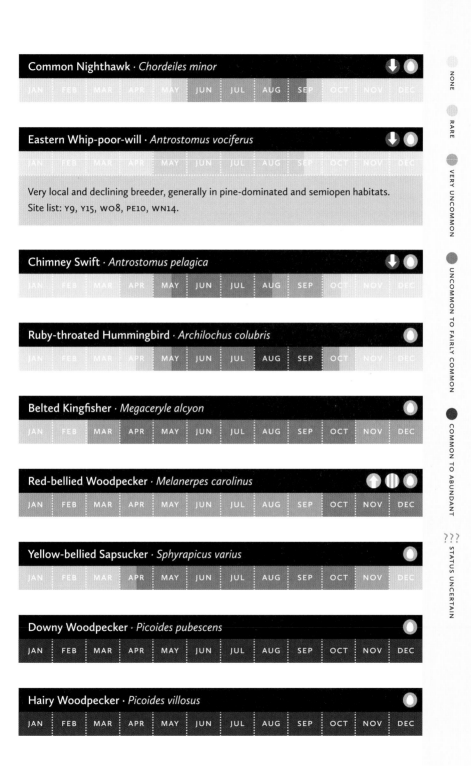

Common Nighthawk · *Chordeiles minor*

JAN FEB MAR APR MAY JUN JUL AUG SEP OCT NOV DEC

Eastern Whip-poor-will · *Antrostomus vociferus*

JAN FEB MAR APR MAY JUN JUL AUG SEP OCT NOV DEC

Very local and declining breeder, generally in pine-dominated and semiopen habitats.
Site list: Y9, Y15, WO8, PE10, WN14.

Chimney Swift · *Antrostomus pelagica*

JAN FEB MAR APR MAY JUN JUL AUG SEP OCT NOV DEC

Ruby-throated Hummingbird · *Archilochus colubris*

JAN FEB MAR APR MAY JUN JUL AUG SEP OCT NOV DEC

Belted Kingfisher · *Megaceryle alcyon*

JAN FEB MAR APR MAY JUN JUL AUG SEP OCT NOV DEC

Red-bellied Woodpecker · *Melanerpes carolinus*

JAN FEB MAR APR MAY JUN JUL AUG SEP OCT NOV DEC

Yellow-bellied Sapsucker · *Sphyrapicus varius*

JAN FEB MAR APR MAY JUN JUL AUG SEP OCT NOV DEC

Downy Woodpecker · *Picoides pubescens*

JAN FEB MAR APR MAY JUN JUL AUG SEP OCT NOV DEC

Hairy Woodpecker · *Picoides villosus*

JAN FEB MAR APR MAY JUN JUL AUG SEP OCT NOV DEC

NONE
RARE
VERY UNCOMMON
UNCOMMON TO FAIRLY COMMON
COMMON TO ABUNDANT
??? STATUS UNCERTAIN

INCREASING
DECREASING
IRRUPTIVE
THREATENED OR ENDANGERED IN MAINE
BREEDS IN MAINE
PRIMARILY COASTAL
PRIMARILY PELAGIC

American Three-toed Woodpecker · *Picoides dorsalis*

? ? ? ? ? ? ? ? ? ? | APR | MAY | JUN | JUL | AUG | SEP | ? ? ? ? ? ? ? ? ? ?

Rare and local resident of the boreal habitats, probably more widespread than believed. Generally easiest to find when nesting—listen for territorial birds drumming in early to mid-spring, and listen for active nests in cavities May–June. Site list: F10, PS5, PS6, PS7, AR10, AR13.

Black-backed Woodpecker · *Picoides arcticus*

JAN | FEB | MAR | APR | MAY | JUN | JUL | AUG | SEP | OCT | NOV | DEC

Fairly widespread in the boreal and boreal-transition habitats, but never common, and often impressively shy and secretive. Generally easiest to find when nesting—listen for territorial birds drumming in early to mid-spring, and listen for active nests in cavities May–June. Occasionally shows in spring or fall all the way down to the coastal plain. Site list: O9, H9, H12, F6, F10, SO6, WN15, PS5, PS6, PS7, AR2, AR9, AR10, AR12, AR13.

Northern Flicker · *Colaptes auratus*

JAN | FEB | MAR | APR | MAY | JUN | JUL | AUG | SEP | OCT | NOV | DEC

Pileated Woodpecker · *Dryocopus pileatus*

JAN | FEB | MAR | APR | MAY | JUN | JUL | AUG | SEP | OCT | NOV | DEC

American Kestrel · *Falco sparverius*

JAN | FEB | MAR | APR | MAY | JUN | JUL | AUG | SEP | OCT | NOV | DEC

Merlin · *Falco columbarius*

JAN | FEB | MAR | APR | MAY | JUN | JUL | AUG | SEP | OCT | NOV | DEC

Peregrine Falcon · *Falco peregrinus*

JAN | FEB | MAR | APR | MAY | JUN | JUL | AUG | SEP | OCT | NOV | DEC

Olive-sided Flycatcher · *Contopus cooperi*

JAN | FEB | MAR | APR | MAY | JUN | JUL | AUG | SEP | OCT | NOV | DEC

Uncommon and local breeder in the boreal and boreal-transition habitats, usually around large, open bogs. Uncommon but widespread during migration at favored migrant traps. Site list (breeding): H12, F10, SO6, SO7, PS1, PS5, AR9, AR112, AR13.

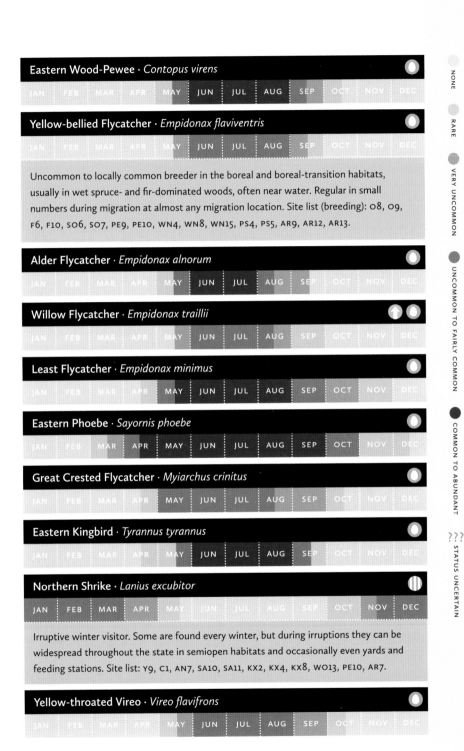

Eastern Wood-Pewee · *Contopus virens*

| JAN | FEB | MAR | APR | MAY | JUN | JUL | AUG | SEP | OCT | NOV | DEC |

Yellow-bellied Flycatcher · *Empidonax flaviventris*

| JAN | FEB | MAR | APR | MAY | JUN | JUL | AUG | SEP | OCT | NOV | DEC |

Uncommon to locally common breeder in the boreal and boreal-transition habitats, usually in wet spruce- and fir-dominated woods, often near water. Regular in small numbers during migration at almost any migration location. Site list (breeding): O8, O9, F6, F10, SO6, SO7, PE9, PE10, WN4, WN8, WN15, PS4, PS5, AR9, AR12, AR13.

Alder Flycatcher · *Empidonax alnorum*

| JAN | FEB | MAR | APR | MAY | JUN | JUL | AUG | SEP | OCT | NOV | DEC |

Willow Flycatcher · *Empidonax traillii*

| JAN | FEB | MAR | APR | MAY | JUN | JUL | AUG | SEP | OCT | NOV | DEC |

Least Flycatcher · *Empidonax minimus*

| JAN | FEB | MAR | APR | MAY | JUN | JUL | AUG | SEP | OCT | NOV | DEC |

Eastern Phoebe · *Sayornis phoebe*

| JAN | FEB | MAR | APR | MAY | JUN | JUL | AUG | SEP | OCT | NOV | DEC |

Great Crested Flycatcher · *Myiarchus crinitus*

| JAN | FEB | MAR | APR | MAY | JUN | JUL | AUG | SEP | OCT | NOV | DEC |

Eastern Kingbird · *Tyrannus tyrannus*

| JAN | FEB | MAR | APR | MAY | JUN | JUL | AUG | SEP | OCT | NOV | DEC |

Northern Shrike · *Lanius excubitor*

| JAN | FEB | MAR | APR | MAY | JUN | JUL | AUG | SEP | OCT | NOV | DEC |

Irruptive winter visitor. Some are found every winter, but during irruptions they can be widespread throughout the state in semiopen habitats and occasionally even yards and feeding stations. Site list: Y9, C1, AN7, SA10, SA11, KX2, KX4, KX8, WO13, PE10, AR7.

Yellow-throated Vireo · *Vireo flavifrons*

| JAN | FEB | MAR | APR | MAY | JUN | JUL | AUG | SEP | OCT | NOV | DEC |

NONE
RARE
VERY UNCOMMON
UNCOMMON TO FAIRLY COMMON
COMMON TO ABUNDANT
??? STATUS UNCERTAIN

INCREASING
DECREASING
IRRUPTIVE
THREATENED OR ENDANGERED IN MAINE
BREEDS IN MAINE
PRIMARILY COASTAL
PRIMARILY PELAGIC

Blue-headed Vireo · *Vireo solitarius*

JAN	FEB	MAR	APR	MAY	JUN	JUL	AUG	SEP	OCT	NOV	DEC

Warbling Vireo · *Vireo gilvus*

JAN	FEB	MAR	APR	MAY	JUN	JUL	AUG	SEP	OCT	NOV	DEC

Philadelphia Vireo · *Vireo philadelphicus*

JAN	FEB	MAR	APR	MAY	JUN	JUL	AUG	SEP	OCT	NOV	DEC

Locally uncommon to fairly common breeder, especially in aspen stands in mountain valleys near water. Be careful with your ID, as Red-eyed Vireos often nest in the same locations and can sound exceptionally similar. Regular if rather uncommon migrant at any favored migration locations. Site list (breeding): O8, O9, F10, PS8, AR13.

Red-eyed Vireo · *Vireo olivaceus*

JAN	FEB	MAR	APR	MAY	JUN	JUL	AUG	SEP	OCT	NOV	DEC

Gray Jay · *Perisoreus canadensis*

JAN	FEB	MAR	APR	MAY	JUN	JUL	AUG	SEP	OCT	NOV	DEC

Uncommon but widespread resident of the boreal habitats. Can become confiding and easy to see at certain locations but is often surprisingly secretive. Site list: O8, O9, H12, F10, SO6, SO7, PE9, PE10, WN11, WN15, PS1, PS2, AR2, AR8, AR9, AR10, AR12, AR13.

Blue Jay · *Cyanocitta cristata*

JAN	FEB	MAR	APR	MAY	JUN	JUL	AUG	SEP	OCT	NOV	DEC

American Crow · *Corvus brachyrhynchos*

JAN	FEB	MAR	APR	MAY	JUN	JUL	AUG	SEP	OCT	NOV	DEC

Fish Crow · *Corvus ossifragus*

JAN	FEB	MAR	APR	MAY	JUN	JUL	AUG	SEP	OCT	NOV	DEC

Common Raven · *Corvus corax*

JAN	FEB	MAR	APR	MAY	JUN	JUL	AUG	SEP	OCT	NOV	DEC

Horned Lark · *Eremophila alpestris*

JAN	FEB	MAR	APR	MAY	JUN	JUL	AUG	SEP	OCT	NOV	DEC

Purple Martin · *Progne subis*

JAN	FEB	MAR	APR	MAY	JUN	JUL	AUG	SEP	OCT	NOV	DEC

Tree Swallow · *Tachycineta bicolor*

JAN	FEB	MAR	APR	MAY	JUN	JUL	AUG	SEP	OCT	NOV	DEC

Northern Rough-winged Swallow · *Stelgidopteryx serripennis*

JAN	FEB	MAR	APR	MAY	JUN	JUL	AUG	SEP	OCT	NOV	DEC

Bank Swallow · *Riparia riparia*

JAN	FEB	MAR	APR	MAY	JUN	JUL	AUG	SEP	OCT	NOV	DEC

Barn Swallow · *Hirundo rustica*

JAN	FEB	MAR	APR	MAY	JUN	JUL	AUG	SEP	OCT	NOV	DEC

Cliff Swallow · *Petrochelidon pyrrhonota*

JAN	FEB	MAR	APR	MAY	JUN	JUL	AUG	SEP	OCT	NOV	DEC

Black-capped Chickadee · *Poecile atricapillus*

JAN	FEB	MAR	APR	MAY	JUN	JUL	AUG	SEP	OCT	NOV	DEC

Boreal Chickadee · *Poecile hudsonicus*

JAN	FEB	MAR	APR	MAY	JUN	JUL	AUG	SEP	OCT	NOV	DEC

Uncommon and often secretive resident of the boreal habitats. Very rare outside of spruce and fir-dominated habitats. Site list: O8, O9, H12, F10, SO6, SO7, PE9, PE10, WN11, WN15, PS1, PS2, AR2, AR8, AR9, AR10, AR12, AR13.

Tufted Titmouse · *Baeolophus bicolor*

JAN	FEB	MAR	APR	MAY	JUN	JUL	AUG	SEP	OCT	NOV	DEC

Red-breasted Nuthatch · *Sitta canadensis*

JAN	FEB	MAR	APR	MAY	JUN	JUL	AUG	SEP	OCT	NOV	DEC

White-breasted Nuthatch · *Sitta carolinensis*

JAN	FEB	MAR	APR	MAY	JUN	JUL	AUG	SEP	OCT	NOV	DEC

Brown Creeper · *Certhia americana*

JAN	FEB	MAR	APR	MAY	JUN	JUL	AUG	SEP	OCT	NOV	DEC

Legend

- NONE
- RARE
- VERY UNCOMMON
- UNCOMMON TO FAIRLY COMMON
- COMMON TO ABUNDANT
- ??? STATUS UNCERTAIN

- INCREASING
- DECREASING
- IRRUPTIVE
- THREATENED OR ENDANGERED IN MAINE
- BREEDS IN MAINE
- PRIMARILY COASTAL
- PRIMARILY PELAGIC

House Wren · *Troglodytes aedon*

JAN	FEB	MAR	APR	MAY	JUN	JUL	AUG	SEP	OCT	NOV	DEC

Winter Wren · *Troglodytes hiemalis*

JAN	FEB	MAR	APR	MAY	JUN	JUL	AUG	SEP	OCT	NOV	DEC

Marsh Wren · *Cistothorus palustris*

JAN	FEB	MAR	APR	MAY	JUN	JUL	AUG	SEP	OCT	NOV	DEC

Carolina Wren · *Thryothorus ludovicianus*

JAN	FEB	MAR	APR	MAY	JUN	JUL	AUG	SEP	OCT	NOV	DEC

Blue-gray Gnatcatcher · *Polioptila caerulea*

JAN	FEB	MAR	APR	MAY	JUN	JUL	AUG	SEP	OCT	NOV	DEC

Golden-crowned Kinglet · *Regulus satrapa*

JAN	FEB	MAR	APR	MAY	JUN	JUL	AUG	SEP	OCT	NOV	DEC

Ruby-crowned Kinglet · *Regulus calendula*

JAN	FEB	MAR	APR	MAY	JUN	JUL	AUG	SEP	OCT	NOV	DEC

Eastern Bluebird · *Sialia sialis*

JAN	FEB	MAR	APR	MAY	JUN	JUL	AUG	SEP	OCT	NOV	DEC

Veery · *Catharus fuscescens*

JAN	FEB	MAR	APR	MAY	JUN	JUL	AUG	SEP	OCT	NOV	DEC

Gray-cheeked Thrush · *Catharus minimus*

JAN	FEB	MAR	APR	MAY	JUN	JUL	AUG	SEP	OCT	NOV	DEC

Bicknell's Thrush · *Catharus bicknelli*

JAN	FEB	MAR	APR	MAY	JUN	JUL	AUG	??????		OCT	NOV	DEC

Very local breeder, confined to stunted spruce-fir forest ("krummholz") on mountains at least 2,800 feet high. Easily heard but often excruciatingly challenging to see, in favored locations while males are singing from early June into early July. Likely regular as a migrant, but extremely secretive and challenging to ID. Beware especially minima subspecies of Gray-cheeked Thrush. Site list: O9, F6, F12, F13, PS2, PS9.

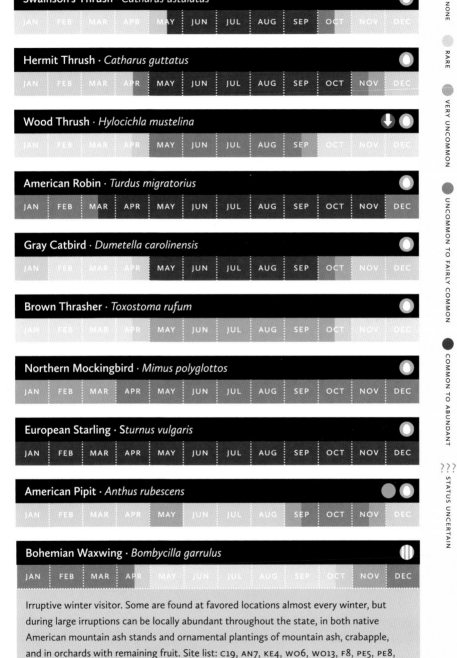

- **Swainson's Thrush** · *Catharus ustulatus* — JAN FEB MAR APR MAY JUN JUL AUG SEP OCT NOV DEC
- **Hermit Thrush** · *Catharus guttatus* — JAN FEB MAR APR MAY JUN JUL AUG SEP OCT NOV DEC
- **Wood Thrush** · *Hylocichla mustelina* — JAN FEB MAR APR MAY JUN JUL AUG SEP OCT NOV DEC
- **American Robin** · *Turdus migratorius* — JAN FEB MAR APR MAY JUN JUL AUG SEP OCT NOV DEC
- **Gray Catbird** · *Dumetella carolinensis* — JAN FEB MAR APR MAY JUN JUL AUG SEP OCT NOV DEC
- **Brown Thrasher** · *Toxostoma rufum* — JAN FEB MAR APR MAY JUN JUL AUG SEP OCT NOV DEC
- **Northern Mockingbird** · *Mimus polyglottos* — JAN FEB MAR APR MAY JUN JUL AUG SEP OCT NOV DEC
- **European Starling** · *Sturnus vulgaris* — JAN FEB MAR APR MAY JUN JUL AUG SEP OCT NOV DEC
- **American Pipit** · *Anthus rubescens* — JAN FEB MAR APR MAY JUN JUL AUG SEP OCT NOV DEC
- **Bohemian Waxwing** · *Bombycilla garrulus* — JAN FEB MAR APR MAY JUN JUL AUG SEP OCT NOV DEC

Irruptive winter visitor. Some are found at favored locations almost every winter, but during large irruptions can be locally abundant throughout the state, in both native American mountain ash stands and ornamental plantings of mountain ash, crabapple, and in orchards with remaining fruit. Site list: C19, AN7, KE4, WO6, WO13, F8, PE5, PE8, WN6, WN8.

NONE
RARE
VERY UNCOMMON
UNCOMMON TO FAIRLY COMMON
COMMON TO ABUNDANT
??? STATUS UNCERTAIN

INCREASING
DECREASING
IRRUPTIVE
THREATENED OR ENDANGERED IN MAINE
BREEDS IN MAINE
PRIMARILY COASTAL
PRIMARILY PELAGIC

Cedar Waxwing · *Bombycilla cedrorum* ○

JAN	FEB	MAR	APR	MAY	JUN	JUL	AUG	SEP	OCT	NOV	DEC

Lapland Longspur · *Calcarius lapponicus*

JAN	FEB	MAR	APR	MAY	JUN	JUL	AUG	SEP	OCT	NOV	DEC

Locally uncommon migrants and winter visitors throughout state, but most often in large farmland areas and coastal marsh/dune complexes. Often seen within flocks of Snow Buntings, especially inland. Also, like the bunting, was once more regular in winter when manure was spread on frozen fields. Site list: Y6, C1, C13, O3, AN7, SA3, SA11, KE12, AR7.

Snow Bunting · *Plectrophenax nivalis*

JAN	FEB	MAR	APR	MAY	JUN	JUL	AUG	SEP	OCT	NOV	DEC

Locally uncommon to fairly abundant migrants and winter visitors throughout state, but most often in large farmland areas and coastal marsh/dune complexes. Traditionally—especially when manure was spread on frozen fields throughout the winter—large flocks were regularly encountered. Now much more regular only in late fall and early spring. Site list: Y6, C1, C13, O3, AN7, SA2, SA3, SA11, KE12, KX4, AR7.

Ovenbird · *Seiurus aurocapilla* ○

JAN	FEB	MAR	APR	MAY	JUN	JUL	AUG	SEP	OCT	NOV	DEC

Louisiana Waterthrush · *Parkesia motacilla* ○

JAN	FEB	MAR	APR	MAY	JUN	JUL	AUG	SEP	OCT	NOV	DEC

Very local breeder, but not nearly as rare as conventional wisdom suggests. Searching the very specific habitat of flowing creeks/brooks with lots of rocks through shaded (especially eastern hemlock–dominated) gullies as they empty into large rivers and lakes have revealed this species to be more widespread in the southern third of the state. Very rarely detected in migration. Site list (breeding): Y10, Y17, C17, O4, AN3, AN4, AN7, SA9, KE2.

Northern Waterthrush · *Parkesia noveboracensis* ○

JAN	FEB	MAR	APR	MAY	JUN	JUL	AUG	SEP	OCT	NOV	DEC

Black-and-white Warbler · *Mniotilta varia* ○

JAN	FEB	MAR	APR	MAY	JUN	JUL	AUG	SEP	OCT	NOV	DEC

Tennessee Warbler · *Oreothlypis peregrina*

JAN | FEB | MAR | APR | MAY | JUN | JUL | AUG | SEP | OCT | NOV | DEC

One of the "spruce budworm specialists," it has declined drastically in numbers over the past decades, but recent upticks in budworm populations should increase the numbers of Tennessee and other boreal-breeding warblers. Now limited mostly to northern Maine. Regular but rather uncommon at almost any migration location. Site list (breeding): PS7, AR2, AR9, AR12, AR13.

Orange-crowned Warbler · *Oreothlypis celata*

JAN | FEB | MAR | APR | MAY | JUN | JUL | AUG | SEP | OCT | NOV | DEC

Nashville Warbler · *Oreothlypis ruficapilla*

JAN | FEB | MAR | APR | MAY | JUN | JUL | AUG | SEP | OCT | NOV | DEC

Mourning Warbler · *Geothlypis philadelphia*

JAN | FEB | MAR | APR | MAY | JUN | JUL | AUG | SEP | OCT | NOV | DEC

Uncommon but locally fairly common in natural clearings and clear cuts within the boreal and boreal-transition habitats. Regenerating stands of forest, especially when blackberry is the dominant understory, seem most popular. Sites are often occupied only for a few years. Rather rarely detected in migration, but possible at most migration locations, especially those with scrubby areas. Site list (breeding): F11, WN15, PS4, PS5, AR12, AR13.

Common Yellowthroat · *Geothlypis trichas*

JAN | FEB | MAR | APR | MAY | JUN | JUL | AUG | SEP | OCT | NOV | DEC

American Redstart · *Setophaga ruticilla*

JAN | FEB | MAR | APR | MAY | JUN | JUL | AUG | SEP | OCT | NOV | DEC

Cape May Warbler · *Setophaga tigrina*

JAN | FEB | MAR | APR | MAY | JUN | JUL | AUG | SEP | OCT | NOV | DEC

One of the "spruce budworm specialists," it has declined drastically in numbers over the past decades, but recent upticks in budworm populations should increase the numbers of Cape May and other boreal-breeding warblers. Now limited mostly to northern Maine. Regular but rather uncommon at almost any migration location. Site list (breeding): F8, F10, SO6, SO7, PE9, PE10, WN12, WN15, PS6, PS7, PS9, AR2, AR8, AR9, AR12, AR13.

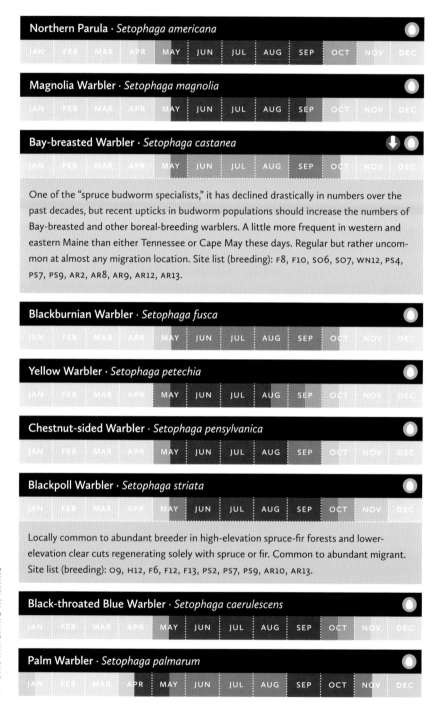

Northern Parula · *Setophaga americana*

| JAN | FEB | MAR | APR | MAY | JUN | JUL | AUG | SEP | OCT | NOV | DEC |

Magnolia Warbler · *Setophaga magnolia*

| JAN | FEB | MAR | APR | MAY | JUN | JUL | AUG | SEP | OCT | NOV | DEC |

Bay-breasted Warbler · *Setophaga castanea*

| JAN | FEB | MAR | APR | MAY | JUN | JUL | AUG | SEP | OCT | NOV | DEC |

One of the "spruce budworm specialists," it has declined drastically in numbers over the past decades, but recent upticks in budworm populations should increase the numbers of Bay-breasted and other boreal-breeding warblers. A little more frequent in western and eastern Maine than either Tennessee or Cape May these days. Regular but rather uncommon at almost any migration location. Site list (breeding): F8, F10, SO6, SO7, WN12, PS4, PS7, PS9, AR2, AR8, AR9, AR12, AR13.

Blackburnian Warbler · *Setophaga fusca*

| JAN | FEB | MAR | APR | MAY | JUN | JUL | AUG | SEP | OCT | NOV | DEC |

Yellow Warbler · *Setophaga petechia*

| JAN | FEB | MAR | APR | MAY | JUN | JUL | AUG | SEP | OCT | NOV | DEC |

Chestnut-sided Warbler · *Setophaga pensylvanica*

| JAN | FEB | MAR | APR | MAY | JUN | JUL | AUG | SEP | OCT | NOV | DEC |

Blackpoll Warbler · *Setophaga striata*

| JAN | FEB | MAR | APR | MAY | JUN | JUL | AUG | SEP | OCT | NOV | DEC |

Locally common to abundant breeder in high-elevation spruce-fir forests and lower-elevation clear cuts regenerating solely with spruce or fir. Common to abundant migrant. Site list (breeding): O9, H12, F6, F12, F13, PS2, PS7, PS9, AR10, AR13.

Black-throated Blue Warbler · *Setophaga caerulescens*

| JAN | FEB | MAR | APR | MAY | JUN | JUL | AUG | SEP | OCT | NOV | DEC |

Palm Warbler · *Setophaga palmarum*

| JAN | FEB | MAR | APR | MAY | JUN | JUL | AUG | SEP | OCT | NOV | DEC |

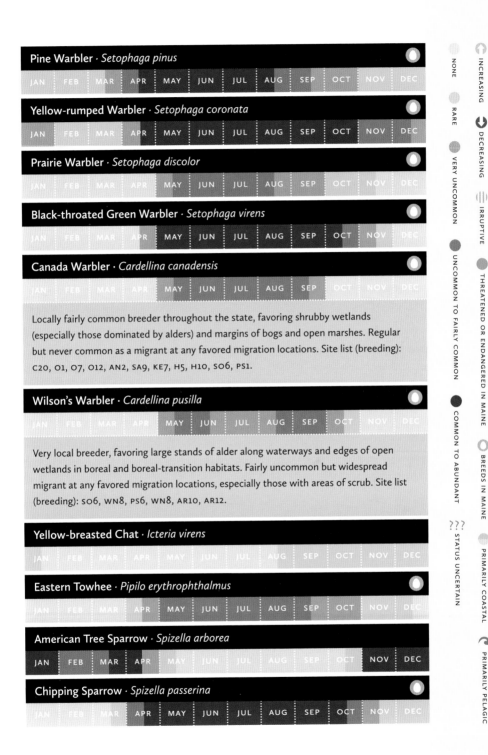

Pine Warbler · *Setophaga pinus*

| JAN | FEB | MAR | APR | MAY | JUN | JUL | AUG | SEP | OCT | NOV | DEC |

Yellow-rumped Warbler · *Setophaga coronata*

| JAN | FEB | MAR | APR | MAY | JUN | JUL | AUG | SEP | OCT | NOV | DEC |

Prairie Warbler · *Setophaga discolor*

| JAN | FEB | MAR | APR | MAY | JUN | JUL | AUG | SEP | OCT | NOV | DEC |

Black-throated Green Warbler · *Setophaga virens*

| JAN | FEB | MAR | APR | MAY | JUN | JUL | AUG | SEP | OCT | NOV | DEC |

Canada Warbler · *Cardellina canadensis*

| JAN | FEB | MAR | APR | MAY | JUN | JUL | AUG | SEP | OCT | NOV | DEC |

Locally fairly common breeder throughout the state, favoring shrubby wetlands (especially those dominated by alders) and margins of bogs and open marshes. Regular but never common as a migrant at any favored migration locations. Site list (breeding): C20, O1, O7, O12, AN2, SA9, KE7, H5, H10, SO6, PS1.

Wilson's Warbler · *Cardellina pusilla*

| JAN | FEB | MAR | APR | MAY | JUN | JUL | AUG | SEP | OCT | NOV | DEC |

Very local breeder, favoring large stands of alder along waterways and edges of open wetlands in boreal and boreal-transition habitats. Fairly uncommon but widespread migrant at any favored migration locations, especially those with areas of scrub. Site list (breeding): SO6, WN8, PS6, WN8, AR10, AR12.

Yellow-breasted Chat · *Icteria virens*

| JAN | FEB | MAR | APR | MAY | JUN | JUL | AUG | SEP | OCT | NOV | DEC |

Eastern Towhee · *Pipilo erythrophthalmus*

| JAN | FEB | MAR | APR | MAY | JUN | JUL | AUG | SEP | OCT | NOV | DEC |

American Tree Sparrow · *Spizella arborea*

| JAN | FEB | MAR | APR | MAY | JUN | JUL | AUG | SEP | OCT | NOV | DEC |

Chipping Sparrow · *Spizella passerina*

| JAN | FEB | MAR | APR | MAY | JUN | JUL | AUG | SEP | OCT | NOV | DEC |

NONE

RARE

VERY UNCOMMON

UNCOMMON TO FAIRLY COMMON

COMMON TO ABUNDANT

??? STATUS UNCERTAIN

INCREASING

DECREASING

IRRUPTIVE

THREATENED OR ENDANGERED IN MAINE

BREEDS IN MAINE

PRIMARILY COASTAL

PRIMARILY PELAGIC

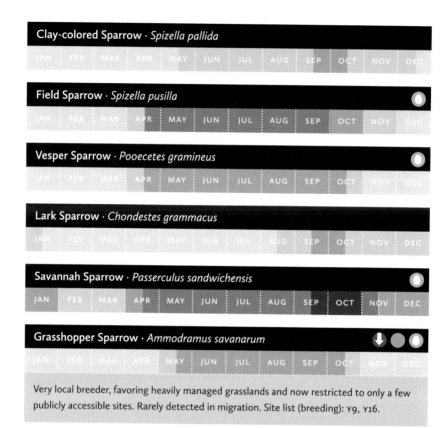

Clay-colored Sparrow · *Spizella pallida*

| JAN | FEB | MAR | APR | MAY | JUN | JUL | AUG | SEP | OCT | NOV | DEC |

Field Sparrow · *Spizella pusilla*

| JAN | FEB | MAR | APR | MAY | JUN | JUL | AUG | SEP | OCT | NOV | DEC |

Vesper Sparrow · *Pooecetes gramineus*

| JAN | FEB | MAR | APR | MAY | JUN | JUL | AUG | SEP | OCT | NOV | DEC |

Lark Sparrow · *Chondestes grammacus*

| JAN | FEB | MAR | APR | MAY | JUN | JUL | AUG | SEP | OCT | NOV | DEC |

Savannah Sparrow · *Passerculus sandwichensis*

| JAN | FEB | MAR | APR | MAY | JUN | JUL | AUG | SEP | OCT | NOV | DEC |

Grasshopper Sparrow · *Ammodramus savanarum*

| JAN | FEB | MAR | APR | MAY | JUN | JUL | AUG | SEP | OCT | NOV | DEC |

Very local breeder, favoring heavily managed grasslands and now restricted to only a few publicly accessible sites. Rarely detected in migration. Site list (breeding): Y9, Y16.

Nelson's Sparrow · *Ammodramus nelsoni*

| JAN | FEB | MAR | APR | MAY | JUN | JUL | AUG | SEP | OCT | NOV | DEC |

Locally common Atlantic coast subspecies *subvirgatus* "Acadian Sparrow" breeds in salt marshes from Southern Maine to the Canadian border, mostly from Scarborough Marsh north. Interior subspecies rare but regular as migrants in grassy areas, wetlands, and coastal salt marshes in mid-to-late fall. Site list (breeding): Y6, C1, SA2, SA3, KX2, WO14, H4, H5, WN3, WN4, WN9.

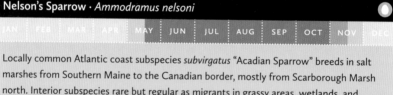

Saltmarsh Sparrow · *Ammodramus caudacutus*

| JAN | FEB | MAR | APR | MAY | JUN | JUL | AUG | SEP | OCT | NOV | DEC |

Locally common but declining breeder in large salt marshes from Midcoast Maine south, but mostly from Scarborough Marsh (but beware of hybrids with Nelson's Sparrow) southward. Site list: Y6, C1, SA2, SA3, KX2.

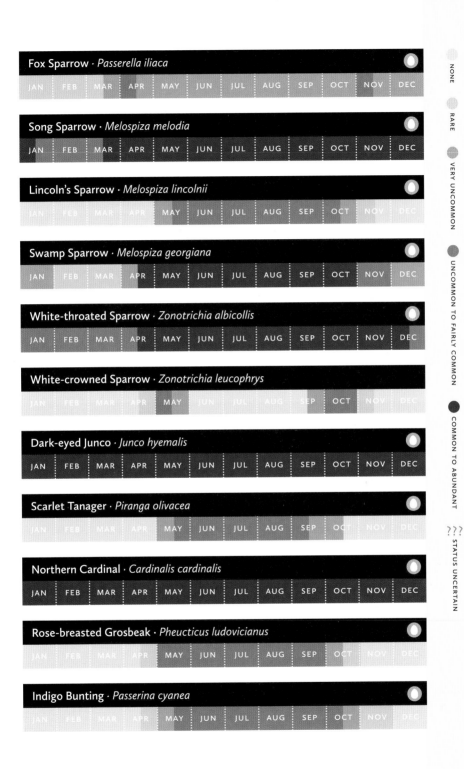

Fox Sparrow · *Passerella iliaca*
JAN | FEB | MAR | APR | MAY | JUN | JUL | AUG | SEP | OCT | NOV | DEC

Song Sparrow · *Melospiza melodia*
JAN | FEB | MAR | APR | MAY | JUN | JUL | AUG | SEP | OCT | NOV | DEC

Lincoln's Sparrow · *Melospiza lincolnii*
JAN | FEB | MAR | APR | MAY | JUN | JUL | AUG | SEP | OCT | NOV | DEC

Swamp Sparrow · *Melospiza georgiana*
JAN | FEB | MAR | APR | MAY | JUN | JUL | AUG | SEP | OCT | NOV | DEC

White-throated Sparrow · *Zonotrichia albicollis*
JAN | FEB | MAR | APR | MAY | JUN | JUL | AUG | SEP | OCT | NOV | DEC

White-crowned Sparrow · *Zonotrichia leucophrys*
JAN | FEB | MAR | APR | MAY | JUN | JUL | AUG | SEP | OCT | NOV | DEC

Dark-eyed Junco · *Junco hyemalis*
JAN | FEB | MAR | APR | MAY | JUN | JUL | AUG | SEP | OCT | NOV | DEC

Scarlet Tanager · *Piranga olivacea*
JAN | FEB | MAR | APR | MAY | JUN | JUL | AUG | SEP | OCT | NOV | DEC

Northern Cardinal · *Cardinalis cardinalis*
JAN | FEB | MAR | APR | MAY | JUN | JUL | AUG | SEP | OCT | NOV | DEC

Rose-breasted Grosbeak · *Pheucticus ludovicianus*
JAN | FEB | MAR | APR | MAY | JUN | JUL | AUG | SEP | OCT | NOV | DEC

Indigo Bunting · *Passerina cyanea*
JAN | FEB | MAR | APR | MAY | JUN | JUL | AUG | SEP | OCT | NOV | DEC

NONE
RARE
VERY UNCOMMON
UNCOMMON TO FAIRLY COMMON
COMMON TO ABUNDANT
??? STATUS UNCERTAIN

INCREASING
DECREASING
IRRUPTIVE
THREATENED OR ENDANGERED IN MAINE
BREEDS IN MAINE
PRIMARILY COASTAL
PRIMARILY PELAGIC

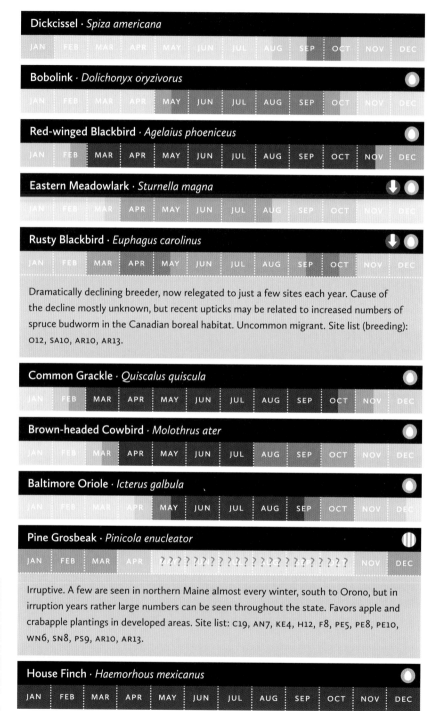

Dickcissel · *Spiza americana*

JAN	FEB	MAR	APR	MAY	JUN	JUL	AUG	SEP	OCT	NOV	DEC

Bobolink · *Dolichonyx oryzivorus*

JAN	FEB	MAR	APR	MAY	JUN	JUL	AUG	SEP	OCT	NOV	DEC

Red-winged Blackbird · *Agelaius phoeniceus*

JAN	FEB	MAR	APR	MAY	JUN	JUL	AUG	SEP	OCT	NOV	DEC

Eastern Meadowlark · *Sturnella magna*

JAN	FEB	MAR	APR	MAY	JUN	JUL	AUG	SEP	OCT	NOV	DEC

Rusty Blackbird · *Euphagus carolinus*

JAN	FEB	MAR	APR	MAY	JUN	JUL	AUG	SEP	OCT	NOV	DEC

Dramatically declining breeder, now relegated to just a few sites each year. Cause of the decline mostly unknown, but recent upticks may be related to increased numbers of spruce budworm in the Canadian boreal habitat. Uncommon migrant. Site list (breeding): O12, SA10, AR10, AR13.

Common Grackle · *Quiscalus quiscula*

JAN	FEB	MAR	APR	MAY	JUN	JUL	AUG	SEP	OCT	NOV	DEC

Brown-headed Cowbird · *Molothrus ater*

JAN	FEB	MAR	APR	MAY	JUN	JUL	AUG	SEP	OCT	NOV	DEC

Baltimore Oriole · *Icterus galbula*

JAN	FEB	MAR	APR	MAY	JUN	JUL	AUG	SEP	OCT	NOV	DEC

Pine Grosbeak · *Pinicola enucleator*

JAN	FEB	MAR	APR	? ?	NOV	DEC

Irruptive. A few are seen in northern Maine almost every winter, south to Orono, but in irruption years rather large numbers can be seen throughout the state. Favors apple and crabapple plantings in developed areas. Site list: C19, AN7, KE4, H12, F8, PE5, PE8, PE10, WN6, SN8, PS9, AR10, AR13.

House Finch · *Haemorhous mexicanus*

JAN	FEB	MAR	APR	MAY	JUN	JUL	AUG	SEP	OCT	NOV	DEC

Purple Finch · *Haemorhous purpureus*

JAN	FEB	MAR	APR	MAY	JUN	JUL	AUG	SEP	OCT	NOV	DEC

Red Crossbill · *Loxia curvirostra*

JAN	FEB	MAR	APR	MAY	JUN	JUL	AUG	SEP	OCT	NOV	DEC

Irruptive. Up to ten "types" in North America mostly nomadic, moving around to take advantage of and breed when favored food sources (perhaps specific to "type") are cyclically abundant. Can breed almost anytime, but most seem to begin breeding in Maine in late winter or early spring. Can be common and widespread in one year, virtually absent the next. Site list: Y15, O8, O9, SA3, KX4, H4, H12, PE10, WN10, PS6, PS9, AR2, AR10, AR13.

White-winged Crossbill · *Loxia leucoptera*

JAN	FEB	MAR	APR	MAY	JUN	JUL	AUG	SEP	OCT	NOV	DEC

Irruptive. More predictable than Reds, White-wings are generally found in varying numbers every other year, but with irregular incursions of large numbers. Can also breed almost any time of year. A conifer-seed generalist, these nomads could be attracted by almost any abundant cone crop. Site list: Y15, O8, O9, SA3, KX4, H4, H12, PE10, WN10, WN15, PS6, PS9, AR2, AR10, AR13.

Common Redpoll · *Acanthis flammea*

JAN	FEB	MAR	APR	MAY	JUN	JUL	AUG	SEP	OCT	NOV	DEC

Irruptive. Generally follows an every-other-year pattern, but recently patterns have become less predictable, possible owing to climate change and its effect on food sources to our north. Irruptions occur when birch and alder crops are poor to our north. Favors those species and bird feeders when they arrive in Maine.

Hoary Redpoll · *Acanthis hornemanni*

JAN	FEB	MAR	APR	MAY	JUN	JUL	AUG	SEP	OCT	NOV	DEC

The northern subspecies (?) of Common Redpoll, it recently retained its independent status; however, the taxonomy and identification are often hotly debated. Birds meeting the description of "Hoary Redpoll" are rare to very rare during flights of Commons (see above).

Pine Siskin · *Spinus pinus*

JAN	FEB	MAR	APR	MAY	JUN	JUL	AUG	SEP	OCT	NOV	DEC

NONE
RARE
VERY UNCOMMON
UNCOMMON TO FAIRLY COMMON
COMMON TO ABUNDANT
??? STATUS UNCERTAIN

INCREASING
DECREASING
IRRUPTIVE
THREATENED OR ENDANGERED IN MAINE
BREEDS IN MAINE
PRIMARILY COASTAL
PRIMARILY PELAGIC

American Goldfinch · *Spinus tristis*

JAN	FEB	MAR	APR	MAY	JUN	JUL	AUG	SEP	OCT	NOV	DEC

Evening Grosbeak · *Coccothraustes vespertinus*

JAN	FEB	MAR	APR	MAY	JUN	JUL	AUG	SEP	OCT	NOV	DEC

With numbers a mere shadow of what they were, this once-abundant winter visitor is now fairly rare, although recent upticks in late summer through winter reports suggests the start of a recovery of the eastern North American population, likely due to the recent increase in spruce budworm populations to our north and west. In Maine, most often seen at feeders in winter but generally found in mixed forest in the boreal and boreal-transition zones in the warmer months. Site list: O9, L1, SO6, PE10, PS6, AR2, AR10, AR13.

House Sparrow · *Passer domesticus*

JAN	FEB	MAR	APR	MAY	JUN	JUL	AUG	SEP	OCT	NOV	DEC

References

American Ornithologists' Union. *Check-List of North American Birds: The Species of Birds of North America from the Arctic through Panama, Including the West Indies and Hawaiian Islands*. 7th ed. Lawrence, KS: Allen Press, 1998. As amended through its 56th supplement (*Auk* 132 [2015]: 748–64).

Appalachian Mountain Club. *Maine Mountain Guide*. 9th ed. Boston: Appalachian Mountain Club Books, 2005.

Behrens, Ken, and Cameron Cox. *Peterson Reference Guide to Seawatching: Eastern Waterbirds in Flight*. Boston: Houghton Mifflin Harcourt, 2013.

Duchesne, Bob. *Maine Birding Trail*. Camden, ME: Down East Books, 2009.

eBird. An online database of bird distribution and abundance. Ithaca, NY: eBird, 2012. http:www.ebird.org.

50 States.com. *Maine Facts and Trivia*. 50states.com/facts/maine.

Infoplease.com. *Maine*. 2015. www.infoplease.com/us-states/maine.html.

Lovitch, Derek. *How to Be a Better Birder*. Princeton, NJ: Princeton University Press, 2012.

Maine Bird Records Committee. "Official List of Maine Birds." 2015. sites.google.com/site/mainebirdrecordscommittee/.

Masterson, Eric A. *Birdwatching in New Hampshire*. Hanover, NH: University Press of New England, 2013.

Newton, Ian. *The Migration Ecology of Birds*. Maryland Heights, MO: Academic, 2008.

Palmer, Ralph S. "Maine Birds." *Bulletin of the Museum of Comparative Zoology* (Harvard University) 102 (1949): 1–656.

Pierson, Elizabeth C., Jan Erik Pierson, and Peter D. Vickery. *Birder's Guide to Maine*. Camden, ME: Down East Books, 1996.

Weidensaul, Scott. *Living on the Wind: Across the Hemisphere with Migratory Birds*. New York: North Point, 1999.

About the Editor and Contributors

Derek Lovitch has made a career out of his lifelong passion for birds. After graduating with a degree in environmental policy from Rutgers University, he worked on avian research and education projects in nine states, from New Jersey to Hawaii and from Florida to Michigan. He also spent three summers as a tour guide on Alaska's Pribilof Islands; he served as tour director in 2003, and organized and conducted the first comprehensive Fall Avian Survey in the islands' history. Derek and his wife, Jeannette, have settled down in Pownal, Maine, and own and operate Freeport Wild Bird Supply, a retail store that caters to birders of all levels. The store serves as a vehicle for Derek to continue to share his enthusiasm for birding, birds, and bird conservation.

Derek has served on his town's Conservation Commission and on various boards and, with Jeannette, founded the Bradbury Mountain Raptor Research Project and is active with many birding and conservation issues in Maine. Yet somehow he still finds time to bird just about every day: whether he is serving as a senior leader for WINGS, as a guide for private clients, or simply working on his local patch list, hardly a day goes by when he isn't in the field.

Derek's first book, *How To Be a Better Birder*, was published in March 2012 by Princeton University Press. He was also the "Tools of the Trade" department editor for *Birding* magazine for six years, and his writing has also appeared in *Birder's World*, *Bird Observer*, *Bird Watcher's Digest*, *NJ Audubon*, and *Winging It*. He is the author of *A Birder's Guide to Whitefish Point (Michigan)* and wrote the text and designed the *Birds of the Maine Backyard* folding guide. Along with birding, Derek enjoys hiking, exploring new natural areas, developing his native plant garden, good food, and beer.

Seth Benz is a transplanted Pennsylvanian who cut his birding teeth at Hawk Mountain Sanctuary, just a handful of miles from his youthful stomping grounds in Berks County. He cites the boisterous Gray Catbird as his "spark bird," based upon a childhood experience that included the discovery of its nest. Beyond birds, his passion for nature and for his eventual career path was nurtured on a gently encouraged diet of fishing and hunting trips with his father. Those many trips helped develop an appreciation for keeping field notes, a reverence for special places, and a desire to experience more of the world. Lured to Maine during graduate studies in 1986, Seth settled here and has worked along the coast of Maine ever since. Along with his wife, Susan, and dog, Sophie, Seth resides in Belfast.

Seth would like to thank Tom Aversa, Margo Carpenter of Hartdale Maps, Rebecca Childs, Cloe Chunn, Scott Hall, Ron Harrell, Cathy Morgan, William Nichols, Buck O'Herin, Annie and Mike Perko, Don Phillips, and Mike and Margie Shannon for their assistance with edits, information, permissions, and other details that greatly enhanced the entries for his chapter.

John Berry has been affiliated with and leads birding trips for Merrymeeting Audubon for nearly twenty years, and occasionally for Freeport Wild Bird Supply. He frequently writes columns for Merrymeeting Audubon's newsletter, including a beginning birder column, and is a board member and officer of the group. John also birds throughout the state of Maine and internationally.

John would like to thank the Brunswick Topsham Land Trust, the Kennebec Estuary Land Trust, and the Bates-Morse Mountain Conservation area for their assistance, information, permissions, and other details that greatly enhanced the entries for this chapter. He would also like to thank the trip leaders of Merrymeeting Audubon who introduced him to many of these locations following his move to this area, especially Chuck Huntington, and to thank his wife, Jane Berry, for editing and improving the readability of the chapter.

Kirk Betts is originally from the edge of the Pinelands and salt marshes of southern New Jersey, but he found himself in the western mountains of Maine some thirty years ago. After seeing a male Common Yellowthroat as a fifth grader, Kirk has spent most of his life studying natural history, even as he worked in various fields over the years. While he relishes memories of mockingbirds on hot summer nights and the raucous chatter of Laughing Gulls at "the shore," Kirk is now most at home atop a mountain at dawn or paddling around the edges of little-visited ponds. Currently, he conducts surveys for Mountain Birdwatch and participates in Christmas Bird Counts, and he has led local bird walks around the Rangeley area.

Kirk would like to thank Derek and Jeannette Lovitch for their assistance with edits, information, permissions, or other details that greatly enhanced the entries for his chapters. He would also like to thank Dorry Shaw for her patience and company during his research for this book.

Ron Joseph retired in 2010 after a thirty-three-year career as a Maine state and federal wildlife biologist. He now leads birding trips for sporting lodges, land trusts, and other conservation organizations. Most of his birding trips are in Somerset County, and his tours for Claybrook Mountain Lodge should not be missed!

Ron would like to thank Don Mairs, Pat and Greg Drummond, and Derek and Jeannette Lovitch for their assistance with edits, information, permissions, and other details that greatly enhanced the entries for his chapter.

Kristen Lindquist is a poet and freelance writer living in Camden; her first published article was a piece on Gray Jays for *Down East* magazine. She has written a natural history column for the local papers for more than ten years and has published three collections of poetry. First inspired by watching waxwings and hummingbirds in her grandparents' backyard, she has been birding her native Maine since childhood. She is a former member of the Maine Bird Records Committee, has served on the board of Friends of Maine Seabird Islands and Merryspring Nature Center, and was a member of the Camden Conservation Commission. Kristen has led bird outings around the state for Maine Audubon, Midcoast Audubon, Coastal Mountains Land Trust, and other organizations.

Kristen would like to thank her husband, Paul Doiron, along with Kirk Gentalen, Evan Obercian, Gail Presley, Don Reimer, and Brian Willson, for their assistance with edits, information, permissions, and other details that greatly enhanced the entries for her chapter.

Rich MacDonald is a self-proclaimed "bird nerd" who started at an early age banding birds (his life "fondled" list—birds he has banded—stands at over 150 species). He has done extensive work studying boreal birds in the

Adirondacks, waterbirds on Lake Champlain, and Bicknell's Thrush in the Dominican Republic. From this base, Rich leads birding and nature tours in the Acadia region, Downeast Maine, and beyond (see his website, www. TheNaturalHistoryCenter.com, for more information). You can often find Rich out and about Mount Desert Island, binoculars at the ready, head cocked as he listens for the birds.

Rich would like to thank Cheri Domina, Aaron Dority, Jim Dow, Matt Haney, Marissa Hutchinson, Derek Lovitch, and Nancy Sferra for their assistance with edits, information, permissions, and other details that greatly enhanced the entries for his chapter.

Dan Nickerson has, as a birder, always been driven to know "what is out there," contributing over the course of forty years to a half dozen *Breeding Bird Atlas* volumes, from Hudson Bay, Ontario, through Quebec, the Adirondacks of New York State, and his home state of Maine, as well as being compiler or participant in an equal number of National Audubon Christmas Bird Counts.

For six years the Maine River Project focused Dan's birding on observation sites along the Androscoggin River. He broadened his study of the birds of Androscoggin County after finding that it was, by one measure, the least birded county in Maine. The invitation to contribute to this book added fuel to his existing fire, and we now have a better understanding of the avifauna of this county, as well as the breeding distribution of several species in the state.

Dan would like to express his appreciation to all those people who, with renewed vigor, have made contributions to our knowledge of the avifauna of Androscoggin County, particularly to the Stanton Bird Club for its historical records and interest in the birds of Androscoggin County, and to Katrina Fenton for her assistance and edits.

Luke Seitz , www.lukeseitzart.com, who created the frontispiece for the book, is an avid birder, photographer, and artist. He has been birding throughout Maine for over twelve years, hitching rides from other birders before he could drive himself. Luke particularly enjoys exploring the boreal forest, searching for vagrants along the coast, and listening to nocturnal flight calls. Now a senior at Cornell University, Luke intends to pursue a career in bird illustration while guiding birding trips internationally.

Luke would like to thank Derek Lovitch for helpful notes and assistance with edits that greatly enhanced the entries for these chapters, and for his first introduction to this wonderful region of Maine—and years of subsequent fantasizing about where Boreal Owls might be hiding. He also thanks Bob Duchesne for publicizing several excellent birding locations in the county, especially Harvester Road in Piscataquis County. And he offers a special thanks to the birding king of Aroostook County, Bill Sheehan, for a boatload of helpful tips over the years; Bill's direct and indirect assistance greatly enhanced the entries for the Aroostook County chapter.

Jeffrey V. Wells and Allison Childs Wells are native Mainers whose families in Maine go back hundreds of years. Both are lifelong birders, and both hold graduate degrees from Cornell University in Ithaca, New York, where Jeff received his MS and PhD and Allison, her MFA. Both stayed on at Cornell, Allison as communications director for the world-renowned Cornell Lab of Ornithology, and Jeff, also at the lab, as director of bird conservation for National Audubon. They returned to Maine in 2004 to raise their child among family and Maine's spectacular natural environment. They are the authors of *Maine's Favorite Birds* (Tilbury House, 2012) and the forthcoming *Birds of Aruba, Bonaire, and Curaçao and How to Find Them* (Cornell University Press, 2016). Jeff is also author of *Birder's Conservation Handbook: 100 North American Birds at Risk* (Princeton University Press, 2007), and editor of *Boreal Birds of North America* (University of California Press, 2011). Allison was coeditor of *Birder's Life List and Diary* and a contributor to *Scholastic's New Book of Knowledge*. Jeff is now senior scientist for the Boreal Songbird Initiative and the International Boreal Conservation Campaign and is a Visiting Fellow at the Cornell Lab of Ornithology. Allison is senior director of public affairs for the Natural Resources Council of Maine. They live in Gardiner, Maine, with their son and two birdwatching indoor cats.

Allison and Jeffrey would like to thank the staff and boards, past and present, of the land trusts and town conservation commissions of Lincoln County for their commitment to protecting land for birds and other values. They are grateful also to their parents and grandparents who grew up in and near Lincoln County and encouraged their interest in birds and nature—many of the sites they share here are places they visited with their parents and grandparents over the years.

Herb Wilson is a professor of biology at Colby College, where he teaches ornithology, marine ecology, marine invertebrate zoology, and evolutionary biology. He and his wife have lived in Maine since 1990. His research interests include the foraging ecology of sandpipers, changes in arrival dates of migratory breeding birds, and the impact of food supplementation on the winter survival of birds. He lives in Waterville during the academic year and spends much of the summer in Lubec.

Herb would like to thank Chris Bartlett, Louis Bevier, Bets Brown, Lisa Dellwo, Charlie Duncan, Bill Schlesinger, and Nancy Sferra for their assistance with edits, information, permissions, and other details that greatly enhanced the entries for this chapter.

Index of Bird Species

For birding sites, see table of contents.

145, 151, 155–56, 179, 184, 227, 231–37, 256, 263, 277, 289, 298, 302, 374, 384, 426, 436; Western, 102, 230

Grosbeaks: Blue, 22, 39, 282; Evening, 348, 367, 402, 413, 425, 464; Pine, 56, 64, 78, 91, 97–98, 126, 140, 142, 160, 330, 338, 354, 361–64, 367, 374, 379, 408, 413, 415, 425, 429, 462; Rose-breasted, 137, 165, 189–90, 196, 246, 260, 266, 272, 312, 314, 335, 378, 461

Grouse: Ruffed, 129–30, 194, 196, 243, 246, 262, 267, 271, 278, 323, 335, 349, 363, 367, 396, 398, 402, 406, 408, 414, 428, 436; Spruce, 1, 118, 121, 287, 294, 296, 301, 309, 315, 317, 324, 333, 339, 349–53, 362–63, 366–70, 373, 378–79, 384, 388, 392–402, 405–6, 408, 411, 413, 426–30, 436

Guillemot, Black, 37, 63–64, 79–80, 155, 171, 182–87, 227–35, 248, 258, 277, 289, 303–6, 370, 374, 376, 379, 384, 444

Gulls: Black-headed, 25, 27, 57, 156, 160, 229–32, 289, 386, 389–90, 445; Bonaparte's, 25, 27, 41, 57, 101, 125, 127, 146–47, 156, 179–80, 229–33, 238, 263, 273, 289, 304, 330, 380, 386, 389, 445; Franklin's, 355; Glaucous, 18, 57, 63, 66–67, 82–83, 139, 142, 159, 203, 206, 219, 229, 234, 289, 309, 342, 359, 361, 389, 416, 419, 446; Great Black-backed, 38, 147, 154, 158–59, 206, 216, 222, 229, 258, 309, 446; Herring, 38, 89, 154, 158, 163, 206, 216, 222, 229, 258, 277, 309, 361, 379, 445; Iceland, 18, 42, 57, 61, 63, 66–67, 69, 82–83, 106, 139, 142, 148, 159, 203, 206, 219, 229, 231, 234, 289, 309, 341–42, 359, 361, 389, 416, 419, 446; Ivory, 68, 306; Laughing, 101, 179, 187, 227, 232, 248, 445; Lesser Black-backed, 27, 41, 57, 61, 73, 89, 152, 155, 159, 163, 203, 206, 216, 219, 231–32, 238, 265, 289, 380, 389, 416, 419, 446; Little, 25, 27, 41, 57, 265, 386, 389–90, 445; Mew, 73, 228, 230; "Nelson's" (Glaucous x Herring hybrid), 139; Ring-billed, 82, 89, 159–60, 163, 206, 216, 222, 229, 258, 313, 361, 445; Sabine's, 26, 355, 386–90; Slaty-backed, 207; Thayer's, 207; "Westbrook," 82–83

Hawks: Broad-winged, 96, 134, 188, 191, 196, 215, 240, 250, 271, 363, 428, 439; Cooper's, 96, 240, 248, 271, 439; Northern Goshawk, 96, 245, 271, 296, 342, 414–15, 439; Northern Harrier, 96, 157, 165, 224, 240–45, 264, 280, 284, 321, 428, 439; Red-shouldered, 96, 129–34, 240, 269, 299, 349, 439; Red-tailed, 96, 164, 206, 219, 238, 240, 264, 270, 337, 439; Rough-legged, 31, 37, 54, 61, 89, 96, 157, 206, 219, 224, 228, 236, 240, 246, 284, 420, 439; Sharp-shinned, 96, 240, 271, 428, 439; Swainson's, 95, 301

Herons: Great Blue, 101, 117, 132, 185, 192, 208, 210, 224, 234, 259, 265, 267, 326, 330, 372; Green, 39,

76, 78, 117, 129, 132, 135, 223, 270, 343–44, 359, 438; Little Blue, 53, 438; Tricolored, 53, 223, 438; Tricolored x Snowy Egret hybrid, 59; Western Reef-, 16. *See also* Night-herons

Hummingbirds: Calliope, 176, 291; Ruby-throated, 268, 306, 449

Ibis: Glossy, 53, 56, 58, 219, 223, 246, 438; White-faced, 53, 56, 58

Jaegers: Long-tailed, 25, 79–80; Parasitic, 63, 79, 233–34, 237, 306, 383–86, 444; Pomarine, 63, 79, 306, 384, 443

Jays: Blue, 452; Gray, 1, 118, 121, 276, 287, 294, 308, 315, 317, 325, 333, 339, 349–53, 365–67, 379, 386, 388, 391–93, 396–408, 411, 413, 421–30, 452

Juncos: Dark-eyed, 48, 116, 157, 250, 300, 324, 338, 348, 398, 425, 428, 461; "Oregon" Dark-eyed, 158

Killdeer, 33, 47, 135, 143, 163, 224, 242, 355, 382, 416–19, 440

Kingbirds: Eastern, 78, 132, 222, 270, 281, 320, 451; Gray, 22; Western, 16, 73, 89, 282, 301

Kingfisher, Belted, 84, 210, 222, 225, 256, 261, 267, 283, 303–4, 449

Kinglets: Golden-crowned, 64, 175, 259, 378, 425, 454; Ruby-crowned, 88, 178, 275, 309, 349, 378, 425, 454

Kites: Mississippi, 33, 95; Swallow-tailed, 92, 95, 175

Kittiwake: Black-legged, 21, 37, 64, 155, 229–33, 237, 299, 306, 374, 383–86, 421, 445

Knot, Red, 40, 383, 441

Lapwing, Northern, 136

Lark, Horned, 23, 40, 55, 61, 63, 68, 86, 103, 113, 126–27, 135–36, 143, 156, 167, 218, 229, 236, 240, 242, 244, 274, 283, 300, 337, 355, 383, 413, 416, 420, 452

Longspurs: Chestnut-collared, 41; Lapland, 16, 55, 86, 113, 126, 143, 218–19, 232, 236, 355, 383, 389, 420, 456

Loons: Common, 25, 37, 60, 81, 84, 97, 123, 132–37, 142, 145, 154–55, 174, 179–80, 184, 217, 227, 233, 236, 239, 248, 254, 256, 260, 263, 265, 275, 289, 302, 322, 330, 344, 346, 357–58, 374, 390, 415, 436; Pacific, 21, 102, 306, 432; Red-throated, 23, 25, 37–38, 97, 102, 145, 154–55, 174, 179, 227, 236, 256, 263, 276–77, 289, 298, 302, 305, 374, 384, 436; Yellow-billed, 80

Martin, Purple, 111, 199, 208, 210, 253, 280–81, 453

Meadowlark, Eastern, 46, 163, 193, 203–5, 226, 280, 462

Mockingbird, Northern, 70, 204, 248, 361, 455